UNCERTAIN VISION

UNCERTAIN VISION

Birt, Dyke and the Reinvention of the BBC

Georgina Born

Secker & Warburg
LONDON

Published by Secker & Warburg 2004

2 4 6 8 10 9 7 5 3 1

Copyright © Georgina Born 2004

Georgina Born has asserted her right under the Copyright, Designs
and Patents Act 1988 to be identified as the author of this work

First published in Great Britain in 2004 by
Secker & Warburg
Random House, 20 Vauxhall Bridge Road,
London SW1V 2SA

Random House Australia (Pty) Limited
20 Alfred Street, Milsons Point, Sydney,
New South Wales 2061, Australia

Random House New Zealand Limited
18 Poland Road, Glenfield,
Auckland 10, New Zealand

Random House (Pty) Limited
Endulini, 5A Jubilee Road, Parktown 2193, South Africa

The Random House Group Limited Reg. No. 954009
www.randomhouse.co.uk

A CIP catalogue record for this book
is available from the British Library

ISBN 0436205629

Papers used by Random House are natural,
recyclable products made from wood grown in sustainable forests;
the manufacturing processes conform to the environmental
regulations of the country of origin

Printed and bound in Great Britain by Clays Ltd, St Ives PLC

Contents

Prologue   *The Anthropologist Among the White City Natives*   1

1   Prehistory: The BBC from Reith to the Tories   23
      'A National Institution and a National Asset'
      A Notorious Syllogism?
      Fertile Competition
      Pluralism and Political Opportunism
      Squeezing the BBC: Placemen and Repudiation
      The Paradox
      Commercialisation and Rapprochement

2   *The Cultural State*   65
      'The Very Model of Socialist Organisation'?
      Patterns of History
      Fission and Fusion
      Reinventing Reith
      The Craft: Situated Ethics and Aesthetics
      Rituals of Inclusion

3   *Accountants and Primitives*   97
      Rationalisation
      Accountancy as Morality
      Accounting Wars
      Virtual Money

4   Trading and Competing   129
        The Flexible Firm?
        Fuzzy Logic: 'Bringing It In' and 'Farming It Out'
        The 'Talented' and the Weak
        The Business: Turning a Blind Eye?
        Policing the Market
        Mixing It
        Trade Wars
        Dealing: Co-Production
        Becoming Entrepreneurs
        Evangelical Entrepreneurial

5   Working and Not Working   179
        Casualising Creativity
        Freelance Fragment
        The Privatisation of Ideas
        Skilling, Reskilling and Multiskilling
        Including and Excluding
        Uncertainty and Creativity

6   New Model Managerialism   212
        New Public Management Ad Infinitum
        Consultancy: Dependence and Prestige
        Adding Value
        Business for Culture
        Accountability for Trust
        Audit: An Intimate Bureaucracy
        Hyperbole and Reduction
        Performing Governance

7   Knowing the Audience   254
        The American Way of Television?
        Marketing Values
        Branding the Real
        Listening to the Research
        A Practical and Interested Ethics
        Researching the News
        Tribes and Punishment
        Authoring Channels

Scheduling Tastes
Telling It Like It Is

8   *Creativity Bound: Drama Group*   302
Centralising Commissioning
Ordering Up Programmes
Genre Unlimited
Drama Bound
Quota Heaven
Profile and Ratings, High and Low
Crafts and Trends
Pitch Culture
Small Cinema and Rapid Response
Social Realism Grows Old
Spaces of Invention
Incommensurable Ethics
The Condition of Value

9   *Framing Democracy: News, Newsnight and Documentaries*   373
Spin, Genre-Bending, and the Crisis of Politics
Democracy and Diversity
Impartiality and Its Discontents
Mission to Control
Centralising News
Collusive Millbank
Emasculating Current Affairs
News as Product
Responsive News?
The Dilemma: Ambivalence
'Casting' Debate: *Newsnight*
A Partial Art: Documentary
Docusoapia
Accessing Truths
Autonomy, Aesthetics, Invention
Mixes and Boundaries

10 Dyke's BBC, Hutton, the Digital Challenge, and the Future   453
   A War, a Death, a Report, and their Repercussions
   Change the Organisation
   Compete to Win
   Sky's the Limit
   Digital Visions
   A Creative Ecology
   Digital Visions
   Auntie's Nanny
   After Hutton

Epilogue *Uncertain Vision*   506
   Re-imagining the Nation
   Point Counterpoint

Glossary   523
Dramatis Personae   526
Full references for narrative quotations   528
Notes   532
Index   548

'The prime condition of a democratically organised public is a kind of knowledge and insight which does not yet exist . . . Knowledge cooped up in a private consciousness is a myth; a thing is fully known only when it is published, shared, socially accessible. The inquiry which alone can furnish knowledge as a precondition of public judgements must be contemporary and quotidian . . . Presentation is fundamentally important, and presentation is a question of art. Artists have always been the real purveyors of news, for it is not the outward happening in itself which is new, but the kindling by it of emotion, perception and appreciation . . . We have but touched lightly upon the conditions which must be fulfilled if the Great Society is to become a Great Community . . . [Then] democracy will come into its own, for democracy is a name for a life of free and enriching communion. It will have its consummation when free social inquiry is indissolubly wedded to the art of full and moving communication.'

John Dewey, *The Public and Its Problems* (1926)

'It was a fundamental principle . . . that everything was to be paid for. Nobody was ever on any account to give anybody anything, or render anybody help without purchase. Gratitude was to be abolished, and the virtues springing from it were not to be. Every inch of the existence of mankind, from birth to death, was to be a bargain across a counter. And if we didn't get to Heaven that way, it was not a politico-economical place, and we had no business there.'

Charles Dickens, *Hard Times* (1854)

The Anthropologist Among the White City Natives

Fly-on-the-Cabinet: the BBC and affection (I)

One of the new experimental directions in the successful prime-time BBC2 documentary strand, *Modern Times*, is exemplified by the film 'Lido'. The director, Lucy Blakstad, gives a day in the life of an open-air public swimming pool in south London. In the course of the day it seems that all human life visits the pool: the lesbian couple, the graceful rasta, black single mothers with their gaggle of kids, the gang of lads. They are portrayed, their mores and prejudices explored, through filmed observation and direct-to-camera monologues and dialogues. Blakstad laces the film with moments of reflection and irreality using slow motion, heightened colour, ambient and repetitive music and sound. It is a new documentary aesthetic, and her film is one of a number of films for *Modern Times* engaged in such fruitful explorations.

Near the beginning of the film comes this sequence. It is early morning and the pool is almost empty. A couple of well-kept elderly men are steadily swimming lengths, stopping every now and then for a chat with the film-maker. 'I'm Sir Humphrey in *Yes Minister*. My job is to be the chief engineer in the engine room of government.' 'Is that quite stressful?' 'Well, yes, it is quite stressful – there's always a lot to do.' Cut to the pool steward checking chlorine levels in the water, and back, longshot, to one of the men, who has begun to dry himself with a towel. His movements suggest he is lowering his costume. Suddenly, he spies the camera filming from the other side of the pool. 'Do you really want this bit?' he says, hesitating. Blakstad, unseen behind the camera, calls coyly back, 'Oh, I didn't know you were going to strip!' The elderly man considers, smiles and – continuing to undress for the camera, revealing some thigh and a bit more too – says decisively, 'Anything for the BBC!' This man is Sir Robin Butler, Cabinet Secretary to the Major government.

*

1

Opening musical minds: the BBC and affection (II)

'He was a musical idol! I first heard a recording of Dizzy Gillespie on a BBC radio show. I was about thirteen and I was already listening to Louis Armstrong . . . I knew about Dizzy Gillespie, and [it was] a recording of his big band from about the forties. It wasn't very well recorded, and the sound was so dense. And I thought, "Oh this Dizzy Gillespie is this avant-garde person, I can't understand it!" I couldn't cope. Then, about two years later, my father got tickets to see Giants of Jazz at the Hammersmith Odeon and I went to see them – it was Dizzy Gillespie, Thelonius Monk, Art Blakey . . . From that moment on, that was it: I wanted to listen to everything of Dizzy's. When he played at Ronnie Scott's I went with a friend. After the show he took me backstage. I had a book of Dizzy Gillespie's transcribed solos, and I remember handing it to him and asking if he could sign it, and I was trembling. Before he signed it he opened it up and looked at all his written-out solos, and he said, "Did I play this?" He says, "I couldn't play this!" . . . I got to know him very well through going every night, and I used to request "Groovin' High". Then one time I went, he made an announcement. He said his favourite fan was in the audience and he was going to play his favourite tune. I looked around, and he played "Groovin' High".'

Guy Barker, Jazz Line-Up, BBC Radio 3, 2000.

*

Gardening the nation: the BBC and affection (III)

With a long day ahead I am taking a taxi into central London. I get talking to the driver. We begin, as so often, with the weather. Not a bad summer, and now the requisite rain and cold. We move to gardening and I confess I am learning to prune. He starts, 'The wife does the garden. I cut the grass, back and front, have done for years. I enjoy it. We both spend a lot of time in the garden'. The conversation continues as we drive down Kingsway. 'Some of the gardening programmes we enjoy; but I don't go for Alan Titchmarsh. There was a wonderful programme ten or fifteen years ago on the BBC; it must have been one of the earliest gardening programmes. There was a lady in a village near Cambridge. She had this marvellous garden that she'd made herself from scratch. Well, at the end of the programme it said: if you want to visit the garden, phone up. So my wife and me, we phoned and got the instructions. One weekend we drove up there with some friends, stopped off at a pub for lunch on the way, made a day of it. It was the first village back on the A10 – where there's a traffic trap and the road curves round. We got there, early afternoon, and there it was. We hadn't said we were coming. We just walked in and up the back – this long thin garden. Marvellous. Not special, like they are today, just done by this lady and full of care, every patch of earth covered with something different. We found her in the potting shed – she spent all her time in there. Her husband and children did the house, the cooking, and she lived in the garden. You should go and visit.'

Diary, 1998.

*

Skills and their erosion: the BBC and trust (I)

I chat to the cameraman attached to *Newsnight* here at the Labour Party conference in Blackpool: Baz, a black guy, who speaks immediately and unprompted of the decimation of the craft base at the BBC through cuts and rationalisation. He's on staff and trained in Drama at Pebble Mill. 'We used to spend half an hour setting up one shot! You could do that in those days – it's unheard of now.' He speaks of how, two or three years ago, there would have been three people in the camera crew, then there were two; now there are just single cameramen and it's very physically demanding. 'There's a guy doing camerawork here, but he's not up to it – really a sound recordist.' Baz says they've lost many skilled craftsmen and are prematurely upgrading less skilled people; the soundman is sent back days later for not being up to the job. Those craftsmen who have left sell their work back to the BBC at inflated prices. Reflecting on my study, Baz says I should take an international perspective. 'I used to work for Newsgathering in Europe and some parts of the Third World. You should see how the BBC is received in Somalia: there, maybe 50 per cent of the population know what the BBC is, what it represents . . .' – he implies that it is trusted, believed, taken to be accurate. He implies too that this is under attack, a passing role. Clearly he has a deep identification with and loyalty to this BBC and its international role.

Diary, 1996.

*

Building civil society in Burundi: the BBC and trust (II)

I am listening to Radio 4's *Today* programme: the rebel ambush of a bus in Burundi has resulted in a massacre of passengers, including Charlotte Wilson, a British aid worker. This kind of event is commonplace in Burundi, which is caught up in a seven-year-old civil war and where the government has a dismal human rights record. Two hundred thousand civilians have died in recent years. A peace accord has been brokered by Nelson Mandela, but it is not holding. Labour MP Tess Kingham, secretary of the All Party Group on Rwanda and the Great Lakes, comments on the situation: 'Massive assistance needs to go into [the Burundi] region to ensure that education, health and government systems are rebuilt, so that people can get rid of this fear of genocide that permeates the area and start to rebuild their lives and a sense of peace. The British government has been part of the donors' conference that took place in Paris this month, and we're hoping now that more aid will go into Burundi to give some sustainable peace . . . The BBC World Service in Burundi has been playing a very big part in helping that peace process by trying to disseminate, in the local language, information about the peace plan to local people, so that civil society can get involved and get behind the peace process. Then, hopefully, pressure will get to the rebel groups which will cut off any support they have and any supply lines, and get everybody behind the peace programme.'

Diary, 2000.

*

Blast the Beeb's bilge: the BBC's critics (I)

'Noel Edmonds, the man who brought us Mr Blobby, has abandoned the BBC in protest at what he calls "dumbing down". If things are too dumb for Blobby, they are too dumb for me . . . We men of moderate opinions are prepared to support the existence of this anomalous nationalised industry, this weird system of taxpayer-funded outdoor relief for 22,000 media folk, even if, in our hearts, we know that Norman Tebbit is right to say that it is full of pinkos. For decades our wrath has been bated by the recognition that it has produced some first-rate stuff. Dimly, inarticulately, we acknowledge that there is some kind of case for public service broadcasting, and we are not sure what would happen if this were left entirely to the market. But when the BBC itself spontaneously forsakes that responsibility, and fills our screens with bilge in the desperate pursuit of ratings, then the compact breaks down. Then we ask ourselves what we are getting, by paying for the last great state media concern in the free world, with its infestation of Lefties; and if the Beeb honchos can't come up with something better than the present offerings, they should prepare for revolt.'

Boris Johnson, 1999.

*

An asinine behemoth run by panjandrums: the BBC's critics (II)

'In an era of broadcasting abundance, why do we need this poll-tax funded, nationalised dinosaur? . . . Commercial broadcasters are becoming increasingly irritated by unfair, state-funded competition aimed directly at undermining their own, often fragile, ventures. The private sector has established ten TV channels exclusively dedicated to children. These channels' struggle to find an audience has cost lots of money and so far produced little by way of return . . . Politicians are becoming increasingly reluctant to defend the regressive household tax on which the BBC depends, or to resist the complaints of commercial broadcasters that the way it is being used threatens to throttle a vital industry in its infancy.'

David Cox, 2001.

*

The BBC is the world's most famous cultural institution, renowned for the quality of its journalism, broadcasting and online services. Throughout its eighty-year existence it has attracted criticism, controversy and political bullying, as well as epitomising the heights to which non-commercial independent broadcasting can aspire. It remains the model for public broadcasters on every continent. It is an institution riven by contradictions, at once liberal and elitist, arrogant and fragile, a cornerstone of British democracy yet replete with internal hierarchies mirroring Britain's broader social inequalities. This book gives an inside portrait of this unique cultural institution, an anthropologist's view of what goes on behind the scenes at the BBC.

But it is also a book about a challenge, one much discussed in contemporary public life: the challenge for the BBC to reinvent itself in response to rapid changes in politics and society, in culture and technology. There is a sense that the BBC, and all that it stands for, is in crisis – although crisis is a cast of mind that has haunted the corporation since its inception. In spring 2004, as I completed this manuscript, the BBC faced the gravest setback in its history: the simultaneous resignation of its chairman, Gavyn Davies, and director-general, Greg Dyke, as a result of serious criticism of its journalism and its system of self-regulation by the government-commissioned Hutton report. Lord Hutton had been asked to look urgently into the circumstances surrounding the death in July 2003 of Dr David Kelly, the government weapons expert. By speaking secretly to BBC journalists of his reservations about the government's case for war on Iraq, Kelly became embroiled in the conflict between the New Labour government and the BBC over the corporation's coverage of the war. As a result of mounting pressure, it appears that Kelly committed suicide, causing BBC–government relations to plummet to their lowest ebb in decades. The present situation finds the BBC in a state of unprecedented vulnerability, and this in a period of heightened risk – the review leading up to the renewal of its Royal Charter, due in 2006.

One aim of this book is to address the question: How did the BBC reach this nadir, at a time of otherwise considerable success? It does this by taking the long view. The central part of the book consists in an analysis of John Birt's controversial tenure in the 1990s as director-general of the BBC, for it is the Birt period that gives the clue to current developments. Birt instituted a series of radical reforms, responding first to political attacks in the period of the Thatcher governments and subsequently to New Labour's highly interventionist style and its continuation of a neo-liberal economic agenda. A central concern of the book is to uncover how the major organisational and structural changes brought in by Birt impacted on the BBC's capacity for programme-making. It therefore dwells at length on the elements and effects of Birt's reforms. The argument is that Birtist management was responsible for eroding the BBC's creativity. In short, the Birt period represents the political subordination of the BBC, a subordination more pervasive and damaging than is apparent from a focus solely on clashes over political journalism, as well as exemplifying New Labour's wider attempts to rein in the public sector. Birt's intimate identification with New Labour was concretised following his departure from the BBC when he gained a Labour peerage and became Prime Minister Blair's strategy adviser. When Dyke succeeded Birt in 2000, he found a demoralised and over-managed organisation. The last chapter examines Dyke's period as director-general, arguing that his determination to supersede Birt's policies and withstand political pressure was necessary, well judged and highly productive. Dyke's changes made the BBC less inhibited and more risk-taking, including in its dealings with the government.

If Birt's tenure as director-general is at the root of the present rupture, it must be placed firmly in context. Well before the current events, a series of longer-term factors converged to create a chronic sense of crisis for the BBC. Among them were the intensifying competition caused by the growth of satellite, cable and digital television and the increasing power of media conglomerates seeking a share of Britain's lucrative media markets. At the same time the corporation came under sustained attack from several sides. Under Margaret Thatcher's Conservative governments the BBC was treated with contempt. Thatcher's visceral dislike for the corporation was compounded by the drive to retaliate against its sometimes outspoken criticisms of her policies, and by a determination to bring it under the iron 'deregulatory' controls demanded by her vision of a strong liberal state. Influenced by the ideas of American right-wing think tanks, Thatcher and her advisers sought to submit British broadcasting to US-style deregulation. Weakened by political criticisms in the 1980s and 1990s, the BBC has also been subject to escalating complaints from rival commercial broadcasters who stand to profit greatly if the BBC falters in responding to new conditions. These rivals have naturally been among the most vocal of the corporation's critics and, with increasing ferocity, they question the BBC's right to exist.

Two further factors fuel the crisis. The philosophy of public service broadcasting, which served the BBC well for most of its existence, evolving to meet the times, has reached a critical juncture. For many, in an era of globalisation and digitalisation, with the decline of national broadcasting systems, it serves no future purpose. Each term in the phrase – 'public', 'service' and 'broadcasting' – has been cast in doubt, undermined by social and technological changes. The BBC is outmoded, our relations with it as drenched in nostalgia and sentimentality as they are with the monarchy or the Church of England. Even if one dissents from this view, there is clearly a need for the values of public service broadcasting to be renewed so as better to meet the demands of a diverse and increasingly fragmented society. Such a change of ethos must be reflected in practice: in the programmes made, the networks and services delivered, but also in the BBC's organisation and its employment practices. Public service broadcasting is a concept larger than the BBC, with a complex institutional expression. Yet the BBC has a special place in the history and the imagining of public service broadcasting. It was founded when there was still a British Empire and when the wireless relied on the thermionic valve. It developed during the period before and after the Second World War when large sections of industry – from the railways to the mines – were under public ownership. What should public service mean and what role should the BBC play in the age of broadband, flexible labour markets, multiculturalism and the 'war on terror'? The BBC's fate, its capacity to reinvent public service broadcasting in testing conditions, is emblematic of the fate of the ideal itself.

The final dimension in the crisis of the BBC is more nebulous; yet it lies behind the previous factors. It is the installation of the language and practice of free-market economics at the heart of public life. Today in government, in the pronouncements of social commentators and influential think tanks, the default position is a profound suspicion of any kind of public intervention. When government looks for models, it looks to private enterprise. A belief in the primacy of markets and their association with competition, efficiency and entrepreneurialism has become widespread. The tenets of neo-liberalism have coalesced into a new common sense. In Britain, the imperatives of markets and enterprise were established during the Thatcher governments. The legacy of that period is clear in the efforts made by New Labour, when preparing for government and since coming to power in 1997, to reshape its former ideological foundations. In its desire to emulate the strengths of Thatcherism, New Labour found it difficult to articulate any positive image of the public sector. While it espoused values of community and social responsibility, New Labour conceived of public institutions only as a variant of business. In this take, when the public sector acts it must always be as if it were a business or in partnership with business; and if it is not working, the cure is to subject it to the disciplines of private management and the market.

But there is an additional destructive aspect to relations between government and the BBC: their entanglement in the disabling disease of spin. In power, New Labour committed escalating resources to managing relations with the media and particularly the popular press. As a leading commentator puts it, 'No previous government had dedicated so much talent and energy to trying to rule through the media.'[1] The media varied in their reaction. In the BBC, given the routing of the Conservative opposition after 1997, there grew a determination to take on the effective role of opposition, to match aggressive spin with aggressive journalistic scrutiny of government. But the result of inflated spin was that after three years in power, 'The spin was spun out'.[2] The seeds of scepticism had grown; the public was now encouraged by the same press that had enthusiastically published the Downing Street Strategic Communications Unit's 'confected articles' to look on New Labour as manipulators and autocrats. The effect was to reduce public trust in government, politicians and journalists, fuelling a wider public disengagement from the democratic process evident in declining participation in local and general elections. The BBC's journalism was to become increasingly troublesome for the New Labour government in the Dyke years; the Kelly affair saw that journalism shift from being engaged with the mechanisms of spin to itself coming under the spotlight as an object of negative spin.

In relations between the Labour government and the broadcasting industry, the continuing dominance of the market model is signalled in a characteristic contradiction in media policy: in the primacy given to competition law, set against New Labour's laissez-faire attitude towards concentrations of media ownership. The tension was plain in the simultaneous roll-out of the 2003 Communications Bill and its centrepiece, the competition-oriented regulator, Ofcom, at the same time as the government exhibited a lack of will to tackle Rupert Murdoch's market dominance in the British press and digital television. Although many Labour politicians remain committed to public service media as the kernel of Britain's civil society, they have found it difficult to disentangle the concept from the carping interests stacking up against it. This was evident in the position taken by Chris Smith, the Labour government's first Secretary of

State for Culture, Media and Sport. Despite being unequivocally for public service broadcasting, because of the conundrums thrown up by the coexistence of a globally successful public media giant alongside powerful private media interests, Smith was driven constantly to intervene. At times his actions seemed guided by the principle that the BBC must be reined in to allow the private sector space to secure its expanded profitability, with issues of competition and fair trading given more weight than the continuing viability of the BBC. Lacking confidence in past values, the Labour government appears unable to conceive of a revivified public media model that would transcend the prevailing neo-liberal terms.

Despite the threatening climate, the BBC continues to attract the affection and esteem of much of the British public and of international opinion. Throughout the 1990s and in the new millennium it has achieved significant success, whether measured in audience figures, awards, entry into new markets or export earnings. The corporation regularly takes the lion's share of the annual professional awards in television and radio. The BBC's Internet and new media activities were launched to almost universal acclaim; 45 per cent of all British Internet users visit the BBC website regularly. It has rapidly become the most used non-portal website outside the United States and is the leading content site in Europe. The BBC's commercial arm, BBC Worldwide, is expanding its operations in the USA and around the world. It ploughs back into programme-making over £120 million a year in earnings. BBC World Service radio reaches 150 million people worldwide and broadcasts in forty-three languages; it continues to play a vital role globally as a source of impartial international news. For all the fierce competition, the BBC's combined share of television viewing is almost 40 per cent of the audience, and its reach – the percentage of the national audience using the BBC each week – is 92 per cent.[3] In 2001, BBC1 overtook ITV1 for the first time since competition began in 1955. Despite the inroads made by new media and multichannel television, the BBC appears to be manoeuvring adeptly in response to rampant competition and technological change.

In light of these achievements, two startling paradoxes face anyone tracking the status of the BBC in the public eye. The first arises when we pose the manifest success of the corporation against the campaign of vilification begun in the Thatcher era, which has intensified in the past decade. Recent years have seen a constant war of words in Parliament and the press concerning the BBC's management and governance, the legitimacy of its funding mechanism, the licence fee, and its right to compete in new markets. Queries are voiced constantly, whether couched in the cool language of business realism or in the jingoistic terms of right-wing populism. Boris Johnson, Conservative MP and editor of the *Spectator*, exemplifies the populist position in almost parodic form. David Elstein, formerly chief executive of Channel 5 and head of programmes for Sky Television, represents business realism. Elstein has been vocal on the contentious issue of broadcasting rights in sport. Disregarding the anti-competitive tactics employed by Murdoch and the anti-democratic effects of the migration of first-class football to subscription television, he portrays their exponential rise as a natural consequence of the unleashing of competition by deregulation. Whatever insane heights are reached by footballers' salaries, whatever the cost of rights to the Premier League, since they are set by market competition they must be for the best. Even left-wing periodicals offer their share of polemic. David Cox in the *New Statesman*, assessing Dyke's first year in office, weighed in with a jaundiced version of the market-based concerns to the fore in New Labour thinking. The impact of the campaign against the BBC by its rivals and political antagonists cannot be underestimated, nor can its cumulative capacity to influence the industrial and regulatory context in which the BBC has to operate.

The second paradox takes us to the BBC's democratic responsibilities. For all the competitive ratings and the range of output, the BBC's services have marginalised the interests and social experience of many of Britain's minority groups. The lack of representation on screen has been matched by the BBC's reluctance as an employer to redress its poor record on equal employment and promotion for staff from ethnic minorities. These linked failures undermine public belief in the BBC's commitment to representing Britain's component cultures and peoples and the mature cosmopolitanism of its urban life. As in previous periods in its history, when criticisms of class and regional bias were to the fore, there are sections of the public profoundly alienated from the BBC. That alienation is in itself a force that turns some audiences towards commercial radio and satellite television – services that appear untainted by alienation since they are based on a simple consumer relation rather than the expectations of citizenship. It is precisely because the BBC claims universality – the right to speak to and for the 'nation' – that it needs urgently to address these issues.

The paradoxes matter in themselves. But they matter also because together they come to the heart of the BBC's struggle. The first paradox is parasitic on the second. The favoured rhetoric used by those – politicians, rivals, pundits – hostile to the BBC is one of consumer choice and diversity, a form of words in which the BBC's failure adequately to respond to the cultural interests of Britain's working class, its youth, its black and Asian populations is dressed up in the now common-sense terms of market-based consumer sovereignty. The cleverness of the campaign waged by the likes of Murdoch and his political allies is to exploit the BBC's cultural–democratic weaknesses to denounce its very existence. The market solution is posed as though it alone can solve the 'democratic deficit' in Britain's media culture.

For all the BBC's genuine achievements, including, most simply, the continued production of a stream of good programmes across a spectrum of genres, the last decade has seen a general degradation in the output of Britain's television system. Such a degradation is also characteristic of some BBC programming, but it is neither led by the BBC nor limited to it. Indeed the reduction in quality is more advanced among its commercial rivals. There are two linked arguments to support the view that the BBC is not leading this trend. First, to justify its licence fee funding, the BBC has to make popular television and it has to show that it is popular among the majority of viewers and listeners by competing, in these shows, for ratings. It has to make popular television in order to win the hearts as well as the minds of the viewing public. This was understood from the outset by Reith; entertainment has always been a vital part of the BBC's broadcast mix, as much as information and education. Second, the BBC has to respond to its rivals, since the popular broadcasters together set the tone of output across British broadcasting as a whole. They create together a broadcasting culture or ecology. The intense competition caused by the proliferation of new channels in Britain has had two overall negative effects. It has caused declining budgets and a blossoming of cheap programming. As importantly, it has caused a rush for the centre-ground of programming, producing a risk-averse broadcast culture in which imitation, populism and sensationalism have become rife. The BBC, which of necessity must follow as well as court public tastes, has been impelled to join the rush downmarket. While these entirely exogenous forces have made their destructive mark, internal pressures during the nineties exacerbated these trends.

Given these problems it is tempting either to consign the BBC to being a relic, or to defend it wholesale against the destructive forces ranged against it. I chose a different route. As an anthropologist I decided to study the BBC from the inside. Was it as inefficient and elitist as its critics maintained? How did it come to make some programmes and not others? Was it more like a bureaucracy or a business? Was it dominated by 'producer interests' or by accountants and management consultants? Above all, how was this old institution meeting the challenge of reinventing itself in uncertain and inauspicious new times?

*

Meet the secretary

It's early days in my negotiations with the BBC before the study begins. Through a friend, my first move has been to contact the secretary of the BBC, the top bureaucrat, whose role is to liaise between the governors and the director-general. We talk, he seems reasonably open, and he asks me to send him my first book. This is a critical study of a well-known Parisian avant-garde computer music institution, in which I employ psychoanalysis and other esoteric intellectual aids. When we next speak, he exhibits the kind of artful understatement that must be a prerequisite for the job. He comments that my book is 'very interesting – perhaps *too* interesting for the BBC'. He says he perceives there may be an openness to my study; in fact the MD of Television has suggestions. Why don't I focus on science programming and the Community Programme Unit? I reply evenly that I had other departments in mind – possibly Drama and somewhere in News. He skips a beat, which tells me I'm on to something, and advises that while he can't encourage me, nothing can prevent me approaching these areas on my own. I do, and in due course, six months later in the case of news, they fall into place. I reflect later on their attribution to me of an extraordinary naivety in thinking I would be confined to two minor, quintessentially 'public service' genres. Instead, I do my best to wade in and feel the currents in the cultural turmoil that is the BBC.

Diary, 1995.

*

The excited eye

'Charles Denton, the BBC's head of Drama, is in a lather of excitement at the impending arrival of Dr Georgina Born, a London University academic who has been commissioned to undertake an "anthropologically based study" of his department. "I have invited her to sit in on any meeting in which I am involved, with free access to any and all paperwork," he announces in a memo to his staff. "I am fascinated by the potential of dealing with Drama as a unique tribe within the Corporation."'

Private Eye, 6 October 1995.

*

'Is that anthropologist woman here?'

I have come to one of the regular Offers meetings in which Drama Group exhibits its wares before the television channel controllers. This one is with Alan Yentob, the

12

charismatic controller of BBC1, considered by some the artistic heart of BBC Television. To me, Yentob has been both wary and friendly; encouraged by the head of Drama Group, Charles, to go along with my study, he has allowed me to observe these and other meetings. Today some thirty people are sitting around a giant table in an anonymous executive suite in Television Centre. Yentob walks in late followed by an entourage of four women. The usual rhythm of pitch and discussion begins. Karl Francis, head of drama in BBC Wales, talks up *Panama Row*, a potential long-running series at £75k per episode, of which Wales is willing to put up £25k. Yentob muses: 'Because of the price range, and the setting in Wales, I'm prepared to look at it very seriously. But there's no point in patronising anyone. The scripts have to be good. We'll look at the schedule. It will have to compete with the successor to *Crown Prosecutor*, currently being reworked – there's only one 30-minute slot available pre-watershed on weekdays.' Yentob adds, of *Crown Prosecutor*, 'The public's still hot for it.' Next up, *The Lakes*: Yentob is very keen, it's almost certain for 'greenlighting'. 'Is Charlie [*Pattinson – producer of recent hit* Our Friends in the North] on board?' George Faber, head of single drama, confirms. Yentob says how pleasing it is that the next Jimmy McGovern drama will be with the BBC: 'It'll be good to have a writer saying nice things for once about the BBC!', a sore spot for Drama Group, and they titter nervously. Discussion centres on the format: what will suit the schedule, six times fifty minutes or one times seventy-five plus four times fifty? This is left hanging and they move to cost. Using the slipstream of good humour, Charles adds casually, 'It's £550k per episode.' Yentob quietly replies, 'I remember when it was £150k per thirty minutes.' But the tension rapidly diffuses and we laugh: Yentob has been reeled in.

Half an hour later, my attention has drifted as I jot rapid notes on a telling exchange that has just occurred. Suddenly I notice a lull; as in a dream, I hear Yentob say belligerently, 'Is that anthropologist woman here?' He fixes me with a stare: 'Look, I don't mind you being here – really – as long as I have copyright in everything I say, OK?' The room is hushed; all eyes are on me. Taken aback, I grin and shrug reassurance, saying nothing. The meeting resumes.

A few days later I meet Yentob. With warmth and an air of vague complicity, he credits my study with weight and credibility. But to start, we fence on issues of permission and control. I remind him of the Offers meeting. Archly, smiling, I say, 'You didn't mean "hard" editorial control, did you?', to which preposterous suggestion Yentob, also smiling, demurs.

Diary, 1996.

*

13

The invisible anthropologist

I'm sitting in on a BBC1 branding meeting. Michael Jackson, now controller of BBC1, smiled at me when I arrived and invited me in. My stock is up. As the meeting closes the head of marketing, Sue Farr, drifts out and pauses in passing, curious, to say hello. I explain who I am and what I do. 'How fascinating! We must meet . . . I'd love to talk,' she purrs. Days later I pick up the thread and phone her office. Can I come and see Sue Farr? We met at a branding meeting, she was keen to talk, I explain. The secretary insists she must check with Sue. Later that day she comes back: could I submit some questions? Sue is very busy, it may be some time. Each week in the following months I fax or phone again. August comes and goes, the summer break. Sue's secretary has changed her tune: she is peremptory and dismissive. Sue wants to find out who I am and who has authorised this study. I say that Will Wyatt, chief of Broadcast, signed off the study. I phone again two weeks later. The secretary says: 'We spoke to several people; no one knows who you are.' I don't get an interview with Sue Farr.

Diary, 1997.

*

I am an unusual social anthropologist, one who works on western cultural institutions. In 1995, I began to research the BBC in the context of the wider television industry. Between 1996 and 1998, with follow-up studies in 2001 and 2003, I carried out fieldwork inside the corporation, the most sustained study of this kind for over twenty years. The fieldwork provides the basis for the analysis that follows. The focus is the mid to late nineties, the mature years of the Birt regime, a period that, even following Dyke's tenure, remains decisive for the state of the contemporary BBC. Sometimes called 'participant observation' or ethnography, anthropological fieldwork is a method that involves living among or hanging out with the people being studied. In earlier times anthropologists were almost entirely concerned with the study of non-western societies, which were often conceived as exotic or 'primitive'. Attention was given to how they were similar to and different from ourselves – in rationality and beliefs, social and economic organisation. Now, most anthropologists recognise that even the most apparently familiar aspects of western culture are susceptible to the same kinds of analysis and are equally strange when given sufficient scrutiny. Whatever the setting, the aim of the anthropologist is to become immersed in the everyday culture, language and thought of the natives, so as to become sensitive to unspoken assumptions and implicit forms of knowledge and belief.

14

Fieldwork is uniquely good at generating two other kinds of insight. It is a sharp tool for discerning not just the unifying features but the divisions, boundaries and conflicts of the society being studied – conflicts so charged that they may be suppressed, or alluded to only in throwaway remarks, or in humour. Fieldwork makes it possible to explore the differences between what is said in publicity or in the boardroom and what happens on the ground in the studio, office or cleaning station. It is by probing the gaps between principles and practice, management claims and ordinary working lives – between what is explicit and implicit – that a fuller grasp of reality can be gleaned. One of the marks of social power is how it enables those who hold it to determine the very framework of what can be said and even thought in a given social space. To understand any organisation, it is therefore imperative to uncover not only what is insistently present, but the characteristic absences and rigidities – what cannot be thought, or what is systematically 'outside'.

These fieldwork tools have been essential in understanding the BBC. Any large organisation, with its internal divisions, its rituals of self-justification, its management pretensions and disgruntled workforce, will yield up at least some of its internal complexities and secrets to anthropological study. The BBC, undergoing permanent revolution and extraordinarily volatile during the later nineties, seemed a good place for an anthropologist to set up camp. My fieldwork focused primarily on two sites in BBC Television. I spent more than a year in and around Drama Group, the largest and most costly production outfit. Drama Group was notorious within the BBC in the later nineties, a troubled place in which many of the BBC's key structural problems surfaced. Drama output is critical for the popularity of the BBC as well as for its cultural aspirations. Increasingly, television schedules are built around popular drama, and the battle between channels is often played out on the territory of popular series and soaps. Drama is also a locus of broadcasters' most ambitious and high-cost programming, so-called 'landmarks' or 'events'. But it has another kind of symbolic importance, since debates over the relative quality of British and American television often focus on drama. In this sense British television drama, and BBC Drama centrally within this, frequently bears the burden of justifying the British system of public service broadcasting as a whole. The state of Drama Group was therefore a prime concern of BBC management.

I also spent several months around the time of the 1997 general election observing the flagship programme *Newsnight*, a hybrid of news and current affairs often considered exemplary of the BBC's journalistic ideals. Famed for its powers of analysis and energetic political interviews, this was a good period in which to trace the programme's political stance and to take stock of shifts within the BBC's journalism of impartiality. Developments around Drama and *Newsnight* provide many of the examples in what follows.

Less intensive fieldwork took in parts of BBC News and factual programming including Documentaries, Current Affairs, the Community Programme Unit (CPU), and the 1997–8 News Programme Strategy Review. Through Drama and Documentaries I had some access to the channel controllers and their offices of strategists, schedulers and broadcast analysts. In each place, fieldwork involved observing and talking to people from all levels of the hierarchy, from script readers, researchers, secretaries and receptionists to the many tiers of BBC creatives and bosses. To gain a broader view of common developments across the corporation I interviewed executives and producers from other parts of the BBC including Entertainments Group, the World Service, Radios 1 and 3, Worldwide and the major regional centres. Occasionally, I did some broadcasting for Radio 3 and so became a full participant. A high point was when I presented, with Geoffrey Smith and Roderick Swanston, Radio 3's Millennium Eve show, an eighteen-hour overview of two thousand years of western music. I kept my parallel selves – anthropologist and broadcaster – pretty much apart. But I also experienced the arbitrary treatment dished out to freelancers – a kind of master/slave relationship – when I presented another show a few years earlier. I thought it was good, but, without explanation, I was never asked back. Such are the travails of the freelancer, and to be able to re-enter the doors of Broadcasting House wearing my anthropologist's hat provided – I admit – a kind of solace.

The research also took a wider perspective, examining the BBC's place in the television industry. I interviewed independent producers working with the BBC as well as representatives from other broadcasters, the regulators, trade unions and trade organisations, and some television critics. I attended industry and policy events, keeping a close eye on the drift of politics and ideas. All in all the study generated some 220 interviews, eight large field diaries, and many files of documents and cuttings.

The task of the anthropologist is to experience the culture from within. But gaining access to the BBC was onerous from the outset and remained taxing throughout the fieldwork. The process of gaining agreement to the study was like waging a military campaign. I planned assaults on several fronts, and finally broke through the defences. The resulting agreement was initially on rather loose terms; 'the lawyers' had been mentioned in an early phone call, but reference to this intimidating totem never recurred. Yet in the Birt period I had no official aid whatsoever from the BBC and repeatedly met barriers; any cooperation I did receive was limited and uneven, and access had continually to be renegotiated. What seemed open to observation often in practice became closed from view. A thread running through the book is my exclusion from a number of places that I wanted to observe. It signals the closure, secrecy and paranoia that suffuses the BBC and its operations, a degree of which may be understandable given the unceasing criticism faced by the corporation. However, with this in mind I had agreed not to publish and to abstain from journalism for some years after the study. The closure reeked of an arrogance often noted by observers of the BBC, and one that belies its rhetoric of account-ability. Inside the corporation the closure was acknowledged, and it resonated with the experience of many staff. As an executive assistant charged with tight-ening control over my study said to me in amazement, 'I can't understand how you ever got in here. This is the most secretive organisation.' While frustrating in the extreme, there was a bleak humour in all of this: the ironies of studying a public institution apparently committed to accountability, but reluctant to have its operations scrutinised; of doing a fly-on-the-wall study of those who make fly-on-the-wall documentaries.

At the same time, I was fortunate in gaining an extraordinary amount of cooperation from people at all levels of the BBC. BBC Scotland, to name one location, made me completely welcome and gave me astonishingly open access. I became a kind of psychoanalyst of the institution, in whom individu-als entrusted private thoughts, theories and anxieties. The BBC was an unhappy place for many staff in the nineties, and knowing that I was interviewing numerous others across the corporation, they hoped I would piece together the larger picture – or, at least, a more integrated account than they felt capa-ble of. Thanks to their trust and the requisite persistence of the anthropologist, the fieldwork proved rich.

*

Openness

I'm meeting Stephen Lambert, editor of Modern Times and a rising star in the Documentaries department. We sit in his glass-walled office having coffee and he puts me at ease. I am going to spend time observing his section in the coming weeks. Casually, he looks at his watch and says he has a meeting to go to. Would I like to come? We set off down the endless corridors of the White City building and emerge at the office of his boss, the head of Documentaries, Paul Hamann. We go in and Paul greets us and bids us sit down. Glancing at some papers he launches into a discussion of Stephen's year: what has gone well, what routinely, what spectacularly. Stephen's first act has been to bring me – the fly on the wall – along to his annual staff appraisal meeting.

Diary, 1997.

*

Thriller

I have hit a slow period. Trying to make the shift from Drama Group to watching the controllers and their teams of commissioners and strategists, things have got sticky and little cooperation is forthcoming. A letter suddenly arrives, apparently from five senior figures with whom I have had contact, although one – the head of Drama Group – denies any knowledge of the letter or its demands. The senders require tighter control over my study. My morale is low and I panic. I read about a woman who made an inside study of the Royal Court Theatre and was prevented from publishing when the theatre management slapped an injunction on her. I decide to take advice. Through a friend, I am put in touch with a civil liberties barrister who gives me his time for free, for which I am enormously grateful. However, in the face of many grey areas, in my eyes he is unable to give me black-and-white advice. It takes me an anxious month to write a four-page reply to the BBC letter, yielding on some issues and reasoning why I should not on others. I never receive an acknowledgement or reply to this letter.

I also contact a senior ex-BBC executive, no friend of the current regime, who almost made it to director-general and will be able to tell me what kinds of tactics BBC management employ to deal with unwanted attention. I meet this man, now running a large cultural organisation, in his plush office. Believing him to be an intellectual, I have brought him one of my books as a gift. With aching condescension, he asks what I am doing. Following my explanation, he smiles in an avuncular fashion and tells me to give up the study. Getting into his stride, he says that BBC management are utterly ruthless, that 'if they don't like what you are doing, they'll do anything to stop you publishing short of running you down in the street'. Dazed, and for all his hyperbole, I find I am the victim of a genre deception! I had thought I was an anthropologist studying a privileged and powerful tribe. Imperceptibly, the ground has shifted under my feet. I am in fact the protagonist in a contemporary thriller set in the media world. Satisfied that he has accomplished a result – warning me off – he bids me goodbye. I've had no offer to intercede, no discussion of the issues; it is hard to believe that he has taken me seriously. Does this indicate, I reflect as I leave, the lack of respect in which academia is held by the cultural establishment?

Diary, 1996.

*

The fieldwork dream

Mid-fieldwork, my access to observe the controller of BBC1, Michael Jackson, and his team had come and gone without clear reason. Jackson and I had met, warmly, several times to discuss terms: yes, I could watch, he could well understand the interest of ethnographic work on scheduling and other controller activities; but could he wield a blue pencil to my writings?, etc. Suddenly his secretary wouldn't answer my calls. I had a dream one night: I am meeting Michael in his office on the sixth floor of Television Centre, where he was famous for having stylish toys – vintage toy cars, juggling balls – on his coffee table, with which he played, walking around, while thinking and talking. We are seated in large sofas talking with several other people; it is an amiable, apparently informal occasion. Suddenly I notice he has five darts in his hand with which he is playing. One by one, he lobs the darts my way in a parabolic arc and they lodge themselves in my ankle – my Achilles heel? It hurts and bleeds. I am shocked. He continues to sit chatting amiably to people. I wake feeling terrified of the subtexts. Am I being toyed with? What vulnerability of mine is he playing on?

Diary, 1996.

*

The book begins with an overview of the history of the BBC from Reith to the ascension of Labour to government in 1997. Chapters 2 to 9 give a portrait of the BBC's functioning in the Birt era, analysing a series of cumulative challenges and obstacles thrown up in the path of programme-making as a consequence of the structural changes introduced by the government and BBC management. These include the internal markets and accounting procedures associated with Producer Choice; the rise of independent production, new business operations and a culture of entrepreneurialism; the effects of casualised employment and of contractual relations between creative staff and the corporation; the introduction of the 'new public management' styled on the private sector, with its habitual recourse to auditing and management consultancy; and the relentless rise of audience research within the BBC. Chapters 8 and 9 detail the impact of the changes on production, focusing respectively on drama and on news, current affairs and documentaries, with a case study of Newsnight. Although aspects of BBC radio are included in the analysis, indicating developments across the corporation, the focus of the book is primarily on television; and the BBC story gives wider insight into the enormous changes that occurred in the later nineties in how British television is made. If the book does not summarise the programme highlights of the Birt and Dyke periods, that remains for the historians. Instead, in later chapters I probe selected areas of programming to exemplify larger issues. The last chapter brings the story to the present. It outlines the changes made by Dyke as director-general and assesses the first phase of the BBC's digital strategies. It considers the conditions that lay behind and the impact of the Hutton crisis. It reflects on the dangers inherent in accelerating government interventions in relation to the BBC. Finally, in the context of the rampant commercialisation and globalisation of broadcasting, the Epilogue addresses the uncertain outlook for the BBC and the future role of public service broadcasting in the twenty-first century.

Throughout the book I make lavish use of the wealth of ethnographic materials. Each chapter is filled with 'stories': interviews, dialogues and meetings, scenes observed, anecdotes and revelations, and excerpts from broadcasts and from other people's writings. Occasionally, I have provided a fictional document based loosely on a real original. The stories can be lengthy, always with illustrative point. They are often allusive or allegorical, and sometimes vaguely confessional. The interviews and field diaries provide a vivid and eloquent counterpoint to the main analytical narrative, but they also carry the narrative forward. More often than not they provide concrete manifestations of the themes discussed; but some are only indirectly related and are intended to give a broader sense of context and of the flavour of the times. Sometimes the stories clash and contradict one another, conveying a sense of debate and disagreement; at other times they confirm one another. There is no temporal unity to the stories: they range from 1995 to the present, although the majority come from 1996 to 1998 and 2001. Interviews have been lightly edited, and to protect my sources they are usually attributed generally via an individual's occupational status or location. Individuals mentioned are sometimes disguised, except when the identity of the person in question is so obvious as to make this meaningless. Quotations from published sources are attributed in notes, with full references given in the end material, and are reproduced by kind permission. All of this material is used with gratitude.

A study like this depends on the help of a large number of people, and I assured most of my informants that I would not name them. I am much indebted to these individuals for their time and confidences. Cathy Wearing and Tatiana Kennedy provided my initial ports of entry to the BBC and Charles Denton let me in, and I remain extremely grateful. Charles Denton, Michael Wearing, George Faber, Ruth Caleb, Suzan Harrison, Kevin Loader and much of the Drama Group, Chris Pye, Mike Phillips, Peter Horrocks, Mark Damazer, Richard Ayre, Giles Oakley, Stephen Lambert, Peter Dale, Paul Hamann, Matthew Bannister, Andy Parfitt, Ken McQuarrie and Colin Cameron were exemplary in their support for the study. Thanks also to Michael Jackson, Alan Yentob, Will Wyatt and David Docherty for generously (if ambivalently) allowing me access. For skilled assistance I thank Geoff Kemp, Caroline Brown, John Bovill and David Steinberg. I am grateful to colleagues in the Department of Media and Communications at Goldsmiths College, London, and the Faculty of Social and Political Sciences at Cambridge University, to the Provost and Fellows of King's College, Cambridge, and the Master and Fellows of Emmanuel College, Cambridge, for their forbearance during the study and its writing up. King's gave me a senior research fellowship to work on the early stages of this book, but I ended up writing another overdue book, and I apologise for this late delivery. A number of colleagues gave feedback and help, for which I thank Steve Barnett, Patrick Barwise, Jonathan Bignall, Jay Blumler, John Corner, John Ellis, Steve Feld, Faye Ginsburg, Michael Gurevitch, Justin Lewis, George Marcus, Brian McNair, Richard Paterson, Steve Pratten, Tony Prosser, Glen Rangwala, Paul Ryan, Paddy Scannell, Philip Schlesinger, Wilf Stevenson, Marilyn Strathern, Janet Willis and Janet Wolff. From the broadcasting industry, for their input I thank Tony Garnett, Bob Towler and John Willis. For responses to the report on which the book is based I thank Carolyn Fairbairn, Peter Horrocks, Will Wyatt and several others. Giles Oakley, Kevin Loader and a number of other BBC and ex-BBC figures commented on the manuscript, and I am grateful for their serious engagement. The Economic and Social Research Council made the study possible. Stuart Weir suggested a source of legal advice and Cyril Glasser generously provided it. Romesh Vaitilingam, Simon Garfield and Patrick Wright gave useful publishing leads. My agent Malcolm Imrie made me feel welcome and has added greatly to what I have made of this work. Geoff Mulligan and Stuart Williams, my editors, have shown immense warmth, patience and commitment.

This book was written in difficult circumstances. David Holzer and family, Nancy Fresella Lee and Peter Lee, Ros Ramsay and Jeremy Gray, Cathy Wearing and Michael Baker, and above all Gustav and Faith Born gave moral support and the use of homes from home. Nicky Manby provided an inspiring place to write via the intercession of Toby and Ginny Farrell. Thanks to Antony Warren, Gill Evans and Peter Baxter for much needed help. Simon Frith was unfailingly supportive, offering wise intellectual and human counsel, and the first reader of an ungainly manuscript. But the hero of the tale is my partner Andrew Barry, who kept the family going throughout with characteristic kindness and fortitude. He has also overseen the project's intellectual zest and coherence, although I alone am responsible for the final cut. For Theo and Clara, I hope this book points in the direction of a better television than they have sometimes encountered growing up, and compensates just a little for my regrettable and repeated absences.

All four of my parents symbolise an era now passing. My late stepfather, George Mully, child of Russian Jewish immigrants to the Bronx, was an innovative director of theatre and opera who took me along to his rehearsals as a child. His legacy is my fascination with creative processes. Sitting at the back of the stage observing his dialogues with actors and singers are formative experiences etched in my memory. My father, Gustav Born, his boyhood marked by exile from Nazi Germany, was brought up in and then enriched Britain's scientific culture. He bequeaths me memories of his creative scientific work and of the importance of unremitting curiosity and good observation. My mother and stepmother, Ann Mully and Faith Born, grew into adulthood at the time of the flowering of the welfare state and became doctors, and Ann also a psychoanalyst, committed to an ethic of skilled care and concern. Together they embody an era when the principle that professional life is engaged in an open-ended commitment to the general social good, manifest always in the particular, was not in question, nor corroded by envious political and bureaucratic attacks. This book is dedicated to them all, with love, admiration and gratitude.

Georgina Born
Cambridge, June 2004.

Prehistory: The BBC from
Reith to the Tories

Reports from the front: New Labour's 1996 party conference

30 September: the Winter Gardens in Blackpool. I am here with the *Newsnight* team to observe this last Labour Party conference before the general election at which, it is widely believed, after eighteen years of Conservative rule in Britain, New Labour is likely to come to power under Tony Blair. I am also here to observe *Newsnight*'s reporting of this critical rite of passage.

From the train up, it has been clear that the mood of journalists is one of an irrepressible imperative – both mischievous and apparently principled – to stir things up. The consensus is that the conference will be uninteresting and excessively controlled. They are appalled by Labour's aggressive stage management and smartness, by the staged spectacle of unity. As one journalist tells me, 'The entire Labour Party now wears tailored business suits!' There are likely to be very few splits. The one exception could be the debate on pensions, an issue stirred up by Barbara Castle and her followers in recent months, who want pensions linked to earnings and not the meaner Retail Price Index. Peter Horrocks, editor of *Newsnight*, whom I meet on the train, says that a split will be avoided by a deal stitched up between Castle et al and Labour's National Executive Committee, in which the NEC will promise to set up a standing commission on pensions once they are in power.

Later, I am in a café and I meet Peter Townsend, veteran sociologist and an ally of Castle's. He tells me the fight isn't over, that he and Castle are not doing deals with the NEC. Wednesday's debate may still involve a big row.

Diary, 1996.

*

Securing the Winter Gardens: the think tank talks sports rights

It's 6 p.m. on the second day of the Labour conference. The leading New Labour think tank, the IPPR, is holding a fringe event on sports rights and broadcasting at the Park Royal Hotel. I walk along the seafront towards the venue. Anna Coote and Gerry Holtham, leading figures in the IPPR, are heading there too. Baroness Margaret Jay is walking from the other direction, elegant and regal; she greets them effusively and joins them. These and similar moments make me realise I am witnessing a gathering of the incipient Labour ruling class, crowding in to be recognised for when the party finally comes to power.

I am a little early, so I sit in the hotel bar before the IPPR event. As I go and get a drink, some old, raddled, well-sozzled working-class northerners are hanging out around the bar. I take out my purse, but one of the men stops me paying and says, 'No, love! It's all on the CCC – you are going to the CCC, aren't you?' The northerners are joking together on the theme of security arrangements for the conference, which are tight and heavily policed. Of an acquaintance, one of them teases, 'Oh, they wouldn't let *him* into the conference! Security kept *him* out!' and they all fall about. It's a heavily ironic laughter and the subtext is clear: that their sort are too lowly, status- and class-wise, to be allowed into the conference by the New Labour security apparatus. There is a weariness just below the surface, and the symbolism they are squeezing out of the joke could not be more politically astute.

As I drink my lager, David Elstein – now chief executive of the recently launched Channel 5, and previously head of programmes for Rupert Murdoch's Sky Television – enters the bar. He warmly hails a large man, who is Lewis Moonie, the Labour shadow heritage and media spokesman, and a young man standing beside Moonie, Labour's shadow sports spokesman. They chat amiably, on first-name terms. Moonie to Elstein: 'How are you? Did you have a good journey?' Elstein: 'Yes, quite a pleasant one, thank you. How did today go?' – meaning Blair's speech to the conference, the big set piece, which is politically critical for Labour – 'How long was the ovation?', and so on, obsequiously. Elstein is smooth, sympathetic, warm to Moonie; I gasp at the mutual attempt to nurture relations between a key media boss and the government-in-waiting's media man.

The debate starts. Those speaking include Will Wyatt, chief executive of BBC Broadcast, Elstein, Moonie, Christina Murroni for the IPPR and a man from the Sports Federation. But the audience is peppered with other media luminaries; for such a small event the room is packed with VIPs. Moonie and Wyatt both speak in support of the 'list' of national events enshrined in the recent Broadcasting Act, which protects them for free-to-air terrestrial channels such as the BBC's. It's only eight events after all, representing 1 per cent of all televised sports. Wyatt adds placatingly that the list should be kept under review, and warns that, while the BBC has found more money for sports rights, there will always be a limit to what it can pay in future for key events. 'Unbundling' is a key issue for policy, he says: the disaggregation of different kinds of rights – for example live, highlights and radio play – so that one can have competitive markets, or specific protections, in relation to each. Moonie and Wyatt both conclude that highlights from all major sporting events should be protected by legislation from being monopolised by satellite and pay television. The lines have been drawn, in a gentlemanly manner.

Elstein, however, who until recently masterminded BSkyB's aggressive strategy of buying up football rights, takes off the gloves. He weighs in truculently, dissidently. The 'list' is problematic; it contains no women's sports! It is a very strange selection of events – take the Derby: what call does it have on the special status of protected event? It's an anachronism. He implies cleverly that the 'list' is an elite one dreamed up by elderly, male, white members of the establishment; it is not a people's list. He agrees with the man from the Sports Federation, who pointed to the vast growth in the value of sports rights: from £2.6 million in 1985, to £85 million this year, to a predicted £185 million next year. It was the BBC/ITV cartel that artificially suppressed the value of sports rights until the arrival of satellite television. Aiming for the jugular, he continues that it was this duopoly – our supposed public service broadcasters! – which deprived football of millions of pounds of revenue at the cost of hooliganism, dangerous stadiums and other ills. In a rhetorical tour de force Elstein has come very close to accusing the BBC of causing or exacerbating football hooliganism and the dilapidation of stadiums that led directly to disasters such as Hillsborough.

There is no way, Elstein concludes, to 'artificially' protect or set up boundaries around certain sports rights. There will always be ways round such barriers, and he talks of technological progress making it impossible to enact such protections in practice. His speech is an almost allegorical account of the inevitability of free markets and of the impotence of regulation in this crucial area of popular broadcasting. The BBC, he ends by implying, should stop resisting the inevitable: it should give up its futile attempts to maintain a presence of popular, national sports on free-to-air television. Of course, there is a deeper meaning to the allegory: the BBC should roll over and die as a popular broadcaster. It can simply no longer compete with pay television.

Diary, 1996.

*

No dissent: the missed film of *Tribune*

10 p.m. on the same day in the *Newsnight* corner of the newsroom: a report comes in from the *Tribune* rally earlier this evening saying that the left-wing MP Clare Short made

a critical speech in which she denounced 'these crushing times when we're not allowed to speak'. She continued by talking of this 'paralysing and constraining political period' in advance of the election which was 'paralysing our creativity' and assisting the political right. The *Newsnight* people are very excited by this first open sign of dissent: they agree that the presenter, Kirsty Wark, or *Newsnight*'s political correspondent, Mark Mardell, should refer to it in their pieces. But Karen O'Connor, the acting *Newsnight* editor in Blackpool, says dismissively that it's just a quote, that Short always hedges her bets. Their real problem is that they have no decent film of the *Tribune* rally. They had a cameraman there, but the BBC News crew said they would film it and share the film so the *Newsnight* crew could go. The *Newsnight* crew left, and now it transpires that the News crew left early and didn't get Clare Short on film!

O'Connor is very annoyed: typical, she says. I reflect that, with all these camera crews here, they manage to miss filming a crucial fringe event, known to be one of the sole likely sources of serious dissent and of critical left perspectives, and coming right after Blair's speech that afternoon. Due to this debacle *Newsnight* – and BBC News – have failed to do their journalistic part by bearing witness to dissent and differences within Labour, and by cracking open Labour's façade of party unity. As these events unfold, I pick up today's *Independent* newspaper and read an article that queries the BBC's need to have four hundred people at the conference. I muse on how strange it is that, for all this manning, there is both duplication of coverage and lack of coverage of significant events such as the *Tribune* rally: a portent of these broadcasting times.

Diary, 1996.

*

'A National Institution and a National Asset'[1]

The history of British broadcasting demonstrates the way that political intervention and political imagination have formed the broadcasting culture of a small but influential nation. It is a history of ideas and of fashions in ethics and aesthetics as they attach to changing technological possibilities. But it is also a history that suggests the importance of recognising the impact of individuals and events. The BBC came into being in 1922 as the British Broadcasting Company, a pragmatic arrangement between the Post Office and a cartel of radio-set manufacturers intended to provide radio content so as to promote the sale of wirelesses. It operated with revenues from a ten shilling licence fee on all sets sold, payable to the Post Office, and from a share of the royalties on each set sold by the manufacturers. The philosophy of public service broadcasting that came to govern the BBC and its licence fee funding began to emerge under the auspices of the Sykes Committee of 1923, set up to consider broadcasting in all its dimensions and the first of many subsequent government-sponsored committees to oversee British broadcasting.

The Sykes Committee proposed that broadcasting should be a 'public utility' and that the airwaves were 'public property'. It rejected the notion both of a commercial monopoly in broadcasting and of direct government controls. Instead, the Post Office was to have indirect controls by licensing any broadcasting station, stipulating its responsibilities and holding it answerable for its operations. As the historian Paddy Scannell puts it, 'The definition of broadcasting as a public utility to be developed as a national service in the public interest came from the state.'[2] It was John Reith, from 1923 to 1926 the company's first director-general and then, from 1927 to 1938, director-general of the British Broadcasting Corporation, who filled in the substance of that definition. Reith's conception remained both influential and controversial over the twentieth century. It is often dismissed as outdated. Reith was, after all, a Scottish Presbyterian and an engineer, moralistic and authoritarian in his dealings and apparently devoid of humour. But the life of ideas cannot be reduced to their author's character or intentions. Despite its paternalist origins, Reith's definition of public service broadcasting repays scrutiny and still has power.

Reith conceived of broadcasting as a social, cultural, educative and moral force. It should entertain, but it is not for entertainment alone; it must also inform and educate. Public service broadcasting should be committed to maintaining high standards and to leading rather than simply following public tastes. It must help to diffuse knowledge and bring the best in human culture into the greatest number of homes. 'He who prides himself on giving what he thinks the public wants is often creating a fictitious demand for lower standards which he himself will then satisfy.'[3] In defining British broadcasting, a primary factor in the thinking of Reith and his peers was their distaste for American commercial broadcasting, its profit motive and market-driven entertainment principle. The British system was to be defined against the American one. In this they reflected the critique of mass culture being propounded at the time by critics across the political spectrum.

In Reith's view, a national broadcasting system must fulfil major social and political functions. One influence here was the Victorian reformer Matthew Arnold, for whom culture was conceived as a way of lessening social divisions and class hostilities. Culture, according to Arnold, 'seeks to do away with classes; to make the best that has been thought and known in the world current everywhere'.[4] Reith portrayed his broadcasting ideal as a means of bringing together Britain's different classes and regional populations. It should reinforce social integration. Live broadcasts of major national events would have the effect of 'making the nation as one man'.[5] The pursuit of cultural values would have intrinsic social benefits. Politically, much was at stake. The first years of broadcasting in Britain coincided with the culmination of the struggle for political equality and the establishment of universal suffrage for all adult men and women; 'the development of mass democracy is closely connected with broadcasting's role in that process'.[6] But the inception of mass democracy brought challenges for liberal theory and profound anxieties for the upper classes and intellectual elites. The problem as they perceived it was the unready state of ordinary people for the responsibilities of citizenship; and the question was how to create the kind of informed and rational citizenry capable of exercising their political rights in a responsible way. Reith and his followers saw public service broadcasting as a central part of the solution. By telling ordinary people about the affairs of government, it would allow the electorate to consider policies and aid the development of a genuine public opinion. Broadcasting would enable people to become interested in ideas and areas of life to which they had no prior access. It would offer not only information but argument and discussion and so provide the means for people to reflect on political and intellectual alternatives. By fostering a reasoning citizenry, it would support the development of an inclusive, participatory and enlightened democracy.

A heady ideological brew underpinned Reith's vision, a combination of nationalism, Victorian ideals of service and of social reform, and the vaunted Arnoldian ideal of middle-class culture and education. But it drew also on the idea of the public interest, a radical tradition encompassing the fight for freedom of speech and assembly, for spaces of public debate and deliberation in which the actions of church and state could be scrutinised and government held to account. This radical movement for instituting the concept of public interest played a leading part both in the victory of representative democracy and, culturally, in the establishment and shape of the BBC.[7]

It was Reith's achievement to turn these ideals into practice. He did this through three central measures, all of which turn on different senses of universality. First, universal availability: a national service meant that the entire population of the United Kingdom should be able to receive a high-quality broadcast signal. Second, there was a commitment to a form of social and cultural universality, in that the BBC undertook to produce both a national and a regional programme service. The audience was conceived both as a unity and as socially and culturally diverse. The BBC was to be an impartial arbiter, assessing the various constituencies and tastes and responding accordingly. Third, there was a universality of genre in the policy of mixed programming. From the outset, BBC radio broadcast a wide range of genres each day and week, including news, talks, sports, drama, religion, light entertainment and a variety of music – both popular and classical. Crucially, mixed programming was not devised purely instrumentally as a means of tempting the uneducated on to better things. For all Reith's high-minded statements about cultural leadership, in practice the corporation soon showed a real commitment to entertainment as an essential part of what the BBC must provide for its licence-fee-paying public. The realisation was that, to achieve its complex ends, the BBC must attract a mass audience and must be truly popular. In the 1930s this policy bore fruit; as one historian notes with some ambivalence, 'by 1934 the BBC was broadcasting more light music, comedy and vaudeville than any other European station'.[8]

The BBC's monopoly allowed a kind of cultural dictatorship, but one that was highly inventive. From the vantage point of the present it is hard to grasp the radical cultural impact of the mixed schedule as national radio first developed. Formally, it was one of the first sustained experiments in the juxtaposition of cultural genres. The audience was offered an entirely new experience in which factual and fictional, high and low, the serious and the humorous jostled alongside one another. Decades later, the critic Raymond Williams portrayed this quality of broadcasting as having ideological propensities in its capacity to seduce the audience and to hide contradictions.[9] But Williams's judgement was too harsh, for this kind of programming has other effects: it enables each genre to comment implicitly on the qualities and the limits of other genres. For the audience, mixed programming offered a first expanded cultural experience that represented something of the increasingly complex and chaotic nature of modern urban life.

The early BBC attempted to tame this potentially unruly aspect of broadcasting. It did so by adopting a 'middle-brow' tone in its light entertainment, a tone that itself embodied a public service mission of socialising listeners into middle-class values of neighbourliness, community and responsibility. Relaxation for the working-class audience must be educative and wholesome; it must avoid excess. The early broadcasters imagined their listeners either as members of an orderly family or as grateful and dutiful citizens.[10] Yet by the mid 1930s this 'uplifting' approach was questioned as a concern arose with what listeners actually wanted. A Listener Research Unit was established in 1936 charged with providing information on listeners' tastes. Audience research henceforth became a vital force in the BBC's internal politics. In discussions of music and variety output, research took the role of representing existing audience tastes to producers. Reithian 'uplift' was a good thing, but only in moderation. As war approached in 1939, struggles arose in the Music department over whether to maintain the commitment to classical and 'difficult' music or increase the amount of popular music to meet changing audience tastes. Adrian Boult, head of Music, fought against the move to 'lighter programming'. He was overruled by the Programme Planning department, which cited listener research and brought in the changes without his consent.

Meanwhile, in entertainment, lessons were being learned from Radio Luxembourg and American radio. The BBC loosened its style and became more knowingly populist, realising that regular entertainment programmes could draw a massive audience. Variety shows, quizzes and parlour games flourished. From 1938, the BBC had a huge popular success with Arthur Askey's *Band Waggon*, a show replete with aural mayhem, inverted logic, surreal fantasy and teasing references to the BBC itself. The show became a cult; its catchphrases passed into everyday language. It 'succeeded in creating a genuinely common culture on the air'.[11] Even in its early decades, the BBC began to produce shows that playfully satirised the corporation, while the organisation itself contained animated reflections on and intense conflicts over its proper cultural role. Paternalist it may have been; but claims that it was unreflectively elitist are put in perspective both by evidence of the early successes in popular programming, and by the attempts made to understand audience tastes.

There were contradictions within the BBC's practice. For Reith, the BBC's de facto monopoly was another core principle, since only with total centralised control could the corporation establish and maintain high standards and sustain its influence. During the later 1920s, despite the avowed commitment to British diversity, this meant the closure of the network of amateur and informal local radio stations that had grown up around the country and flourished alongside the BBC. In this way the BBC effectively converted British radio into a centralised medium as opposed to its earlier form, a form that approximated Bertolt Brecht's dictum of the 1920s that radio could become a democratic network of two-way communication and politicisation. By incorporating local stations in the name of the 'national interest', the BBC diminished the representative and diverse character of early British radio. As a result, by 1930 local radio had disappeared; British 'cultural diversity' was in the hands of five BBC regional centres that were institutionally and culturally subordinate to the BBC in London. Yet the BBC regions resisted that subordination, and clashes over programming occurred throughout the 1930s. Debates, dissent and dissatisfaction about the nature and the degree of representation of the regions and nations by the BBC have continued to the present.

Equally contradictory is the relationship between the BBC and the state, which spills over into the corporation's stance on politics. A critical factor in the political character of the BBC is its constitutional status. The BBC's existence has depended from the outset on a Royal Charter, renewed every ten years subject to parliamentary review of its performance. The Charter specifies the BBC's objectives, functions and financial operations. The BBC is a public corporation overseen by governors who act as 'trustees to safeguard the broadcasting service in the national interest'.[12] The Board of Governors is responsible for broad matters of policy and strategy, and for oversight of management. Constitutionally, 'the Board is the BBC. It holds the legal title to BBC property.'[13] The governors are appointed on the recommendation of the government. Not only the periodic renewal of the Charter and the make-up of the governors, but the financing of the BBC is also dependent on the state. The level of the licence fee and ultimate regulation of any additional income-generating activities are in the hands of the state. If the government is at odds with the BBC or wants to exert pressure on the corporation, it has these three formidable weapons at its disposal. Time and again in the BBC's history, they have been used.

Yet the BBC is not formally a direct instrument of state. While the government keeps it on a short lead, as an institution the BBC has a real autonomy, deepened over the decades by the growth of a powerful and recalcitrant professionalism. For all their awareness of the governors and the impact of external pressures, BBC journalists and programme-makers are not simply the creatures of the governors of the day, let alone of the government. Hence the inherent tension within the BBC: part child of state interests, part watchdog on the state. But there is another central tension, and this concerns the accountability of the BBC. Despite its tethering to the government and its apparatus of self-regulation, according to one authoritative commentator for much of its existence the BBC was not 'even indirectly accountable to Parliament' and lacked 'effective accountability'.[14]

A Notorious Syllogism?

In the fragile earliest years of the corporation, Reith faced the problem of state control. At the time of the General Strike of May 1926, in a memorandum to senior staff explaining the BBC's pro-government tone and controversial internal policies (such as the directive that 'nothing calculated to extend the area of the strike should be broadcast'), Reith wrote that 'since the BBC was a national institution, and since the government in this crisis were acting for the people . . . the BBC was for the government in this crisis too'. In this 'notorious syllogism', Reith appeared to elide government interests with the interests of the people and of the nation; yet the strike had been declared illegal by the High Court and there was little space for manoeuvre.[15] Months later, negotiating the terms of the first charter, and in subsequent years, Reith fought furiously for the BBC's right to deal with politics and 'controversy' in its broadcasts. His stance was that, to be trusted as an independent source of information, the BBC must provide listeners with news and debate on public and political matters. In November 1926, in the first charter, this right was curtailed by a nervous Parliament; but in March 1928, the government relented and granted the BBC greater latitude to deal with controversy.

Historians of the BBC have different views on Reith's achievements in the 1930s on the critical question of the BBC's independence and the political stance of its journalism. Jean Seaton maintains that the BBC's political culture was laid down in its early years. She characterises the BBC's stance as a 'denial of politics', arguing that Reith despised politicians and believed the BBC should be above politics.[16] Under the continuous pressure of the government, she comments, 'the General Strike marks the end of the propaganda based on lies and the start of a more subtle tradition of selection and presentation . . . The BBC emerged from the crisis with an ethic of political neutrality . . . expressed as much in the tone of its broadcasts as in any formal regulation.' Throughout the 1930s, Seaton says, a pattern recurred in which 'the BBC was forced to pass off government intervention as its own decision'.[17] She points to unhealthy links with the Foreign Office and the civil service at the same time as the corporation sought to become part of the establishment. Seaton argues that these processes fed the emergence of a culture in which 'journalists stopped being passionate advocates [and] saw themselves rather as independent professionals, and their writing as a nego-tiated product of conflict between partisan views'. In this culture, 'politics was an activity which only happened between major political parties. Two kinds of politics never reached the air waves: divisions within parties and the expressive politics of the street.'[18] Seaton illustrates with telling incidents middle-class producers' awkwardness when having to deal with members of the working class or trade unionists. The implication is that the BBC's professional journalism of impartiality and of the mediation of party politics was born of defensiveness and expediency. It is a journalism that was formed by over-close relations with the state; and it is a journalism that, over decades, has aided a widespread depoliticisation.

Paddy Scannell and David Cardiff portray a more complex set of forces during the 1930s. They trace the waxing and waning of the Talks department's attempts to offer independent insight into major social problems, such as unemployment and poverty, through new forms of eyewitness reportage. By the mid 1930s, faced with government displeasure and under the pressure of charter renewal in 1935, caution took hold and 'there was a marked retreat from dealing with contentious issues'.[19] The same result was evident in the BBC's failure, despite internal advocacy, to take an independent stance from the government in the later 1930s by preparing the public for war – a failure that caused widespread dismay within the BBC and which the then ex-head of News criticised as a 'conspiracy of silence'. The BBC's quiescence and its collusion in the suppression of dissent contributed to 'a vacuum at the heart of public life'.[20]

Yet this state of affairs was not a foregone conclusion. There were repeated attempts by BBC programme-makers in the later 1930s to offer independent assessments of the coming crisis, such as 'the strenuous efforts in those final months before the war to alert the public to the true implications of Munich by trying to bring the opponents of appeasement . . . to the microphone'. But these initiatives were constantly thwarted by the combined weight of government, Labour Party 'opportunism' and the 'crass blindness of the conservative listening public'.[21] For Scannell and Cardiff, BBC journalism in this critical early period crossed the line between imaginative independence and expedient conformity, but it did so under pressure. Ultimately, the result was a culture of compromise and complicity in the face of government powers to impose its definition of political reality.[22]

The most damning evidence of the democratic shortcomings of the early BBC comes from the Second World War. During the late 1930s, the BBC became closely implicated in the management of Britain's foreign and domestic affairs. It played a large part in the development by the state of powerful tools of news manipulation, tools which long outlasted the war. In 1939, BBC executives were involved in founding the Ministry of Information, the government's propaganda machine, for which the BBC was in some ways a model. Throughout the war the corporation was closely scrutinised by the MoI, although great reliance was placed on its capacity for self-censorship: 'the BBC embraced a strict censorship as to the manner [sic] born'.[23]

The BBC's supreme skills in propaganda are shown by its external broadcasting services during the war. Memoranda recording debates within the

BBC's Turkish Service and between its policy advisers and the MoI, for example, convey the imagination and expertise expended in the rhetorical management of 'truth'. Turkey was a neutral country, and the memos reveal an acute awareness of the different strata of the Turkish audience and their importance in determining the response of the Turkish state. Some are devoted to the relative merits of positive or negative propaganda. Others give editorial guidance: care must be taken to maintain the BBC's image of impartiality and truthfulness in contrast to German propaganda. One memo offers a list of dos and don'ts: 'Every opportunity should be taken of giving London date-line reaction to major domestic events inside Turkey. / Every opportunity should be taken of giving emphasis to (favourable) news tending to throw importance on Turkey's status as a friendly neutral. / It is important to project the uninterrupted progress of "peaceful" scientific and cultural development in this country. We should establish our lead as a "humanistic" nation.'[24] What this material reveals is the care taken during the war to maintain a façade of disinterested truth-production, one that covered over highly interested military–political purposes and workaday collaboration between the BBC and the state.

Such insight into the debased nature of the democratic functioning of the early BBC must be weighed against a more diffuse achievement. In its early decades the BBC was almost singularly responsible for creating for the first time in Britain a 'national culture', a unified sphere of public experience. The new 'general public' created by broadcasting gained access to a series of previously restricted forms of entertainment and sport – the Cup Final, the Grand National, Wimbledon – and to previously exclusive political, religious and cultural events – royal weddings and funerals, coronations, political speeches, services from Westminster Abbey, the King's Christmas broadcast. 'Such broadcasts unobtrusively stitched together the private and the public spheres . . . At the same time the events themselves, previously discrete, [were] woven together as idioms of a common national life . . . Threaded through the year [as] a tapestry of civic, cultural, royal and state occasions', they formed a calendar of public life.[25] These transformations in the nature of collective experience together led to the emergence of a public cultural life, one constituted by broadcasting.

In assessing the balance sheet of the early BBC, what is striking is the attempt by many commentators to close down this contradictory reality, either by damning the BBC for its collusions and cowardice or by eulogising its manifest social and cultural contributions. Yet the tensions in the balance sheet cannot be resolved: the record reveals both the democratic and the counter-democratic record, and potential, of the BBC. As historians show, critical to the BBC's democratic leanings is its capacity for internal reflection on its policies and actions and their effects. This capacity has taken two forms. It is shown firstly by the many BBC professionals who struggled to pursue enlightened practice or to respond to new social or cultural developments in the face of political obstructions or corporate inertia. But from 1926 to the present, the reflection has also taken an institutionalised form in corporate meetings, and particularly in the central ritual of the BBC: the Programme Board. In the early years this weekly meeting of bosses and heads of departments was the place where the content of schedules was debated and given shape eight weeks ahead. But it was also a place for collective commentary on the previous week's programming, discussions that could get 'extremely caustic'.[26] Renamed the Programme Review Board, this meeting still takes place. It has lost the function of forward planning but consists in a group reflection on the output and wider policy issues arising. It is the BBC's high-level forum for communal debate. The existence of such forms of reflection are important indicators of the degree to which the BBC permits self-criticism and internal dissent, and good measures of the democratic health or otherwise of the BBC as an institution.

*

Hamilton's half-hour: Newsnight plays a role

10.30 p.m. on the second day of the Labour conference. With the whole of the media pack, I am watching Newsnight on one of several televisions suspended around the newsroom shared by all the news broadcasters here. Everything has stopped and everyone is staring intently as Jeremy Paxman, live in London, interviews the Tory MP Neil Hamilton who is at the centre of the Cash for Questions scandal. He is accused of receiving cash from businessman Mohammed Al-Fayed, the owner of Harrods, in return for asking questions in the House of Commons. Also being interviewed is Hamilton's chief accuser, Guardian editor Alan Rusbridger. It is an astonishing piece of television, with Hamilton holding forth without inhibition and Rusbridger occasionally exploding with sheer fury. Among the hundred or so journalists the atmosphere in the newsroom is as one: extreme excitement as Newsnight willingly assists Hamilton to bring himself down. Why he ever agreed to do a live interview with Paxman and Rusbridger no one can explain. Those around me are aghast, astounded by how it is going. Peter Horrocks grins broadly, speechless at Hamilton's folly.

Today is also the day of Tony Blair's speech. So earlier in the day there was much discussion among Newsnight's editors and producers: which story should lead, Blair or

Hamilton, Labour triumphalism or Tory disgrace? Nonchalantly, Horrocks told me that Hamilton would go first and Blair second – a decision guaranteed to rile Labour's spin machine. The Hamilton interview does indeed push Blair's conference speech to the margins of the programme.

On the way to eat after transmission, Horrocks shares some professional tricks. He tells me that Hamilton nearly walked off the set in London a minute before they went on air because he objected to the use of the word 'discrepancy' in the opening package about the scandal. Hamilton gave an ultimatum: either the word must go or he would. Horrocks laughs as he explains that Paxman got the word past Hamilton by telling the soundman to go and fiddle with Hamilton's microphone just as the package was being replayed in the studio.

Diary, 1996.

*

The tide turns, the blue Sun sets

Next day, the third day of conference, I enter the newsroom to find all the journalists crowding round the television screens to watch the BBC *One O'Clock News*. The lead item is the escalating scandal around Neil Hamilton. Ian Greer, formerly Britain's 'top political lobbyist', who was implicated in the scandal through supplying cash to Hamilton on Al-Fayed's behalf, is being interviewed. He goes over the top and accuses Al-Fayed of being a liar; it gets quite racist in tone. The journalists are united: gleeful, guffawing at Greer's excessive self-righteousness, amazed at his gall. They love watching him squirm. They love the fact that the political scene is under their scrutiny, and the power they hold.

I bump into Mark Mardell, Keiran, a *Newsnight* producer, and Raj, the cameraman. They are off to interview Trevor Kavanagh, the political correspondent of the *Sun* newspaper, Britain's most popular daily and part of Murdoch's News International group. They are doing this, Mardell explains, because the most significant thing about the coverage of Blair's speech nationally has been the *Sun*'s entirely positive endorsement of it. I follow them, and we find Kavanagh in another section of the Winter Gardens reserved for the press. Kavanagh says smoothly that the *Sun* wasn't alone, that all the right-wing press were very impressed with Blair – the *Daily Express* and the *Daily Mail* too. He says that Blair appeared to be truly a leader-in-waiting with many policies thought through, although for their money there remain certain areas of policy that need firming up. He mentions the disarray of the Tories and how the Hamilton corruption saga is now implicating many more Tory MPs, stressing this as a cause of disaffection with the Tories. As we walk away I am reeling: the *Sun*, it seems, is now unequivocal in its support for New Labour and in its rapid distancing from the Conservatives. History is crystallising before my eyes.

Diary, 1996.

*

Fertile Competition

In 1955, when the BBC finally faced competition from the new commercial television channel ITV, it faced its own likeness. ITV was to be supervised by the Independent Television Authority, a public body similar to the BBC's Board of Governors whose members were also appointed by the government. The ITA's remit required the ITV contractors to inform, educate and entertain and to produce programmes of quality and balance. Like the BBC, the ITV companies had a ten-year licence and came under periodic review. The nature and extent of advertising were strictly controlled and a rigid separation was made between programme content and advertising, preventing commercial interference. Yet, while the ITV contractors in some ways emulated the culture of the BBC, they were owned and run by entertainment moguls like Lew Grade and Val Parnell. Under these figures the ITV companies helped to create a new mood in British television, one that was livelier and more responsive to the changing culture of British working people. In turn, ITV's popular awareness affected the BBC. British television 'acted as the barometer of the great attitudinal shifts of the 1960s',[27] but it also contributed to those cultural shifts.

The BBC / ITV duopoly provided a particularly benevolent environment for creative television. It rested largely on the integration of production and broadcasting; each influenced the other process, and production bosses had some creative autonomy and some say in decision-making. Thanks to the growth in viewing, the additional revenues from colour television and the general economic expansiveness of the 1960s, both bodies were well financed and of a size and scale that ensured a strong training base for the British industry. Dissidents from the BBC found a natural home in the ITV sector, causing a sense of broader social representation within British television, while the cultures of the two sectors were unified through a constant movement of personnel between them.

The advent of ITV did not immediately decimate the BBC's audience. Indeed, the BBC is credited with providing more memorable programmes in this period; and throughout the 1960s, it was the BBC that innovated more in terms of new genres and new directions within old genres. Nor did the start of

ITV have much effect on the overall growth of the audience, which rose most sharply in the preceding years, in particular when the BBC televised the 1953 coronation. But by the end of the 1950s, the signs were that working-class audiences were threatening to desert the BBC, particularly because of its scheduling of serious and minority fare throughout prime-time as part of the Reithian mix. In the era of competition such scheduling had to change. Throughout the 1960s, the BBC and ITV vied to innovate across a number of programming areas. Each developed particular strengths and echoed in different ways the wider social and cultural changes, notably the erosion of class differences, the rise of youth cultures and the growing affluence of post-war Britain. There was no simple division of high and low between the two providers. The BBC proved stronger and more innovative in sports and children's television. It took up the challenge of rock'n'roll with Juke Box Jury. It oversaw innovative real-life comedy from the mid 1950s with shows like Hancock's Half Hour, a trend that continued into the sixties with Steptoe and Son and Till Death Us Do Part. And with That Was The Week That Was, the BBC explored a vein of sophisticated satire and comment. ITV, on the other hand, expanded television's repertoire of light entertainment with variety shows and showbiz spectacles. It imported a rash of American cop shows and Western series. To recover massive start-up costs, the ITV schedules contained 'giveaway' quizzes such as Double Your Money and Take Your Pick – shows that were cheap and attracted huge audiences, but which the BBC declined to copy because they were considered outside its remit.

The creative fertility of the structure of limited, well-funded competition in this era is well displayed in the dynamics of television drama. ITV pioneered a number of new genres. With Emergency Ward 10 and Coronation Street it initiated two soap opera forms – the medical soap and the regional working-class soap – which still dominate the schedules of mainstream British channels. The Street went on to be the most successful ever British prime-time serial. With Danger Man, The Avengers and The Prisoner, ITV began the fantasy espionage form; and with Armchair Theatre it achieved the transition from televised studio theatre to the single television play, a genre that responded increasingly to contemporary experience. The BBC took up the mantle in both popular and 'high end' drama. Z-Cars began the genre of 'grim and gritty' police series that remains a centrepiece of British television. While in the area of single television dramas, The Wednesday Play led a new filmic turn, exploring the social realism of recent British cinema and expanding upon it with a new generation of writers and directors.

The benign impact of competition is equally evident in innovations in television news. From 1946 to 1954, BBC television news consisted in photographic images accompanied by a faceless voiceover – radio news with static pictures. When in 1955 ITV's dedicated news organisation, ITN, came onstream, it was unencumbered by a radio past and set about constructing television news as a dynamic journalistic and visual form. The news presenters employed to the full their journalistic authority. The intention was to compete with the press for scoops and exclusives, and film footage became the core of news reports. Compared with the BBC, politicians were treated less deferentially. Ordinary people figured in 'vox pops' or street interviews; and the regional basis of the ITV companies meant a greater commitment to local news than the BBC, with its metropolitan bias. In 1957, the BBC bounced back with Tonight, a nightly magazine programme that mixed politics, current affairs and light entertainment, and emulated ITN's pace and verve. Its style was familiar and iconoclastic, and its reporters became television personalities. In 1958, under a new chief, BBC News itself finally learned the lessons of ITN and adopted a more televisual approach. Through the weight of competition, ITN's impact was to reinforce the independence of television news in general. The maturity of television news as a genre was signalled by the huge audiences for the filmed coverage of the 1962 Cuban missile crisis, from which point television news has remained the British public's preferred news medium.

Competition in the late 1950s and 1960s was limited, and it took place between two vertically integrated, large and well-funded organisations. Critically, while there was competition for audiences, the two sides of the duopoly did not compete for revenues; nor was there internal competition for revenue between the regional ITV companies. Indeed, the revenue base grew at a significant pace, a situation that continued until the high inflation of the 1970s. ITV was awash with advertising money; it paid higher salaries and funded programmes at higher levels than the BBC, pushing up programme costs across the industry. Combined with the cultural expansiveness and democratising tendencies of the period, the result was rising creative standards and innovation across the range of genres, particularly in, but not limited to, popular programming. How much these changes can be attributed to the structure and funding of British television and how much to the cultural and ideological flavour of the times cannot be known. But it is well to be aware of the creative response made by television to such benevolent conditions.

*

The golden opt-out: duopoly and difference

GB: 'How would you sum up the area of drama in which you work?'

'Well, it has tended to be original, to be writer-led, and it has been able to have its head in terms of what it attempts. It made its own genre, and until quite recently the premium was on the content and quality rather than pressure about the size or make-up of the audience. And the BBC allowed this tradition to persist, largely because there were criteria for justifying its existence – criteria that weren't commercial returns or size of audience. The BBC's strength during the years before the whole industry was systematically challenged by Mrs Thatcher was to be allowed a sort of golden opt-out. The duopoly was like a mirror in which ITV and the BBC were allowed to live by their own rules of survival, politically sanctioned, outside the ordinary laws of the market. It was a very peculiar system, the engine of public service TV, and it was socially licensed. And that social licencing is now undermined from the outside, both politically and technologically, through the fact of multichannel.'

GB: 'People have described the duopoly period to me in terms of a common culture, because ITV was staffed by people who were ex-BBC or floating between the two . . .?'

'Yes, there was a profession in common. There were drama people who never crossed the line, but they were the exception. Certainly, the times I worked with ITV, it was at their invitation because they were trying within my field to excel against the BBC. That process of always looking at each other while competing was what defined it. The attitude of people like David Puttnam to me was that there was something illicit about being able to make good costly work without having to fight for the right to make it in an economic market, as he had to with movies. My situation was slightly jealously regarded by people like David: "It shouldn't be that easy", you know, "we should all have to prove ourselves in the jungle." That's rubbish. If you can create conditions where the jungle doesn't intrude, which is what public service TV did, and if the results find a collective endorsement from society, well, fine. And something of that has been destroyed and thrown away.'

Senior producer, BBC Drama, 1997.

*

'I won't show your material on my channel': Commodities and the birth of Channel 4

GB: 'Wasn't this an era, in the seventies, when there were networks of small scale funding – through local government, regional arts associations, the British Film Institute,

40

the Arts Council, even the trade union movement, and then joined by the early Channel 4 – which supported a film culture that has since disappeared...?'

'Absolutely. The independent film movement, which emerged in the late sixties out of the counterculture, was avant-gardist in both its politics and aesthetics. In the early seventies disparate groups and individuals organised together in the Independent Film-makers Association. If you look at the IFA's founding articles, there's a statement from Aubrey Singer, then controller of BBC2, saying "I won't show your sort of material on my channel". In retrospect that was hardly surprising, but then it was the stimulus for people to say: OK, if we can't work for TV, we'll have to work outside TV. And that's what we did.

'The guiding principle of the sector was what came to be called "integrated practice". You did everything: you did the research, scripted, trained people, you produced, you distributed, you got the feedback from audiences to make the next project. That's what distinguished us from mainstream televison. It was community film-making, organised around independent workshops with the focus on representing those national and regional voices that were marginalized from mainstream TV by their politics, their ethnicity or cultural interests. And we always had one eye on what was happening internationally, as similar film movements were developing the world over. So we saw American, Latin American and French material and our films were shown abroad.'

GB: 'Then Channel 4 came . . .'

'Channel 4 came, partly as a result of the Annan Committee, partly as a result of pres-sure from people like ourselves who wanted to make different material and show it on television. And partly in the end because Thatcher wanted to stimulate a new economy of independent facilities and independent producers; she wanted to break the duopoly. But for us it was an opportunity to introduce new voices to television and change the way TV was made.

'During the mid seventies we'd done research papers for the DTI, for Michael Meacher when he was under secretary for film, to set up a regional workshop structure for film and media production and distribution. These were the proposals that the IFA fed into the Channel 4 group. The independent film sector was split between those who were happy to work for the new Channel 4 under a normal commissioning rela-tionship, and those who argued for what was called the Workshop Declaration, whereby the workshop retained copyright in all its work, and the TV company matched local and BFI funding to enable that integrated practice to go on. Under this model the TV company had the first option to broadcast, but the workshop retained all the other rights. A lot of people worked in that way.'

GB: 'Wasn't there resistance from the trade unions to this kind of small-scale collective practice?'

'We were all active within the ACTT, and the ACTT not only accepted it, but negotiated it with Channel 4 and was a signatory to the agreement. It was a real intervention in the union, and the notion of collective ownership that we worked with was an intervention in traditional ideas of copyright. We also tried to intervene in the way film was written about, and certainly changed the way we related as film-makers to the communities with which we worked, where we showed our films…'

GB: 'A rather totalistic intervention! When you say writing about film, was this linked to the journal *Screen?*'

'It was. There was an interplay between *Screen* and the sector, primarily through the agency of Clare Johnson, Paul Willemen and Rod Stoneman – who later became a commissioning editor for Independent Film at Channel 4. People moved between theory and practice – Rod was primarily a theorist, one of the few people who made the move that way. Mick Eaton used to write for *Screen* and is now an established writer. Sue and I and two others set up *Commodities*, which was a series of six films, a history of the world as seen through its primary commodities – coffee, tea, sugar, oil – and through them telling the story of the development of world capitalism from early Amsterdam to the financial futures markets. It was four years in development and production – much too long in traditional TV terms. In the end it was shown on Channel 4 in the summer of '86. It got a real mix of audiences, about one million. It's still distributed internationally.

'*Commodities* was a huge project. We shot it in Colombia, Brazil, Zimbabwe, India, Sri Lanka, Hong Kong, China, Holland, England – mad in retrospect. We really weren't equipped to deal with a project on such a huge scale. We combined fiction with documentary, graphics and archive film; we harnessed all the audio-visual materials to create a synthetic whole. We worked with local film groups, writers and theatre groups around the world. When we went over budget and over schedule, the Channel started intervening quite heavily in how we were working. It was a case of TV-cost-control-hierarchy meets anarchic, not to say an anarchist, film-making collective. TV wants a determined schedule, a determined budget and that's it. Feature films are in some ways more flexible. It was a painful learning experience, but in the end immensely valuable for many of those involved.'

Executive, BBC Drama, 1996.

*

Pluralism and Political Opportunism

When the Conservatives came into government in 1979, they inherited both the BBC / ITV duopoly and the legacy of the Annan Committee, which between 1974 and 1977 had deliberated on the next development in British television. A third national channel had been awarded to the BBC in 1962 by the Pilkington Committee, which criticised the early performance of ITV and decreed that it should shoulder stronger public service obligations. BBC2 began in 1964, and by 1980 the share of audience between BBC1 and BBC2, on the one hand, and ITV, on the other, was roughly fifty fifty. The report of the Annan Committee gave voice to a number of criticisms of the state of British television that had been rumbling since the late 1960s. It appreciated that the broadcasting institutions, partly through the expanded recruitment into broadcasting that occcured in the 1960s, had absorbed much of the self-conscious unrest and new cultural expressions of that decade. But it also attacked the complacency of the duopoly and took the view that these developments issued a challenge, that broadcasting should be 'opened up'. 'At present, so it is argued, the broadcasters have become an . . . unelected elite, more interested in preserving their own organisation intact than in enriching the nation's culture. Dedicated to the outworn concepts of balance and impartiality, how can the broadcasters reflect the multitude of opinions in our pluralist society?'[28]

The Annan Committee had been effectively lobbied by two groups keen to see a change in the organisation of British television. On one side were disgruntled programme-makers working for the BBC and ITV, who for some years had been pressing for a space for independent production. This group contained both those who felt politically and ideologically constrained as employees, and those who perceived the value of their ideas and were keen to develop production companies as businesses that would in future sell to various distributors. On the other side was a complex alliance of politically left-wing critics of the duopoly, a group that reflected the growth of trade union militancy within broadcasting, a rising awareness on the left of the politics of gender, race and ethnicity, as well as the leftist orientation of the new academic disciplines of film, media and cultural studies. The duopoly was portrayed by this group as representative of narrow establishment interests and as excessively close to the state. Instead, the leftist alliance called for a more plural, democratically accountable and bottom-up alternative system. The interests of the different lobbies converged in a series of demands and visions focused on the future fourth channel.

The Annan report reflected the influence of the lobbies. It argued strenuously for greater pluralism in broadcasting, to be embodied in the new channel, while leaving the existing structure of the duopoly intact. Annan proposed an Open Broadcasting Authority that would act as a publisher and draw programming from a new independent production sector. The sector would bring in social groups previously under-represented in broadcasting; it would be a fount of diversity and of new ideas. By advocating a pluralistic model of public service, the Annan report made a radical break with the past, while retaining the principle of British broadcasting as a public service. The impetus behind what was to become Channel 4 therefore represented a curious coalition of interests. It elided three strands of ideas. One was the notion of increased autonomy for existing producers, enabling them to develop perspectives that were previously off-limits; another was a belief in the importance of greater social diversity in the population supplying programmes, as a means of boosting innovation and diversity; and the third was a belief in the uses of small, independent programme sources, outside the broadcasters' direct control. It was an ambiguous model that pointed towards both small businesses and leftist production collectives, both of which arose during the 1980s to serve the channel. The ambiguity, and the elision, attest to the labile, essentially opportunistic political coalition forged around the movement for Channel 4.

Following Margaret Thatcher's election victory in May 1979, the Queen's speech gave a commitment to the new fourth channel, but under the control of the existing regulator, the Independent Broadcasting Authority. That summer, independent producers put to the government their case for a substantial share in the new channel's programming. A telling shift occurred in the language of the debate. Increasingly, they stressed the entrepreneurial and economic dimensions of independent production, and the potential for independents to become prosperous players in international programme sales in the manner of their American counterparts. Moreover, the rising video, cable and satellite industries would soon require content suppliers, a role the independents could fulfil. Such a sector would diversify production, and it might provide a lever to break the restrictive closed shops of the broadcast trade unions. The independents' arguments were persuasive not only to the public-service-friendly Home Secretary, William Whitelaw, but to the free marketeers of the far right.

In August 1979 Jeremy Isaacs, soon to be the first chief executive of Channel 4, gave the MacTaggart Lecture at the Edinburgh International Television Festival. In it he offered a prescient vision of the new channel, specifying that it should aim for a variety of audiences, especially significant minorities not yet catered for, and a 10 per cent audience share. 'I hope, in the eighties, to see more black Britons on our screens in programmes of particular appeal to them and aimed at us; more programmes made by women which men will watch; more programmes for the young, for the age group that watches television least partly because so little television speaks to them.'[29] Another contender for the chief executive job also gave a speech at the festival: one John Birt, controller of features and current affairs at LWT. Birt made a more radical pitch. The pluralistic fourth channel offered 'an opportunity for us to listen to the raw, unfiltered, immoderate and sometimes angry views of those excluded'.[30]

Soon after, Whitelaw outlined the government's plans for Channel 4. In a speech to the industry he employed a language and dwelt on a set of concerns that are striking in as much as they were soon to be submerged beneath a rising tide of free-market thinking that would dominate the next two decades. The channel should bring innovation, Whitelaw said, and greater opportunities for creativity in television. It must extend the range of programmes, serve minority and specialised audiences, and provide educational programming. It must complement and not engage in ratings rivalry with ITV. The largest possible proportion of programmes must be secured from independent producers. This imaginative cultural and industrial vision was underpinned by an equally imaginative funding solution. The fourth channel was to be paid for by a levy on the ITV companies, and the size of its budget would not be determined by the revenue raised by advertisements shown on the channel. Whitelaw stressed how this solution avoided competition for revenue. For such competition would lead inevitably in the direction of a drive for audience maximisation, with destructive consequences for the quality of the new channel, ITV and eventually also the BBC. With its focus on enhancing the well-being of diverse audiences, and how this could best be served by positive regulation of the preconditions for creativity in production, the architecture of the fourth channel was the culmination of the public service paradigm that had prevailed in Britain for more than fifty years. With hindsight, it seems extraordinary that Channel 4 was brought into being in Thatcher's first term; that it was suggests that Thatcherism as a political ideology was still taking shape.

Channel 4 began operating in 1982 and in the remainder of the 1980s offered a range of challenges to the televisual status quo. *Channel 4 News* broke the mould of television news with an extended early-evening programme that went beyond events to examine causes and background. The strand *Diverse Reports* allowed new perspectives to be voiced, free of the duty to create 'balance' within one programme. Attention to plural interests and communities was embodied in strands such as *Out on Tuesday* for gays and lesbians and *Union World* for trade unionists, and in the output of the Multicultural Programming Unit. *Film On Four* was a feature-film slot based mainly on co-productions, and the channel went on to play a leading part in the revivification of the British film industry. Channel 4 became the first channel systematically to mark television's coming of age as a medium by recycling its canon, with shows such as *I Love Lucy*, *Sergeant Bilko* and *The Munsters*.

The channel's most experimental initiative — a legacy of the radicalism of the 1970s — was the cultivation, under the Independent Film and Video Unit, of a workshop sector. On the basis of sustained funding, the workshops had the brief to train people from under-represented groups in video production, so as to generate new kinds of programming. Here was the link between broadening the social profile of producers and heightening diversity in output. A number of innovative black and regional film and video collectives arose such as Sankofa, Black Audio Film Collective and Ceddo.[31] For a few years their output gained a viewing on Channel 4, fuelling an extraordinary opening of television's aesthetic. For the first and only time it was possible to speak in the mid 1980s of an avant-garde in British television, sometimes integrating aesthetic and political invention, at other times driven simply by polemical intent. The results were uneven but occasionally spectacular. It was a moment that was soon to pass as Channel 4 veered on to the tracks of mainstream programming.

The transformation of Channel 4 during the late 1980s and 1990s reflects the changing times. By the later eighties the independent sector was maturing and concentrating around the more successful companies; increasingly, its leftist origins were displaced by the independents' concerns as small- and medium-sized businesses. A number of leading independents were based on the control of 'talent' or entertainment stars, causing a focus on the development of star vehicles; while some of the BBC's most acclaimed producers left to start their own companies. In 1993, the channel began to sell its own advertising, creating just the competition for advertising revenue between Channel 4 and ITV that Whitelaw had been at pains to proscribe. With the added impact of Michael Grade, chief executive from 1988 to 1997, the result was a relentless shift in a populist direction, with greater reliance on soap operas and imported American series, and declining space for the kinds of different and minority programming characteristic of the channel in its first decade. By the later nineties, under pressure of intense competition, there was a focus on the lucrative upmarket youth audiences that are highly attractive to advertisers, and an increasing similarity between the schedules of Channel 4 and its rivals.

Despite these changes, a striking legacy of the early Channel 4 is that independent production has come to stand in general in British television for innovation. Independence is now seen as the space preferred by 'talent', and enterprise is thought to be synonymous with creativity.

*

The ITC speaks: 'Public service? No such thing'

'The best brains in Britain have struggled for years to find a definition of public service broadcasting. They have all failed – because there is no such thing . . . Public service TV is what, at any moment in time, the public wants it to be . . . Public opinion is dynamic . . . We should monitor and trust those changing views – and ensure our policies and regulation reflect the best understanding of them.'

Robin Foster, ITC head of strategy, 2001.

*

Squeezing the BBC: Placemen and Repudiation

Following the founding of Channel 4, a new era in broadcasting policy opened under the Thatcher governments. Thatcher's first administration left the BBC and ITV largely alone, with the exception of criticisms of the BBC's coverage of the Northern Ireland crisis and of the 1982 Falklands War, and growing interference in appointing BBC governors. The new policies began to emerge in the mid 1980s. There were three central planks, each notably absent from the earlier paradigm represented by Annan. First, the virtues of liberalised market competition, linked to a concern with economic efficiency; second, a commitment to fostering the industries stemming from the new technologies of cable and satellite, and media convergence; and third, the aim to encourage national broadcasters to think globally and to compete on the international stage.

The concern with convergence – specifically with cable's capacity to deliver telecommunications as well as broadcasting and interactive services – fed the growing perception that broadcasting formed part of a rapidly expanding and potentially profitable information technology sector. The government started to conceive of television in terms of technologically driven industrial policy; and in 1983 the Department of Trade and Industry awarded eleven regional franchises for cable, mainly to operators from the United States and Canada. The early British cable industry failed to flourish, and it was only after 1990, when the cable operators were permitted to offer telephone services as well as a range of broadcasting channels, that it began to take off. Similar liberalisation occurred in relation to direct satellite broadcasting. After a shaky start and severe economic and technological difficulties in the mid 1980s, the British operator, BSB, was taken over by Rupert Murdoch's Sky, giving Murdoch an unregulated bridgehead into British broadcasting. By 1991, the BSkyB package was offering almost entirely American programming and movies, to which was added Murdoch's growing control of sports and football rights. As the British cable and satellite industries developed, they formed one flank of the rising governmental intent to break open the broadcasting duopoly and boost competition in British broadcasting.

Such developments, and the increasing emphasis on competition and efficiency in the face of globalising tendencies in the economy and technology, must be seen in relation to the wider politics of Thatcherite neo-liberalism. The Conservatives had gauged the public's dissatisfaction and fatigue with the social and economic problems of the 1970s, with inflation, industrial unrest, inefficient public services and repeated state intervention. Under the influence of right-wing economic thinking, the Tories determined to lessen state controls and free business from excessive 'bureaucracy'. The new economic era was to be led by private enterprise; privatisation and marketisation were the panaceas for the reputedly underperforming state-owned and -controlled industries. Leanness, competitiveness and efficiency were the driving concepts in production, while on the demand side notions of consumer sovereignty took hold. Together the two formed a market-based discipline that would drive economic recovery and growth.

In the mid 1980s government attention turned to the duopoly and led to calls for the BBC and ITV to improve efficiency and cut costs. To enforce greater efficiency, the government squeezed the BBC's finances. In 1985, the Home Secretary granted a much smaller increase to the licence fee than the BBC had sought. In 1987, the next Home Secretary declared a 'double squeeze' on the BBC's funding by indexing the licence fee to general inflation, a lower rate than inflation in broadcasting, and by starting that indexation from a lower baseline than the BBC had requested. In 1991, the government set the licence fee increase at 3 per cent below the increase in the retail price index, and in the two subsequent years it was indexed to the RPI. Overall, there was a significant fall in the real income of the BBC.

Political criticism also escalated as the government and the Tory Party attacked certain programmes as biased or otherwise unacceptable. The attacks were repeatedly picked up and amplified by hostile coverage from the Tory popular and broadsheet press, including those from Murdoch's stable. Two instances among a number from the mid 1980s will illustrate. The first was a *Panorama* from 1984 called 'Maggie's Militant Tendency' which concerned extreme right-wing infiltration of the Tory Party, infiltration that had been documented by the Young Conservatives. The broadcast led to a lengthy legal process when two Tory MPs issued writs for libel. The BBC eventually settled out of court and paid damages; the director-general, Alastair Milne, who was inclined to allow the case to proceed, was ordered to settle by the acting chair of governors. The incident marked a serious rift between the director-general and the governors; for the BBC it amounted to a constitutional crisis. A second instance was a documentary from 1985 in the *Real Lives* series that gave a sympathetic hearing to a prominent member of the IRA and to an 'extremist' loyalist. The Home Secretary, Leon Brittan, took the unprecedented step of writing to ask the BBC not to show the programme, and the governors complied, again over the heads of Milne and his Board of Management. The BBC's editorial independence had been utterly compromised and a strike of BBC staff ensued. It was the nadir of Milne's period as DG; within months he was fired by the new chairman, Marmaduke Hussey.

Another instrument for controlling the BBC had been apparent from the first term of the Thatcher governments: increasing intervention in the appointment of the BBC chairman and governors. In 1980, 1983 and 1986 the government appointed its own people as chairman, and in 1981 the Thatcherite ex-editor of *The Times*, William Rees-Mogg, as vice-chairman. Rees-Mogg was to wield great power and embodied patrician disdain for the BBC. The 1986 chairman appointment, Hussey, was backed directly by Thatcher and Norman Tebbitt and was highly political; it coincided with the height of government antagonism towards the BBC and a determination to enforce reforms. The extent of Hussey's political patronage was revealed when, for the first time in BBC history, he was awarded in 1991 a second term as chairman. But the majority of those making up the Board of Governors in this period also reflected Tory interests. Hussey was able to garner near unanimous support for sacking Milne and for other moves, some of them contentious, including the appointment of the accountant Michael Checkland as Milne's deputy and then as director-general, and John Birt as Checkland's deputy and subsequently as director-general.

In this hostile climate, a committee was set up in 1985–6 under the free-market economist Alan Peacock to consider whether the BBC should be funded by advertising. It was the aggressive outcome of the pressures being directed at the BBC by the government and spoke of Thatcher's intention to privatise the corporation. The committee's findings set the framework for the most significant changes in British broadcasting in the next decade and a half; from its views derive many of the received opinions that still dominate the broadcasting debate. On the committee with Peacock was the right-wing financial journalist, Samuel Brittan. Together they championed the notion of consumer sovereignty, and they did so with an eye to the multichannel future. Consumers were the best judges of their own interests, they proposed. Consumers, and not producer elites, should decide on the character of broadcasting. It followed that the optimum funding mechanism for future broadcasting services was subscription, not advertising. The Peacock report deplored the dual monopolies of the BBC, which received the licence fee whether audiences liked its services or not, and of ITV, which could charge what it wanted for advertising.

In the face of such free-market arguments, the BBC mounted an energetic defence of the licence fee as superior to the alternatives in supporting public service broadcasting. In doing so it had the united support of the then chairman, Stuart Young, and of the management; Young, although a Thatcher appointee, developed during his tenure great respect for the corporation. In the end the BBC's arguments prevailed. By a narrow margin the Peacock report resisted the government imperative to find in favour of privatisation. It did, however, recommend greater economic discipline for the BBC, and subscription funding in the medium term. The report took a sceptical view of the meaning of public service broadcasting, claiming that even the broadcasters were unable to give a clear definition. Such scepticism remains a favoured rhetorical device of the commercial lobby in broadcasting.

If the Peacock report restrained the Thatcherite desire fully to commercialise the BBC, through other recommendations it constructed a framework that would eventually bring similar results, but less directly. Three of its less trumpeted findings laid the groundwork for the 1990 Broadcasting Act. Echoing a paper issued in 1984 by the Adam Smith Institute, an influential right-wing think tank, the report recommended that licences for the ITV regions should in future be awarded on the basis of competitive bids in an auction rather than being allocated, as hitherto, on the basis of quality and proposed services; to introduce competition into the advertising market, it suggested that Channel 4 should sell its own advertising; and to stimulate greater competition both in production and between broadcasters, it proposed that the BBC and ITV should be required to buy 40 per cent of their programming from the independent production sector. Each was a significant change. Together their impact was to be revolutionary.

The 1990 Act was the apogee of Thatcherite deregulatory reform in broadcasting. It brought in a host of measures the overall design of which was massively to stoke commercial competition – between the broadcasters for audiences and for advertising revenue, and between producers for commissions. Moderating Peacock, it required the BBC and ITV to commission 25 per cent of their total programming from the independents. Channel 4 was to become a public trust and from 1993 it would sell its own advertising. A new commercial terrestrial network, Channel 5, would be licensed by the new broadcasting regulator under the same terms as the ITV companies, to begin operation in the later 1990s.

But the centrepiece of the legislation was reform of ITV and of the existing regulator, the IBA, considered necessary because of the IBA's strong public service history and its resistance to purely commercial imperatives. The Act proposed to auction the ITV licences to the highest bidder, subject to the applicants passing what was termed a 'quality threshold'. Since there was no upper limit to the auction, the bidders might be tempted to saddle themselves with ruinous payments and, if successful, would be under pressure to reduce broadcast operating costs. The IBA was to be replaced by a 'lighter touch' regulator called the Independent Television Commission, with an overview of commercial terrestrial television – ITV, Channels 4 and 5 – as well as cable and satellite. The IBA had owned the ITV transmitters and was legally ITV's publisher, with a right to preview and direct responsibility for the quality of ITV's output. The ITC, however, was to be a licensing authority with a more diffuse and distant supervisory role. Its remit clearly spoke of the deregulatory thrust of policy and the aim of installing commercial competition at the core of the industry. But from the start it was ambiguous just how 'light' the ITC's touch would be when monitoring the content of programmes and schedules. How much would it be empowered to intervene when standards were not met by its licencees? By what measures would it effectively enforce its programming and quality requirements?

The 1990 Act epitomised the political paradoxes of the Thatcher governments, fuelled as they were by a repudiation of all public provision and of the philosophy of the welfare state. This was an administration engaged in legislating away the powers of the state, authoritarian in its rejection of the paternalist state. The one symptomatic resistance to the free-market paradigm was the debate that occurred as the bill went through Parliament on the issue of the quality threshold. To maintain the standards of British television, a forceful alliance developed between the IBA, the Campaign for Quality Television, led by programme-makers with the backing of some ITV companies, and a number of MPs. The BBC failed to give support, a mark of its political timidity at the time. The alliance fought fiercely over two years against the nugatory proposals outlined in the government's White Paper and for the quality threshold to be given real substance.

The result is revealing: after ten years of Thatcher's premiership, on this issue of immense cultural and political concern, the government gave way. It greatly strengthened the programming specifications that the ITC would oversee. It also delegated to the ITC the statutory power to detail stringent programming requirements and to award the ITV and Channel 5 licences on the basis of a series of tests, including thorough scrutiny of the financial probity of applicants. It may appear that the 'lighter touch' prescribed for the new regulator had been compromised. In actuality, throughout its existence, the ITC seemed reluctant to exercise its controls and sanctions to the full. It grew intimate with the industry it was supposed to police, signalling a general problem with the model of specific industry regulators. The predictable result of the legislation, combined with the growth of cable and satellite, was the unleashing of rampant competition and pressures to maintain ratings and cut costs across British broadcasting, a situation to which the BBC was impelled to respond. Given these forces, and the feeble regulatory will of the ITC, by the mid 1990s the cart was leading the horse: the commercial companies made an increasingly populist running, while the ITC panted along behind. Britain's erstwhile public service ambitions were subordinated to the vaunted ideal of market competition.

*

The World of Coronation Street: more gathering of the clan

It's early evening of the third day of the 1996 Labour Party conference. I have come to a fringe event, 'Licence to kill?', on the future of the BBC organised by Arts for Labour. It is being held in a Blackpool attraction: The World of Coronation Street, a copy of the set of Coronation Street built at about three-quarters actual size. While we wait for things to start, we wander into the Rover's Return and throw ourselves on to settees in the characters' living rooms. Even for a theme park it's weird: a simulation of a simulation of a reality that no longer exists. When cultural theorists speak of postmodernism, they surely mean this. The broadcaster Laurie Taylor opens the event, criticising Labour for lack of attention to the arts, culture, the BBC. Where, he asks, is the robust defence of the licence fee? He speaks of the need for more investment in the BBC, citing research that shows reduced funds bring falling audiences and lower domestic production. He talks of the need for Labour to take a stance on these issues.

The debate begins. After a few openers, Alan Yentob stands up from the audience and speaks of the importance of the BBC selling its brand around the world. I glance over at Yentob's part of the room and see that he is sitting next to David Puttnam, the film producer and Labour peer, and my friend Colin MacCabe, head of research at the British Film Institute. Gus MacDonald, managing director of Scottish Television [*and soon to be made a Labour peer*], is nearby too. The room is packed with eminent media folk.

Then Jack Cunningham, Labour's shadow Heritage Secretary, speaks. He is defensive and irascible. He refuses to respond to a lobby asking for assurance that Labour will reduce the licence fee for the elderly and those on income support. He says firmly that all major change at the BBC ought to be prefaced by consultation, but doesn't say how or with whom. Yet he will not be drawn when asked whether Labour will hold a consultation process on their arts policies.

Diary, 1996.

*

Fantasy British politics: fish and chips with MacCabe and Mr Heffer

Later that evening Colin and I sit in a hotel awaiting his friend Denis MacShane, like Colin a Marxist in his youth and now Labour MP for Rotherham. MacShane arrives and says excitedly that he has arranged to meet up with some right-wing journalists for a meal. We can tag along. They are a succulent bunch: they include Simon Heffer, ex-*Daily Telegraph* columnist, now of the *Mail*, Anne Applebaum, associate editor of the *Evening Standard*, formerly deputy editor of the *Spectator*, a female television journalist, and Boris Johnson, assistant editor of the *Telegraph*, [*soon to edit the* Spectator, *and from 2001 Tory MP for Henley*]. Heffer and Johnson are fat and middle-aged before their time; the women are tough, thin, spiky and good-looking. All wear dark suits. We troop out and cross the dark streets and alight on a welcoming chippy.

It is bizarre. MacShane seems totally, animatedly at home among these right-wing journalists. He is in his element! He sits with Johnson and the women at one Formica-topped table, while Colin and I sit at another with Heffer, who has apparently warmed to Colin. He responded to Colin's introduction in the hotel by saying, 'You taught me semiotics at Cambridge!', and the ice was broken. He confides that he has just completed a biography of Enoch Powell of one million words which will not be published before Powell's death because he has had access to Powell's personal papers. I hold my breath as they negotiate Britishness and race, but without cause; they are happily, intensely engaged. It emerges that they share a deep interest in philology – in the foundations and history of the English language. Over cod and chips and mushy peas, passing the vinegar, we talk this out. Occasionally we stray on to difficult terrain. Heffer opines that he

53

doesn't think there's anything wrong with black English dialects except when they're illogical. Colin and he almost get less than affable over the question of whether there can be a British West Indian culture, and over Mrs Thatcher's contributions to education. However, they agree fulsomely on their hatred of John Major and on the need for proper English teaching in schools – grammar, spelling and so on. Illustrating the urgency of the latter, Heffer mentions en passant that he is reviewing a recent book on the Queen, and says it's pretty interesting but has some awful grammatical gaffes.

It seems clear that MacShane wants to cosy up to these key right-wing media figures, no doubt partly to milk them for Tory gossip. But the cosiness across what have been viciously drawn political lines seems to speak also of a simpler interest and enjoyment. The fact is that these members of the two-headed political and media class are fascinated by one another, close and at home with one another. 'Political differences' are put in perspective as their shared social and cultural territory moves to the fore.

Diary, 1996.

*

The Paradox

Many observers have noted the paradox facing the BBC, and any licence-fee-funded public broadcaster that aims for universal audience address. It stems from the need to justify its funding mechanism, often criticised as a regressive tax. Since 1955, BBC television has had to compete with ITV and then with others. Yet while it is not engaged in commercial competition, the result of the BBC's drive for legitimacy is the same: it has to be popular and it has to demonstrate its popularity. The recognised conduit for such a demonstration is the ratings game. But the BBC cannot stop at this; competitive ratings are necessary but not sufficient to justify the licence fee. The BBC must provide a range and diversity of programming. It must offer mass-appeal programmes, but it must also serve minority audiences and those unattractive to advertisers, who are under-served by commercial television. It must engage in creative risk and innovation. It must provide those genres that are currently out of favour but have value in themselves or may be about to become popular. The BBC, in other words, has to achieve what commercial broadcasters do and much more.

One of the striking effects of increased competition in British television since the early 1990s has been the growth of contradictory criticisms of the BBC among its antagonists. On the one hand, when the BBC is successful in its popular output or new services, it is accused of commercialism or of simply chasing ratings. As such it does not merit public funding. Yet this is to mistake necessary legitimation for commercial purpose. The complaint continues: by offering popular programming and successfully entering new markets, the BBC is betraying its public service orientation. Instead of competing, it should focus on filling gaps left by the market – the 'market failure' model. The last rhetorical flourish in this line of argument is to accuse the BBC of unfairly entering and trading in what are properly commercial markets through the use of its public monies. Yet the BBC is not a profit-oriented body. Its earnings are ploughed back into its public operations, for audience benefit, while the production standards supported by its substantial budgets set positive benchmarks for the industry, again to public benefit. The argument that the BBC is popular, for which read commercial, and that it should not be, ignores the additional cultural and social ambitions that it bears and the wider benefits it brings.

On the other hand, if the BBC abstains from competing in popular output, the chorus immediately retorts that it is a minority broadcaster and unsuccessful in the mass arena. As such it does not deserve universal public funding. Lowbrow, highbrow; damned if it does and damned if it doesn't: the complex functioning of the BBC – its purposefully mixed cultural economy – is travestied in these carping refrains. From the early 1990s to the present, versions of these tautological complaints – both of which are directed in reality at destroying the BBC – have consistently rumbled through the broadcasting debate.

*

Red Castle: the frail, the theatrical and the politically possible

The third afternoon of the Labour Party conference: in the main hall the pensions debate is due to start. But just today they inserted before it a rally called 'Operation Victory' led by a video full of anti-Tory propaganda, followed by John Prescott, deputy party leader, giving a humorous rallying speech and awards to party activists. It's a thinly concealed attempt to boost unity before the potentially divisive pensions hot spot, and to remind the floor of the need to support the NEC policy on pensions. I am watching from the camera balcony, perched high above the hall.

There's a big hum when Barbara Castle enters the conference hall and walks, assisted, with dignity to take her seat. She is very old and immensely frail but dressed head to foot in fighting, socialist red. She sits in the front row and a crowd of photographers advance and continue snapping relentlessly, as though mesmerised by her aura, presence, significance – is this the last effective representative of Old Labour, the last potential destabiliser of New Labour 'unity'?

Suddenly two women appear; they talk to Castle and help her up. Very slowly, she walks with their support behind the stage; Blair – who had been on stage – has also disappeared. Are they talking last-minute deals? Castle seems almost to have been hustled away. Fifteen minutes later Blair is back on stage. Castle is brought out again and put in a different position, ready to speak from the floor. The debate proceeds: mostly cautious, 'unified', advancing the NEC's position. Finally, one man gets up and speaks in support of Castle: he reels off a list of ways that money could be found to boost pensions, mainly by scrapping various defence and military projects. It begins to feel as though the occasion might almost become a real as opposed to a staged debate. Another speaker calls for backing for Castle's proposal, linking pensions to earnings, and is applauded. He ends, and Castle claps too for the first time. An elderly woman gets up to speak and again supports 'Composite 11', Castle's pension plan. She calls for a card vote here, now, in the hall, and she gets a clap. On the platform behind her Prescott begins to pull faces, to look theatrically 'anxious' and 'despairing' – he rubs his brow and face, as though to convey to the hall that they mustn't show divisions. It's one of his party tricks. Castle sits there, frail and unmoving, herself a symbol of the elderly whose fate they are deliberating.

The open debate starts. Second up, Castle moves to the platform and speaks: passionate, humorous and deadly serious, timed to perfection, playing her audience. She is vitriolic in her attack on NEC policy and on Harriet Harman's approach. She says the party leadership has been 'fencing with statistics'. She refuses the idea of a post-election commission to review pensions policy and says there must be a commitment upfront to linking pensions to earnings. Blair, Brown, Harman and Hattersley are on stage listening, and Blair and Brown periodically get up and stalk around, authoritative and apparently concerned. Castle speaks for six minutes, twice her allowance, and she gets a standing ovation. The third speaker happens to be a pensioner who speaks eloquently for the NEC and against Castle. The next day Gerald Kaufman admits that this was 'not unplanned'. Harman winds up the debate, low-key but firm, extending hands to Castle and Jack Jones, veteran trade unionist and Castle's ally on the pensions fight. Harman says they can be involved in the NEC's recommended review of pension policy, starting 'now'. The debate goes to a vote, and the result will be known tomorrow morning. Shrewdly, New Labour has taken the opportunity for yet more PR: like a loving family it has demonstrated its capacity magnanimously to absorb internal dissent and to value its difficult, radical elders. Conference closes for the day.

10.45 p.m.: I return to Newsnight at the Winter Gardens and watch the programme go out in the main newsroom with Jeremy Vine, Keiran and several others. Kirsty Wark is interviewing Barbara Castle. It is rather strange; they are seated talking at a set dinner table. Wark asks Castle, 'Has it been a gruelling week?' and Castle replies that it has, with little sleep and little to eat – 'At least you've given me a meal!' she says gratefully to Newsnight, and with only the hint of a smile. Someone comments that Castle has been neglected this week, that Labour haven't looked after her properly, gave no one over to supporting her: unpardonable. If true, it's a strange enactment of the very neglect of the elderly that she and others are contesting.

11.30 p.m.: I go with the *Newsnight* team to the Imperial Hotel, Labour's HQ and the poshest hotel in Blackpool, for drinks. Intense security. Inside, old-style glitz; everyone who is anyone in media and politics is here, and all links between. I spot Leighton Andrews, whom I have met as part of the BBC policy machine but who moved there from Welsh politics [*and will soon move out again*]; Charlie Whelan, Brown's spin doctor, and so on and on. The Imperial is the key site of collusive social networking between political and media elites. As I leave (and I leave soon because I am utterly on my own, with no one even pretending to include me), in the front lobby I am forced to squeeze past John Prescott and Tony Blair. What I am struck by, above all, despite my short-sightedness, is how extremely smart and classy are their suits: they both sport dark evening suits which *glow* with expense.

The next morning I watch the outcome of the pensions vote. The result is announced by Robin Cook, today's conference chair. It is 33 per cent for Castle's composite, 66 per cent for the NEC's position and the promise of a review. On this crucial vote the NEC comes out on top; a show of a modicum of internal democracy has succeeded in reaffirming party unity. Labour is surely all set for power.

Diary, 1996.

*

Commercialisation and Rapprochement

In the early 1990s, under the Conservative government of John Major and in the period leading up to charter renewal in 1996, the political climate grew gradually less hostile. In a context in which neo-liberalism had permanently changed the foundations of British public life, Hussey, Checkland and Birt manoeuvred the BBC to become the quiescent organisation that successive Tory governments had desired. There were two main elements of reform. The first was to bring the BBC's journalism under greater control so as to reduce further the political flak aimed at the corporation. As deputy director-general from 1987, Birt was given the task of unifying and disciplining the BBC's News and Current Affairs departments. He introduced an approach termed 'mission to explain'. It emphasised the need to give news stories a methodically researched analytical context in order to provide more journalistic depth and superior understanding. One feature of the merger was the closure of the Current Affairs department's Lime Grove buildings, physically distant from the news base in White City, a distance that symbolised its independence from the body of the BBC and its own creative tradition of investigation and analysis. Yet as well as centralised control, Birt's reforms also resulted in increased status and budgetary autonomy for the combined operation, fuelling tensions between News and Current Affairs and the channel controllers.

The reorganisation was accompanied by intensifying managerial caution, as borne out by incidents in which programmes were cancelled or delayed under the threat of government displeasure. In January 1991, at the start of the Gulf War, and against the convictions of the editors, a sensational *Panorama* was blocked which revealed that Britain had supplied Iraq with a massively power-ful piece of armoury, the 'supergun', on the grounds that public opinion would not tolerate the story at a time when British servicemen were going to war. And on the eve of the 1992 general election campaign, a *Panorama* entitled 'Sliding Into Slump' was pulled, in which Britain's economic problems were laid at the door of the former Conservative chancellor, Nigel Lawson. The con-tentious explanation given was that the programme was 'a little backward looking'.[32] Such acts stoked alienation among BBC journalists, while current affairs, confused by the dual message of Birtist analytical seriousness yet political emasculation, began an identity crisis which lasted throughout Birt's tenure.

The other legacy of Thatcherism for the BBC in the 1990s was continuing pressure to meet the financial shortfall produced by a continuing real decline in income. From the early 1990s, and gathering pace after Birt became direc-tor-general in 1993, the response was for management to embrace the full panoply of neo-liberal economistic themes: markets, competition, efficiency, the pursuit of commercial activities and international markets. All responded to both the Tory imperative to become commercially oriented, and the need to supplement licence-fee income.

The language of 'efficiency' translated as cuts. In 1990, Checkland reported that £75 million could be saved through cuts by 1993; and later that year a government consultancy proposed that a further saving of £131 million could be made by 1996. Job losses were a major component, and in both the BBC and ITV these were speeded by the introduction of the 25 per cent independent production quota decreed by the 1990 Broadcasting Act, which led to escalat-ing competition and outsourcing of production. Between 1986 and 1996, the BBC lost approximately 5,000 permanent jobs in television, while in fewer years the ITV companies shed about 7,000 jobs, and more as the ITV sector became increasingly concentrated through the later 1990s.

Before the 1980s, the BBC earned a small commercial income from its print operations, such as sales of the *Radio Times*, and from overseas programme markets. In 1987, Checkland backed a massive expansion of the BBC's commercial division, BBC Enterprises, aiming to increase its profits almost threefold between 1988 and 1993. New businesses were absorbed and numerous new tie-in magazines launched. The magazines received free on-screen promotion, prompting complaints of unfair trading from the BBC's print competitors. As a result the BBC was censured in 1992 by the Monopolies and Mergers Commission. BBC Enterprises also diversified into areas – pub games, credit-card authorisation – with no connection to programme-making. There began a searching internal debate on the proper nature and limits of the corporation's commercial activities. The conclusion emphasised the importance of the BBC's commercial extensions being linked to its core broadcasting and media activities, and the need to protect the corporation's 'brand image'. An additional problem was that BBC Enterprises, despite its ambitions, was not particularly effective or profitable as a business.

Some commercial expansion responded to the growing internationalisation of television. Following the launch of CNN's twenty-four-hour international news service, executives from BBC World Service radio decided that they should be competing in international television too, building on the immense journalistic resources of the World Service. The result, from 1991, was World Service Television News, distributed by various satellite carriers. It was the first of the BBC's commercial channel ventures and in its first years unquestionably bore economic risks. The next year the BBC took a stake in a joint venture with Thames Television and the American cable company Cox to launch UK Gold, a commercial satellite channel that ran classic television and used parts of the BBC's programming archive. As competition grew, deals were struck with Murdoch's Sky satellite channels in order to secure certain types of popular programming, particularly sports. In 1994, BBC Enterprises was relaunched as BBC Worldwide under a new chief executive, Bob Phillis. Phillis announced a goal of raising 15 to 20 per cent of licence fee revenue in due course from commercial activities. But as the operations gathered pace, critical questions began to arise over the separation between the corporation's publicly funded and commercial activities, and the extent to which commercialisation might contaminate the independence and creativity of the BBC.

In parallel, the corporation experienced another radical change: the marketisation of the BBC. There were two wings to the process. The 25 per cent independent production quota created an external market in programme supply. Henceforth, in-house BBC producers were required to compete against independent producers to win commissions for programmes on the BBC television channels. On the other hand, to stimulate efficiency and bring further savings, Birt introduced an internal market to the BBC under a policy, piloted from 1991, known as Producer Choice. Given the uncertainty following Major's ascent to power, and with charter renewal looming, Producer Choice had as much political as economic significance. In the same period, the government was encouraging the introduction of internal markets throughout the public sector, particularly in the National Health Service. With Producer Choice, not only did the BBC pre-empt possible government action, but it showed itself to be zealous for marketisation. When the Major government issued its 1992 Green Paper The Future of the BBC, although it questioned almost all aspects of the BBC's future, it did not push advertising as a solution and it applauded Producer Choice and the steps taken to improve efficiency. In its wake, in April 1993, Producer Choice was launched throughout the BBC. Despite this, the corporation remained on a short lead: the licence fee increase continued to be set at the rate of inflation.

Commercialism was not simply an economic imperative. It took hold in the collective consciousness of those working for the BBC. In 1991, Checkland set up a series of internal task forces; one was titled 'The BBC: The Entrepreneur'. Its report reveals the political expediency behind the wholesale adoption of the language of entrepreneurialism: 'Beyond the needs of the consumer, there is a need to run with the political tide. Entrepreneurialism was a requirement of the 1980s and will still have an important part to play in the public sector in the 1990s. The BBC's involvement in commerce signals that it is part of the market place'.[33] By the mid nineties the combined effect of these developments was to install a culture of entrepreneurialism throughout the BBC, one that was manifest in the smallest of everyday interactions as much as at the highest levels of corporate policy.

In 1994, as part of the process of charter renewal, the government published a White Paper that endorsed the BBC's initiatives. The White Paper specified for the first time as priorities for the BBC both increased commercial operations and the growth of foreign markets. In this way the corporation would be poised to lead Britain's move into global media markets and to spearhead the UK's international competitiveness. It would forge a presence for Britain in the international multimedia industry. The directive was affirmed by the BBC when it published in 1996 the policy statement Extending Choice in the Digital Age.

As the political thaw gathered pace, one criticism remained. It concerned the BBC's structure of self-regulation, in particular the role of the governors.

Ironically, given the way the Thatcher administrations had used the governors to manipulate the BBC through imposing political placemen, the argument was made by the Major government that the corporation lacked real accountability. The governors were both too interfering and unaccountable to the general public. For all the statements of purpose and other gestures at accountability, in the nineties this question refused to go away. The settlement under the Major government was that, in return for its enthusiastic engagement with commercial expansion, cost cutting and a new focus on accountability, the BBC would find a supportive government. Privatisation was off the agenda. The licence fee was guaranteed until 2002, and a government press release praised the BBC's 'rich tradition of high quality public service broadcasting'.[34]

The 1996 Broadcasting Act set the framework for the arrival of digital television. At the same time it responded to widespread concerns over Murdoch's dominance of satellite television and his growing media power. By the nineties a political consensus had developed to the effect that, in order to stake a claim in the international information economy, Britain should nurture large media groups. The question of cross-media ownership therefore arose, and specifically whether newspaper groups should be allowed to buy stakes in British terrestrial television. It was a sign of the times when, in the process of the Bill, New Labour took a more deregulatory stance than the Conservative government. Its thinly veiled rationale was to remove the obstacles preventing the biggest newspaper groups, in particular Murdoch's News International, from entering terrestrial television. In the lead in to the next general election, Labour were keen to attract the support of Murdoch's papers. In the event the government line prevailed.

Two other parts of the Act attempted to contain Murdoch's predatory plans, in the process signalling critical future policy issues. In an era in which competition had achieved the status of a transcendental truth, Murdoch – one of Mrs Thatcher's favourite businessmen – had become adept at basing his market power on anti-competitive strategies. Murdoch used classic techniques: of technological advantage, and of vertical and horizontal synergies. On the first, the act attempted to limit his controls of the 'digital gateway', the technologies giving access to digital channels – controls that were a direct extension of BSkyB's virtual monopoly in British satellite television. On the second, the Act targeted Murdoch's content strategies. His tactics in buying up the live screening rights to football's Premier League for his premium subscription channels, to be promoted by his five national newspapers, amounted also to the establishment of anti-competitive tie-ins. Movies and live sports were the content that drove consumers towards satellite television. The pay-TV revenues generated by exclusive control of sports rights had become a key means for Murdoch to repay his huge satellite start-up debts. The BBC became embroiled when, in the 1992 auction for football rights, it suddenly deserted its former partner ITV for BSkyB, contributing £4.5 million to BSkyB's total bid of £60 million per annum over five years in return for weekly highlights.

The Premier League's main reservation about dealing with BSkyB had been the very limited audience it would reach via satellite. By joining BSkyB, the BBC delivered to Murdoch the universality craved by the Premier League clubs. The temptation to try and tame the devil by appeasing him had, it seems, become irresistible for the BBC. The corporation was heavily criticised for reneging on its ties with ITV, for selling its universality cheap, and for giving up on the goal of keeping the national game on national channels. In response to these moves, the 1996 Act tightened a policy of 'Listed Events' established by the 1990 Act. The legislation prohibited certain major national sporting events from being shown exclusively on subscription television, including the Olympics, the Wimbledon tennis finals, the FA Cup Final and some test matches. Despite such restraints, the market value of football rights continued to grow exponentially. The next auction, in 1996, saw the contract for live television rights soar to £185 million per annum.

The Tory transformations of the BBC were increasingly controversial in the worlds of broadcasting and culture. To a host of critics they represented a Faustian bargain: the political subservience of the BBC in exchange for less government aggression. Prominent figures engaged in passionate public denunciations of the corporation's direction under Checkland and Birt. In 1992 Michael Grade, chief executive of Channel 4, formerly controller of BBC1 and a leading voice in British television, accused the governors of adopting a 'policy of political appeasement' and of bowing to the 'political mood of the times'. He was followed by the BBC's senior radio correspondent, Mark Tully, and Dennis Potter, the distinguished television dramatist.

For all the market rhetoric, the BBC faced a crisis in the early 1990s due to declining ratings particularly on BBC1. Milne's period as director-general had been a time of relative ratings success, with the BBC holding up at 46 per cent against the combined 54 per cent share of ITV and Channel 4. By 1991, BBC1 was at an all-time ratings low, and they continued to fall. A new soap opera, *Eldorado*, was produced despite opposition from Birt, who at this time favoured taking the BBC upmarket. In the event it was a disaster, and signalled the corporation's difficulty in gauging the popular mood. As competition bit in, and as the critics continued to bray, executives became increasingly aware of the huge significance of popularity, as measured by ratings, for the legitimacy of the BBC. The result from the early 1990s was a preoccupation among those charged with overseeing key genres – drama, light entertainment, comedy and sitcoms – with finding popular shows that would ensure competitive ratings.

At the same time, given the rise in commercial activities and the imminent arrival of multichannel television, there was felt to be a critical need to redefine the BBC's aims and ethos. A series of high-level statements of public service purpose began to be issued by senior management from the early 1990s, each reflecting twists in the debates raging among executives inside the corporation. The statements oscillated between advocating the market failure model – the BBC as 'filling the gaps' and concentrating on the 'Himalayan peaks' – and the Reithian model of universality and mixed programming.

The first statement, Extending Choice (1992), took the high road. It spoke of the BBC providing services of 'distinction and quality' and of serving a 'clear public purpose' in the new broadcasting market. The word 'popular' was barely present. The position it represented was speedily revised. In 1993, with BBC1 showing its lowest ratings for almost a decade, Alan Yentob, acting controller of BBC1 and BBC2, and the new managing director of radio, Liz Forgan, announced the half-time results of an audit called the Programme Strategy Review (PSR). Yentob and Forgan's statement spoke of the BBC giving excessive attention to the 'ABC1s' or middle classes, to the neglect of those from lower socio-economic groups. It amounted to a swing back to a commitment to Reithian universal provision centred on strong popular programming. Soon after, several new creative leaders were brought in: Yentob as controller of BBC1, Charles Denton in drama and David Liddiment in entertainment. The systematic attention to improving popular output began to yield fruit. Despite intensifying competition, by mid 1994 BBC1's share of viewing was 33 per cent and climbing.

In 1995, another attempt to redefine the corporation's purposes, People and Programmes, set out a new paradigm. It married the PSR and its overview of current programming with the most extensive audience research ever carried out by the BBC. Criticising the BBC's over-reliance 'on its own judgement of audience needs', it adopted the language of consumer satisfaction and spoke of the need to respond to changing tastes as well as to the new marketplace in talent. A detailed appraisal of the BBC's output in all radio and television genres followed, with a series of undertakings to increase range, diversity and quality for both minority and majority audiences.

The new managerial vision was completed by Extending Choice in the Digital Age (1996), which stated the BBC's intentions to move into digital terrestrial television and to use it primarily to augment its public service offerings. Cable and satellite, by contrast, had been conceived by the corporation mainly as vehicles for commercial development. The document also gave a new rationale for the BBC's expanded commercial operations, arguing that they formed part of a 'virtuous circle' in which commercial earnings fed revenue back into programming and services for the national audience, supporting high quality. The resulting output would, in turn, further boost international sales. In the same year, for the first time in over a decade, the BBC had the confidence to argue for a real increase in the level of the licence fee to fund new services and the entry into digital. In the meantime, Birt proposed to deploy 'efficiency savings' as well as the revenues from selling off the BBC's transmission services to fund the new initiatives.

By the mid 1990s the growth of cable and satellite, the unleashing of commercialism at Channel 4, the coming of Channel 5 and the first stirrings of digital television had together effected a massive reorientation of British television. Competition in the industry had rocketed, while the combined revenue base had not grown to match. Moreover, the ITC believed in a hands-off approach. As a result there were more primarily commercially-oriented channels competing for audience time than primarily public service ones. In the space of a few years the centre of gravity in British broadcasting had shifted. The BBC came increasingly to be seen in exceptionalist terms, while the frenzy of competition in low-cost programming between commercial broadcasters drove a rise in sensationalism and populism across the industry. Faced with this, and with the consequent conditioning of audience tastes, the BBC had little option but to emulate the prevailing character of popular programming. In any case, in a deregulated industry it was competing to buy programmes from the same powerful production companies as its rivals.

Birt, as director-general from 1993, had developed a vision in which the marketisation of the BBC and its growing entrepreneurialism were conceived as ways both of seeing off political criticism and of producing a BBC fit for intensifying competition. Did Birt save the BBC from death by privatisation? Probably. Did he have little option but to pick up the gauntlet and reinvent the BBC in terms acceptable to the prevailing political climate? Probably. Was his regime overzealous in adopting the culture of market liberalism and its attendant managerial techniques? The answer lies in comparing BBC management's own statements of public service purpose with what was actually going on inside the corporation in the nineties.

The Cultural State

At the coal face, 1960s

'Universal deference was paid to the image of the producer as responsible for the "real job" of the Corporation, as the creative person, as the worker at the "coal face"; administration was accorded a subsidiary role – even by administrators . . . So the self-effacing, supportive, even cosseting demeanour of administrators towards programme staff often carried with it some compensatory mannerisms and a slightly adult–child tone in observations about them or a manipulative, organising attitude.'

Tom Burns, *The BBC.*

*

Teletext hierarchy

I am standing in the lobby waiting for a lift in Television Centre, late for an interview I've arranged on the fifth floor. Beside the lift, as in many BBC buildings, hang television screens showing a stream of teletext information put out by the BBC's internal communications department – responsible also for publishing the weekly internal magazine, *Ariel*, wittily dubbed *Pravda* in the corridors and editing suites. I glance up and scan the usual mundane news spots. The sixth floor tea bar will close at the weekend for refurbishment. The Queen is to visit the BBC Experience exhibition at Broadcasting House. At the Royal Television Society awards last night BBC programme-makers swept the board; there follows a list of BBC winners. Suddenly the name of an executive flashes up on the screen and with it the news that he has been promoted from *Director* of Strategy, Television, to *Controller* of Strategy, Television.

As I watch over the months, I see that each day such redesignations – minute and opaque adjustments of status, probably auguring jumps in salary – are the surface manifestation of a relentless machinery of naming and renaming that drives BBC management and its fine-tuned structure of control. After months in the BBC the meaning of this naming game and of the constant shifts of status and territory become clear. Those who are winning are repeatedly reshuffled and renamed by those in power. Those who are not stay nominally still. The BBC is truly run by a *nomenklatura*. Ordinary staff are asked mutely to witness and concur with these obsessive renamings. It is the kind of display of hierarchy guaranteed in any organisation to stoke nothing so much as massive indifference.

Diary, 1996.

*

The grapes of Reith

We are waiting in a suite at Television Centre, some twenty-five people from Drama Group and I, for a BBC1 Offers meeting to begin. Alan Yentob is running late, we have been told, and good-humoured banter fills the waiting time. Suddenly the door opens and, emperor-like, Yentob sweeps in accompanied by an entourage from his BBC1 Planning and Strategy Unit, mostly women. One of the women is bearing a large gilt dish on which are arranged luscious fruits, apparently carried over from a previous meeting, from which Alan selects the odd grape or plum as we move through the agenda of ideas for potential commission.

Diary, 1996.

*

'The Very Model of Socialist Organisation'?

The Italian Marxist Antonio Gramsci, reflecting in the early 1930s on the state and civil society, wrote that 'every state is ethical in as much as one of its most important functions is to raise the great mass of the population to a particular cultural and moral level'.[1] He might have been designing the normative basis of the Reithian BBC. From a different perspective, writers influenced by Michel Foucault argue that liberalism has been characterised by the project of inculcating a responsible, ethical and normalised citizenry.[2] This stress on the combined ethical and cultural project of modern government is telling when we consider the BBC, the incarnation of such a project: the government of culture. In another telling phrase, the BBC has been described as 'more like a minor nation state than a business'.[3] It has its own distinctive ethos and

66

language, and its own quasi-tribal structure of loyalty, identification and division. In 2003, it employed 27,000 people and had an annual budget in the region of £2.7 billion.[4] The BBC, then, as a 'cultural state' within a state on which it is dependent.

What kind of organisation is the BBC, and why does it matter? Why should we be interested in what it is rather than what it produces? There are three related reasons why the BBC's character as an organisation matters. Above all it matters because it affects what is made. The way creative practices and processes are organised, and who gets to make programmes, powerfully influence the extent to which the BBC is able to fulfil its public service broadcasting ambitions. The second reason it matters is because the BBC is a social microcosm. As a major public employer, the social character of the BBC – the way it treats its workers, the degree and the forms of hierarchy that it embodies, and the representational adequacy of its population – is itself a political issue.

But it matters also because there has been a loss of faith in public sector organisations, and since the 1980s governments have looked to the private sector for models of good practice. In earlier periods the situation was reversed. During the later nineteenth century it was the state-owned network industries – the railways, telegraph and postal services – that pioneered the rationalised modes of industrial organisation, the planning, forecasting and coordination skills, that were later taken up by private companies. These industries were perceived to be the leading organisations of their time. Their huge scale and geographical scope demanded centralised control, and they were seen as naturally linked to modernising government. In Britain in the mid twentieth century, the BBC had a special role to play; it was repeatedly used as a model of the public corporation. The Crawford Committee set up in 1925 to consider the future shape of British broadcasting when deliberating on the nature of the BBC gave the first formal consideration of what a public corporation should be and how it should be run. But public sector organisations came to embody even higher aspirations. For the Labour left, the Post Office, the NHS and the BBC 'were seen as prefigurative, their methods and values ultimately designed to spread to the whole society'. Hugh Dalton, a prominent Labour politician in the 1930s and 1940s, considered the BBC 'the very model of socialist organisation'.[5] This was a time when the social character of leading organisations was taken as a measure of the condition of the entire society, and public enterprises, with their well-developed social purposes, were the leading organisations.

By the 1980s the public status of the BBC weighed heavily the other way, and in the early 1990s Birt famously derogated the BBC as a 'command economy', justifying the embrace of markets and private sector management techniques.[6] One legacy of Birtist revisionism was a profound ambivalence towards the BBC's own history and achievements. Under Birt it became unacceptable to speak positively of the BBC's past.[7] Indeed, a concern with the past and any attachment to it became a source of scorn, as a narrative of the BBC's erstwhile complacent decline became established as an orthodoxy.

The chapters that follow redeem a view of the BBC as a social microcosm that provides a compelling portrait not only of the state of the public sector, but of Britain's public, working and ethical life. For the contemporary BBC offers an acute example of what has been productive and what corrosive in the introduction of markets and business practices into the public sector and in the tilting of its mixed economy towards private sector mores.

*

The history man

I have been waiting for months to get my first one-to-one interview with Michael Wearing, the producer and impresario who has been responsible for some of the greatest television drama of the eighties and nineties. *The History Man, Boys from the Blackstuff, Edge of Darkness, Middlemarch, Pride and Prejudice, Our Mutual Friend, Our Friends in the North*: Wearing's career encompasses some of the most innovative and radical work in television. He is now head of BBC drama serials. Mike has been friendly across many a crowded Drama Editorial Board. He has included me in his scene, allowing me access to his people. But he is immensely busy and, it turns out, shy, as am I when finally I get to the appointed hour. Mike wants a cigarette and has gone out; I am ushered in to wait in his room in Centre House with its view of the brutal contours of the M40 flyover as it cuts through west London.

I notice a set of Asa Briggs's five-volume corporate history of the BBC sitting on his shelves, a history commissioned by the BBC. This surprises me. Mike Wearing is no corporate man; his demeanour and politics do not lead me to expect such an interest or such an identification. Bemused, when he gets back I ask whether he finds the volumes a good read. Mike smiles widely, laughs and says he has never read them. He explains that the set is supplied to all BBC executives to adorn their bookshelves as part of the corporation's standard executive decor. We speculate that, presumably, it is intended also to school the officer class in the arcane workings of BBC power and status. For all he cares, Mike shrugs, the sacred text might just as well have some use as a bookend or as the case for a handy whisky bottle.

Diary, 1996.

*

Patterns of History

How does a huge organisation with an ethical project such as the BBC comport itself? How are values transmitted and unity achieved, and yet its essential creative and intellectual vitality – the capacity for original and dissenting thought – maintained? The BBC is a restless institution. Increasingly influenced by management theories, under constant political surveillance and ten-yearly parliamentary appraisal, it has repeatedly reinvented itself.

Old institutions can have short memories. In the BBC's case this is so despite Asa Briggs's official history. Indeed the Briggs history's relation to the BBC mirrors the BBC's own ambivalent relation to government. It is at once an independent history, officially sanctioned but produced on sufferance; yet in its sympathetic portrayal of the high politics of the BBC, providing little cause for sufferance. Asa Briggs and Tom Burns, the sociologist who studied the BBC between the mid sixties and seventies, provide some memory, including evidence of recurring patterns in the corporation's attempts at self-reform. From the thirties to the late sixties, the BBC consisted of a number of directorates or divisions with the character of 'baronies' – a term commonly used to convey the extremely hierarchical, vertical organisation of the BBC, in which powerful department heads ruled unchallenged over their designated programme territory. Reith's organisational policy aimed for centralised administration and unified control, but independence in the running of production or 'output' departments so as to prevent uniformity and encourage diversity in the making of programmes. It was a highly segmented organisation with few horizontal links between the vertical directorates, with the exception of the Board of Management at the top executive level.

A curiously wide set of institutional analogies have been offered for the BBC. Edward Heath, when Prime Minister, likened it to a university, with its 'wayward and contrary "creative" people'; in marked contrast, Sir Michael Swann, on becoming chairman, concluded that the BBC resembled nothing so much as the armed forces with its 'clear cut network of people all doing their jobs in a tightly controlled way'.[8] Burns sees the BBC and its mode of arm's-length governance as the very model of the public sector quango.[9] Many have commented on the civil-service-like qualities of the institution, with its cult of the flexible and gifted generalist and its character over decades as an

Oxbridge-based, apparently meritocratic but closed society consumed by the internal politics of promotion.

From the early years of the BBC these qualities were compounded by the internal divisions and conflicts that mark any large organisation. Intense rivalries existed between the output departments, and an 'unending game of prestige-poker' occurred between different services and specialisms. The rivalries were individual as well as collective and a 'markedly status-conscious attitude' prevailed, with 'gruelling competition to gain the edge over others in technical qualifications, or in expertise, or in flair, or in artistic insight'.[10] Particularly in the early decades before competition, departmental rivalries amounted to an ersatz form of such competition, one that helped to sharpen purposes. Corporate management acted as referees or arbiters. The introverted rivalries point also to the extremes of solipsism and narcissism that are still to be found in the BBC, qualities that might be further linked to what Burns identifies as the 'autistic world' of the corporation stemming from the endemic pressures and fears that an error or misjudgement may damage its public image, and thus its wider interests.[11] Given the BBC's moral authority, self-importance and sheer scale, the solipsism is a purer form of the self-absorption to be found in the broadcasting industry as a whole. It is as though broadcasting's status as a parvenu profession, combined with its high visibility and glamour, produces a curious mixture of intense, defensive insecurity and arrogance. Such a stance has survived broadcasting's passage from dubious cultural occupation to wealthy and glittering establishment profession.

Equally characteristic of the early BBC was a split between its 'creative' and 'administrative' sides, the balance of power shifting in different eras. A long tradition, dating from Reith's first reorganisation in 1933, protected the corporation's ' "creative workers" from the responsibilities and preoccupations of administration'.[12] In the sixties and seventies, according to Burns, administration became subordinate in status to the creative departments and colluded somewhat resentfully in that subordination. Administrators were self-effacing and deferential to producers, who in turn were divested of any financial or managerial consciousness. Burns's sardonic comments on what he portrays as an artificial split between the creative and the administrative speaks of his disillusion, from the vantage point of the seventies, with the blinkered and unworldly privileges of the BBC's elite producer class. A similar criticism surfaced in harsher ideological guise in the eighties free-market attack on BBC elitism. Partly as a consequence, relations between production and its management continued to be a central preoccupation of the BBC throughout the nineties, and the theme permeates this book. In fact, the creative and the administrative are intimately bound in broadcasting, and management's task must be to achieve the optimal form of integration to serve evolving creative and normative goals.

Evidence of further recurring patterns comes in Burns's account of the corporate reorganisation at the turn of the seventies which came hard on the heels of severe economic pressures and which, for the first time, drew in management consultants. The reorganisation foreshadows later developments under Birt, and it set in place roughly the organisation that endured until Birt's major restructuring of mid 1996. Between 1960 and 1975, the BBC's staff grew from about 16,000 to 25,000, the level it has hovered near ever since. The relentless rise in staff numbers, increasing rates of pay and rising programme costs, compounded by inflation, caused a serious financial squeeze. In 1968, with relations between the BBC and the Wilson government already uneasy, the corporation approached government for an increase in the licence fee, the third request in as many years. In this unpropitious context senior management appointed McKinsey and Co. as part of a show of its earnest intentions to exert greater financial discipline.

The result of the McKinsey-inspired seventies reorganisation was to move financial and practical management from the central administration to the 'product divisions', Television, Radio and External Services (the World Service). Overall financial responsibility was to be held by the managing directors of these divisions. To achieve better financial accountability within the divisions, responsibility was further devolved. Each programme proposal was to be accompanied by an estimated statement of costs, to include both corporate overheads allocated by a new central resources department – the use of staff time, equipment, studios and other BBC services – and cash costs such as writers' and performers' fees. Producers and editors were given financial responsibility for all programme-making under their charge. The changes ushered in an awareness of the cost basis of programming across Television and Radio, from executives to assistant producers, that Burns calls revolutionary, although leading figures from the period contest the view that awareness was lacking before.[13] Personnel functions were devolved and for the first time engineering and technical staff – cameramen, studio and sound engineers, lighting specialists – were placed within production directorates. From this period, too, dates a convention whereby the majority of senior management jobs were held by people with programme-making experience; 'at long last', Burns says, 'output was clearly on top and no longer on tap'.[14]

A continuous cycle was installed, which still operates, in which the planning of programmes for each channel and service became systematically organised around a new ritual, the twice-yearly 'Offers' meetings. In these meetings the channel controllers and their teams of administrators, financial advisers and, later, strategists took a view of the future direction of the channels about two years in advance, and sought programming from producers to fill the schedules in accord with their vision. In turn, production department heads came with a series of costed programme proposals or 'offers', each containing details of the intended genre, format, style, key performers and writers. Controllers later came back with a response to each offer: 'yes', 'no', 'perhaps, with this condition', 'too expensive', and so on. The planning cycle brought together the three central elements of the turn-of-the-seventies reorganisation: financial discipline; forward planning, in which individual ideas were integrated into a prediction of the bulk programming requirements for each channel; and a management system to monitor costs and operate the planning.[15]

The seventies reorganisation anticipated Birt's reforms in numerous ways, in the emphases on rationalisation, management and planning, and greater financial probity. Power was ceded by the 'barons', the production department heads, to the managing directors of Television and Radio, the channel controllers and their chief accountants. The reorganisation therefore brought greater central control, although, critically, the process of commissioning programmes was not so centralised. Burns comments that it resulted in top management losing the confidence of large sections of BBC staff, a disquiet interpreted characteristically by management in terms of a 'failure of communication'. Yet Burns criticises such language as an attempt to gloss over the unleashing of unprecedented internal opposition and distrust within the corporation, which he links to the growth of a managerial obsession with monitoring the performance of subordinates.[16] By the nineties, this aspect of the culture of the BBC had expanded and taken a new, systematic form in the guise of auditing.

Burns's account of the BBC touches only in passing on another continuing element of the BBC's organisation: the complex structure of internal divisions, of which the organisation is fundamentally composed. This structure has always been an essential feature of the BBC, and a dynamic and changing one. But in the minds of programme-makers and executives, the wider broadcasting ecology is also experienced as a universe structured by perceptions of likeness and difference, unity and opposition. At the highest level, in relation to other broadcasters, the key factor is the closeness of the rival broadcaster to public service commitments or, indeed, its opposite – unalloyed commercialism. For much of the nineties, for many BBC programme-makers working in minority and experimental genres such as arts, access programming or some areas of documentary, Channel 4 was considered the main, often benevolent rival. For those working in the large audience and popular genres such as drama series and entertainment, ITV was the natural competitor. Those producing popular series, for example, mourned the day that Nick Elliott became ITV Network Centre's head of drama, walking away from an equivalent job at the BBC, for at ITV he was seen to deploy his talents in ways that BBC drama could only envy. Meanwhile, documentary producers working for BBC2's *Modern Times* strand looked to Channel 4's *Cutting Edge* as the opposition. The constant attrition of the ratings war on such strands was one measure of hostilities — hostilities, however, that existed back to back with a sense of regulated common purpose, striving competitiveness and sometimes grudging mutual admiration. Above and beyond quasi-tribal rivalries this was a universe of common, if differentiated, public service commitments.

Into this balanced conceptual universe from the early nineties parachuted the industry *arrivistes*, cable and satellite. In 1997, the start of Channel 5 — brash, populist, low budget, and at times reasonably inventive within those considerable constraints — added to the unbalancing of existing arrangements. In combination, the new broadcasters caused a change in the known universe: from now on ITV and Channel 4 had one face turned to the new populist wing of the industry, another face to their public service obligations. For the BBC the balance shifted uncontrollably; it was increasingly out on a wing. In entertainment, leisure and daytime programming, the BBC was faced by a range of low-budget rivals whose production values were rapidly becoming established as the norm. For ITV and Channel 4, Channel 5 and Sky came to be perceived as competitors, not only for audiences but for programming and revenues. During the later nineties, there was a significant change in the nature of the competitive dynamic between similar strands across the broadcasters. Where productive rivalries had formerly resulted in raising the game on both sides, as the nineties dragged on and budgets were squeezed, such fruitful competition morphed into baser and more cynical imitation across a number of genres.

Nonetheless, it is striking that, to the present, in industry forums held under Chatham House rules, when faced with the prospect of radical revision to this still-regulated universe, that sector of British television committed to public service — the BBC, ITV, Channels 4 and 5 — continues to express common interests and unified values. Only Murdoch's Sky stands outside the consensus.

*

The Rivals: the documentary debate

The 1997 Edinburgh International Television Festival: a session called 'The Rivals' in which key strands from rival broadcasters reflect with an audience of professionals on the state of the genre in question. Today Stephen Lambert, editor of BBC2's *Modern Times*, and Charles Furneaux of Channel 4's *Cutting Edge* are in conversation about contemporary documentary, with critic Gillian Reynolds in the chair. Their exchanges offer model insights into the genealogies, competitive positioning and creative aims of documentary. Reynolds opens with the bare facts: *Modern Times* gets an average rating of 2.9 million, *Cutting Edge* 3.4 million; both air about twenty programmes a year.

LAMBERT: '*Cutting Edge* was set up in the early eighties by John Willis and Peter Moore, and occupied the middle ground of popular documentaries. *Modern Times* began in 1995, taking the *40 Minutes* slot, which had been edited by Eddie Moerzoff. Michael Jackson [*controller of BBC2*] said he wanted a rival to *Cutting Edge*, but also to do things differently: for directors to stamp the mark of authorship on their films, to produce a body of work distinctive to them, to make the films enter public debate in a way they weren't then doing. We gave people in our department the space to explore and experiment – like Mark Phillips and Daniel Reed. The aim was to bring on talent, to be bold and ambitious, to do things with a signature; but also to use better known directors such as Peter Dale and Susanna White, to whom we gave the freedom to play with form; and Paul Pawlikowski, who does docudrama. I see *Modern Times* going in two directions: either very stylish "film" films, or very intimate films on DV [*digital video*] that are filmed over a very long period, and that allow close relations to develop between film-maker and subjects.'

Lambert shows three clips: 'Quality Time', a film on the problems of childcare for middle-class parents via a portrait of several families and their troubled encounters with their nannies; the dinner party scene from 'Mange Tout', Mark Phillips's film tracing the relations between developed and developing worlds through the life history of the luxury vegetable, which Lambert compares with and judges superior to a similar scene from Paul Watson's notorious 'The Dinner Party'; and a scene from 'Saturday Night', shot cheaply in black and white with a poetic voiceover, an empathetic and experimental portrait of young people's hedonism and drug use.

FURNEAUX: 'Our department at Channel 4 puts out 150 hours of television a year, of which only twenty hours is *Cutting Edge*. We have just three people in the department – check if you don't believe me! Dealing with the independents means responding to very variable quality, style and tone. We call our strands "anthologies", since it would be difficult to produce such a polished visual style as *Modern Times*. So we make a virtue of that and go for diversity. We can be flexible; if we commission a film, and it goes in a different direction than anticipated, we can put it in a different strand.'

He shows three clips, the second from 'The Grave', a harrowing film about the exhumation of bodies from the civil war in the former Yugoslavia, which was moved between strands and which, he says, 'wouldn't have gone out on the BBC – but there is an audience out there for this; it got 1.5 million'; and the third an 'arresting form of observational film about people who complain about things. It's about capturing the dramatic moments in our lives as they happen – and that's what I think we want to do in *Cutting Edge* which Stephen wouldn't do.'

REYNOLDS: 'I want the essence of *Modern Times*, Stephen: how mainstream are you?'

LAMBERT: 'We're "mainstream" in being the main popular documentary slot on BBC2 in prime time: BBC2's average share is 11 per cent, and we get 12 to 13 per cent, a younger and more female audience than the rest of BBC2. We help to correct the channel's male bias.'

REYNOLDS: 'It's visually very beautiful; you stress aesthetic qualities rather than journalistic ones, don't you?'

LAMBERT: 'I do think they're visually strong. But we also do other kinds of film, where the energy's not going into the look but into capturing the story unfolding.'

REYNOLDS: 'They're very intimate, but they're also cool . . .'

LAMBERT: 'I like a bit of voyeurism. I like "cool". I like the odd cruel joke – these are qualities I like.'

REYNOLDS, *turning to* FURNEAUX: 'Is there a house style in *Cutting Edge*?'

FURNEAUX: 'No, visually this is impossible to achieve because of the diversity of independents working to us. I envy Stephen his editorial "authorship", that he can stamp a look on the strand. *Cutting Edge* is more ordinary, it has more straightforward narratives than *Modern Times*. I want it to be welcoming and friendly, not cold or voyeuristic. The ratings matter to us: after *Friends*, *ER* and *Brookside*, we are about the fourth dependable ratings-puller on the channel, and we get co-productions. So we are very valuable. I asked our advertising department what would be the revenue implications of putting *Modern Times* in the *Cutting Edge* slot, and they said it would involve a loss of £1 million a year!'

LAMBERT *(retorts):* 'For me, *Cutting Edge* is not risk-taking enough, and this is evident in the fact that it shoots fewer films than us on DV. At one time it was very homogeneous in style – the same voiceover, the same Aston style. It seemed to be going over the old *40 Minutes* cuttings book . . .'

REYNOLDS [*chuckles, agreeing*]: '. . . and the old *This Week* cuttings book, and old *Daily Mirrors* . . .'

She invites questions from the audience. *Modern Times* appears to be controversial and to be riling its professional circle. A film-maker targets Lambert: 'Modern Times puts entertainment before insight, and even then it's usually limited to middle-class human insight. Too often it's the middle classes laughing at the working classes.' Another man says: 'Within a few minutes of the start of "Quality Time", I know who's the goodie and who's the baddie – it's too predictable.' And another: 'It would be better if the films were focused on the subjects of the film, rather than being so concerned with the author's voice and perspective.'

At the close, rivals Lambert and Furneaux find common ground by considering the threat to quality documentaries represented by the recently erupted rash of docu-soaps.

FURNEAUX: 'ITV's documentaries have lost their way; they are too caught up with docu-soaps. On the other hand, it's marvellous that the last episode of *Driving School* [*a hit BBC1 docu-soap*] got 14 million! I'm ambivalent about the success of docu-soaps and what it does for documentaries.'
LAMBERT: 'The explosion of factual programmes on BBC1 is great; it has a lot to do with the relatively less well-performing output from drama and entertainment. But the continuing decline of *Network First* on ITV is very sad and a warning to us all.'

Diary, 1997.

*

Me too drama: ITV, the popular novelist and us

It's late; the Programme Finance Committee in Drama Group has run on, and we are now going through the details of the drama development budget. Every payment made for script development and acquisitions has to be passed by this committee. We have come to a proposal to spend £75,000 to buy an option on the latest novel by one of Britain's leading popular novelists. There is discomfort and incredulity in the room; the figure is queried: 'You cannot be serious!' jokes one. A department manager weighs in, defending it persuasively, comparing it with comparable fees paid by ITV, which she knows about first-hand: 'Sixty or sixty-five thousand were standard for ITV; that's what she was paid for options on the earlier adaptations, and this is only slightly higher, after all. It's a question of whether we want to do it, the first time the BBC will have made something by her to rival the series on ITV, and remember, that delivered 16.5 million!' She finesses the opposition and justifies the spend by reference to the potential for huge ratings and a productive mimicry with ITV. It works: the spend is passed; the option is taken out.

Diary, 1996.

*

Fission and Fusion

Within the corporate body of the BBC, another structure of fission and fusion exists. In each programme area, staff have a powerful belief in the central importance of and the contribution made by that genre to the BBC's public service mission. This is accompanied by a palpable sense of rivalry towards adjacent genres: current affairs sceptical of the intellectual value of news, while the newsroom sees current affairs journalism as lumbering and slow; news and current affairs anxious about, and keen to learn tricks from, the successes of documentary; entertainment keeping a close eye on daytime leisure shows; Radio 4 producers watchful in relation to Radio 3 talks and features, Radio 3 producers wary in turn about the rise of cultural programming on Radio 4; the Community Programme Unit concerned about the bowdlerising of its access techniques by the higher-profile docu-soaps. The distinct identity of each production area, expressed in a scepticism towards rival departments and other parts of the BBC, is vital to the BBC's well-being. It fosters internal diversity and the space for dissent and debate – essential preconditions for an independent and innovative production culture.

In the Birt era there were two further axes of division within the corporation. The first and most serious posed Birt's Corporate Centre against the rest. Corporate Centre was widely perceived to be a bloated stronghold of centralised administrative, policy, strategy and corporate relations departments, and to have grown out of all proportion under Birt in response to political pressure. Corporate Centre was therefore associated by many staff with political expediency and even appeasement. Its Policy and Planning Unit, set up in 1987, was seen as part of the increasingly elaborate apparatus for monitoring programme-making and rebuking those who threatened to offend the political class. A new post of controller of editorial policy, attached to Policy and Planning, was given the brief of troubleshooting across all genres and developing new journalistic guidelines. In the nineties Corporate Centre also became the source of the burgeoning managerial initiatives – efficiency drives, auditing directives, accountability requirements – that regularly chastened production departments. Yet Corporate Centre itself is said to have cost £90 million a year to run.[17] There was therefore intense resentment among production departments towards the expensive, unproductive and disciplinary managerial carapace that they carried, a burden manifest in the 15 per cent corporate overhead levied on parts of in-house production.

This axis was cross-cut by another, dividing the News and Current Affairs (NCA) directorate from the rest of production and broadcasting. News was regarded, sometimes admiringly, sometimes jealously, sometimes with frank disbelief, as the elite intellectual corps of the BBC. Even in the late eighties, recruitment on to the news training scheme favoured recruits from Oxbridge and a couple of elite modern universities. In the nineties, newsroom management still boasted of the high numbers of recruits from those who had taken history firsts at Cambridge. It was believed that DGs, channel controllers and senior executives had come disproportionally from the ranks of NCA, and often from the ranks of the flagship programmes Panorama and Newsnight. For this reason, because of news's perceived central importance to the democratic purposes of the BBC, because of its close contact with government and politicians, and because of Birt's background in news and current affairs and his apparent privileging of these areas, it was widely held within the rest of the BBC that NCA had a hotline to the DG's office and, more broadly, to power. NCA was pilloried as excessively serious, pompous and self-regarding, as intellectually unyielding, and as supercilious and uncomprehending in its attitudes towards the corporation's entertainment and popular sides.

But news was seen as having other privileges too. With its guaranteed schedule slots, it stood outside the rough and tumble of the internal competition for commissions and schedule time, and was uniquely beyond the channel controllers' reach. And when Producer Choice and the independent production quota took hold in the early nineties, alone of all genres news was exempted. Given the sacred principles of independence and impartiality, according to management dictum, news should not have to compete against external suppliers.

There existed, finally, rivalries and ideological divisions within the larger BBC production groups and departments, between their component units. Drama Group in the mid-nineties, for example, contained internal tensions between the Series, Serials, Singles and Films departments, rivalries that echoed with the historical tensions between the mass-oriented and popular-cultural dimensions of the BBC and its more middle-brow, high-cultural and literary–artistic elements. If Series, responsible for soaps like EastEnders, appeared unashamedly devoted to the popular end of drama, while Serials, Singles and Films were associated with more writerly projects, in fact by the nineties the differences between the genres were subtler. And while these distinctions played a part in internal rivalries, the real motor of competition was the imperative to win commissions and get programmes on screen.

BBC staff existed in a shifting universe of identity and affiliation, rivalry and enmity. When faced, as a producer in the Community Programme Unit or as a film-maker in *Newsnight*, with lower budgets and reduced output due to the efficiency savings being channelled into setting up BBC News 24, internal antagonisms were honed. When the flagship political discussion programme *Question Time* was pushed to the fringes of prime-time by expanding late-evening light entertainment, current affairs producers quipped ruefully about the BBC's declining serious purpose and the unstoppable rise of celebrity quiz shows. Yet a higher level of integration was evident in current affairs producers' acknowledgement that, critically, the BBC must compete in prime-time and must therefore match the popular mix of rival channels. And when in 1996 the World Service was faced with cuts to the autonomy of its newsgathering operations and their rationalisation within the centralised Newsgathering department, staff from all over the BBC, united by a common ethic and common outrage, joined the wider hue and cry against the sacrifice of this remaining symbol of internal pluralism, internationalism, local expertise and connectedness in the BBC's journalism.

*

All the people

'The definition of public service broadcasting is really complicated. For some, it means broadcasting funded out of the public purse, and they ally that to news and education. For me, the long tradition of public service broadcasting has been an integration between the classic trilogy of inform, educate and entertain: that you do one to help you do the other, and you aspire to the highest quality in all genres. We set a standard for everything. And increasingly, the thing that marks out public service broadcasting is that it's on the side of the people: *all* the people. It's not interested in niches for their own sake, in providing shareholder value. It's interested in nothing else than providing enlightening and creative programming to audiences. The BBC stands for innovation and diversity in programme-making; and the problem is that if we are not there, the market will not provide these things. You can't withdraw from the market if someone else is doing, say, popular drama. Public service is always about teaching audiences that there's further to go within a genre, more to explore.'

David Docherty, deputy director of BBC Television, 1998.

*

Fantastic interactive

GB: 'So what is the public service rationale for what you're doing here?'

'I'm not good at the standard BBC-type official answer, but my personal one is this. Every interactive service that we've so far launched on the three digital platforms has been, I believe, the best of its kind. BBC Text is simply better than anything else on offer, on all platforms. We've taken analogue text services way into the digital age. Our service on DTT is exponentially better than the rivals. On satellite, I got a call from Skytext on the day we launched . . . which just said, "Congratulations, a fantastic service! We're going back to the drawing board." Everything we've heard from the public so far has been, "Wow, this is great." So what's our role? It's quality. We know now that other broadcasters and platform owners are running around trying to match what we've done. It sounds horribly snotty, but we have set the benchmark for interactive TV standards in this country. Now, we're in a privileged position because we don't have to squeeze money out of this medium, and we're very, very aware of that privilege. So what do we do in return for using public money to launch these services? We make sure they are bloody great. We are setting the quality standards – no, that really is pompous, we're helping to set the quality standards for this platform. If that isn't a public service rationale I'm not sure what is.'

Manager, BBC interactive television project, 2001.

*

The Poetics versus *The Sweeney*

'I've always been passionate about public service broadcasting; I have immense respect for the BBC, its history, its standards and aims. So I'm amazed, and grateful, to find myself working inside the BBC now. It's extraordinary, if you think about it, how identified I am with the place, given that I'd never worked here until eight months ago, and that I came in as a lowly script editor. In the eighties and early nineties I worked for independents, never for the BBC, and for Central and Channel 4. So I was very familiar with how they operated. The BBC was still a very old-fashioned, closed operation then. I applied for a job as a junior script editor years ago; I didn't get it. I was interviewed by four men, and they asked when I'd last read Aristotle's *Poetics*! I was stunned. Then they asked what my favourite popular drama was, and I obviously should have said whatever the top BBC series was at the time. But I said *The Sweeney*. And they practically fell on the floor having heart attacks because people who work for

80

the BBC didn't make programmes like *The Sweeney* or watch *The Sweeney*, because it was clearly unspeakably common and vulgar.'

GB: 'What was your recent interview like? Why the difference?'

'It was with George [*her boss*] and Charles Denton. Charles asked if I'd ever fired anyone [*we laugh*] – rather curious; it was for a job that didn't actually come into existence, a manager who'd have to hire and fire. George asked me easy things like what makes a good script. I'm being sarcastic: it was bloody impossible. I gave really gormless answers. Then he said, "Would you have made *Four Weddings and a Funeral?* – which was also impossible; well, given its success, how could I say "no"? But I can remember liking him, and that was the main thing.'

Script editor, BBC Drama, 1996.

*

Reinventing Reith

Until recent years, for all the organisational divisions, because the BBC's social purposes and ethical basis are real, unequivocal and long-standing, the corporation had been a way of life for many employees, in whom it inspired unusual devotion and who approached their work almost as a vocation. The robust identification of many staff with the BBC provided the organisation with an implicit but resilient unity. It was an identification with myriad registers, according to the position occupied within the BBC. It commonly took the form of contemporary, still vital enunciations of the Reithian discourse of serving the public, justifying the licence fee, universality, high standards, quality and integrity of output and so on.

In the nineties, the Reithian discourse in fact had two expressions. It circulated still as an official managerial rhetoric in publicity and public relations, internal and external rituals, internal and external documents – a Reithian icing on the new managerial cake. But it was also spoken informally with commitment and emotion by many individuals at all levels of the institution, and often in the context of their angry denunciations of Birtist management – for destructive cuts and casualisation, excessive bureaucracy, destroying the BBC's creative base, shifting the output in a crude commercial direction, being flaccidly middlebrow, neglecting popular tastes, not delivering on cultural diversity, or for failing effectively to reform the BBC's finances and for being profligate with the licence fee. In this counter-discourse, it was senior management and its proselytising initiatives that were perceived as having undermined the corporation's capacity to fulfil its central democratic purposes and ethical ideals. Reithianism therefore bore both official *and* informal, oppositional inflection. Ambivalence was woven through the counter-discourse, whether in acknowledgements of the failings of the BBC's past or in its idealisation. Indeed, Reithian principles were often articulated by individuals in critical or self-critical reflections on those principles being only imperfectly realised, or under threat, or betrayed. But such varied, informal critical articulations attest to the strength of the ethical ideals. They amounted to a continual reworking and reinvention of the Reithian ethos for contemporary conditions, in reaction to what was perceived as its current managerial debasement. A first theme for reflection was the functioning of the institution itself, taking in such questions as employment conditions, money management, internal cynicism and the BBC's overall cultural limits.

*

Little old ladies in Lambeth

'I was in a staff job until last year and then I was put on a one-year staff contract, and now I'm on a development deal – employed per project. It isn't satisfactory. The continuity of the BBC is very valuable. That's because you're here, known to be in the building, working on several things. You had an example when you walked in: a young writer whose script has been sent to me, a very original piece of work. I can get someone here to read it, and I can give the guy pointers what to do. Now if he gets the revised script in, it's taken, what?, fifteen minutes of my time – of BBC time. And if that comes up with a really good script, it's time well spent. You can't do that when you're not here. I get a lot of unsolicited scripts; those two piles are unsolicited scripts waiting to be read . . .'

GB: 'It must be difficult, losing a staff job. You get different views, people defending a contract basis because of this idea that creative people ought to feel insecure or they won't come up with the goods.'

'That's rubbish. I'm not saying people should be on staff for life. But I do think here, where it's people's licence fees, it should be very carefully used, because it's public money – little old ladies in Lambeth are paying their licence fee, and they want that money on the screen. People work far better with some degree of continuity – not security. I don't think one is any less creative; I think you're more so, because you have openings available to you.'

Producer, BBC Drama, 1996.

*

Vested interests and expense accounts

'That's incredibly sad about the BBC now: the fact that everything has become completely "expense account", without any of us being able to chart the moment. I remember Betty Willingale, who produced Tender is the Night, which was a mega American co-production, and she used to get the bus! And we could never take people out to lunch unless we'd cleared it for more than five pounds. So you could buy a writer a sandwich and a beer in the Bush and that was it. And suddenly, in the last three years, the spend has rocketed on non-programme stuff. It's absolutely shameful, the level of expense accounts, taxis and so on that we use. You know, Paul Williams, who's a producer, and I had a day trip to Cannes with the head of department: that kind of behaviour, it's all being paid for by the licence fee. Another microcosm of the whole thing was when I was talking about both Sheila and myself having vested financial interests in our own editorial decisions: once the BBC goes down that route, it's a catastrophe.'

GB: 'It's completely in contradiction with greater financial probity, isn't it?'

'I could cite example after example . . .'

Executive, BBC Drama, 1996.

*

Corrupting the BBC: heritage, taste and style

'It's really easy to get sucked into the BBC culture of constant complaints, of thinking that public service is not an inspiring term or an inspiring set of values. It's incredibly easy to become middle-aged. One of my constant worries is, have all my edges been polished off, so there's nothing spiky about what I'm commissioning? It's really odd because lots of the values of public service are things like honesty and trust and freedom. Public service in broadcasting should stand for freedom from commercial constraints, relative freedom from ratings constraints; it should stand for honesty and integrity, for cutting edge, and promoting culture for its own sake rather than because of the dictates of an advertising agency. Those are exciting things that lots of under-thirty-fives, the area I'm supposed to specialise in, absolutely engage with. But as soon as you put them in a BBC context, for some reason they develop added values that are corrupting, like heritage, and past, and gravitas, and affection. There's this constant idea that people need to feel affection for the BBC. The idea of having affection for an institution is an approach that most under thirty-fives these days can't relate to. I certainly can't.'

83

GB: 'I see, and the earlier words you used – gravitas, heritage . . . – you didn't mention nationalism, but that soft cultural nationalism . . . ?'

'It's really odd, isn't it? If I was black I would be so angry with the BBC. Why the hell should I pay a licence fee? The Sky licence fee is £320 a year, triple the BBC's, and you don't get the five radio stations and the five TV channels and the Internet sites. You just get Sky One for that. Yet I would still relate more to Sky One than the BBC if I was a young black kid, because the BBC doesn't speak in the way I speak, it doesn't have the music I listen to. The most dangerous cultural thing in the BBC for me is when people start to reject something on the grounds of taste or style. They'll say, "I'm sorry, it's just not stylish" or "It's just not tasteful". Of all the things that are difficult to argue against, it's almost impossible to argue that something is stylish when your boss feels it's unstylish. And for a West Indian community, what they believe is stylish is often seen as tacky by a white middle-class community – the jokes they listen to or the comedians they like. Similarly, that kind of glitzy working-class Asian culture that seems to be obsessed with gold and necklaces, and I suppose a stereotypical Jewish culture: they seem "styleless". And when you remove things because they're "styleless", you're effectively removing a whole set of cultural values that a non-white audience could absolutely relate to. Do you know what I mean?'

BBC youth channel executive, 2001.

*

The Craft: Situated Ethics and Aesthetics

Informal reworkings of the Reithian ethos were most prevalent in relation to the BBC's central practices: the production of programmes and development of services. A continually evolving Reithianism animated the BBC's production cultures, as for decades it had informed the shared craft of British broadcasting. For each kind of programming the Reithian ethic had a different inflection; it formed part of the collective expertise and implicit knowledge of programme-makers. Drama, comedy, entertainment, sports, current affairs, documentary, arts, science, access programming: each genre had a history marked by partic-ular ethics and aesthetics, themselves subject to reflection and renewal, each forming a dynamic community of ideas. The BBC's production departments and their output formed part of these histories, connecting them to a wider professional world beyond the BBC and to common, genre-specific concerns.

For BBC programme-makers, the attempt to forge knowing links between generic pasts and imagined generic futures was their primary mode of professional engagement. So the desire to innovate in the look or tone of a particular genre, or the inclination to tweak a rival's successful format, or criticism of others for failing to deliver on a necessary BBC commitment to popularity or distinctiveness: all speak of how, for producers, the task of reinventing the Reithian ethos was inflected through a concern with the nuances of particular genres. Such a stance was, again, often articulated through self-criticism or criticism of others for imperfectly meeting the ambitions of the public service ideal. Reflection was as much a property of collective debate and disagreement – in editorial meetings, or the weekly review of output, the Programme Review Board – as of consensus. The state of popular or historical drama, cutting-edge comedy, online news or interactive television: all were subject to both individual and collective reflection.

*

I believe in the craft

GB: 'You have a problem with Alan's [*controller of BBC1*] editorial tastes: in what way?'

'I think that what Alan believes is popular TV is the *Sun* on TV. I think the more you make stupid product, the more you create the audience. The more you pander to unsophisticated taste, the more that taste becomes unsophisticated. And I don't believe that popular TV should be allowed to become stupid. It doesn't need to be *Pets Win Prizes* or *Noel's House Party*. I'm not a snob. I think good drama, good light entertainment have a massive place in popular culture. But it's insulting the stuff he puts money into and that he defends – it's not even as if 25 million people were watching! So there's no justification. TV is the most important medium in the world, and if you don't give it the respect it's due then you're a fool. I believe in the craft and I respect the popular audience, and the problem is that so many people who work here in TV don't respect the audience. What they care about is numbers and "excellence" – you know, "critical excellence".'

Producer, BBC Drama, 1996.

*

Crossing genres: trouble with trouble

GB: 'Your company seems almost to have cornered the market in this extremely risky, near the edge, cross-genre comedy. People single out Chris Morris and *Brass Eye* as the most radical stuff happening in this area . . .'

85

'Chris Morris was rejected by the BBC. We made a pilot and Michael Jackson looked at it when he was controller of BBC2, and he didn't want to commission it. He didn't like it ethically; he had a problem with the celebrity interviews. I was surprised because Michael commissioned Dennis Pennis, and *he* goes out sticking a microphone under celebrities' noses without their permission. Michael put *Brass Eye* up for the Programme Review Board recently. Afterwards I had a conversation with him, and I said, "Maybe the BBC of the late nineties is not a very good home for the troublesome maverick, the iconoclast," and he said, "Is that true? Well, it shouldn't be, that's something to think about." When we were making *Brass Eye* for Channel 4 there was a very strong sense of "It's our remit to do things that cause trouble". You never get that in the BBC now. I've never heard anybody at the BBC say, "Let's stir things up." The BBC, ironically, as the licence-fee-funded non-commercial channel, is obsessed by ratings, focus groups, research, with BBC1 beating ITV, BBC2 beating Channel 4. Obsessed. *Brass Eye*'s first episode played to a very modest audience, and I said to the commissioning editor, "Nobody watched it," and he said, "Who cares?" You never hear that at the BBC, and you should.'

Executive, independent production company, 1997.

*

Slave trade

GB: 'What projects are you currently working on?'

'I'm working on a six-part serial which I very much hope I'll get to make, a bodice-ripper by Philippa Gregory called *A Respectable Trade*. She's a feminist, socialist historian who writes romantic novels, and this is the best book she's written. It's a story set in the late eighteenth century about an impoverished governess whose last chance is to marry a Bristol trader. He turns out to be a slave trader, which is fine by her, and he marries her so she can train his slaves, so he can sell them for more money. And through that the whole British slave trade is explored, the extraordinary scale of it, about which so little is generally known. She falls in love with one of the slaves, of course, so you have that power relation played out. And I'm also preparing a drama documentary, something I came across through *A Respectable Trade*, because I've been reading to try and find modern equivalents, because it's so hard to imagine. I came across the story of this Pakistani boy who was in bonded labour and was promised a law scholarship to university; and all this happened, and then he was shot dead, in Pakistan. I want to make a film about his life to get to the whole issue of child slavery. The story was in the papers last year. The writer has done a very good treatment, we researched all last year. He's an American called Jeffrey Lewis; he wrote and exec'ed a lot of *Hill Street Blues* . . .'

Producer, BBC Drama, 1996.

*

To affirm the existence of diverse critical and self-critical reflections on the part of producers is not to say that the resulting programmes were exemplary. The existence of these deliberations, while necessary for creativity, does not guarantee it. Moreover, it is plain from these quotations that the corporation was as susceptible in the later nineties as it ever was to the culturally middlebrow, that some of the BBC's central historical weaknesses – problems of risking extremes of satire, or of intervening creatively in popular culture – continued to pose serious challenges. Yet without the driving force of the interweaving ethical and aesthetic reflexivities described, the BBC's output would not have the character that it does. The ethical stance is potentially productive: it *may* have effects in practice.

Rituals of Inclusion

The integration of the BBC depended also on a number of core rituals of unification. These staged events, performances of collective reflection on the BBC's output, often had the sanctimonious tone characteristic of BBC public address, even when they were for purely internal consumption. Through these rituals, senior management projected a momentary illusion of flattened hierarchy and inclusion, diffusing norms and judgements and unifying the culture around its 'higher' missions. In the later nineties those slender events held with the BBC's own proletariat bore the impossible burden of compensating for the everyday, cumulative alienation of staff from Birtist management. One such annual ritual, for all television staff, was the Network Television review of the year, a reflection on the 'achievements and challenges from 1995 to 1996 and key issues for Network Television in the coming year'. A different level of integration was vested in the weekly television Programme Review Board, in which production heads sat with television's managing director, the channel controllers and a few guests to consider the past week's output, both the BBC's and competitors'. But the BBC was adept at staging rituals of inclusion even beyond its borders. On various pretexts, executives and governors held selective consultations with different sects of the British establishment, self-consciously co-opting influential opinion, and being seen to do so. These consultations had the effect both of including these establishment orders, if temporarily, within the BBC – spinning elaborate webs of connectedness – and of repeatedly resecuring the legitimacy of the BBC, a task with as much internal as external importance. Something of the insecurity of the corporation is gleaned in the need to ground the BBC's self-belief in such repeated performances of securing legitimacy. Something of its arrogance is evident in the way these encounters were so knowingly or cynically staged, and the cynicism so readily disavowed.

*

Consulting widely

We are in a meeting in the early stages of the News and Current Affairs (NCA) directorate's Programme Strategy Review, a huge exercise that will examine over the coming year the entire corpus of news and current affairs output on BBC1, BBC2 and Radios 1 to 4. The exercise is driven by three objectives: the need to understand better the channel strategies within which news and current affairs programmes must now sit; the need to reflect on the public service dimensions of news and current affairs and consider how they might evolve; but the main emphasis is on the need to understand audience wants and expectations of news and current affairs. The news PSR is being led by the deputy head of NCA, Richard Ayre. He has explained to me that the Broadcast directorate has already improved its understanding of audiences, and the aim is to instill the same knowledge in NCA, 'to tell us how the portfolio should change'. An elaborate system has been put in place: five of the rising stars of news and current affairs have been seconded to run teams looking at each area of output; weekly steering group meetings will be held to review progress. Early meetings dwelt on how to undertake the task, and planned a massive programme of audience research.

A couple of weeks in, and our meeting has alighted on the problem that word has spread about the PSR around the news and current affairs programmes, causing disquiet and curiosity, but that staff have as yet been neither informed nor consulted. Richard confides that at a recent staff lunch 'a very senior TV news journalist collared me and said [*in a pompous, Oxbridge-type voice*], "When is Steve Hewlett going to consult me about TV news output?" We smile, and Richard says he took from this that they must consider how to create a sense of wide involvement among the workforce, judiciously, so as to convey that key people are being consulted. Steve Hewlett, editor of *Panorama*, responds that it is imperative to start informing colleagues.

Over sandwiches for lunch, Richard asks who 'on the outside' should be consulted about the PSR for ideas and suggestions. Mark Wakefield suggests Philip Whitehead and Michael Grade, and there is a discussion of the PR problems raised by consulting Grade. Richard and Steve counter that he cannot be approached; he would use it mischievously to make trouble for Birt and the BBC. Richard asserts, 'I'd like to rule out consulting our competitors – enemies if you like – before our "friends". Let's keep away from the media industry for now; let's consult other opinion-formers. I've always said, of the three groups to consult – ourselves, the audience and the chattering classes – it's us and the audience that should carry most weight. But there is a place for the chattering classes – or whatever you call them.' Steve: 'This exercise is about the audience. But at this stage, I think we should be both audience- and expert-focused. At best, you can get out of it the PR benefit of showing you've consulted opinion-formers. Say we're talking of getting rid of *Panorama* and the *Nine O'clock News*, then we need to prepare the ground by talking to that group.' Richard recalls genially that he was invited to a dinner last year by the Archbishop of Canterbury, who proceeded to give a diatribe on the role of the media, especially the news, in the moral breakdown of society. 'It was rubbish, but fascinating – and he sounded off. That kind of thing is basically a political exercise, pure PR. I think we should be seen to consult with a group of the "great and the good" soon: say, three vice-chancellors, a couple of professors, some captains of industry and trade union chiefs, church leaders and senior policemen . . .' They knock around how to stage the consultation: should they go individually and talk to these people? Attend professional events? Finally, they alight on the idea of holding a series of five or six dinners at Broadcasting House under Chatham House rules, each with about ten of the 'great and the good', where they will be invited to air their ideas and criticisms. Someone adds, 'It must be dinners, and they must have plenty to drink – so as well as going away pissed, they'll really feel they've been listened to.'

A few weeks later, one hot summer's evening, I find myself seated with about eight others in an executive dining room in Broadcasting House, accepting too many drinks and talking volubly about news and current affairs programming, while our good-humoured host, Steve Hewlett, chivvies the conversation along. Opposite me is seated the pro-vice-chancellor of Cambridge University. On my right sits Anne Atkins, religious broadcaster. On my left is a very senior policeman, and beyond him an industrialist. None of the guests appears to have particularly well-formed views about news output, and Hewlett does not appear to be taking any notes . . .

Diary, 1997.

*

Come together: Network Television's review of the year

There's a light disco beat; there's a buzz in the air. Several hundred people are crowded into TC1, one of the main studios in Television Centre. It's the annual review of the year for all the staff of Network Television. The format follows any live studio show: the floor manager is preparing the audience, feel-good music is playing, and a video rolls with the 'Highlights of the Year'. Will Wyatt, MD of Network Television, Alan Yentob and Michael Jackson, controllers of BBC1 and BBC2 respectively, are standing in the aisles greeting people, chatting and smiling, affable and relaxed. The 'Highlights' video gives short out-takes from the year's hits: in drama, *Our Friends in the North, Pride and Prejudice, Casualty, EastEnders, Hamish Macbeth, Hetty Wainthropp Investigates, Persuasion, The Sculptress*; in documentaries, *The House* and others; in comedy, *Mrs Merton, Reeves and Mortimer, They Think It's All Over*.

Will opens, exuding satisfaction and corporate confidence to the troops: the average reach per week for BBC television in the last year was 94 per cent; 50.2 million people tuned in on average each week. Combined share is 43.4 per cent, and BBC1 added 0.2 per cent share compared with ITV. BBC2 also added share and overtook Channel 4. The headlines for the year: the revival of popular drama, from both London and the regions; factual successes; improvements in children's programming after a problematic '94–5; success in comedy output; and an unbeatable Christmas schedule. And setbacks: sports rights – 'We've lost a couple of key events, but kept a number of others'; staff reductions in drama, factual, music and arts, and children's; and the commissioning moratorium – 'We had to slow production down; we were making too much programming too early.' Marks of progress: 'We met our cash targets; we were on budget for the third year running; we made 119 extra hours of programming; we managed competitive programme pricing; and we made less use of repeats. The commissioning process is not pleasing everyone, I know, but . . .; and we placed our first bundle of programming with another broadcaster, Children's BBC on Nickelodeon. For all these marvellous achievements, I bring fulsome congratulations from the DG and governors to you all'. There is applause.

Alan takes over for BBC1. 'We've narrowed the gap with ITV and kept our place as satellite encroaches. Our competitive showing indicates the value we're giving our audience: we're doing what they want. Strategy has helped, despite all the paperwork; we've been taking more notice of the audience – a major achievement. Commissioning has had to be more calculated, and that irritates you all as programme-makers, I realise. But it has results. We've had an incredible revival in popular drama – *Silent Witness, Ballykissangel, Dangerfield, Hamish, Hetty* – but we've also had range in drama: *A Mug's Game, Rich Deceiver, P and P* building on the success of *Middlemarch* and *Chuzzlewit*; *EastEnders* acting as a brilliant launchpad for the sitcoms; and *Casualty* sustaining itself. The key challenge is reinventing the strands, keeping them strong and alive. In features, we need occasional big events. In entertainment we need a better showing, although this is a troubled area across the industry. But *Noel's House Party, TOTP* – both have managed to be self-critical, to reinvent themselves successfully. In the schedule the 7 p.m. slot is still a tricky one. The other difficult area is late evening, post-watershed, or as they say in the States "post-peak", where the audience continues to grow. In sport, none of us wanted to lose the FA Cup or the Grand Prix, but we're working on the golf. The Events department delivered good coverage of VE and VJ days. And in children's we've seen superb improvements: we won everything in the latest awards – unheard of for years!'

Now Michael comes in for BBC2. 'Thanks, everyone, for a good year. Share is up 0.5 per cent, the highest for BBC2 in ten years; and BBC2 is the only terrestrial channel to extend its reach – that means we connected with youth and women to an unprecedented degree. Highlights: in autumn *The Death of Yugoslavia*, in winter *Our Friends* and *The House*, and all year *Modern Times*, *Picture This* and *Fine Cut* – excellent documentaries. We had some good single dramas: *Priest*, *Streetlife*, the *Love Bites* trilogy. *Our Friends* was without doubt the contemporary drama event of the year. *This Life* made a good start and will return. *Degrees of Error* and *Ghostbusters* were a bit disappointing. *Horizon*'s 'Fermat's Last Theorem' was the key single documentary of last year. The highest audience for the whole year was *Wallace and Gromit*. Aims for the coming year? The core aim is for BBC2 to have the greatest range of all the networks. More sitcoms are needed to attract the young audience, and we need more ideas for our Friday evening comedy zone. Challenges? Weekdays after *Newsnight*: we need something better for this slot. Saturday evening needs attention. We want ideas for African and Caribbean programmes. We need low-budget contemporary drama, to allow more voices on to the channel, and simply more drama. And we want to create a Sunday youth zone.'

Will returns, commenting on press coverage: 'We got an outside company to measure the amount of publicity achieved by different broadcasters for their new year launches, and the BBC beat the competition by sixty/forty! What improvements are we after in the coming year? Better talent management, especially in entertainment and comedy. New services are coming on-stream – joint subscription channels with partners. There's the "Smart TV" initiative about using new technology to achieve savings and employ better ways of working. We must eliminate deficits in production: I have to ensure we have the right size and shape workforce in each area. The resource base must fit. We're introducing new directorate-wide policies on relations with Worldwide and with the independents, and the new rights agreements are almost there. And finally, accountability to our audience: we have to look after our audience better. We need to watch out for breaches of the taste and decency policies – a couple of these occurred this year pre-watershed and they must be avoided. And we must attend to the new rules on impartiality; all those in production must be aware of the revised Producer Guidelines.'

The speeches are over. Will takes questions, which are televised on the screens suspended around the studio. Mike Leggo, head of light entertainment, asks, 'What share should we be aiming for, in strategy terms, to justify the licence fee in future decades with increased competition?' Alan replies, 'It's silly to give a figure, because when there's a less good year, people criticise and complain'. He adds defensively that planning and strategy have been very helpful and are also made up of programme-makers, countering any implication that strategy will impose unrealistic expectations on producers. Lorraine Heggessey asks, 'How important are the documentary strands?' Michael responds, 'They are incredibly important: they brand the channels.' Paul Hamann comes in: 'How can we make sure, given Smart TV, that all our departments really start using the new technologies?' Will replies, 'We need to have a learning culture here', and Michael adds, 'We all know some of the best new shows have been across genre' – implying the new digital video technologies foster this. John King says, 'We've achieved better communication with the audience, but we still don't seem to know what they want.' Alan disagrees: 'We have a strong research base now; but creativity also has its place. Both research and intuition are needed.' He adds, archly, 'I've got lots of paperwork – shall I share it with you?' John continues, 'But don't we need it more continuously?' Will replies, 'I'm strongly considering commissioning a tracking study that would allow us to keep in touch with the audience – what they like, what they think of us – as a stimulus. I've got a pilot with me now.' Jana Bennett asks about promotion and presentation: aren't these becoming more important? Alan: 'Yes, they'll need more resources. The channels will have to be branded.' Michael adds, 'The promotional airtime we have is extremely valuable. It's worth millions. We need a properly thought through policy on on-screen promotion.'

Will winds up: 'Join us for lunch! There are demos of desktop editing and DV technologies for those interested. Thanks for a smashing year! Not a bad medal, this year's achievements, to have among all the medals on your chest!' As we leave, we are handed a sheet asking for feedback: 'It would help us to plan these events in future if you could answer the following questions: 1. What aspects of the briefing did you find particularly interesting or useful? 2. Were there any aspects that could have been improved? 3. Please add any other comments on the briefing.'

Diary, 1996.

*

Collective reflection: Programme Review Board, 1996

A large room in the basement of Television Centre, Wednesday morning: the weekly meeting to review the output on BBC and rival channels. Last week we were given a sheet with 'homework' for today: two shows for 'essential viewing', and a number of 'highlights of the week', selected to indicate new directions, current hits or problematic areas. Will Wyatt is chairing with obvious authority, with Michael Jackson alongside. Thirty-five or so department heads are ranged around the table with papers and coffees, some hunched after late-night schmoozing, some vaguely self-conscious. Most of them are in their forties and fifties, five are women, and one is not white. A show at this meeting has both the air of having arrived among the BBC's senior executives, and the risk of being seen as overambitious, a goodie, a swot. The pace is brisk, but dis-cussion can be leisurely – the meeting often lasts an hour and a half. Ken Trodd is here, producer of the Dennis Potter television plays and considered a maverick in the BBC. We have already talked, and before the meeting begins Ken leans towards me and con-fides that there's a lot of sensitivity about who is invited to Programme Review and who not, and about the distribution of the minutes – detailed weekly records of judgements formed and given, a kind of ongoing historical memory of BBC bosses' commentaries on programming. Until quite recently the minutes were sent to all producers, then it suddenly stopped. Producers feel disinformed. Ken is sure cost was not the reason, but the corporation's characteristic paranoia that the press might get hold of the minutes and use them against the BBC. 'It's about the British establishment's (ergo the BBC's) obsession with secrecy.' For Ken, the BBC is a metonym for the establishment.

Will welcomes us, and starts with the announcements: at the recent BAFTA craft awards the BBC took eight out of eleven, and he congratulates those involved, particu-larly those on *Persuasion*, which swept the board. A new award has been announced, the Dennis Potter New Writer's Award. 'Great news! *Reeves and Mortimer* won the Golden Rose at Montreux! And congratulations to Mark Damazer, who's just been announced as the new head of weekly programmes in News and Current Affairs'.

Will turns and commands a young woman at his side, 'Linda: the figures' (as in 'Bernie: the bolt'). Linda is a BBC1 business analyst, and it is her job to take the assem-bled dignatories through the weekly figures from BARB, the British Audience Research Board: the ratings. Linda has about five minutes, and there is a lot to cover. BARB pro-duces a booklet each week which sets out the four main channels' ratings against each other in the form of a graph, with percentage of audience share and gross millions for every quarter-hour over twenty-four hours each day. Everyone in the room has their large BARB booklet open, and we pore conscientiously over the graphs as Linda talks through them. Her rap resembles nothing so much as a running sports commentary, fast and upbeat: highs, lows, competition to note, abnormal moments, expectations confirmed and confounded, when ITV or 4 did well and when they didn't. When the ratings are problematic, Linda adds in the BBC's own measure of AIs – the appreciation index, a crude qualitative indication of how much the available audience liked a pro-gramme. 'For BBC2 this week, low ratings were often balanced by high AIs – take

Murder One: it got a 2.8 per cent share but the AI was 79 per cent.' She gets to Good Friday: 'Viewing up 6 per cent on last year!' When Linda finishes Will asks Michael to comment. 'A good week . . .' and he continues by praising *FDR*, a documentary series on the US president which is doing amazingly well for the genre.

We come to the homework, focusing this week on two factual shows representing genres that are in the ascendancy. The form is that Will announces the programme to be discussed and then summons people from around the room to give an opinion, which they usually give in a snappy thirty seconds. Often, when Will asks for views, several individuals confess that they 'missed that one', and it takes a few shots to elicit a comment. '*Home Front*: Sandy?' *Home Front* is a DIY show on BBC2, an example of the makeover genre that has begun to colonise the mid-evening schedules. The main concerns are the qualities of the presenter and how practically useful is the information. Michael Jackson steps in: 'This is a success story; it's become bankable over three seasons. The current series is reaching its stride. Doing up the house over several programmes is a great idea because it becomes a kind of soap.' The producer, Daisy Goodwin, gets a right of reply; she defends it but is ambivalent about the presenter; 'there's a fact sheet!' Will winds up: 'Excellent.' Daisy adds seductively, 'We could do more', to which Michael retorts, 'Oh, you will.'

Will moves us along. '*Making Babies*: Lorraine?' This is a fly-on-the-wall documentary series on IVF treatment, following three couples through the process. It is the BBC's first venture with the consultant gynaecologist and peer, Robert Winston. Lorraine answers sincerely, enthusiastically, 'from my own experience: I know several couples going through fertility treatment. In my household we went on talking about the pros and cons of IVF for an hour after the programme.' She adopts the persona of the ordinary viewer, just another mother watching telly. Others weigh in, taking a professional stance: how contrived some of it felt; that some of the subjects were playing to camera. Concern is expressed over whether sufficient scientific information is given, and whether fly on the wall as a genre can meet these demands. Ethical issues are raised: is the series too intrusive in the emotional lives of the couples? One of the couples later split up; a camera captures one of the women, who has started menstruating, crying while expressing profound disappointment that IVF has failed. Several people agree that it was nonetheless 'gripping television'. The producers field the implied criticisms: 'Staginess was how some of these people behaved – true life is more stagy than drama!' 'And it wasn't actually a science documentary . . .'

The homework over, the next phase begins: a trawl through last week's *Radio Times* to select key programmes for discussion. Will calls out programmes, but anyone can join in. *Rough Justice*, the investigative current affairs series, on the Carl Bridgewater case: Paul Hamann, head of documentaries, comments that his department is preparing a dossier on the case in support of the *Rough Justice* team, to pass on to Michael Howard, the Home Secretary. Will, implicitly affirming the BBC's public service role, mutters 'Jolly good.' *Modern Times*, the BBC2 documentary strand, a film called 'Flatmates': several people speak in strong support. Will says, 'It made me feel glad that I'm an old man!' Michael champions it, teasing, 'It made me envious!' Paul sums up, paying tribute to the film-maker, Lucy Blakstad, who is 'consummate at this style of documentary.' The *Ant and Dec Show* from the Children's department: Will starts, 'We've had a lot of calls from viewers on this one – is the sexual innuendo under control?', and he probes whether the programme is right for the schedule slot it inhabits. The commissioning editor from Children's, Rod, declines to offer a defence. Will reproves him: 'We look to Children's to take care of this, Rod . . .' and leaves it there. Next up, ITV's coverage of the golf: several people applaud how the psychological tensions were brought out. Will remarks on the ad breaks: 'Less intrusive than usual.' He invites a non-golfer to comment. Michael volunteers: 'Superb – that rare moment when sport moves over into drama.'

A hiatus; then back to the *Radio Times*. Lorraine offers comments on yet another show. So far she has owned up to watching most of the programmes discussed. Quips fly, teasing her: 'Not going out much, Lorraine?' 'Got a boring social life?' She laughs and protests, 'I've just been watching some telly!' The joke plays on the irony that, for these TV professionals, one does not watch television except by default, if one is not doing something more important. Nothing, it seems, is more embarrassing than to be seen to have watched too much television.

Michael assesses negatively a UFO-type real-life documentary on BBC2: 'Pity the title is so Discovery Channel-ish'. Samir Shah, head of political programmes at Millbank, speaks of a late-night political show with coverage of Tony Blair in the USA. 'He only relaxed as the show went on. So if you want to see a politician talk straight, like ordinary people, you'll have to stay up very late!' and all laugh at the implied self-criticism of the generally abstruse tone of the BBC's political coverage. The *Gaby Roslin Show* on Channel 4: two women slag it off. 'Plugs, predictable – everything it said it wouldn't be, including the sofas!' Peter Watkins's film *Culloden*: a thirty-one-year-old drama-documentary, highly controversial when it was first made, which had its second ever showing on BBC2. Michael leads in, effusively: 'Wonderful drama. It very much deserved this outing. Two and a half million watched.' It was preceded by *Rebellion*, a documentary on the Jacobite rebellion in Scotland that lay behind the Culloden massacre. The executive producers of the history doc are here. They outline the programme's aims, and Will and Michael laud this too. Finally, *The Works*, a new BBC2 arts strand. Kim Evans, head of music and arts, defends it: the concept is to do stories around music and arts that bring in a new audience. This one was the story of an American skyscaper with major structural faults; it focused on architecture as practice. Michael is cautious: the title is surely a problem? 'We need to work at branding this one, so that people know it's an arts programme.'

We are nearing the end; the new BBC2 drama *This Life* is mentioned. Michael turns to Will, saying, 'We should do this,' meaning it should be given as homework for a future Programme Review. Smiling, Michael comments on the *Radio Times* promo of it as a 'comic drama': 'My only problem with this show is that it's not comic, and . . .' a consummate pause . . . 'it's not very dramatic!' Several people laugh. Michael commends 'two good shows on Channel 4', signalling that he is watching the opposition, and that he is magnanimous. Michael has a mythical capacity for metabolising television output. He seems to have seen everything, causing people on his BBC2 team to wonder when he finds the time to watch. As one commented, 'He watches TV fast.'

The meeting winds up; people hover in pairs. I say hello to Samir, whom I met when starting my research and who was open and friendly. I explain a problem I am having with Mark Damazer, now head of daily news programmes. Mark has said that I can watch news operations, but that I will have to leave the room when delicate political issues come up – spin doctors calling in, clashes with politicians, that sort of thing. Samir suggests a solution, a tactic he says journalists often use: 'Strike a deal: offer Mark editorial control for *those* bits – and then get in there. After the event, a long time after, the issues will be less pressing and he probably won't bother to exert strict control. For God's sake, he'll have moved jobs three times by then!'

Diary, 1996.

*

Such rituals of unification and of collective reflection both performed and real, with their displays of authority, status and jostling for position, fuel the integration of the BBC, binding the workforce into an *internal public*. The rituals exhibit a preoccupation with discerning and affirming the BBC's proper stance as a public service organisation, often dressed with BBC piety. Throughout the nineties they continued to take place, apparently in keeping with BBC history. But in terms of the individual, while Reithian reflection continued to be characteristic of staff throughout the BBC, as other values were cultivated by management, and as changing employment patterns eroded the corporation's career and training structures, on which their identification had been built, the ethical identification of many staff with the BBC had become almost a latent one. It was being undermined.

Accountants and Primitives

Macho overspend

'Among the male drama producers there's a simple rule of thumb: the higher the overspend the greater the prestige.'

Female producer, BBC Drama, 1997.

*

Profligacy and trust

'You trusted the people you worked with. But we can never return to that idyllic way
of working, because that suggests a system in which people have accepted downtime,
and it's apparent that the finance heads are not going to finance downtime. And that
may well be right. When I arrived here there was a system that horrified me, in fact it
was throughout the BBC: that the production staff were on overtime, and they were
largely, well, "self-scheduling". Once you're cheating, you're cheating. They could be sitting around when there was no filming going on for several months on full salary, making
massive amounts of overtime as well. Most of the AFMs on my productions made more
money than I did. You'd try to limit the hours they worked and make your schedules
tighter, but even then it was amazing. And that's changed now.'

Producer, BBC Drama, 1997.

*

Flying high: a maverick outfit

'I went with an idea to do an *Arena* about a journey up Broadway. They sent me over
to research it, and I came back and they said, "Why don't you do it?" even though I

didn't know one end of a camera from the other. Now *Arena* was very particular, but it was that fantastic period in the BBC in the mid eighties when . . . you know, I was twenty-five or twenty-six, and there I was on a plane to New York, and sitting in a hotel waiting for the crew to turn up, and I hadn't got a clue, not a clue.'

GB: 'But the crew taught you?'

'Completely, yes. *Arena* was a maverick outfit based at Kensington House, and Alan was very much part of that. It was an extraordinary place the BBC at that time; you could do whatever you liked. I remember Nigel coming in with an idea, "We should do this," on a Friday morning. And that afternoon I was on a plane, and the next day I was filming it in New York with my brother working as my assistant because he just happened to be there . . .'

GB: 'Was it partly that this was Alan's little empire, so he could protect people and there was a lot of freedom and space within that?'

'Partly, but it was also partly that there were no proper cost controls – well, within certain limits there were, but it was so loose, so vague. And because there were so few checks and balances, there was freedom to be imaginative in the way you ran the place. In the *Arena* cutting rooms those films were really put through the rings, and that was Alan's legacy. When he was editor of *Arena*, he liked to cut through the night. Anthony and Nigel inherited that mantle, so it was incredibly labour-intensive. We'd be there weeks and weeks, nights and nights. One Christmas I remember Alan coming in and asking the editor how much overtime he thought he was going to have to put in for, and it being X amount; and Alan pulling out wodges of notes, you know, "Take this!" It was an extraordinary place to work. I mean, ask Alan about his Heinrich Böll film which has still not been cut; the rushes are still in some vault, and he was just too busy to ever get round to cutting, but he shot it.

'Another time, I was presented with two documentary films on Andrei Tarkovsky which Alan had bought as head of music and arts as acquisitions from some distributor, and I was told, "Here are two films, an hour long each; cut them down to a fifty-minute *Arena*." Tarkovsky had just died and it was a straightforward brief. So I watched them, and it was clear that he'd been totally ripped off. There were two films, but they had the same material edited in different ways. That was how I got my first bit of directing: suddenly we were meant to be transmitting this Tarkovsky tribute in two weeks' time, and though they'd apparently bought two hours of stuff, there was nothing there. I ended up going to Paris to film Tarkovsky's death mask arriving, Tarkovsky's wife at the funeral, that kind of thing. Somehow we saved it.'

BBC producer, 1996.

*

Lime Grove and Kensington House: innovation

'The great innovations in television have come about because of the existence of well-funded groups of producers, both in the BBC and ITV companies. Among the most remarkable of these were the BBC's Lime Grove studios and Kensington House, which initiated . . . between 1957 and 1980 most of the accepted genres of the medium: the magazine programme, the documentary series, the various styles of political interview, the filmed reporter-led feature, the dramatised documentary.'

Anthony Smith, 1994.

*

Rationalisation

During the 1990s, as Birt ascended to power first as deputy director-general and from 1993 as director-general, wave upon wave of rationalisation and reorganisation swept over the BBC. The prototype was Birt's construction out of three independent departments of a unified News and Current Affairs directorate for both radio and television on arriving at the BBC in 1987. The troublesome Current Affairs department, responsible for some of the most serious clashes with the Conservative governments, was absorbed and its Lime Grove base closed. This was followed by a further consolidation of the diverse sources of news reporting into a centralised Newsgathering department feeding all news programmes in television and radio. In the mid nineties a policy of 'bi-mediality' was introduced, modelled on the bi-medial NCA, in which radio and television production for each programme genre, which had hitherto operated in separate departments, were required, if unevenly, to integrate. With all the changes, the ostensible aim was to reduce duplication by achieving synergies in the development of ideas and use of personnel. But the result was a relentless centralisation that undermined the sources of independence and diversity in the BBC's culture and its output. The ambiguity of purpose was evident in the reorganisation of NCA, which was widely taken at the time to be a disciplinary measure intended to rein in those elements of news and current affairs that were considered 'out of control'.

The marketisation of the BBC was a further stage in this process. It proved to be the one with the most far-reaching effects in transforming the culture of the BBC. The policy of Producer Choice began, with the intention to install an internal market in the BBC; and following the 1990 Broadcasting Act's injunction that the BBC must buy 25 per cent of its programming from the independent sector, the early nineties saw the growth of an external market in programme supply. To devise the huge organisational changes necessitated by Producer Choice, Birt drew on the assistance of five management consultancies – Deloitte, Coopers & Lybrand, PriceWaterhouse, Ernst & Young and Kinsley Lord – signalling the growing power vested in management consultancies. The culmination of these developments – a kind of auto *coup d'état* – was Birt's sudden restructuring of the corporation in June 1996, the largest reorganisation in the BBC's history. Overnight, the BBC was carved up into six new directorates. The most significant change was the construction of an unprecedented split between the new Production directorate, containing all the programme-making departments in radio and television, and the new Broadcast directorate, within which sat the management of all the radio and television networks. In constructing the Production directorate, a further rationalisation reduced the number of production departments from thirty-six to eighteen. At a stroke the former structure, which embodied cooperation and dialogue between channel controllers and in-house producers, was replaced by one in which their relations were to be governed by the concept of the market.

In parallel with these shifts the BBC faced continuing economic pressures. To ameliorate the financial crises, and fuelled also by marketisation and management's embrace of a new accounting rationality, a series of complementary initiatives took hold. On the one hand, commercial expansion before and after the relaunch of the corporation's commercial division in 1994 as BBC Worldwide. On the other hand, the selling off and closure of BBC services and departments, cuts to existing departments, and on the employment front a shift from permanent, career-grade staffing towards increasing use of freelance and short-contract staff, particularly in production. Chronic instability took hold as the reforms gathered momentum. The phrase 'permanent revolution' was repeatedly used by anxious staff. The thinking behind Birt's policies was made plain in a lecture in March 1993:

> 'Auntie – like so many other large organisations in the public and private sectors in the post-war years – became a vast command economy; a series of entangled, integrated baronies, each providing internally most of its needs . . . Territorialism often stifled initiative. Nothing was transparent, everything opaque. It was Byzantine in many of its structures . . . Creative freedom was frustrated.' [1]

Closures, cuts and reduced budgets were legitimised by the reigning values of the Birt period: the importance of 'efficiency' and the necessity of pursuing 'efficiency savings'. Several factors fuelled the new language and the imposition of markets. Not only was the 1990 Act in place, but a decade after the start of Channel 4 there had grown around the channel a flourishing sector of independent production companies and facility houses to service the independents. These companies were eager to do business with the BBC, and they provided the competition against which the BBC's activities in the same areas could be market-tested. The early nineties were, in addition, a period of growing political sensitivity for the BBC given the lead-in to Charter renewal in 1996. Following the government's 1992 Green Paper, *The Future of the BBC*, which required the BBC to provide 'value for money' and 'urged the BBC to improve its efficiency',[2] the dominant theme in the public debate on the BBC's future became the corporation's efficiency or lack of it. The external concerns were matched by the views of chairman Hussey, who considered the BBC shockingly profligate and favoured tighter financial controls and faster staff reductions than Michael Checkland had delivered as DG. A common hope among staff was that the implementation of Producer Choice and similar policies would 'enable the BBC charter debate to be fought on programmes and the rationale for having a BBC, rather than on its efficiency'.[3]

Just one striking exception to the cumulative marketisation and rationalisation occurred during the nineties. A policy adopted in the lead-in to Charter renewal pulled boldly in an entirely different direction, stoking diversity and decentralisation. It followed a report in 1993 by the former director of radio, David Hatch, who spent two years drawing up recommendations through consultation with the BBC's outfits in the regions and nations. A new policy of 'regional proportionality' decreed that henceforth, 33 per cent of all network television output must come from the BBC centres in Bristol, Birmingham, Manchester, Scotland, Wales and Northern Ireland. The regional quota proved extraordinarily fruitful over the decade in opening up new sources of creativity in these centres, and in giving the regions and nations a higher profile on the main channels. Yet, given the prevailing free-market ethos of the television industry, the quota was treated ambivalently by BBC executives; in industry events they blanched as commercial competitors accused them of having recourse to dubious Stalinist measures.

*

'Bringing rationality to the primitives': the mission

GB: 'So what is Producer Choice?'
'If you look at the early literature on Producer Choice, it was a new way of managing

resources. In the old days, the resource departments managed themselves: studios, outside broadcasts, technicians. Producers bought into them but not with any strong purchasing power. You could never measure what resources you needed, and the people who ran resources were empire-building. They staffed up to capacity; they had taxis waiting on the rank. And this capacity was building up and up without any way of asking, "Is it efficient?" Just before Producer Choice there was a Resources Review, which was John Birt and a crowd of heavies wandering around the resource departments saying, "You've got too much of this and that." So Producer Choice was a way of sizing the resource capacity, teasing out what the real production demand was by means of the internal market.

'And wasn't that happening already, you say? Didn't the BBC historically manage its resources quite well? Well, if it had studios it would manage them well on paper. But once you started to peel off the surface, you'd find they would pad out the schedule. I remember walking around the TV studios with a director and he was saying, "They *lie* about the studios; they're always telling you they're busy. But when you wander round, the place is empty half the time." They were busy on paper. So when the TV show *Holiday* saw the price of a studio for its links, it said, "Bugger me, we could send Judith Chalmers to Spain and do the links from there cheaper." Once they saw the true cost they could make decisions. That was the principle, and that was why it was called Producer Choice. If they could buy it better outside, let them do it, and that would shrink the in-house resource base to the right size. Then it trickled up to doing production business plans, and tracked throughout the production systems, working its way up the organisation.

'Our task was like bringing rationality to the primitives. I'll give some background. British TV is very peculiar. The early BBC was designed around an army concept of having everyone "under orders": you don't need specialists, you need soldiers who can add up, who can cook. That created a very isolated culture, a bit like the Lost World – the plateau where dinosaurs roam. When ITV started, it took a lot of people from the BBC, and one of the fundamental tenets of the BBC was that you couldn't have creative people worrying about money, that being completely oblivious to what you're doing financially somehow makes you a purer, nobler human being. That was the way both ITV and the BBC ran. For many years the BBC had to strain to do what it wanted to do. Then Wedgwood Benn introduced the colour licence, and his attitude was that only the rich were going to be able to afford it, so make it expensive, a tax on the rich. But in fact colour TV spread like wildfire. This place had money pouring in, and the issue was not "Let's make every pound go as far as it can"; the issue was "What can we spend it on?" As bad as that. A spend culture grew in the BBC up until the eighties. ITV had money pouring in too; they had a monopoly on advertising and a tax structure which included an Exchequer levy on profits; so they had no strong profit drive. Because of the duopoly you also had a strong union presence in both companies; if there were problems money was just thrown at them.

'So you had the BBC where everyone wandered around in a financial vacuum, and ITV where money didn't matter and if you had a problem you bought it off. The BBC had an incremental budgeting system where it divided the cake up on day nought – the Network TV slice, the Regions slice, the Radio slice – and then adjusted the cake every year. They kept transferring between these walled directorates that were jealously guarded, and great rows took place. My first contact with BBC production was in the early eighties; I met producers who said, "We only control a third of our budget," because production was narrowly defined: it was the bits of cost that *weren't* this or that. For budget purposes you'd have a series of arduous meetings with people arguing. There was no basis for consensus. That's incremental budgeting: an incredibly inefficient financial management system. But there was so much money anyway, the only problem was where to spend it and making sure that the costs were charged to the right directorate.

'The old BBC accounting rules are a disgrace. I'll quote one bit: "The reporting of programme costs is on completed programmes." It's historical, so the only action management can take is to make changes to the planned production. If anyone over-spent they'd just stop commissioning programmes. Completely retrospective, no *proactive* management at all, and no one thinking there's anything wrong with that. I've had people saying, "Of course we manage our money; I sat down when I finished *Persuasion* and I added up everything we'd spent"! Programme-makers were given a "programme allowance", like children – "give them an allowance"; whereas the central-ised functional bits were controlled on the sixth floor of TVC in a department called Financial Planning, with a system that broke down spectacularly in 1992. I came back from holiday to find that the financial system had fallen apart. In the previous financial year, Network TV had overspent by £60 million, and nobody could understand how. The crisis hit the press; finance directors left the BBC, found jobs in Switzerland. It was traumatic. Checkland was still DG; the next year, January 1993, John became DG. All that is to paint a picture of an organisation running, really, on the economics of a tuck shop.'

GB: 'Was it possible to reconstruct the logic behind the crisis that year?'

'You could never find anybody who could tell you the whole picture. Lots of people knew bits and the systems had developed over years, and the logic of it failed. It was systemic; the systems were there to manage production as narrowly defined, with a lot of poor basic assumptions. I knew when I came in that the systems we had to get in place for Producer Choice had to be radically different, but I didn't realise where we were starting from. I hadn't calculated down to ground-level behaviour quite what it would mean when you start looking at the way people manage money. I have a much fuller picture now. You had people with a very strong view that they understood money. But the demonstration of it was absent. So in the early work on Producer Choice we started by getting the concept of a business unit in place, explaining what it was. That was hugely resisted. I had to yell at people, "Of course you can do it." We were carving the place up into business units and telling them, "This is a profit-and-loss account, this is a balance sheet, this is how your activity fits in." We also had to make sure the rest of the organisation understood, because they obviously didn't; and there was no firm point to convert everyone from. I was the first accountant into programme departments that were spending £600 million.'

GB: 'There were no financial managers?'

'No, and yet the people all, bless them, thought they managed their money! They said, "We don't need accountants because we do it all already." So at the start of Producer Choice we gave them some examples of the new business units and new financial systems to run, and it quickly became obvious they couldn't cope. Then they understood that they needed accountants, and so we brought in fourteen accountants. Fourteen in after me to this lonely place. It then became obvious that the whole place was not being managed properly. It was decided to create the Groups – Factual, Drama, Entertainment – by grouping like areas of output. So the three drama departments were put together, and Charles Denton came in to run Drama Group. We met, and I was telling him how far we'd got with Producer Choice, and he asked if I could work for him. I liked Charles. I'd always felt guilty that when working with the programme departments we'd always put Drama in the "too difficult" file, because they were impossible. And I felt this is not acceptable, one has to go in there and sort it out. So I came in.

'We took a year and looked outside the walled city at what was happening in the rest of the world. There was a much more sophisticated financial environment outside, and we adopted the Channel 4 model. Channel 4 started with a film industry approach: you put a budget together, you come to us as financier, we crawl all over it, our cost controllers assess it, we agree it, you go off and manage it, and you take a financial risk if you don't bring it in as agreed. So we decided in Drama Group we'd have proper budgets; we'd make producers responsible for the budgets; we'd have systems to deliver proper control to the producers; we'd have cost controllers whose job is to make sure the producer gets a fair budget to start, and once it's in they monitor it from a distance; and we'd have a new Programme Finance Committee, the PFC, that would sit there with everything being reported to it. So that it's all clear, open and accountable.

'If you track the changes down to programme level, you find significant differences in the shape of the production team. The old structure was the head of department, who was editorial, head in the clouds, couldn't be bothered with money; a department manager whose job spec wasn't a "best use of money" type spec; it was just "make sure you've got enough"; they were like squirrels. And then on each show there was the nark, the associate producer, whose job was to report anything untoward, and if there's a problem report back to the manager. And the manager would have a line into Planning. In the new system we put in place you have the producer, an associate producer to run the production, and the production accountant to do the sums. The producer has that double support. And the cost controller's job is to ensure that the producer has the right budget to make the show, from a distance, professionally detached, not emotionally involved. To get it to work we gave the producer a full cash budget, not just entitlement to spend with a series of credit cards, as before. The producer is therefore in charge editorially and financially, which in the past BBC producers haven't been, although independents have. When I came into the Group producers thought their job was to do everything, which is why they were such a depressed lot. And that is a huge behaviour change.

'In order to make this work we had to come off BBC financial systems and institute our own accounting system. Developing this system I sometimes found myself fighting the rest of the BBC: "This is mad! You're trying to be different!" But actually drama is demonstrably different; you're saying to people, "Here is six million pounds." In the real world that's the turnover of a small business. You need to know how to manage it, and you've got creative people around who can bankrupt you. Making a drama you pay for every single thing you see on the screen. It's hugely expensive. The BBC doesn't realise the difference between programmes costing £250 an hour for local radio and Drama Group's half a million an hour. Different scales of operation require different financial systems. It's been almost overwhelmingly difficult; there are times when I think if I was being rational I would just stop. It's no different to what Murdoch did; he didn't try and reform Fleet Street, he shut it down and opened something new in Wapping. OK, he had people bussing up and down for years, and demonstrations and riots. But he got there in the end.'

Finance executive, BBC Drama, 1996.

*

I knew what my budget was

'When I was editor of *Sportsview* or *Panorama*, I knew what my budget was, I knew what my resources were, I knew when I was going over budget or when I still had money in hand. When I was controller of BBC1, I knew what my budget was. There was a very simple way of saving money when the financial year came round: you ran a few more feature films, you ran some repeats; that was the way to save money.'

Paul Fox, 1994.

*

The overspend?

A Drama Editorial Board close to the end of the 1995–6 financial year. The chief accountant of Drama Group speaks of his overview of the end-of-year accounts, saying gravely, regretfully, that Drama Group is currently overspent by £1 million. I am sitting next to Mark Shivas, head of BBC Films, and we are looking together at his copy of the accounts. He whispers to me that at first glance there are two glaring errors in the accounting of films, and films is just one of several sections making up the total accounts. One of his shows, down for £1.2 million, hasn't yet been made, and another show has £80,000 down that hasn't been spent. Mark is puzzled and bemused. There may be no debt of £1 million at all.

Diary, 1996.

*

Accountancy as Morality

Producer Choice rested on a conviction that the BBC lacked mechanisms for knowing, and for proving, that it was financially rational. In this view its producers were spendthrift, and the BBC's resources were used extravagantly. The internal market mechanisms ushered in by Producer Choice therefore installed a split between the BBC's production and resource departments. Henceforth, producers could compare the cost of in-house resources against those available in the external market, and were permitted to choose between them. In this way internal costs, hitherto shrouded in mystery, would be rendered visible and market-tested. Producer Choice was expected to yield substantial savings which, it was proposed, would be ploughed back into new services and programme-making. In the late eighties, Checkland had asked television management to consider whether programmes could be made more cheaply without adversely affecting quality, and a consensus resulted that 15 per cent savings could be made if producers were given more freedom and choice.[4] The changes required the introduction of new accounting systems and the allocation of monetary values to all internal transactions. The rigours of the market, it was believed, would lead to lower expenditure, cutbacks in overheads and less wasteful use of resources. Inefficiencies would be squeezed out of the system.

Producer Choice was first piloted, in 1991–2, in the Television Film Services department housed at Ealing Studios. Almost immediately there were redundancies, including some of the best technicians, who left to go freelance. This was a pattern repeated many times among the BBC's staff technicians, the best of whom, having taken redundancy, were commonly hired back as free-lancers at higher rates than when on staff. Other absurd patterns emerged: by the second year of the Ealing pilot, when payment of overheads kicked in, it was obvious that Television Film Services would be unable to meet the payments without making a loss. The studios were eventually sold and parts were hired back by the BBC on terms favouring the new owners that, under Producer Choice, were not permitted to BBC resource departments. The pilot was broadened in 1992 to include the department housing many craft services: costumes, make-up, scenery and set design. Losses were forecast for the second year's trading. In order to break even, compulsory redundancies were made and the BBC's make-up training scheme was closed. The resource departments were enjoined to test their value against the wider market. Yet paradoxically, unlike their competitors, they were not allowed to engage in work outside the BBC. In microcosm, the pilots revealed many of the inequities of Producer Choice.

Producer Choice also *redescribed* the corporation. The BBC was now com-posed of 481 business units or cost centres, each of which could in principle trade with any other. As the number of transactions mushroomed, legions of bureaucracy grew to meet the administrative demands. By the following year, in recognition of the excesses, the number of business units was reduced to under two hundred. A new accounting rationality supervised the operations of the business unit structure and it became pervasive. The layers of accountants managing the system were natural proselytisers for the new world view, which rested on a number of assumptions. These assumptions involved a funda-mental reframing, both conceptual and practical, of the economic functioning of the BBC. But the reframing functioned at the same time as a new morality within the corporation, one spread with missionary zeal by the accounting cadre, and one that was highly critical of what was seen as the wasteful and libertine past. These moralistic attitudes stoked the ruthlessness with which the new culture was implanted. The assumptions of the new accounting rationality-cum-morality can be condensed into two basic principles.

The first principle was that all economic behaviour must be accounted for within strictly bounded units of time and of activity. To transgress these boundaries was to transgress the bounds of accounting rationality, a rational-ity equated with economic reason itself. The key dangers, or sins, opposed by this principle were that of viring – the carrying of costs or budgets across dis-tinct units of activity, such as productions or departments; and the carrying of

costs or budgets across units of time – most commonly, the carrying forward
of debts across the end of the financial year. Time and again, the accountants
attempted to enlighten production departments and to instill the virtues of
bounded discipline: couldn't producers see that viring between headings, or
carrying costs forward, amounted to cheating, even lying?

The second principle centred on the necessity of foresight, a form of
financial enlightenment aimed at instilling a kind of anticipatory discipline.
Foresight was to be embodied in proper financial planning. In the accountants'
view, the previous system of balancing budgets *post hoc*, through trimming or
carrying over, lacked rigour and integrity. It was, again, not truthful. Moreover, it could not forewarn against the dangers of poor functioning of the
system. Foresight, through the detailed projection and intricate planning of
financial activity, aimed to tame all risks. If the accountants could model and
prescribe optimal financial behaviour, surely that was to the good for all concerned. If it also generated more employment for accountants, so much the
better. The watchword was professionalisation.

The accountants encountered extraordinary resistance. For production
departments commonly conceived of their budgeting across these boundaries
through operating a *redistributive* logic. If one programme went over budget, to
compensate another would be tweaked to come in under or a cheap acquisition would be made. If one strand became overly expensive, another strand
would be reined in. If one department was so small or made such risky or
minority programming that it could not be sure of earning enough to cover its
overheads, it would be cushioned by being grouped for accounting purposes
with a large department with a handsome income that could more than absorb
the extra overhead. It was precisely this organic integration in the service of
editorial ambition, with its mechanisms for dealing with eventualities borne of
creative risk and the pursuit of quality as much as profligacy and misjudgement, that was targeted by the new accountancy. The two systems amounted
to radically incommensurable economic world views.

The many small irrationalities of Producer Choice have become notorious:
the excessive library charges for borrowing CDs, which led producers to go
and buy them individually rather than use the central music library, in turn
undermining the viability of the BBC's libraries; the £10 charge for using the
BBC's News Information department, which caused news and current affairs
producers to phone their press colleagues for information; the charges for bed
and breakfast accommodation so high that World Service staff found rooms at
the Waldorf Hotel cheaper; the extensive paperwork that was as heavy for
trivial expenditure as for large transactions. After 1993 such bizarre 'market'

customs regularly filled the columns of *Private Eye*. Moreover, it was plain that the 'market' was in reality a *quasi-market*: the rules were different for those outside and inside the BBC.[5] Indeed, in significant respects they were skewed in favour of those outside. The high centrally imposed overhead – 15 per cent of programme budgets in Drama Group – was a burden that many business units struggled to support, while their external competitors were not so burdened. Independent producers, when bidding against in-house producers for programme commissions, were required to carry less than one-third of the overhead carried by the BBC departments. The fact that the overhead subsumed the costs of escalating bureaucracy added insult to injury. Producers found that there were arbitrary limits to the market and to their 'choice': faced with high rents for BBC office space, they were not at liberty to rent elsewhere or take lower-standard accommodation. The BBC's exceptional strengths stemming from its integration and huge scale, such as its training schemes and craft specialisms, were not valued sufficiently to be exempted from the harsh market dynamics; many folded as they were found to be 'uneconomic'. The divisive 'choices' facing producers meant that, by choosing to buy external facilities or resources, they knew they risked undermining other BBC employees' jobs. Above all, compared with external competitors, in-house resource and production departments were handicapped by being prevented from trading outside the BBC. They faced a monopoly buyer.

The combined impact of external financial pressures, Producer Choice and the new accounting culture, with its fetishism of efficiency, was to make cuts and closures routine. Each year new targets were set for efficiency savings; each season brought casualties in terms of the closure or absorption of formerly independent production units. The cumulative effect was a devastating erosion of morale and of belief in management's commitment to, and its ability to secure, the BBC's public service purposes. Widespread cynicism, both angry and bemused, swept through the corporation. To be sure, the collective mood was leavened by the more surreal and comic aspects of Producer Choice. But faced with budget cuts, job losses and department closures, the levity was superficial. The identification of many staff with the BBC now took root in a collective contempt for senior management.

*

Rationing pronunciation

A basement recording studio in Broadcasting House. I am here to record a script I have written for Radio 3's Saturday morning show, *Record Review*. The CDs I am reviewing are all of contemporary music. Most of the pieces are composed or played by foreign-named artists, so I am grappling with a large number of Polish, Japanese and Estonian names, and I am in difficulty. The producer has contacted the BBC's central pro-nunciation unit ahead of time, and for some of the names he has a list of correct pronunciations. But others have been left off his list. We try a few takes with me intel-ligently guessing the pronunciation, but it doesn't work. Why, I ask, can't we go back to the pronunciation unit and get the remaining names emailed over to us right away? The producer looks down at his shoes, sighs, and explains that under Producer Choice, for each word he asks the unit to clarify, the programme budget is charged £12. He simply can't afford to consult the unit further on this programme. I am left to guess some more.

Diary, 1996.

*

Squeezing the flagship

It is a sweltering evening in July 1997 and I am visiting the Broadcasting House studio of *The World Tonight*, Radio 4's late-evening news and analysis programme. Of all the news programmes, it is perhaps the one most committed to international affairs and sus-tained, intelligent analysis. We are gathered for a meeting with Richard Clemmow, head of daily news programmes bi-media, and his deputy, Steve Mitchell. They are coming with information about 'major processes of change hitting television and radio daily news'. Before they arrive the atmosphere is one of foreboding and barely repressed anger. Word has already spread around NCA that further efficiency savings are being imposed on all news programmes. This programme has already shouldered its share of cuts and there is disbelief that it can survive much more.

Richard and Steve arrive and Richard sets the scene: changing markets, more and more channels, a proliferation of outlets. Budgets are inevitably getting tighter; it's going to be more difficult to deliver the same quality. Steve then gives the headlines. The News Programme Strategy Review is in train: it's about seeking a greater understand-ing of audiences, pretty much ignored by NCA till now. James Boyle, newly appointed controller of Radio 4, is conducting a Radio 4 review; Steve has been involved since the start and assures them that *The World Tonight* 'has nothing to fear from the review'. Co-siting: Birt has announced a policy of bringing radio and television news together in a new building in White City, a plan that is meeting fierce opposition from radio journalists, whose work will be relocated from Central London. Richard says the plan is moving into high gear. ENPS: this new online system for the whole of NCA, to replace the existing BASYS, is being piloted in Bristol and is on course to be rolled out next year.

We come to the heart of the meeting: cuts. Richard takes over and speaks gravely, taking them through some landscaped, bullet-pointed Corporate-Centre-styled documents that lay out the reasoning. Tony Hall, chief executive of the directorate, is looking for 32 per cent efficiency savings over the next five years. It's inevitable that in some departments that will involve staff cuts. *The World Tonight* is already the smallest daily news programme team; but he explains that it is likely to have to cut staffing from the current level of seventeen to just twelve. Richard asks somewhat rhetorically, hinting at his own scepticism, 'Can you deliver this quality of programme at that staffing level?' One of the team replies forcefully, 'No!' Richard says, 'We'll talk about this . . .'

The room is heating up; *The World Tonight* journalists are becoming physically agitated with dismay and anger. It is worse than they thought. In passing, Richard alludes to an earlier round of efficiency savings in the directorate in which, he says, Tony Hall offered to find higher cuts than asked by Corporate Centre! In this way he appears to distance himself by painting Hall as a super-ideologue who takes painful policies further than necessary; Hall's nickname in NCA is the 'head prefect'. Richard continues that the overall aim across the directorate is for staffing levels to be constant, implying reassurance that any staff cut from the programme will be redeployed. Staff will reduce in certain areas and grow in new areas, especially continuous news with the start of BBC News 24. Steve takes over and talks about the need for new efficiencies, multiskilling, the use of new technologies, and savings stemming from bi-mediality. The message is: retrain to retain your job. Richard, in a feeble attempt to rally the troops, winds up that across the whole of daily news they made £4.5 million savings in the past year.

Discussion begins. Some hang back mutely. Others weigh in, unable to disguise their hostility and sense of betrayal. A long-standing presenter questions whether, given rolling rationalisations and cuts, the programme will survive with its own separate editor and production team. Richard demurs; the programmes will remain distinctive even if synergies between programmes increase. A journalist asks despairingly, 'Isn't the game of "savings" unending? Won't they just keep making more cuts?' Richard answers by saying that it would not work for them to resist the savings directive at this stage. It is a rational process and must be followed through diligently, not obdurately. He assures them that if, at a later stage, the cuts seem to be threatening quality, he and others will go to Hall and Corporate Centre to resist. A producer argues, 'We in radio have already made a lot of savings through the introduction of digital technologies; we've been ahead of TV in this, and our staffing is far lower. But staff costs are proportionally higher for radio news than TV. Isn't it true, then, that staff costs are going to be more under attack in radio with the new cuts?' Another journalist picks up the thread: since budgets are far smaller in radio news than in television, imposing the same percentage cuts on both radio and television inevitably has more devastating effects on radio than on television. How, he asks, can Hall justify this crazy approach? Richard concedes that he may have a point. A reporter ends bitterly, referring to the channelling of savings into the new BBC online services and News 24: 'There are so many reputations on the line, they won't allow the new initiatives to fail, will they? They'll become a black hole, eating up money.' Richard exhorts them once more to 'look rationally to find savings, by eliminating duplication . . .' The meeting ends.

Diary, 1997.

*

Accounting for difference: absorbing the CPU, shedding minority programming

'I'll explain why I was pushed out, which happened during '97–'98. Before the 1996 restructuring the old Factual Group contained four departments including mine, the joint Community Programme Unit and Disability Programme Unit, Documentaries, Science and Features. And although mine was a smaller department, in terms of numbers of programmes and budgets, in hierarchical terms I had parity with the other department heads. In the 1996 restructuring Birt introduced the Broadcast/Production split and the Production directorate was created. Amazingly, when the first wave of reductions in production departments took them from thirty-six to eighteen, my department survived but on very different terms. The CPU was still in some ways autonomous, but it was put in the same business unit as Documentaries. As head of the CPU, I retained editorial autonomy, could pitch to the controllers and get programmes commissioned; but I was now answerable in managerial terms to Paul Hamann, head of Documentaries.'

GB: 'What was the managerial control about then?'

'It became more and more blurred as time went on. Between '96 and '98, I never knew what was going on behind the scenes. I used to get leaks from people who were worried on behalf of the department about what was being done behind my back. Ultimately in 1998 the CPU was absorbed into Documentaries. It was going to be a full absorption, but there was a vociferous campaign of protest inside and outside the BBC which was very embarrassing for the chief executive of Production, Ron Neil. I think this protected the CPU, which survived in some sort of institutional form. It was also gratifying because some of the protest was against how I had been treated, which was a disgrace, Kafkaesque. The biggest issue given as formal grounds for the absorption was purely financial. The system of accounting that had been introduced to production

112

departments when they became business units included a system of charging back overheads as a percentage of the total department budget. As your budgets shrink – and in the five years I was head of the CPU our budget shrank by 50 per cent in real terms, mainly through annually imposed efficiency savings – it becomes harder to recover the overheads. The critical point is that our overheads were easier to subsume when we were in the Factual Group, as the overheads could be spread across the four departments. And although there was some protection when we became part of Documentaries in the restructuring, we were more exposed. There was no adjustment for the difference between high- and low-cost departments, so the overheads took a larger chunk out of small departments like the CPU. It just became harder and harder to recover our overheads on a shrinking base of programme budgets; they become unrecoverable.

'At the beginning of the financial year '97–'98, we were on course for a deficit of about a third of a million. By November, when I was summoned and told the CPU was to be amalgamated into Documentaries, we had already reduced the deficit to £79,000. We had pulled it back an enormous amount through gaining more commissions and by finding cuts; we were chopping out whole lines in the budgets. We never had any downtime, no time when staff were not assigned to a particular programme, and very little "think time" for new ideas. We were surviving on the commitment and good will of the staff, who were knackered.'

GB: 'What was your staffing like?'

'We had fifty or sixty people in the department. We had the highest productivity per person of any factual department in the BBC, the best cost per hour in programme terms in factual. This was with none of the advantages of departments like Features, with long-running studio format shows like *Esther*. We won four major awards that last year, including a major European award and the CRE Race in the Media award, the third time we'd won it. By any objective standards we were doing well – leaving aside any philosophical issues about what the BBC should be doing in minority programming. Yet because we had a deficit, we had to go. So in November '97 Paul Hamann told me that my job had gone and the CPU was to be absorbed into Documentaries. I asked to see Ron, and he said, "Your deficit is too high," and quoted figures that made no sense to me. I said, "In the larger scheme of things, for the sake of very low-cost programming, is a deficit of £79,000 such an intolerable burden for the BBC?" He said, "Yes, well, we have to be seen to be efficient."'

GB: 'To what do you attribute this? You seem to be saying that in the late Birt period they couldn't see the public interest beyond bizarre accounting structures that delivered "efficiency"?'

'I think the BBC was then, and is now, schizophrenic. We all want to have huge ratings, we all want to be public service; there are times when you can't be both so you have to make choices. Ron Neil's sense of the public service remit was a very traditional one: strong and independent journalism and a broad range of programming. But in my opinion he had no interest in what we do: in minority programmes, in disabled viewers and their needs, and no sense at all of the importance for the BBC and the social significance of there being large ethnic communities in Britain. He didn't seem to recognise the issues, or understand the language we were using.'

Former head of the BBC's CPU/DPU, 2000.

*

Cross-subsidy

'Before the merger of the four drama departments, Serials always overspent spectacularly, when it was Michael Wearing and the department manager on their own. Singles and Films were a bit of an overspend, but not so drastic, and Series always came in under. There was about an £8 million surplus on Series the first year I was here . . .'

GB: 'So a cross-subsidy happened between the departments?'

'Yes, and it was pernicious.'

Senior accountant, BBC Drama, 1996.

*

Accounting Wars

The experience of Drama Group exemplifies the impact on production made by the new accountancy and by Producer Choice. As Producer Choice gathered pace, questions arose as to whether Drama's existing structures could adequately administer the rigorous market processes that it entailed. Drama's large scale and high budgets made it a test case for the introduction of tighter financial management, with the aim of disciplining what were considered to be its lax and amateur methods. From 1993, the new head of the Group and chief accountant initiated radical changes, to be spearheaded by tiers of accountants.

The previous hierarchy of financial administration in drama centred on a department manager or chief assistant, who oversaw all non-editorial management under the direction of a drama genre head, and associate producers attached to each production. To this had recently been added production executives, whose role was to supervise the financial management of several productions under the charge of each executive producer. The relationship of these personnel to producers and creative figures tended still to be one of fealty, of devoted subservience to creative aims. In 1993, management accountants were brought in to work alongside the department managers. In 1994, a centralised finance control process began, embodied in the weekly Programme Finance Committee (PFC), through which all major financial decisions had to be passed, and a large new department, Drama Finance, grew to service it. In 1995, a slew of accountants known as cost controllers were installed to monitor every production. The new staff began to impose entirely new accounting practices, and existing forms of financial management were no longer recognised as legitimate. A crisis erupted as the drama department managers and other staff protested. For them the imposition was aggressive and unilateral; it undermined the existing flexible and cooperative relations between managers and producers. For several years previously, the staffing of drama production and resources had been severely cut; against this background the surge in accountants was seen as indefensible.

Civil war broke out. For more than a year, parallel processes of financial management coexisted. Each represented a competing rationality. The accountants championed the new framing and planning procedures; the department managers and their teams continued to employ their redistributive, compensatory logics. The drama department heads, their executive producers and producers continued to work with the original teams, and successful efforts were made to isolate and freeze out the new accountants; while on their part, the management accountants and cost controllers tried determinedly to exert their authority and controls. The bizarre stand-off was manifest at lunchtimes in the cafeteria. One or two tables would be occupied by a group of unfashionably dressed people, among them a number of young British Asians. These were the outcasts from Drama Finance, invariably hunched together laughing, orderly but defiant. They were ignored by the rest of the lunchtime crowd, whose behaviour made plain that the accountants lacked the cultural élan to become truly part of Drama Group.

*

Unnecessary, unproductive management

'Before Charles was head of Drama, Mark Shivas was head of Drama, but he was also head of Films. Until Charles we never had a hands-on head of Drama; it was a position people occupied as well as something else. They were mopping up the Group needs as well as running an output department. As a result of Charles's appointment we have seen the appointment of the masses of financial staff. We have seen the absorption of Drama Personnel into Drama. We have seen Linda Stone come into Drama, the creation of Margaret Smith's job, the proliferation of admin staff looking after safety and schedules. We have seen the creation of the Drama Production Centre. That's why we can't recover our overheads – because they have become bloated.'

GB: 'An enormous ballast of personnel . . .?'

'Absolutely. Unnecessary, unproductive management. The wrong way.'

Department manager, BBC Drama, 1996.

*

Turmoil: parallel management

'There's a culture here which is difficult to break: "We know what we're doing, we know how to make drama, we're professionals, specialists; why are we always under attack?" As managers, we were asked to become business users, to do a business plan. Then we were given a management accountant; then suddenly the following year, the management accountant was working for a huge new section called Drama Finance because, it was implied, we weren't doing it properly. A lot of people suffered badly as a result – unnecessarily, because most of us pride ourselves on being professional and financially accountable. The appointments were made with no consultation in a spirit of confrontation. And these changes are not just within Drama Group; they have occurred right across Network TV. There is a problem with Drama Finance: compared to the way they do things, the way we do things seems unrobust. We tend to say, "It'll be about like that". We talk in halves, whereas for the Finance people it's either two or three but there's no half. It's a different attitude. Accounting on a drama production is not an exact science. But Finance's attitude is "This is appalling! They don't know what they're doing; we'll have to tell them." It's dictatorial. If you want to manage a pro-gramme, including controlling its costs, there has to be one person doing it because any financial decision has editorial implications and vice versa. So the parallel structure is not designed to function well.'

Department manager, BBC Drama, 1996.

*

Single drama was the most vulnerable of drama genres in this period. Its budgets were among the highest in television, between £600,000 and £1 million
per hour, but its ratings were unpredictable. Despite its prestigious reputation
as the most literary of drama genres, in the newly competitive climate single
drama had an uncertain role in the schedule. It could not be relied on, as could
series and serials, to bring the audience back repeatedly to a channel. Singles
were being inexorably drawn towards theatrical film, an area in which, while
the BBC had a track record, it had still to consolidate its international presence.
The fact that in television terms Singles budgets were very high meant that the
department was under intense pressure to deliver sure winners, whether in
ratings or in 'profile', that is, critical acclaim or renown among the cultured
classes. In combination these pressures threatened singles producers' capacity
to experiment or innovate. But the Singles department's editorial culture was
highly developed, ambitious and knowing, and a key strategy used to support
such risks was to take a view not of each individual project but across the entire
slate of singles productions. In this way, sure-fire successes could be balanced
against the odd experimental project, high-cost star vehicles against cheaper
ideas using new writers. The technique generated a bit of precious autonomy
for Singles in planning their output.

In this context, the department manager fought strenuously to retain flexibility in singles' budgeting. Alone of all the drama genres in the mid nineties,
Singles received annually from the controllers a budget for the total output of
the main singles strands on BBC1 and BBC2. This meant that the manager was
able to vary each project and adjust the budgeting across the strands as a whole
during the year, as long as the outcome balanced. This allowed flexibility in the
use of money to reflect critical editorial judgements about investment, risk,
quality and compromise. Moreover, the controllers would often decide during
the year to alter the mix of singles projects, according to scheduling needs. But
this flexibility was under attack: the accountants required the manager to adopt
their method of budgeting for individual projects with no adjustment after the
initial allocation, so as to come within the boundaries of project and of time
decreed by the new accounting procedures. For the manager, allied with the
department's editorial staff, this would utterly corrode the creative autonomy
of Singles.

The rival sides in the accounting conflict were encapsulated by the oppos-
ing rationalities deployed by the Singles manager and the department's
management accountant. In the mid nineties the two were supposed to be

working cooperatively to reform the financial systems. But mutual incomprehension fuelled an ideological stand-off. In talking about the fight over accounting processes, the manager expressed a general indignation that the supposedly rigorous accounting was so unevenly applied. Three years into the new regime the much contested budget for drama development, which paid for early stages of script writing before any drama project could be 'green lit', had been made neither transparent nor properly disciplined; the drama producers had yet to be trained to meet the requirements of the new accounting; and significant anomalies continued to arise, such as where the cost of paying for the Group's core producers should be met. All things financial in Drama continued to be in flux.

*

Irrational rational: conflicting accounts

'As far as Charles [*head of Drama Group*] is concerned, the agreed budget at the PFC is the one that we work to, and never any variance shall be agreed; variance is bad programme management. Now I come from a very disciplined background in which, when a budget is agreed, that is the budget; but that doesn't take into account the editorial decisions that George [*head of Single Drama*] and David try to make in order to enhance a drama. Let's take a hypothetical case, say *Mansfield Park*. We agree the total budget with the PFC. Having agreed the budget, we go into pre-production and suddenly Laurence Olivier agrees to play the main part. Now we weren't planning to have Olivier in this film, but of course, to have him would enhance the production. George could say, "No, that's the agreed budget and I'm not going to enhance it," or he can say, "What if I agreed an extra £20,000 for Olivier, what would that do to the rest of the mix?" And at that point I would say, "If you took the £20,000 for that, we could make sure that we did the other single drama TBAs for less money." And I think, editorially, both George and David should be entitled to do that within reason – although there comes a point when you have no money and no flexibility left.'

GB: 'This is specific to Singles, isn't it, because you have control over your own total strand budgets for *Screen One* and *Screen Two*, whereas Serials and Series don't . . .?'

'Correct: we have a total fixed budget. About two or three years in advance we know what incomes we're going to get from the controllers of BBC1 and BBC2, and George will agree the number of films we're going to deliver. In February, I was about to have my meeting with Planning to agree prices and titles, but we then changed the mix following discussions between George and Michael Jackson about how he sees the BBC2 schedule going. So the mix is up in the air, and then all the money changes. The ongoing battle I have is to get Charles and Drama Finance to recognise that we are actually balancing our money within the whole strand; we don't work to individual budgets. Charles's point is that when a budget is agreed at the PFC, if you don't keep to that budget it is poor programme management: "Look, you in Singles have overspent to the tune of a million pounds." My reply is, "No, we're delivering at exactly the right price. Sure, we've altered the budget from when it was first agreed at the PFC, but this wasn't done without pre-planning for how we are going to afford it."'

GB: 'And isn't this how production budgets always tend to work, that they have to develop to some extent during the actual production process?'

'Certainly in singles they tend to because there are unknown factors: casting and income. Drama Finance's argument is that "artificially" inflating the budget if extra income comes in is wrong; just because there's extra income doesn't mean you should increase the budget. I think there's a happy medium. In some cases you wouldn't inflate the budget; you'd say "Great, that reduces BBC2's inject and leaves me more money to put elsewhere where it's needed" – which is also important for us in Singles.'

GB: 'It sounds as though co-production money can fall into place late on.'

'Absolutely, another difficulty here: because of Worldwide, and because of the arm's-length negotiations that go on, quite often the additional income is not agreed till you're three-quarters of the way through production. That happened on *Deacon Brody*, one of our current *Screen Ones*. We agreed a budget of £1.3 million – about £300,000 above the strand average – knowing that we would get some co-production. We also knew we could take money from the other *Screen Ones* for next year if necessary to afford it. It isn't unrealistic, because some of this year's *Screen Ones* have come in at £800,000 or £850,000. And now we've found £230,000 co-production, so there is hardly any overage and I can adjust the TBA figures upwards again. We make those adjustments constantly. Another method we use to make the mix add up financially is to go for an acquisition, because they're cheaper. Say George spends a million each on a couple of films, to compensate he will undoubtedly go for an acquisition, which only costs £250,000, so as to be able to deliver the number of titles he's agreed with Michael.'

GB: 'It seems that Finance are resisting acknowledging the degree of financial and editorial autonomy you have here. But Annie [*department manager for Series*] seemed to be arguing for the same general principle at PFC, even for Series: that there has to be flexibility to deal with unforeseens – the director is lousy, the star storms off – and that therefore good production management must take into account these eventualities . . .'

'Correct. And if we did budget on a project-by-project basis, in the way Drama Finance want, that would inevitably have an inflationary effect. If we are only allowed what is agreed at the PFC, I would want to keep the budgets up that are being agreed there, rather than trimming them down to the level that I realistically think we can aim for. To me, it's better to agree a PFC budget of £620,000 knowing that it's tight, and as production develops ask for an extra £15,000 to get the film completed, than to start with a PFC budget of £700,000 just to make sure of contingencies. To me, that is good management.'

GB: 'It sounds like an argument for devolving budgets because that allows you to take financial responsibility.'

'But that's what I think my job is, Georgie! If it isn't, then what the hell am I doing here? Don't get me wrong: I think it's incredibly important having a recognised Programme Finance Committee that acts as a formal finance forum to agree budget decisions. But in theory, we're not asking them for anything, because it's our money. In practice, I think Charles and Keith would say that it *isn't* our money – and that's the central problem. PFC allows us to bring them into the loop. How would they know that we're doing as many co-productions with HBO if we didn't take it to the PFC? Take *Deadly Voyage*, a movie costing £4 million, but only £1 million to the BBC: now, isn't it clever of us to have got the HBO deal, so Michael can have a £4 million movie on BBC2 that only cost him £1 million?'

GB: 'How does development money fit into all this?'

'It's utterly mad. It's handed out across the Group, not allocated per department. Therefore the departments haven't had to build the discipline of managing their own money. They just go to the PFC and say, "I want to develop this project," and get a yes or no. We need a devolved budget structure that means each department manages its development, and the decisions are based not only on editorial matters but also on financial restrictions. Then development would be much more focused. It hasn't been managed this year, and that's why we are notionally £1 million over. But it's been clouded by the fact that £X million of the £6 or £7 million development pot has had to pay for the Group's core producers and script editors, who haven't been able to be recovered anywhere else.'

GB: 'So there's an emphasis on discipline via the PFC for production, but not for development. That's why you all sit round the table discussing development, having no idea whether claiming another X thousand pounds for the latest Mary Wesley book is . . .'

'. . . A lot of money or not a lot of money, yes. Or what it's doing to the global development budget. It's one of the ironies: Charles and Keith have been in place for three years, yet there's no proper management of development. We need reports on an annual and a departmental basis.'

GB: 'There's a sense in your Singles meetings that when Stuart [*the Singles management accountant*] brings out his accounting papers near the end, George ostentatiously wraps up the meeting. Is this expressing the fact that none of you are really going to listen to him?'

'It's my duty as department manager to go through those papers with Stuart, because our production executives will look at them and say, "These don't bear any resemblance to our figures", and I'll go, "I know, he does X Y Z." We do take into account Stuart's papers; George relies on me to go through them to make sure there isn't anything awful there, because Stuart's figures – not mine – are the ones that go into the business plan and to the PFC. Stuart wouldn't dream of giving them my papers, because I'm not a qualified accountant. It's a political thing.'

GB: 'So you have to harmonise the two sets of accounts and make sure they tally. It's strange: Stuart still hands out his accounts to everyone, even though no one takes any notice. It's like a ritual gesture of defiance – that everybody should see his papers.'

Department manager, BBC Single Drama, 1996.

*

Stuart, the Singles management accountant, had been one of the first to enter Drama Group in the new regime. He passionately upheld the value of the principles of financial probity and rational accounting that he had been appointed to instil. Contemptuous of what he saw as the arrogant, lazy, class-imbued, producer-driven culture of the BBC, frustrated by the resistance and isolation he suffered in carrying out his job in Singles, he wrote detailed, perceptive and in some ways sympathetic analyses for his Drama Finance colleagues of the history of the Drama crisis. His notes centred on the handling of financial discrepancies, and mercilessly found wanting the previous mechanisms for managing money. But the analyses speak also of disillusion and conflict with the financial management coming from Corporate Centre, whose support for the individual accounting system adopted by Drama Finance appeared to be waning in favour of a new wave of centralisation.

*

Revolution, counter-revolution

'Creating new structures will always be harder than maintaining the status quo. It was clear that we would face suspicion and misunderstanding from "creative" people unused to contact with accountants ... In the past Planning dispensed programme budgets to departments but ignored actual costs as reported. Production departments adopted a variety of strategies when explaining actual costs against budget. These included: denial – the accounting records were denigrated as being inaccurate and local attempts to monitor costs claimed to be the "real" results; disagreement – resource costs in particular were seen as arbitrary and inaccurate; and false accounting – when all else failed, costs for an overspending department could be charged to a programme which was underspending ... Management accounts were compromised by the devices they employed to obscure overspends against budgets ...

'Thus the introduction of Producer Choice was a revolution within Network Television which sought to introduce proper financial accountability to a financially primitive organisation ... But all the attempts at reform have met with incomprehension and resistance within the Group. Accountants were generally marginalised and excluded from most key financial areas; the result was the creation of parallel universes with departments using two sets of figures ... Unfortunately, we do not seem to have many friends outside either. The impetus for reform seems to have run out of steam; most of the initiatives from Corporate Centre since then appear to be counter-revolutionary, principally MIDAS which proposes a central finance scheme. The current approach is clearly in favour of centralisation. This despite Network Television having the most inadequate financial controls I have ever come across: the illegality of false accounting and tax evasion has been considered justified if it is for programmes and not for personal gain.

'Conclusion: We must make a missionary effort with senior management outside Drama Group, especially in Corporate Centre.'

Management accountant, BBC Drama, 1996.

*

Virtual Money

Stuart was not interested simply in chastising the production departments. His analyses pinpointed also a larger set of forces behind production's difficulties in meeting set budgets. This took him into a discussion of the fantastical way that money moved around the BBC through a five-step chain of internal virtual transfers, none of them, even after Producer Choice, concretised in cash exchanges. A tariff set in Corporate Centre, on the basis of crude projections of gross costs per genre per hour, formed the basis for the division of the licence fee income into chunks to be sent to different parts of the BBC. The Broadcast division then set a target price to allow money to be allocated more finely according to the needs and deserts of each radio or television network. The finance planning team for each network then translated the target price for each genre into a contract price negotiated with the production departments – that is, what the network would 'pay' for any commissioned programme. The production departments then allocated a budget to each production team for particular commissions, a budget which may or may not have been close to the contract price handed down by the channel. And the fifth stage in the process was the actual cost of the production when it was completed. The chances of systemic errors occurring in such a game of economic Chinese whispers must, as Stuart pointed out, have been substantial.

A critical disjuncture in the virtual chain occurred when a channel, by setting the contract price, dictated the budget available to production, since the channel controllers held all the cards and could choose to remain oblivious to the pressures on producers to meet high expectations and the additional costs this may incur. 'Overspends' were always seen as a property of the production team, not of unrealistic contract prices set by controllers. But in a deeper way Stuart identified the magical qualities of the BBC's economic functioning, a theme pursued by a senior ex-BBC programme executive when reflecting, as an independent producer, on Producer Choice:

*

'Lies!', £2.1 billion in, £2.1 billion out

'The BBC's whole position is that they can make a programme cheaper than independents like me; but they can do that because they don't know how much it really costs. They never have done and they still don't know . . .'

GB: 'Even after Producer Choice?'

'They don't have a clue. I was speaking to Tony Hall recently. I said, "Tony, we haven't a clue how the BBC's financed. As an independent, I now know everything about how my programmes are costed. I know what it costs because I write the cheques." The BBC? No idea. I don't even know how much I paid for the computer on my desk at the BBC. I can tell you exactly how much this one here cost because I wrote the cheque for it. That's the difference. In the BBC a new computer would arrive on my desk, ordered by the head of computers, but at what cost I never knew. Why did it happen? Why did I get an upgrade? I didn't ask for it. And so the BBC will tell you they can make a programme cheaper in-house. It might be cheaper, you haven't got a clue, but it will be subsidised.'

GB: 'Did Producer Choice have some kind of cultural effect in terms of increasing cost-consciousness, and was it productive in that sense?'

'Yes, it absolutely did that. You've got to encourage an awareness of costs at the BBC, and Producer Choice was a big shift in that direction, huge, but easy in the sense that there was zilch cost-consciousness before, so any movement was an improvement. It went too far. People lost trust in it, and also it was scuppered by a completely inefficient finance system. There were seventeen different finance systems, it was too big a job.'

GB: 'And they had to bring in a bevy of management consultancies to try and sort all the finance systems out . . .'

'And they could never do it. I'm not sure that the BBC *can* actually be rescued in that way. It's grown too organically to be deconstructed and put back together in a way that's efficient. The systems are too complicated. Television had a different system from Radio, Radio from World Service; they were different from Regions, and different parts of Regions had different systems from each other, and BBC1 had a different system again. It was just a complete bloody mess.'

GB: 'But in the end, surely somebody was balancing the books? Somehow it all comes together . . .?'

'I've never known the answer to that question; I always just assumed that in the end someone's balancing the books, but I'd love to know whether somebody really is. Baker Bates [*the former BBC director of Finance*] was there for a long time and he never did sort it out. Look at what happened to Marconi: with an organisation like that you think somebody must have balanced the books, but discover that nobody did and that it's actually bankrupt. I mean, I don't even know where the BBC banks! How does the money, the actual cash, move around the BBC? How does the licence fee money arrive, and in what way does it become real inside the BBC?'

GB: 'And the auditing process didn't produce convincing directorate accounts which could then add up?'

'I wasn't convinced by the information. I don't think our information was solid enough. It was an exercise. I think partly John [Birt's] approach was that the very act of doing it helps focus the mind. I'm sure that's true – the very fact that you had to start worrying about money meant that people started worrying about money. That meant it had some impact, but whether the numbers were robust . . . John was always banging on about it, but just looking at my own numbers: sometimes you were £100,000 over or sometimes you were £400,000 in the black, because someone multiplied by two and divided by three. And you'd think, "What the hell's all this? What's the reality?" The reality for me now, as an independent producer, is simple: what's in the bank balance? I look it up, there it is. If I spend and it goes into the red, I stop. What's the bank balance of the BBC? With any big corporation, it's other people's money, isn't it? For anyone working for a big corporation it's "Let's have a bigger television set", "Let's have five TV sets and a VCR", "Let's upgrade". I don't think there's anybody in the BBC who cares, who really cares, about the money. Just go to any BBC lig: who's paying for that? I was invited to the Proms by the BBC a few weeks ago: a car picked me up, took me to the Albert Hall, they fed me, took me back home. That's a licence-fee-worth of car, isn't it?'

GB: 'As far as I could see, under Producer Choice, you were sitting in Drama Group or Entertainments, and you were making a big effort to cost aspects of above-the-line and below-the-line budget. But then the overhead came in, and it would be totally opaque. Nobody could tell you why you should carry that 15 per cent, which would take you over what the indie bid was.'

'But in the BBC you didn't work to real money, in that you know you have X thousand pounds to make a programme. Instead, you'd know you have ten days' shooting and three weeks' editing; that's real. Then Tony says "I want 10 per cent more out of you", so suddenly you only have eight days' shooting and two weeks' editing. So you have that kind of awareness of costs, but it's not real money.

'You know, 11 September happens and in the BBC the money all turns up to cover it. Where did that come from? As an independent I just sit and watch it because I can't do anything about it. The BBC is geared up somehow to do it, quite rightly; but that means there's a hole through any managing director saying, "There is no money, it's all gone, it's all in the output" – lies! Of course there's money, because you can send everybody out on 11 September, when it matters. So everybody knows that in the end there's something somewhere. I wouldn't call that profligate, although management continue to spend. In a £2 billion organisation, I doubt that cars cost that much; the big money still goes on programmes. But it's a cultural thing, an attitude to financing. In a very general way I think Producer Choice had an impact on people, made them more cost-conscious. Now it muddles along, but somewhere at the top it must all work out in the end, mustn't it? £2.1 billion must come in, £2.1 billion must go out . . .'

Executive, independent production company, 2001.

*

By 1996 the cost controllers had gone from Drama Group, defeated. The new accounting went into abeyance, and an uneasy peace prevailed. But more direct and brutal ways were used to bring Drama into line with the new ethos. Cuts in the later nineties devastated drama staffing; producers were put on project-based contracts, and the Drama Production Centre was closed. The former internal body of committed and collaborative drama talent was eviscerated. What remained was a skeleton crew for commissioning and development. The dynamic of merging departments into ever-larger business units rolled inexorably on, eroding autonomy and providing the rationale for further cuts. Where in 1998 Documentaries had eaten up the CPU, for example, in autumn 2001 the department of Leisure and Factual Entertainment merged with Documentaries and a further spate of redundancies was announced.[6]

The profits and losses resulting from Producer Choice are possible to state but, like the BBC's own accounts, they are impossible to 'balance'. Producers spoke of both its destructive and its beneficial effects. They regretted the closure of departments unable to operate as independent business units, the casualisation of the workforce and shedding of jobs, the depletion of central services, and the many arbitrary limits and petty annoyances of what was in reality an ideological construct, a quasi-market. Many spoke also of the benefits of some downsizing, of choice between suppliers and of greater economic realism. But the relentless budget erosion spearheaded by Producer Choice had real effects. While there may be no necessary correlation between higher budgets and high quality in broadcast output, there is a limiting point; and among television professionals in the later nineties, cumulative budget cuts were perceived as the dominant factor in declining programme standards.[7]

*

How low can you go?

GB: 'Isn't one of the key problems for Drama in the last few years that you go to the channel controllers with a budget for a show and they treat it as inflated, as something to be bargained with, rather than assuming you've done your damnedest to cut the budget right back?'

'It's a real problem, and not just for our part of Drama. Broadcast has been trying to cut the budget for *EastEnders*, for instance, even though the on-screen value of that is so high to them, and its place in the schedule is so valuable. Whereas I have a feeling Granada sells *Coronation Street* at a higher than purely cost level to ITV Network

Centre, and are then able to cross-subsidise their other shows when they need to – period drama, for example, which is hugely expensive to make. I think *Moll Flanders* was one they were saying had cost lower than we believed. Last autumn all this pressure was coming from Broadcast: they were saying can we do period drama for even less money, and actually period drama is a complete nightmare, we're in trouble on most of them, we're always having budget problems. The earlier the period the harder it is, because you can't get the right architecture in the background, so you have to build more. *Ivanhoe*, for example – we had a lot of problems with that budget.'

GB: 'On *EastEnders*, I was at a debate at the Television Show recently on the question of how low the budgets for the major soaps could go. Corinne Hollingworth, Jane Tranter, executive producer of *London's Burning*, and others were talking, and their view was that there's a bottom line of about £40,000 a half-hour below which quality would be compromised too much: "The broadcasters are crazy if they think we can keep on cutting." But Mal Young, in charge of Channel 5's *Family Affairs*, said he'd happily have a go with lower budgets.'

'The BBC income in reality is reducing. But *EastEnders* is the wrong programme to be having an argument about budgets. We've really pretty well squeezed out all the things we can, so we'll have to do different sorts of drama if we want to make it for less. We didn't used to make as much period drama as we do now, and that's the highest cost drama. There are contradictions: I remember when *Extending Choice* came out, we all read it, and Michael and I looked at each other and said, "Surely they can't afford this policy?", because they were talking about increasing the amount of period drama! Now you can get quite high amounts of co-production money from North America to support that, but it still costs a lot more to the BBC than contemporary drama – closer to £1 million an hour, rather than £500,000-ish.'

Department manager, BBC Drama, 1997.

*

How much did the efficiency savings yield financially to be diverted into new services as well as new bureaucracies? Birt claimed in September 1993 that Producer Choice had brought £100 million savings across the BBC in its first year, predicting that this would rise to £175 million by the third year and would continue at that level. In 1996, he said that the BBC had saved £500 million since 1991 through efficiency savings and staff cuts. He anticipated a further 15 per cent savings in the coming three years, but despite this he noted a shortfall of £300 million stemming from the costs of bringing in digital television services.[8] The savings were huge and, certainly, Birt's expansive plans for new services were supported by them. But they may have come at unacceptable cost to the BBC's main networks. In 2001, a persuasive argument was made that, via Producer Choice and the efficiency drive, Birt 'starved the main analogue stations of money and lavished care and cash on digital channels which, in spite of the investment, didn't pull in any ratings. BBC1 is still paying the price for that error.'[9] Nonetheless, Birt presciently reshaped the organisation, preparing it for the new landscape wrought by digitalisation, preparations that were far in advance of the BBC's terrestrial rivals. To draw out the lines of reason retrospectively is not to deny the collective pain caused by the reshaping, nor is it to ignore the risk that such a reorientation might have proved unfruitful. But Birt trusted BBC staff to rise inventively to the challenge of new media; and in this, as measured for example by the calibre and the success of the BBC's Internet operations, he was proved right.

Producer Choice and the new accounting rationality were the stick. The carrot – the seductive element in the BBC's marketisation, with the more insidious effects – was the installation throughout the BBC, courtesy of the intensifying impact of the independent production quota, of a new culture of entrepreneurialism.

4

Trading and Competing

Three steps to the controller

'To an outsider, last summer's restructuring seemed totally incoherent. There was an appalling lack of consultation with department heads. Considering that the BBC at a very senior level stands for the cult of good management, their way of treating people is disgraceful. That the restructuring could take place overnight without anybody being consulted is amazing! Why is Birt never held to account for changing a whole organisation without taking soundings from anybody in advance? You have a situation now where Alan Yentob is director of programmes, Ron Neil is in charge of Production, and then they appointed Paul Jackson as head of Entertainment Group, without any consideration of where that leaves the people running each department. So if you're [a department head like] Geoffrey Perkins or John Plowman, from being one step away, you're now technically three steps away from a controller. I don't want to see BBC production disappear in entertainment; there are reasons for retaining a production base. But I don't see any strategy to do this. What's gone on in drama is even worse. They've just casually let drama disappear; it's melted like snow.'

Managing director, independent production company, 1996.

*

Let's face it

'You know, speaking now as an independent and as someone who worked for years inside the BBC, they didn't go far enough with Producer Choice. That was the moment to completely break up the BBC, separate out the broadcast end from production, and make in-house production into a very large independent. It still ought to happen! Let's face it, the BBC's main problem now is staving off the independents, since that's where the best work and ideas are coming from.'

Independent producer, former BBC producer, 1996.

129

*

The cream of the ideas

'Unfortunately the best ideas tend to come from independents: they can cream the best ideas from writers because they pay more, because the PACT contract used by the indies is structured so that on the first day of principal photography the writer gets 100 per cent of his fee including a buyout of all the other rights. Whereas under the BBC contract the writer gets no payment for other rights until those rights are owed to him; in other words he'll get sales when the sales are made, repeats when repeats are made. So if you were a writer, wouldn't you rather go with an independent? That's why they get the cream of the ideas. And that's one of the main reasons we at the BBC do too many independent productions, far more than the 25 per cent quota.'

Department manager, BBC Drama, 1997.

*

The empire's closing down

GB: 'In the entertainment area, the BBC's commissioning rate for independents is very high, about 50 per cent, isn't it? Is that inevitable?'

'Well, I'm sure there's an awful lot of programmes made in-house that you could point to, and a lot of them are perfectly good. But you're right that in-house is trapped in a long-term sense of decline. It's like being in the Colonial Service when the empire's closing down. The trend is against you, and that's a big problem for the BBC. I don't have an answer; I'm happy to coexist with in-house production. If we didn't coexist then maybe some of that feeling directed at in-house producers of "You've got to find something to fill the seven o'clock Friday slot" would devolve upon us, and I'm really glad someone else has that problem. There are occasions when independents feel they're at a disadvantage against in-house production. But it works in many ways in the opposite direction.'

Independent producer working in entertainment, 1997.

*

The Flexible Firm?

The impact of Producer Choice has been widely discussed. Less known are the tangled web of consequences for the BBC of the 25 per cent independent production quota introduced in the early nineties, which link closely with the effects of Birt's restructuring of the corporation in June 1996. This chapter probes that tangled web, tracing the extraordinary repercussions of the twin developments. The prevailing political consensus is that the advent of the independent quota is one of the few unequivocally constructive changes to hit broadcasting in the last decade. Here at last are demonstrated the beneficial results of forcing a sluggardly public body to match up to external competition. Given that the quota applies also to ITV, the more general argument is put, as it was at the start of Channel 4, that the market in programme supply continues to prise open the stranglehold of the giant duopolists, increasing the diversity of Britain's television output, enabling enterprising new voices to enter and to create businesses in television production. The consensual political faith in markets finds its apogee in this lauding of the independent sector.

Producer Choice was seen by many inside and outside the BBC as an ambiguous measure that put in place the preconditions for privatising parts of the corporation if this proved politically opportune.[1] As the independent quota kicked in during the mid nineties, the flavour of the times led New Labour policy analysts to propose, in the name of efficiency, clarity and fair trading, the need to break up the BBC into its component parts so that they could trade transparently with each other. In this tidy conception, the market model behind Producer Choice would be followed through at a meta-organisational level. As the BBC channels were now buying a considerable proportion of programming from the independent sector, the Channel 4 publisher–broadcaster model was portrayed as the new norm. For some analysts, it followed that the privatisation of the BBC production departments might be a logical step, enabling BBC producers to sell their programmes beyond the corporation. At the very least, the argument went, it was necessary to separate the BBC channels from the production departments so as to put in-house producers on the same footing as independents when pitching programmes.[2] In the first years of the independent quota, a number of independents had complained that the BBC production heads faced conflicts of interest in having to represent to the buyers, the channel controllers, proposals from both their own departments and their competitors, the independents. This was by no means a consensual view. Some BBC production heads and independents denied the existence of significant conflicts of interest; others considered there to be benefits in close links between production departments and independents. Nonetheless, the 'conflict of interest' doctrine took hold and, apparently providing evidence of just that contamination of market forces by the messy pragmatics of coopera- tion that the policy analysts abhorred, provided a final justification for the restructuring.

In this context, Birt's restructuring remade the BBC pretty much in the image of the New Labour analysts' recommendations. The most extensive reorganisation of the BBC in its entire history, it came out of a year-long exer- cise by the management consultancy McKinsey to devise the BBC's ten-year strategic plan. The restructuring sliced the corporation horizontally, replacing the integrated television and radio directorates with the new BBC Broadcast and BBC Production, which were intended to become separate trading bodies. The bi-medial Broadcast contained all the television and radio networks, and Production all the bi-medial production departments. The in-house produc- tion departments would henceforth compete with independent producers on a level playing field to sell programmes to Broadcast, driving down costs and honing efficiency. Whereas in the previous, vertically integrated BBC, channels and production departments sat side by side in Television and Radio and co- operated in planning the output, now a streamlined commissioning apparatus based in Broadcast and backed by teams of market analysts and strategists would determine channel strategies and schedules, to be filled by Production as required. The strategy and planning apparatuses had grown from the early nineties; the restructuring sanctioned and enhanced their new power.

Astute industry observers, however, were not slow to note the irony that just as the BBC was disaggregating and discovering the joys of 'flexible specialisation', its commercial competitors were reaggregating. By the mid nineties the ITV companies were engaging in mergers and buying steadily into production capacity. As the BBC struggled with the complex forces unleashed by the independent quota and the restructuring, the same com- mentators were stressing the manifold benefits of large, vertically integrated producer-broadcasters: lower transaction costs, reliability, regularity, trust- ing and cooperative relations between distributor and producers, economies of scale, the ownership of rights for exploitation across diversifying channels and the accumulation of a rights archive − increasingly central to the global media economy.[3]

Birt's restructuring, secretly prepared and announced without warning on 7 June 1996, posited neat and supposedly rational solutions to the conun- drums thrown up by the external market. In tandem, the restructuring and the external market appeared to improve organisational structure and generate clean competition. But the planning of the restructuring by Birt and the management consultants was skin-deep. Within days it became obvious to many of those affected that numerous unavoidable organisational complexities had been given little thought, and that the details of how the restructuring would impact on the functioning of large parts of the BBC had not been addressed. A chaos began which lasted months. Indeed, a year later critical structural difficulties in Drama Group had not been solved; some had worsened as a result of the restructuring. For all the strategic thinking, the ensuing months saw a spectacular and sustained failure of practical management at the top of the BBC and in the leadership of the directorates.

A cascade of interrelated problematic developments ensued. The external market exacerbated a growing belief on the part of BBC senior management that the independents were superior to in-house production, the key source of innovation and talent. In some programme genres the independents rapidly became the preferred source of programming. Executive conversation extolled the pleasures of hanging out in Soho and spinning deals with independents over expense-account lunches, partly as an escape from the grey Birtist vistas of Shepherd's Bush. The elevation of the independents fuelled a self-fulfilling cycle: an outflow of BBC talent in a number of key genres, including drama, entertainment and factual, given producers' belief, confirmed by managerial practice, that talent was valued more highly when it stood outside the BBC. Ambitious BBC producers soon realised that the best strategy for advancement was to 'move outside' or threaten to leave for an independent, Channel 4 or ITV in order to increase their perceived value to the corporation. To be a 'BBC lifer' became a statement of contempt, and one that colluded with the ageism now rife within the BBC; both legitimised the shedding of a generation of long-standing producers. The net result was that in some programme genres – particularly entertainment and drama – the 25 per cent quota was much exceeded, so weakening the BBC's own production base in these genres, since in-house production departments now had to win commissions in order to justify their ongoing staffing and resources. All of this fuelled staff fears of rapid downsizing and of the privatisation of production, generating insecurity and low morale, in turn causing more producers to leave. There was also a pull factor. BBC staff who had left to set up successful independents were known to be the beneficiaries of higher earnings than those docile bodies who remained. The challenge issued by the market seemed to taunt those staff who chose to stay. Increasingly, admiration was reserved for the indie trailblazers.

The example of Drama Group shows how devastating these forces were when combined with Producer Choice, and how they fuelled a vicious circle.

Between 1992 and 1995 in-house production dropped from 74 per cent to 54 per cent of the BBC's total drama output. In the same period Drama Group's costs rose by 32 per cent, most of the rise attributable to staff costs. Staff producers were being made redundant or moved to freelance contracts, while the main areas of staff growth were accountants and managers. The combination of increased staff costs with a £35 million decline in in-house production, according to a financial executive, caused a projected loss for the group in 1995–6 of £5 million. The loss included increased downtime for staff – likely to augur further staff cuts – and the 'pernicious effects of the artificially low overhead recovery rate for the independents', which in turn elevated the overhead coverage that in-house was required to achieve. It was a war of attrition. Drama Group could not win.

The restructuring systematically disempowered BBC Production vis-à-vis BBC Broadcast in a number of additional ways. It set up an unequal market. While the independents were free to sell programmes to any broadcaster, for in-house production BBC Broadcast had a monopoly as a buyer: a striking example of the arbitrary limits set to market operations. In-house production departments continued to carry high central overhead charges in their budgets, dictated by Corporate Centre, which were three or four times higher than the equivalent for independents. Independents were thereby favoured in competitive programme areas. Under the restructuring the bulk of licence fee income flowed to Broadcast; with no autonomous income, production departments could reproduce themselves only on the basis of winning commissions in what was effectively a skewed market. Given Production's lack of financial independence, a central concern was access to the development funds that would allow in-house producers to give seed money to new ideas and new writers. The tale of Drama Group's experience of development funding is an allegory of the fallout of the restructuring. The funding of development had been messy before. The promise was that the restructuring would simplify procedures, devolving a certain amount to each department to ensure their autonomy, and otherwise being centrally controlled in Broadcast so that producers could make bids to a central pot. In fact, the funding of development became a gigantic fudge, more complex and less available than before. In the face of these combined forces, a devastating demoralisation swept through the production departments.

*

Tartan Big Bang meets Big Bang

June 1996. I'm visiting BBC Scotland. It's three weeks after the restructuring, which has come to be known around the BBC as both 'Big Bang' and 'Year Zero'. A small group of top executives is meeting to discuss the aftermath of the restructuring, to feed thoughts back to Colin Cameron, BBC Scotland's head of television, who will soon draft BBC Scotland's response to Corporate Centre. Everything is unclear, there is immense confusion, and the talk often goes round in circles. Earlier today, Colin announced in Scotland's Television Editorial Board that there will be a major restructuring of BBC Scotland in the coming week – an event that his co-executives Mike Bolland and Ken McQuarrie immediately dub 'Tartan Big Bang'. Mike reports on his genres, arts and entertainments: 'When I met the head of Ents in London this week, he said that he no longer considers himself to be representing Scottish Ents, but only London in-house. It seems we in Scotland are suddenly seen as competitors! The key questions are: will the transition be fast? That will be easier. And will the regions sit in Broadcast or Production? It seems Broadcast, but nothing is certain. I'm not sure it's even been considered! I had to beg the head of Ents's secretary to let me see the controllers' channel overviews. It's all so secretive. If we get marginalised, how will we know where the free schedule slots are to pitch for?' There is great anxiety that the 33 per cent regional quota will be rolled back in the fallout of the restructuring. Scotland would lose its right to pitch for a privileged share of the network, and with it the basis for all the cultural and economic growth they have been fostering here. So far they have received no reassurances. Mike speculates, 'As long as we keep up the quality ideas, they'll go on taking our stuff: that's surely the key challenge.' Ken sums up: 'I'll write a memo saying we need to flag up regional proportionality and not let this get lost.' But the big question remains: how will Tartan Big Bang interface with Big Bang? No one, it seems, is telling.

Diary, 1996.

*

Management as neutron bomb

It is late 1996, five months after the restructuring, and everything remains supremely confused in Drama Group. Almost all the critical issues impacting on how the drama departments will operate have still to be clarified or even, it has become plain, decided. For Drama, the restructuring has an apocalyptic quality. Everyone knows that Birt has removed all certainties; but nothing has come in to fill the vacuum. It is management as neutron bomb. There is paralysis and seething frustration. We are in a Drama Editorial Board and it seems that today a few things might become clearer. Charles Denton, former head of Drama Group, has left. The acting head reports that 'the new head of Drama Group, when he or she is announced, will be bi-medial and will embrace a larger territory including radio drama and the World Service'. Michael Wearing and Mark Shivas, the two most experienced and respected editorial heads, have received letters from the chief executive of BBC Production informing them that there is still time to apply for the job of CE of Drama Group, but Michael muses, 'What's really going on in this letter is evasive. It looks as though we're being required to reapply for our own jobs.' The acting head reports that there will henceforth be two rather than one Business Affairs departments, in Broadcast and Production. The drama executives are sceptical: 'Surely that risks two sets of business practice competing with one another, let alone unnecessary duplication of jobs?' Michael comments that such duplication will ensure that production departments continue to carry huge overheads, like before – one of the problems the restructuring was meant to overcome: 'What a bloody mess.'

The acting head continues that leading figures in Broadcast have made clear that when disputes arise between Broadcast and Production, Broadcast will be the moderators; the final power will reside with Broadcast. They move to discuss the interface between the drama production departments and Broadcast, which is only just emerging. Drama's independent commissioning group will move into Broadcast; and the proposal is that the drama units from the national regions – Wales, Northern Ireland and Scotland – will also move into Broadcast, while London in-house and Birmingham will sit within Production. No one understands why. Several people express concern about the fragmentation of editorial purpose that will ensue; there seems to be a common desire to retain an integrated Drama Editorial Board.

The discussion moves to the future of development funding after the restructuring, the means of early script development, the most critical issue for the drama editorial heads, since only with access to autonomous development funds can the departments sustain an individual approach and take risks. The acting Drama Group head, reading from a document, begins inauspiciously: 'There's to be a new joint Programme Board overseeing development on which key people from Broadcast and Production will sit – [with irony] a very grand board indeed. It will oversee a total of £14 million development money across the BBC, and this will be divided four ways: £1 million to the regions, £3 million to the controllers for what is called "Targeted Development", £6 million to Production for "General Development", and £4 million to the director of programmes, Alan Yentob, for "Strategic Development"'. Those present absorb the new dictum. Then someone asks, 'But where do we go to float ideas? To Alan or Michael? Or will we have to go to both separately?' 'All our time will be taken up chasing after various uncoordinated development pots! It's a nightmare.' 'We'll spend even more time going to meetings.' 'The whole thing will collapse within months.' Hysteria mounts. The terms are opaque: 'What do they mean by "strategic", "targeted" and "general"?' The acting head reads out the definitions provided; they are highly bureaucratic and they overlap. It's impossible to know what they mean. One editorial head responds, 'It's a classic fuck-up. Instead of making a clearer structure, as we were promised, they've built this appalling edifice simply to defend certain people's interests.' Another is incredulous: 'This is chaos. We were told the restructuring would deliver simplicity: we'd just pitch ideas to Broadcast direct. Now we find it's all more complex, with more points of contact than before. And where will the indies go to pitch? To Michael, or Alan, or us in Drama, or the indie commissioning group? Where?' The acting head doesn't know. She sags, defeated: 'It *is* more complex than before, isn't it?'

Someone asks, 'Why has Alan got £4 million to play with?', and gets boiling satire in reply: 'It's a deal with Birt: he's been bought off.' 'He revived the fortunes of BBC1 so they took away the channel! They couldn't sack him, so they've given him £4 million instead!' Someone presses the acting head: 'Who wrote the document you're reading from?' Another teases, 'There isn't an author!' Others continue to press: 'Why was there no Drama input?' The chief assistant replies that there was input from Drama, but declines to say by whom. She and the acting head refuse to say who is behind the document. Bureaucracy, secrecy, defensiveness: in the face of a debacle, the classic BBC vices prevail. Development funding will be more Byzantine than before, with ominous implications for the creative well-being of drama and production at large.

Diary, 1996.

*

In-house 15 per cent, indies 5 per cent: overhead blues

'All of us in drama production feel we have to try and reduce the central overhead from 15 per cent of programme budgets, which is ridiculously high; the indies are only being charged 5 per cent. Ever since the restructuring our overhead is supporting a centralised admin structure, and what is that structure doing? There needs to be a radical look at the BBC overheads, and there's actually an overheads project being run now across the corporation. But the problem is, the people involved are far removed from production management. So they've said things like IT should be a programme charge, which makes sense to the extent that you get charged for the number of computers you have in a production. But what's not sense is that the corporate IT policy has imposed this new high-powered desktop rollout on us all. Now if you were an independent and you were setting up your programme, you wouldn't go for a Rolls-Royce solution to your IT problems; you'd go for what you could afford. Our 15 per cent overhead also includes things like BBC Club subsidies and a crèche facility, which are valid costs, but they shouldn't be handed down to programmes. Those things aren't in an independent budget; they're not getting any benefit so we can't charge them. But half our shows probably aren't getting any benefit either. By contrast, the publicity budget is very important to the programmes, yet they want to control publicity corporately. I agree with that in terms of responding to stuff in the press. But in terms of publicising a programme, producers should be able to make decisions like hiring a publicist, or getting journalists to interview stars for the press pack. It doesn't make sense that it's corporately held, and it means we end up with a double spend – we augment the publicity department's budget even though we're not meant to. Well, it's not actually disguised, but it doesn't particularly show up on the information we send across to Finance in TV Centre. . . .'

Department manager, BBC Drama, 1997.

*

Fuzzy Logic: 'Bringing It In' and 'Farming It Out'

Despite the apparent clarity of the in-house/independent distinction, on which the external market rested, in practice the boundary between in-house and independent production became fluid in response to economic pressures. A range of clandestine, technically illegitimate measures developed, their outcome resting on the respective power of the BBC and the particular independent involved, to enable the system to function. Independent productions had to be paid for in cash, whereas for in-house production the cash outlay was much less. When cash resources were low the in-house production heads, with collusion from the controllers if they wanted the project in question, would try to persuade – or exert pressure on – the independent to 'bring the production in-house', thereby saving cash outlay. But the opposite also occurred: since independent productions carried a lower overhead than in-house, the same project might be delivered cheaper by an independent. Some productions, particularly in the drama departments, were therefore 'farmed out' to independents to take advantage of the differential and save money. Bizarre variations on these themes developed: the proxy independent; the tax-break project; the BBC born-and-bred producer who would be serially placed with inexperienced or unreliable independents to secure similar conditions on a production as if it had been made in-house.

The pressure, and the temptation, to engage in such activities was compounded by the new trading arrangements between Broadcast and Production. Even before, the channels had begun to offer budgets for expensive commissions, such as high-cost dramas, that were lower than their estimated cost to in-house production departments. Following the restructuring this manoeuvre became systematic. It gained the spurious legitimacy afforded by the 'clean' separation of Broadcast and Production. Now a moralism prevailed: if a production department could not bring a project in at the target price offered by Broadcast, it could only be due to indiscipline. Responsibility for forcing productions to engage in clandestine ways of reducing costs was firmly shed by Broadcast and was seen to lie exclusively with Production. In fact, such pressures led some production departments not only to send the pressures on down the chain, to the independents, in the ways mentioned; it also led them to seek co-financing or co-production deals to meet budget shortfalls – more unofficial activity antithetical to Birt's clean structural divisions.

*

The proxy independent and the pyrrhic victory

'I've worked both in-house and increasingly, in recent years, for independents. And I get vehement about the BBC because of one experience, a film I produced for Drama Group in Ireland. There was no real reason to film in Ireland because it was set in Dorset and London. But basically, we ended up going to Ireland because we could get a big tax break if we filmed there. And in order to qualify for that we had to set up an Irish company, so that was what happened: we set up an independent. What made me very angry was that I only did it to make the project happen for the BBC. But having done so, during the production the attitude was "It's your baby", and the BBC back-up disappeared when difficulties occurred. It was partly to do with what was going on internally politically at that time, which was a pretty unpleasant power struggle between on one side the accountants, and on the other the production executives and managers. We were filming and the Section 35 tax deals were being administered by the accountants, and the production was being overseen by a production executive; and the accountants felt miffed when they were told they had to cop a cheque for half a million quid and they refused to do so, because they felt it needed investigating. The result was that the production was jeopardised. I was getting phone calls from the bank saying, "We're going to start bouncing your cheques." The whole thing was about to go to the wall, and I was caught in someone else's battle. I'd been mandated by the BBC to spend a budget, and it wasn't being honoured.'

GB: 'You're saying that to get this project made, to get that tax break which made it cheaper, you had to set up as a kind of proxy independent?'

'Yes. It was really nothing to do with independent production. The production "became"

139

independent. It was happening a lot in singles. There was at that stage an overhead charge to in-house productions to cover central costs of, I think, 14 per cent; for independent productions the overhead was 2.8 per cent! Making the project go independent was a bookkeeping manoeuvre, purely notional; it was far more affordable. But it was part of a system that was not working. There's a telling anecdotal detail on this story. We had a rather fine cast – John Fortune, John Bird and Peter Capaldi, who'd just won his Oscar for a short film. To save money we managed to persuade most of them to fly from Stansted rather than Heathrow, and to stay in a relatively cheap hotel. Then, when the difficulties blew up, this delegation of BBC accountants flew out to Dublin; needless to say they flew via Heathrow and they stayed in a hotel that we had actually rejected for our cast as being too expensive! It really grates, you know? There were four of them! And a secretary! And I had to ask, why the secretary? Well, they've all gone from the BBC now, but then so have most of the drama producers. So it's a pyrrhic victory.'

Drama producer, 1997.

*

Rights and wrongs

'We do a much higher percentage of indie productions than we ought to. The problem is that independent productions are cash-flowed; they contract all the talent, they book the crew, they manage the production, they send us cost reports and progress sheets, and if everything goes OK they are responsible for delivering it to the channel. For that they get paid their production fee, and the amount of work we do is a lot less than for in-house, so the overhead we levy on indie productions is only 3.2 per cent. The more independents we do because of their better ideas, the less chance of us being financially viable because we only recover 3.2 per cent on those budgets. It's a vicious circle. So the drive to bring projects in-house is to ensure that we can actually cover our costs, or we'll go under.

The other point is that projects that come in-house and use more in-house production and resource staff are projects on which we also keep the rights, because they've been generated from within the Drama Group. That means we're contributing towards the BBC's archive of programme rights, and we're ensuring a financially healthier BBC in ten, twenty, thirty years. The majority of independent productions that go through the Series department are licence deals, and on those deals we retain no rights at all, except for one UK transmission. So when we see something that's come through an independent, we may say, "You should come and do this one in-house." Now that deal will work on a sliding scale depending on how much has been invested by the indie. If they're bringing an idea and nothing's been spent on it, it's not so difficult. If it's been developed by a very small independent, they might be persuadable. If it's been developed by a big independent who've cash-flowed the development themselves, it's virtually impossible. There's nothing in it for them, so why should they?'

GB: 'Can I push you: if there's an independent who's got on an idea, but lacks the resources to make it themselves, then there may be a reason to bring it in-house? Is the bottom line that the smaller indies face a monopoly buyer in the BBC, which is quite a coercive situation?'

'Well, it's not legal to coerce them into doing it in-house. But I think if they want to make the project, and if it's already been to the ITV Network Centre or Channel 4, then they may have nowhere else to take it. And then it could be that the only way we can fund it is in-house because of cash-flow restrictions. That happened in this department last year, because we only had £121 million of actual cash to spend. An independent production of course is all cash-spend, whereas an in-house project is about fifty-fifty, so bringing it in-house helps us to do more programmes.'

Department manager, BBC Drama, 1996.

*

The 'Talented' and the Weak

The independent production sector had undergone major changes by the mid nineties, a decade and a half after its inception as a cottage industry feeding Channel 4. They interacted with larger structural changes in the industry: the falling costs of production with the new digital audio-visual technologies, the multiskilling of production staff, and the move on the part of the major producer-broadcasters towards short-contract employment. But the structure of the independent sector reflected above all two forces: the regulatory compulsion embodied in the 1990 Act's independent production quota, which meant the broadcasters had to trade significantly with independents, and the rising value in the industry of 'talent' – star performers, writers, producers, filmmakers and directors.

With an expanding number of channels and with the broadcasters obliged to compete for their products, certain independent production companies were able to use their talent base to build strong financial foundations. As these strong independents matured as businesses during the nineties, intensifying competition caused concentration and stratification, and the sector effectively divided in two. The top stratum contained a group of companies, based often on the control of talent, for whom that control guaranteed great bargaining power with the broadcasters. The most powerful of these independents could more or less dictate terms to buyers like the BBC. As a consequence, contrary to free market expectations, the independent quota was accompanied by substantial inflation in the cost of talent-led and popular genres, such as entertainment, popular drama, light factual and leisure.[4] In these genres in-house programmes became cheaper than those of the independents; while to undercut the independents' stranglehold, the BBC and other producer-broadcasters faced the challenge of continually replenishing their talent pool.[5] The lower stratum contained the majority of small and medium-sized independents, who occupied a relatively weak position in dealings with the broadcasters. In genres such as documentary, small independents led an uncertain, project-by-project, hand-to-mouth existence. They had to chase commissions, and were often impelled to accept them on nearly unviable terms. For the small independents, the broadcasters held all the cards.

*

1997: the view from PACT

'As the independents' trade organisation, we're broadly in favour of consolidation within the industry, because it makes for a more efficient market. But most of our effort is directed towards the smaller companies, because they tend to need us more than the large companies. Where we can, we encourage companies to merge; we act as a kind of marriage broker on occasion. As broadcasting in Britain becomes a less regulated, more market-driven economy, the wisdom of being a larger company becomes more apparent, and the prospects for survival as a small company become tougher. Production companies are starting to drop away or to merge.'

GB: 'I read a prediction that the number of independents would drop from a thousand to about a hundred in the next few years . . .'

'Rubbish. The only way that could happen is if Channel 4 changes its strategy. You've got probably 250 companies supplying the BBC, ITV and Channel 5 each year. And then you've got Channel 4, which dealt with something like 535 companies last year. Now, as long as Channel 4 has that editorial policy, which is driven by its remit for diversity, there are going to be 535 little companies. They are not going to disappear. If Channel 4 says they're only going to deal with fifty companies a year, it will change overnight. But until that happens, it will consolidate a little, but there will still be margins where people can grow companies and get into the business.'

GB: 'But didn't Michael Jackson say when he was at BBC1 that it would be easier to deal with fewer suppliers? I think his point was that, for creative reasons, it's very useful to cultivate a relationship with a good independent. Now he's going to be chief executive at Channel 4: do you get any soundings that he's going to go that way with Channel 4?'

'I think that will be his natural inclination. But it's a tough one because of Channel 4's remit and its very broad range of programmes. If like Channel 4 you want to be at the cutting edge, you have to take your ideas where you can find them. And there's a basic question about where really innovative and new ideas come from. Do they come from large production companies that are themselves institutionalised and have their own orthodoxy and culture? Or do they come from a madman sitting in a cottage in Wales with a brilliant idea that he puts on a word processor? And quite a lot of Channel 4's programmes still come from those people.'

GB: 'Interesting: I don't hear many people putting this defence of Channel 4 any more. A lot of people are arguing that the output is really not that distinctive.'

'Well, yes, but be careful, because that's not to say Channel 4 aren't getting new ideas. They get something like 30,000 programme ideas a year! Who's to say what is or is not buried in the big file marked "Reject"? If Channel 4's output is not distinctive, when there are a thousand production companies in this country all pitching programmes, there's more likely to be a fault with the commissioning team than with the supply side. There's a massive oversupply, which can only be good for the channel. If they can't sift the wheat from the chaff, that's a problem in their own house. It's important to realise that there are two things that drive any independent producer: one is ideas, and the other is economics. That's the dichotomy that Channel 4 and the BBC are grappling with. It's not an issue for ITV or Channel 5, which have taken the same path, which is to say, "We would rather work with a smaller number of suppliers who have particular expertise in prime-time products." All they want is to go to a brand-name company that makes good shows. BBC and Channel 4, because they are public service channels, have to be more interested in the variety and diversity of their schedule, not simply the ability to deliver the numbers.'

GB: '. . . And therefore, you're implying, they ought to have a commitment to enabling a plural market of suppliers to exist.'

PACT executive, 1997.

*

2001: the indies' choice

'We do a lot for Channel 4 and BBC2, that's where I put most of my effort.'

GB: 'The received view of the independent sector now is that you either do what companies like Wall to Wall or RDF are doing and move into higher-volume throughput, diversify into entertainment or drama, grow and become a medium or big indie, and then there's pressure to be gobbled up by a larger company; or you stay tiny, the proverbial indie with the fax machine in the front room, which barely makes ends meet. You say you're managing to find enough business and to produce a flow of high-quality documentaries?'

'Yes, there are lots of us independents who do that. Blakeway does it, I do it. You can stay small. It depends why you're doing this, what's the purpose of your business. Conventionally, the purpose of a business is to make money, and the product is simply the vehicle for this. Certainly, if you're owned by shareholders, the drive to increase shareholder value must become the only purpose of the business. If you own a company like this, a limited company fully owned by me, then all that matters is "can I make a living out of it?" If you're relatively successful you can make a perfectly good living, until you fall out of fashion, in which case you die. But the only way you can make a living is by who you know. You couldn't survive, you wouldn't get the commissions, if you didn't have relationships with the key commissioning editors. I go back twenty years with almost everybody senior in British television from being at the BBC and before that at LWT. That's when I met Greg Dyke, and all those people from LWT in the eighties are still significant players in the industry. The people I met in the BBC, whether it's Tim Gardam or Michael Jackson or Mark Thompson, I've known for ten or twelve years.'

GB: 'Isn't it a generational thing, because as the big organisations fragment those networks of people who know each other well are going to become more tenuous, aren't they? Right now, you act here as a broker for complete newcomers who come in with a film . . .'

'Absolutely. But you have to keep it up. I see much of my job as networking, as keeping in contact with the key people. In four or five years there's always a huge turnaround in who's got power in television. But you also have to build an identity, a track record: you have to believe that if your programmes are good enough they are going to commission you. And my company has done lots of quite successful programming. It has a name that people will listen to, just as Diverse has, or RDF. British television is a cottage industry, a few people in London, so the one thing that's difficult is for new companies to break in, because they find they just can't get through the door. Even I have so many people writing to me that I just can't see them all. And if I can't see them, what's it like when you're sitting inside Channel 4 or the BBC?'

GB: 'Do you have permanent staffing, or do you bring people in on a project basis?'

'I have a staff of seven, production management, infrastructure and editorial. For individual programmes I'll often buy in the producer and researcher. You have to take the risk. Because of the staffing structure and overheads, such as rent on this place, I have to make several hundred thousand pounds worth of business to cover my costs. If I think too hard about it I'd just run into a corner and stop. What I do think, though, is that I'll *make* it happen. If David Lloyd or some commissioning editor rings me up and says, "can you do this?", I have the people to make it happen. You have to take a leap, have several projects on the go. You generate something, you get the reward for having taken the risk. You can make a perfectly good living on that basis.'

GB: 'So the cries from the independents and PACT that the current funding basis of cost plus a production fee is insufficient, and that indies should be rights owners now . . .?'

'It varies for different kinds of production. Most of my programmes don't have much secondary value. They are domestic documentaries; so if I get £170,000 revenue for a first showing, that's probably 95 per cent of the total revenue for that programme. The prospect of selling to a new network is nil. The standard Channel 4 deal is a production fee, about 15 per cent of budget, plus your costs. So I cover my overheads. And it depends how well you run your company. I only know the final profit and loss at the end of the year, though obviously I manage it over the months. It works. I could make a really, really good living if I moved out of central London and down to Croydon. But I don't want to move to dreary, bloody Croydon. It's my choice.

'If I was RDF, a big organisation with lots of staff, which has to keep the turnover going, and which has formats, the rights of which have significant value beyond the first terrestrial transmission, I would absolutely be going in their direction. British TV still hasn't locked into the idea that production costs aren't the same as value – that the cost of making a Mars bar is quite different from its price. I can completely sympathise with the bigger indies that have real value attached to their output. If the film I've just made, which does in fact have secondary value, was my normal stuff, I'd say to the channel, "Hang on, it cost £170,000 to make, but it's actually worth £400,000 when you look at its sales potential. So if you want all the rights, pay me £400,000. I'll make it for £170,000 and I'll keep the profit."'

GB: 'You're implying that there's a dual structure, that the commissioning editors who know what you're interested in producing know that you're not into profit maximisation or making formats; so they know they can come to you for a terrestrial show and not worry about the additional work to sell things around the world. They get their quality show and that's the end of the story.'

'Exactly, and I position myself as being available for that kind of stuff. I mean, if I had a fantastic format that was going to sell around the world, then I might get into all that other business. I would get into it in a proper strategic way. But personally, I'm not into that.'

GB: 'You're saying really it's a matter of *choice* as to how much you decide to conceive of the indie as an expanding business?'

'Yes. Endemol and Television Corporation, these are big businesses, the purpose of which is to make money, and you make serious money by developing ideas that have sales potential around the world and that can be exploited around the world in a number of different ways.'

GB: 'But you wouldn't make a value judgement that those programmes – reality shows, format shows – are poor television?'

'No, they're quite watchable; obviously a lot of people watch them. I understand the proposition those guys are on about, that the value of their shows is more than their cost, and I think the BBC and Channel 4 have to recognise this. But there's another big danger. The big indies are rumoured to be offering a deal to the broadcasters, one that trades off the independent quota for retaining rights. They'd say to the BBC and Channel 4, "You give us our rights and we'll forget about the independent quota." Now the quota is incredibly important. We mustn't lose it. If you want to keep the industry innovative and fresh then the big businesses should move out of the independent sector. They should lose their indie status. Sometimes they behave like predators on small indies. I was recently working on an idea with a scientist, and the scientist was bought up by a large indie who took him on a £5,000 freebie; they stole him and the idea. They have money to throw around and it's difficult to compete. It shows the success of the indie sector that these companies grow. But they should get out and small indies move in, so the sector is continually refreshed, because it needs to have the small and creative outfits that add that extra zing to the market.'

GB: 'People from the broadcasters, including Channel 4, now freely admit that they're doing most of their business with the top ten indies. In the past, Channel 4 used to publish as part of its annual report a graph showing the total number of indies they'd worked with during the year, and who'd got how much work. It was a telling graph, because it always concentrated on the major twenty companies, say, but there was a huge tail as well. Now they've stopped producing that graph.'

'Sure. I think that may get worse, because one of the other things the big indies do is cross-subsidise. They have some bit of the operation that's highly profitable and that subsidises the stuff they really want to do or that the broadcasters want, so they can offer it at a price the smaller indies can't match. I've heard that one indie makes a lot of money duping Continental porn. They could then use that money to undercut other producers. You can make a lot of money on porn if you want to go down that route.'

GB: 'I gather that porn is a major factor driving broadband uptake in Europe.'

'Well, there you go. How do we know that some of the big operations aren't doing that? If you're into making money you stop worrying about the product.'

Managing director, independent production company, 2001.

*

The Business: Turning a Blind Eye?

During the later nineties there was further significant concentration of the independent sector. A number of the most successful independents were bought up by larger, sometimes international cross-media groups. In return for financing, they no longer enjoyed the autonomy of dedicated creative organisations. They had become business subsidiaries. But the high profile and the extraordinary riches accruing to the successful independents sent a signal to the rest of the independent sector: these could also be yours! Think international, not national! The sector was increasingly dominated by business logics, the inexorable drive to compete, and the search for higher productivity and profits. Entrepreneurialism became the presiding value. The example of Bazal Productions is instructive. Bazal was responsible for a number of the hit new leisure and hybrid leisure–gameshow formats, including *Changing Rooms*, *Ground Force* and *Ready Steady Cook*. These were relatively cheap entertainment shows which from the mid nineties, along with the rising docu-soap genre, began to fill the early- and mid-evening schedules. In 1990, Bazal was acquired by Broadcast Communications, which later became Endemol UK, part of the Netherlands-based entertainments group Endemol, a company focused on aggressive international expansion and a specialist in selling television formats throughout the world. In 2000, Endemol UK created the reality gameshow format *Big Brother*, which became the year's biggest television success. In the same year, Endemol was itself bought up by the Spanish-based Telefonica group, an international telecommunications and media giant. Endemol UK is Britain's largest 'independent' producer.

Meanwhile, the smaller and less powerful independents and those companies resisting such logics settled into an unhealthy dependence on the broadcasters. Their dependence was signalled in the late nineties by the BBC's tendency to operate unsatisfactory terms of trade. While the corporation apparently offered a flexible range of rights arrangements to its suppliers, the practice fell far short. Many independents found that the corporation would not allow them to retain the majority of rights in their programmes; if they insisted, they might lose the commission.[6] A vicious circle ensued: the larger companies had the advantage and could mop up the available commissions, reinforcing their grip. Smaller independents claimed that their ideas were stolen and resurfaced as the property of a large independent, or their presenters were bought out by a wealthier company.[7]

The stratification of the independent sector together with the burgeoning business ethos had worrying repercussions. Both the large, successful independents with business plans and profits to deliver, and the small independents dicing with economic insecurity, had overwhelming incentives to offer the broadcasters sure-fire popular winners. Both poles, the powerful and the dependent, were motivated to head for the centre-ground of programming.[8] In conjunction with the new, schedule-led commissioning process, the system of outsourcing favoured safe commissions, formulaic output and populism. These factors fed directly into the cloyingly imitative broadcast schedules of the later nineties.

With the successful independents perceived as key talent brokers and as creative powerhouses, the BBC became increasingly keen to attract their leading figures to join the corporation as executives. New risks of conflicts of interest arose. It was rumoured that, when wooing talented independent producers, the corporation might turn a blind eye if they continued to hold external interests in the companies being commissioned. Indeed, on occasion such producers might be commissioning their own former companies. More directly questionable practices were also rumoured to occur, such as the BBC executive who, when given a commissioning role, received a substantial loan from an independent producer in the same programming area. He was exonerated but demoted. Less seriously, the same informal networking and lobbying continued to operate between commissioners, independents and in-house production heads as before. Given the powerful forces outlined, then, the restructuring did not greatly enhance the open market. Stories continued to circulate of the controllers making direct contact with their favoured sources of programming, circumventing the laborious 'open market' system.

In 1997, when the low-budget Channel 5 launched, it announced that, to secure bulk programming at low cost, it would commission programmes from a small group of 'preferred suppliers', a potentially contentious arrangement that was, however, uncontested by the regulator, the ITC. This was soon followed by talk among senior management in both the BBC and Channel 4 of moving similarly to a list of 'preferred suppliers': selected independents who would enjoy favourable bulk output deals and sustained relations with the commissioners. By the late nineties, under chief executive Michael Jackson, former controller of both BBC2 and BBC1, Channel 4 was operating this way, with a significant proportion of its prime-time schedule coming from a few established independents.

As a result of the escalating kudos of the successful independents, a mindset based on a curious associative logic became pervasive in the industry. In it, 'independent' was conflated both with 'entrepreneurialism', a term condensing the ideology of heroic, risk-taking, inventive business, and with 'innovation' – both a legacy of the early Channel 4, and an effect of the flood of talent into the sector. Entrepreneurialism was conflated with creativity itself. The mindset fuelled even more the chronic self-doubt, unleashed by the managerial revolution, that was raging through the BBC.

*

Interview postponed

Part of my brief is to research relations between the BBC and the independent producers from whom it now commissions a considerable amount of programming. I am trying to interview one of the two or three leading British independents, an extremely successful company which, through its clever brokering of talent, has cornered the market in certain areas of sophisticated British comedy. It happens that this company is also the locus of a potential conflict of interest, a situation well known in the industry and, when mentioned, accompanied by sighs and longueurs, but little appreciated beyond the columns of *Private Eye* and the small world of British television. In recent years one of the former directors of the company moved inside the BBC to head up a BBC department.

I phone and fax several times to arrange an interview with the managing director. I am told that – uniquely among those I have interviewed – she wants her lawyer to be present. The date is arranged. The day before, her assistant calls and says the MD cannot meet me; something has arisen that demands her attention. We rearrange. The day before, again the assistant calls to say that something urgent has come up. Again we rearrange. Again something comes up. The pattern continues. Each time, the first four or five times, the problem seems genuine. Finally, after the eighth cancellation, I give up. The leading indie has led me up the garden path.

Diary, 1997.

*

Increasing productivity: the drama dinner

I am at a dinner party being held by some researchers investigating 'best practice' in the UK television drama industry. Several drama luminaries have been invited. As the drinks flow, shop talk gets going. One mogul, the managing director of a highly successful, sitcom-producing independent, laments that 'Kevin Lygo [*head of Entertainment at Channel 4*] is only looking for star-led entertainment projects, while Peter Salmon [*controller of BBC1*] is a populist out and out!' He regrets the absence of ambition, and wishes the commissioners would welcome more unusual fare. But he is out of temper with his peers. Another mogul takes issue with this research project's focus on Britain, saying, 'What we really need is information on the international industry: how is it that the Australians produce soaps for far less than we can?' He implies forcefully that the primary concern should be economic, that this is the only information worth garnering in the age of global competition. A third executive, who in the past took charge of Granada's soap *Coronation Street*, says the first thing he did when he came to the *Street* was check out the production process: how was it organised? He talks of having stream-lined many elements of the process – continuity, shooting, scriptwork. And triumphantly, he comes to the punchline: that it resulted in higher productivity. 'When I finished we were making twelve and a half minutes of final on-screen film per day, as opposed to the seven minutes when I arrived.' In the discussion of 'best practice' it seems that lower budgets, international competitiveness and higher productivity are the chief preoccupations of these representatives of the drama industry.

Diary, 1997.

*

Travesties of the market

An ex-student of mine has become a television researcher, working for various independents. As is now the custom, he earned nothing the first months, staying at his parents' flat in St John's Wood and clawing his privileged way into the industry. Amused by what he is discovering, he is not yet socialised into the routine cynicism of the TV profession. He reports that Channel 4 operates a clandestine list of 'top ten' producers

150

who must be used on commissions. Programme ideas are never genuinely exposed to 'open' competitive tendering. Rather, commissions are fixed through patron/client relationships: 'It's like Versailles!' he marvels. When working for a favoured indie, a commission on a particular topic is often followed by a package from the channel containing research on the same topic undertaken by an indie which has been unsuccessful in gaining the commission.

Diary, 2000.

*

Small indie woes

I am talking to a creative figure about the state of the industry. For many years he has run his own small independent production company. 'It's not really worth developing ideas to pitch to commissioners: too much work, too much uncertainty. If you do offer ideas, they're plagiarised. The indie producer's role, if you're a small- or medium-sized indie, has been reduced to that of a line producer. The commissioner insists on taking all the casting and crewing decisions; they want to be in not only on the final cut, but the rough cut! All the creative decisions are taken away. What's left are the simple technical jobs – which is not why I'm in it. There's little creative or financial incentive, so why go on?'

Diary, 2000.

*

Policing the Market

Another effect of the independent quota was further expansion of the bureaucratic apparatus required to administer markets by the BBC. In particular, there was a need to police 'compliance': adherence by independent producers to the proper financial, legal and editorial or creative standards when supplying programmes. As indicated by the eruption of a series of fakery scandals in British television during the late nineties, enforcing compliance in a fragmented industry is no easy matter.[9] In the prior vertically integrated British system, the existence of common professional ethics and standards was supported by common institutional cultures, internal training and limited competition – unifying dynamics that were undermined as a consequence of deregulation.

Following the restructuring, Broadcast was meant to supervise legal and financial compliance for every independent commission. But despite the core

151

restructuring aim of vesting all management of the independents in Broadcast and of severing contact between the independents and Production, because of the lack of production expertise among Broadcast staff some production departments were charged with monitoring editorial compliance, just as they had before. In drama, for a year after the restructuring, Broadcast continued to rely on the drama production departments not only for managing editorial compliance but for financial management of the independents as well. The arrangements were complex, partial and unsatisfactory, highlighting the fictional character of the vaunted separation of Broadcast from Production.

There was another problem. While Production continued to have oversight of editorial compliance, in practice it was not always possible to enforce. The executive producers charged with supervising the compliance complained of the difficulty of controlling powerful independents, some of whom engaged in a cynical show of compliance while pursuing their own agenda. In turn, this undermined the BBC's ability to ensure the quality and integrity of its output, a crucial factor in the fakery crises. One illustration of the BBC's difficulty in ensuring compliance was the 1996 drama serial Rhodes which, at a cost of £10 million, was one of the most expensive television dramas ever made. Rhodes was an embarrassing critical and ratings flop. The commission had gone to a leading independent, Zenith, which had close links to a senior BBC Drama executive and which had an excellent track record. The production had been entrusted by Zenith to a documentary film-maker who had never made television drama before. But because of Zenith's reputation, the BBC's enforcement of editorial compliance had been light. To the extent that it could be explained, the failure of Rhodes was commonly attributed to this nexus of causes.[10] But an alternative perspective came from some independents, who experienced the compliance codes as a spurious means of the BBC justifying excessive interventions in their productions. In their view, the whole concept of editorial compliance played out the exhausted refrain of the BBC's putative editorial superiority.

*

Founding myth and fig leaf

'I don't buy this stuff about "editorial compliance". In reality, notions of editorial compliance are used partly to bolster the myth about the BBC's editorial strengths, and partly as a kind of a fig leaf for BBC Production, so that the staff who work there can remain under the impression that there are still things they can do better than the independents. It's an absolute fallacy. I mean, legal compliance for *Have I Got News For You*: of course that's an issue. But that's something that's done between Hat Trick and the BBC lawyers. There's no executive producer inside the BBC with any more skill than the staff at Hat Trick about working out through hard experience what is and isn't acceptable in terms of defamation in a topical satirical quiz show.'

GB: 'Sure. And you're querying, I think, the way the BBC has such a sacred investment in the higher qualities of its own editorial culture?'

'Yes, that's neatly put. Yes.'

PACT executive, 1997.

*

The BBC plant

GB: 'It sounds as though in the last few years you've been almost a BBC producer who's been loaned out to independents to inject some "BBC editorial values" into their productions. You've also been paid by the indie, haven't you?'

'Yes, when a BBC producer goes outside I guess the idea is they can improve, or ensure, the quality of the independent's output, and therefore legitimise it to some degree. It's overseeing the production. It's basically, "We've got somebody in there who we trust," and the BBC don't trust the independents very often. Quite rightly, it has to be said!'

Drama producer, 1996.

*

Rogue indie[†]

It's that point late in the Drama Editorial Board when collective reflection occurs on current issues. An executive producer requests advice on his run-in with a prominent independent drama supplier, a company called Moonlight led by a powerful figure, Ron Littlewood, which is currently making four major shows for BBC1 and BBC2. 'Basically, I have almost no control over Moonlight, even though we've inserted a BBC-paid script editor into the process: he produces detailed script notes but they are simply ignored. The two projects I'm overseeing are not good enough, and I'm having enormous difficulty getting them to make changes. So the shows are threatening to come in very sub-standard.' He continues that such powerful indies feel invulnerable; they have

[†] Names and details have been changed.

significant protectors in the BBC. He is plainly pointing to the channel controllers, with whom some of the deals have been directly struck. 'A couple of weeks ago I told them I wanted some changes to a script before shooting. They didn't respond. Finally, the day before the shoot, they called me to a meeting at 11.30 at night! I asked for the changes, and Littlewood, the director, all of them kept arguing, until finally Littlewood said, "This seems to be a major hang-up for you, Tim, so we'll do it for you, though I don't see why. It's just a matter of taste." But when the rushes came through, the changes they'd agreed weren't there! They made a fool of me. But worse, the show is going to be crap – and he knows he can get away with it. The only way I can exert control is by threatening to stop the cash flow – which I *do* threaten, quite regularly. But I can't do it every week or the whole thing will grind to a halt. We should never work with this lot again.' How, he ends, can these rogue indies be controlled? A colleague from Business Affairs recalls watching Littlewood strike a deal with a drama executive in two minutes: 'It was overwhelming. He bulldozed that deal!'

The discussion moves to a larger problem stemming from the restructuring: the bizarre terms of trade for independents being drawn up by Broadcast, which have been leaked. Under them, Broadcast will commission and finance the independents, but Production will be responsible for overseeing compliance with BBC editorial and creative standards. Those present express horror at the proposals, which promise to make situations like the one with Moonlight even more intractable. One of the drama heads explodes, 'Production will have all the responsibility but no power! No financial controls, so no tough sanctions to pull on recalcitrant indies! It's ludicrous.' Alan Yentob, now director of programmes, is attending; he listens sombrely and comments, 'Things like this are problems for the BBC to address *together*. You must stop conceiving of everything as "us" versus "them", Broadcast versus Production.' No one seems convinced. Almost six months after the restructuring, the case of Moonlight and the difficulty of ensuring compliance suggest that basic structural issues impacting negatively on both Drama Group and drama output may not even have been perceived by senior management, let alone solved.

Diary, 1997.

*

Compliance confusion: nonsensical management

GB: 'It's weird, this notion that you can have an editorial compliance overview which is quite separate from financial management, isn't it? And that you in drama production can exert this?'

'It is very strange, yes. I think it's because it's been devised by management consultants, who've packaged these things as separate. Broadcast don't know what's going to hit them. The indies are generally very cooperative, but the situation can cause serious heartache. There's one indie project right now with major financial problems which is slipping between the cracks, and we're about to start shooting. This independent was suggesting editorial cuts to help the financial position, but the cuts just aren't acceptable. The project's been commissioned with certain expectations, and if they start cutting all those expectations away, what's the point in doing it? So it's all coming home to roost, and we just pretend, the production executive and I, that we work for Broadcast on this show. We've asked who they want us to report to and nobody has clarified that, and the situation is spiralling very fast. I've written to Broadcast today saying this is my view of the situation, and if you're not prepared to live with a potential overspend, you ought to consider pulling the show. It's Broadcast's money, but we're being asked to manage it here in Drama Group.'

GB: 'But this is a year after the restructuring. Isn't it strange that this key structural issue hasn't yet been sorted?'

'Yes, and it diverts us in Drama from what we should be doing; it's a heavy workload, and independents take a different sort of management. There's a further problem: there's a period show we're looking after which is technically in development as an independent, very close to being commissioned, and there are huge budget variances. I'm concerned that in the course of me doing the financial management on it someone may say "there's a conflict of interest," as though it's in my interests to spoil this show. I hope people will see I'm not doing that, that I'm trying to be honest, but there is such disagreement between us and the indie over what the show should cost. But of course it shouldn't be us monitoring indie budgets, it should be Broadcast.'

GB: 'You're being quite restrained, because as drama people have said for ages about the restructuring, the only benefit in it for in-house drama was to shed some of this hidden labour, and not to have to carry the burden of managing the independents.'

'We do think it's wrong. Managing the indies, you have to be tough. One indie got really upset and said they were going to complain to PACT about me because I was driving down their costs – but that's what I'm here to do! It's a business deal: we can't give them everything they want; we don't give our own programmes everything they want. Here in Drama we've learned a lot in the last five years about dealing with the indies. But how are Broadcast going to build up that expertise? My concern is that the independents could do rather well at the expense of the BBC.'

GB: 'I heard you just now dealing with another indie over a financial problem on their show, and the producer is wanting to get straight to the controller, Michael Jackson, to appeal; and you're meant to mediate between the two parties. It's a tricky position for you.'

'Yes, and that's an independent we have strong ties with. But the problem isn't confined to indies. On an in-house show recently the controller wanted a particular star actor, and the perks involved in casting him put the budget in a different league: stunt doubles, Winnebagos, drivers, first-class accommodation and so on. So we said to Broadcast, "If you want to cast that actor, you should set aside a contingency of £200,000." And they came back and said would we accept £100,000! To which I replied it wasn't a negotiating position. In fact, it'll work out at just over £100,000 because we've done better deals than expected. We try to be responsible, but there's a notion with Broadcast that I'm bargaining all the time, and I'm not. I consider myself working for the BBC generally; I set realistic expectations, and I expect them to trust me.'

GB: 'So on the one hand Broadcast now think they have a trading relationship with you, so they can bargain. But on the other hand they devolve their financial management on to you, and having done that, surely they ought to trust your figures? Doesn't it make sense for the financial management in Broadcast to be done by production executives, like those you work with now?'

'It might, but in this department we only have two, and we're swamped. But this was always our concern about the restructuring: the escalation of jobs. The BBC talked about the Broadcast/Production split as reducing management and bureaucracy, and in reality that isn't the case. It can't be when you split the functions. I find it terrifying, the number of jobs you see advertised.'

Department manager, BBC Drama, 1997.

*

Mixing It

During the nineties, with the falling real value of the licence fee and encouraged by the government, the BBC grew its commercial activities in order to augment its income. Given this commercial expansion, as well as greater internal and external competition, how did the public service and commercial sides of the BBC coexist? Three further areas attest to the problems thrown up by the restructuring and by the BBC's operations as a mixed economy: issues of the control of rights, co-production and the growth of self-competition.

The control of rights epitomises the contortions attendant on the BBC's mixed economy. After the licence fee, rights sales are the corporation's largest source of income. The critical question of where rights should reside in the BBC is much reinforced by the multichannel environment, since with expanding services and budget squeezes, the sale of rights to high quality content has become a major source of income and of cultural influence. As a public body, the BBC is not permitted to trade and profit. Only its commercial subsidiary, BBC Worldwide, can legally do this. In the years before the restructuring, Worldwide had a monopoly on rights sales. As sales increased, revenue flowed back to the BBC and, reinvested in new programming and services, escaped tax. This arrangement drew charges of unfair trading from the BBC's competitors. As a consequence, in the 1996 Charter renewal process, the government insisted that fair trading policies and commercial guidelines be introduced by the corporation. A central part of the solution was the setting up of a department within the BBC called the Rights Archive. Through the mid nineties, the archive existed to hold uninvested programme rights, test their market value through sales to third parties, and on this basis 'sell' rights to Worldwide for onward external sale.

The archive was thus a fascinating anomaly: a pseudo-trading entity set up to translate the BBC's non-commercial activities into commercial ones. It acted as a kind of buffer zone or contamination chamber that legitimised the process whereby public service products were morphed into fully-fledged commodities. The archive was also the gateway to the BBC for companies wanting to buy licences to exploit spin-off products from the BBC's core brands. It was therefore responsible for ensuring the quality standards of these deals since, as commercial operations grew, it was considered essential that the BBC's brand should not be sullied by inappropriate activities or dubious commercial associations. With an exponential growth in commercial licensing, policing the brand became a challenging and consuming task. But if the archive attempted to smooth out the contradictions of the BBC's mixed economy, it did little to quell rivals' complaints that the corporation gained unfair commercial advantage from its publicly funded programming and strong brands. The question of fair trading, the problem of constructing appropriate limits to the commercial exploitation of its products, and the need to maintain the quality of its expanding product range, continue to vex the BBC.

*

Monopoly to fair trading

'The Rights Archive was set up at a time when – well, when isn't there a time of great change and great politics here? Historically, Worldwide had a monopoly on all the BBC's intellectual property assets; the only way in which a third-party publisher could get access to a BBC programme was by licensing it from Worldwide. Then the Commercial Policy Guidelines came along and spelt out what commercial activities the BBC ought to be in and those it should not. For the first time the guidelines recognised that Worldwide was not capable of exploiting every programme; so the archive was set up as an alternative route to market. In the old days there were two ways Worldwide could get access to programme rights: they could invest up front, but even if they didn't invest, they still gained the rights to a variety of contracts as post-production deals. Sometimes they paid some money for the rights, but often they didn't. The problem was that they were getting state aid through the licence fee, a subsidised product, and were therefore competing unfairly in the market against commercial publishers. Well, those were the old contracts, and we got rid of them. Now under the Rights Archive, when licensing to Worldwide for post-production rights sales, there are thirteen separate contracts reflecting thirteen kinds of rights that, when they are unbundled, can potentially be derived from any programme – video, TV sales, books, magazines and so on; and if Worldwide invest pre-production, they get all the rights. Each agreement seeks to license to BBC Worldwide as the partner of first choice, because we own them – not only the income they pay back, but the net income as well because we're their parent. But the agreements set out clearly at arm's length the rates that should be paid. The primary purpose of what we've done is a defence against attacks of unfair trading. It was a Charter prerequisite that we had to introduce fair trading, and this is the mechanism.'

BBC commercial executive, 1997.

*

Contamination: brand new troubles

GB: 'I was just at a meeting of Michael Jackson's BBC1 marketing team where they were discussing a campaign to brand BBC1 and improve how it's perceived. It was fascinating because they were talking about how the Corporate Centre has its own universal BBC brand campaign, which is also carried on the channel; and how there's a tension between this corporate branding and what the channel wants to do. What are the issues, what's brand thinking about? Is there *one* BBC brand, *one* identity? Or is BBC Drama moving, with *Silent Witness* and similar dramas, more and more into classic commercial TV territory, so the whole BBC identity, and the BBC's difference, is bleeding away, as the commercial instincts get sharpened up?'

'There's certainly a huge tension between the Corporate Centre, and their desire to maintain corporate brand identity, and a growing understanding that there have always been lots of different brands in the BBC. If you look at the BBC children's brand in the sixties, you knew when you turned the TV on, or picked up the BBC children's books, you were going to get *Watch With Mother* and so on, and then in the seventies with *Noggin the Nog* against ITV's *Tiswas*, you knew clearly what the children's sub-brand stood for. So it's not a new thing. What's new is that the people running the production departments now are more sophisticated in their analysis of what their products combine to offer as a brand proposition. Some of them have marketing backgrounds, so they have a much clearer understanding of how to manipulate a brand. And the commercial exploitation of our programming, both in terms of product and in terms of distribution, has given rise to much more debate about brand than there ever used to be.'

GB: 'Tell me about this key tension I was trying to bring out: that, whether it's Channel 4 mimicking BBC2 or vice versa, or BBC drama trying to compete on the territory of ITV popular drama, the desire to compete for ratings and sales generates a blurring of the brand, doesn't it?'

'Yes it does. You turn on the TV at ten o'clock tonight and you could be on BBC2 or Channel 4; they're almost exactly the same in the nature of the programming. Well, is that a bad thing?'

GB: 'But doesn't this mean that the brand is a kind of illusion? Isn't the attempt to brand an attempt to say "this is different" when there is no difference?'

'Well, I think some people would answer that the brand isn't an illusion because the ten o'clock slot on a Friday night is one brand, and it used to be just Channel 4's. If you were at Channel 4 you would almost certainly say, "That was our brand, but it's been nicked." That was an accusation levelled at Michael Jackson when he was running BBC2, and frankly, to be accused of that is quite flattering. It would be considered a success. I'm not sure what the problem is.'

GB: 'OK. Let's talk about your meeting earlier with BMG about a video rights deal on some recent BBC dramas. If I understand right, you queried a clause where they were asking to sell the rights on to subsidiary distributors around Europe, and your view was that it was problematic because, presumably, you trust BMG – you know they're a high-quality outfit with good retailers – but you didn't want them selling the videos on to a street vendor in Istanbul or something?'

'That's right. There are two business issues here. One is purely financial. We know the people at BMG very well. They're part of Bertelsmann, the second biggest media group in the world; so you're not exactly exposed to risk when you're licensed to BMG. But if they sold the licence on to some crap company in Mexico or something, you start to lose the guarantees that you're going to get paid. That's the first issue. The second is that, if they sell on the rights, you lose control of the product. When I was at Enterprises years ago, for example, we had an agreement with a Scandinavian producer to take our product, package it up and sell it on, and we always approved the packaging and normally the advertising. But there was one awful occasion when we weren't sent the packaging, and it was a kids' drama video aimed at ten- to eleven-year olds. When we finally saw the video, on the back of the box next to the blurb for the children's drama was an advert for *A Clockwork Orange* and for some ghastly pornographic thing. Now it could be disastrous for the BBC to be associated with things like that. We had it pulled straight away, and because we had a direct relationship with the Scandinavian distributor we were able to say, "We'll sue you, we'll have our rights back." Another example was when I sat on a panel to judge bids from various distributors for a video special of *They Think It's All Over*, the sports quiz. It's an independent production but we own a large element of the rights. There was a shortlist of two, Polygram and BBC Video. Both companies presented their financial and marketing proposals. But one of the criteria in considering which to do a deal with was that Polygram have a lot of comedy on their roster, most of it of the blue variety – the Roy Chubby Browns of this world. So the question was, do we really want *They Think It's All Over* being sold cheek by jowl with Roy Chubby Brown? Or wouldn't it be better to sell it to BBC Video where it can sit next to *Fawlty Towers* and *Blackadder*? From my perspective it was actually a very important issue.'

GB: 'So one mechanism for protecting the brand is that you assert quality control, since the BBC logo is on it and you don't want to be associated in marketing with things that are clearly against BBC values. There's a danger of contamination?'

'Yes, there is. We always do quality control. Even with subsidiary deals you can have controls through the principle licensee, BMG in this case; you can try to force them to put mirroring provisions in their contracts with any sub-licensee. So it's not the end of the world if they want to sub-license, and from time to time it is acceptable. We agreed that BMG would sub-license within the BMG Group, which is an international business.'

GB: 'So in a way there's a tick list of multiple criteria you're thinking about: financial security, design, guilt by association, and so on . . .'

'Yes, and there's a gradation. When we're licensing book deals we insist on approval of the text, for instance. We've done a couple of books on *The Archers* recently, and we insist on having copy, and it goes off to the programme producer to be read, and we'll make changes if need be. In this case what we're licensing is *The Archers* as a trademark; there's a huge amount of protection around *The Archers* as a brand. We've done something on the *Today* programme recently, and again there's great sensitivity as to how you use that. The Commercial Policy Guidelines lists whole swathes of areas that we can't tackle, lots of merchandising groups we can't go near. We are not allowed to use the BBC brand to give another company a commercial advantage over others, for example. There was a big issue some time ago when we licensed a company to use the BBC brand on a blank videotape on the grounds that the quality of our programmes is very good, so if it's got the BBC name on it, it's going to be good-quality videotape. And indeed it was. But finally, quite rightly, we were told it wasn't an appropriate deal because it wasn't an extension of our core business. All it did was give TDK or BASF or whoever it was a marketing advantage over their competitors by the use of our brand.'

GB: '. . . And earn the BBC some money . . .'

'. . . Quite unacceptable: earning us money in the final analysis is not good enough. There are times when we have to turn down very lucrative deals on the grounds that they're not consistent with our brand image and with our remit as a public service broadcaster.'

Executive, BBC Rights Archive, 1997.

*

Fair dues and Teletubby cakes

'As we all know, the BBC is vulnerable to the charge that it uses the licence fee to gain unfair commercial advantage. So it has a department called Policy and Planning which tries to police programming. You should see the knots they tie themselves in. As we rolled out our *Ready Steady Cook* merchandise they told us no licensed BBC products should carry retailers' logos on the packaging. Then we found a *Top of the Pops* Easter egg with St Michael on it. "Oh, it shouldn't have happened." Then we found a Teletubby cake with Tesco on it. "Oh, we'll review the policy." They told us BBC products can't be licensed exclusively. Guess what? That cheeky *Top of the Pops* egg was exclusive to M & S. They told us food licensing was not acceptable. Then we found Pingu cereal and Noddy biscuits. "Oh, 'traditional' food licensing is acceptable, but not off the back of a food series." They told us there should be no question of endorsement of alcohol or gambling. Then we found *The Fast Show Live* being sponsored by Carlsberg and an *EastEnders'* slot machine. Need I go on? It's a mess that's cost us hundreds of thousands of pounds.'

Peter Bazalgette, chairman of Endemol UK, 1998.

*

Trade Wars

One of the gravest consequences of the restructuring in the later nineties was the eruption of serious internal conflicts between Production, Broadcast and Worldwide over the ownership and sale of rights and where the resulting income should flow. A series of factors exacerbated these conflicts, which had been brewing for years, among them Broadcast's control of licence fee income and its setting of programme prices at levels perceived by Production to be artificially low; and the policy that Production had no call on the rights to the programmes it produced, which were formally held and negotiated by Worldwide, with revenues returning primarily to Broadcast. Denied market incentives, Production was, once again, disempowered. These factors required Production to find additional sources of income to make up its programme budgets. But rather than turn to Worldwide for additional financing against international sales, as might be expected, Production took the view that Worldwide was often commercially inept and its rights dealing in some genres poor. It believed that Worldwide misjudged commercial potential and often undersold rights. This resonated with a larger judgement in the industry that Worldwide lacked commercial nous, a handicap linked by critics to what they perceived as the BBC's continuing antipathy towards all things commercial. The future chief of Worldwide, Rupert Gavin, himself summed this up when he likened the challenge of organising commercial operations within the BBC to running 'a brothel from inside a monastery'.[11]

In these circumstances, and against the BBC's own commercial policy, Drama Group and other production departments set up their own teams to seek co-production deals and rights sales to meet shortfalls in commissioning budgets. They enjoyed the collusion of the channel controllers, whose interests were also served by getting programmes made at higher budgets than they were willing or able to offer. These unofficial trading activities were contrary to the BBC's commercial policy. They set up self-competition for rights sales and a potential anarchy of rights trading within the corporation. Yet they were entirely understandable, given the structural arrangements faced by Production. Significantly, the co-production deals being arranged by Drama Group, while meeting immediate production needs, let go of rights in perpetuity. This was against the long-term interests of the BBC as a whole. Worldwide's deals, in contrast, were mainly for limited-term licences, under which rights eventually returned to the BBC. In this sense Worldwide represented the BBC's long-term

interests. Either way, Broadcast was the winner. If Worldwide sold rights officially, it gained revenue towards its commissions. If Production sold rights
unofficially, it gained subsidised programmes.

In light of these chronic divisions and unofficial activities, a new executive
body, the Rights Agency, was created in 1997. The aim was to arbitrate the
competing rights claims between Production, Broadcast and Worldwide, to
foster discipline and coordination in external trading and mitigate the conflicts
attendant on the BBC's growing commercialism. The problems inherent in the
rights issue continued to surface, for example in the BBC's negotiations in
1997 to create a partnership with the American-based Discovery Channel to
co-finance factual programmes. The discussions were lengthy and threatened
repeatedly to break down due in part to the sheer complexity caused by the
involvement of several rival parties from within the BBC.

*

The rights stuff: conflict and fragmentation

GB: 'Senior people from Worldwide have acknowledged to me the historical distrust
between themselves and the production departments when dealing with commercial
exploitation.'

'It's always been a problem. In 1986 co-production was part of Television. In 1987, the
chief executive of Enterprises took that co-production unit from Television and set it
physically in Woodlands in an attempt to make them talk to Enterprises. It didn't work.
Then Worldwide took over most of the co-production function; the staff moved into
Worldwide. But it was soon realised that they were too distant from production, so
they were given desks in production. Then in the mid nineties it swung the other way
again: Drama and Factual got business development managers; the deals were again
being done in production. You can see we have been round the circle. I think the Rights
Agency is the best attempt yet to crack it.'

GB: 'Hasn't the restructuring exacerbated these structural conflicts over rights? Isn't
this shown when someone like Susie in Drama Group tries to make deals independently from and in competition with Worldwide . . .?'

'Production want to be treated as independent programme-makers. They want to have
a production fee; they want to own and sell the rights and handle their own co-
productions. And Birt has said, "No, Broadcast own the rights, Broadcast will give you
a rate card to make a programme, and you're on risk to make up the shortfall."

Production have always borne the risk and will continue to bear the risk. To my mind the intention of the restructuring last year was that Production would have even less power. Broadcast was to be the powerhouse; it would own the rights and set the direction. But that's been chipped away at. The gang in Production have said, "This isn't fair. You in Broadcast can buy programmes from us in Production or you can go out to market, but we're not allowed to sell to the market. We're wholly dependent on you, and you can put us out of business." In the end it comes down to politics. I think Birt should say, "Stop all this, Production. These are the rules: you don't own rights, you cannot license to market; and yes, you might wither a little on the vine." Now Birt is not saying that, so what we've got instead is the Rights Agency. It's designed to be a vehicle for cooperation and generating relationships, a fast arbitration mechanism to resolve disputes and establish case history, which will be hugely useful.'

GB: 'The sale of rights is the main additional source of income after the licence fee, right? With the restructuring, it seems that everybody wants that rights income because there's no security – the feeling is everyone must fight for their own territory, pay their own way. So once you disaggregate, there is no unity and no overview being imposed. Why on earth don't they impose one?'

'Well, maybe Birt felt he'd imposed enough last year and wanted to let the big boys sort it out for themselves. It's not a new problem though. In Network Radio, for instance, the old structure was similar to the Broadcast/Production split. Matthew Bannister, as controller of Radio 1, used to pay a price for a programme to a Radio 1 production department, and then he'd find out after that they had co-production finance. When you added that to what he'd paid, the production had made a profit! It used to drive Matthew mad. So in principle the restructuring does provide the opportunity for clarity. But there's been a void since, and in the area of disposal of rights and financing programmes, nothing is clear and the factional fighting is worse than ever.'

Executive, BBC Worldwide, 1997.

*

Making an anomalous profit

A BBC1 Drama Overview meeting; two of the channel management team, Pat and Katherine, have talked us through the coming year's budget which, with the quota calculations, sounds very tight. Charles, head of drama, responds, 'Well, those are your figures. Our aim is for Drama Group to make a profit on some of our successful productions, such that the net payment from the controller plus any external co-production comes to more than the Group's costs. So there's a profit.' Katherine

164

seems puzzled; she apparently has no idea what this could be about. It's certainly against official policy. She asks rhetorically, 'But why would you want to make a profit?' Charles says evenly, 'So that we can offset that profit against the deficits we run up due to the risks we want to take on projects that are less bankable.' Katherine and Pat are mute.

Diary, 1996.

*

Dealing: Co-Production

During the nineties, Britain's balance of trade in television worsened significantly. To a large extent this resulted from the growth of multichannel television and the appearance of a rash of niche channels reliant on mainly American acquisitions for their programming, compounded by inflation in the cost of Hollywood films and premium US entertainment. The poor balance of trade became a major concern of the government. But rather than attend to the main cause, rising imports, the government issued a call for British producers to develop their international trading, increase exports and grow as global businesses.[12] For the BBC the political message was plainly that it should become more commercial and international in its outlook. These pressures occurred in a period when funding was flat while services were expanding. In response, co-production and co-financing deals rapidly became established as the norm, particularly as a means of subsidising national broadcast commissions in high-cost areas of programming when the channel controllers could not provide full funding. Without such co-production or co-financing, certain genres, such as drama serials and single films, would simply no longer have been made.

The rising reliance on international co-productions was one of several forces in the later nineties that tended to erode producers' autonomy and capacity to take risks. But it is a mistake to consider the creative outcome of co-production as predictable. However real the pressures for formulaic 'mid-Atlantic' or 'mid-European' programming, evidence from film and television in the nineties suggests that international markets do not necessarily bring a dilution of British content. Moreover, British broadcasting executives were fully aware of the contradictions between serving a national or local audience and orienting production towards international markets, and their priority remained national. The tension was between local cultural needs and international economic challenges. Probably the main impact of the stress on international markets in the later nineties was the drive on the part of the large, business-oriented independents such as Bazal/Endemol to develop highly profitable populist programme formats that could be reversioned and licensed throughout the world. It is these companies more than the British producer-broadcasters that led the way in superseding national differences in favour of global populism. Since these same powerful companies retained their attractions and their hold over the BBC and other broadcasters, they continued to exert considerable influence and to place their programming on favourable terms on Britain's channels.

The need to secure co-production as a way to subsidise core channel funding became more and more obvious to BBC production executives in the later nineties. Educational events were held at which producers new to the demands of co-production were made aware of the criteria according to which programmes were more or less likely to succeed in securing a deal. In 1996, Drama Group was lectured in this way by its own in-house co-production manager on factors favouring co-production. Producers and executives were sufficiently new to the game that such a lecture was seen as necessary, and it was met with interest, amusement and just a little cynicism. Increasingly in commissioning meetings, mention of possible co-production funds became a key technique used by producers and executives to reel in a controller's interest in ambitious projects. They began to use the technique unashamedly.

*

Unreal trading

The close of Drama Editorial Board. Charles, head of Drama, asks how the drama regions are dealing with the problem of having to underwrite their own productions – that is, how they are coping with the increasing number of shows that overspend. One regional head says that his most successful series, a centrepiece of the prime-time BBC1 schedule, is overspending by £90,000 per episode. Charles offers to help using Drama Group funds. The story opens the floodgates to a string of complaints from other drama heads about underfunding by the controllers and Worldwide's lack of effort in selling their shows. Robert, the Northern Ireland drama chief, says, 'I walked into Worldwide's drama marketing department yesterday, and there were no *Ballykissangel* posters up! This is a show that did 14 million last week – they should be selling it hard.' Another chips in: '*Dangerfield* is selling all around the world – it's been sold to France for £750,000 – but the production team doesn't see any of that money. We get nothing back from Worldwide.' Charles confirms the worrying larger picture: 'It's a fact that about 90 per cent of our shows now need underwriting because they're overspending beyond their notional controller budgets.' Andrea, head of drama in Scotland, agrees: 'The controllers' budgets are increasingly unrealistic; they don't relate to the rising real costs of shows.' Charles: 'To give them their dues, the controllers are having to find savings of 6 per cent this year. But we can't even fund *Casualty* and *EastEnders* next year at the price they're offering.' Someone adds, 'We shouldn't need to under-write all the time. Where do their figures come from?' A veteran concludes, 'When we know that a show they say costs £200,000 actually costs more, we should reject the whole deal – but of course we can't. They'll simply take it to an indie.'

Diary, 1996.

*

The co-production tutorial

A Strategy and Planning Overview meeting with executives from BBC1 and BBC2 and Drama Group. There has been lengthy discussion of the BBC2 drama slate, and then of BBC2's finances, which are a cause for concern. 'Efficiency savings' mean that the aver-age cost per hour of drama must drop from the previous year's £474,000 to £420,000, and next year even lower. The BBC2 finance manager says that 35 per cent of BBC2 drama is set to come from the independents – an optimistic target, she adds hastily, as last year the percentage was far higher. The hit series *This Life*, made by the celebrated independent World Productions, is repeatedly presented to in-house producers as a paragon: it cost just £175,000 to £200,000 for each forty- to fifty-minute episode and is taken to blaze a trail in high-quality, low-budget drama.

With the news of domestic funding squeezes ringing in our ears, the next part of the meeting opens. Susie Gold, the manager charged by Drama Group with seeking international co-production funds, gives a presentation using overheads on what co-production is all about. She compares the different genres. Co-production for series and serials is relatively static. There is usually only one series being co-produced at any time – it was *All Creatures Great and Small*, then *House of Elliot*, *Silent Witness* and *Dalziel and Pascoe*. In serials, recently *Ivanhoe* and *Nostromo* attracted substantial funds. But single drama is seeing great change, with bigger deals for a smaller number of shows; two HBO deals each worth £1.5 million pushed up the total in recent years. Susie puts up the total drama co-production figures: from £3.7 million in 1990–1, it reached £8 million in 1995–6. US revenues hover at around 93 per cent, and a bulk deal with the American A&E channel is Drama Group's primary source of co-productions.

She moves to a discussion of formats: the length and number of episodes. The first requirement, Susie emphasises, is to fit into the formats acceptable to the majority of global territories. Most broadcasters have less flexibile scheduling than the BBC.

Formats that work include three or four times a hundred minutes, as in *Dalziel and Pascoe*; six times fifty minutes, as in *Silent Witness*; thirteen times fifty minutes – 'Volume! In series everyone wants volume and we rarely deliver it! Why is that?'. Four times fifty minutes for serials, which can be re-edited to various lengths; and ninety- to hundred-minute movies also work. 'And duration no-no's? Thirty-minute series; seventy-five minutes of anything; long opening episodes – which we routinely do in serials; and episodes with different durations. Take *Our Friends in the North*: a third of the income from distributors went on reversioning it to show abroad.'

Susie turns to content. 'What are international markets looking for? Classics sell, as serials or singles: on *Tom Jones*, for instance, we raised £2 million of a £6 million budget from A&E and Worldwide.' But only certain classics sell: Jane Austen does, Dickens does not – 'it's too dark'. 'International themes sell – a good example is the single on the Nick Leeson story, *Breaking the Bank*.' And, she continues, broad, internationally recognised genres sell: sci-fi and fantasy; family shows for seven o'clock at the weekend – 'something we never do, I wonder why?'; vehicles for talent – writers, actors or directors, including 'anything using Jimmy McGovern or Tara Fitzgerald'; mystery and detective themes; action and adventure, and high-concept drama.

'What isn't fundable? What can't be sold?' The collective mood takes a turn for the worse as, under this heading, Susie reels off many of the themes of recent Drama Group output. 'Social issues drama won't sell abroad: it's a very British genre, although it can be sold as theatric films; soft and gentle drama, such as *Pie in the Sky* or *The Missing Postman*, are, again, very British; domestic themes, as in *Common as Muck* or *Casualty*; character-driven series, like *Hetty Wainthrop* and *Hamish Macbeth*; and drama based on quirky British humour, like *Cardiac Arrest* – although we have just sold this to Japan. I wonder what they'll make of it?'

Susie outlines various financing options: there are the international distributors, CTE, Brite and ITEL; there are equity investors like Irish Screen, Baltic and Harvest; there are co-production pre-sales as with A&E, WGBH and HBO. Video rights can be sold through Polygram, Pearson and BMG. Publishing and music publishing deals can be done with Boxtree and HarperCollins. She ends: 'We always offer Worldwide first option; but there's so much output these days, there are huge opportunities to sell elsewhere.' The meeting is into its third hour. Some producers look stimulated, others are slumped over. Now there is no excuse for them bringing a seventy-five-minuter to the next Offers meeting. And if they want to do social realism, they will have to cut their cloth to suit.

Diary, 1996.

*

In light of the internal conflicts over the control of rights, one of the main tasks of the Rights Agency became the arbitration of disputes between Production, Broadcast and Worldwide over co-production. In Rights Agency meetings reviewing potential co-production sources for documentaries, collective distaste was shown for the editorial dumbing-down, such as increased visual sensationalism, that was evidently required by an international commercial partner with which the BBC was developing massive ventures. But market pragmatism prevailed. The rules of the game had changed, and there was the will to do the best under the new circumstances. New opportunities had also appeared, such as the return of the international documentary feature film, an important new market and one the BBC hoped to get into.

Rights Agency discussions revealed that co-production cannot be reduced to purely economic calculation. Co-production relationships have to be cultivated; indeed, they are likened by those involved to creative partnerships. There is a need to harmonise editorial values, but this may fail or result in severe compromise. Co-production commonly requires the integration of talent from the co-producing nation: the casting of star performers or use of a local director. Finance may be offered by a foreign distributor on one production as a loss leader in order to secure a preferential relationship with the BBC on other deals. Political imperatives sometimes operate, superseding commercial considerations. Long-standing partnerships tend to be favoured over new ones, trusted partners over industry arrivistes. In the meeting described below, I watched as the combined interests of Worldwide, Production and Broadcast to sell rights to a high-bidding newcomer so as to secure a costly drama were threatened by Corporate Centre's politically determined insistence on doing a less lucrative deal with a sister Commonwealth public service broadcaster – apparently unaware that this meant the production would not proceed. Here, loyalty (or cronyism?) stood implacably opposed to the liquidating forces of the market. Yet in this case, without the operations of the market, there would have been no creative project.

*

In the Red : dealing and compromising

A Rights Agency meeting in the White City building. Round the table are Mike, representing Worldwide, Chris and Brendan, for Production, Jonathan, a lawyer, and Susie, Carolyn, Paul, Kevin and Oliver, commercial managers from Drama Group, Entertainment and various parts of Factual. We are here to share information and to go through a list of projects so as to knock out the optimal rights arrangement for each. The atmosphere is genial, constructive and – yes – efficient. It seems there is a will for relations to improve and conflicts to be overcome.

Fiction first. *In the Red*: a Malcolm Bradbury murder thriller. Carolyn says Worldwide has offered £70,000 co-production and the controllers have given £550,000 per episode – 'not bad for a contemporary piece' – and they all joke that Worldwide's offer is not so low that they can go back and complain. A&E and WGBH have been approached and are not interested, so there will be no American investment. Worldwide don't want video or publishing rights, so Carolyn asks if she can sell these elsewhere? Mike and Chris agree.

Next up, a *Screen One* drama, Andrew Davies's *Getting Hurt*. Susie reports a budget shortfall of £300,000. One commercial partner, Belgravia, is asking for Australian rights to be thrown in for an extra £100,000 which, she puzzles, is surely excessive. But Belgravia argue that it would add value to two other BBC shows they've already acquired, through cross-promotion. Overall Belgravia are offering £250,000, a valuable injection to the project, and Mike sighs that they can't afford not to take it: 'Without this cash the project just won't get made.' But, he continues, the Australian Broadcasting Corporation, the Oz equivalent of the BBC, have been told they can have this show by another part of the BBC, 'so ABC will be very pissed off if the deal goes to Belgravia.' Chris teases, 'Bags you tell Bob Phillis!', implying that the deputy DG will not want to offend as big a partner as ABC, and a sister PSB at that. Susie comments that Worldwide and ABC have not offered much; their bids are simply not competitive. Carolyn asks whether she has seen sales projections by Belgravia and ABC, but she hasn't. They can't understand the huge discrepancy between the offers. Eventually, they concur that Belgravia's bid is probably higher than rational commercial calculation on likely sales. Mike says this kind of situation is a major problem for the BBC; it should be discussed at board level.

Two single dramas are discussed, *King Lear* and *Wives and Daughters*, both to be made by the producer of *Pride and Prejudice*, both requiring co-production. *King Lear* will cost between £650,000 and £740,000; £500,000 is on the table from the Performance strand, and Alan Yentob has agreed to underwrite £100,000 more against a future US co-production deal, while Worldwide has offered £40,000. *Wives and Daughters* will be sold as a package with *Lear*, but they are blocked as Alan hasn't yet commissioned it, and he is now away. I reflect that those present are acting as midwives to the various projects and parties, the objective being to ensure that finance is secured and rights sold on to the best possible advantage – but with a first duty to Production that the finance is there to get the thing made.

They move to a key structural challenge. It stems from the existence of two parts of the BBC which compete for music entertainment projects. One is Radio International, a branch of Worldwide with its own outside broadcast vans which record concerts to sell on. Then there is the Music Entertainment department within Production, which does similar recordings of major pop concerts and sells various rights packages for TV, radio, video and audio. This department is trying to close a deal with Oasis to record a mega concert of theirs; Chris and Mike suggest to Carolyn that she encourages them to close the deal. She reports a series of confusions in this and other projects about who people are dealing with when they are told it's a 'BBC project'. The two bodies are approaching people independently and competitively; it's chaos. Chris and Carolyn ask about the line management for Radio International; Mike replies that it's in the 'too-hard-to-resolve basket'. Radio International reports up through Worldwide's Music department to the CE of Worldwide, Dick Emery; it has strong managerial backing. Mike and Chris are to meet Dick tomorrow and will raise the problem.

The discussion shifts to factual co-productions, which necessarily involve the Discovery 'JVP' or joint-venture partnership, the bulk deal to co-produce factual and documentary programmes by the BBC and Discovery. The JVP is almost finalised but not signed, yet Discovery are already invoking it in various questionable ways. They dis-cuss *Rhythm of Life*, a series commissioned by Music and Arts and made by an indie, which means it lies outside the JVP. But Discovery are claiming that it does come under the agreement and have thrown their considerable weight around, making increasingly unreasonable editorial demands. The collective view is to go back to Discovery and agree to some of the changes requested, as long as Discovery proceed on the basis of the original deal, including rapid payment. Jonathan, from a legal perspective, adds that he's very concerned they clarify with Discovery now that normal co-production deals allow for consultation but do not give Discovery final editorial clearance. They must hold out for this principle or a dangerous precedent might be set; after this story every-one solemnly agrees.

They move to consider the *Natural World* strand from the BBC's Natural History Unit. Stranded docs, it seems, come under the JVP. The case they are discussing is a three-part series made by an indie, *Dark Heart of Africa*, the status of which is ambigu-ous: it can be seen as either part, or not part, of the *Natural World* strand. It was commissioned by the strand management, but has been made as a miniseries and branded separately. The issue is particularly fraught for indie commissions like this series, since they come under the JVP only if they form part of a larger strand. Then I click on what is at stake: clearly the BBC cannot be seen to act as a commercial agent for its indie commissions, that is, for companies who are rivals to BBC Production. Yet Broadcast has an interest in ensuring that extra financing is also found for its indie commissions, thus enhancing its own funding. These are powerful and contradictory pressures. As they review the JVP, Brendan leans in and cautions that budgets for par-ticular projects must not be shown to Discovery; a sales negotiator for Factual says

Discovery have been asking to see budgets ahead of signing deals. This must be resisted; there is a risk of revealing their hand. I muse that, in this room at least, the BBC is certainly acting like a fully commercial animal.

They turn to *Under the Sun*, the ethnographic film strand, also part of the JVP. Oliver reports that the controller of BBC2 wants to change the remit: it must become 'glossier, lighter'. The archetype for the new feel is a film called *Painted Babies*, and the strand editor is keen on this direction. But Paul reports that on a film currently being edited, *Kung Fu Monks*, Discovery are pressing for more violence, 'for kicks and blows every ten seconds!' There is cynical laughter. The controller has asked them to find lots of co-financing, but there is an anxious consensus in response: 'There's no history of finding co-production for this genre.' Jonathan adds grimly, 'It looks like he's trying to kill the strand off.' All agree that it's a classic snooker: the controller signals he's not interested by setting the commercial side an almost impossible challenge.

As we close, the Music and Arts commercial manager bursts out, as though incapable of repressing any longer an unexpressed truth, that they all know how difficult – how incredibly picky and fussy – Discovery are editorially. It will lead to major problems in future on the JVP. 'Just imagine what would happen if Discovery had got to grips editorially with *Rhythm of Life* . . .', he poses rhetorically, implying that if they had it would be horrifying, beyond the pale.

Diary, 1997.

*

Becoming Entrepreneurs

With the independents' success in winning commissions hanging over their heads, and under pressure from the quasi-market conditions described, the BBC production departments strove to become intensely entrepreneurial in the later nineties. This was evident in the growth of another pronounced form of self-competition within the BBC: the tendency for different departments to head for the same programme areas. Commissions for currently successful genres – docu-soaps, leisure and lifestyle, classic drama adaptations – began to be chased simultaneously by several production departments. Indeed, with a similar dynamic operating among the independents, both in-house and independent producers targeted the proven centre-ground of programming. One sign was a wasteful duplication in development across the production departments. Another was the reduced commitment to seeking out innovative and unusual ideas and less popular genres. The degree of imitative desperation in the search for successful commissions was partly an index of the rising tide of independent commissions in several prime-time genres. It was also a measure of the frantic search among department heads and producers for commissions that would secure work for their production teams. For some departments, such as Music and Arts, the word was simply that the genre failed the competitive ratings test and would be scattered to the edges of the schedule; the challenge issued was to reinvent arts programming for the new environment.

But these negative dynamics do not do justice to the transformation. A cultural change began to crystallise, answering the long-standing taunt that the BBC was constitutionally uncommercial. A new seduction, a collective hallucination, imperceptibly took hold: the notion that even BBC producers could play the market, could join an indie, could copyright an idea, could pitch and sell; and moreover that to do so, to be seen to do so, and to be seen to be successful in doing so, were sexy. In themselves these actions attracted esteem. Prowess in gaining commissions, hybridising popular genres and achieving ratings became the stuff of cafeteria gossip and corridor talk. Good fortune in being headhunted by a major independent brought enormous prestige. Many informal moments revealed producers' admiration for those individuals who had gained promotion, or had attracted enviable outside job offers, on the back of masterminding a high ratings show. In the context of widespread cynicism and demoralisation, playing the new entrepreneurial games, with the chance of gaining recognition and real rewards not only within the BBC but in the larger world, offered a new source of consolation and exhilaration, a pleasurable challenge – and one in inverse proportion to any slavish identification with the BBC. There was a libidinalisation of entrepreneurialism.

*

The golden girl

I'm having lunch in the White City café with Giles, Debbie and Bob of the Community Programme Unit. It's a break from a long editorial meeting. As we jaw, a woman walks past. They hail her warmly, call out 'Congratulations!' and she comes over smiling. They talk for a few minutes, and she goes. They explain excitedly that she is Lorraine Heggessey, presently one of the most blessed figures in BBC television. She became famous as the brains behind the ratings winner Animal Hospital, a key show in the development of the new popular documentaries, the building blocks of what is emerging as the new mid-evening schedule template for both BBC1 and BBC2. Not only did Lorraine create the series, but she had the instinct to insist, against the weight of higher opinion, that it should be fronted by Rolf Harris, at the time widely considered a has-been. The recipe has been an extraordinary success, and Lorraine's soft public service populism is seen as inspired, magical, and much to be emulated. But her achievement does not end there; it has been crowned by a double whammy. In recent weeks rumour had it that she had been offered a major executive role in a leading independent – her salary would treble, at least! But soon after, another rumour spread like wildfire: the BBC was fighting to retain her by making a counter-offer, a giant promotion. She would head up a major department. Days ago she was confirmed as the new head of Children's programmes. [*Indeed, Lorraine Heggessey's rise to power proved to be unstoppable. In 2000, she became the first ever woman controller of BBC1.*]

Diary, 1997.

*

Opportunities

The annual overview meeting of the Documentaries department: over a hundred people are gathered in a conference room in the White City building. Paul Hamann, head of documentaries, is congratulating them all on a stunning year, 'the third year we've been singled out as the strongest production department. We *lead* in the Annual Report!' Proudly, he reels off the trophy of their current huge slate of commissions: they have twenty-four series in production for BBC1 and thirty-six for BBC2. In passing, Paul mentions a series called *The Brain* 'which we're trying to keep from science'. He continues, 'Our only concerns are that we're not reaching enough young people on BBC1, so we've commissioned audience research on this; and we need more observational soaps for BBC1 that aren't about children, animals or hospitals!' This touches a nerve and Paul's tone changes as, confidingly, he alludes to one of the most significant recent events in documentaries: 'The Jeremy Mills business was about the worst thing that could happen to us this year. But I've dealt with it the best possible way: I've got Jeremy and his team, Richard and Nick, signed up and working for us for the next year and a half.' The tale is a salutary one. Jeremy Mills was a BBC producer responsible for one of the biggest BBC1 hits in recent years, the documentary series *Children's Hospital*, a show which, along with *Animal Hospital* and another of Mills's major in-house hits, *Driving School*, created the new docu-soap genre. This year Mills left the BBC along with two others from the same department, Richard Bradley and Nick Catliff, to set up their own independent, Lion Television. They began immediately to sell back programmes to the BBC, it was rumoured at far higher prices than had they been made in-house. Mills was fêted as a buccaneer, an exemplary entrepreneur, his earnings vastly bigger for having moved outside the BBC. To prevent Lion from taking their valuable shows elsewhere, the BBC had attempted to tie them in by offering Lion a bulk output deal. [*In subsequent*

174

years, Lion continued to pour docu-soaps into the BBC1 schedule, among them Paddington Green, Hotel, Castaway 2000 and The Heat is On. In this way, Lion rapidly became established as one of Britain's most successful independents.]

Paul continues by speaking of the Discovery deal, 'which will bring new opportunities to us all. I also met the chairman of Flextech last week – very exciting.' He hands over to Margaret, the department manager, who plugs the new Flextech joint-venture public service and commercial channels being developed: 'Lots of new avenues for programming, and for commercial ideas too.' Paul talks of the exceptionally good relations they are enjoying with the controllers. Ron Neil, chief executive of Production, has asked him to come up with suggestions for the whole of Production about how to cultivate such relations and maximise commissioning opportunities, 'but this may mean giving away our tactics to rivals, so I have reservations'. Drawing the meeting to a close, he enjoins them not to slacken off with bringing new ideas, warning against complacency and spurring them on to even greater efforts.

Diary, 1997.

*

The classics database

Sally, Single drama's development executive, is meeting George, head of Singles. She reports that her readers have started an online database of 'classics', that is, literary works that may be suitable for adaptation. George: 'Great – have you shared it with Suzanne and Kevin?' Suzanne and Kevin are executive producers from Serials, home of the majority of BBC classics. Uneasily, Sally says no, that she has asked several times for a copy of Serials' classics archive, but Suzanne has failed to deliver. They exchange wry smiles. George says, 'Fine, then do your own database and make sure Serials can't access it!' Months before, it emerged that both Singles and Serials were working on scripts for *Mansfield Park*; soon after, both departments and BBC Children's were found to be developing treatments for *Jane Eyre*. It seems interdepartmental rivalry is so strong it prevents the kind of routine coordination that would avoid duplication.

Diary, 1996.

*

Doubles and rivalries

It's the day before the BBC2 Offers meeting for the Community Programme Unit, and we are in a day-long editorial to hone the pitches that will be made to the controller,

Mark Thompson. The CPU badly needs commissions. Giles, the CPU's head, recalls Michael Jackson saying to them in the last BBC1 Offers meeting that his target rating was nine million. This concentrates their minds; the vast majority of CPU output will continue to go out on BBC2. We are working through the CPU Offers brochure, a glossy document detailing programme ideas intended strictly for the controller's eyes. Kath says the designer of the brochure asked her recently whether they had thought about releasing the Offers document on to the Internet or – even worse – the BBC Intranet! Everyone gasps, feigning horror. Kath reassures them that she told the designer where to get off. I ask why releasing the brochure on to the Intranet is such a problem, and Sue replies, 'It would blow the confidentiality of our ideas! Rivalry within the BBC, you see, with departments like Docs, Factual, even Music and Arts, is a far greater problem for us than competition with the outside.' The phone rings, and Giles speaks for a few minutes. 'It's Alan Yentob; he wants a copy of our Offers document. He's sending an assistant to collect it.' Everyone is excited; Alan is showing interest. Then someone recalls that the assistant is a problem: her husband is an indie producer to whom she may leak ideas. There is unease, and they consider how to get the brochure to Alan in other ways.

They discuss the first two ideas, *The Duel* and *Chain Reaction*. Debbie points out that they are rather similar – 'What if the controller only wants one of them?' They decide that *Chain* is the better idea. *6 on Risk*: six films on risk to be fronted by Perri 6 of Demos, a charismatic figure from an influential New Labour think tank. Debbie warns that Mark Thompson might consider this not to be CPU territory, since it overlaps with current affairs and political programmes: 'Come on, *Newsnight* are *always* doing Demos!' *The New Entrepreneurs*: Giles reflects, 'It's the community service movement meets collapse of the welfare state meets *Video Diaries*, isn't it?' Kath warns that Glenwyn Benson, head of adult education, is pushing a similar network proposal, *Social Entrepreneurs*, so there's a problem of rival ideas. Giles urges Bob to stick with it. Last up, *The Nash*: Ian explains that it has several narrative strands, 'some continue throughout, some are resolved in one episode – like a soap, in fact just like *Animal Hospital*!'

Diary, 1997.

*

Evangelical Entrepreneurial

By late 1999, the end of Birt's time as director-general, 40 to 50 per cent of the BBC's television entertainment and 35 per cent of its drama and factual programming were being supplied by the independent sector, and relations between Broadcast and Production continued to be troubled. In recognition of the loading of the system in favour of the independents, and in view of the need to support the BBC's production base, a concession was eventually won. An informal output deal operated from 1997 in which Production was guaranteed a minimum of 60 per cent of all Broadcast commissions.[13] But by then the damage had been done. The conflicts unleashed by the BBC's marketisation, and the corrosive effects of commercialisation, competition and disaggregation as they were stoked by Producer Choice, the independent quota and the restructuring, had caused a disintegrating unity of purpose inside the corporation. They had eroded the BBC's efficiency, the creative autonomy of its production departments, its quality standards and public service orientation. Above all, they had dislocated the former ethos of creative cooperation and trust between the channels and production arms. The BBC's well-being and its capacity to be inventive were undermined. Its components had little incentive to work in integrated ways for common public service ends. Instead, a great deal of collective energy was expended on internal battles and bureaucratic solutions, to the detriment of creative focus.

In terms of programming, the independent quota and the restructuring together favoured an intensely competitive dynamic leading to ever tighter mutual imitation across individual programmes, strands, genres and channels. As low morale swept through the production departments, the entrepreneurial independents became a model. The infatuation with ratings, the evangelical belief in an entrepreneurial spirit, drove both independents and in-house producers to cannibalise existing genres and to develop repeated mutations of hit shows. In some production outfits, entrepreneurialism was rife at the expense of other, more salient values. Rather than being harnessed to public service aims, entrepreneurialism became a goal in itself, allied to the desire to win high ratings. Where ratings had once formed part of the public service calculus, now the populist category error took hold that ratings were sufficient in themselves. Since the continued staffing and resources of production departments depended on securing commissions, it is perhaps understandable that entrepreneurialism drove out other values. It became a mode of survival, a necessity in order then to be able to pursue adventurous work. The irony is that as an entrepreneurial dynamic became dominant, creative 'respite' became increasingly rare; the imagination required to do more than simply hybridise existing shows tended to atrophy. Occasionally, the chemistry worked fortuitously in creative ways. In the BBC regional centres, with the 33 per cent regional quota, entrepreneurialism became a means to public service ends. For BBC Scotland and Northern Ireland, fulfilling the quota required that they compete successfully against well-established drama and entertainment outfits for network commissions. In time, this stimulated the development of the local skills base, bringing regional issues and talent, and greater cultural diversity, to the screen.

The BBC's infatuation with markets was ideologically led and politically imposed. It generated a new value system in which entrepreneurialism was conflated with creativity, while in reality it led to overcrowding in the centre-ground of programming and ever purer imitation of the BBC's rivals. This imitation is often interpreted as evidence of the supremacy of populism in the late Birtist BBC and of a terminal cynicism. But this is to mistake symptom for cause. Rather, it was the inevitable result of the structural changes described, as well as of the BBC's continuing conviction that to retain legitimacy, the corporation must be popular, and that to be popular it had little choice in current circumstances but to ape commercial television.

The greatest irony returns to the big picture. Research on the competitive environment of British television shows that, while commercialism permeated the industry by the later nineties, there was no necessary correlation between increased competition and 'efficiency' in terms of more programming for less cost. Indeed, a direct consequence of increased competition during the nineties, particularly from satellite broadcasting, was a substantial increase in the price of some kinds of programming, particularly those linked to talent and sports rights. The relative efficiency and quality of independent as opposed to in-house production remain to be proven and vary with genre. Economies of scale, the capacity to scrutinise expenditure and control quality, and the importance of retaining rights for exploitation across a range of media all favour in-house production. As the BBC disaggregated, international media markets saw accelerated conglomeration. Distributors bought up production companies and studios for their programming and rights libraries; powerful content providers bought into networks to secure and expand their outlets and to benefit from cross-media synergies. Globally, deregulatory measures aimed apparently at increasing competition and choice have led to mergers and concentration.[14]

In this light, while the independent quota was an instrument of its time, albeit one in which rhetoric and reality were continually in tension, the BBC's restructuring must be judged a spectacularly misguided and self-destructive adventure.

Working and Not Working

In-house *The House*

One of the celebrated highlights of BBC television in 1996 was a documentary serial called *The House*. Filmed inside the Royal Opera House, Covent Garden, it was a fly-on-the-wall account of a period of mounting crisis, and gained notoriety for a scene in which managers were shown planning to sack a member of staff. *The House* represents one of the proliferating sub-genres of documentary in this period, what might be called 'power fly-on-the-wall'.[1] At the time that *The House* is being transmitted, I am talking to a senior television executive when Alan Yentob, controller of BBC1, enters the room to speak to him, not realising I am there. Surprised, Yentob shoots me – the ethnographer-cum-documentarist – a look, smiles, and says, 'Ah, Georgina! Shall we stage a sacking for you?'

Replete with irony, the subtexts are multiple and rich in meaning:
- That he knows that I know that one of the main causes of criticism of BBC management is for its callous shedding of staff, a symptom of marketisation and of the wider casualisation of the industry;
- That I should take this encounter as a teasing sign that, unlike his own documentary film-makers, I will not be given access to such controversial and 'private' managerial moments within the BBC;
- That he and I both know there is a contradiction in the BBC demanding this kind of access for its own film-makers while itself resisting such access, a contradiction the BBC seems willing to risk being publicly aired through my research;
- And that, despite the BBC's claims for the professional realism of its factual programming, 'documentary realism' is a tenuous affair and might involve judicious staging.

Diary, 1996.

*

The first lie

A routine meeting between Paul Hamann, head of Documentaries, and the editor of *Modern Times*, Stephen Lambert. They're discussing a film which, it seems, has been long in the making. Paul asks Stephen how it's progressing; a tense moment, and then they laugh collusively. Stephen, smiling, collects himself and says it's coming along and it's good, but implies that it's very slow. Paul teases him, 'That's the first time you've lied in front of Georgie!', and goes on to explain that the director is the partner of a top BBC executive; so however slow she is, however wayward, there's absolutely nothing they can do about it.

Diary, 1997.

*

Casualising Creativity

One of the most striking developments in the broadcasting industry in the eighties and nineties was the casualisation of employment, evident in the drift away from permanent staff jobs and towards a reliance on short term contracts and freelancing. This change had impacts far beyond the BBC. It was a core feature of the restructuring of the entire British broadcasting industry, one determined by government policies which from the late eighties sought to deregulate labour markets, reduce the power of the trade unions and break up the large integrated producer-broadcasters. The 1990 Broadcasting Act's imposition of the independent production quota was a central tool. The symbolic importance of the broadcasting industry for Conservative governments was plain when in 1987 Mrs Thatcher famously attacked British television as 'the last bastion of restrictive practices'.[2]

In broadcasting, the result of government pressures to adopt 'labour flexibility' was plain: staff numbers in the major broadcasters plummeted, and short-term and freelance employment became commonplace. Freelance status had long been a feature of certain creative jobs in broadcasting, but it now became pervasive. Independent production companies had always relied on freelance labour beyond their small core editorial teams in order to respond to changes in demand. Where in 1979 almost all employment in television was accounted for by staff jobs in the BBC and ITV, by 1989 39 per cent of all employees were freelance, and by 1994 this figure had risen to 54 per cent. From a peak in the mid nineties, the percentage of freelance employment fell in the later nineties to around 45 per cent, and it has continued to hover at around this level.[3] This shift is probably the single biggest change in the structure of British television in the last twenty years.

The BBC was greatly affected by these trends. Under the impact of Producer Choice, the independent quota and the broader political and ideological climate, wave upon wave of department closures, outsourcing and privatisation took place over the nineties: the winnowing of technical staff in BBC Resources between 1991 and 1998, when it was privatised with a staffing level 5,000 below that of the early nineties; the privatisation of transmission in 1995 with the loss of 1,100 jobs; the outsourcing of financial management to a private company in 1997 with the loss of 700 jobs; and a reduction in production staff across departments over the nineties of about 3,000, with the exception of news, the staffing of which grew to accommodate new services such as BBC News 24. Reductions in labour costs through cuts to core staffing were an inevitable result of the budget cuts imposed by efficiency drives. Downsizing, redundancies and casualisation were relentless features of the reorientation of the BBC under Birt. Staff producers and production-related craft workers became endangered species; in 1996, over 50 per cent of all BBC Production employees were on short contracts. In the later nineties management announced the intention to reverse the trend towards freelance working, and by 2001 the figure had dropped to about 35 per cent. Over the nineties it is estimated that the BBC lost at least 7,000 and possibly as many as 10,000 permanent jobs.[4]

But such losses were not the only source of change in the social composition and the employment base of the corporation. As producers and technicians were required to adjust to the uncertainties of the external labour market, there was an influx of managerial personnel. Accountants, lawyers, consultants, strategists, commercial managers, business analysts, marketers and market researchers were brought in. Filling out layer upon ramifying layer of middle and senior management, they became the new permanent staffing of the BBC. This chapter and the next chart the changes in the social make-up of the BBC and the consequent transformations in the values of the corporation. What was it like to work for the BBC in the later nineties? How did the changing context influence people's capacity for creative work?

Casualisation was accompanied by both market realism and a 'tough love' moralism. Times had changed; new competitive conditions meant new realities. Programme-makers, it was believed, had become complacent and lazy under the old dispensation. They were like snails hiding from the light. The insecurities and rigours of the market would boost creative energies and lessen any unhealthy dependence on the BBC.

*

The logic of the BBC animal

'One of the key things we did in our reorganisation of Drama Group was to have cost controllers working across both independent and in-house productions to get cross-fertilisation of ideas. And the nearer you get to working in an independent mode, the more you get all sorts of benefits like you can lend your staff out to people if they're not busy, or you can buy people in off the market. Faced with this the logic of the BBC animal is, "I'm needed because I work the BBC way. If I work the way everyone else works, what is unique about me? I could be replaced!" You've got to break that fear; these people need to think, "I'm good at what I do. I can learn new ways, and then if the BBC ever tosses me out I can get a job elsewhere." They don't think that way, and you see people in a state of shock. One of the things we've done recently is say to producers, "We're not having you on the payroll for ever if you don't produce anything. We're going to pick you up when we need you for a project." It's quite a cruel place at the moment. It's terrifying the level of individual angst.'

Senior manager, BBC Drama, 1996.

*

Contract calculus

GB: 'The outside perception is that staff jobs are disappearing and that people are being put on short contracts. Has there been a radical shift?'

'In Drama, producers have either been on freelance contracts, employed by the project with certain tax advantages, or they've had the odd staff contract of fixed-term duration. When Charles came three years ago we tried an experiment. People kept moaning about the insecurity. So we decided to give a core of the best producers three-year fixed-term contracts. With some it worked OK; but others appeared to lapse into inactivity more than before. We couldn't charge them against programmes because they weren't producing any. So the message was we can't sustain this because it costs us horrendous amounts of money in downtime. Then we thought, "Maybe what they need is something longer than a project but less than three years. Maybe they need to be driven, to have a degree of insecurity to chivvy them along." The number of independent commissions was rising; and money was being wasted in development. Some in-house producers drifted on for ever, developing ideas the BBC would never want in a million years. So now we've gone to a three-contract model. If you're instrumental in the development of projects and you're part of the small editorial team, you get a one-year contract. If you're project-driven, you get a contract for the length of the project. And if you're just developing, you're on a freelance contract working from home, and we'll pay a modest fee.'

Manager, BBC Drama, 1996.

*

News: staff cuts and flexibility

'This programme is losing 30 per cent of its resources. It can only mean job losses and a very different type of radio news programme. A few of us were asked to sit down months ago to discuss how you could produce it on 30 per cent less money. The only conclusion was that there had to be fewer staff, because in radio that's by far the greatest cost. We talked about the options: longer discussions, less reporting. I think people fear a whole type of broadcasting going. I hope it will be retained as part of the variety, because without that the BBC is in danger of losing its distinctiveness. It has to keep, across its different brands, if you like, some kind of BBC identity, which is to do with reliability and ethics and integrity and truthfulness in the news. Otherwise, there's nothing to distinguish us from commercial competitors. What will go are packages with reports from abroad, perhaps the programme having its own reporters; my role might disappear. You won't have, as you do now, reporters going out, recording sounds, speaking to people and putting together a piece that contains impressions of where they've been. There'll be greater dependence on the Newsgathering department. Last week I went to Dublin to do a piece; three days of work for eight minutes of radio. That's very labour-intensive. In future I doubt there'll be the money for that. I'll be moving on anyway, because these days that's the way things are; you have to be flexible.'

Reporter, BBC radio news, 1997.

*

As commissions went to the independents and departmental cuts bit in, production executives sought frantically to attract commissions to their departments in order to maintain some core staffing and the viability of in-house production. In turn, this stoked competition for commissions, exacerbating self-competition within the BBC and the tendency among all departments to head for popular programme territory and currently fashionable genres.

183

*

Stretching the brief: cuts and commissions

'The budget of the CPU/DPU is about £6 million a year. But there are cuts coming down. We've been cut every year for the last three years; the message that everyone is getting from the controllers is that there will be no expansion in BBC production. I just assume we get cut 5 per cent every year. And the cuts come from staffing. Until last year, my area of the CPU had a guaranteed sum to spend for the financial year, which was the subject of negotiation between me and the controller of BBC2 about what we'd spend it on. The new controller has changed that system, because the channel planners didn't know if they were going to get six half-hour documentaries or twelve late-night chat shows, and they want to know in advance. So the basis we're now working on is that we have no guaranteed output at all, beyond what we get at the next Offers meeting. It's a big change. When I came back from leave, the first thing I had to do was hold a meeting with core staff to say, "From November you have no security of employment. BBC2 has *Video Diaries* and *Video Nation*; they've got enough documentaries going on elsewhere. They may not want anything more from us." In which case we'd close and everyone here is finished. That's new for some of my staff. I've been thinking of places I could go in future. I would not like to work in Music and Arts, even though a lot of my interests would take me in that direction. It's partly because it doesn't know where it's going. It isn't sure whether it's doing the Proms and the odd eclectic piece, or trying to make arts programmes that people might watch. The ethos seems to be one of uncertainty.'

GB: 'When I visited Music and Arts, the executives put across this idea, which seems increasingly common in other departments, "Oh, we'll do populist pieces, popular design programmes, we'll compete on *Changing Rooms* with *Home Front*; we'll do the heavyweight single presenter pieces like Andrew Graham-Dixon's *History of British Art*; we'll do the Proms; we'll do the whole range. It's postmodern." Is that uncertainty, or incoherence, or being entrepreneurial? Isn't it a result of the pressures that are setting all of you in-house to compete with each other, especially in the lower-cost leisure and light factual entertainment area? That's where the big commissions are coming from, isn't it?'

'For the staff it's bewitching and bewildering, because to work on an Andrew Graham-Dixon is fantastically different from working on *Home Front*. There's a sense that you get put on to *Home Front* when you haven't got anything else to do. That's where the lack of coherence is. *Home Front* has nothing in common with *Last Night of the Proms*, nothing at all. Yes, Music and Arts have done *Home Front*, quite rightly, because they can get some commissions, earn a bit more, stock up and support the higher-cost pro-grammes.'

GB: 'It occurred to me when I watched you all preparing for the CPU's Offers meeting in May, aren't you also tempted into diluting the remit of this department in chasing commissions?'

'Yes, absolutely.'

GB: 'You were talking about a BBC1 commission you wanted to get, a film following the Olympic rowing team in the period leading up to the Olympics. I can see that's a potentially interesting and popular show, but in what way is it distinctively CPU? Isn't it partly the product of you guys, understandably, wanting to play the competition game?'

'Yes it is. It's about us wanting to get more commissions and we will go absolutely any-where we possibly can, particularly BBC1, to get more commissions. I can justify the *Olympic Gold* idea within our remit: entering into the personal dynamics, the marital traumas, the training – quite a different perspective from the usual sports coverage. But I'd be the first to admit it's stretching our brief. Yes of course we are all fighting for that ground, fighting from where we are.'

Executive, BBC Community Programme Unit, 1997.

*

Revolving doors

'All the long-running strands are now up for renewal every year, commissions for these strands have to be bid for competitively even internally. It leads to anomalies. For example, Features had a long-running strand. It went up for recommission, and Arts programmes won the bid, so the strand migrated to Arts. Features made redundancies. Then it emerged that people had been made redundant by Features only to be re-employed on short contracts for the strand in Arts two weeks later! We call it the revolving-door phenomenon. Right now they do everything humanly possible to stop people having permanent contracts. The managers like the power it gives them.'

Union official, BECTU, 1997.

*

Freelance Fragment

The high incidence of freelancing and short-contract employment among the BBC's production staff had repercussions both for those individuals and for the organisation. For employees, freelance status often entailed an extreme degree of fragmentation in their working lives. It became common in the nineties for production staff to be engaged for years on serial contracts of two or three months' duration, often with bouts of unemployment, bouncing between the BBC, a range of independents and perhaps some of the larger commercial companies. In such conditions it was difficult to concentrate on the present job as effort had constantly to be made to find the next contract. Working relationships were sustained for short periods, inhibiting any cumulative build-up of creative dialogue or collaboration. Give the chronic insecurity, the individual freelancer's relations with the current employer became a microcosm of the relations between the insecure independents and the broadcasters: the need to secure another contract militated against risk-taking or originality and towards the need to flow with prevailing trends. Countering this, of course, was the need to stand out from the many rival candidates for any freelance position by cultivating individuality.

Since relations between freelancer and employer were only passing, there was no incentive on the part of employers to offer training or support the professional development of such employees. Indeed, as permanent staffing decreased in the BBC, the corporation's commitment to training atrophied. By the later nineties the decimation of training had become a central anxiety of the broadcasting industry.[5] The problem was compounded by the tendency to save costs by employing freelancers for only a limited part of the production process. In this way they were prevented from seeing projects through and learning on the job, an informal apprenticeship that had been possible when junior staff had permanent status. Moreover, freelancers were often given repeated contracts at the same grade, with no career progression. Rather than creative engagement and growth, freelance work in production offered a highly circumscribed experience.

*

Hard News: narrative of a working life

'I'm now an assistant producer on a three-month contract in BBC Documentaries. My first job in TV was as a researcher. Having been told I didn't have any experience I was then straight in and had a huge amount of responsibility with no guidance whatsoever. No one explained anything to me. In fact, in my working life in the independent sector I've been assigned four or five work-experience people to train. It just sort of happens. Nobody shows you what to do.'

GB: 'Which company was this?'

'Zeno Productions, researching an education series for Channel 4. I welcomed the opportunity, went at it all out. The first contract was ten weeks, followed by another contract at the same company. But at the same time a series editor I'd been writing to, who edited *Europe Express* at Diverse, had been encouraging me. She went to another company and asked me to come, so that was the next project: *Hard News*. I was senior researcher, a quantum leap! That was followed . . . this could be a long journey, from '92 to '97 if I go contract by contract . . .'

GB: 'So you've had a lot of short contracts?'

'Oh yes: I've had four or five contracts a year, in lots of different independents, typically for two or three months each. Very fragmented. Often they'd try to keep the budgets low, so they'd hire you for eight weeks and then realise they couldn't deliver the documentary in eight weeks and say, "Could you stay on for a couple more?" All this time I'd be trying to find another job, always interviewing, sending my CV out, reading the trade press, developing ideas, trying to get lucky. I was also doing a lot on the side to supplement the salary. Then it was just lots of experience in different places. You have to adapt to each person's different methods, and being junior, you are always the person who is adjusting.'

GB: 'It's an unstable history you're painting, working for different people every few months . . .'

'Yes it is. Next I worked for Wall to Wall. I'd been writing to them for years because I was interested in lots of their output – *Vive La Différence*, *The Media Show*, *For Love or Money*. Eventually, I was taken on for a development contract of six weeks, and that show was commissioned at Cannes; and after that I was interviewed again internally. It was a big project, six programmes. I think that gave them a bit of faith that I could be trusted. You always have to prove yourself, with each different person, no matter how much experience you've acquired. That project finally went out on Channel 4. On that I was still a researcher and I developed it with the AP [*assistant producer*] from Jane Root's idea. After that I did another six-part Wall to Wall series for BBC2; I was hired as a researcher from May to November, and during that project I got stroppy and insisted on getting an AP credit or I'd leave. They said it couldn't be done, so I left. But they needed me, so I came back in January as an AP. That was how I won the AP credit, but I've had to make an issue of it ever since. It became a well-established pattern. From then on I was seen as difficult because I would stick to my position even if it meant being out of work.

'That was also my first encounter with the BBC, because that series was for BBC Manchester. So we had access to all the BBC resources and that made me hungry to work for the BBC. I suddenly saw the research libraries, the archives and resources you could draw on, everything opening up as a possibility. I began to realise how many doors were opened by the BBC name. Then a director I met at Wall to Wall was asked to do something by that BBC department again and he hired me, and that was my first internal BBC project. It was amazing. I was the AP for twelve weeks, working on a fifty-minute episode. A major breakthrough. We had about three weeks' preparation on location and we did all the research, and then flew back and did it again for real with the crew and presenter, and then had a week to wrap. In that project it was explicit that I was not required for the edit, which I accepted as I was delighted to be doing it. But then I thought: I'm never going to learn to direct if I can't get in on the edit. As a result, the first time I saw that programme was when it went out. In those conditions there's no personal development possible.'

GB: 'So you did the pre-production, the shoot, and you're working closely with the director. But once the shoot's over you're out. When it's this fragmentary, how can you develop?'

'It's hit-and-miss. And the pay issue is so tricky. I got quite uppity when I found all these boys were getting paid significantly more than me. So around that time I got quite tough negotiating. But I've been constantly amazed by the low pay people have offered. Then there'll be situations where you'll ask for something preposterous and they'll buy it. It's quite random.'

GB: 'Hasn't the BBC been more predictable than the independents? You now have an AP grade here, don't you?'

'But Georgie, I don't know what grade I'm on. I don't know if I'm well paid or not as a BBC AP. I have no idea of the internal structures. All I know is that I've negotiated a particular contract with my unit manager and that bears some resemblance to what I was being paid in the independent sector. But in fact I had to take a pay cut to work at the BBC, and their first offer was derisory. So I finished that project in mid '95 and had a horrible three months out of work; and everyone told me I'd been arrogant. I took that on board and was more humble pie-ish. But I don't think I've done myself any favours, because I'm now more or less where I was before, except I'm here free-lance in the BBC. I was recently offered, for example, a travelogue for Channel 4 by a well-respected independent. They wanted to pay me four weeks' pay, a £2,000 buyout, for six weeks' work, again with huge amounts of responsibility. Really poor money.'

GB: 'You're conveying being trapped in a rather masochistic position . . .'

'[*Laughs*] I actually think I have quite good self-esteem, but that's the irony. Last year, when I was determined to get into the BBC, I was really masochistic; over seven months I was interviewed twelve times: nine times by people in Documentaries and History, twice by BBC Bristol and once by BBC Manchester. And I was working all that time as well. I bashed my head against this wall regarding the BBC. I saw a lot of people and took a lot of rejections. I left quite a long period before I put myself forward for the BBC again, because after all that I just couldn't take it.'

GB: 'So why this massive draw to the BBC?'

'It's this idea of the resources and the support offered by the BBC, and the personal development that should be possible, because of the greater quality of your work. Given that there's a structure in place here, you're not so dependent, as you are in the independent scene, on friends getting commissions – and then, as happens quite a lot working for independents, they divert your salary into setting up an office or buying an extra computer!'

GB: 'Is there a wider view among your friends, who've worked for independents, that the BBC – whether in reality or fantasy – provides the basis for career development, so people want to come here?'

'Definitely, especially when people on all sides are saying, "Hold the children thing." I mean, it's absolutely inconceivable to think of having kids working in the independent sector. And that bugs me. I'm close to thirty now.'

GB: 'But what about the other big companies, Granada or . . .?'

'I've had no experience of those companies. I suppose there's LWT. But there's a quality issue: if you want to make programmes about money called *Dosh*, and about girls going topless in Ibiza . . . It's a different concept of programme-making. If you're interested in making things that are worthwhile, it's got to be the BBC. This is very subjective. Above all, there's the opportunity for more continuity here in the BBC; there's more going on, more career opportunities. Soon I'll have worked here – let's see – eight months, on three contracts: my longest ever stint anywhere, the most continuous! My longest in any one place with any one director.'

Assistant producer, BBC Documentaries, 1997.

*

Liberating freelance

'When I began in TV it was all staff, all unionised, and it was hard to get in. The minute Channel 4 and the independents started, you didn't have to be in the union. It liberated a lot of people for work in TV. I started off as a staff person at Channel 4; but the minute I could I went freelance, because I hated the idea of being in a job that told me when to have my holiday. And because the money was always very good, you could live for a few months while you were looking around for the next one. There are certain jobs you go into knowing you're going to be secure, and there are others you go into know-ing you're not. You don't go into advertising without knowing that you burn out pretty quickly; all the glamorous jobs are high risk. I do think employers owe people some sort of security because you can't work well if you're permanently insecure. Security helps you make the right decisions. But there's too much security. I mean, a two-year contract is wonderful; that's the longest I've ever had! That's just the sort of security I need to do this job.'

GB: 'Do you feel, then, that the recent news that Drama Group is letting go of a number of producers and script editors, or changing their contract basis, is justified?'

'Absolutely, it needed to happen years ago. We all carry people when – no fault of theirs – there isn't enough for them to do. If the marketplace says we need the rights to a book, and the rights are brought to us by an independent, then that's who we go to. I genuinely believe that you can't carry people, because in the end it's not good for them. They'll be passed over again and again, and how demoralising is that? They'd be better off doing something else. It's hard for me to be sympathetic, because you choose this job: as a producer you have to be hungry, to fight for your projects, to sell yourself.'

Executive producer, BBC Drama, 1996.

*

The Privatisation of Ideas

The exchange of ideas in employment is immensely sensitive to the conditions of work. In secure conditions of employment, ideas tend to be exchanged rel-atively freely: when a majority of workers are permanently employed in an organisation with a powerful sense of common purpose, it fosters a striving and solidary work culture, whatever the internal competition and division. By contrast, in situations of insecure employment workers are necessarily attuned to the need to seek the next job. Collaboration may be inhibited because of the temporary nature of the contact and the contract. The public qualities of the workplace are weakened. Ideas are effectively privatised; they become a currency by which future employment may be transacted. Intellectual property issues become pervasive in workplace politics; legalistic concerns can prevail over substantive creative ones.

During the nineties the BBC witnessed such changes. As freelance status became common among programme-makers, it became plain that they had little incentive to contribute ideas to the corporation. Ideas were their means of attracting another commission and thereby employment. Ideas were withheld. In parallel, the BBC became hawkish about its stake in the ownership of ideas. If a producer who had since left, or who had been made redundant, was on staff at the time of forming an idea, then, so the reasoning went, that idea was the property of the BBC and could legitimately be exploited.

The privatisation of ideas and consequent inhibition of creative exchange were grave developments in themselves. But they were also symptoms of a deeper malaise. The new employment patterns threatened to erode employees' identification with the BBC. Since the BBC offered no long-term commitment to the freelancer and little support in terms of training or employment benefits, so the freelancer felt no commitment to the corporation, imaginative or otherwise, beyond the current short contract. Casualisation caused dissociation and inhibited healthy dissent and the voicing of criticisms. It stoked a 'climate of fear'.[6] The BBC's capacity to generate in its employees a sense of collective identification with and loyalty to the public service ethos at its core was attenuated by the new contractualism. Opportunism and the new entrepreneurialism seeped in to fill the vacuum.

*

Necromancy: conjuring ideas[†]

A Drama Editorial Board: there is discussion of a show, *The Necromancer*, focused on the contractual status of its producer, Paula, who was made redundant in the latest wave of Drama redundancies two months ago. Now she's back involved in the show, and there's an urgent question: under her redundancy terms, can she be re-employed straight away? The manager from Drama Personnel is non-committal; she asks whether the ideas behind the project were developed while Paula was still on BBC staff. A couple of people assert that they were, so that it is legitimate to go ahead with

[†]Names and details have been changed.

developing the project here, with or without Paula. The BBC can claim rights in her ideas. Paula's employment situation is left unclear.

Diary, 1996.

*

Schedule D ideas

It's AOB, the end of a Drama Ed Board. Tim, an executive producer, raises a critical problem he's finding with gaining access to new ideas. Key producers are coming to him with good ideas, he says, but they are now freelance or coming to the end of their current BBC contracts. So they are being instructed by their agents not to share ideas, but to sell them on to the most interested party. Tim adds that the project-based contracts and development-based pay now being offered by the BBC are considered risible. At this rate the flow of ideas into Drama Group may simply dry up. It's a major problem, he finishes, arising from producers' changing contractual situation: what can be done? The challenge hangs in the room; no solution is offered.

Diary, 1996.

*

Insecurity: having babies, selling ideas

'When I was on rolling contracts, as far as I was concerned the BBC owned all my ideas. Then I realised that I was facing short contracts, and then I was down to three months. It became clear to me that if you're only on three months, and if the BBC doesn't want your idea, it's in your interests to try and sell it to other people. And actually I'd had a difficult time at the BBC: I'd been employed continuously for about ten years, mainly on rolling contracts. That's my defence, and that's why I'm happy to reveal the contradictions of my own position. So I sold a format to Carlton, which Rob Morris commissioned, and since I'd been on short-term contracts when it had been developed, I'd kept a right in the format. I then got a job in Drama Group with a three-year contract – my first ever. I went on to PAYE, rather late, and for the first time had pension rights and the kind of employment stability that's quite rare in our business.

'Then, in a meeting, I mentioned this format to Alan Yentob. He jumped at it, and it went right into production. Admittedly, the amount of money I got from it was small. But the point is I myself had rights in a project that I raised at a meeting. It wasn't right. It was a good project, and I could justify it till the cows come home. But I knew there was something wrong in my position, and probably the only proper resolution would have been not to take acceptance of my format rights. But then you think, if the show becomes a runner, and my contract is only for three years and then I may be out, you know . . . So it's complicated, and this kind of situation is happening again and again. It's one reason the BBC finds it hard to attract the best people to take in-house jobs, since they often face conflicts over outside interests in businesses or formats. But if people were made to think about it, they would probably trade those interests and rights in return for security of employment.'

GB: 'From what you say, only a shift away from short-term contracts would redress the problems you're identifying. In your own history, as long as you are insecure, that takes precedence and there is no ethical dilemma. You sold an idea at a certain time for completely understandable reasons, but then it kicks back when your status changes.'

'Yes, but at the same time I see my own personal morality bending as a result of the atmosphere. You're tempted to take taxis on the BBC for non-work things. You can always justify it in the way executives do: "My time is incredibly important, it's not worth my while waiting for a bus," and so on. But each time it happens I feel it very clearly as traducing the public service ethos, and it worries me, it preoccupies me.'

Producer, BBC Drama, 1996.

*

Skilling, Reskilling and Multiskilling

Given pressures to reduce budgets, one of the main solutions adopted by BBC management, along with the rest of the industry, was to encourage the adoption of new digital technologies in various stages of the production and editing processes. News was particularly subject to changing technologies. Not only filming, recording and editing, but the core news databases giving access to international press agencies and other information sources, as well as the internal databases used by each programme, were being upgraded and, it appeared, harmonised throughout the news operations. Across the production departments, digital technologies were seen as offering new opportunities as well as major cost reductions, primarily through the replacement of certain skilled jobs. In radio the studio manager's role was superseded as journalists were enabled to assemble and edit their own material. In television documentaries and some areas of drama, a spectrum of jobs in the filming process were rolled into new practices that could be accomplished by just one or two people using digital video equipment. The changes were not purely instrumental. Word spread rapidly in the mid nineties that the independents were using DV technologies to create an exciting new look, and at low cost. In drama and documentary the hand-held *vérité* look became fashionable again using DV camcorders. A range of cheap factual sub-genres sprouted on the basis of the new medium; and in drama the independent World Productions led the field, using Digi Betacam to film a sequence of hit series – *Cardiac Arrest, This Life* and *The Cops* – with a strong naturalistic feel.

The technological shifts required the remaining workforce to retrain in new skills. Concepts of reskilling and multiskilling became part of the every-day lexicon as programme-makers were encouraged to think that technology meant they must never stand still. The adoption of a bi-medial approach in news and other areas of production brought additional pressures, particularly for radio employees to remain in touch with technological changes in televi-sion. A generational divide opened up as younger employees, who had been initiated early into the new contract-based, bi-medial, multiskilled mores, took naturally to the digital environment, while some older workers found the need to adapt a skill too far. Those who did reskill faced greater intensity of work, covering what had previously been the work of two or three people. With union agreements torn up, their time was bought out wholesale by the week or month rather than regulated according to the former codes of work-ing day plus overtime.[7] The multiskilling entailed by digital technology threatened the loss of certain arts, such as those of the dedicated editor, and eroded the benefits wrought by the former marriage of particular skills in collaborative creative work. But the technology also brought gains: new ways of working as the former job boundaries melted and reformed, requir-ing new kinds of collaboration among smaller teams; new creative possibili-ties such as, in documentary, long-term filming of complex stories and greater intimacy with the films' subjects; and the opportunity for groups out-side the broadcasting organisations who had never made films for television to do so.

*

In the shadow of television: bi-media news

'There are bi-media News jobs being advertised at the moment. But there's a failure here in radio to help people adapt to flexibility: if you get to a certain level in radio and you haven't done television, it's very difficult to move across – and that's expected now. You can have someone who's been editing *The World At One*, who's highly experienced and bright, but they can't go and do an equivalent job in television. The danger is that you get too far up the radio ladder. Then, symbolically, we in radio are being moved from Broadcasting House to the new bi-media building at White City. Now, Broadcasting House has been the home of radio news since the BBC began. To go and live in the shadow of television, if you don't have television skills, is frightening. I'm lucky that I spent time in television before I came here, so I have basic TV skills.'

GB: 'Do people go the other way and routinely move from television to radio news? Is it asymmetrical, with TV people coming to radio considered to be skilled enough?'

'The technical skills as a radio producer are much easier. All you need is to be able to edit. But increasingly the distinction we have now – where in television you go into an editing suite and a VT editor will cut your piece with you – that will go as television moves to desktop editing. It's just starting to happen; twenty-four-hour news is pioneering it. Then your only worry will be, have you got all the skills for the different sets of technology that are being brought in.'

GB: 'But with the technology constantly changing, if you are multiskilled and bi-medial, are you going to have to keep on top of shifts on both sides, TV and radio? It's a tall order, isn't it?'

'Certainly, in the bi-media world, there's a shelf life for how much longer I can stay in radio without going back to television, because I need to keep my skills up to date there as well. The move we've made in radio into digital editing is the biggest shift in the time I've been working, as well as the loss of jobs it entailed. Most of the studio managers were made redundant as a result. Two were given the opportunity to retrain as journalists, and one applied for jobs as a journalist, but he doesn't want to take a pay cut to climb another ladder. But if he doesn't, he's out.'

GB: 'Doesn't the BBC owe the studio managers to keep them at the same salary, if it transfers such skilled people over to another job?'

'No, it doesn't think it does. And when programme budgets are being squeezed, if two people apply for a job and one has a different background and is more expensive to hire, you can see it's probably too risky to hire him. The decision to maintain salaries can only be made on an organisation-wide basis; but in the BBC now, you have no sense that anyone keeps an eye on your career development. In terms of where I was five years ago and where I'll be in five years' time, that's entirely driven by me, despite the fact that the BBC has invested a lot of money in me. So the motivation for lots of radio people going into twenty-four-hour news was to get in at the beginning of a reskilling process; they'd get access to TV skills which they would then be able to use elsewhere.'

GB: 'How does the new digital editing work? What are the benefits?'

'It saves money, both in removing the SMs and in studio time. Instead of recording interviews on reel-to-reel tape, editing them and handing them over to a studio manager, going in and reading my scripts and they would play it in, now I do the whole process myself. I go out and record on to a CD using a hand-held digital recorder; I come back and plug it in to my PC. You can select material from a CD, the radio, tape, whatever. You feed them into your digital editing system and work with the material. The advantages? As a reporter I find it satisfying knowing how I want a piece to sound and having the means to manipulate it myself. You've got the potential for four layers of sound, but it takes a while to get that degree of subtlety. What you lose is the SM's skill, because a good SM will say, "I don't think that works, I can't tell what that man's saying." They give another input, both on a technical level and in terms of making sense of things. A good SM is another ear, a listener. They can often interpret an idea into the final broadcast version better than the journalists. And now we've lost that input.'

Reporter, BBC radio news, 1997.

*

Working differently

GB: 'Has the digital video technology you're using in the CPU made production cheaper?'

'*Video Diaries* has used camcorder technology for six or seven years. Its team were by far the earliest users in the BBC. You work in a totally different way. With the old film crews, they had to work all the time because you were paying; it was like a taxi meter running. With DV there's no crew; the assistant producers are trained to use it. Originally, when DV was heralded as bringing fantastic cost savings, the notion was that one person would do everything: camera, sound, interview, come back to the office, stick it on their desktop and edit it. Well, that's a fiction. It's very hard for one person to do both camera and sound on anything other than an interview; and even then it's difficult to run the camera while getting a decent interview out of someone. It's two separate jobs. And on editing, it's not simple. The pioneering DV series in the arts area, *How Buildings Learn*, tried to do their own edit and gave up after a couple of months and got professional editors in. There was something about bringing in an independent eye at that stage to look at the material which is crucial for creativity and for making things accessible.'

GB: '. . . Let alone the timing, the craft skills and aesthetics skills, which an editor brings . . .'

'Absolutely. So yes, there are savings but they are not as magical as people believe. With

DV the tape's cheaper, the cameras are £1,000 not £30,000, you can crew it differently and editing's faster. But it completely knackers people, because at the end of the day, instead of going back to your miserable little bed and breakfast in Walsall and thinking "What are we filming tomorrow? Did we get the right shots? Have we still got parking?", which is what an assistant producer would normally do, now you've got to do all that and then you've got to do the log, check your tapes, number them up, colour-code them and make sure they're OK. It's two jobs. It's hard.'

Executive producer, BBC Community Programme Unit, 1997.

*

Including and Excluding

The BBC's culture of employment militated against creativity not only because of the anxieties and uncertainties stemming from casualisation and the new technologies. It continued to be weighed down by its historical social biases, and in particular by the corporation's inertial inability to respond to the late twentieth-century reality of Britain's multi-ethnic and minority populations. Recruitment into the BBC, career consolidation and pathways to promotion continued to be disproportionally captured by those from traditional elite and establishment backgrounds – the private schools and top-drawer universities – and this was accompanied by movement through typical networks of patronage and influence. Of course, any single biography might fail in some detail or other, through the marks of genuine individuality, to conform to the pattern. And there were variants, notably the lower-middle-class grammar-school girl or boy who made good – a feature of the nineties executive generation. But this is not to say that the pattern did not exist. While it is impossible to point to such tacit routes and networks in any but the most generalised terms, their reality is engraved in the experience of those excluded, those whom the system leaves with little doubt as to their being 'not an insider'. These people, if they got into the BBC, might well fight for a space, and they would frequently leave.

*

I'm middle class

'I'm middle class, public school-educated, did English at Oxford – typical BBC, although why I haven't made it into management yet I don't know! After Oxford I worked as a freelance journalist, and then started at the BBC with a six-week contract as a researcher on *Panorama*.'

Producer, BBC Current Affairs, 1997.

*

Archetypically BBC

'I'm a Londoner, went to a private girls' school and then to Oxford – archetypically BBC! I had several years on *Newsnight*, which at times was nightmarish. It put me off production for ever.'

Senior BBC manager, 1997.

*

Officer class

'I'm upper-middle class. My father's an ambassador. I was brought up as a diplomat's child at private schools, flying out most holidays to my parents in whichever location they happened to be in. I spent a long time between school and university travelling the world, trying to decide what I wanted to do; and then I went to university, to Edinburgh. But I spent most of my time doing student journalism. When I left Edinburgh I joined ITN on their graduate trainee scheme, and then I went to *Channel 4 News* as a producer and then as a programme editor. The overall editor was Richard Tait, a former editor of *Newsnight*. I left *Channel 4 News* about two years ago, joined the BBC and spent three months in the newsroom and then joined *Newsnight*. This time last year I was promoted to a programme editor on *Newsnight*, and two months ago I left and joined *Breakfast News*.'

Assistant editor, *Breakfast News*, 1997.

*

People connections

'My father's an academic. I went to a fee-paying school, and to Durham University; my grandparents funded a fee-paying education. I didn't think of being a journalist until I'd left university. I was a magazine journalist for a while, and then trained at the BBC on the broadcast journalists' scheme. Now I'm an acting assistant editor on *Newsnight*; I do the job but I've not been promoted yet. As part of the training I worked on *Panorama* for three months, then *The World Tonight* for three months. Then I got a job on *Panorama* as an assistant producer. It was on the cusp of Tim Gardam leaving; I was given my job by Mark Thompson when he became editor.'

GB: 'Right, the *Panorama* succession is Tim Gardam, Mark Thompson, Glenwyn Benson, then Steve Hewlett, isn't it? From *Panorama*, how did you get here?'

'The connections are almost always to do with people. I was an AP there for three years. Then I went to *On the Record* as a producer for two years. Peter Horrocks was the deputy editor of *Panorama* when I was first there and I got on well with him. The guy who took me on as a producer on *On the Record* was David Jordan, who'd replaced Peter as deputy editor of *Panorama*, with whom I also got on well. Then I got alarmed about what was happening to *On the Record*, and I was bored, anyway. I knew Peter was here at *Newsnight*, and I'd talked to him about whether I might move here. So I had a kind of level transfer to *Newsnight* from *On the Record*.'

Acting assistant editor, Newsnight, 1997.

*

Making good

'I was educated at grammar school in Sheffield, the last intake before it went compre-hensive. My parents came from the working class – their families worked in the steel-works – and they strove to better themselves and now live comfortably in a suburban semi in a leafy suburb. So my upbringing was lower-middle class, I suppose. I went to Nottingham University, but I didn't like it and spent a lot of time doing drama, and got a very poor degree, a third. My association with broadcasting happened because a guy in the year above me at university went to work at BBC Radio Nottingham and seemed to be having a good time. So, while my ambition was to be a theatre director, as a back-stop I wrote to Radio Nottingham and asked if they had any dogsbody work, and they offered me a contract for £3,000 a year to be a reporter, and I took the money! I've always liked radio; as a child I used to make my own tapes from the radio.'

Radio executive, BBC Broadcast, 1997.

*

Hell music

'My father came from a large rural mining family in Somerset, my mum was from a posh Victorian family from Gloucestershire. I went to a comprehensive school in Bristol,

199

technical college, then drama school to do a production course. Sport was my main thing as a child. My parents didn't have any money but we had real value systems, so we didn't have a TV and my father would play classical music all the time; we all had to listen to the Third Programme. It was a very austere upbringing, coal fires, like something from the nineteenth century, really. I used to go to bed early some nights to listen to *The World Tonight*; it was a way of accessing the world, like the Internet now for kids. I loved Radio 4, but when I was a teenager I had pop music very badly as well – or "hell music", as my father would call it.'

GB: '"Very badly", I like that. So your father really threw you into it.'

'Yes, the fact that, really, he didn't understand. I listened to Radio Luxembourg, Radio I and Radio 4; the Third Programme was imposed on me. I used to listen to *Newsbeat* at lunchtime, and envisage myself working there; and when I listened on Sunday nights to features on Radio 4, I wanted to make those sorts of sounds, I imagined myself going out and talking to people. I was completely smitten by radio. So I became a Radio 4 producer, and now I run much of Radio I.'

Senior executive, BBC Radio I, 1997.

*

ZAPU, GMG, and exclusion

'In 1976, during the summer of punk, I was sitting with about a dozen other people in the dingy basement of a building in Great Portland Street directly across the road from Broadcasting House. The room was furnished with audio equipment which even then was beginning to look quaint . . . We had been invited to take part in something which had the characteristics of a parlour game. We were given various sheets which consisted of twenty questions. On one sheet there was a list of initials: UNESCO, ZAPU, SOGAT. On another, a list of people currently in the news around the world: Isabel Péron, Hafiz al Assad, Kakuei Tanaka. Our job was to identify the newsmakers, spell out the initials, et cetera, et cetera. But the stakes of this particular parlour game were high – a place on the BBC's coveted news trainee course, one of only twelve on offer each year.

'In the afternoon we were taken to another part of the building where at an oval table sat an intimidating panel of five besuited men who grilled each of us for about half an hour on our views of the BBC and the politics and culture of Britain generally. In my case they were particularly keen to hear my views about *Bad News*, the controversial study from the University of Glasgow Media Group, which had been published the previous year accusing the news organisations of systematic bias against working people and trade unions in their news bulletins.

'I didn't get a place. To this day, I don't know if they failed me because of my sympathy for the radical critique of television news or because I didn't know what ZAPU stood for. I wanted desperately to work in television, and more than anything else I wanted to work for the BBC.'

Alex Graham, chief executive of Wall to Wall Television, 1993.

*

The BBC is keen to present itself as a purveyor of best practice in employment. One form taken by this concern in the nineties was the corporation's apparently strong commitment to policies promoting equal opportunities. The BBC adopted an equal opportunities employment policy in 1983 and set itself achievement targets in 1990. In the early nineties the Equal Opportunities department was proactive, well funded and independent, with the direct backing of top management. Under a dynamic leader, several minority training schemes were instigated including a black journalists' scheme, a Television Training Trust scheme and trainings in post-production and editing. The Television directorate set up a Directorate Implementation Group (DIG) for equal opportunities, a unit with a director, a research budget, bimonthly meetings attended by some department heads and a quarterly internal magazine.

Michael Jackson, when controller of BBC2, became chair of the DIG, raising its profile. Jackson spoke of the need for strategy and goals, and for an action plan. In meetings, there was a clear understanding that overturning biases in employment was intimately linked to achieving greater cultural diversity in the BBC's output and to changing the representation of minorities on screen. Under Jackson's leadership, sophisticated academic research was commissioned in 1995 both about the representation of ethnic and other minorities on screen, and about the responses of different minority audiences to those representations. Initiatives were taken such as the appointment of an executive producer for African–Caribbean programmes dedicated to creating a 'university of black talent' within the BBC to achieve 'high quality black programmes made by high quality black programme-makers'.[8] Jackson commissioned strands like Black Britain and experimented with black zones on BBC2 like the A Force, a themed evening of black entertainment shows made by BBC Manchester's African–Caribbean Programme Unit.

But following this dynamic period, in the later nineties the budgets were rolled back and optimism declined. The Equal Opportunities unit was brought within the Personnel department and became an outcrop of management. Training could be targeted, but jobs could not be. The corporate focus became narrowly legalistic, to avoid prosecution for flouting equal opportunities leg-islation, as opposed to the former concern with positively furthering equality. Meanwhile, casualisation and the fragmentation of career trajectories had the paradoxical effects of opening up the BBC to a more diverse workforce while at the same time worsening the conditions for those employed. The most remarkable result of the equal opportunities initiatives was a transformation over the decade of women's position within the BBC, with a steady rise in the proportion of women in senior and middle management.[9] But in relation to ethnic minorities and to disabled people, it was plain in the late nineties that the battle against biases both in employment and in the output was not being won. Quotas for ethnic minority employment were generally being met. The BBC could claim in 1999 that 8.1 per cent of the workforce were ethnic minorities, exceeding its own 8 per cent target.[10] Yet for all the appearance, the corporation had not become more inclusive and representative of ethnic minorities, and in private people at all levels freely admitted this. The mono-culture of the BBC tacitly but strenuously resisted change.

*

Not brown-nosing

'I'm a freelance producer and a part-time consultant and lecturer. My father is a jour-nalist and my mother was a teacher. I consider myself mixed race, African and English. I went to further education college and then became a trainee journalist on a local news-paper, then went to local radio on *Black Londoners*, and then went into television doing *Black on Black* for two years with LWT for Channel 4. After that I went to Granada and worked on *Union World* for two years. Then I went to the BBC on *Ebony* at Pebble Mill as a director and producer, and then I went on the BBC directors' course at Elstree before joining *Newsnight* as an assistant producer. I had two and a half years at *Newsnight*. I then left and became a sort of independent, doing a drama-doc for ITV, as well as some docs. After that I decided to go into lecturing. So I was in the BBC for three and a half years. At *Newsnight* I was allowed to produce films, but I was never made a producer. It was unheard of for APs to do that and not be promoted to a producer. I produced investigative news stories and I had different contact lists, not just MPs: trade unions from my time at *Union World*, ethnic minorities from *Black on Black* and *Ebony*. I had a more critical approach to journalism. I'd never just do a story that was already in the press, so a lot of the stories I did ended up in the *Guardian* or wherever, I suppose because they were reasonably original.'

GB: 'What do you think blocked your promotion at *Newsnight*?'

'I think mainly because I wasn't an insider; there were three or four of us who weren't insiders, politically or in terms of class background. I hadn't been to university, certainly not to Cambridge or Oxford where most of them had been. I was not white; I was not southern middle-class. There were others: a guy from Burnley, another who was lower-middle class and hadn't been to university. It was quite public school. I remember making a decision early on that I wasn't going to brown-nose. There were those who arrived and immediately they were brown-nosing, desperately having lunch with the editors. People arrived who had a leg up, from top families, who were obviously looked upon with favour. As a mixed-race person, race has always been central for me, and of course I rode on the racial bandwagon to some extent post-riots. I've always been interested in those issues. But I've also been very wary and didn't want to be ghettoised by staying on "black" programmes. When you talk to black journalists, despite the equal ops clause at the BBC, the vast majority are still in black programming. Lots are in local radio, but once they grow up, they don't end up in the mainstream in senior positions. With the odd exception – the Trevor McDonalds – they end up in senior positions in black programmes. There are always the exceptions.'

Former assistant producer, Newsnight, 1997.

*

Blocked: cutting the umbilical cord

'My parents came from the Caribbean in the late fifties. My father worked in tailoring, and my mother works for the health authority. I went to the local comprehensive. I loved school. After that I did part-time college and at the same time joined the BBC as a secretary. If you were black at that time, you'd go to university and come out not quite sure who you were. So I did my honours degree gradually, in applied sciences. I wanted to make documentaries on what was happening in the sciences and technology.'

GB: 'Did you join the BBC as a secretary in order to try and move into production?'

'That was the only reason I joined the BBC. It took me an awful long time to move, because at the time the BBC was a really closed shop: extremely backward, extremely sexist, extremely racist. I was put in engineering and it took me four and a half years to get into radio. It was really, really difficult; people would find all kinds of excuses. But you knew what the reason was. I persevered and fortunately went for an interview at Radio

London, where I became a production secretary on a magazine show. That's how I managed to get into production. The producers allowed me to go out with the reporters and make programmes, do reports, write bits of script, edit. However the station manager, who was a very open man, didn't want anybody employed as a secretary to move on up the station. So then I moved into TV, as a production assistant in the Education department. Education became my core department for fourteen years, but I went off and did other attachments. Eventually I came to Drama, two years ago, on attachment as a script editor. The first year I was still on staff; then I took a contract. Prior to coming here I had been planning to leave the BBC; the opportunity came up to take voluntary redundancy and I decided to go for it. But then the Drama opening came up, so I took it part-time and freelance.'

GB: 'Why did you want to leave the BBC after, what, fifteen years?'

'I wanted to leave a long time before because I'm a trained studio director, a trained film director, a producer, I'm very good at getting projects off the ground, and my skills were being underutilised. They weren't appreciated in my department and I'd had enough. It was such a negative place; budgets were constantly being cut, and they were cutting the wrong people. The lazy people on fat salaries were staying, people who knew nothing about the outside world, and it was reflected in the programmes.'

GB: 'What happened to your contract status when you took the Drama attachment?'

'That's touchy. When I first came to Drama, I was getting the same salary. But last year when I took the script editor job on contract, Personnel said I must take what the other script editors earn, which was quite low. So I took both a freelance contract and a drop in pay. Maybe I was naive. But I wanted to be on contract, to divorce myself from the place, to cut the umbilical cord.'

GB: 'Why did you come to Drama? You said you wanted to make documentaries?'

'Long-term, I wanted to produce feature films, so coming here was linked to that ambition. Drama is very different, I had a lot to learn: working with writers, scripts, a different medium. I'd done some drama outside, as well. For ten years, between 1983 and 1993, as well as working in the BBC I was part of a group called Ceddo, a film and video workshop.'

GB: 'I know about Ceddo. I was at the Edinburgh TV Festival when they had the screening and debate about the Ceddo film that got dropped by Channel 4, *The People's Account.*'

'Well, I was a founder member of Ceddo. It was based in north London. Outside the BBC that was always my work, my interest. I'd leave the BBC after work and go straight down and spend my evenings there. So with Ceddo, I'd always been involved in film.'

GB: 'At Edinburgh, Channel 4 didn't really have a good account of why they didn't screen the Ceddo film. It sparked a fascinating debate about production values – I'm sure you know: the production values were not what Channel 4 expected; and the people from Ceddo were eloquently stating the case that the cloak of production values can actually be a way of talking about content, and the fact that it was an uncompromising piece of film, a powerful statement.'

'It was. It was about the Broadwater Farm riots, if you remember. At the time of that film, the establishment view had been given. The Ceddo film had the people from Broadwater Farm commenting on their situation, the non-establishment view. The riot was about those people deciding enough was enough, and they took to the streets. Channel 4 expected a nice cosy "debate" in the film, and it didn't get that. Yes, the production values weren't brilliant, but how could they be? Some of it was shot in the middle of the riot. And then we went back the next day on location talking to people. It was real, that's what was actually happening.'

GB: 'Wasn't Ceddo part of the wider group of black workshops working for Channel 4?'

'Yes, we all knew each other. Ceddo was the one that operated most as a workshop, allowing people in. Black Audio fulfilled the training remit later on. Sankofa was really like an independent company; those people have gone on to have individual careers – Isaac Julien's a big director now. Ceddo had a lovely place, half the floor of an old school building in Tottenham. We had two 16mm editing suites, a low-band pneumatic suite plus VHS area, offices, a big hall; we showed Spike Lee's first hit, *She's Gotta Have It*, to a crowd of about three hundred people.'

GB: 'In the next generation is Britain going to see, like in the States, some big names making it in black television and black film? Is it gathering pace here?'

'I hope it's gathering pace or, you know, Georgie, what are we doing here? We're the first generation to have come through TV and the media. It's not going to happen with us, but inevitably it will come. We've paved the way; look at the rising numbers of black people studying at college. And with the new technology there's a rolling ball that can't be stopped. Anyone can go out with a Hi 8 camera and shoot something over the weekend. It's distribution where the shutters come down. But I've had to fight for every opportunity at the BBC. It's fine if you're white, male and middle class, from Oxford or Cambridge. As a black woman it's a different story. I was directing for three years before they allowed me to go on a proper course. I *fought* to direct, through the union. I had a case up against the head of department. What used to happen was, although you could direct, they didn't give you the job title or the money until you'd been on a training course. The head used to allow me to do the work, but wouldn't let me do the training, so I couldn't get the money – until we threatened to take him to court. We all knew what the real reason was, but until you confront somebody it carries on – keeping certain people down. One of the reasons I was with Ceddo was that while all this was going on, I could go outside and make films anyway. I could say, "Don't tell me I can't do this, because here is the evidence." The producers I worked with here were very supportive. At that time I was the only black person working at that level, a staff assistant producer, in the department; the only other black people were a production assistant and one or two clerical people.'

GB: 'I've seen leaflets lying around for the black and Asian caucus; is there now a move to have a specifically black representation within the BBC?'

'Yes there is, and there are more black people around the last three or four years, so you can actually do that. I think people get involved for two reasons. Some find they can use the Black Workers' Group to their advantage in terms of getting noticed and career building. Others are just normal people who do a job and find, like I did, that they're being held back. A lot of black people here find themselves on shorter contracts than their white counterparts. They're not sure whether that's normal or whether they're being paid right; they need to share information. So it's used as a support network. The equal ops scene has also become big in the BBC. I think it's a sincere exercise. The previous head, an Asian guy, managed to court the different heads of department without threatening them. There's a wind of change. But I'm leaving.'

Script editor, BBC Drama, 1996.

*

A very nervy organisation

'From the late eighties there was a Black Workers' Group set up by black staff who wanted to share problems and strategies for dealing with them. One issue was that in the last few years it was the Afro-Caribbean members of the Black Workers' Group that had some influence on programming strategy with Michael Jackson; the Asian members had less of a voice. There's always that tension. It's the age-old problem with race relations: you want to drive equality issues forward together, but there are also special cultural concerns you want to see happening in relation to particular communities, and sometimes you resent being put in the same bag. And that's valid; we're different. Michael's idea with this input was that you needed to move away from "problem-centred" black programming and have a whole variety of black inputs into different genres – entertainment, drama, whatever. I think his idea was that he could grow a black entertainment talent base like the Americans did. That's why he focused on the Afro-Caribbean community – he saw it as being similar in some ways to the American black community, and therefore you could develop innovative entertainment as Cosby and others have done in the US, with *The Fresh Prince of Bel Air* and so on.'

GB: 'Has the equal ops policy been successful now, at least on the employment front?'

'There have been a variety of problems. A year ago, at the end of Sarinda Sharma's reign at Equal Ops, the targets that had been set had been exceeded for ethnic minorities and women, but not for disabled people, and not necessarily at every level. But then the budgets were cut, you know: "You've reached the targets; surely we don't need these expensive initiatives any more." Whenever targeted adverts were run there were complaints from the Freedom Association, various Conservative MPs and so on. They would write in to say, "Why is the BBC favouring black people? Isn't this racism in reverse?" The BBC is very sensitive to this sort of campaign. A couple of years ago Sarinda noticed that black people were getting to assistant producer level but they weren't moving up to producer level; so he tried to arrange a trainee producer attachment for one of the assistant producers in TV. There was a legal challenge to it by the Freedom Association. Herman Ousley had just been imposed as head of the CRE [*Commission for Racial Equality*], and to show how fair he was he made this case a *cause célèbre* and said he wasn't going to let the BBC flout the law, whatever the good intentions. It was a real political botch-up around a genuine attempt to break the glass ceiling and get black people into senior levels that were still eluding them. That incident tainted other efforts because management got nervous.'

GB: 'What's shocking is that something like that can scare the BBC so much.'

'The BBC is a very nervy organisation, as you've probably found. It's particularly wary of public lobbies with a certain establishment profile. Out in society there's a concerted campaign saying positive action of any kind is unfair, think tanks like the Centre for Policy Studies, figures like Roger Scruton and Melanie Phillips. Anything to do with equality is politically correct and should be shunned. In response, the clubbishness that was such a problem in the BBC is now reasserting itself with a vengeance. The BBC tradition of the old boy network has become the culture of the whizz-kid, equally elitist and exclusionary. The clubbishness is about having certain favoured skills; when you write a report, for instance, do you write it in landscape with bullet points as Birt and the management consultants prefer, or do you write something worth reading in portrait? It's about recruiting people with a similar culture, in your own image. A lot of work has been done on this aspect of corporate cultures in the equal ops field, the way people are comfortable with others who lock into the same references without long-winded explanations, cultural references that are really about their own ethnicity and gender.'

Senior black BBC employee, 1997.

*

Race, class and the BBC

I'm standing by the lifts in an entrance hall in Television Centre. A large, burly, clean-cut white man, a buildings manager I guess, is gripping the arm of a thin black man, a cleaner I presume, speaking to him as though he were a child or stupid: 'See that? There! Na, there! *That* one – it needs cleaning. *Today!* It's not good enough, is it? *Is it?'* I take the lift to the sixth floor, the executive level. I walk around the circular corridor seeking my next interview. Black women and men caterers are in a special sixth-floor kitchen, preparing delicacies for some executive event. As a rule backstage is black at the BBC; front of stage is white. Routine harassment, routine racial hierarchy: at last McPherson has created a name for it.

Diary, 2000.

*

Everybody's doing diversity

'My experience in this country has given me a deep understanding of racism and its impact. I arrived here in 1958 at the age of eight, and understood for the first time that I was black and that there was something not OK about being black in Britain. McPherson of Cluny put his finger on the malaise of British society with his definition of institutional racism.[11] The main response to McPherson has been to bring on a euphemistic word called "diversity". Everybody's doing diversity. Don't get me wrong, I'm not against diversity; it's about synergy, creativity; it contains all the possibilities of a new society in Britain and in Europe. [But] the word diversity has been hijacked by many institutions to avoid the issue of equality of opportunity; most organisations have fudged the issue by jumping over equal opportunity in pursuit of diversity. Those in power curtail the opportunities for others to find a place, to make a contribution, to feel valued. But the organisation that allows that culture to persist is stunted. My question to the BBC is, how long do you have to listen before you take action? As a black consumer and licence fee payer, I will not comment on your service delivery in terms of under-representation and stereotyping. All I will say, Sir Christopher, is: I think I'd like a rebate.'

Beverley Barnard, 2000.

*

Uncertainty and Creativity

Creative nuclei: the wellspring of ideas

'Television devours ideas which stem either from individuals or from teams which have worked together over a long period, whose members spark ideas from each other. The nature of teamwork is immensely important, not only in the sense that it is a team – writer, director, designer, cameraman, sound engineer, lighting engineer and others – that finally puts the programme on the air, but in the sense that the television organisations consist of creative nuclei from which ideas spring by contact, argument, collaboration.'

Stuart Hood, 1970.

*

Exile

Mandy, a former BBC drama producer who left to go independent, tells of a generational shift in identification with the BBC. Her generation of producers, those under 40 in the nineties, were on the cusp: they began with a strong identification with the BBC ethos, but over the nineties it was dismantled. They were given no secure, sustained relationship with the organisation; having had rolling contracts, she was asked to go freelance. 'It's an industrial structure of employment, not collegial. There is no reciprocity between the BBC and oneself'. For her and others Drama Group had been 'a very fluid web of power relations. We were all anthropologists, Georgie, all outsiders trying to understand the place. The proof that you had read the organisation well was if you landed a huge commission.' In her view it is those producers who most embodied the public service ethos in Drama who have left. 'No one will go near the place. There's a complete absence of creative autonomy. Can it be rebuilt? I'm pessimistic.' The philosophy binding the BBC, she says, can have no intrinsic meaning for those with a tenuous relation to the corporation; it is held 'in brackets'. The public service ethos belonged properly to an older generation, for whom its meaning was bound up with solid employment and long-term identification. She recalls meeting an ex-controller who left under Birt, who asked with feeling, 'like an exile, "How *is* it at the BBC now?"'

Diary, 2002.

*

What is the BBC? The loss of common memory

'There's no database of past documentaries any more that I know of; there was one in radio, with probably twenty years of documentary output on it, but it isn't being kept up. So if you want to know about what was made in the past, it's the memory of the older producers or nobody really knows. That raises important questions, like: what is the corporation, what is the BBC, if you lose that common memory, because you have a staff that is temporary? What remains of the institution? If we're all operating like little independent companies, or commissioners, then why do we bother to sit in one place in White City? We used to talk about the learning and training, the atmosphere and the commonality of the whole project. But all these young film-makers coming in here in their twenties, their memory probably starts with *Modern Times*. They may not even register the existence of *40 Minutes*, let alone any earlier documentarists. The fact of there being any history or thought about the medium doesn't exist for them; they're not educated and have little to draw on creatively. So what is the end result of this? It's short-termism. There's the personal thing about the end of career development, but there's also the corporate thing – what does it mean? What is at the heart of the BBC?'

Executive producer, BBC Documentaries, 1997.

*

If the new working environment in television was a predictable corollary of intensified competition and marketisation, this does not imply that it was either well considered or inevitable. In the BBC, downsizing could have been achieved without recourse to the much increased use of freelancing. Greater thought might have been given to the likely negative results of casualisation in terms of eroding the webs of loyalty, trust, mutuality and commonality spun both between creative workers and between them and the corporation. And the erosion of ethical identification, or at least a greater ambivalence, among creative staff could surely have been foreseen as a natural consequence of the BBC's declining commitment to those employees. But in the mechanical thinking of management under the one-dimensional sign of flexibility, such obvious forms of damage were not perceived or were not given due seriousness. Under Birt, the BBC was guilty of ignoring just those factors that historically favoured the BBC as a locus of creativity.

Recent research offers a wider snapshot of the impact of the new working environment in the television industry, focused on the unprecedented uncertainties and risks faced by programme makers, risks that have been passed on by the large organisations. If it needs detailing, uncertainty in employment is greatly disliked. It is a major cause of stress. Women face freelance status more than men, and find it more stressful. Because of uncertainty, workers are impelled to diversify their sources of income; a significant proportion consider leaving the television profession, particularly experienced workers. They are likely to be replaced by young, less experienced employees new to the industry, who are happy to work almost unpaid at least in the early stages. Not only is this likely to be detrimental to the quality of output, but it favours wealthier entrants and decreases the meritocratic and democratic characteristics of the profession, curtailing both social diversity and the invention that such diversity brings. The existence of trust and of collaboration between talented individuals, the freedom to take risks and make mistakes are seen as crucial elements in fostering creativity. Competitiveness is seen as an irrelevance. But a third of freelancers believe that short contracts make them cautious about bringing new ideas to their work, and as well as shrinking budgets, short contracts are seen as the major cause of a reduction in the quality of television programmes.[12]

These conditions, rampant across the profession in the nineties, were plainly contrary to both the public and the professional interest. In the BBC, however, the centrifugal ejection of creative professionals from the corporation's core was matched by an equally controversial development, one that further compounded the erosion of trust: the insinuation of the new managerial cadres.

New Model Managerialism

The culture of integration

'Programme planning in the sixties was a small group of people, about eight or nine of us, who in good old BBC bureaucratic and civil service tradition were a "secretariat", but had all been programme-makers before. It was a great BBC boast in those days that the people who were scheduling the programmes, running the channels and controlling finances and resources were all people who'd made programmes. By definition and by instinct they knew the problems involved; so there was a culture of integration.'

Former BBC producer, 1997.

*

Pitching the pitch: Drama Group's own consultant

I've been inside Drama Group a few weeks, and I learn that a resident management consultant appointed by Charles Denton is to hold a closed session with the drama department heads. The aim, it is rumoured, is to teach them how to pitch ideas in commissioning meetings – an increasingly critical skill in the marketised BBC. The plan is met with reluctance and cynicism from several drama heads, who refuse, but are required to attend. While Charles has said that I have complete access to Drama Group, he says I can't attend; this meeting will be too sensitive.

Some days later the management consultant phones me. He has heard about my work and is enthusiastic to know more. Can we meet and swap notes on our analyses of the organisation? Surely an anthropologist is doing something very similar to what a consultant does?

Diary, 1996.

*

Enough of this madness: the ludicrous crucible

'You see it all the time; you keep coming upon it in editorial boards where the frustration with the BBC and its initiatives and strategies and visions is so huge. Duke Hussey rang me last night to say he was sorry I was leaving, and could I tell him why? And I said one of the major reasons is that I'm fed up to the back teeth with the constant streams of strategies and initiatives and restructurings and performance reviews which come out of Corporate Centre and are imposed downwards from it in a centralist way. [*Impersonating Marmaduke Hussey:*] "Yes I quite agree, so am I." I thought, "Christ, Duke, you are the chairman, and if you feel that then why does it keep happening?" It feels regularly like we are living in a ludicrous crucible of management theory here, as kind of specimens. It shouldn't be half my job to keep my own department safe from these initiatives, yet it appears to be. If Network TV resisted as a whole, we might be able to defeat the BBC's worst corporatist tendencies. We should say, "Enough of this madness. If we get it wrong change it. If we're getting it right leave us alone." Why on earth would anybody do otherwise than trust the people they'd employed in a senior job to get on and do that job?'

Senior production executive, soon to leave the BBC, 1996.

*

New Public Management Ad Infinitum

The BBC had for decades been perceived as highly bureaucratic. But during the nineties the nature of the bureaucracy changed through the introduction of new kinds of professional management, bringing with them new values. Producer Choice, the independent quota and the volatile employment market together necessitated a rapid increase in management to oversee them; and the fracturing of the BBC's ethos consequent on these changes stoked further the need to monitor the performance of individuals and departments. Tiers of financial, legal, personnel and administrative apparatuses grew to handle the new operations. Moreover, in response to the expanding channel portfolio and burgeoning concern with marketing, the mid nineties also saw the growth in many parts of the BBC of management focused on strategy, planning, market analysis and market research. In each area management consultancy played a leading part; consultants arrogated to themselves the role of the BBC's elite intellectual vanguard. Senior executives began to rely on management consultancy both internally, as a number of consultants were hired on staff, and in terms of near permanent contractual arrangements with external consultancies such as McKinsey.

Two further developments fuelled senior executives' voracious appetite for new modes of management. Mindful of past political difficulties, there grew inside the corporation a formidable machinery concerned with managing the BBC's relations with the political class and the various levels of government with which it had to interact. In the era of increasing management of political public relations, the BBC had also to be remade in this mould. But another development had greater repercussions for those working in the BBC. This was the now-global concern with implementing processes of accountability, part of a general shift in government away from central state controls to indirect controls exercised through a variety of regulatory and self-regulatory means. From the late eighties government demands for accountability had become a central plank of public sector reform, and auditing a core means of delivering it. The idea of auditing leaked from its origins in financial management to become a term subsuming a range of monitoring and assessment practices, or 'rituals of verification' as Michael Power terms them. There followed an 'audit explosion' as such practices became common in public and private organisations.[1] The new public management, of which Birt's BBC came to be exemplary, borrowed the conceptual framework of business administration. Notions of cost control, financial transparency, performance measurement and value for money coalesced into a 'vague normative space'. Citizens were recast as consumers empowered to demand that public services achieve certain standards and operate economically, efficiently and effectively: the 'three Es'. Auditing was the instrument for checking that such requirements were actually met.[2]

In Britain, one form taken by this development was the Major government's 'Citizen's Charter' initiative and its particular conception of public sector accountability. The 1994 White Paper *The Future of the BBC*, the culmination of the debates leading into the 1996 Charter renewal, made the influence explicit: 'The BBC should operate its public services according to the principles of the Citizen's Charter. It should make clear the standards to which it will aspire in a new statement of promises to its audiences.'[3] The exhortation stood in for any more strenuous intervention, and the specified instrument for delivering accountability was a relatively trivial one. Notably, the White Paper ignored the central problem of accountability that had been identified in the debates: the BBC's governance arrangements. Birt, however, reacted in a characteristic manner by doing not only what was necessary but much more. Over the nineties he responded to the larger spirit of the new public management by implementing a host of managerial reforms centred on accountability and auditing. The BBC grew evangelical concerning the new managerialism. It sent top executives on training courses at the elite American business schools. In 1993, it began a dedicated MBA for BBC managers run by the University of Bradford's Management Centre. It poured money into the new systems for saving money. The rising expenditure on management at the same time as closures and cuts in production and resource departments resulted in new depths of cynicism and anger among employees. The scale of resentment was proportional to the scale of managerial excess. In the Birt years, spending on Corporate Centre approached £90 million a year, a figure that excludes the additional planning, strategy and accountancy functions that grew in each directorate.[4]

While Birt's managerial initiatives augured a new focus on productivity and accountability, they had corrosive effects on the culture of the BBC, stoking hierarchy and division. As production departments were stripped down and resource units privatised, the experience of many staff was that the executive esteemed consultants' expertise more than the skills both of existing managers and of journalists, programme-makers and technicians. As strategy and accounting departments proliferated around the BBC, it stoked general indignation at what was perceived to be a wasteful duplication of unproductive and non-essential functions. For critics, the proof was the bloated 24 per cent of annual income devoted to running the BBC as opposed to services and content.[5] This suggested that the Birtist infatuation with management trends had become an end in itself and that the BBC had become subject to almost uncontrolled managerial growth. The erosion of trusting cooperation, the profligate duplication of functions, the imposition of a mechanical and aggressive managerial discipline: these were the complaints of programme-makers by the mid nineties.

*

Where does the trust lie?

'The question is fundamentally: where does the trust lie? It's to do with whether the people in Drama Group are trusted, with their specialist knowledge, to advise the generalists and make decisions. At the moment initiatives come down from the controllers' offices and they haven't been thought through. They don't trust us to manage our own affairs; we simply can't plan what we're doing. There are too many people built into the decision process. It was easier when there wasn't a huge edifice – finance, planning and so on – over there in Network Television, because now the edifice is moving into action. So on the one hand you've got the drama specialists, and on the other you've got a second layer, the kitchen cabinet.'

GB: 'When you say "kitchen cabinet", isn't it the case that the DG has set up a policy and planning unit around him, a supervisory body over the different directorates?'

'Oh, if you go back to the DG you've got a bigger problem because [sketching a diagram] you've got the Board of Management level, which includes Policy and Planning, and the director of Finance and IT, Rodney Baker Bates, who's got a huge edifice of corporate finance people with analysts and strategists and God knows what. So you've got strategists and analysts there [pointing to Policy and Planning], and you've got strategists and analysts there [pointing to Finance and IT]. Then when you come into Network Television, the channel controllers are supported by this huge planning and scheduling outfit – the David Docherty empire – which has finance, planning, strategy, and various other bits. And then you've got Drama Group, which again has oceans of people analysing and cost-controlling.'

GB: 'So there seems to be three levels of duplication – inside Corporate Centre, Network Television and Drama Group?'

'Well, yes. And as far as the finance and planning people are concerned, we in drama are second best. They're crawling over budgets with everybody else – with cost controllers, chief assistants, executive producers, producers and production staff. No one can actually tell you what the budget ought to be, but the world is analysing and controlling things! There are more and more people telling David and the channel controllers what they should pay; but they are also making judgements – which they are probably least able to make. What on earth have you got all these people for?'

Senior manager, BBC Drama Group, 1996.

*

Corpulent corporate: planning and strategy ad infinitum

GB: [I am poring over a corporate diagram, trying to make sense of the complex highest levels of management] 'The Corporate Strategy Unit: who's that? Are you with that?'

[Patiently, as if to an idiot:] 'No, I'm part of the Corporate Affairs directorate which is largely . . . well, in most places it would be called Corporate Communications; it's concerned with politicians, media, marketing, and so on. There is a directorate of Policy and Planning which deals with regulatory and policy issues, corporate strategy, engineering policy, editorial policy and so on, and that's headed by Patricia Hodgson. But the key person in corporate strategy is Robin Foster, who joined the BBC about the same time as I did. He was at NERA before, the economic research consultancy. And he's . . . well, I think the title is controller of corporate strategy. Colin Browne – with an "e" – is my boss, director of Corporate Affairs. He was at British Telecom until he joined here two years ago.'

GB: 'And then there's planning and strategy . . . but David Docherty is only strategy for Network TV, right? His role is . . . er, can you give me a sense of what his brief is?'

'Yes, well, to be honest I'm not entirely . . . I mean, David's looking at planning programmes on air; he's looking at scheduling, at how the audience thinks about programmes, what the need of the schedule is, creating a balanced schedule, those kinds of issues. Look, the key thing we've tried to do is build up that planning and strategy expertise within each of the directorates, so they will become less reliant on consultants and the BBC is more able to do it internally.'

GB: 'Right, so Radio has planning and strategy, News and Current Affairs has something . . .'

'. . . Absolutely, and Regions has something, and Worldwide does, and Education does and so on. Listen, [*looking ostentatiously at his watch*] I think my next meeting is about to begin. . .'

Executive, BBC Corporate Affairs, 1996.

*

Consultants

'Consultants: they borrow your watch to tell you the time. It's in their interests to paint as bleak a picture as possible. The more complex they find it, the longer they can be in, the higher their fees. When they come in they know nothing; they have to get all that information. If an insider proposes a solution nobody listens. But when it comes with the weight of McKinsey or Coopers & Lybrand, and the BBC has paid tens of thousands for it, it carries almost unnatural weight.'

BBC television finance manager, 1997.

*

Consultancy: Dependence and Prestige

Despite the myriad forms taken by the new management, it was the expanding but shadowy use of management consultancy that most drew the fire of critics.

Consultants became the locus of a negative mythology, one fuelled by Birt's reticence in the early nineties about making public their cost. When in 1994 he revealed that £6 million had been spent on consultancies in the previous eight months, adding that it was not otherwise possible to estimate how much had been spent on them in recent years, the paradoxical character of the new management was confirmed.[6] Consultants, proselytisers for merciless financial scrutiny within the corporation, could not themselves be financially scrutinised. Later, the sums emerged. It is estimated that about £22 million a year was being spent on consultants in the nineties. In 1997–8 alone, £28 million was spent on 'external advisers', of which £4 million went to McKinsey, £3 million to PA Consulting, and £1.8 million each to Ernst & Young and KPMG Management.[7] One commentator notes, 'By the late nineties, even the management consultants employed by the BBC were advising that the BBC employed too many management consultants'.[8]

But the paradoxes of management consultancy did not end there. In-house BBC audit staff complained of another in relation to an international consultancy brought in to create a computerised audit system for Broadcast: that the consultants were completely unaccountable. Alone of all the BBC's contractors, they neither worked to a fixed contract and budget, nor were their objectives set out in advance so that the results could be assessed. Rather than a transfer of skills, the staff argued, a culture of open-ended dependence on consultancy had developed, which became more insidious as consultancy became woven into the fabric of management politics. With Birt leading from the front, executives developed a habit of employing consultants as a means of courting political influence and winning battles. In an insecure managerial culture consultants could be used both to advocate and lobby for a desired policy or action, adding a veneer of disinterested sanction, and to blame if such a policy proved to be misjudged. To control a budget sizeable enough to support consultants became a symbol of prestige and seniority.

The cynicism and distrust directed at consultants by BBC staff at all levels stemmed in part from their disproportionate cost, in part from their dubious politicisation, and in part from their role in the management of unwelcome change. Consultants were sometimes sent in at little notice to recalcitrant departments as shock troops, with a brief to sort out grand and ill-focused difficulties.[9] As the BBC faced a vastly more complex competitive environment, the suspicion arose that senior executives' repeated recourse to consultancy was both consequence and symptom of a dysfunctional management culture. Birt's apparently confident, at times authoritarian management style, with its twin tactics of obsessive micro-management and sweeping macro-management, were seen by some as veiling a weak and defensive reality. For all the efforts spent on cultivating the new management in the BBC, incoming consultants and executives puzzled over the continuing absence at the end of the nineties of what they termed a 'smart' managerial culture. The irony was that the attempts at change that appeared to have failed rested in large part on the saturation use of management consultancy.

*

Not managerially smart

'When I was at the BBC I felt it was an organisation that was not managerially smart. I was not learning as much as I would in the commercial world about being a manager.'

GB: 'Tell me in what ways the BBC was not managerially smart.'

'One reason the BBC has difficulty is that the money comes top down, from the licence fee, rather than seeping up through successful programmes. So unless you've got a way – techniques like cost per viewer per hour analysis, which looks at how many viewers you're getting for the money spent – it's difficult to sort it all out. In the end, the leaders at the top of the BBC should be held responsible for the way they set up and manage or do not manage. But games would go on and heads weren't always bashed together to resolve them.'

Management consultant, former BBC strategist, 2001.

*

Micro-managed indecision

'The BBC decided that they needed a public service online effort. Birt used McKinsey to do a public service online brief, and McKinsey put together a high-level business plan for BBC Online that wasn't actually of great quality. It was bizarre; the McKinsey people took me out for lunch in spring '97, and as we talked I sketched on the back of a napkin an organisational chart and some suggestions on what things would cost. When I joined the BBC soon after and looked at the McKinsey strategy documents, they'd used the diagram I'd drawn on the napkin!

'As BBC Online got going, a key question was: what should be commercial and what should be public service? We wasted a year and a quarter trying to define this. The problem was there wasn't a strategic authority who could decide. We never got a coherent answer. If I come to you and you're my manager and the choice is stark – do

219

this or do that – I expect a clear answer. I found the BBC organisationally dysfunctional; the internal structures, the flow of information, the way people behaved, were designed *not* to give clear answers to problems. And this despite the fact that in Broadcast Online alone we were spending £150,000 a month on McKinsey. John Birt didn't need to know about particular IT issues; what matters is that you have decision-making processes and enough trust between the people who are operating, and clear guidance, and then we'll come to the right result. The BBC can't think like that. The managers don't have the tools to deal with unfamiliar situations; they're inflexible.

'Since the BBC is a public service organisation, I felt it was important to use our money wisely. But we had too much money; we wasted it. The BBC was spending £2.6 million a year just distributing the content. That's an enormous sum, so we got a competitive tender for distribution from the company that did it for Yahoo. Their bid was £300,000 a year, one-ninth of what we were paying internally. We spent a year and a half trying to persuade senior management to let us change. They got McKinsey in to do a benchmarking, and the McKinsey benchmark involved the consultant and me sitting down one evening, knocking a paper together and it being the same argument I'd presented to the Board of Management nine months earlier, saying we don't need to be spending this much. Even with the imprimatur of McKinsey they didn't listen. Money was being misspent; I could repeat that example many times . . .'

GB: 'You're pointing to the contradiction that in these days of Producer Choice, you weren't allowed to go to market for this major tender . . .'

'Yes, and the same happened with accommodation, and with our technical requirements, and it damaged morale. Internet businesses are designed full of newfangled ideas like virtual corporations, so we worked all the time with outside partners. But the BBC constantly tried to force us back inside, which meant we couldn't get the tools we needed. Even with high-quality people, somehow the organisational inertia prevented things from happening. They didn't have the confidence not to micro-manage. John Birt would tell us he didn't like the blue on the site's front page! We'd have been better off with none of senior management's time and more autonomy. It wasn't as if we were suddenly going to start putting pornography on the BBC website. We needed not to be producing papers and documents three or four times a week.'

Former BBC Online executive, 2001.

*

Adding Value

Although there was safety in numbers, consultants and strategists inhabited an uncomfortable niche in the BBC, powerful, but distrusted by the creative community. They could hardly remain immune to the criticisms of their role and of the overgrowth of management. Each had a considered response to the criticisms; each developed a rationale for the contribution, the 'added value', offered by their particular skills to the BBC's 'core work'. Generally, consultants aimed to be useful by doing what they felt was not otherwise being done. They made long-term, in-depth analyses of the BBC's operations and outlook. They made analyses that delivered counter-intuitive or unpalatable conclusions, for example by interrogating the balance between a creative project, whether programme or new service, its cost, and its likely audience impact – which is to say a formula for assessing 'value for money'. Or they positioned themselves to link up disjointed aspects of the BBC's functioning, trying, for example, to calm the ructions thrown up at the interface between commercial and public service activities when the corporation engaged in ambitious new ventures. There was unquestionably a growing need for strategic thinking, central as that is to all fast-moving industries in the technological economy. The problem for critics was the excess and the arrogance of consultancy, its sometime inaccuracies and woeful misjudgements – as with the restructuring – and the way the shift in the balance of power within the corporation symbolised a crisis of trust in those professionals engaged in the BBC's primary work.

*

Not McKinsey: people implications

'I trained as a consultant and joined the BBC in strategy for Network TV. But I was involved first in the McKinsey ten-year strategy overview, which lasted a year and resulted in the restructuring and the BBC's ten-year plan. That was in large part written by McKinsey based on workshops with the relevant units. I felt strongly when I was in Network TV that there was no point making a career there if they continued to use McKinsey, because one was just being undermined.'

GB: 'So there was McKinsey, then there were other strategy people – like yourself – who were employed as BBC strategists. McKinsey were on job-specific contracts, weren't they?'

'I think so, although McKinsey projects tend to be "We'll sort of do this, and it'll sort of cost this many millions". The ten-year strategy exercise was huge, partly because all the fiefdoms wanted to get an impartial view. That was an argument for using McKinsey. But as an internal resource you think, "Why should I invest energy doing strategy if someone else is then going to do it?"'

GB: 'So there *was* duplication going on at that time?'

'Let me be clear. Some of the McKinsey consultants were outstanding. The consultant working with TV was very involving; not all consultants are the same. When an organisation uses consultants, the key issue is how we consultants position ourselves. Consultants need to *add value*. So I focused on implementation, because McKinsey don't do implementation, McKinsey don't think about how to communicate strategy to programme-makers, they didn't think about the people implications of the restructuring. That was an area where I could add value. But if the BBC uses McKinsey, yet you have all these strategy people in-house, there must be overlap.'

Management consultant, former BBC strategist, 2001.

*

Not rocket science: systematic strategy

'In 1992 to '93 there was a small corporate strategy function; four or five of us worked very closely with John Birt on lots of pet projects.'

GB: 'The impression one gets is that under Birt, strategy blossomed everywhere.'

'Absolutely. A lot of the blossoming of strategy came from the corporate strategy diaspora. The people who ended up doing strategy began in Corporate Centre and then formed working relationships with the directorates – with the baronies as well as the king, as it were. People came into corporate strategy, and then went out from the centre to set up little strategy groups in the directorates: in TV, News, Worldwide. Some started out in the baronies. In Editorial Policy there was a fair team, mostly editorial people, mainly from News.'

GB: 'Can you explain for the layman what the brief of strategy was? It was not politics and regulation, it was not editorial policy, so what was it?'

'It was about all the other aspects of the BBC. What I did was essentially about helping John understand what his business managers weren't telling him about their businesses. The projects we did weren't rocket science; they were about taking a systematic approach to understanding the performance of BBC services. To say, here's what the pattern of output has been for BBC1 looked at systematically over time; to help understand why the BBC performs less well or better than our competitors in the TV market; or what impact the proliferation of local commercial radio services is having on the radio business. It was basic market context stuff really, and allied to that helping to define the BBC's role in the evolving ecology to feed into discussions with the DCMS. We did long-term studies of audience trends, of the differential role of various types of programming in the schedules. We got into classic BBC problems such as the lack of good returning popular drama on BBC1. On that, John wanted to say, "Look, this has gone on for ten years; here's some more depth as to why it's gone wrong. Can we have a dialogue in Performance Review as to how you, Television, are going to address the strategic challenge?"'

GB: 'I was around Drama Group between '95 and '97; what if I said they and the controllers were obsessed with the ten-year problem of the need for hit popular dramas and new soaps? Wasn't Jonathan Powell across this as controller of BBC1 before that? Look at *Eldorado*.'

'No, no, it developed out of our painful strategy meetings with Drama Group in '93. Nobody likes being told they haven't delivered any shows that have had more than three series in ten years. But it was essential if we were going to grasp the scale of the problem and acknowledge that radical change was necessary. In Entertainment there are still people going round saying, "If we gave these sitcoms another couple of series they would succeed." Utter bollocks. Our analysis allowed us to show there have been no successful sitcoms that did badly in their first series. Only with our analysis could we have the discussion properly with Entertainment.'[10]

Senior BBC strategist, former management consultant, 2001.

*

Value for money: audience share per investment

'One of the early strategy analyses I did was on entertainment, while a strategy colleague looked at drama. We took a historical perspective, which hadn't been done before in the BBC. The drama findings were intriguing. At that stage BBC-originated popular drama had been under-performing ITV in terms of hit rate, in terms of audience size, for 10 years. We originated fewer new series, and of those we got one hit in ten, where ITV got two or two-and-a-half hits in ten.'

GB: 'Are you talking strictly about ratings at this point?'

'Well, that's audience performance, and arguably that is the appropriate measure when you're making popular drama for BBC1 or even BBC2, where they try to have some popular ones as well as the costume dramas and the Poliakoffs. If you're then going to adopt a strategy that says, "We've been underinvesting in drama", but even when we were investing more than ITV our hit rate was lower, why would you get any greater success by pouring more money in? I remember a calculation that was quoted to me after the analysts ran the numbers for BBC1 when they got the recent new money. The fourth episode of *EastEnders*, they predicted, would add to BBC1 in total somewhere between half a point and one point in audience share. That episode costs, say, £25 million a year. The rest of the new drama investment, a great deal more money, let's say of the order of £100 million, would add 0.1 of a share point, because of the hits and misses. When you see the numbers, where do you think they put the investment?'

Senior BBC strategist, 2001.

*

Business for Culture

Not only the numbers of management consultants but the values they brought with them proved controversial. During the nineties, consultants played a prominent role in the importation into the BBC of auditing and accountancy practices derived from the commercial sector. Strikingly, these practices came to be associated in the minds of senior management with accountability *per se*. Tighter financial probity was posited as the cutting edge of a broader cultural change that would instil greater discipline in relation to the corporation's obligations to its licence fee payers; ensuring value for money became the core of the BBC's democratic role. In this way financial discipline took on the cast of a new corporate morality, and one that threatened to displace the former ethical centre of the BBC. The determinedly complex cultural purposes of public service broadcasting were flattened in this mentality to commercial measurements: 'value for money', equated with 'audience performance', equated in turn with ratings and audience share, came to stand in for value itself. The displacement is evident in documents and speeches from the later nineties that attest to the wholesale adoption by senior executives of the concepts and lexicon of business management. They show how a concern with the quality of output and related questions such as the conditions for creativity have been marginalised, while the term 'business' has become ubiquitous as the standard shorthand for the corporation. An illustrative speech by a leading strategist in Corporate Centre, an overview of the BBC's audit processes to a major institution in the field, centres on 'Measuring the BBC's Performance' through identifying three overall objectives – 'Managing the Business, Driving Strategy and Accountability' – which are then assessed against key performance indicators (KPIs). The language is indistinguishable from commercial management, and there is pride in the accomplishment:

'There's a real need for KPIs or performance measurement statistics, and the real test for most managers is, does this help you in running the business? Across the BBC there is a huge amount of interest in very detailed performance indicators collected quite often on a daily basis. For instance . . . the overnight ratings which are sent round electronically every morning . . . tell us how well the previous evening's television schedule has done, how we've done in audience share terms compared with our main competitors, and increasingly we're looking at particular target audience groups as well as the total audience. We also have some continuing financial performance indicators and some operational indicators which managers need just to run the business.'[11]

This summarising account, which dwells on the challenges of identifying performance measures for an organisation such as the BBC, eventually alights on four sets of KPIs. Just one of them – Learning and Growth – touches on issues of 'innovative programming, cultural patronage and so on',[12] and later again, 'innovation, creativity, distinctiveness, and [the BBC's] educational role'.[13] No expansion is given. 'Measures that looked at creativity' are briefly mentioned, and they are interpreted quantitatively and equated with 'the number of new ideas that are coming out each year in terms of programmes or services'.[14] Pushed to the margins by the persistent focus on the challenge of developing measurable indicators and robust management techniques, these crucial issues are made residual: emptied of substance, emptied also of managerial attention. In this vision of the BBC, its cultural and public service purposes and the problem of how better to fulfil them are barely mentioned. They are placed beyond the frame.

The displacement is there also in a telling discussion in the same document of the benefits of the BBC's adoption in the mid nineties of a 'more strategic approach' to Radio 1: 'If we had decided for one of our radio stations to focus on a particular audience group, which for Radio 1 would be the fifteen- to twenty-four-year-olds, it is that group we are interesting in focusing on as far as performance is concerned . . . We've identified a real strategic target, [and] that's what we now want to measure.'[15] What is notable in this account is the lack of any attention to the decisive factor in the reorientation of Radio 1: the invention of a new public service rationale, known as 'New Music First'. This rationale, centred on a more contemporary aesthetic mix, required Radio 1 to shed its dated top-forty persona and become a station oriented to new kinds of popular music by breaking unknown artists and bands and giving slots to electronic dance and hiphop genres that had previously not been aired.[16]

The difficulty of making the BBC conform to the terms of contemporary business management is revealed in the reflections of strategists and consultants distributed around the BBC directorates. They spoke in retrospect of what they saw as the ill fit between the 'intangible', 'nebulous' nature of the BBC's aims as a public service organisation and the standard techniques used to identify strategic targets and assess outcomes in business. Their reflections show how, according to the now reigning business values, the BBC is by definition anomalous, its former purposes epiphenomenal. After all, they cannot readily be measured. For the consultants, steeped in the norms of business, the BBC can only be conceived of negatively; it is not an 'ordinary business'.

*

Intangibles and variables

'As a public service organisation, the goals the BBC is attempting to achieve are more complex. They're not as easy to measure as profit. It has a purpose beyond that. The BBC, like all public service organisations, has a difficult job trying to deliver things that are slightly intangible. Some objectives you can measure, some of them you can't, and there is a very large number of objectives to juggle. In television it has to do with programming ambitions for different audience segments, regional programming, the indie mix – there's a whole range of variables, and it's difficult to make priorities, so it's a difficult management task.'

Management consultant, former BBC strategist, 2001.

*

Not a profit-maximising entity

'In any ordinary business you've got a financial year-end where you weigh things up. Performance Review was an attempt to do that, but it foundered partly because of John's fondness for mind-boggling detail, and partly due to the difficulty of defining objectives and measuring performance because of the BBC's nature as a PSB rather than a profit-maximising entity. That's a problem that continues to exist for the BBC.'

Senior BBC strategist, 2001.

*

What Birt accomplished through an expansion of the layers of senior and middle management was a transformation in the prevailing values of the BBC. As the concerns of business management met the new entrepreneurialism, they threatened to overwhelm the ethos of public service broadcasting and its diverse local expression in the services and production departments. Consultancy played a leading role in building the new management apparatus which, originating in Corporate Centre, sat hierarchically above and supervised both production and commissioning. The new management had bulk; it formed a significant part of the BBC's population. The BBC's future was effectively being conceived by those with little connection to its driving ethos. The legacy was an antagonistic split between many of those in programme-making and the new management, a split made evident daily in countless differences of language, focus and ethic.

*

McKinsey boys go digital: inside Murdoch's walled garden

July 1997: I am sitting with a small group in the office of Mark Wakefield, head of the politics unit in the current affairs section of the White City building. We are waiting for two young men, McKinsey consultants who 'work in strategy at Corporate Centre'. They are coming to give a presentation of the broad strategic outlook for the BBC regarding digital and interactive television and the future of BBC Online. They are travelling all over the BBC. When they arrive, Mike is the dominant personality, but both are fiercely smart in grey suits, striped shirts and ties, with identical Franz Schubert glasses, the hip 'young executive' look of the moment. Mike introduces himself bullishly by way of a classic corporate genealogy of his patrons and trials: 'I'm from McKinsey; I worked with Michael Starks on digital terrestrial options; then for Patricia and Dominic Morris on the Sky negotiations. Recently I've been at Online with Ed Briffa.' He talks us through a forty-eight-page Corporate Centre strategy document, densely written in bullet-pointed 'landscape' – famously Birt's preferred format; indeed, legend has it that it's the only format he will read. In the future the BBC will be on every platform: digital terrestrial television [DTT], digital satellite and digital cable. The view is that DTT will be the main carrier to go for, but that satellite will win out over cable in the UK.

Mike moves on to talk about BIB, British Interactive Broadcasting, a commercial joint venture between Murdoch's BSkyB and others formed earlier this year: 'At present the development of infrastructure for interactive services on digital television is yielded to

BIB. Government's view is to allow BIB to carry the risks rather than publicly funded R & D. BIB are very keen to work with the BBC,' for example by carrying a new interactive service, BBC Inform. For the BBC to be part of the BIB Internet site it will have to pay. It will also have to buy space from BIB to build interactive services around its channels and programming. Moreover, if BBC interactive services are to be free, the BBC will be required to pay via a licence bought from BIB. The BBC will have to pay BIB for every concession. I ask, 'Is this the privatisation of Internet delivery on digital TV in Britain?' Mike smiles and answers glibly, 'Yes, I'm afraid. Oftel is very sympathetic to BIB.'

We examine diagrams setting out various potential scenarios between BIB and the BBC, and the future suddenly looks strange. But the consultants' genial, high-octane delivery doesn't falter. In relation to interactive news services, Mike mentions almost casually that BIB will favour Sky News over the BBC: 'the BBC could be locked out of some content areas'. On the next page we see a mocked-up interactive TV screen with the Sky logo emblazoned across the top, alongside a commercial sponsor, above a list of interactive services: Shopping, Games, Travel and so on, and – yes – the BBC, sitting above Internet and Email. The following page has a similar diagram, this time showing the BBC as one of series of options within BIB's 'window box'. The next has the BBC sitting inside BIB's 'walled garden': here, the BBC no longer even has a presence in the main on-screen menu; it is a sub-class of the Internet and Email option. The consultants tell us, but they don't want to dwell on the massive ironies, and the dubiousness, of what is being outlined: a universe in which the BBC becomes a sub-brand – equivalent to Dorling Kindersley or Cartoons.com – within BSkyB's BIB. It is a future in which, to reach the BBC's services, one will have go through the gateway designed by BSkyB's subsidiary BIB; in which the BBC will appear as a little icon set within BIB's 'walled garden'. It is a future in which access to the BBC will be subject to the commercial controls of its most dangerous rival. But despite grim faces around the room, nobody presses the point, and the consultants drive us merrily on through the forty-eight-page dossier. For we are above all about business realism now, aren't we?

Diary, 1997.

*

Surreal winter interlude: 'I Will Not Complain'

A dark, late Friday afternoon in January, and I am preparing to go home. In my borrowed office the phone rings. A man introduces himself. He has heard that there is an anthropologist studying the BBC and is fascinated and excited by the news. He is a management consultant and happens to be visiting a friend at the BBC, and he says that he too uses anthropology as part of his repertoire of concepts. We must have much in common. Could we meet, and now, as he is leaving tomorrow for foreign parts? Reluctantly, I agree. Ten minutes later he knocks.

Anthony runs a company called I Will Not Complain International, Inc., based in Tokyo, Beijing and Shanghai which specialises in training business people for leadership, teamwork and success – what is called 'experiential management training'. The glossy pamphlet explains: 'I Will Not Complain creates training programs that challenge people to go beyond their perceived boundaries, to work with others to solve problems and to experience success . . . The I Will Not Complain name has its origins in an expedition undertaken by [the] company founder . . . in the jungles of Papua New Guinea in 1985. During the expedition food ran short and one member of the group complained incessantly, ruining morale and hindering the group's ability to overcome the challenges it was facing. When the company was founded the name was chosen to inspire course participants "not to complain" and to pull together to overcome the challenges of the modern business environment.' The pamphlet's motif is a repeated image of a lonely 'tribesman' leading a train of camels through the desert.

Assuming a camaraderie of philosophy and purpose, Anthony hands me the latest brochure for IWNC's 'program for advanced executive training', titled 'In Pursuit of Primary Knowledge'. The exotica multiply: the document is subtitled 'Understanding Tribes, Trees and Territory and the role of shields, feathers and spears in modern organisations'. Over the page it continues:

'If humans have been organising and surviving for millions of years then . . .
. . . why are so many managers and employees so confused about what their organisation is and what it needs to do
&
. . . why is every new corporate strategic plan so complicated?

Do you think the answer might be that organisations have been making simple concepts far too complicated?

Your first Tribes, Trees and Territory Question:
Can you name who in your office has earned his or her spears?

If you know the answer then you are tapping into your
Primary Knowledge

How strong is your Primary Knowledge?

Shields – Feathers – Spears & Power – Wealth – Status

Shield = Power: Those who **willingly** protect you by using their bows and arrows for you if need be.

Spear = Status: The sign of **genuine** authority which must be earned. It can never be bought or sold and is seldom thrown away.

Feathers = Wealth: What you have earned through **recognised** hard work or giving and thus have the right to give away.

Quote from the village: "A big man has many feathers, a bigger man can give away his feathers."

The document drones on, with scratchy caricatures of 'tribal territories' featuring hunting grounds, the Sepik River, crocodiles, the cassowary and breadfruit tree. I listen, read, humour Anthony. Charlatan or madman? His primitivist corporate fantasies leave me speechless, vaguely scared in the gathering gloom. Is this the lunatic fringe of management consultancy? Or is consultancy engaged routinely in traducing the concepts and data of social anthropology and using them to milk Asian businessmen? Still speechless, I wave Anthony farewell.

Diary, 1996.

*

Accountability for Trust

From 1994, senior management's introduction of accountability and auditing policies gathered pace. A series of official statements were published, *An Accountable BBC* (1994), *Governing Today's BBC* (1997) and *The BBC Beyond 2000* (1998), a kind of political marketing beamed outwards to convince the government and the public of improvement and change. While purporting to be about increased public accountability, the developments responded to the political critics of the BBC's mode of self-regulation. Auditing and accountability took on the vital task of shoring up the legitimacy of the BBC, part of Birt's defensive pact with the political class. But the documents had another purpose. As Michael Power points out, auditing is an ill-defined set of practices, a 'collection of pragmatic and humble routines'.[17] There is a yawning gap between the practices and the normative claims resting on them. Official statements therefore bear the additional weight of binding the disparate, in some ways unconvincing routines into a whole that *does* effectively legitimise. The scale and complexity of the BBC's accountability practices were remarkable; and compared with what went before, there is no doubt that during the nineties the BBC attended scrupulously to the challenge to be more publicly responsive and open in its dealings. They took three forms: self-regulation, which in turn subsumes both externally oriented and internally oriented regulatory practices; and external regulation – the various governmental, parliamentary and legal powers that oversee the BBC's operations beyond the Board of Governors.

The external powers to which the BBC is subject are extensive and in the nineties they mushroomed, largely in reaction to escalating calls by competitors for scrutiny of the BBC's activities. They included periodic renewal of the Charter; regular scrutiny of the chairman and senior executives by the Culture Select Committee; ministerial appointment of the governors; the setting of the BBC's budget by the government via the licence fee; presentation of the BBC's annual reports and accounts to ministers and Parliament; review by the several National Broadcasting and Advisory Councils; scrutiny of output and handling of complaints by the Broadcasting Standards Commission; annual financial auditing by an external firm; and potential appeal by complainants to the Office of Fair Trading and to European law on competition issues. Additional powers coming into play include tighter scrutiny of the BBC's appointments and operations after the Nolan Committee recommendations; post-devolutionary interest stemming from the Scottish Parliament and its equivalents in Wales and Northern Ireland; and the implementation since 2000 of the 1998 Human Rights Act. In 2000, the government announced its intention to exercise even more strenuous oversight of the BBC's operations. Detailed scrutiny was given to the BBC's proposals for new digital services both before approving their launch and afterwards; key here was the 2002 Lambert review of BBC News 24, which criticised the governors' 'perfunctory' supervision of the new service. This amounts to a formidable array of external regulatory instruments. What is extraordinary is the apparent lack of governmental concern over the cumulative effects of requiring the BBC to answer for such a large number of responsibilities to such a range of different outside institutions.

Externally oriented *self*-regulation processes, many of them dating from the mid nineties, also formed a complex texture, gathered under the rubric 'Listening to the Public'. They included the BBC's Programme Complaints Unit, and 'The BBC Listens', a governors' initiative which aimed to review, 'from the point of view of the audience', all services every four years. The process, it was claimed, 'ensures that the Governors are fully aware of public opinions and concerns'. Public consultations were staged in relation to most major changes to services. BBC Online offered information and requested public comments on the annual report and other statements. A Fair Trading Audit Committee monitored the boundaries between public service and commercial activities and compliance with competition regulation. Two governors' seminars were held each year, consultations on topical issues such as the Digital Future, Taste and Decency, and the BBC and Children.[18] But the centrepiece of the BBC's external accountability drive, required by the 1994 White Paper and dating from 1996, was the annual Statement of Promises, a booklet posted to all licence fee payers which '[challenged] the BBC to do better' by listing strategic promises to the audience and reporting back on last year's undertakings.

In combination the various initiatives amounted to a frenetic and highly visible performance of self-regulatory activity. They combined genuine gains in self-examination and reporting with elements that had the inescapable air of simulations of openness. On the one hand the Statement of Promises trawled through significant figures: in 1999–2000, for example, that 80 per cent of peak-time BBC television programmes were original, or that eight in ten hours of BBC television were made in Britain.[19] On the other hand, its rhetoric tended to be self-congratulatory and placatory, closing down enquiry. The gap between sweeping promises and unprovable claims invited incredulity. Moreover, the routing of public feedback into the documents was obscure and appeared ineffectual. To ordinary viewers the welter of accountability instruments could seem bewildering, and the litany contained in the Statement of Promises like a placebo standing in for real response to real public concerns. Yet however gestural or grandiose, the initiatives undeniably represented an attempt to redefine the relationship between BBC and public for a post-Reithian era.

*

Our Commitment to You

'We promise to be accountable and responsive.'

BBC Statement of Promises, 1997–98.

*

We promise to . . .

'BBC: Twelve Promises:

- We promise to refine the mainstream music policy on Radio 1 to ensure it appeals as strongly to young women as to young men . . .
- We promise to devise programmes which respond to devolution and political change in Scotland, Wales and Northern Ireland . . .
- We promise to focus on our obligation to represent all groups in society accurately and to avoid reinforcing prejudice in our programmes . . .
- We promise to report our performance against all the specific promises, continuing commitments and standards set out in the BBC's Statements of Promises.'

BBC Statement of Promises, 1998–99.

*

Standards were high

'Our Performance Against Promises for 1998–99:
Standards were high overall, and the BBC met its specific promise to:

- Represent all groups in society accurately and avoid reinforcing prejudice in our programmes. Positive action to broaden the range of programme contributors included the introduction of the BBC's Diversity Database, giving programmes access to over 2,000 individuals and organisations representing minority interests and backgrounds.'

BBC Statement of Promises, 1999–2000.

*

Audit: An Intimate Bureacracy

Two documents constitute the core of the BBC's internally oriented self-regulation: the Producer Guidelines, which set out for programme-makers the professional standards and ethical codes underpinning the BBC's output, and the Commercial Policy Guidelines, giving the rules adopted by the BBC on fair trading. Under the impact of the new managerialism and the call for account-ability, to these were added a collection of self-audits, and by the middle of the nineties there grew a dense, overlapping and cyclical series of auditing processes at every level of the corporation. Of all the managerial initiatives, it was these that creative staff found most onerous and that obtruded most on their work. They included periodic Programme Strategy Reviews throughout the corporation lasting a year or more, sometimes involving workshops for all staff; Annual Performance Reviews for all departments, which took several months and required the production of exhaustive documentation; and monthly and quarterly statements of purpose and account by each programme editor. Audit encompassed even the mundane. The BBC toilets were audited by a Toilet Housekeeping Checklist hanging on each door, on which cleaners had several times a day neatly to note the details of their visits by time and task. On every table in the BBC cafeterias sat a card on which customers were enjoined to offer assessments and criticism, the better to improve services. The culture of audit flourished in Birt's BBC. In these processes, as in its marketisation, the BBC self-consciously constructed itself as a showcase of managerial best practice. To this end auditing required a second-order professionalism, a parallel hierarchy of audit managers whose function was to monitor the broadcast professionals. Under their tutelage auditing was not just performed, it was zealously experimented with, enhanced and expanded. Those audited were required to internalise and 'own' the experience. No sooner had one audit process been completed than, eliciting feedback from the auditees, another cycle began.

*

Recursive audit

GB: 'You mentioned the aim of making Annual Performance Review come closer to the needs of each particular department. How are you going to find out how to design the APR differently?'

'Well, at the moment we're information gathering, having a post-mortem-stroke-ideas session with each of the directorates to say, "What do you think are the problems with Annual Performance Review? How would you like it to be different?" Or, "Tell us what you're doing to redesign it yourself." We will then, depending on what state the directorate is in, work more or less closely with them. The idea is to get them thinking, if they're not already, about what strategic objectives they want to map out, and to use Andersen on designing the templates.'

GB: 'Getting them to set their own forms and goals for Performance Review . . .?'

'That's right, but then commenting on it and checking that it fits the BBC's needs. At the same time we're developing with Andersen's help a corporate framework where we're saying, "What are the BBC's aims? How do they break down?" We're at the stage of thinking how to measure them. This is about things like: we must protect the brand, we must serve all licence payers, we must make sure we're balanced regionally, all those things. Most of the measures would be things we'd expect to be owned by a directorate. So there'll be a sort of extraction of their own goals.'

BBC internal audit manager, 1997.

*

Audit squared

A Programme Finance Committee in Drama Group. Some fifteen executives are poring over the fine details of every drama spend and financial commitment, an apparently rigorous auditing process. An unknown woman is sitting next to Charles, head of the Group. A few minutes in, he introduces her: she is an auditor from Corporate Centre, and she will be observing this and other meetings. Charles is polite but his body language betrays a stiffness in reaction to the infinite regress that characterises his bosses' infatuation not only with auditing, but with auditing the auditors.

Diary, 1996.

*

Mystery audit

A Drama Editorial Board, late on. The executive producer in charge of *Silent Witness* complains wearily that an audit is being carried out on this successful series. This is despite the fact, she says, that the producer has acted impeccably and everything is well within budget. The auditors are questioning every aspect of the budgeting, and they are making suggestions that mean the show wouldn't be delivered until September, when it's due for the schedule months earlier. The executive is pissed off. 'Who are these auditors?' she demands, 'Does anyone know?' The chief accountant knows nothing. Nor does Charles. No one, it seems, knows who they are or who has sent them.

Diary, 1996.

*

Hyperbole and Reduction

The Annual Performance Review offers a microcosm of the workings of the audit culture. It required the preparation of a highly detailed self-assessment of the past year's activities by each department. In Drama Group, the APR documentation for 1995–6 was handled by two managers who, with secretarial help, worked almost full-time on the process for four months. The resulting several-hundred-page dossier was an uneasy amalgam of routine attempts to meet the demands of the audit genre – with its bullet-point layout, assertive style and language of 'objectives', 'aims' and 'achievements' – and a set of brief but frank reflections on the knots and difficulties faced by the Drama departments over that challenging year. The dossier thus combined the reductive yet hyperbolic qualities of audit-as-PR with potentially valuable revelations. Even when heavily clothed in audit-speak the initial dossier included fragile attempts to communicate concerns up the line to top management. But as it was passed up the hierarchy and subsumed into the larger process of review, the APR of Network Television, the Drama dossier was progressively condensed and critical messages to management tended to be squeezed out. The result was a set of self-evident statements, rendering the exercise effectively meaningless for drama staff. The generic won out over the specific, form over substance. The serious concerns of Drama Group were folded into 'due process', apparently as a substitute for effective response by senior management.

*

Objectives for 1995/96

'The following . . . of Network Television's objectives were specific to Drama Group:
(i)   Enhance the quality and impact of single drama on both channels and of contemporary serials on BBC2 . . .
(ii) Work to improve the quality control of BBC drama; ensure drama production is delivered as specified; and that suitable contractual arrangements are in place to protect returning series . . .
(iii) Continue the initiative to ensure that the BBC's pre-watershed policies are observed . . .'

Annual Performance Review document, Drama Group, 1995–6.

*

Audit and its characteristic style also infused relations between parts of the BBC. Months after the 1996 restructuring, BBC Broadcast produced a booklet for internal distribution titled What is BBC Broadcast? to explain to the rest of the BBC how it would operate. Even in apparently functional writing of this kind, the language and claims were hyperbolic and sanctimonious, closer to PR than to self-description. Given the commissioning chaos being experienced daily by producers, the distance between the reality and the rhetoric of clarity and transparency in commissioning made the document ironic to the point of insult.

*

What is BBC Broadcast?

'• BBC Broadcast puts the audience at the centre of its thinking.
• Its overall aim is to provide the best possible value to the audience, thereby improving the public perception of the BBC's services and of the licence fee as the means of funding them.
• To do so it seeks
    • to remain the most watched and most listened to broadcaster in the UK
    • to provide services which in their quality, range and integrity add up to something special, something different from all its competitors . . .
• BBC Broadcast guarantees to programme-makers that its commissioning system will be:
    • formal and contractual
    • consistent
    • clear
    • transparent
    • fair
    • timely
• We will constantly and publicly monitor our performance in all areas to ensure that we become the industry leader in good commissioning behaviour.'

BBC Broadcast, document sent to other directorates, 1996.

*

Auditing is the central technique of the new public management; as Power explains, audit becomes routine when 'accountability can no longer be sustained by informal . . . trust alone but must be formalised'.[20] It embodies a number of paradoxes amply demonstrated by the BBC, paradoxes which tend both to reveal and to exacerbate the loss of trust. The logic of audit means that auditing itself comes to be audited; the phenomenon is recursive and self-reinforcing. The only thing that cannot be queried, however, is the rationality of audit itself. Auditing claims to deliver an ideal of transparency in organisations; yet the audit process itself is often opaque, closed to public scrutiny. While auditing promises solutions to particular organisational and sectoral problems, it deals in standardised language and methods and in the reduction of complexity and specificity. The criteria of effectiveness for audit are vague, which leads to heavy investment in 'due process', exacerbating its formalistic and intrusive nature, which further eats away at trust. But audit's most pernicious effect is that 'targets that seem measurable become enticing tools for improvement'; audit changes organisational cultures by conjuring into being and magnifying in importance the very parameters that it claims neutrally to 'discover' and measure.[21] At a time when audit has never been more prevalent and powerful, there is an irresistible drive for the 'is' – assessment and measurement – and the 'ought' – normative goals – to converge, annulling the entire exercise. Such fatal ironies, widely perceived by BBC staff, subverted senior management's wholesale investment in audit.

If audit purported to systematise the Reithian ethos by giving it measurable and self-critical form, it had other latent, but nonetheless critical, functions. Externally, in the face of continuing questioning of the BBC's governance and self-regulation, it was aimed at fending off public criticism and pre-empting government intervention by depicting the BBC as an irreproachable organisation, one engaged in exhaustive monitoring of its efficiency and rectitude. Whatever the content, audit acted as a public sign of morality and a source of legitimacy.

Internally, audit ostentatiously performed assessments of the performance of departments. In doing so it provided the justification for painful managerial decisions such as departmental cuts and closures. For many employees it amounted to the new face of bureaucratic domination, a travesty that in its reductive genericism failed to represent real difficulties and occluded genuine reflection. For all the effort expended on making auditing a fine-tuned 'bureaucracy of intimacy' sensitive to 'local' departmental needs,[22] audit, its processes and results, floated in a parallel universe to the one inhabited by those subjected to it. Audit therefore embodied what the anthropologist Pierre Bourdieu has called *symbolic violence*: the imposition on a group of cultural or symbolic forms that have no basis in that group's own experience and culture, but to which, as a consequence of legitimate domination, it must conform.[23] That such symbolic violence was being perpetrated as a consequence of the Birtist desire to appease the corporation's political masters deepened the injury. Audit formed yet another link in the chain of forces that was eroding the BBC's store of collective trust. The hurt was multiplied by the way the audit burden was felt to reflect not only an indifferent senior management, but a governance system that failed to perceive or turned a blind eye to that unhappy situation.

*

RAPping the audit

Charles Denton, head of Drama Group, is calling the Drama Editorial Board to order:
CD: 'OK, let's discuss RAP [*a new financial audit*]: how many people are aware of the detail of all this? Could any regional drama head say how their region intends to take submissions to RAP? Are they going on an electronic link, or via London here, or have you no idea how the bloody thing works?'
BB: [*a regional BBC drama head*] 'I think that's a fairly fair assessment.'
Laughter in the room. Throughout this discussion, a crazed hilarity prevails.
CD: 'I see, you have no idea and don't want to know. Has anybody heard of RAP?'
AA: 'A large bunch of papers arrived on my desk on Monday, but I haven't read it yet.'
DD: 'We had that presentation, didn't we?'
CD: 'We did. [*Patiently, starting from scratch*] RAP is "Resource Analysis Project"; the idea is that in future we will be expected to offer for our projects electronically against a matrix of in-house cost drivers.'
More helpless laughter.
DD: 'I've heard it so many times before . . .'
EE: 'What the hell does it mean?'
CD: 'The idea is that we, at the point of delivery, record the actuals against those drivers . . .'
EE: 'Isn't this what we normally do with cost reports, except we'll have do it electronically?'
DD: '. . . And it will go direct to Finance Planning in Network Television . . .'
CD: '. . . And Finance Planning will get inside the whole process and try to become pseudo-producers themselves. It's agreed that it's going to happen; I've got a really ratty note from Will saying "For God's sake stop obfuscating, get on and cooperate."'
FF: 'Wasn't there some debate about the system that should be used, because most of our outside folks use Movie Magic[†] and there's a BBC-type system we're using, and now it's going to be a third system that has to be used?'

[†]Movie Magic was an online accounting system widely used in television production outside the BBC

CD: [*Dripping with irony*] 'Yes, there's going to be a huge increase in work.'

FF: 'They're trying to make it homogenised. Because every time you bring in a freelance producer or production manager who wants to use Magic, you get confused because they're used to keeping track of their own costs on their own system. If you then have to translate it either they lose track of the real costs, or you have to employ a third person to type all this stuff in.'

CD: 'All that is true and we're going to do that.'

AA: 'We're going to employ third people? It's a job-creation scheme!'

BB: 'This is a parallel system to what already exists . . .'

DD: 'The idea is they will have complete access to our actuals to inform negotiations for the future; so if they see on the system that we're spending £550,000 on a project, they'll begin negotiations using that as a base. It doesn't necessarily mean you'll get 550; it means they'll say "Why did it cost 550 this time round?" and "Let's see how you can reduce that." [*Sceptically*] They claim they'll be in a better position to make cases to Corporate Finance for extra funding . . .'

EE: 'Why don't they just ask us what it cost afterwards?'

BB: 'Eddy, you're such an innocent . . .' [*Laughter.*]

AA: 'It wouldn't cost enough money to do that!' [*Laughter.*]

CD: 'It wouldn't employ enough people . . .'

FF: [*Defiantly*] 'Well, we're not going to submit *EastEnders* in the RAP form.'

AA: 'Couldn't we all just work on Movie Magic?'

DD: '. . . It's loony, it's loony . . .'

CD: 'OK, we're the first production area testing this out. I was on the Steering Group and I argued passionately against it, and ended up with another of those corporate reports saying "We have consulted widely, people are generally in agreement . . ." So here we go.' [*Resigned laughter.*]

Discussion at BBC Drama Editorial Board, 1996.

*

Bullet-point bull

A Drama Editorial Board: We are checking the final draft of a huge document, drawn up by a managerial sub-group, which presents the Drama Group's self-audit results for the first round of the 1995–6 Annual Performance Review. Charles, head of Drama Group, is trying to run the meeting soberly, but the atmosphere is one of total alienation and disinterest. The creative heads probe the language of audit with anarchic humour. Mike, head of Serials, laughs at a bullet point which claims they have 'enhanced the quality of contemporary serials on BBC2': 'I remember how *that* happened! Michael

Jackson commissioned *Our Friends in the North*, and the next week he was able to add that phrase!' – which is ludicrous, he implies, since everyone in the meeting knows he'd had to fight for years against controller disinterest to get the serial produced. Charles consoles, calling the APR just 'a ritual dance', and reads another bullet point: '"We have improved the quality control of BBC Drama" – can anyone tell me what the hell "quality control" means in terms of drama?' Hilarity, and no one bothers to reply. Another drama head points wildly to the smiley faces covering the pages of assessment: 'Who did this? The whole of BBC management is now assessed by smiley faces!' and the room collapses in powerless mirth.

George, head of Singles, notes that the document boasts of a new 'accelerated train-ing scheme for producers who could hold their own in an independent environment'. He comments sardonically that 'this amounts to training BBC producers to go out and work as independents!', alluding to the increasing outflow of producers nurtured by the BBC. [*Within a short time George would himself leave to set up his own independent pro-duction company*.] Charles says, 'John Birt wants Drama to pilot an Independent Advice Panel as part of Performance Review.' He mentions the three names Birt has proposed, adding that he knows them all 'quite well'. George comments with amusement on one of them, playwright David Hare: 'I wonder what he'll have to say about the play of his that went out last year!' – hinting that there just might be a question of propriety in using a BBC writer to review the BBC Drama Group. . .

Diary, 1996.

*

Strategists talking to strategists

'There is little doubt that the Performance Review process never worked. It was always an onerous thing you did at the end of the year rather than being part of a business cycle.'

GB: 'I saw it being exceedingly cynically complied with, causing bad faith and a lot of work.'

'I would acknowledge that. It was painful, it never got embedded in the business. It became a heavy, over-rigid and formalised process. The absurdity of the early Performance Review got cleared up, but it never became a completely bought-in process. It was fundamentally divorced from the business. It was the likes of me being sent out to work in the directorates, communicating with our counterparts back in Corporate Centre, as opposed to it being intrinsic to the operations of the business. Strategists talking to strategists.'

Senior BBC strategist, former management consultant, 2001.

*

Performing Governance

Despite the manifold doubts about audit as an instrument of internal accountability, it gave senior management a crude take on what was going on within
departments. Who, then, would ensure the accountability of senior management itself? How could the performance of the BBC executive be judged? This
was apparently a job for the governors, the cornerstone of the corporation's
self-regulation. But how well did they perform it? How robust was the BBC's
system of governance?

In fact, any expectation that the governors would monitor senior management encounters serious obstacles. Throughout the BBC's history two linked
criticisms have been levelled at the role of the governors, and both remain
apposite. Both derive from the 'lack of any properly codified guidelines for the
precise conduct of the Board of Governors. Exactly what their duties were . . .
was entirely a matter of convention'.[24] Both criticisms centre on the governors'
relation to the executive, and the chairman's to the director-general, and
whether an appropriate boundary or distance exists between them. The first
concerns whether the chairman and governors interfere too much in senior
management affairs, particularly in programme issues and policies, so compromising the editorial independence of the executive. Case studies of the
governors intervening to cancel or modify programmes before transmission
are wheeled out in evidence; but any reckoning is ambiguous, since every case
of interference can be matched by one of resilient independence.[25] The second,
related criticism is that by failing to be sufficiently independent of the executive, the governors fail also in their obligation to represent the public interest
vis-à-vis the BBC, and so in their duty of ensuring public accountability.

On both counts historians and commentators have often been equivocal,
conceding too fondly that the separation of governors and executive is an ideal
more honoured in the breach.[26] In the standard account, the governors act as a
kind of Janus-faced human medium of translation between the BBC and the
public, standing for and allied to the public when dealing with management,
standing for the BBC and allied to management when dealing with government. Yet each side of the equation is wholly unsatisfactory. As critics have
recognised from the earliest decades of the BBC, the 'great and the good' who
comprise the governors have had little in common socially and culturally with
'the public' that they affect to represent. But it is the second part of the equation that is more troubling, and that has been neglected. For if the governors

are allied to senior management when they represent 'the BBC' to the outside world, they are rendered incapable of representing the interests of the *rest of* the BBC – the workforce, the programme-makers – in relation to management.

In the nineties, this was the most serious challenge facing the governors in their capacity as representatives of the public interest: the need to temper the managerial excesses that were eroding the corporation's collective identity and weakening its creative bases. But the principle is a general one: the governors, if over-identified with the executive, are unable to monitor to what extent senior management are enhancing or inhibiting the conditions necessary for the BBC to engage in the range, quality, ambition and integrity of programme-making and services that are its *raison d'être*. In short, they are unable to secure the public interest since that is synonymous with the BBC's creative well-being, a critical point often overlooked in favour of political independence. This was the test signally failed by the governors during the Birt years. Certainly Marmaduke Hussey, chairman from 1986 to 1996 and a Thatcher appointee responsible for bringing Birt to the BBC, was excessively hands-on and appeared to blur the constitutional boundary between governors and management.[27] For all his complicity, the quote near the start of this chapter and his autobiography indicate that Hussey became disillusioned with aspects of Birtist management. Nevertheless, precisely because of the lack of appropriate separation, events suggest that the chairman and governors in these years were unable effectively to monitor, question and *require changes in* the policies of senior management.

*

Superlatively vague governance

'Given the superlatively vague definition of their constitutional position, it is difficult to see how [the governors] can bring any new light . . . [They] are trapped in an impossibly contradictory situation. For the most part, they have accepted the compliant, consultative role the director-general, and the corporation generally, needs of them. They speak, publicly at least, for the corporation to Parliament and its agents, to the press and public at large, and not as the chosen guardians of the public interest vis-à-vis the corporation and its activities. How could it be otherwise? For the true situation is represented by a simple adaptation of Reith's fatal remark in his letter to Baldwin at the time of the General Strike: "Assuming that the BBC is for the public interest, and the governors are appointed to serve the public interest, it follows that the governors must serve the BBC too".'

Tom Burns, *The BBC.*

*

Calling the shots: from the horse's mouth

'I was beginning to suspect [DG Michael Checkland] wasn't making much progress because he didn't really want to. The 1 per cent savings per annum that he had been achieving were just not enough, but try as I might I couldn't push him further. He flinched from the difficult decisions which would extend this efficiency drive and make it bite. Moreover, I wanted the impetus to come from him in order to avoid any suggestion that the governors were calling the shots ... About three years into my time at the BBC, the electricians called a strike ... [John Grant, an SDP MP] said he could act as a mediator ... and that Eric Hammond, the general secretary of the ETU, would like to meet me. This was familiar territory, so I said I'd ring back shortly. I called Mike Checkland and told him. He made it clear he didn't think such a meeting was the job of the chairman. It was his responsibility ... "Look, Mike," I said, "I know this business, I know these people ... I really think you should let me do this. Just give me the parameters of the issues."'

Marmaduke Hussey, *Chance Governs All.*

*

It was to correct any impression of a lack of independent oversight, and to buttress the BBC against charges of insufficient accountability, that there arose over the nineties the armoury of external regulatory mechanisms described earlier, mechanisms in which the governors were fully implicated. Despite their scale and complexity, however, they failed to address the core problems: the lack of separation between governors and executive, and the Board of Governors' lack of effective sanctions if the executive was found to be in breach of its responsibilities. Two more features of the system stoked the situation by rendering the governors out of touch. First, throughout the BBC's history the stance and the composition of the governors have been conceived in the civil service tradition of the 'philosophy of the amateur', a model in which gifted, usually Oxbridge-educated generalists are employed to make judgements that are not burdened by too much knowledge.[28] Second, because of their closeness to management, the governors lack independent sources of information and research on and insight into the organisation. This was revealed in the mid nineties in the language used by staff in Corporate Centre. They spoke of 'running the governors', 'keeping the governors informed' and 'making sure the governors are happy'. They enthused about an innovative 'listening strategy . . . a relatively new idea of saying that the governors must have a mechanism by which they actually listen to the audience', that 'they shouldn't just rely on the contact through management but should take a view independently'.[29] The governors come across as thoroughly managed, as utterly dependent for their information on the largesse of the executive.

*

I know nothing at all

'I know nothing at all about broadcasting, but I can learn . . . Specialisation is one of the most dangerous tendencies. It has given us experts, not wise men.'

Lord Tedder, governor and vice-chairman of the BBC, speaking in 1949–50.

*

Meet the governors

It is lunchtime at a governors' seminar. The congregation floods into the reception area. Sobriety is discarded and an awkward sociability develops between the professional insiders – the broadcasters, journalists and members of the political and cultural elites – and the few outsiders whose function it is to stand in for the 'public'. Myself neither fish nor fowl, I collect a plateful of food and a glass of wine. I'm slightly at a loss where to stand. I spot a middle-aged lady also on her own and introduce myself. She is Margaret, a governor and an ex-headmistress, and we begin to chat. Soon we are joined by a middle-aged man, Adrian, also a governor, who opens by admitting cheerfully that he comes from an entirely different world to broadcasting – something to do with water – and doesn't know why he should have been chosen as a BBC governor, except, he supposes, for his managerial and business experience. The air is genial and open. I ask Margaret and Adrian whether they ever watch Channel 5, Sky or any of the other satellite and cable channels to get a sense of the competition. They say, disarmingly, that they don't. Margaret continues, 'We can't actually get cable or satellite at home – can you? The BBC provides us with nothing, except free copies of the *Radio Times*!' and they laugh. Adrian adds, 'But every week, a truck appears with a large bag of documents – we get everything written down!' They chuckle again. Margaret reflects, 'In Reith's day, the governors were all given a radio – a wireless; *that* I know . . .'

Diary, 1997.

*

245

Questions about the system of governors do not end there. For all the efforts made in the later nineties to be more publicly responsive, some of the mechanisms were unconvincing. The governors' seminars, for instance, were staged encounters, their audiences packed with the jaded ranks of 'opinion formers'. While a great deal of statistical audience research was cited, little attempt was made to bring in a representative range of members of the public. In its place the seminars substituted a few individuals plucked from the ready-made 'public' supplied by the Community Programme Unit's *Video Nation* series. Like the Statement of Promises, the seminars had the surreal, dual quality of being both genuine attempts to attain greater public accountability through open debate on significant issues facing the BBC, while in execution amounting to performances of 'accountability' that short-circuited contact with a broader public. The seminars were insular affairs, the BBC talking to its immediate circle, almost to itself.

*

Consulting the 'public'

I am attending a governors' seminar held in public rooms on the higher floors of the White City building. These occasions are ostensibly exercises in public consultation and accountability in which a topical theme is taken, presentations are made, and those invited get to debate and to ask questions of BBC executives and governors. The 'public' invited to such events is a curious one. The formula seems to be: take plenty of BBC executives, add a bevy of public figures – politicians and members of the Lords, ministry officials, regulator personnel, journalists, media critics, educators, religious leaders, people from business, management and the arts – and spice with a dash of contributors to *Video Nation*. The latter are an eclectic bunch. Across several seminars I note: the telephone engineer, the personnel clerk, the supermarket supervisor, the warden of a home for the elderly, the engineer and retired engineer, the retired teacher, the NHS Trust chairman, the retired tea planter, the private caterer, the graduate, the unemployed office manager, the pensioner, the retired colonel and his wife, the Belfast GP, the unemployed woman from Newcastle and the ten-year-old schoolboy. I know their occupations because they are flagged in the guest list. Among the public figures present at this and other seminars I'm amazed by the predictability of the names. It's like some central casting list of the British establishment: Melanie Phillips, Janet Daley, Polly Toynbee, Andrew Neil, Ian Hargreaves, Christina Odone, Brenda Maddox, Baroness (P. D.) James, Jane Asher, Joanna Trollope and her husband Ian Curteis, Rachel Billington, Lord Dubs, Lady Howe, Baroness Hogg, David Hare . . . right and left, great and good.

This seminar is on Quality, Values and Standards: The Future of Broadcasting Regulation. The first session is an address by Professor Lisa Jardine, cultural historian, broadcaster and daughter of the philosopher Jacob Bronowski, whose *Ascent of Man* is a television classic. She stresses the extraordinary maturity of viewers and the need for programmes that engage, enhance life and 'renegotiate the tendency to passivity'. But, she says, the BBC is poor at addressing social and cultural diversity, for example at meeting the news interests of working-class women. There are questions, then coffee. The second session opens with *The Armchair View*, a filmed compilation of viewers' opinions on regulation and censorship which uses members of the *Video Nation* group, asking who regulates for whom? It is followed by a panel discussion with four senior executives, who sit on stage in front of us watching the film: Will Wyatt, CE of Broadcast, Patricia Hodgson, director of Policy and Planning, Matthew Bannister, director of Radio, and Philip Harding, controller of editorial policy. The moment is powerful: as we watch, the BBC sees 'ordinary people' talking back. But it's also controlled; nothing has been left to chance. In the film and discussion, regulation is the key word. I wonder: is the day just a political exercise aimed at demonstrating that the BBC's self-regulation is alive, responsive and well?

In the last session James Naughtie, moderating, notes a certain complacent consensus in the room on quality. Will anyone disagree? he pleads. A young woman from *Video Nation* comments tartly that no wonder there is a consensus; the composition of the governors' seminar does not exactly represent a broad cross-section of the population. Naughtie pursues the theme, asking his bosses whether the BBC has improved its employment profile in terms of greater representation of the non-white, the non-middle class and the non-middle-aged. Tom Gutteridge, of the independent Mentorn Barraclough Carey, picks up the ball and throws it to the chairman, Sir Christopher Bland, asking how many of the BBC's top executives are black. Bland says, 'Not enough', but doesn't have a figure; he points vaguely to one man in the room. Then he throws the challenge back, and Gutteridge boasts, 'In MBC, three out of eight!' Birt speaks for the first time to say that women are increasingly well represented throughout the BBC, but that for ethnic minorities it's not such a good story. The young woman comes back sternly: 'The seminar's been arrogant and inward-facing; the BBC sees itself alone as the centre of values and standards in British broadcasting. So what was presented as a wide-ranging debate on quality and standards across the industry has degenerated today into a self-congratulatory discussion about the BBC.'

Sir Kenneth Bloomfield, the governor for Northern Ireland and former head of the civil service in Belfast, wraps up with an eloquent commentary in which he lauds the recent BBC1 documentary series, *Provos*, made by Peter Taylor, which gives the history of the IRA and Sinn Fein. Alluding to Jardine's opening thesis, Bloomfield argues that it marks the maturing of the BBC's audience, who are now ready to take more controversial material on Northern Ireland. He rests a defence of the BBC's self-regulation on this: for him the handling of the series shows the BBC's capacity to sense and respond to changing public values at its best. The seminar ends. Later, I pull out a review of *Provos*. It gives a different take. Desmond Christy comments, 'Is there another country in the world where its public broadcasting company would give hours of prime time to the people who have been murdering that state's soldiers and citizens?. . . It will probably be the only detailed history of the Northern Ireland conflict that many viewers will ever watch and they will learn next to nothing about the Protestant view, or of the majority of Catholics who don't support the IRA. Does that really help anyone?'[30]

Diary, 1997.

*

As well as questions about the external contacts made under the sign of 'public accountability', there were doubts about internal processes and about the effectiveness of governor interventions. If it appeared from the bulletins of the Programme Complaints Unit and the governors' seminars that self-regulation was robust, that was not necessarily the experience of programme-makers.

*

Rubber teeth ruling

'Here's why I am still here. There were several films in the strand, and before transmission we referred them up through the controller of editorial policy and the controller of BBC2. Well, after they went out there were complaints from viewers, which the Programme Complaints Unit responded to, investigated, and defended the programmes. Then there was a Broadcasting Standards Council complaint, which we don't respond directly to; the Complaints Unit does. The BSC judgement was that we shouldn't have transmitted the films. Because of that it was referred to the governors. Then I had a phone call with the secretariat, the people who service the governors, telling me off the record that the governors had decided that the films should have been neither transmitted nor defended, that the BBC, once there was a complaint against them, should immediately have apologised. In fact, I had to instigate the phone call to the secretariat myself, because I hadn't been contacted; I had to ask them what the judgement was. That was the last I ever heard of that saga. But just for fun I'll show you a *Daily Mirror* cutting with chairman Bland saying that any producers found to be in breach of the BSC would be summarily sacked. Well, I'm still waiting!'

GB: 'Your point is that Stephen, the controller of editorial policy – hasn't he since become head of the BSC? – that he and Michael Jackson didn't find the films problematic?'

'They were both happy. Stephen was clear that they were at the edge of what we can transmit; two of the films were of particular concern for him. One was about drug use; the other was about criminal behaviour. On that one he asked for one little bit to be removed so that we wouldn't be charged with teaching people how to steal. So there were differences between the rulings. And my own experience was that the governors' ruling had rubber teeth; it wasn't followed through. A different pose in public and internally. It seems odd.'

BBC producer, 1997.

*

Is it getting better?

A Drama Board; it is devoted to discussion with the Independent Advice Panel appointed to assess Drama's Annual Performance Review and the past year's drama output. The panel consists of playwright David Hare, journalist Peter Fiddick and TV writer Dorothy Hobson. Present are the drama heads and executive producers. The atmosphere is one of engagement and enquiry. Hare opens: 'The Birt revolution is always defended by the notion that it will deliver more money for programme-making. And that ultimately means money for drama, because that's the key challenge for the BBC, the most costly genre and the most prominent for the audience. So: we're here to see if that *is* what's really happening, and whether – crudely – drama is getting better on the BBC. That's what the governors have charged us to check out.'

Mike Wearing weighs straight in: 'The problem is, how do we assess whether drama is "getting better"? At present in the BBC it's basically advertising and commercial criteria that hold sway – numbers, ratings – as well as the audience appreciation index. What criteria do we use to assess quality? There's no sense under the current regime of how BBC drama might contribute to the national dramatic culture.' Hare and others agree that the best work of the year, two singles – *Life After Life* and *Streetlife* – were buried on BBC2 and should have been heavily promoted and put out on BBC1 as theatric films: 'They were the best output in British *film* for the whole year!' Hare continues, 'You're in the hot seat here, with a very varied output. The standard of music is often low, and dialogue can be poor – take *Roughnecks*.' An executive producer adds, 'Let's face it, *The Family* was done purely for ratings.' Hare criticises *Hamish Macbeth* as poorly written, as though by a team, part of a swathe of programmes that seemed as though they were 'made in the Moulinex'. But Andrea, in charge of *Hamish*, defends: 'It was

249

written by a key new writer, Danny Boyle, but with help in later episodes.' They talk through *Dangerfield*: 'I inherited this one, and I agree it's bland,' admits the executive producer. 'The strange thing is, it was brought by a writer who really wanted to do it, having found an area of GPs' work – with the police – that no one had written about. But it got flattened out in the making and ended up like a corporate video for the Warwickshire Tourist Board! Dreadful . . .', and all laugh in agreement.

Hare and Hobson eulogise *EastEnders* and *Casualty*, saying the oldest soaps are still the best. Robert, drama supremo from Northern Ireland, poses the big question: 'Should we be doing what we are trying to do? That is, both quality work and ratings-led work?' Jo, head of Series, counters, 'Come on, nobody pitches work to the controllers that they don't believe in.' Hare responds, 'You're poised somewhere between the old BBC model, with the focus on "distinctiveness", and the American model – *ER* and others that are written by teams and are extremely expensive.' He suggests that the source of problems with poor popular shows like *Hamish* and *Dangerfield* is that they lack a sense of unity, of being overseen by a single writer. There's discussion of a reluctance on the sixth floor to nurture popular series through the early stages. All agree that the BBC has failed to build the schedule around popular drama in the way ITV did over the last decade, which reaped amazing results. But Fiddick demurs, 'I wouldn't want BBC1 to go any further into soap territory.' Drama heads Jo and Tony argue passionately that the problem is that popular series are still looked down on at the BBC.

Ruth, the acting head of Drama Group, astutely identifies the core malaise: 'The drama output this year is reactive, led by the controllers' responses to what "ought" to be made, rather than being led proactively by creativity, by giving producers some autonomy, as used to happen. The fight is to keep the control here in Drama, and to keep doing singles – which are under threat.' Others chime in: 'There's been a centralisation of power in Alan's and Michael's hands.' 'What you're seeing this year is "pitch drama".' Robert muses, '"Distinctiveness": it's a difficult concept. The controllers want to play both games – getting ratings and doing "distinctive" drama, that unique BBC focus on risky, innovative drama. Take *The Hanging Gale* on the Irish famine, which Alan put on BBC1 even though he thought it'd only do 2.5 million.' Hobson adds, 'But Alan should have known that anything with the McGann brothers in it would do well.' Hare winds up; he says the panel *understands*, that the point of the report they've sent to Corporate Centre is to give fuel to Drama Group's case that they should have greater autonomy from the controllers, that the controllers should not intervene so much in commissioning – as was reported as being the core problem. 'Our aim above all is to help you fight your corner on these issues.'

Diary, 1996.

*

Sackcloth and ashes

A Drama Board following the end of Annual Performance Review. Ruth, acting head of the Group, announces a BBFC conference on screen violence this September. 'Does anyone want to attend?' Groans, especially when she mentions that it will include 'an international group of academics'. She winds up by reading from a memo summarising the DG's response to Drama's Performance Review. All present feign attentiveness. There are banalities: the need to develop only the most promising scripts (with heavy sarcasm, 'What a great idea!'); the need to police the watershed more fiercely (at which the head of Series jumps in mock shock at the disciplinary term 'police'); and the need for care so as not to transgress against taste and decency. The Group's attention is brought to three complaints against BBC Drama upheld last year by the BSC. Ruth and others ask rhetorically, 'What do we do when these complaints are upheld?' Mark, head of Films, shoots back, 'Sackcloth and ashes' – that is, penitence, that is, he plainly implies, it's all pretty meaningless, there are no real sanctions. Drama Group, the memo continues, should give full consideration to and continue to discuss the findings of the Independent Advice Panel. Groans again at Corporate Centre's effortless passing the buck in terms of responsibility for Drama's present troubles back to them. . .

Diary, 1996.

*

In 1935, the political scientist W. A. Robson, an expert on the new public corporations, made a perceptive diagnosis of the BBC. Robson praised the corporation for its successes and its constitution, but he criticised the Board of Governors as 'too old and respectable', the BBC's regional policy as too centralised, and its 'controversial' programmes as too cautious. 'The BBC is almost overburdened with a sense of responsibility. One sometimes has the impression that because it is not answerable to one particular body it feels itself to be answerable to everyone for all its actions.' Robson stated that the BBC had 'only the vaguest and most remote contact with its listeners'.[31] A year later the corporation opened its Listener Research section, and audience research has continued ever since. But the corporation continues to be racked by anxieties over its responsibilities and accountability, anxieties that find expression in a strange combination of remoteness yet frenetic appeasement.

What is glaring about the BBC of the nineties is the imbalance between, on the one hand, the under-resourced and largely unreformed traditional mechanisms of accountability in the guise of the Board of Governors and, on the other, the excessive resources poured into the intrusive audit and accountability instruments wielded by the executive over its workforce. Power was held by senior management effectively unchallenged by the governors, whose regulatory oversight appears to have been impotent on the issues that mattered most. Trust and creative autonomy were replaced by processes of audit and notions of accountability conceived simplistically in terms of a contract between the BBC and its public. But despite the genuflection to the public, the critical linkage in that contract was absent: that is, the accountability of BBC management to its creative staff, the executive's duty to promote – not erode – the conditions that allow integrity, creativity and innovation in programme-making to flourish.[32]

The evidence from the nineties suggests that when significant internal conflicts arose – over the excesses of Producer Choice, the new management, the control of rights, or between Production and Broadcast following the 1996 restructuring – the governors were either insufficiently informed, or incapable of intervening independently of senior management. They were unable to scrutinise and overrule the policies of the executive, one of their principal roles. They could not do so because they formed part of the same defensive regulatory shield set up by the BBC against external criticism and government intervention. The lesson is one for the very concept of self-regulation. As serious was the governors' inattention to the weakening of commitment, identification and trust that stemmed from casualisation, and to the pervasive drift in the BBC's public service ethos stemming from these changes and from the business values championed by influential parts of management. The consequences for the BBC were grave. The governors were too closely allied to and dependent upon the executive, an unhealthy symbiosis that stoked the cynicism of staff and that remains a pressing issue for reform.

For all the high-level statements of public service vision issued by senior management over the course of the nineties, their preoccupations and the policies they unleashed worked in a contrary direction. Questions of how the BBC's programming and services might be reconceived and what new guiding values they should espouse were given low priority and displaced by other dominant concerns: efficiency, markets, value for money, audit and accountability. While these concerns might well form part of a redefinition of the practice of public service broadcasting, they were not articulated in these terms and stood more as ends in themselves. Serious problems were caused by the way these 'autonomous' values were pursued. Management had its face turned towards the concerns of the wider political culture; there was a vacuum in terms of reanimating the particular social and cultural values of the BBC as a public service broadcaster.

Did the new model managerialism improve efficiency, productivity and accountability? The question is difficult to answer since one of its main effects was to alter the very terms in which efficiency, productivity and accountability were understood and judged. But the rubric of accountability signalled another cultural change within the organisation. It elevated 'the audience' or 'the public' into an object of the BBC's enquiry and the source from which it must seek approval. Indeed the clearest managerial articulation of a new definition of public service broadcasting centred on an enhanced role for audience research. The questions are whether the public was more adequately under-stood and represented than in earlier decades, and whether the practice matched the rhetoric.

Knowing the Audience

The shipping forecast

The poet Seamus Heaney is standing beside a lighthouse on a windswept dockside under a louring sky. He faces out to sea. Before reciting the opening lines of his 'Glanmore Sonnet', he says to camera: 'The voice that read the shipping forecast had a terrific strength about it, a terrific certitude. It also conjured up the threat of gale. So you felt secure, in a sense, listening at home. It was a form of poem, really:

'Dogger, Rockall, Malin, Irish Sea:
Green swift upsurges, North Atlantic flux
Conjured by that strong, gale-warning voice
Collapse into a sibilant penumbra
Midnight and closedown. Sirens of the tundra,
Of eel-road, seal-road, whale-road, keel-road, raise
Their wind-compounded keen behind the baize
And drive the trawlers to the lee of Wicklow.'

[*Offscreen: the Greenwich time signal*] Pip, pip, pip, pip, pip, piiip.
[*Cue*]   Seventy-five years of the BBC.
        BBC: You make it what it is.

BBC seventy-fifth anniversary corporate video, 1997.

*

On audience research and the mass

'If you don't believe in good television for a mass audience, you don't belong in television. There was a kind of narcissism in [the old BBC] Drama; producers would do their own thing, and brought that to the controllers. Producers were too autonomously-driven; they didn't concern themselves with what the audience might want. Now, schedulers are much more competitive: there is more of a research basis than before. This was an eye-opener for me – and so the aim of [audience] research is to educate producers about what the audience might want. Producers come to some research groups, and they get feedback that way. It's useful to see popular programmes deconstructed, good for my education. It's useful to know the mass audience's prejudices, useful as a tool for popular drama – educative, not prescriptive. Comedy is much more unpredictable; shows wax and wane. In comedy the best things don't fit into received categories; there are no genres. How do you account for [the success of] *One Foot in the Grave*?'

BBC1 executive, 1996.

*

The American Way of Television?

The way British television is made was revolutionised during the nineties. The model was the American system. For the commercial US networks, marketing plays an integral part both in the conception of channels and in determining their output. The schedule is planned with the input of marketing and market research, and programmes are ordered up to fit the schedule template. The recent successful US cable and terrestrial channels, such as Fox, MTV and Discovery, pioneered brand-driven television; they were seen as more fully modern and professional in their operations than the British networks. As the marketing-led model caught on, it swept not only through the BBC but, via the BBC, through other European public broadcasters as well.

A number of forces took the BBC in this direction. Intensifying competition, the growth of multichannel broadcasting and the wider drift of the industry towards the model of cross-media companies caused a huge increase in advertising spend among the BBC's competitors. Marketing, branding and cross-promotion grew in significance. The Sky channels benefited from cross-promotion through the News International newspapers, while MAI, then owners of the ITV companies Anglia and Meridian, merged with Express Newspapers, also providing opportunity for cross-promotion. Channel 5, launched in 1997, became the first British terrestrial network to be built around a brand identity, one encapsulated in the slogan 'modern mainstream'. Many in the BBC felt impelled to respond to these developments. The corporation's launch of new commercial and public service channels and of BBC Online necessitated a new attention to planning the market positioning of channels and services, their identities, and their differentiation from each other. Here the marketing and strategy machineries came to the fore, while branding became a tool for delivering their visions. The shape and content of the schedule would now have to conform at a high level to the encompassing brief delivered by marketing and strategy. To this was added the pressure for more 'efficiency' in the financial planning of channels. By determining the schedule at the centre and dictating what could be spent at each point, the goal was to reduce wasteful expenditure on the development of programmes that had little chance of getting on screen.

The final element in the picture was the growing importance accorded to market or audience research. There was a telling duality in the BBC's use of research. On the one hand it played a key part in the centralised planning of the new marketing-led schedules, techniques at the heart of commercial media. On the other hand, audience research was portrayed as a powerful way to promote greater public accountability. It would allow the BBC to understand how its viewers were being well- or under-served, their desires fulfilled or ignored. Research and marketing were seen by their advocates as playing a critical role in transforming the BBC's culture, forcing what had been an introverted and narcissistic organisation to look outside itself. At the same time, the rationales of marketing were leavened by an awareness of the expanding parameters of creativity within the organisation. Creativity was becoming multi-layered. Now not only programme-making, but the design of each network and of the total portfolio of BBC services were conceived as creative practices. At base, in the face of continuing questioning of the licence fee and the threat of its non-renewal, marketing aimed to set out very clearly in the public domain the BBC's public service 'proposition'. If this was the American way of television, the intention was to remix it with the British commitment to broadcasting's democratic and cultural potentials.

*

Perfect Day

LOU REED: *'Just a perfect day, drink sangria in the park . . .'*
BONO: *'And then later, when it gets dark . . .'*
SKYE: *'. . . We'll go home'*
DAVID BOWIE: *'Just a perfect day . . .'*
SUSANNE VEGA: *'Feed animals in the zoo . . .'*
ELTON JOHN: *'Then later a movie too, and then home . . .'*
. . . Andrew Davis conducts the BBC Symphony Orchestra emotively . . .

BOYZONE: *'Oh it's such a perfect day . . .'*

LESLEY GARRETT: *'I'm glad I spent it with you . . .'*

. . . Lou Reed plays air piano . . .

BURNING SPEAR: *'Oh such a perfect day . . .'*

BONO: *'You just keep me hanging on . . .'*

THOMAS ALLEN: *'You just keep me hanging on . . .'*

. . . BRODSKY QUARTET: *Dud dud dud dud dud, dud dud dud dud dud, dooo . . .*

HEATHER SMALL: *'Just a perfect day . . .'*

EMMYLOU HARRIS: *'Problems all left alone . . .'*

TAMMY WYNETTE: *'Weekenders on our own . . .'*

SHANE MCGOWAN: *'It's such fun . . .'*

. . . Sheona White plays a mournful break on the tenor horn . . .

DR JOHN: *'Just a perfect day . . .'*

DAVID BOWIE: *'You make me forget myself . . .'*

ROBERT CRAY: *'I thought I was someone else . . .'*

HUEY: *'. . . Someone good – yeah . . .'*

IAN BROUDIE: *'Oh it's such a perfect day . . .'*

GABRIELLE: *'I'm glad I spent it with you . . .'*

DR JOHN: *'Oh such a perfect day . . .'*

EVAN DANDO: *'You just keep me hanging on . . .'*

EMMYLOU HARRIS: *'You just keep me hanging on . . .'*

. . . Courtney Pine plays a sax solo over the BBC Symphony Orchestra . . .

BRETT ANDERSON: *'You're going to reap just what you sow . . .'*

VISUAL MINISTRY GOSPEL CHOIR: *'Reap, reap, reap . . .'*

JOAN ARMATRADING: *'You're going to reap . . .'*

LAURIE ANDERSON: *'. . . Just what you sow . . .'*

VISUAL MINISTRY GOSPEL CHOIR (O/S): *'Reap, reap, reap . . .'*

HEATHER SMALL: *'You're going to reap just what you sow, yeah . . .'*

TOM JONES: *'Oh, you're going to reap just what you sow-ooh-oooh . . .'*

HEATHER SMALL (O/S): *'You're going to reap just what you, what you sow, yeah . . .'*

[*Cue*] Whatever your musical taste, it is catered for by BBC radio and television. This is only possible thanks to the unique way the BBC is paid for by you. BBC: You make it what it is.

'Perfect Day', BBC corporate promotion video, 1997.

*

Marketing Values

In the tailwind of the 1997 award-winning promotional video, 'Perfect Day', marketing emerged as a powerhouse within the BBC. A cover of the classic Lou Reed song, 'Perfect Day' was exemplary in marrying sophistication and gut appeal. It could be enjoyed in many ways. Its hyperreal and ironic visuals drew on the grammar both of music video and of the English art-house film, *The Draftsman's Contract*.[1] Its multi-ethnic cast took in household names from every musical style, old and young, female and male. Its lyrics spoke in a double metaphor of music's and the BBC's capacity to give us a perfect day, to keep us hanging on, to make us forget ourselves, to make us think we are someone else. They ended with a good ol' evangelical homily: that in life we reap just what we sow, which, through the final promo message, was linked with the inherent morality of the licence fee as a contribution to sustaining the greater cultural good. The sounds, the switching between voices and voice styles, effected a cross-genre but seamless kind of soul, a hummable, danceable but poetic whole. 'Perfect Day' managed to link the BBC as the soul of Britain's musical and media culture with soul music as the symbol of musical healing. It became a paean to the BBC's hybrid cultural and social aspirations, its ability to weave the black with the white, the national with the international, the sublime with the mundane. Ironically, it could achieve all this only by shedding any association the original song had both through its author and its use in the film *Trainspotting* with drug-taking – another, less benevolent source of heightened experience. The promo video was itself both art and product. 'Perfect Day' was released as a CD and raised £2.4 million for the BBC's Children In Need campaign.

The escalating importance of marketing within the corporation caused ructions as various organisational configurations were tried out to find its optimal location. Should it be located in each directorate? Should marketers sit within the controllers' ambit? Reflecting the instability, marketing and publicity were restructured in the mid nineties under McKinsey's guiding hand. In addition, rivalries broke out with the burgeoning strategy departments over which of the newly ascendant disciplines should take precedence. Was strategy a function of marketing or vice versa? Audience research, formerly an autonomous department, was the love child torn between them: should it sit in marketing, or alongside the channels, or in strategy?

The seriousness attached to the marketing push was evident in galvanising internal documents issued by the Television directorate which decreed, for the internal public, the marketing plans that should drive all presentation, promotion, publicity and public relations activities. The intention was to unify these efforts to ensure the propagation of 'a defining "vision" of how we wish to be perceived'.[2] Marketing was to be coordinated with the strategy for BBC Television. It must integrate an understanding of the corporation's overall competitive strategy, the positioning of its brands and customer needs. The aim of the coordinated activities must be a long-term communication strategy which 'consistently signals value to licence fee payers'.[3]

In the marketing plan for 1996–7, following a brief analysis of the changing competitive context, the marketing objectives for Television were set out, including the need to engage the audiences then most distant from the BBC – lower socio-economic groups, young people and female viewers. Stress was laid on 'needs mapping', an experimental research project designed to understand the needs of audiences, so as to serve them better. A series of more specific objectives was then given for BBC1 and BBC2, followed by a list of 'ideal brand perceptions' for each channel, pointing to their intended distinctive qualities. It was noted that these were qualities the BBC would like the audience spontaneously to attribute to each channel, but that considerable work remained to be done to consolidate the branding. BBC1, branded 'Our BBC1', was to be a channel of broad appeal, the nation's premier channel; it should be perceived as entertaining, engaging, trustworthy, authoritative, contemporary, warm, welcoming, elegant and so on. 'My BBC2', by contrast, should be perceived as topical and relevant, diverse, playful, modern, challenging, surprising, able to take risks, a channel of ideas. Certain values – being accessible, innovative, intelligent and stylish – were repeated as desired features of both. Despite the importance attached to branding, there was, then, a lingering incoherence in the attempt to delineate distinctive brands, a problem that surfaced in another guise in marketing meetings concerned with defining an appropriate hierarchy of BBC brands.

*

Crown Jewels and nested brands

Michael Jackson, controller of BBC1, has invited me to a branding strategy meeting. When I enter the meeting on the sixth floor of Television Centre, it has a hushed and concentrated air. Austerely elegant women and men of about thirty line the twilit room, draped on sofas. The women wear red and grey. The meeting is a 'Concept Overview' to discuss a new branding campaign for BBC1. A video of various brand concepts is being shown; it's followed by slides showing options for a new channel logo. Voices are low, hesitant, serious. A few words spoken are taken to say a lot. How to time the roll-out of both the new concept and the new logo? It would be too much to do both at once. Two people hint at strenuous rivalries between different parts of the BBC. Corporate Centre, they complain, are using some of the best comedy clips for the corporate marketing campaign, 'the same clips we want for BBC1!' Someone responds, 'But the perception at Corporate Centre is that it's we at BBC1 who are using too many of the Crown Jewels' – meaning the best takes from hit comedies, sitcoms and soaps. The meeting dwells on the contradictions of creating a brand identity for BBC1 which is distinctive, when it is likely to be in tension with the overall corporate brand – which is being carried on BBC1 as the main mass channel, and which those present discreetly ridicule. The challenge is clear: how to work out these nested brands, these competing identities within the whole?

Diary, 1997.

*

One story exemplifies the ambitions of the marketing-led approach in the mid nineties: the repositioning of Radio 1. Matthew Bannister, one of the authors of the 1992 paper Extending Choice which argued for greater diversity and innovation in the BBC's pop music output, became controller of Radio 1 in 1993. His task was to shift the station away from its dated profile and make it again a youth music network. Radio 1 had aged with its 1970s audience; its listeners were now in their mid thirties and forties. The station had an air of malaise. In the context of a massive expansion in commercial radio, and of repeated calls for Radio 1 to be privatised, what was the justification for the BBC intervening in the market for popular music radio? The repositioning required painful changes: the shedding of a generation of core personalities and presenters and the adoption of a new music policy, one that came to rely heavily on independent suppliers. But the paramount challenge was to reinvent the station's public service 'theology', as Bannister called it. The new theology, conceived in light of the revised target audience, would form the substance of the Radio 1 brand, and from it would proceed both programming and the detail of marketing. In the new marketing universe, the public service purpose of Radio 1 became, in effect, a facet of strategy and marketing.

Radio 1's new theology was condensed in the phrase 'New Music First'. The aim was that the network should become a showcase for up-and-coming bands and reflect current trends in a way that the collusive duo of the record companies and commercial radio would not. Through its independence from commerce, the revamped Radio 1 should find and nurture new talent, delivering it in due course to the market. It should take risks and innovate by exposing its audiences to unfamiliar musical genres. And it should have a range differentiating it from commercial stations by containing, alongside its musical mix, news, documentaries, features, and social action and information campaigns on issues of relevance to young people. Independence and integrity – those age-old BBC values, imaginatively reinterpreted – were the watchwords.

*

Stacked heels and sycophancy

'Radio 1 had stayed petrified in the mid seventies to early eighties; the DJs had become a laughing stock. There were blokes with crap haircuts wearing bomber jackets and stacked heels. Music tastes had changed. Kiss FM came along, and genre stations were starting up; big musical forces were at work for young people. Rave happened in the mid to late eighties and was completely ignored by Radio 1. There was an exponential growth of commercial radio, now some 180 stations. The network was living in a world of its own, a world it had created in its heyday when 22 million people listened. The music industry had no motivation to challenge Radio 1's producers and DJs. The station was almost a mirror reflecting the industry back to itself; sycophancy and money and promotion washed around. Producers were taken to lunch and their programmes were praised; the industry just fed the status quo. The station was driven by powerful personality broadcasters who were laws unto themselves. Many of those involved were lazy and un-self-critical. It was all pretty sick. Now, I can tell when a record is a cynical piece of crap or when it's good, and I *hated* the old Radio 1. It stood for everything that was bad taste; it didn't stand for music. So when I came to the BBC I listened to the pirates. Every time you came in contact with Radio 1 it was just offensive. I did listen to John Peel, but he was tucked away somewhere and they weren't proud of him.'

Executive, BBC Radio 1, 1997.

*

The nugget: what are we for

'To change the station, we had to free ourselves from where we were. The very first thing you have to do is understand what you're for, define your vision – as the brand people say, your technical values and tonal values. It all comes from defining the brand: once you've done that you can create your world with those values in mind; it makes decisions on content easy. So we talked and talked, went to presentations about the market, until we had distilled what we were for. We had a couple of goes at getting the

261

schedule and presenters right. But before that we had to ask: which audience? What sort of pop station should the BBC have? As the pop market has grown old it's become sophisticated. You have to find your place in it. As a public service we couldn't serve just one musical genre. Virgin and Capital were serving the older audience. But at that time, what did the BBC do for young people? Bugger all, actually; they're future licence payers and it doesn't know how to reach them. That led us to say: Radio 1's got to be for young people; it's got to be mixed genre; it's got to lead by playing more new music, encouraging new British artists and DJs and investing in live acts. It's got to be about the young experience and that passion for music. That's what distinguishes us from the commercial market, which is about maximising share with Tina Turner records. So our vision statement, which we settled on after a year and a half of experimenting, was Radio 1 as the UK's leading contemporary music station.

'Then we had to overhaul the schedule, to make it match the target audience's lifestyle. That's about being consistent, having proper junctions and flow, deciding how many sequence programmes you have. Lead and reflect: Radio 1 leads and invests in new music in a way the market won't, whether it's a rap show that encourages UK rap to become an authentic thing for black kids, or a new indy band discovered for the evening session. The Oasis story is a good example: Radio 1 picked them up in 1990 when nobody else would play them; the sound they made seemed ragged and noisy. Only Radio 1 had the clout and investment to give them sessions and let them play live. Then what have we got? A world phenomenon, a band that's generating a huge income for the UK, and we've served our part in that triumvirate of the business, the audience and Radio 1. To reposition ourselves we ruthlessly changed everything, from the faders in the studio to on-air talent and presentation. But once you've got the idea, everything feeds off it, your marketing, your live shows, the producers you employ, the sounds you make, the bands on your playlist. The hardest thing was to get that nugget, that thought: what are we for.'

Executive, BBC Radio 1, 1997.

*

To help deliver this ambitious programme, a new marketing manager was brought in. The management team worked in an integrated way, using the panoply of market research and strategy skills to transform the network. The repositioning was perceived as highly successful and as a model for the rest of BBC Radio.[4] In 1997, Bannister was promoted to director of Radio with a brief to lead a strategic consideration of the entire structure of BBC radio output.

*

Roll over Radio 1

'Matthew wanted Radio 1 to be repositioned as a youth music station again, and it was exciting. Marketing is very important to him. So I joined as marketing manager in June 1994 when he'd made changes, the audience had started to go down rather dramatically and Dave Lee Travis had left very noisily – a traumatic period, when we weren't sure if it would work. Matthew involved me totally in all creative decisions, in scheduling and presenter and policy decisions; it was a collaborative relationship. After I arrived we identified fifteen- to twenty-four-year-olds as our target. Marketing gave us the confidence to focus on that group, in the music we played and the risks we took with the schedule. That age group are quite sophisticated, and if you focus down even more, we're talking eighteen- to twenty-one-year-olds. They're into NME, Loaded, the Sun. Chris Evans brought them in, but so did the evening session, the specialist genre shows and the live music. Well, the demographic shift has been achieved, reach and share have grown, and our biggest improvements are among the fifteen to twenty-four-year-olds – they find more that they like. But 48 per cent of our weekly reach is among the over thirties, so we've still got that older audience as well.'

GB: 'What you're doing with your brochure and the poster campaign . . . they're using something like old typewriter print. What's the idea? The style is almost early sixties.'

'It's really just a way of making it look more interesting. When I came everything had a different look: the DJ cards were different, the programmes did their own promotional stuff, and the logo was four colours, which looked naff. It was a disparate and fragmented image, still very end of the pier, which is where Radio 1 and the Road Show brand were positioned then: DLT, funny boxer shorts, Mr Blobby. That's the one thing we all say when we get drunk: if we were really honest with ourselves, and we were really going for the eighteen to twenty-ones, we'd get rid of the Road Show. It appeals to the younger-end family groups and Radio 1 loyalists. We've made it a bit cooler and slicker; we've put on new bands, and before I joined they tried taking it into inner-city Liverpool, into urban centres. But it didn't work. It's still about being on the coast on a sunny morning, Western-super-Mare and places like that, a holiday atmosphere.'

GB: 'It shows you have a split audience. The eighteen to twenty-ones are growing, but you've still got this older, kids and mums and dads audience, and then the students staying up all night as well . . .'

'Yes, it is difficult. When I first joined I thought it was an almost impossible task, selling something that was one thing in the day and another thing at night. My initial thought was to make two brands out of it. But for a total repositioning the daytime product had to change as well, so we could talk about Radio 1 as a unity. That only started to kick in when Trevor Dann came; he made the changes to the music policy on which the whole thing had to rest. For the advertising campaign we had a pitch. I wrote the brief, and it was "This message has got to come from within; it can't be about bolting a cooler image on to Radio 1. It's got to be a slow job of conveying conviction for the music from within." The successful advertising agency thought up the line "Radio 1 As It Is", which we now use. The agency came in and lived here for a month talking to people and getting quotes on tape. It was important that it wasn't just presenters, but people behind the scenes as well, because the station's image then was a bunker full of old men in jumpers who had lost their way and were gloomy about the future – that was the impression.'

GB: 'So they did a kind of anthropology of Radio 1?'

'Yes, it was a bit like that, getting to know what was actually going on inside the station. The bits of film in the promo video were footage from a documentary company who came in and shot behind the scenes for two months, fly-on-the-wall. The campaign was trying to create a better vibe about Radio 1. After that, when Chris joined, we got some positive coverage in the tabloids and music press. The atmosphere was more positive, so we then went on to talk about the shows.'

GB: 'There's an interesting analogy between Radio 1 and Michael Jackson's BBC2. He says it's a channel that should bring everyone in at some point to the schedule; and Radio 1 is now a kind of genre patchwork, which also tries to bring particular music fans to particular shows.'

'That's exactly what our latest advertising, based on research, is about. It's going for non- and light listeners, and it's accepting that they won't listen in the daytime, but they really like rap music and think Tim Westwood is the epitome of cool but they don't know he's on Radio 1; or they really like dance music and respect Pete Tong, but they don't necessarily listen to him on Radio 1. So it's bringing them into the schedule at times that fit with their musical taste and then almost telling them to go away at other times.'

GB: 'On market research, Andy [*Parfitt, deputy controller*] talks passionately about knowing his audience: "I know what a twenty-year-old is doing on a Saturday night: what music they get ready to go out to, what they play in the car, what they fall out of a club at three in the morning to . . ." Where does he get that?'

'I'm in charge of feeding back research: we have awaydays where I do an update on the latest audience research. Mostly it comes from Network Radio Research, the internal BBC function. But that is very demographics-led, very dry and quantitative. It doesn't give you a sense of people's emotions and passions. The best insights come from outside focus group companies; they bring it to life. Informer, a company specialising in qualitative youth research, did a lot of brilliant work for us on fifteen to twenty-fours before we developed the last burst of advertising. I've also used a freelance advisor on trends and attitudes on some projects – he works for Channel 5 as well. Everyone else uses BARB data, which I find mystifying – relying on research that everyone else has access to. You want insights you can own yourself. Other youth brands – Nike, for example – use really interesting creative processes to arrive at marketing ideas. We also use a quantitative brand tracking study to prove effectiveness, and that shows we've seen huge positive shifts in the associations with Radio 1. The funny thing about the BBC is that they don't like their audience; they see them as somehow problematic. When reach increases there's a warm feeling. But when it decreases there's a sense of "Why can't these people see that they should be tuning in?"'

GB: 'Can marketing help bring people to programmes they might not otherwise go to? Isn't that one element of the public service role?'

'Yes, but it can only help so far, which goes to the key issue of marketing being involved in product development. You can only bring someone to a product they want to consume, or that they might try once. You can bring them to Radio 3, for instance, at an accessible point in the schedule; but as soon as they're assaulted by a spectacularly alienating presenter or a difficult slot, that's that. We'd like to help the other networks by bringing the marketing perspective. But BBC processes make it so tortuous – the huge quantities of documents get in the way of clarity.'

GB: 'So what are the main challenges to address in marketing the other radio networks?'

'It's to look with Matthew, as director of Radio, at the whole portfolio of networks, their complementary fit, their core target audiences and respective positioning, because those are by no means clear. Matthew wants to say, "These networks don't have a positioning, and they should." It's difficult and painful, because we're sweeping in and trying to do something new.'

Marketing executive, BBC Radio 1, 1997.

*

Branding the Real

With escalating competition and less dependable audience loyalty, it was widely accepted within the corporation that marketing, promotion and publicity were increasingly central to securing the BBC's success. In the multi-channel era, and with the BBC offering a growing diversity of services, the consensus was that branding had a crucial part to play in distinguishing the BBC from its competitors, providing a basic unity in diversity, and reinforcing the perception of the BBC as reliable and trustworthy. Promotion had the added role of leading audiences across the expanding range of services, from radio or television to online and interactive options. If marketing's heightened profile provoked doubts, it was because of a sense that marketing traded in truisms and was insufficiently informed about the complexities facing the corporation. In marketing presentations, Drama Group were quick to sniff out weaknesses; the ostentatious but brittle professionalism of marketing executives was scrutinised mercilessly for any signs of a less than total command of the challenges for drama.

*

Trial by trailers

Sally, a marketing manager, has come to the Drama board with a marketing report. 'I work to Tina in presentation, and Karl and Paul in publicity.' Ignoring the gathering clouds of collective boredom, she briskly sketches the competitive environment, the task of presenting to licence fee payers the value for money represented by BBC services, and the need to boost brand campaigns and on-air trailers. These will be effective because of the astonishing reach of BBC1. 'I came here from Proctor & Gamble, and we'd have given our back teeth to advertise Fairy Liquid on BBC1!' Sally says Channel 5's activities will pose a challenge to Drama in the coming year. Charles rouses himself and shoots back, 'From what we know of their plans – and we've heard direct from Corinne Hollingworth, their head of Drama'[5] – they're doing eighteen hours of drama a year plus a low-budget soap. We do 360 hours a year. How much of a challenge is that?', implying: do these marketing people know their brief? Sally, slightly fazed, replies that Planning and Strategy think this is likely to be the situation. She continues with the main challenges for Television: the need to attract lower-class women viewers, now underserved; the task of boosting the BBC's audiences in the North-West, Scotland and Northern Ireland; the challenge of securing sports rights; and the need for 'landmark' shows which unify all categories of viewer.

Moving on to 'Our BBC1', she highlights the need to promote Sunday-night period drama. Charles picks her up: 'Surely not just period drama? In Drama Group we believe in a mix, period plus hard-hitting contemporary drama. We want to avoid BBC1 being perceived as a "heritage" channel with "theme park" drama.' Sally backs down, but makes the mistake of mentioning *Pride and Prejudice* and *Ballykissangel* in the same breath. The drama executives snicker: '*Ballykissangel* isn't period drama!'

Sally goes pink and soldiers on, but falls straight into the next hole. 'On channel per-ception, "My BBC2" has huge image problems.' She talks of poster campaigns, like Channel 4's, to raise its profile with youth, and she identifies BBC2 as 'the writer's channel'. 'But why isn't BBC1 the writers' channel?', the drama executives query immediately, rejecting any such crass account of the distinction between the two net-works.

Andrea says, 'Our biggest problem is getting a decent audience for drama on BBC2. We make great drama; it seems perverse that we don't promote it.' Sally agrees, but Robert presses her: 'On-air promotion is incredibly important, but we're told there's a ceiling on how many trails can be shown without pissing off the audience. Will your report lead to an increase?' Sally demurs: there will be no increase, but more care with what is promoted. Charles persists, 'Is Alan still resistant to trailers for BBC2 on BBC1?' Sally hedges: he is, but less strongly. She stresses the importance of off-air campaigns; but the current off-air budget is £500,000 – peanuts, and everyone nods in agreement. 'The trouble is, until now Will has spent all his money on programme-making . . .' She tails off, aware of another faux pas. It doesn't go down well here to argue that money should be drawn from programme-making into publicity. Sally comes to the market-research-based guidelines for the 'ideal brand values' for BBC1 and BBC2, and lists the values associated with each. A drama head teases her, querying the contradictions and banalities of the brand values. 'Aren't these terms equally applicable to both channels? What the hell do they mean?' Sally stands her ground. Charles draws the presentation to a close and thanks her, adding pointedly: 'We wish you luck in *getting more money*!' After she leaves he adds, a little vexed, 'It would help to have some money before you write up a report of that scale. OK, now let's get on with the real work . . .' and they begin to tackle the drama development slate.

Diary, 1996.

*

Another problem also dogged marketing. A brand would be defined as symbolising certain values and proposed as an ideal, only for the reality of a channel or service to fail to live up to the vision. A disjuncture existed between image and output. In the later nineties Radio 1 and BBC2 showed this characteristic slippage: both were networks branded for a young audience, while their programming was demographically eclectic, far from exclusively oriented to youth. By sleight of hand a patchwork schedule targeting a range of demographics would be subsumed within a channel identity ostensibly aimed solely at the elusive young audience.

*

Schizophrenia and hearts and minds

'Despite what we've achieved with Radio 1, I'd admit there's an element of image and brand leading reality. One of the basic rules of brand management is that your product should be consistent and consistently match up to the values that you claim. We've got a slight over-claim problem, because if you switch on our station with your head full of all the things we talk about, our posters and promos, the reality doesn't always match up to our claims. The daytime programmes are a real problem, because there's still that schizophrenia about having broad appeal and less angular stuff on then. We've failed to get hold of the hearts and minds of our mainstream presenters, so that when they speak they live our world, if you like. It's a real problem if you sell somebody the idea of you, and then they sample you and you're no good. We haven't got enough daytime presenters who are young and vibrant enough, who *live* our values.'

Executive, BBC Radio 1, 1997.

*

The most significant effect of the rising influence of marketing on the culture of the BBC was that under the impact of brand-thinking, the guiding values of the corporation and of each of its services had now to be consciously formulated and *performed* by branding, where before they had been part of the collective subconscious. As the employment base fragmented, the former embedded ethos of the BBC was being replaced by the instrumental processes of marketing. One result of this process was a perceived danger of *artificiality*: of the 'bolting on' of cool, or of surface changes hiding a truth 'behind the scenes', or of a failure 'to get hold of hearts and minds'. The question was then how to render the new relationship to BBC values *authentic* and lived – via a kind of auto-anthropology, perhaps, or through exhaustive qualitative market research. In the end, there was no escaping the need to render the reality behind the brand inherently valuable – by providing good programmes and services. If the broadcasting industry in the nineties had begun to believe that the multichannel world required greater consumer trust, and that branding was the way to build it, then BBC professionals were haunted by an awareness that the more trust is marketed, the less substantial it seems; that the audience does not trust the 'trust' produced by branding, and may be right not to do so. For it rests on an elementary category error: that image can stand in or compensate for reality.

*

Habits and tastes: audience research c.1936

'From the mid thirties on there was a renewed emphasis [in the BBC] on the domestic context in which listening took place . . . A special Fireside Number of *Radio Times* in November 1935 affirmed the home as a retreat burrowed deeply away from the pressures of work and urban life . . . Radio was beginning to play a significant role in the organisation of work and leisure. In the later thirties, the Programme Planning Department [began] to adjust daily output to chime in with the time routines of day-to-day life. In this they were immeasurably helped by the establishment of Listener Research and the information it began to supply, from 1936 onwards, about listening habits and tastes. Information was needed in order to have reliable data about who was (and who was not) available for listening, where and when. For the planners Listener Research very quickly became an essential aid in organising output.'

Paddy Scannell and David Cardiff, A Social History of British Broadcasting.

*

Autism and complacency? Audience research c.1963–73

'For the professional broadcaster, appreciation of the service he gives is mediated by the enquiries carried out by a department of the BBC – Audience Research. [But] there was, as one senior official commented, "no evidence of people at the top of the Corporation knowing, or indeed caring, what the audience makes of the service it receives" . . . There are reasons for the constraints put on Audience Research, and these are not the irresponsibility, or arrogance, of broadcasters. The pressure on those responsible for programmes is such that deeper analysis of audience reactions would amount to an intolerable strain . . . The autistic world of commitment and belief which producers and broadcasting as a whole can create around itself is liable to be construed as complacency . . .Yet to regard the apparent imperviousness to outside criticism shown by officials in the BBC as a sign of complacency seems ludicrously inappropriate. They are perpetually concerned with "quality"; many are self-critical to the point of hypersensitivity.'

Tom Burns, The BBC.

*

Listening to the Research

The BBC in the nineties was not just steeped in the managerial audit culture; auditing also became central to its relations with its audiences, as increasingly sophisticated methods of audience research were embraced by the corporation. Research using large-scale survey techniques began in the BBC in 1936. Such a belated commitment might be interpreted as proof from its earliest years of the BBC's lack of interest in its audiences. But in fact the corporation was 'a pioneer in the emerging field of opinion sampling and market research'.[6] Reith, initially reluctant to admit research because of the perceived threat to quality that it might represent, gradually gave it his support. In the late thirties it took in the listening habits of different parts of the population by region, gender, age and social class, and their tastes for different kinds of output, with variety receiving particular attention. By 1961, BBC Audience Research was described as 'probably the largest department of its type maintained by any broadcasting organisation in the world'; and in the years following the start of competition in television, its statistics were the stimulus for the programming brought in to raise the BBC's ebbing share as a counter-offensive against ITV.[7] The quantitative measurements summed up in ratings and relative audience share were central to the British television economy, for both the BBC and ITV, from its inception.

Accounts of the impact of research differ. In the corporation's first decades, according to Paddy Scannell, audience research provided the foundations on which were built increasingly effective forms of programming. For Tom Burns, however, observing in the sixties and seventies, research was invariably disavowed in the culture of anxious professionalism that characterised the BBC; not complacency, but extreme defensiveness masked by professionalism were rife. For recent critics, the statistical abstractions behind ratings lead broadcasters to objectify audiences, obviating any more adequate reflection.[8] There is some truth in all of these accounts, but the developments around research in the later nineties point to entirely new problems.

For decades Broadcasting Research, as it came to be known, was a dedicated department independent of vested interests which carried out its own 'objective' surveys of the audiences resulting from programmes and policies, with a direct line to the director-general. In 1981, the BBC and ITV jointly set up an integrated body, BARB (Broadcasters' Audience Research Board), to provide the surveys that generate ratings and share figures. Other BBC research functions remained in Broadcasting Research until the early nineties, when the department began to be shrunk in size, with many of its operations devolved to, and sometimes duplicated by, the planning and strategy outfits in the directorates. BR's independence was undermined as a new model took hold, in which research should be close to and functional for Television and Radio management. The new relationship between research and its 'customers' or 'users' was to be one of intimacy. The devolved research units produced an increasingly copious supply of information on audiences. Together with the BARB data, it amounted to an almost overwhelming flood of abstract information. Overnight, weekly, monthly, quarterly and annual audience data cascaded from the burgeoning research outfits and had somehow to be metabolised into practical sense by those making scheduling and commissioning decisions.

*

Perched on the controllers' shoulders

'When David Docherty came in '91 or '92 to Broadcasting Research, he immediately argued that in a competitive world, if research is going to make an impact, it needs to be here, in TV Centre. It was delicate because it was breaching the sovereignty of Broadcasting Research. Before then, the culture in Television didn't have research as part of its operation. Jonathan Powell was controller of 1, and Alan was Controller of 2, neither of them particularly interested in research. David persuaded them, and they began to see the benefit of having professionals along. David provided a sort of intellectual leadership; he set up forums where people could argue things through at the same time as giving the controllers support and providing a structure in which they could exercise their creativity. It's a tricky role for the researchers because our first duty is to be true to the data; we can't afford to go native, and it can be extremely uncomfortable when we have to bear bad tidings – say, on a controller's pet project. The purpose of having a broadcasting analysis function here in Television is to be a conduit for tailored research, to get very close to the controllers and schedulers, so as to provide information that bears on their worries. The broadcast analysts are perched on their shoulders; they're privy to all deliberations and decision-making, so they can interrogate the evidence, whether through BARB data or by commissioning ad hoc research. Creative people are still suspicious that we're leading towards making programmes by numbers, which we're not. My job is to review progress at channel level, and to produce monthly, quarterly and annual reviews of our performance which contribute to Annual Performance Review. Where the analysts work at a microlevel with the schedulers and controllers, I work at a macrolevel from the top down, diagnosing strengths and weaknesses: how are we doing this year compared to last year? How are we doing vis-à-vis the competition?

'The technology we now have to interrogate data compared with a few years ago is amazing. I can do it all through this machine, sitting here, where a few years ago I needed a mainframe. The volume of data available now is absolutely vast, overwhelming. And you can cut it whichever way you want, so it's fascinating to interrogate it. But such is the volume that the amount of time I have to *think* about what is being produced is much reduced. The data we have is pre-processed into databases by Broadcasting Research: one is the quarter-hour database, which is average viewing every quarter-hour by channel through the day for a range of demographic breakdowns – gender, social grade, age; the other is a database providing audience estimates by programme, again by a whole range of demographics. Then there are databases for regional analysis.

'The first audience information we get here is the day after transmission. It arrives in this office at 10 a.m., and by 10.30 it's been emailed to all the people that matter, about sixty customers in the organisation. The telex screens carry the weekly round-up. It's the overnights that are the currency because what was on last night is fresh in your mind, so you can make connections between audience and programme; whereas if you wait for the Grey Book with the weekly BARB figures to come out in ten days' time, you can't remember which week was which. I've developed ways of displaying the overnight data so that a controller can get a picture of yesterday's prime time viewing on one page. This one was for Monday: there's BBC1 compared with ITV, BBC2 compared with Channel 4, a satellite figure, and then summaries of our share in peak and all hours, and for daytime. But that's only one version. We have another that focuses on children's audiences; we have a third that breaks down the audience every quarter-hour in demographic terms; and a fourth that compares performance yesterday with the same channel's performance the same day last week and the same day last year. And we have a version that we don't yet send out – it's ready when anybody wants it – which is share of viewing in satellite households.'

Senior executive, BBC Broadcasting Research, 1996.

*

The Transparent Audience

The intensification of audience research in the nineties coincided with the BBC's weakness in popular programming and the perceived need to compete more effectively in this area. But it also related to several other developments. Research was portrayed by senior management as a central means of promoting accountability because it allowed the BBC to know its audience better. It would strengthen the corporation's capacity to deliver value for money by reducing outlay on unlikely winners. It would empower the BBC to hone its public service offerings to provide what audiences actually want and need, rather than what producers think they want and need. For some internal critics it followed that research was a powerful weapon in the ongoing war of attrition against what they saw as the elitism and paternalism of the producer-led culture of the BBC. More constructively, the commitment to research, when combined with a public service orientation and with attention to minorities and to audiences unattractive to advertisers, was seen as forging a new ethical conception of public service broadcasting, one that institutionalised, in however fragile a way, a kind of cultural democracy by suffusing the organisation with understandings of the views and habits of its publics.

If the goal was little different from that of listener research in the thirties, the nineties saw innovation in how it was to be achieved. Not only was research to be intensified and made integral to scheduling, commissioning and production, but the reams of quantitative measures were to be augmented by qualitative research and specifically by focus groups, which became the method of choice. By dealing in less objectifying quasi-conversational techniques, focus groups were believed to proffer a subtler, more humanising knowledge of audiences than ratings, and to throw light on the meanings and emotions attached to broadcasting. They were used to research a range of issues: channel strategies, scheduling decisions, whether to commission or recommission existing shows, concepts for new strands and popular series, pilots and first episodes, controversial storylines, character developments or plotlines, and changes to existing series.

*

Reassurance

'We in the controllers' teams go away for a few days with the controllers three or four times a year, and at those meetings the broadcast analysts will have been analysing where the share is falling or rising and can we do anything about it. There are two analysts for each channel. One examines the BARB data, looking at trends, at what ITV or Channel 4 are doing, as well as individual programmes: how did *The Generation Game* do compared with last year? The second analyst, who's Paula for BBC1, commissions and interprets qualitative research. She's majored the last two years on popular drama, and that was quite new. Drama will be the first to admit they were resistant; they'd grown up in a BBC culture where it was "Trust us, we're the professionals, we know what the public want". And patently it wasn't working because we'd been a long time between hits.

'You can use qualitative research in many different ways. You can test a concept before you make it, as we did for *Dangerfield*. We talked to various groups about the idea, storylines, who might be in it. We'd commissioned the series but the scripts weren't there, so the research was to see in what direction it might go to ensure success. You can use focus groups to help decide where to play a new series in the schedule. You can use them after a series has transmitted to inform the next commission. Alan will say, "In principle I want to recommission; let's do focus groups to test where to take it." Sometimes, because of drama's long lead time, you have to recommission before it's transmitted, as we had to with *Ballykissangel*, so we didn't have the comfort of the 14 million audience it eventually got. That was a departure, and Paula talked drama through it so skilfully that other producers are now asking for focus groups to see how to refresh their series. Alan was pleased with *Ballykissangel*; it would have had to have been damning research for him not to have gone with it. He just wanted the reassurance, because, you know, a priest: where can that possibly go? The public are very sophisticated; they watch a lot of TV, a lot more than some BBC producers or, dare I say it, controllers! It's always reassuring to hear them echoing the professionals. The danger is when you get a total non-meeting of minds, when the producer can't understand what the public's saying. But focus groups are only a tool; they're not the only means by which Alan recommissions a major drama. The judgement is informed by lots of other things as well: how good the scripts are, the producer, the peer-group buzz, none of which is scientific, but they all add to the understanding. We are spending *vast* sums of money . . .'

Commissioning executive, BBC1, 1996.

*

Among executives and programme-makers, and within Drama Group, there were both cynical and sympathetic responses to the rising power of audience research. For some, audience research was seen as tied to the ratings game, and ratings were a cynical hook for popular legitimacy and, increasingly, for legitimacy within the BBC. Research-led ratings fodder was fine as long as it formed part of a mixed programming economy that continued also to permit creative risk and ambition. But for the champions of audience research, it was a useful means of reminding BBC elitists that the most valuable output is quality popular programming, since this alone serves the neglected 'C2DEs'. From this perspective, research enhances the BBC's responsiveness to the mass audience, seen as the prime democratic duty of the public broadcaster; Reithian purposes sit in harmony with an enhanced popular vision delivered by audience

research. Employed in this way, research amounted to a mode of cultural accountability, and for its advocates it was this that gave it a central role in the revivification of public service broadcasting. Occasionally, confrontations occurred between the two positions. In the following BBC1 overview meeting, those presenting focus group findings and others intrigued by the research encountered the largely mute resistance and disaffection of those who felt they had 'heard it all before' and who questioned whether the advocates of research really 'know anything about drama'. For all the potential significance of these means of listening to audiences, the trite nature of the research results fuelled any incipient producer scepticism.

*

'What Makes a Good Drama?'

A Drama strategy overview, and Paula is presenting a summary of focus group research. 'I'm going to canter through key facts learned from the last three years' research on fifty-minute series.' Using bullet-pointed overheads in landscape, deploying viewer quotations and referring to both BBC and ITV series, she describes the typical Popular Drama Viewer as an armchair expert with high expectations, seeking involvement and escapism. She speaks of viewers' categorisation of drama into types: action, realistic, plot-centred, easy watching, calm, soapy, psychological, far fetched, demanding or cosy. Granada's *Cracker* and *Prime Suspect* have set the benchmark for demanding dramas. Under the heading 'What Makes a Good Drama?', she lists viewers' ingredients for success: good characters, involving storylines, believability, a good plot, it 'makes you think or doesn't make you think', stimulating emotions (tragedy, excitement, mystery or humour), or an interesting location or setting. The overhead ends with the observation: 'NB: Viewers tend to have a simplistic view of drama, but a sophisticated appreciation of the programmes themselves.' She turns to perceived weaknesses in BBC popular series: lacking credibility ('The police don't do drugs raids like that!' of *Back Up*); the need for more suspense; predictable storylines (of *Bugs* and *Hetty Wainthropp Investigates*); not accessible ('I just felt distant from it' of *Out of the Blue*); characters not likeable or not adequately developed; problems with pace (of *This Life*), or insufficient tension (of *Crown Prosecutor*); needing more oomph ('It's a *Morse* for thick people with a sense of humour' of *Dalziel and Pascoe*); being formulaic (of *Dangerfield* and *Madson*); and 'no politics please' (of *The Ambassador*).

Paula turns to the positive: what must a first episode deliver? Keen viewers, she explains, look for: an introduction to the main characters; an idea of the kind of stories they can expect; an indication of pace and depth; and a talking point. She quotes a

viewer, 'The first episode has to be really spectacular to make you think, "I want to watch that again next week".' Alan Yentob reinforces the importance of first episodes, as *Rhodes* showed by getting it so wrong, 'or even the first two episodes – we should hold a seminar on that'. Under 'Strengths' for Drama to build on, Paula lists: realism ('It's got to be true to life'), but 'the unrealistic is accepted if giving viewing pleasure'; access to a new world, allowing viewers to explore (as in *Band of Gold*, which gave an experience of 'the "worst" of society safely'); easy viewing, light-hearted family drama (*Hetty* and *Heartbeat*), adding that in this context there should be 'no sex and violence please'; topical subjects; a desire to see skilled professional characters (*Casualty*, *London's Burning*); and a desire for glamour (*Berkeley Square*) or high production values (*Ballykissangel*).

She focuses on medical and police dramas, crowded markets which appeal for the 'human drama surrounding a crisis'. *Casualty*, still the main prop of BBC1's Saturday evening, is 'an institution'; it gains 'tremendous respect'. Viewers feel moved by its emotional range: 'Saturday night wouldn't be the same without it.' *Peak Practice*, a key ITV medical drama, is seen as realistic and uplifting: 'It manages to be gritty and still look pretty.' *ER* has upped the quality ante, but the feeling is that *Casualty* 'is what our hospitals are really like'. *Cardiac Arrest*, however, played on fears and many viewers thought it an unacceptable representation of doctors and nurses; they want to see heroism more than satire. Turning to police dramas, Paula identifies three types: real (*Cracker* and *Prime Suspect*), nice (*Hamish Macbeth* and *Heartbeat*), and soapy (*The Bill*). Few are thought to be bad, but there is fatigue and a wish for something different. A BBC1 peak-time crime series, from an independent, draws critical comments from viewers. Alan admits ruefully, 'It really only had one plot, didn't it, which they repeated every week.'

They turn to a central problem: Sunday nights. 'As well as *Heartbeat* there's going to be a new episode of *Coronation Street*'. How to tackle this unbeatable combination from ITV? Alan says, 'Not with drama! We're going to grow something elsewhere, and when it's going well, we'll move it suddenly.' Michael Jackson adds that Sunday nights demand 'the "must see", as they say in Burbank'. Jane, an executive producer, muses, 'To what do we attribute the incredible success of *Darling Buds of May*?' A colleague offers, 'It's a family show; all the family could sit down together on a Sunday evening . . .' but Jane continues, subversively, '. . . and *not think*! It was about *not* having to think!' She is drowned out as several people insist that a crucial function is fulfilled by dramas that give enjoyment without confronting people with 'all the problems of the world'.

Paula's presentation culminates in summarising maps of audience tastes. Viewers' perceptions of key dramas, derived from focus groups, are mapped in the space marked out by two axes, one representing a continuum between 'Action/Hectic' and 'Calm' dramas, the other between 'Character-based/Soapy' and 'Plot-centred' dramas. The map suggests that ITV has extremely strong showings in three of the four quadrants, for

example in the area of 'Action : Plot-centred' dramas (with *Cracker, Taggart, Band of Gold*) and 'Calm : Plot-centred' series (with *Morse, Kavanagh QC, Prime Suspect*). The message is plain: the channel management is requiring the drama producers to target their projects more precisely to the quadrants of the taste map apparently under-exploited by the BBC. Faced with the maps, producers stare bemused or with head in hands: how to translate them into creative ideas? The room is charged with ambivalence. Some of those working on popular series are stimulated. Those working at the 'high end' of drama appear reluctant and disengaged; later, they despair at the way these and other forces are felt to be sapping their creative autonomy. A development executive asks, *faux naïf*, 'In drama, we usually think in terms of a platitude: the need for "character-driven plot". So how come you've got 'Character-based' and 'Plot-centred' as two ends of a spectrum? Aren't they interrelated?' Michael replies firmly that this is how the *audience* perceives the shows. Paula says the head of Series has been given the research results to bear in mind for next year's Offers; someone quips, sardonically, 'Oh, I'm glad you've got them in mind, Jo. . . .'

Diary, 1996.

*

Getting closer and doing fantastic business

Things are going better for Drama Group. Some of the new popular series are getting the ratings. I'm waiting in an antechamber for an audience with the chief of Broadcast, Will Wyatt, when one of the foremost proponents of research as a weapon of anti-elitism within the BBC exits from Will's room, almost dancing on air. 'Georgina! How nice to see you! You're still in Drama? And aren't things going well! *Ballykissangel, Hetty, Silent Witness* are doing *fantastic* business. It's years since performance has been this good! We're getting closer to what the audience wants. The test for me is always: is this something my mum up in Glasgow would want to watch?'

Diary, 1996.

*

As external and internal competition heated up, research became a key currency in the politics of commissioning and scheduling. It was used at times to overcome controller vacillation, or to settle disagreements. For producers, positive research was seen as an effective way to lobby for attention 'on the sixth floor', among the controllers, with the hope of securing a commission. Research was also deployed by the controllers, sometimes insensitively, to

explore their own hunches or justify their preferences. The advocates of audience research shifted uneasily between claiming its predictive efficacy, and disclaiming that it was used deterministically. The process was very similar to that described in the anthropologist Evans-Pritchard's classic account of the Azande people's predictive use of the poison oracle, and the role of 'secondary elaboration' in explaining failures and contradictions.[9] When research proved wrong in predicting ratings or critical success, it was forgotten or the methods were disowned (the focus groups were badly designed, the questions inappropriate, the setting unconducive). When research proved right, it was 'owned'; it 'did the business'.

*

E, F and Z: Hertfordshire lads won't watch it!

'The BBC had to do what it hates and agree to a second series of *Hetty* before the first had gone out, because of Patricia's option. By then we had a fine cut of the first two episodes, and on that basis the BBC should have been able to make up its mind. Time was when it would have trusted its own opinion. But now they decided to do research, when I was already heavily into pre-production, and it was very negative. Yet if we had changed the second series according to the research, given that when the first series went out it was a winner by anyone's standards – our average audience was 10.96 million at 9.30 p.m. on a Wednesday night – what would Alan Yentob have done? Babies and bathwater come to mind. When the research came in, Alan wanted episode one re-edited. In the first series we were asked for a seventy-five-minuter; but by the time we came to go out, Alan hated long first episodes. So we got it down to sixty-eight, and it improved. But then some of the flak was that some of the editing looked dodgy; well, yes, because it was crash-edited! This was my first encounter with this sort of thing, but I do know that other people have been speechless with rage, as I was.

'There were six focus groups in three venues. I went to the first and last two, in Cheshunt and Stockport. They were guided discussions, and they'd seen the first episode before with the BBC logo taken off, so one of the questions was "Where do you think this is going to be shown?" The view up north in Granada land was "This must be BBC because it's not good enough for ITV", which says a lot for Granada generating loyalty among local viewers. They were very aware of Granada's status in drama. *Band of Gold* and *Cracker* had gone out; Granada were riding high. In Cheshunt they were supposed to be BC1, males, twenty to thirty. There was one B, the rest were C going on D, and a couple were E or F or even Z if you could get there. And that was the first thing that hit me: the BBC had paid good money to find out that eight twenty-year-old

men in Hertfordshire weren't going to watch a series about a sixty-year-old Lancastrian housewife turned detective. Well, there's a surprise! On that first group my notes said, "Seven male chauvinist pigs and one solicitor," and as they left the solicitor said to me, "What were the criteria for being on this panel: being racist, sexist and misogynist?" – this is one of the panel! One of the comments was "It's about the north, I don't like the north". Another man only watched sport on Sky. What was he doing on the panel? I sat in on four groups with thirty-two people, and of those I reckon twenty wouldn't have known where the Channel 4 button was, and thirteen wouldn't have known where BBC2 was, you know?

'Well, with the research being so depressing, when the overnights came in for the first episode, I can't tell you . . . you'd have thought we'd won the lottery. The relief was palpable. Then you think, how could they have got it so wrong? But they said they *didn't* get it wrong. So then you doubt the research entirely, and it goes back to it setting up a phoney situation. I was called in for a debriefing session. It was Yentob, me, Michael Wearing and the executive producer. They did a presentation, and it was like someone taking something you're proud of and dismembering it in front of you. Of course there were faults, and we all agreed we must try and do better in the next series. But they criticised things like the way Hetty dressed; a lot of people said, "People don't dress like that." Well, yes they do; my costume designer went and sat in markets and coffee bars and watched Lancashire go by, and that's what Hettys wear in the winter in Lancashire.'

Producer, BBC Drama, 1996.

*

Seven out of forty-four isn't bad

'The first I heard about the research was when I went to a meeting when the programmes were delivered, which I thought was to discuss the transmission date. But I found it was a huge meeting with all the BBC1 dignatories and heavies to hear about some research that I didn't even know had been done. When I sat down and the woman started I said, "What is this?" and Charles said, "It's the broadcast research." "What research?" "Didn't anybody mention it to you?"

'It was 1994, the first or second time they'd done it. It was like standing there in front of all these people, hearing the most negative report on the programme you could possibly think of. So I asked how the research was done. They'd sent a tape of episode one to fifty people, and asked them to watch and write a verbatim report on what they felt about the programme. Forty-four responded, and they divided them into focus groups and brought them together and showed them samples from episodes two and three and then asked their opinions. There were criticisms of the episodes for being the same, but they'd chosen silly excerpts. Then the music came up: they'd asked the respondents, did they like the music? No, they didn't like the music. It turned out that *seven* people did not like the music when asked in the groups, and that nobody had put that in their initial reports. It was very individual music, and seven out of forty-four isn't bad. So I said, "That's pretty good"; but they said, "Oh no, it proves you've got to change the music."

'I came out feeling deeply frustrated and angry. I was almost in tears. Charles came running out and said, "Look, they're always negative." As I got up the woman presenting gave me a summary of the research, but when I got into the tube I found I'd also picked up the verbatim reports. I told my assistant here to reanalyse them and we just couldn't see how they'd reached that judgement on the music. When you analysed the remarks, it came out completely different to the BBC's findings. I sent our analyses to the controller, who didn't respond. We had to change the music, which delayed the delivery; so the series went out late in a summer slot, which probably dented the ratings. But our analyses turned out right when we got the ratings. The BBC had predicted less success on the basis of the focus groups. We were the first programme for some time to have beaten ITV, and nobody said, "Thank you, well done"; nobody at all phoned us from the BBC.'

Independent drama producer, 1996.

*

A voguish political tool

GB: 'Two producers I've spoken to were miffed about the focus groups done on their series, rightly or wrongly, and both reached for criticisms of the method.'

'Sometimes we get it wrong: either the communication breaks down, or the sample wasn't right. Most embarrassing is when a controller commissions research about a programme, and the production department also commissions research on it, and there's no communication, so there's effectively competing research coming up with slightly different answers because the questions and methods were subtly different – which is embarrassing, quite apart from the waste.'

GB: 'You're implying, as programme-makers hint, that they sometimes commission research as a political tool, to show the controller, "Look, this is going to solve this problem for you" . . .'

'That's right. If production departments want to pitch an idea, and if they've got the money, they sometimes do research. One of the strengths of the old regime, when

Broadcasting Research was the only source of authoritative research, was that this kind of thing didn't happen. These days it *can* be a political tool; I freely admit it has become rather voguish. The controllers are enamoured with it. We try to argue to the controllers not to do research in a clandestine way, and to involve the producer if we're researching a programme, because, apart from anything, you're likely to get better research if you get a brief from the producer as well as the commissioner.'

GB: 'But you imply that it *has* been clandestine in the past, that you've sometimes done research to check a project out and only later told the producer?'

'. . . Or not! But it's rare because there will be tears; this place is as leaky as a sieve.'

BBC research executive, 1996.

*

Researching the News

Under the growing influence of marketing and strategy, the long arm of audience research began to reach even those parts of the BBC that had hitherto been immune to its attractions, notably the combined News and Current Affairs directorate. In 1997 the chief of NCA, Tony Hall, set up the first audience-research-based review of its entire output, with the aim of increasing understanding of audience expectations and of seeing how the portfolio might change. In consultation with Broadcast, the review would probe the place of news and current affairs in the context of changing channel strategies and expanding news services, and would reconsider NCA's public service obligations, which might be in tension with, say, channel pressures for competitive ratings. The News Programme Strategy Review, as the project was called, was modelled on the PSR conducted in Television and Radio in the early nineties; it paid homage to what were seen as the benefits accruing from Broadcast's innovative attention to research and 'massively improved understanding of the audience', as a news executive put it.

The News PSR exemplifies the way audience research became installed as a force for cultural change within the organisation. If the historic democratic function of BBC News centred on the duty independently to inform public opinion, it was thought that the PSR would supply a missing contemporary element: the duty to respond to the public's changing attitudes to news, by 'enfranchising' them via the representations of research. Combining introspection and exhaustive research, at times the News PSR appeared genuinely to be guided by how best to achieve the new democratic remit. At other times, it seemed to be ruled more by the BBC's unceasing thirst for legitimation: to be seen to engage in such a process was, perhaps, sufficient. Enormous resources and efforts were put into thinking subtly and intelligently about the complex issues posed by the review; awareness was shown of methodological pitfalls. Yet for all this, the research process risked riding roughshod over subtlety and qualification in its relentless, instrumental momentum.

*

What is research? Which audience? What is politics?

May 1997: an early planning meeting of the News PSR. The deputy head of NCA, Richard Ayre, and his strategist are sitting with five up-and-coming editorial figures from different sections of NCA who have been chosen to lead the review. Each has been allocated an area of the review to supervise – daily TV news, radio news, current affairs, political programmes, and other specialist areas – and each has a team of five colleagues working under them. They are discussing the programme of audience research at the heart of the PSR, which will encompass a large-scale 'usage and attitudes' survey, and then a round of focus groups to look closely at the issues raised by the 'U & A'. Mark Wakefield, editor of *Public Eye*, says his group is trying to locate previous research – focus groups on *The Midnight Hour* – but it has disappeared. Anne Koch, editor of *The World Tonight*, says her group is developing its methodology. They don't yet feel they understand what audience research is about, and they are trying to decide which specialist area to focus on – indeed, what should be included in the 'specialist' category.

At this point two researchers from the market research company RSGB, who will carry out the U & A, join the meeting. Larry, the spokesman, says the aim is to gain insight into how people consume news and how it fits with other areas of life. The survey will focus on three tasks: identifying general factors in the audience's relations with news; the factors that consumers see as most important in drawing them to the BBC, and how they see the BBC in comparison with its competitors; and grouping the audience into different segments according to key factors in their news consumption, a more meaningful exercise than standard demographics, he asserts, and gives the category 'time-pressed professionals' to illustrate. At this the team giggles, 'That's us!' Larry continues that before the U & A they feel the need to get a richer, more qualitative awareness of how people experience news media, which will allow them to refine the survey. He proposes the insertion of a new first phase of focus groups to get at this rich linguistic and behavioural data. The survey, to be preceded by a pilot, will involve 2,000 interviews across the country, a representative sample by region, age and class (though he does not use the word), but skewed to 'upmarket' social groups – a decision he doesn't explain. Then, he says, they'll do a third stage, a qualitative study of what people did yesterday: asking them to recall their news consumption hour by hour, a closer account than the usual generalisations. The findings should be ready by late August, at which point another – fourth – phase of focus group work can begin.

Someone criticises the summer timetable, pointing out that news agendas in July and August are atypical. Someone else asks what the criteria will be for analysing the social segmentation. Can they have the data in a form that will allow them to 'recut' it in ways not envisaged in the RSGB findings? Larry is evasive, answering that their main criteria for segmentation are availability and types of news media used – but that they could take some additional criteria from the team. Richard Clemmow, from daily News, queries the methodology: is it inductive, taken from the data, or deductive? Larry says it's initially inductive, drawn from number crunching. Several people probe the decision to skew the survey towards upmarket audiences: why? Larry replies that there will be more of them interviewed, but that this data will be analysed proportionally as part of the total population; he doesn't answer the main question. The same people pursue it: 'Isn't the whole aim of the exercise to look into those areas of the audience, the young and lower socio-economic groups, that we don't serve well? Or are we simply researching those who are already our audience?' The News strategist weighs in, assuring them that there is no problem because the research will sample the whole population, non-viewers and viewers, downmarket and upmarket alike. Richard Ayre asks, 'Can we attend the focus groups?', and there's a buzz of excitement. Larry says this would cost more, as it means hiring a viewing facility with two-way mirrors.

Steve Hewlett, editor of *Panorama*, raises the question of what is the real competition for each area of output; for *Panorama*, for example, is it news or even documentaries more than other current affairs programmes? Larry brushes this off; he seems not to understand the importance of the research tracking the rapidly shifting boundaries between genres in news, current affairs, documentary and factual. The team, however, pursues the discussion of genre, which ends with the strategist briskly asking them all to supply, in relation to their own area of output, a list of programmes within the genre boundary, and those close to but outside the boundary. Someone interjects: 'But should we be taking a supplier or a consumer perspective on genre?' There is discussion of doing focus groups on cable and satellite homes and on the 'regional dimension': 'We should be doing something on Scotland, the North and so on.' The strategist relates his as yet unsuccessful attempts to get hold of research from Scotland: 'I sent an email, but the reply probably got stopped by customs! Seriously, I know the head of News strategy in Scotland; he'll be helpful' – to which someone quips, 'So there's still hope for the Union!' The exchange plays on rising tensions with BBC Scotland, given Labour's commitment to devolution and BBC Scotland's much publicised wish for greater independence from London.

Mark Wakefield, whose group is looking at political programmes, raises what is for them the crucial question: 'What do people mean now by "politics"? There's the narrow definition, party politics and Westminster, but increasingly there are wider definitions and understandings in use.' Larry mistakes Mark's point, responding: 'Yes, we must be careful, because with the general election, politics will be more prominent in people's minds than is normal.' He fails to grasp Mark's observation on changing conceptions of the political, particularly relevant to young people – one of the key groups underserved by NCA output. This critical issue is therefore unlikely to be registered by the RSGB research. The two researchers leave, and over coffee Steve chats to me about the origins of the analysis of statistical correlations in Francis Galton's work on the relations between physical and moral attributes, one of the sources of 'scientific' racism. He and I reflect on the dangers of ill-judged interpretations of statistical correlations. Wrapping up, Richard Ayre says a key aim of the PSR must be to establish an ongoing review of output; and immediately people tease, 'Yes, with daily meetings!', 'No, two a day, surely?' – comments, dripping with irony, on the BBC culture of endless meetings and continuous self-review. Sian Kevill of Millbank raises tentatively the PSR's budget. Richard reassures her, 'Don't worry about that now; we're here to consider what we need to know. We'll think about budgets later.'

Diary, 1997.

*

Tribes and Punishment

One project was the apogee of the BBC's cultivation of audience research in the later nineties. Known as '100 Tribes', it was developed by Planning and Strategy in Broadcast under its leading figure, David Docherty, and gained the imprimatur of the powerful Policy and Planning unit in Corporate Centre. Docherty had been the driving force behind the expansion of research, and had a reputation as an *éminence grise* through his influence over the controllers and other Broadcast executives. The impeccable aim of 100 Tribes was to gain a 'deep understanding of the behaviour, attitudes, wants and needs of our audience', so as to identify both underserved groups and how they could better be served by the BBC, and future opportunities for the BBC to exploit.

100 Tribes was megalomaniac in its scope and lofty ambition; it circulated in a 250-page dossier. The project developed '"smart demographic" group segmentation' by analysing which clusters of demographic and lifestyle variables had the strongest influence on media consumption, and specifically on BBC usage. Ten distinct macro-groups subsuming thirty-one sub-groups

were identified. For example, Young Solos, representing some 1.1 million individuals, subsumed three sub-groups: Single Young Career Men, Single Lads and Young Independent Women; whereas Golden Agers, some 5.6 million, subsumed Older Cosmopolitan Men, Older Male Traditionalists, Older Cosmopolitan Women and Older Female Traditionalists. The project threw light on critical issues, such as how the different groups fared on *real* value derived from the BBC, measured in terms of the cost of BBC output that they consumed, as against the BBC's *perceived* value to them. The analysis zeroed in on those groups – mainly younger, mainly lower socio-economic groups – 'at risk' for the BBC. Yet despite the claim that the research identified meaningful clusters of characteristics for understanding BBC audiences, it contained telling inconsistencies, such as striking differences in attitudes towards the BBC between some of the sub-groups within the same macro-groups.

Whatever its merits, within a few years 100 Tribes became notorious as an intellectual exercise that failed to connect with the productive elements of the BBC. It was the ultimate face of a back-room philosophy that placed audience research in prime position and chided those programme-makers who failed to absorb its lessons. At worst this was a punitive philosophy that saw its role as answering back to decades of BBC producers' putative arrogance and abuse of their creative power, by inverting the order of things. Now 'the audience', speaking through the strategists and analysts, would tell producers what was what. Ironically, 100 Tribes seemed to ignore a golden rule: that television audiences are not strongly segmented, since the most popular programmes in every genre attract more viewers from all social groups.

*

100 Tribes

'Sometimes the strategic approach clearly went barmy, like the 100 Tribes project, which was rather cleverly conceived, saying, "Let's try and understand media consumption using a needs-based framework rather than some unsatisfactory sociological construct." But it gained its own horrifying momentum. It was incredibly detailed, a very easy way of churning out for the director-general a vast amount of analysis, which was at the same time great and useless, because it didn't have any meaningful, practical and implementable consequences to feed back into production or commissioning. At the point of commissioning, particularly with television, your ability to target demographically is limited. It's very broad brush. Your audience is younger or older, richer or poorer, north or south; and anyway – and this is the funny thing about television – more of every single group watches a successful television programme.'

GB: 'This is what Patrick Barwise and Andrew Ehrenberg proved, didn't they?'[10]

'Yes – a brilliant book: Paddy Barwise came and talked to us just the other day.'

Senior BBC strategist, 2001.

*

No creativity left

'We were asked to do research for a potential drama on the Crown Prosecution Service; we were given a number of storylines to examine with the public, and pictures of actors to see what parts they could fill. It would have been much better if some writer had simply taken that story and made the characters live. As it was the writer followed the research slavishly and produced a dead series – *Crown Prosecutor*. What you need to do is take the risk and make things, otherwise you get dull, formula TV. On ITV you see it night after night; it's so safe there's no creativity left. But it also means research doesn't have the independent authority it used to have.'

Executive, BBC Broadcasting Research, 1996.

*

The BBC's engagement with qualitative research in the nineties followed a history in which producers knew their audiences mainly through ratings abstractions or vague intuitions that formed part of a shared professionalism. Many commentators on this history have argued that closer understandings of audiences in the service of the BBC's public service goals would be progressive, and might correct the tendency for producers to be concerned primarily with peer judgements. As I was carrying out my ethnography of the corporation, ethnography became the favoured method of the cutting-edge market research firms, and executives began to commission ethnographic studies of targeted groups to gain a glimpse of the entire pattern of lifestyle and consumption practices. There is no question that qualitative research does generate more humanising representations of audiences than ratings; and in this light, focus group research had the effect of enriching what might be called the corporation's internal public sphere. More than ever before, the BBC's audiences became an object of collective interest, reflection and debate.

Yet the BBC's reliance on research in this period brought novel delusions.

The first was the assumption that focus groups come closer than ratings to providing a transparent window on to 'the audience'. In reality, focus groups offer a substitution in which a social 'part' bears the weight of representing the social 'whole'. But what is this whole? Nothing more than a sociality which the research both conjures up as a fantasy and keeps at bay. As much as ratings, the focus group performance of the 'social' acts as a controlled and instrumental encounter with broadcasting's 'others'. Of course it has another pay-off: through its apparently ethical and unmediated nature it boosts the BBC's legitimation. The corporation's embrace of research was akin to what the philosopher Jürgen Habermas has called the 'social psychological liquidation of public opinion'.[11] Instead of fostering an active and critical engagement on the part of its publics, the BBC rendered those publics in terms of inert 'tastes' or 'needs' to be measured and manipulated.

The second delusion is framed by the question: can focus group research help to foster creativity and invention in production in any but a trivial sense? The answer is no, on several counts. As I have shown, the quality of audience insights delivered was often achingly banal. More importantly, research examines existing tastes for past programmes, which can frame spaces for attention but does not help to generate new ideas. Production is, inevitably, both processually and imaginatively prior to consumption, and creativity cannot be enhanced by crude understandings of existing audience tastes. To be perceived by producers as ignoring these truths was a grave mistake of senior management in the nineties. If BBC producers were guilty of arrogance, management seemed unable to see that a tyrannical elitism could easily be replaced by a tyrannical populism that took 'actual audience tastes' as its justification. Propelling the rise of audience research at this time was an unholy alliance between the critique of producer elitism and the neo-liberal doctrine of consumer sovereignty. Both formed part of a slew of forces that tended to weaken and displace creative responsibility. Rather than strengthen accountability, the use of research in this period, by undermining creative responsibility, eroded the BBC's capacity to carry out its central obligation: the production of high-quality programmes.

The late nineties saw signs of recognition among senior management of the threat posed to creativity by the deterministic use of research. There was a rolling-back of its more imperial ambitions in relation to production, and the 'punitive' moment passed. But research continued to be central to the design of networks and schedules, where it could be used more productively.

*

Try this!

'The difference between us at Radio 1 and commercial operators is that, while we need to understand what people want, we try to leap ahead, to be creative in tackling what they might want in future. If you were applying to run a commercial radio station, you'd survey the market, find a niche that wasn't being served, ask those people what they want and design a service to meet it. Whereas here I try to gain a sophisticated understanding of people's lifestyles and aspirations, their place in society, and then I let loose the best programme-makers I can find to respond. When you understand people's lives, you can design services that take them forward. We are the professional broadcasters; the audience couldn't have designed the Chris Evans show – they didn't know they wanted it till we thrust it on them saying, "We know you aspire to anarchistic values; we know you like mavericks. Well, we've found one who, by the way, is also funny. Try this!" And it works.'

GB: 'But isn't market research often used to tie you very closely to existing audience tastes?'

'The worst thing that could happen to the BBC is if we started designing cynical formats aimed at allowing us to tick boxes for particular groups that aren't being served. And there is a danger, you will find that approach going on in the BBC. When I took over at Radio 1 we looked at the fact that we were failing miserably to contact ethnic minority listeners. The knee-jerk BBC response is to say, "Let's do a programme on the problems of being black in Britain." But I thought, what kind of music do these people care about? Who are their icons? Let's get those people on and the programme will appeal much more broadly; and it will also show the black community that we care about their music. To put on a worthy discussion programme on being young, black and British would have been formulaic. Knowing that we're not contacting black people is very good for us, a salutary experience; doing no market research is hopeless. Doing research and then using your judgement to respond is incredibly important.'

Matthew Bannister, controller BBC Radio 1, 1997.

*

Authoring Channels

The chemistry of BBC Television in the later nineties came to fruition in the design of channels, which in turn had to be translated into daily schedules. The 1996 restructuring streamlined the structure: now strategy, marketing and research informed the schedule, while the needs of the schedule determined commissioning. Marketing and branding required that the values the channels were intended to embody were made explicit. But in the multichannel environment, it was imperative to formulate not only the networks' identities but their differentiation from each other, projections summed up in the notion of *positioning*. For the main BBC networks, the controllers sat astride these forces, and the newly centralised commissioning apparatus placed responsibility fully in their hands. The controllers' role, backed by teams of strategists and analysts, became that of creatively authoring channels, of insinuating their personalities into the complex planning logistics that keep a channel on air. A discourse attributing a channel's success or failure to its controller had long existed; under the new conditions it became pronounced. If gifted controllers justified the epithet, there was also greater potential for individual misjudgement in managing a channel. By contrast, for the new BBC niche pay channels, positioning was more impersonal, given by strategic analysis. Channel identities became the focus of a tension between authorship and marketing 'science'. Yet for all this, increased competition in the nineties exacerbated the rivalry between BBC1 and ITV, BBC2 and Channel 4, resulting in greater sameness. The drive to 'close the peak-time and all-hours share gaps' was given precedence, particularly for BBC1, constraining authorship and impeding both channels' capacity for difference.[12]

*

The rich mosaic: the BBC2 overview

Mark Thompson, newly appointed controller of BBC2, is holding an overview for Drama Group. He pays tribute to Michael Jackson, his predecessor: 'Under Michael the schedule became more coherent, with breakthrough programmes like *This Life*, *Crow Road* and *Soho Stories* – all envied by other broadcasters.' He outlines his vision for the channel and the role of drama in it: '2 must aim to be the most original channel on British TV, its programming rich in range and texture, a rich mosaic of different kinds of programmes appealing to different kinds of people, but adding up to something special for everyone. A mosaic also within genres. I want 2 to remain the third most watched UK channel, to extend its reach especially to young and female viewers. Take *Crow Road*: that was very successful in reaching out to previously untouched viewers. I want the best singles and serials, and the best leisure programmes – we want to stay the market leader here. I want 2 to excel in storytelling, not only in serials such as *Our Friends in the North*, but in documentaries like *The House* and *Modern Times*. I want 2 to be salient, the channel with the most impact, the most talked about: this is how it can be special for licence payers.

'My task is to simplify the schedule and help the public understand what we're doing, because in the multichannel age if you aren't clear, people won't find you. We have to put in place a schedule based on real audience needs and programmes that will have maximum impact. Weekends need reviving; people watch repeats of *Have I Got News For You* because there's nothing else on! The 6.30 p.m. slot is underfunded; we use cheap US programming, *Star Trek* and so on. If competition hots up we may have to attack that spot with original shows. Above all, we need to experiment with new form and talent. George and I are discussing new formats, say a fifteen-minute drama stripped through the week. But experiment must be strategic; take *American Visions* – that was expensive, but very important for us. I have to say, the BBC2 schedule is still compromised by internal BBC politics, by historical commitments and past deals. This has to change.

'Drama is mainly there to create impact on 2. In recent years there's been a rather stable mix: a classic adaptation, a major contemporary serial, and if we add *This Life* or its successor *Project X*, an ongoing narrative strand. One surprise for me is finding how little contemporary drama is in development now. I want to bring in new writers, to have more adaptations of contemporary novels and plays in the vein of *Buddha of Suburbia*, *Oranges Are Not the Only Fruit* and *Our Friends*. I'm not so interested in three- and four-part thrillers like *Degrees of Error* or *Signs and Wonders*; they don't deliver like they used to. I want all singles to move towards bundling or trilogies, like the *Wicked Women* strand, which was a meretricious bit of marketing but worked well – it held its own against ITV's *Moll Flanders*. That raises whether, with BBC1 and ITV doing big classics, we should still do them on 2? The situation on commissions for '98–'99 is open. At present for '97–'98 we have *Holding On* as a key contemporary piece, plus Frank Deasy's *Looking After Jo Jo*. But there's some uncertainty about one of our main commitments, Rushdie's *Midnight's Children* . . .'

Diary, 1996.

*

The conversation: the BBC1 Overview

A BBC1 Drama overview: Michael Jackson, who recently became controller of 1, is telling Drama Group how he sees the channel developing and what role drama can play, against the backdrop of a persisting sense of crisis around the genre. He begins with a summary of audience perceptions drawn from research. 'BBC1 *is* the BBC: an authoritative, national institution – professional, serious. It's the first choice of viewing for ABs, second choice for all others. If you ask a middle-class male, he sees BBC1 as uplifting, reliable and disciplined, where ITV is a good time, "a friend you go out with on a Saturday night". In drama, BBC1 is period drama, world-class actors and production values, whereas ITV is action, pace and everydayness. ITV has risk-takers, *Cracker* and *Prime Suspect*; but it also has warmer drama in *Soldier Soldier* and *Heartbeat*. So: BBC1 needs more of the everyday and more risky drama. I want BBC1 to be inclusive. The word I'd use to sum up what I want the channel to be about is *conversation*: characters in conversation with one another, and with the audience; that the channel sparks off conversation in the viewing community, the family . . .' He cites *EastEnders*, *Animal Hospital* and *Vet School* as exemplary. It is not lost on this audience that the latter two are docu-soaps.

Michael continues: 'I've been catching up on the past couple of years' drama output. Successes? *EastEnders*, absolutely brilliant, fantastically inventive; *Silent Witness*: great use of a star, meaty stories; *Ballykissangel*: brilliant first episode; *The Sculptress*: a great idea, serials stripped over a week or weekend. Problem shows? *Rhodes*: you felt in the first episode, why should you care? *Bad Boys*: comedy drama, one of the most difficult genres to get right; *Writing on the Wall*: a co-production . . . Somewhere in the middle: *Hello Girls*: well produced but no plot, and blown out of the water by the fifth episode of *Brookside*; *No Bananas*: a difficult format, and little new to offer on the Second World War; *Dangerfield*: an air of gloom. There's a problem with Saturday evening after *Casualty*: this needs work. And what about ITV? It's drama output is in flux. *Peak Practice* and *Soldier Soldier* are on good form; it's copying the BBC with classics – *Emma*, *Moll Flanders*; and *Sharman*, with its car chases, was really formulaic. ITV's soap strategy? A fourth episode of *EastEnders* and a third of *Emmerdale*.' But Michael makes a Freudian slip, substituting *EastEnders* for *Coronation Street*, implying that he may be thinking about a fourth episode of *EastEnders*. He smiles quizzically.

Michael hands over to Rosemary, his scheduler: 'We have four aims for the channel. First, that BBC1's share is maximised; second, that the range and mix of programmes is right; third, our public service commitments; and fourth, to make our programmes into hits! Each of these four is vital. Let's look at recent changes in the peak-time schedule. At 7 p.m. to 9 p.m., the question is how to schedule against the soaps. Thursday is a case in point. *Top of the Pops* was losing out against *Emmerdale*, so to counter the new third episode of *Emmerdale*, which starts in January, we've moved *Watchdog* against it at 7 p.m. and we're building it in advance. We also use inheritance: we know exactly who the audience are for *EastEnders*, so we try to follow it with something appealing to the same audience to prevent them switching over to *The Bill* at 8 p.m. We're trying factual storytelling with *Animal Hospital*, and it works: women and children stay with us! We've really damaged *The Bill*. If we look at the nights of the week: we can't do drama on a Monday; *Panorama* blocks it. Tuesday: a key evening for drama, although the football's on for six weeks in the autumn. One of our main problems is Friday night: the combination of *Coronation Street* and *The Bill* is a huge challenge. We used to have *Tomorrow's World*, but that's the wrong feel; we know it's women driving the viewing on Friday. We're trying *Hetty*, it should do well. Saturday is family viewing; Sunday is for watching together, an "event" evening. Tactically, we try to pinpoint the weaknesses in the ITV schedule, and to hone our knowledge of who is watching when; the demographics are critically important. There's always an audience, for instance, to be garnered when the football's on ITV or when they offer us a 9.30 p.m. junction. But my main problem as a scheduler is the *9 O'Clock News*. I just wish it wasn't there . . .'

Diary, 1996.

*

UKTV: channel identities and consumer expectations

'Driving all the strategic decisions on the BBC getting into pay TV on cable was a killer graph, from about '95 but updated annually, which presented a fifteen to twenty-year forecast of the total value of the UK television market. It plotted how the lines of advertising, subscription and licence fee went through time, and showed us that even if the BBC keeps a fair share of the terrestrial audience, it will lose so much of the total TV revenue that it won't be able to stay in the market for sports and film rights and so on. We took it to show that there was an absolute necessity to get into commercial activity in order to protect the public service aspect. That was the paradox: it was an "and/both" strategy; "either/or" was just not an option. The decision was to get into a joint venture with Flextech, which became the UKTV channels. In designing the shape of those channels, we used the "smart demographics" research to populate our understanding and identify groups that were underserved. We had maps of viewer needs. There were broadly two axes, from "sit-up-be-informed" through to "lounge-back-be-entertained." The former wanted news, current affairs and factual: "I want information; I want to trust the source, to be enlightened". Cable and satellite channels are genre-based. As a consumer you know Discovery is about animals and nature, but you don't know much more. So the research was important for the UKTV plans as a way of considering the competitive landscape and asking, what do we want to stake out? Will the channels be meaningful for a purchaser? It's about branding, positioning, giving a coherent identity to a channel that in some way meets consumer expectations. But the programmers knew this stuff intuitively; the research simply turned editorial intuition into an analytical, numbers-based thing.'

GB: 'What was the genre breakdown that you decided to go for with the UKTV channels?'

'There's a number of channels. The first was UK Arena with Roly Keating. Roly then became head of programming for all the UKTV channels. He came from Music and Arts, and UK Arena grew around music and arts. It wasn't ever going to get a large audience, but it would do very well with advertising because of its high ABC1 focus; and for the cable operators it was a differentiator for our UKTV package compared to other channel providers. It was an appealing upmarket channel, summarising all that's unique about the BBC. But it could only be part of the mix. The next channel was UK Horizon: it was documentaries, animals, natural world, natural history, David Attenborough, that sort of thing. A competitor to Discovery, head to head; or as it turned out, not so head to head, because Flextech didn't want to throw money at something that competed directly with their own major channel.'

GB: 'In other words, Flextech had something of a conflict of interest?'

'To an extent, but it's one of those conflicts of interest that any genre-channel provider will face. It worked out in a continuing need to schedule UK Horizon in a complementary way, by not putting money in the same slots and programming as Discovery were doing. That had flow-backs for the BBC: it meant our funding partner, which was also a competitor, would put more money into the venture; it also meant we found out about their schedule and didn't throw our shows away. UK Horizon did OK for audience, but UK Gold – which is entertainment and drama – is doing best. It's a repeats channel, but a fresh one. Then there's UK Style, which is leisure, lifestyle, gardening, homes and cookery; and there's a channel associated with Radio 1 called Play UK. The channels are bundled, so as a purchaser you'll typically be offered a tier with them all in. A channel provider like Flextech makes money from the cable company paying it an amount of money per subscriber per month for the package, and then advertising. But it's the subscriptions that really make money, so you have to tempt the cable operators to take your package. For UKTV, for instance, the research on the channel mix said that adding in the Radio 1-oriented channel made the package far more interesting to young people, so the bundle itself could be valued more highly; it added far more value than it cost. All the channels are primarily repeats and archive programming, with not that long a delay. The price structure for rights is: the fresher the programme, the more a channel has to pay. Origination in all the UKTV channels is slowly growing, but to launch we couldn't afford to originate. The rights negotiations were complex, but also successful since they allow the BBC to – in McKinsey language – sweat its assets.'

BBC strategist, 2001.

*

Scheduling Tastes

Scheduling had always been akin to narrative editing writ large. In the nineties it became the point of integration for television's expanding components: strategy, marketing, branding, research, publicity, financial planning, talent management, commissioning, production, accounting; and as all of these bear on the broad editorial judgements that in turn inform practical decisions on finer details of genre and format – on what will be shown. An art as much as a science, scheduling condenses all the complex logistics of television. In the alchemy of scheduling, long-term and high-level strategic objectives must somehow be transformed into a continuous and successful broadcast flow – into gold. On the back of a substantial planning apparatus, its BBC2 practitioners in the era of Michael Jackson's controllership depicted the late stages of the scheduling process as fuelled by mood and flair through dialogue with the controller, evident in a concern with range and variety, colour and wit, mining a seam or changing pace. As one scheduler confided, 'Sometimes it's all popular, over the top; then it's vulgar; then we decide to be difficult, to resist tastes; sometimes we get very "public service" and high-minded. It's partly to do with Michael's frame of mind.' Despite the overwhelming evidence of imitation between the schedules of BBC2 and Channel 4 in the later nineties, BBC2's scheduler demurred from any simple explanation: 'I know the Channel 4 scheduler, but we don't talk. The only time I remember we talked was to avoid running operas back to back at Christmas. There was a bad moment: they accused us of using cynical copycat tactics. But it's not in our interests to schedule like against like. If we put our gardening programmes against theirs, we just split the audience for both.' Protesting too much, and focusing on the placing of programmes, this overlooks the forces propelling both channels towards very similar content. In scheduling meetings, the pressure of balancing many variables, of condensing masses of detailed decisions into limited time, of predicting audience tastes, and of exercising editorial judgements appropriate to the channel's personality could all be glimpsed in the genial rough and tumble. The considerable responsibilities were shared through collective speculation, through a distributed intelligence. If the meetings were playful, that was perhaps the only possible response to the seriousness of scheduling's task of making judgements without end, many of them with huge financial and human repercussions, in the face of extreme uncertainties.

*

Finding *Steptoe* and losing *Mrs Merton*: scheduling BBC2

Michael Jackson's office on the sixth floor of Television Centre: a BBC2 scheduling routine. Michael is hovering, making calls, while his scheduler Adam, Adam's assistant Jack, the BBC2 commissions manager Tim, the finance manager Jan, her assistant and I sit on sofas eating sandwiches. The atmosphere is laid-back, with much joshing and participation; Michael's understated role is that of presiding intelligence. When it gets going the meeting lurches rapidly between items, almost in the manner of free association. Discussing programmes, people switch between presenting themselves as 'ordinary fans' and connoisseurs. The repartee is laddish; someone jokes about an American ad they saw about condoms for dogs. When Michael finally sits down there's a review of the planned schedule for weeks 20 to 22, most of which is mapped out on a chart, but there remain spaces such as the feature film slots. Michael and Adam dip into a list of acquired films from which they select something for each slot. 'What did this one get on its previous showing?' Adam goes out to check. 'In 1993, 3.3 million'. Michael's impressed. Week 21: there's concern about the sports. Adam points to a George Best evening, and says that Best didn't turn up for the recent press preview – at which there is mirth, as this is so perfect for his image. Michael spots a scheduling problem: 'Why aren't we hitting the 10 p.m. junction here?' Adam passes him the longer-term overview, which shows 'what we're up against' in explanation. They move to a new series on British architects which still needs a title. Everyone chips in: '*Public Property*?' 'Too seventies; it sounds like an Open University unit.' '*Building Sights*?' 'Not bad.' Michael raises *Oprah*: what to do with it? He wants to extend Esther Rantzen's talk show. 'While I was in Cannes I thought of running *Esther* four times a week, or three and a "best of" on Friday'. His plan is to run *Oprah* at 2.10 p.m. and *Esther* at 5 p.m. in the prime-time afternoon slot where *Oprah* used to be. Jan says she'll look at funds to see whether they can afford both.

Michael says to Adam, 'David has some ten-minuters made of offcuts of the VE and VJ day celebrations, interviews with veterans. They sound interesting.' Adam says, 'We could use some ten-minuters'. 'We've also got three of those animation compilations – let's put them on late night, stripped across a bank holiday weekend or something.' Adam takes note. They move on to discuss the ending of the Grand Prix. 'We'll need to know how much share we'll lose when that ends. We don't want to replace a sport that gets six million with one that does 600,000.' One idea is to replace it with a popular natural history programme, 'an elephant series or something'. Michael asks in passing, 'Does anyone know the date of the anniversary of the royal wedding – Charles and Di?' Jack replies, 'It was July '81'. Michael leaves it hanging – presumably pondering what can be done to mark the event at the appropriate time, part of the concern to register major national events in the popular mind. They come to *The Proms*: Jan speaks of an underspend last year. This year, BBC2 is signed up for six concerts plus the *Last Night*. They discuss how to finance this: 'We're insisting on cheap interval fillers. And we might tape one or two, but do the rest live.' Jan says they need a meeting with Kim Evans, head of Music and Arts – can Michael find any time in his diary? It's difficult: eventually he finds a free half-hour.

Michael asks Jan about switching channel funds away from one factual programme to another. A commission, *A to Z of Horror*, has come in, but he doesn't like it and wants to commission a new one. 'Factual will be pissed off.' 'But they'll get the new commission, which should placate them.' Michael gets out a list of programmes he's been sent by Worldwide for which they intend to sell six-month licences to other broadcasters. He asks whether there are any that BBC2 wants, so they shouldn't be sold: *Clarissa*, *Thérèse Raquin*, *The Monocled Mutineer*? Nobody objects. *Boys from the Blackstuff*? They agree to keep these rights, and the same for '*Allo 'Allo!*, *It Ain't Half Hot, Mum* and *Howard's Way*. They turn to *Nostromo*, an expensive co-produced classic serial to be shown this autumn. Adam has seen preview tapes. 'It's very slow, not action-packed – I'm speaking as your ordinary viewer.' 'Is it "epic"?' 'Um, sort of.' No one has read the book; Michael: 'I've read *Heart of Darkness* . . .' They are unconvinced: 'Who'll watch it?' 'Conrad fans?' 'People from Drama Group?' They move to *This Life*. Last night's episode had a steamy sex scene in the lawyers' office. Michael and Jack say it's improving: 'Something happened!' They discuss a gap in week 20's Friday-evening schedule. What to put in it? Michael stalks up and down, throwing out ideas, in dialogue with Adam. '*Hi-de-Hi*?' 'Great, a bit of kitsch.' 'Then let's go to *Up Pompeii*, continuing the kitsch theme.' 'And before them?' '*Steptoe and Son*? No, not right for that audience.' '*Citizen Smith*?' 'No.' '*Happily Ever After*? That'll be a whole kitsch run.' Eventually they agree: 'Let's do a run of the six lost *Steptoes*, and bill it like that.' Michael phones John Whiston to do the deal; he is the BBC executive who controls these shows – recently discovered, never-before-shown pilots of classic comedies.

They move on, looking at the longer-term schedule: where to place *Screen Two*, a run of six single plays for Saturday evenings? Once decided, Michael says 'George [*head of Single drama*] should be pleased: we're hammocking it.' Michael shoots questions at Adam, ticking off things he has to check: 'Is *Death of Yugoslavia* episode six in the schedule?' 'Yes.' 'Is Terry Venables in the schedule?' 'Yes.' 'Have we sorted Esther Rantzen's contract?' How to brand a certain feature? 'Let's discuss it with Jeremy.' Michael asks how the snooker is going; Jack fills him in on the latest twists. Adam: 'I saw *Clash of the Titans*.' 'How was it?' 'Brilliant.' Jack: 'Michael, we need to place the Grand Prix highlights on Sunday.' 'Fuck. How?' They move everything around and drop *Animal Dramas* to make room. They knock around a slate of design-related programmes coming up this summer: films on Charles Rennie Macintosh and William Morris; coverage of the Design Awards. Brand-think kicks in: 'It's a *Design Summer*!' They talk about a

Susie Orbach show, *Talking to Susie*, to go out soon, a 'popular therapy talk show'. Orbach was famously Princess Di's psychotherapist. They've seen a pilot and are uneasy; they seem sensitive to press coverage of a trend towards 'media therapy'. *Mrs Merton*: Adam reports that repeats are scheduled for August. Michael: 'Is there an issue of her going in future to BBCl?' 'She wants to go to either BBCl or ITV.' Long faces.

The meeting is winding up. Jack turns on Michael's TV. A snooker star is featured in a news spot; he's been given a suspended ban for assaulting a press officer. Michael didn't catch his name, and Jack begins a game, testing Michael's knowledge of BBC2 sports. Who is he? Michael can't guess. Jack, reproachful: 'Michael! It's Ronnie O'Sullivan!' Michael raises final touches for BBC2's Annual Performance Review submission. Adam passes him a briefing about how BBC2 has increased its share in satellite homes. Michael asks Adam to draft him a note about how BBC2 has met the challenge of marking 'major events facing the nation'. Jan asks Michael to give her a note on the importance of comedy on the channel. Michael dictates: 'Comedy is vital to BBC2 in attracting a younger audience that does not otherwise naturally find a home in the channel . . .' and he adds, a touch bitterly, 'in the manner of *The Mrs Merton Show*.'

Diary, 1996.

*

Telling It Like It Is

Uncertainty is the only rule in broadcasting, and the controllers and strategists did not always get things right. This became plain when they subjected themselves to the discipline of feedback from audience research. In 1997, when ethnography had become the vanguard of consumer research, BBC2 and Radio 1, both concerned with renewing their appeal to young people, commissioned joint research from a company specialising in the method. The resulting research was frank in its appraisal of both networks' chosen strategies. Matthew Bannister, whose repositioning of Radio 1 had been lauded, faced an analysis that relentlessly probed his thinking and forced it to move on. If the debrief was uncomfortable, it demonstrated one of the most fruitful potentials of research: not to conform to executives' preferred outcomes, but to act as a resistance and an irritant, with the effect of opening up debate and rendering strategy contestable.

*

Understanding young people

A debrief led by two researchers from Informer, Sophie and John, who have carried out eight focus groups and observational research to gain a background understanding of the media use of fifteen- to twenty-four-year-olds, as well as to explore their views of BBC2 and Radio 1. The intention is to draw out editorial and marketing implications for the networks so as to maximise their appeal to this core target group. Sophie starts with the headlines: that young people use media to define and evolve their self-identities, and that they classify all 'items of media' – music, TV and radio – by the extent to which they embody one of two values, two ends of a spectrum: the 'allure of the mainstream' or the 'myth of the underground'. The 'underground' is about transgression, difference, individuality; the 'mainstream' about pleasure in familiarity and belonging. Young people are drawn to both, and they experiment with different roles. There's a constantly evolving tension between the two, and over time things can move across. But no media experience can embody both. The implication for the BBC is that the identity of any service must unequivocally embody one of the two mindsets. And the problem, John explains sternly, taking no prisoners, is that neither BBC2 nor Radio 1 follows the rules: they send mixed messages. The situation is complicated by the BBC brand as a whole being identified as mainstream, heritage, the national, whereas some BBC programmes are identified as underground. But this isn't insuperable: young people understand that contradictions can exist between the overall brand and specific products, that the 'product within the brand' can be different. The question posed to the BBC is how to use the contradictions to work with its sub-brands, or how to change the overall corporate brand.

Sophie continues that young individuals bring together a wide range of identifications, according to different needs. The same individuals move between mainstream and underground: they'll read the News of the World and the Guardian, watch Blind Date and listen to jungle on Cool FM. Irony is common, as in watching Blind Date 'as an outsider'. Television and radio themselves have properties as media. TV gravitates to a mainstream space identified with the national, universal, public, familiar, comfortable, accessible and reliable; but it can also be slow, boring, safe, censored, stale and predictable. Radio is underground: it is individual, spontaneous, private, raw, fast, specialised, authentic and owned; but it can also be inaccessible and sporadic. The bad news is that BBC2 and Radio 1 are both perceived as having a range of shows spread across the spectrum, with very little pattern. They have no clear positioning in the terms in which young people process media experience. Mark Thompson, recently arrived as controller of BBC2, bursts out: 'But we've been scheduling well-defined zones for young audiences – like Friday evening – for years! It doesn't seem to have got across!'

John zeroes in on BBC2. It has, he says, a very confused brand image. Its access points are relatively arbitrary, driven by particular programmes, with little sense of higher order. He introduces some maps of viewer perceptions and classifications of television, ranged between two axes – 'My World' versus 'Their World', and 'Reality' versus 'Escapism' – which produce four quadrants. BBC2's news programmes and most of its documentaries are located in 'Their World/Reality', the quadrant of least interest to young people. This space is seen as boring, irrelevant, serious, for older people, as lacking edge, shock and glamour. For young people, *Newsnight* is a particularly negative obstacle, 'but at least they know where it is, so they simply switch over between 10.30 and 11.15 p.m. to 1 or 3 or 5.' John points to the quadrant 'My World/Reality' as lacking in all British channels, although Channel 4 does it best. Too many BBC2 factual programmes are seen as lacking topicality and closeness to young people's lives. But there is great opportunity here. The tone should change to be more humourous, fearless, opinionated, personal and confrontational; and the aim should be to take underground values but represent them in the mainstream. Young people want more programmes on 'My World', on their politics and on issues they 'own': on drugs, street crime and breaking into cars, life on housing estates, environmental politics. The *Cook Report* on drugs, Radio 1's shows on drugs and Channel 4's 'Pot Night' were all highly valued. Matthew quips, 'Oh, you mean more leisure shows!' and there is laughter. The quadrant 'Their World/Escapism', characterised by glamour, fantasy and relaxation as in the Oz soaps and US sitcoms, is not likely to suit BBC2, John cautions; while BBC1 is seen as the natural home of 'My World/Escapism', involving zany humour, parody, the familiar and comfortable, in the guise of British sitcoms and comedy. BBC2 struggles to convince here, because it's too intense and fragmented. Apart from mining 'My World/Reality', à la Channel 4, and improving how BBC2 'explains itself' to the viewers, Sophie and John have little to offer: 'BBC2 is a strange channel, strangely positioned'.

They turn to Radio 1. Radio is a background medium, fitting into people's lives. Young people are attracted to clearly branded stations with distinctive identities because this allows an understanding of the core proposition. And branding is principally achieved by a combination of one musical genre and DJ reputation. The exception is chart stations, which can cross several genres as long as they are all linked to charts, which itself becomes a kind of genre. Usually, says John, station identity, musical genre and DJs form a virtuous circle, reinforcing each other. But Radio 1 fails to fit this model; the circle is full of tension. The overall BBC brand is in tension with the 'new music' proposition, which is in tension with the DJs, not all of whom are credibly committed to new music. Radio 1 also spans a number of non-chart genres, reducing its coherence. A minority of listeners, John concedes, can reconcile that the same station can be both generalist and specialist, that it can be about both the BBC brand and underground music; they even allow that Radio I takes more risks than other stations. But there remain serious problems. 'New Music First', the central concept of the relaunched Radio I, is flawed. It is distrusted by the audience: 'It's not credible for all genres; there is no "cutting edge" in some musics.' The 'new music' rhetoric is seen as either: a) referring to indie/Brit pop/grunge music, i.e. music out of the John Peel stable – and Matthew concedes that this *was* really the genesis of the relaunch; or b) it's seen as a cynical front for remarketing an ageing radio station, to make it seem up to date. For the majority, Radio I is in such conflict with the usual rules of radio that at best they try to relate to it through specific DJs, and at worst they dismiss the station entirely through its BBC associations. It needs unifying personalities to help people in, says John: a Chris Evans, a DLT or a Simon Bates. Matthew and others groan loudly with dismay: this is just the structure they dismantled, while Chris Evans left recently following a noisy falling-out. Must they really grow some powerful presenters of this kind?

Sophie points to three possible ways forward. Radio I could become a single genre station, like Kiss FM or XFM: the indie/Brit pop station, perhaps. But this contradicts its remit. It could 'challenge the rules' by changing how people relate to radio and establishing a unifying theme that transcends musical genre. Or it could 'evolve the rules' in the way already being attempted, by offering a number of genres and 'multiple propositions' driven by time of day, generalist in the daytime, specialist at night. If so, marketing has to help more: the genres must be clearly signposted, and the proposition explained to the audience. Sophie stresses how a DJ's authentic passion for a genre can help enormously: 'Chris Evans was brilliant at this, wasn't he?' Matthew says nervously, 'We'd better get him back then.' 'You need to raise the profile of the new DJs; put Mark Radcliffe and Danny Rampling on TV, get them known as personalities, like Chris. Don't put underground DJs on TV; this contradicts the message. But do give TV exposure to DJs who are perceived as moving into the mainstream.' Matthew and Mark turn apprehensively to each other, as though facing an arranged marriage. Matthew: 'Well, Mark?'

Diary, 1997.

*

The development of marketing and branding required that some of the guiding values of BBC services were made explicit, in a way that previously they had not been. Research added a dimension of controlled reflection, apparently routed through understandings of 'the audience'. If the conflation of techniques for selling products with the conception of public service ideals is seen as troubling, the beneficial effect was to render such ideals a conscious object of collective deliberation. At the same time these processes ushered in dangers of banalising those public service values, reduced as they were to a branding vision, and of their reification. The question is the sufficiency of the discourses of value to their tasks and objects. When used fruitfully in the authoring of channels, to unify and 'populate' a channel's *Geist* and to complexify the mechanical directives of strategy, the approach was vindicated. When used punitively to batten down and curtail the particular and expansive imaginative engagement required by good programme-making, marketing and branding were revealed in all their bathos as a wholly different order of 'creativity.' Productive in their place, the problem was that they were wielded by the new layers of management intent on justifying their existence and augmenting their influence and powers within the organisation. If channel identities were defined through strategy and marketing, how was this translated into the pro-duction of programmes? And how did it impact on programme quality?

Creativity Bound: Drama Group

Self-criticism

Drama Editorial Board: discussion alights on *Dangerfield*, a popular series built around the life of a Midlands police surgeon that's intended to 'solve the Friday evening problem' and dent ITV's share. It reeks of design by focus group, although the idea came from a writer. Ruth, acting Group head, is upbeat: 'The figures are getting better!' But there's a unanimous sense that something is wrong. Tony, whose Pebble Mill unit produces it, reflects, 'It's doing about nine million, but a series like this in its fourth year ought to be doing ten.' A colleague comments, 'It's slow-moving; but then a lot of ITV drama is slow – look at *London's Burning* or *Heartbeat*. For women viewers it's a show about a vicarious experience of a new man, a new area of life, isn't it?' Tony: 'The research shows women find him decent but sexy. We've tried to think of new angles – two narrative lines at once, side narratives; we brought in a new writer to beef it up, but it's not meant to be beefed up! The personal life stuff is just awful. You can't be too ambitious when it's carefully designed not to be ambitious.' They ask Jenny, who has worked at ITV, what Network Centre would do with it. 'I don't think we'd have recommissioned. Marcus would have said it's too smooth and middle class.' Ruth jumps in: 'Should it be more working class, then, with more edge?' There is palpable ambivalence towards this ratings puller they have spawned.

Diary, 1996.

*

Midnight's Children, episode one – The recce

September 1996: The Serials department is turning Salman Rushdie's novel *Midnight's Children* into a BBC2 drama. The project is in early stages. It has not yet been 'green-lit', but the controller, Mark Thompson, is keen as it will provide an 'event' for 1997–8 and mark the fiftieth anniversary of Indian independence. If it is to be made in time, the pressure is on to develop scripts and research its feasibility. Director Dan, producer Pete and executive producer Ed are discussing a recent recce in India, where it will be filmed. The aim is to draw the large cast mainly from Indian actors and non-professionals, and to collaborate with local crews. The politics are tangled. Rushdie is still the subject of the post-*Satanic Verses* fatwa. He is also a personal friend of Alan Yentob, now director of Television. It is a project of vast ambition: it will be the first British television drama of this scale to employ a primarily non-white cast.

Dan speaks of the difficulties they faced in India: cultural differences, intense factionalism; everyone selling their friends and putting down the competition. He reports that Indian stage sets are 'cardboard and emulsion', with no sound sync possible. 'You're shooting on stage one and they're building stage two!' Ed: 'Difficult conditions in which to achieve BBC production standards, but appropriate for Indian films, where they're usually after glitter.' Dan: 'It's tricky; if we're not careful we'll be three months in and it'll all fall apart.' He talks eloquently of the problems of dealing with their Indian counterparts and the need to create partnerships, 'Not an imperial structure where the BBC imposes controls.' Dan recounts a dinner party thrown in their honour by the head of an Indian advertising agency, the parent company of the Indian co-production partner. Games of male bravado were played and 'florid egos' displayed; they were required to drink flaming whiskies – all very tense and public school. Ed reflects on how cultured are the Indian elite, 'Almost better-read and more cosmopolitan than we; they all speak three languages!' Dan remarks on the problem of deference, how hard it is to approach people politely. 'You ask how one is expected to behave, but they say what they think you want to hear!'

Money: Ed says BBC2 look likely to come up with £4.2 million, 'But we should aim for £4.5.' The budget will be about £5.5, so there's a million to find. An American alliance led by a British director is interested in co-financing; Mike Wearing is meeting him in LA. Ed reports on tricky negotiations with Salman. Alan called last night to tell him off for not consulting Salman on the choice of director. 'I nearly lost my rag. Salman had been consulted when we had a shortlist of two. There was no real problem.' Still, he has written contritely to Salman. They move on to casting; will a certain British actress be able to work with Indian non-professionals? They've got Indian casting scouts tracking down theatre groups which might provide people to use. They're looking for locations all over India and in parts of Pakistan. The logistical challenge is huge.

Diary, 1996.

*

303

Just a minute: carry on commissioning

'Radio 4 producers still chatter nostalgically about the times when you could have a bright idea for a programme, pop into the controller's office, make a brief pitch, and then walk away with a straight yes or no. That was long before the invention of the new commissioning process, which involves sufficient paperwork and layers of decision-making to suggest that one is not so much asking permission to make a short series on Britain's remaining lighthouse keepers as tendering for a new nuclear power station ... Whenever malcontents gather in the eighth-floor canteen to complain about the failure of their latest proposal – failures that nowadays can mean the non-renewal of a short-term contract – they find mutual consolation in concocting fictional scenarios involving the rejection of some of Radio 4's most successful strands. "I regret that your suggestion for a programme in which people are required to speak for one minute without hesitation, deviation or repetition has been rejected by the commissioning panel because of its failure to meet the appropriate demographic profile."'

Laurie Taylor, 2001.

*

Centralising Commissioning

Television in the nineties was a classic instance of the paradox that an increasing concern with marketing and brand differentiation develops at the same time as, with intensifying competition, real differences decline. If television exists at the interface of integration – the scheduling of programmes into channels – and differentiation – the production of programmes in a variety of genres – then, to optimise the vitality of any broadcasting organisation, that interface must not inhibit the creativity of either process. But in the BBC of the later nineties the situation was far from optimal. Integration became centralisation, and it disciplined production, compromising freedom and diversity in programme-making. Here we see the most serious effect of the Birt period: the erosion of the creative autonomy and confidence of BBC production. A key cause, compounding the forces already outlined, was the newly centralised structure of commissioning. This chapter tracks these developments through their effects on the creative functioning of Drama Group. It begins to ask, through the tale of BBC drama, how to conceive of value, and therefore quality, in television.

*

Creative devolution c.1967

'The BBC functions on a system of devolution. A producer is given full powers in making a programme. On him rests the final judgment of what is right and seemly to present to his audience. If he is doubtful on any point he may refer his problem to his superior, who will either make a decision or refer the matter higher. Judgements are not based on written laws – although there is a code of practice. In part, they are based on precedent and tradition; but precedents can be ignored and traditions questioned or modified.'

Stuart Hood, 1967.

*

Authoritarian permissiveness: the controller's view c.1973

'I operate on the principle that I will push my vision of what the network should be like as hard as it can be pushed: that's to say until my force meets an immovable object. What I always say to producers is, "If I don't like your idea, I shall say so. If you persist in a rotten idea, I shall refuse it and refuse it again. But if you go on making the case, I will give in." Because in the end, producers are the people who make programmes, not controllers. So it's a mixture of authoritarianism and permissiveness.'

BBC radio network controller, in Tom Burns, The BBC.

*

Organising freedom

'There was more freedom in the late seventies; producers had an enormous amount of freedom. The BBC could afford to allow you to experiment, to fail. It doesn't seem able to do that now; the amount of drama is much less, and drama is used pretty much to get the ratings. I joined drama in the early seventies after the creation of BBC2. It was recognised that the complexities of planning two networks would need a stronger power base for production, so that each area – drama, light entertainment, features – would be strong enough to *argue* with the controllers. The controller would tell them what he wanted and then let them go off and do it. That was it.'

Former producer, BBC drama, 1997.

*

Boffin-led unrealism c.1996

'Before Producer Choice, annual planning consisted initially of editorials where creative heads would see the controllers and dream about what they'd love to do. Money wasn't on the agenda, it was creative free flight: "What shall we do? Let's have another series here." Then rationality started to prevail. Offers were put in and departments tried to put sums of money against those titles. You'd end up with offers costing three times what was available. Then you'd go through a nasty process where realism would dawn, and finance people would say, "We can't have this" or "This is too expensive." So what was supposed to be a creative process was incredibly inefficient; it didn't start by trying to get the best for the money available. It took two years to get the organisation thinking the new way. It took even longer to see that, in order to know what Drama is making in the coming year, we need eighteen months' foresight. It was a completely new concept; till then there was a production strategy but transmission was an afterthought. Now, the most important thing is the transmission strategy: you decide what you want in the schedule and make programmes to fit, to deliver what you want them to deliver. The BBC was a production-led, boffin-led organisation; now it's marketing-led. It's like a lot of British industries: they used to make toys without thinking what kids like to play with!'

Finance executive, BBC Production, 1996.

*

The unprecedented centralisation of commissioning in the BBC of the later nineties was a corollary of the importance accorded to marketing, strategy and financial planning. As the new accountancy gathered momentum and converged with marketing, a critical dimension emerged: a less-known aspect of Producer Choice devised by Corporate Centre strategists called the tariff-based programme funding model. Rather than simply the production of programmes, now the entire output of the television and radio networks was to be scientised according to the logic of financial planning. Network output had always been planned in advance; but when the accountants and strategists applied their panoply of forecasting skills to schedule planning, they identified a critical question: what was the audience share being delivered for the tariff associated with each schedule slot? The tariffs had been based on estimated cost per hour for each genre. But Birt's BBC was founded on an inherent distrust of any figures, such as cost per hour per genre, stemming from the erstwhile producer-led 'command economy'. Far better to use as a yardstick figures provided by market analysis and untainted by producer reasoning: quantitative audience data, a calculation of the audience available for any schedule slot at each point in the day. In some parts of radio this was productive. Now it was possible to ensure that high-cost programming was not thrown away at times when audiences are low, but scheduled to attract the most listeners. But in prime-time television the effect was different. Given the pressures to maintain or increase audience share while finding 'efficiency savings', it was a small step to discover that similar share could be achieved by lower-cost genres. At one mechanical stroke 'value for money' was improved. But the result was to cement schedules into a lowest common denominator logic: if it was possible to get an equally good audience for a slot with a cheaper show, then that's what should be done. In television this mechanism became Broadcast's way of disciplining Production to push down budgets. But it was also a key force behind the proliferation in the nineties of low-cost genres in prime time: leisure and lifestyle programming, docu-soaps, game shows and reality TV.

Centralised commissioning had other profound effects on the organisation of creativity. It was the logical culmination of the 1996 restructuring, with its split between Broadcast and Production. The restructuring streamlined commissioning and placed all the network teams in Broadcast, from where they could commission at will from independents or in-house, unimpeded by the loyalties and consultations formerly owed to their production colleagues. Henceforth, responsibility for commissions lay solely with the controllers, with marketing and strategy their natural allies. Now, the controllers had an eye for market context and demographics more than an ear for programme-makers. In Broadcast, the rationally planned, market-led schedule was king. The result was a less distributed and devolved structure of decision-making, with little space for the particular expertise of genre production heads or for ideas to flow up the hierarchy and be nurtured through dialogue. Such things would contradict 'fair trading'. If controllers were able to exercise greater individual vision in shaping channels, producers and production heads were disempowered, their creative latitude curtailed.

It was not always so. Previous decades saw acute sensitivity within the BBC to the balance between central control and devolution in the origination of ideas. Production heads cooperated and argued robustly with controllers, bringing ideas from producers and editors, with varying degrees of autonomy and authority in decisions over what would be made. Producers themselves had de facto slots to fill. The relationship was dialogical, the hierarchy looser, and the effect greater diversity in the sourcing of programmes. The amount of devolution altered in different periods. Tom Burns describes growing ideological diversity within the organisation in the sixties and seventies, encouraged by competition as well as wider cultural currents. Producers spoke of greater freedom and, decades before the tariff-based funding model, more awareness of the relationship between audiences and cost.[1] The burgeoning diversity made it into the schedules because decisions were taken by controllers in 'continual discussion with heads of departments and even individual producers'.[2] Devolved commissioning in this era brought heterogeneity and risk. The result, evident in a rash of irreverent current affairs and satirical shows, was a 'liberal dissolution' of the pre-war ethos, a reinvention of Reithianism for new times.

The centralised commissioning of the later nineties meant ideas had to travel via editorial boards and finance committees, via the advocacy of production heads and executive producers, to the controllers. The layers of decision-making caused bottlenecks, which led to breakdowns in relations with the creative community. The controllers became editorially directive, intervening at the level of ideas, casting, writers and even scripts, reducing producers' creative independence and leaving them closer to line producers. Certain projects continued to merit closer, cooperative development, but this had become exceptional and now took place across an organisational divide. As development was disciplined and brought closer to commissioning templates, producers were less able to spend time and money on developing projects not tied to immediate schedule goals. The kind of fertile dissent over creative directions that feeds diversity was attenuated. Centralisation threatened the system's capacity for risk, experiment and difference.

*

The mantle of 'freedom'

'The lobbying of controllers for commissions goes back to the impact of the independent quota. The criticism of the old BBC was that it needed democratising, that there were a small number of socially homogenous people making creative decisions. So you break that up, you say "Everybody can pitch in." But that just pushes it down the line: now someone has to say, "*That's* better than *that.*" Ten years ago in Singles you had ten or twelve producers with some degree of autonomy, each with two or three slots a year they could make. There were arguments with the head of department; if you wanted to produce something he didn't like, you arranged it so that you had no alternative, you busked it. Eventually he'd say, "Prove me wrong." If a producer had a passion, it could be translated into action. So varied stuff got through the system. And with a dozen people making decisions, if you had a project as a writer or director you had a dozen ports of call. Now the number of gatekeepers has reduced drastically. There's an extraordinary paradox. Ostensibly, by introducing independent production you suddenly have a hundred different sources – "Let a hundred flowers bloom." But actually, decisions are now made by one or two people; in Singles it's down to the judgements of two people. I'm sure they try to be heterogeneous, but you can't escape subjectivity. The situation is ludicrously disproportionate; the controllers, George and Michael, disappear under this mantle of "freedom". There are so many ideas they can't digest them. They constantly turn up at meetings apologising for not having read things; stuff is not read for ages. That leads to major disenchantment for writers. Paula Milne said at Edinburgh, "When I wrote *The Politician's Wife*, the BBC was the last place I'd have taken it," and there's a long list of writers who feel the same. It's about the long turnaround time, decisions that make no sense. It now seems simply to be about who's in favour and who's not. The idea was that the independent quota, the market, would make the system more open. If anything it's more closed. And for a body like the BBC that's unsatisfactory.'

Producer, BBC Drama, 1996.

*

The frail creator and the paraphernalia

'In the past, as a producer you might say to a new writer, "Not this one, but I'll commission you to do another." Now you can't. If I want to pay a writer £500 for a rewrite it has to go through layers of decision-making. There's been a disastrous centralisation which means that the pivotal position of the producer has been completely eroded. In the contract I used to have, it said I would do three films a year, and then it was largely down to me – budgeting, legal stuff and so on. The opportunity to do *Pennies From Heaven* came in the period when they tried to get rid of me; they'd banned *Brimstone and Treacle* but they came back saying, "Do something else." They probably wanted one sixty-minute play, but Dennis said, "I want nine hours." We'd make things bigger than they wanted. It was a privilege of riches. When I was producer of *Play for Today* and said to them, "Dennis wants to do a six-parter," they said, "All right, but you'll have to cancel six other plays." They didn't say, "We'd rather hedge our bets; maybe this whole Dennis Potter thing will fail." They gave me the opportunity, and then Dennis and I went away for a period of research and experiment. It was total freedom with everything to lose. Nobody was interested in seeing anything until we wanted to show them. No accountant came near us; there weren't committees or executive producers. Now all that paraphernalia has got between the frail creator and what ends up on screen. There's so much it interposes. One simple difference is volume. When I felt guilty about

309

cancelling the six other plays, there were about twenty-six original plays or films on BBC1 a year. Now there's eight if you're lucky, with all sorts of compromises in making them. The difference is enormous, and the pressure on those plays is extraordinary.'

Producer, BBC Drama, 1996.

*

Emasculation

A Drama Ed Board: there is mutinous fury that the controllers are marginalising Drama executives from the circuit of contacts, decision-making and commissions. 'Alan and Michael – the people with all the power – are holding creative meetings, colonising the talent, and purposefully have no Drama people there at all!' 'Why does Birt hold meetings with the indies without inviting any of us?' 'They're cutting our legs off, so they can commission everything!'

Diary, 1996.

*

Picking up baby

A story is circulating among the drama producers, following the commissioning power vested in Alan Yentob as controller of BBC1 by the restructuring. An independent producer, so it goes, has managed to get his infant a place in the same nursery attended by Alan's child, with the aim of orchestrating the sort of informal and friendly contacts, as they collect their offspring at the end of the day, that may spark a relationship and so smooth the way to potential commissions.

Diary, 1996.

*

Ordering Up Programmes

The rationalised system of the later nineties took the physical form of channel 'commissioning briefs' distributed to both independents and in-house production departments. Based on market analysis and financial planning, these booklets laid out schedule 'needs' in the guise of pre-conceived templates. The briefs warned that they were intended as 'a guide . . . not a prescription', that 'primarily it is . . . the quality of ideas that determines whether or not a proposal is commissioned', and that 'the main aim is to speed up the com-missioning process'. Yet their substance was to set out for each schedule slot detailed targets for genre and editorial type (for instance, 'Drama series: con-temporary drama with a lighter feel; this slot is closer in feel to the weekend than other weekday drama slots'), day, time, delivery date and season ('Midweek: Friday, post 2100, week 14/'98 to week 13/'99, all seasons'), length and number of episodes ('Duration: 50, eps per strand: 6–12'), and budget and potential co-production ('Target price range: £450k–£550k; third-party investment for this genre varies, but 6% of cost is regularly achieved; programme costs will range from £475k–£580k'). For BBC1, to these were added 'available audience' (for a Friday evening drama series in the mould of *Dangerfield*, '24 million'), expected demographics ('Primary focus: all adults; Secondary focus: women (older bias)') and minimum ratings ('35% – 8 million').[3] Sometimes the demographic would be broken down yet further into gender, age and socio-economic groupings (for a con-temporary drama series, Sunday pre-2100, competing with ITV's *Heartbeat* or *A Touch of Frost*: 'male 45%, female 55%; children 11%, 16–34s 22%, 35–54s 30%, 55+s 37%; ABC1s 43%, C2DEs, 57%').[4] The BBC2 drama briefs, in con-trast, set looser audience targets: 'Our strategy is based on supporting the widest range of ideas and talent rather than meeting specific demographic targets. Nevertheless drama can play a special role in speaking to women and younger viewers . . . BBC2 will continue to commission some drama which . . . will only achieve relatively low audiences. As a general guide, however, we would expect [peak-time drama] to meet or exceed the channel's average audience share of 11%.'[5]

This approach to scheduling was the BBC's invention; it took commercial practices to an extreme. For all the provisos, the briefs delivered a double coup. Programme concepts were first crudely formatted, then programming could be 'ordered up' to fit the templates. The templates provided a basis for disciplining producers over format, budget and expected audience or demo-graphic; the onus was on producers to justify deviations from the projected norms. On the one hand the booklets made schedule plans explicit and available to all, equalising opportunities between independents and in-house. On the other hand the effect, combined with the economic pressures on both in-house and independents, was to encourage a shift in the mindset of the entire production community towards thinking in ever more standardised terms. Apart from any resilient creative in-house traditions, the main exception to the dynamic were those successful independents, based often on the control of talent, who wielded power over the controllers and, if they cared to exercise it, retained a certain creative freedom and the capacity to resist the template logic.

*

Ordering up laughs

GB: 'There's much talk now about the commissioning booklets which set out schedule needs and budgets and so on per slot. Are they helpful?'

'Not much, for an independent. It's useful to see a broadcaster's thinking. But in comedy and entertainment you can't be too prescriptive. You can't say, "I want a late-night comedy sports quiz programme." Those are the limits of all forms of research and focus groups: nobody knows what they want until it's put in front of them. I've been to seminars for independents where the controllers said, "I need good stuff for seven o'clock on a Wednesday, for seventy thirty on a Wednesday, for eight o'clock." But TV programmes don't come about like an advertising brief! That's the cart before the horse. They come about when a very talented person has a great idea they really want to do, and a production company puts that together as a package and takes it to a broadcaster. Broadcasters will tell you that's the most exciting thing as well – the idea they never thought of, someone coming in and saying, "Why don't we do a comedy sports quiz programme?"'

GB: 'I can relate to that, but BBC Broadcast is now laying enormous stress on the market-research-driven prediction of schedule needs. Is it overbearing?'

'Partly; but it's far more onerous for in-house producers than for us. If you're in-house, you've got an obligation at Offers meetings to come up with a number of ideas. The great thing about being an independent is that nobody obliges you to do anything. I went to see the controllers a month ago and they said "We're looking for this." We then bear that in mind when developing projects. It's not overbearing. As an indie you have a relationship with a broadcaster, you don't contact them for nine months, then you ring up and say "I've got an idea." That's far more interesting for both parties than the monthly meeting where the controllers say, "Have you cracked my problem of seven o'clock on a Friday yet?" I probably can't crack seven o'clock on Fridays, and I'm glad I don't have to! I've never been to these hideous Offers meetings where fifteen people sit in a circle pitching ideas at the controller. It sounds worse than death.'

Managing director, independent production company, 1997.

*

The absence of censorship

'Risky drama is no longer conceived, let alone made. The industry has swallowed wholesale the invitation to self-censor – as many of us feared when the controllers reiterated the mantra that what we called censorship was legitimate editorial control. Today, controllers no longer get nasty surprises when they sit down with preview tapes because they pull the strings as early as the commissioning stage. "Producer Choice" is a bitter joke: producers had infinitely more choice when it was in their offices that dramas were commissioned, cast and put into production. On the one hand, British teledrama finds itself in a continuum with Hollywood feature product, calculating how a piece about racketeering in Rhondda will play in Peoria. On the other, schedulers want proven success: familiar ingredients, stars, sequels, spin-offs and revivals.'

W. Stephen Gilbert, 1998.

*

Safety first

'Safety first is the network rule. The safest, easiest formula is that nothing succeeds like success . . . but success anxiety reduces many a fertile idea to an inert object . . . In head-long pursuit of the logic of safety, the networks ordinarily intervene at every step of the development process. It is as if there were not only too many cooks planning the broth, but the landlord kept interfering as well. More often than not, commerce defeats not only art but commerce itself.'

Tod Gitlin, *Inside Prime Time.*

*

Genre Unlimited

In his account of the operations of the American commercial networks in the eighties, Tod Gitlin analyses the techniques – the 'logic of safety' – employed to ensure the return of audiences and so continuing financial health. Ideas are generated in one of three ways: through spin-offs, new shows based on characters or actors from existing hit series 'whose appeal is pretested'; through copies, which reproduce a winning formula, and which raise the teasing question of distinguishing mere clones from the kinds of imitation and variation that inhere in most forms of creativity; and through recombinants, the hybrid splicing of elements from proven successes. In the US, network competition has raised these processes, he says, to the level of self-parody.

By the later nineties the dynamics outlined by Gitlin, mixed with due moralism, were prominent within the BBC. Indeed, they were taken as a positive sign of the BBC having absorbed the productive populism of the times. At risk was the capacity to pursue other values and to imagine shows outside the logic of safety. Intense competition, the drive to secure ratings for legitimation, and the infatuation with entrepreneurialism cranked up the imitation across programmes and channels. Producers were led to cannibalise and hybridise existing shows and to develop repeated mutations of hit programmes, resulting in formulaic output across all genres.

One prominent symptom was the spate of spin-off soap opera and docu-soap series filling BBC1 in the late nineties, such as the spin-offs from *EastEnders*, *Casualty* and *Paddington Green*. The main strategy for competing in prime-time of the last BBC1 controller under Birt was to extend existing popular hits, 'the bankers', in this highly generic way. Another symptom, in all channels, was the new prevalence of reality TV, which married sensational and voyeuristic content to a logic both of international formats and of proliferating slightly variant copies. At the end of the nineties, 'success' in the British industry had begun to be weighed in terms of the capacity to devise such formats. *Big Brother*, the globally successful Endemol format aired in Britain on Channel 4, was only a prominent instance of this trend. In the BBC the rationalisation of scheduling and commissioning caused similar dynamics at the level of schedules and channels. It honed further the existing mimicry between BBC1 and ITV, BBC2 and Channel 4. Now, even single strands and sub-genres were tied into ever more intense imitative rivalry: BBC2's documentary strand *Modern Times* against C4's *Cutting Edge*; BBC1's 'dark, regional police thriller' *Out of the Blue* against ITV's *Liverpool One*; in daytime, BBC1's talk show *Vanessa* against ITV's *Trisha*. The centralised commissioning structure permitted no resistance: as a senior producer put it, 'The controller is god.'

*

'Innovation' tales: formats, copies, the law, and gold

'Forget *Big Brother* and *Popstars*. *Survivor*, as [Charlie Parsons] constantly reminds you, is the "original and best", a British creation that British TV executives never had the courage to commission. It's hardly surprising. On paper, the concept is mad: 16 people are sent to a desert island, forced to compete with one another by carrying out challenging tasks, and told to vote each other off before the last person standing walks away with £1 million. Planet 24 [*Parsons's company*] sold an option on the rights to Endemol, the Dutch format house, but Endemol never made the show. A Planet 24 executive quit to go to Endemol, which came up with the *Big Brother* format. Parsons believes the events are directly linked and robbed him of being the first to conquer the reality TV kingdom. Parsons took Endemol to court in a case that drags on still. At the moment, he is appealing a ruling that *Big Brother* is not a copy of the *Survivor* format.

'Parsons suggests that there is a wholesale racket in British television where ideas are routinely stolen by TV executives. Some might wonder why he doesn't just sit back and rake in the cash. Who cares if he came up with the idea first if he's making millions in the process? He believes *Survivor* was the victim of an unwillingness to innovate. "There was an astonishing wall of resistance." Apart from [in] Sweden. So a series called *Expedition Robinson* was made and it fast became the nation's top-rated show. It started to be noticed around the world and the US network CBS took it up. *Survivor*, the US version, was the startling number one hit of the summer schedules last year, and Parsons struck gold. Even there, lawsuits have flown: CBS now claims that a Granada format, *Boot Camp*, airing on Fox, is a copy of *Survivor*. Once the show became a hit in the US it was not long before it was taken up here. When Parsons and [Lord] Alli sold Planet 24 to Carlton – a deal that made them millionaires – they cannily hived off the *Survivor* rights to a separate company. Parsons also believes that the BBC's *Castaway* series is a *Survivor* copy. Oh yes, and Channel 4's *Shipwrecked*. Perhaps the creator of *Coronation Street* should sue the guy who came up with *Emmerdale*. Where would it all end?'

Matt Wells, 2001.

*

Lashed together: recombinant factual

'A new series this week actually invites viewers to watch paint dry. *Big Strong Girls* (BBC1) is a daytime DIY show which has several sequences of emulsion losing its moistness. The series seems lashed together from bits and pieces of other projects. As the title indicates, the greatest debt is to the cookery series *Two Fat Ladies*. Like their culinary predecessors, the *Big Strong Girls* are a studiedly eccentric double act requiring the upper dress sizes. [But the show] copies its overall format from the consultancy genre which increasingly dominates factual television. In *Can't Cook Won't Cook*, a top chef remoulds a kitchen novice. In *Changing Rooms* and *Ground Force*, the houses and gardens of the public are turned over by experts. In *Big Strong Girls*, a man identified by his wife as a DIY disaster is given a respray. One of the most notable trends in factual television [during] the last decade has been the way in which lifestyle shows have raised their audiences by borrowing techniques from game shows and drama. The consultancy series inject tension through one of two formats: either Time Trial (the recipe or house must be completed by a certain deadline) or Pygmalion (an incompetent will be transformed by mentors).'

Mark Lawson, 1999.

*

Midnight's Children, episode two – A writer calls: honouring and humouring Salman

A production meeting for *Midnight's Children*. Dan, Pete and Ed are joined by scriptwriter Will, the script editor, designer and casting director. The group is meeting Salman for the first time; he is expected soon. Ed says time is tight: the controller wants *MC* delivered for Christmas 1997. The plan is to start filming in four months. Ed: 'Budget work is continuing. Of the potential co-producers, Brite has offered £600,000, and Media Asia are interested in a distribution deal that would get it on Indian TV.' Will asks when they'll know if it's green-lit, and Ed replies, 'It's really already decided, given the political weight for this project at the top of the BBC. They think it's fantastically different and innovative. If we ask BBC2 for £300k more, they'd be crazy not to put it on the table.' Will says there's now a script for Part One, and adds apprehensively, of Salman, 'There'll be tension, as there always is adapting an ambitious novel; but if we're reassuring, it should be OK.'

Salman enters and there are warm hellos. He mentions that he's writing a screenplay, and that *A Suitable Boy* is being filmed for Channel 4. Salman: 'The cultural attaché of the Indian Embassy went to see my publisher and said the government [*of India*] is very excited about this project – "It's going to be a marvellous year for India!"' Dan reports meeting a senior Indian civil servant in Delhi to talk about the production, and the only thing they objected to was a scene set in Kashmir. Everyone laughs as they plot how to get the Indian minder drunk the night before the crucial scene; 'I imagine it's pretty easy to keep people off the set over there?' Salman, smiling, concurs. Pete and Dan say they expected the Indian government to put up resistance and set lots of conditions, but so far this hasn't happened, 'And so far, without a single bribe!' Salman looks suitably amazed. Dan reports on the dinner party with the Indian co-producers at which, at the climax of the toasts, it was announced that 'We have gained possible, potential, close to permission from the government!', and there was an enormous cheer. He interprets that this seemed tantamount to getting permission, or perhaps the best one could expect. Ed tells Salman about the challenge, central to the project, of setting up

316

cooperative structures between the BBC and Indian production teams, like on *Gandhi*. Dan tells of the risk of being rushed in post-production due to unrealistic channel demands, and foresees a case of 'Do you want it *good*, or do you want it *Thursday*?!' Ed says that, if they're green lit before the co-production funds are confirmed, BBC2 may underwrite the gap: 'Me and Pete have to guarantee that it'll come in on budget, and we'd commit professional hara-kiri if we did that before the finance is secure.' It will cost £1 million per hour, 'but that's still less than Jane Austen. And this is far more ambitious, somewhere between *The Killing Fields* and *Arabian Nights*!'

They discuss the potential syndication of *MC* by Indian commercial stations. Discussion turns to Doordarshan, the Indian state broadcaster. Salman regales them: 'It was like the Ministry of Truth. And then came satellite, and suddenly there were lots of different channels around and Doordarshan had to change. A friend of mine became head of news. His major innovation was to suggest that a journalist should go and comment on events. Before, they sent only a cameraman and sound recordist; the voice-over was given by the politician being filmed! He lasted a year before he was sacked . . .' Dan speaks about the look he wants for *MC*. The aim is to shoot in several states to find appropriate settings. They will use 35mm film and some computer-generated images. 'There's magic in the book, *braggadocio*, and I want to capture this spirit. I don't want it to be simply a period piece.' He sketches for Salman some ideas for a scene set in a tower inspired by an Escher image, an endlessly ascending staircase. He describes a non-realist approach to several key scenes: 'I want to keep the wit of the text, to do them with a twist and catch the audience unawares.' He and the designer talk of transforming images: a boy's bedroom turns into a parliament building, 'The child has created the parliament building in his head.' Salman laughs: 'I love all that. It's not unflashy, *Midnight's Children*, at points. It needs to be cinematic.' Dan: 'People in India said to me that you'd taken a lot of things in the novel from Hindi cinema. Is that true?' Salman says he can't remember, 'I finished it in 1979. But Bombay is the centre of Hindi film-making, and I have watched a lot of Hindi movies. Take the baby-swapping: that's of course a wonderful melodrama, very much from that genre. So there are a few conscious borrowings, and no doubt unconscious ones too.' Dan asks about the club scene: there's always one in Hindi movies. 'Can I use some Hindi songs in that scene? I'd like to have a big musical set piece; would that be in the spirit of the thing?' Salman is pleased: 'It would certainly help to sell it to the Indian market.' They discuss the idea of casting a Bollywood star, to which Salman enthuses colloquially, 'Major big shit!' He adds that some of his family were in film in Bombay, so it was around him as a child: 'Movies and cricket. That's what you can't get away from, growing up in Bombay.' Dan reports that some Indians with whom he spoke commented that there were always four storylines in Hindi movies, and they'd found all four in *MC*: '"That's what Salman was doing in the book," they said.' Salman, amused, isn't saying.

They come to the scripts. Will speaks of doing well, but needing to find further cuts. Dan speaks up for a strong visual interpretation of the book; they need to translate the literary into the visual. It's not an easy text to bring the audience into. Salman responds passionately, giving his own experience of finishing the book: 'I thought then, who will want to read this? No one, just members of my family. But then it sold 600,000.' He speaks of the double reception of the book. 'In India it was read naturalistically, as history; in Europe it was read as fantasy, fabulous, a fairy tale. In India it was the familiarity that people liked – an old man once came up to me and said, "I could have written that! I know those things,"' and we laugh. 'But in the rest of the world it was liked for the unfamiliarity. It needs to work in both ways, naturalistically and as fairy tale.' All agree. Dan says the task now in scriptwork is to understand the psychology of the boy. But Salman expresses anxiety about the cuts to the script: 'It might become a comic strip.' Dan responds that the challenge is to pick out the key moments which move the narrative along, and they discuss how to capture the novel's spirit without the detail of the novel. Salman explains how he tried in the book to capture the sense of the crowd, the crowd being the overriding symbol and the first impression of India. How to express this in the text? He decided to do it by a sense of crowding the storylines, by giving a 'crowd' of events and perspectives: it's there in the writing itself. He implicitly issues a challenge to Dan and the others: can they keep this *feel* of the text in the film? I think immediately of the potential for formal narrative innovation in the mould of Fellini's *Satyricon* or Pasolini's *Oedipus Rex*, films in which just such a jostling of storylines occurs, cutting across each other, suddenly falling away, dissolving, or rising up unexplained – techniques I find marvellous. But neither Dan nor anyone else picks up the implied challenge; instead Dan speaks firmly of the need to keep the narrative focused on essential developments.

They move to consider art deco as a key visual and architectural motif in the film, concurring on how well this will work. Dan and Salman are very taken by the 'fabulosity' of the novel, how this needs to be expanded in the film. Dan growls, Groucho Marxish, 'And I want three elephants!', satirising the movie mogul's approach to shooting 'Indianness'. Salman mentions another structural feature of the book, that at one level it takes place within the span of one day. He says this is a deep element, one that was in his head when writing as a way of bringing unity. He asks them to bear this in mind, subliminally, 'and then you can ignore it' – as perhaps he felt they ignored his point about the crowd being emblematic of the novel's form. They talk of Kashmir: the book opens there, and Salman speaks eloquently of Kashmir's beauty, the weather, the deep winter. But all agree that it's too risky to film there; there are half a million Indian troops, and tanks everywhere. The film will be experienced as being about Bombay, and they discuss how to convey the essence of the city, the look of different districts. Finally Dan poses the question: 'What relation would you like to have to the project?' Salman replies even-handedly that there can't be too many drivers in this car. He'd like to see final scripts and to be consulted and informed about what's happening. Dan says he'd value his advice; the relationship is being warmly cemented. 'I'll need to know how much licence I can take with those Hindi songs . . .' and Salman says, 'Oh, that will be fine. I have a very vulgar heart.' Winding up, in his new advisory role, Salman gives a donnish exegesis on the goddess Kali. He speaks of his relationship now with India; this winter he makes his first trip back since the fatwa and he is concerned about a media circus. Ed raises, humorously, the idea of him having a part in the film, at which point Salman mentions a leading role he's recently been offered. Ed: 'OK, you've got the part – but we don't pay much.' Salman: 'I know.'

Diary, 1996.

*

Drama Bound

In the later nineties Drama Group was a huge and expensive body spanning the most popular television to the most abstruse, with an annual budget somewhere under £200 million. It was composed of four London-based departments, Series, Serials, Single plays and a small Films unit, and four energetic regional drama outfits based at BBC Northern Ireland, BBC Scotland, BBC Wales and BBC Birmingham at Pebble Mill. Series dealt with long-running series and soaps, largely the popular, most ratings-driven kind of output. Serials was the home of limited-duration serials, often based on literary adaptations, as in the classic serials adapted from Jane Austen or Dickens, but also contemporary adaptations and original contemporary dramas. Singles was the department charged with the legacy of the single television play, usually considered the most writerly, high-cultural drama form, most able to cultivate innovation and risk-taking.

Rivalry existed between the departments, particularly Singles and Films, which Singles appeared keen to subsume. Drama Group also hosted small spaces of alternative work, as in the Black Screen initiative in Singles intended to nurture black talent. Where the London genre-based departments were mainly oriented to in-house production – and after the 1996 restructuring were restricted to this – the regional outfits worked across the genres and could executive produce both independent and in-house projects. Of necessity they were entrepreneurial, and for once to productive effect as an increasing amount of regionally inflected drama hit the networks.

The history of BBC Drama is commonly identified with the BBC's 'Golden

Age', the creative heights reached in the sixties under director-general Hugh Carleton Greene, which in drama gained added impetus from the leadership of the impresario Sydney Newman, as well as with the continuing tradition of inventive radical drama of the seventies and eighties. Drama lived up to its luminous history with a mixture of resilience, compromise and irony. Yet while there was a healthy scepticism towards notions of a 'Golden Age', as the Birt reforms bit and prevailing values shifted uncontrollably, it was widely believed that Drama faced changes more destructive than at any point in its history. Several orders of problems faced Drama Group in the later nineties. First, through a few spectacular flops it had become associated with failure, particularly in popular drama. Industry lore was that ITV had built its highly competitive schedule around popular drama: the soaps *Coronation Street* and *Emmerdale*, and series such as *The Bill*, *Peak Practice* and *Heartbeat*. In mid 1991, BBC1 had its worst ratings since the mid eighties, and the BBC's relative weakness in popular drama was seen as a key cause. Jonathan Powell, BBC1 controller, determined to sharpen the channel's popular appeal and set in motion several drama initiatives, including a second episode of *Casualty* and a new soap, *Eldorado*. Birt scuppered the former, and despite positive audience research, *Eldorado* was a disaster. With ratings plummeting, it ended after just one year. For all the ambitions to the contrary, there seems to have been a kind of desert in popular drama in the late eighties and early nineties. Yet *EastEnders* and *Casualty* continued to perform well, disturbing any simplistic account. Since then, popular drama has been seen as the core of the BBC1 schedule and as central to the BBC's legitimacy. As a result great attention was paid in the mid nineties to the genre, causing an unsteady renaissance. But the legacy of the crisis was a low tolerance on the part of BBC senior management towards drama failures.

Drama executives perceived a deep ambivalence underlying Corporate Centre's response to the drama difficulties. Did the Birtist vision of the BBC include drama? Despite its belief that it embodied the best of the BBC's modernising tendencies, Drama Group was frequently chided by senior magagement for being out of line or insufficiently striving. The message from the controllers was that London Drama, in particular, was troublesome, that they were more interested in talking to those untainted by the past – to the independents, Glasgow and Belfast. Trumping these difficulties were the incessant managerial reforms, including the deleterious structural changes aimed at production departments which, given Drama's vast scale and high cost, bore down fiercely on the Group. These changes caused constant organisational turmoil and a devastating demoralisation. In response, Drama became a locus both of accommodation and of struggle and dissent.

In hostile conditions, the heart of Drama Group was the biweekly meeting of the Drama Editorial Board chaired by the Group's head, at which all departments were represented along with Group management functions. In these meetings the culture of the Group was marked by sharp and sometimes petty rivalries, but also by constructive cooperation and solidarity in the face of external pressures. Drama continued to support a vibrant editorial community, one that grappled self-consciously with contradictory demands. The board was the site of collective editorial debate and preview; its discussions gave a sense of connection with the history of the genres and of conversation, in shorthand, between different tendencies. The board was where Corporate Centre policies and managerial directives impacting on the Group were worked through. Here the complexity of reconciling and implementing those policies, Drama's immersion in internal and external politics, and the chronic uncertainties thrown up by all of these were made plain – as shown by the histories of major dramas of the period such as Midnight's Children and Our Friends in the North.

From 1993 till his departure in 1996, the editorial board was run by Drama's head, Charles Denton. When he left, largely in protest at Birtist reforms, there was a prolonged interregnum as, it was rumoured, every leading figure in television drama approached by the BBC refused the job, which was seen as a poisoned chalice. A respected drama executive, Ruth Caleb, took the helm until Alan Yentob, then director of Television, and Colin Adams, a senior manager, provided further temporary cover. The leadership of Drama remained unsettled for some years.

*

Just say no

January 1997: I'm meeting one of the leading creative figures in British television drama. Over a decade ago he began as an assistant floor manager at the BBC. Now, he explains, 'I've just turned down for the second time an offer to become head of BBC Drama.'

Diary, 1997.

*

Excess and resentment

I'm speaking to a senior figure who left BBC Drama years ago and heads a rival outfit. He gives his diagnosis of its ills: 'Drama has been put in the position of having to respond to the editorial judgements of a couple of arts journalists. It's a very conspicuous area of output, and expensive; success and failure are magnified. What has hurt it above all is the BBC's inability to tolerate failure. Look at their inability to stand by *Rhodes*, their barely suppressed anxiety about *Nostromo* even before it went out! It's very damaging. With that volume of drama, a third will be bad, a third will get away with it, and a third will be exceptional. You have to back programme makers and nurture their confidence. And it's gone. I used to sit on Programme Review Board: the other departments, especially Documentaries, saw drama as a land of make-believe, as *additional* to the public service remit. There was a single, *The Hummingbird Tree*, a classic BBC adaptation born of the Commonwealth tradition of writing, about racism and cultural conditioning in the Caribbean. Dead-centre BBC values. It got great reviews and respectable overnights. But the other departments couldn't stand it. There was resentment because it cost £1 million. For them drama represents excess; it's a fiction, fluff, lacking a good critical culture, and a poor relation of theatre and film. This is what you're up against in the BBC.'

Diary, 1997.

*

Quota Heaven

A supreme expression of the complex imperatives under which Drama Group laboured was its difficulty in integrating the several quotas to which it was subject. First, Drama had to implement the statutory 25 per cent independent quota. In parallel, it had to implement the 1993 regional quota, the BBC policy that aimed to raise the proportion of network drama made outside London to 33 per cent. Finally, to stem the tide of independent commissions and buoy up in-house production, an informal policy from the mid nineties decreed a 40 per cent 'minimum output guarantee' (MOG) for the London in-house departments. In editorial board meetings, executives struggled to reconcile the quotas, an extraordinary rationalisation that tried to enforce a mix of 'market' and 'culturally representative' forces, each with distinct moral and political foundations. Lengthy debate occurred as to how the independent 25 per cent intersected with the regional 33 per cent; or what defined a regional independent company; or whether Belfast could legitimately claim ownership in all Irish projects, and Glasgow in Scottish projects; or how a regional drama should be defined – by its Highland setting and Scottish content, in other words what it represents, or by its BBC Scotland executive producer or production team, that is, by whom it is made? The terms appeared opaque, and at times the situation veered towards the farcical and unmanageable.

*

Quota catch-22

GB: 'So, the indie quota, the regional quota, and now the MOG: how do they all square?'

'It's very easy. By law 25 per cent has to be provided by independents across the genres. The BBC also decided that a third of all output will be made in the regions, on the reasonable grounds that the BBC is funded by the country and that there are regular complaints that the networks are metropolitan-dominated. Of that 33 per cent, 20 per cent has to come from the national regions – Scotland, Wales, Northern Ireland – and the rest from the English regions, which for us is Pebble Mill. Twenty-five per cent of the regional 33 per cent has to be made by indies, and of the remaining 67 per cent, from London, twenty-five per cent must be indie as well. But in fact they closed down Belfast's production resources, so almost 100 per cent of its output will come from indies. Scotland has also closed a lot of its production resources so around 75 per cent of its drama is from indies. Wales is about fifty–fifty; only Pebble Mill has a balance of sixty–forty in-house to indie. So we might well reach a point where all the drama indie quota comes from the regions. Unfortunately, most of the major production companies are not in the regions, but in London.'

GB: 'Aha! A catch-22. Or will the BBC reinvest in production in the regions?'

'No, there's not enough money. They won't go back to having production staff because, well, they've only just got rid of them. They made them redundant at exactly the same time they agreed to build up regional production. The decisions were made by different people. It's appalling.'

Senior executive, BBC Drama, 1996.

*

Complexity

Kate, a planning chief from Alan Yentob's BBC1 team, has come to the Drama Editorial Board to fill in the Drama executives about the controller's budget targets for 1997–8.

323

She distributes documents and projects overheads, in which Venn diagrams with over-lapping circles set out the various intersecting quotas that will impact on the allocation of drama budgets for that year. She begins: 'The total target drama spend for BBC1 and BBC2 is £159 million, of which £47 million is for the regions, and of that amount £28 million is for the "national regions" – Wales, Northern Ireland and Scotland – while £19 million is for Birmingham.' She continues at breakneck speed: 'So, £112 million is left for London, of which £10 million will go to *Casualty* and £30 million to *EastEnders*. That leaves £72 million for the rest of London drama output, of which we assume about 40 per cent will go to independent production. That leaves £44 million in the pot for all non-Elstree London in-house production. Clear?' As she finishes the Drama executives gasp, baffled by the quota calculations and by their implications: there is much less money than anticipated. Mike Wearing and Karl Francis, head of Drama Wales, look aghast. Someone asks how an indie working in the 'English national region' is being defined. Kate replies, 'Currently, an English regional independent is defined as having a production base' – and someone interjects, 'But there's no agreed definition yet of what a "production base" means!'. Kate presses firmly on, '– as having a production base somewhere outside the M25.' The room is in uproar; 'This is corporate managerialism gone crackers!', says a veteran.

Diary, 1996.

*

Map and ruler

A Drama Ed Board: we are discussing a serial being developed with one of the hottest properties of the moment, Jimmy McGovern. As with all writers, McGovern's strengths are demonstrated by a genealogy of his work. From the 'nursery slopes', scripts for Channel 4's soap *Brookside*, he progressed to write what are by consensus some outstanding dramas: the BBC film *Priest*, the Granada series *Cracker* and drama-documentary *Hillsborough*. This new serial, *The Lakes*, is set in the Lake District. With McGovern involved it is bound to be made; the controllers are utterly enamoured of him. Earlier, we've touched on the need to fulfil the regional quota, and Tony, the Birmingham drama head, picks up the theme: 'I really think *The Lakes* would be made best at Pebble Mill.' Charles, often concerned to support the London in-house depart-ments, says, 'Hang on! We've got to consider it for London in-house.' But Tony stands his ground, and they all start vying. Andrea, head of Drama Scotland, teases, 'Let's get the map and ruler out! I'll bet the Lake District is midway between Glasgow and Birmingham. Perhaps we in Glasgow should do it?', to which Robert, Northern Ireland drama supremo, adds, 'Well, it's only a hovercraft ride away from Belfast,' implying it

324

could equally well be made by his outfit. The room is full of helpless mirth. The struggle to win commissions and justify funding, and the lack of clarity over criteria for regional status, tangle and spin hilariously out of control.

Diary, 1996.

*

The consequence of the weighty carapace of reforms and policy directives bearing on Drama Group was severely to curtail creative autonomy. Two signs, evidence of the decimated morale of creative personnel, attest to the malaise. There was a steady outflow of leading younger producers and executives to work in the independents and in film. At the same time the reactive commissioning culture, lengthy delays in decision-making and restrictive conditions for creativity damaged relations with external talent. Writers were increasingly alienated. They might wait months for responses to scripts, only to be given mixed signals, or for the details of a commission to be reneged on. Star writers, on the other hand, could experience the opposite, existing commitments swept aside to accommodate them.

*

Alienation: the writer's complaint

Alex, an established writer, is adapting his own well-received novel as a drama. I watch an early script meeting in which his work is discussed by two executive producers: where filming might happen, the number of episodes, issues of character. The meeting is warm but unfocused. Months later a letter arrives from Alex to one of the executive producers:

Dear Ian,

I would be grateful for some news about my adaptation. It's now two months since I sent you the revised 1st episode. My agent has written a series of letters and has phoned a number of times, but we don't seem to get any response from you. Can you please explain why? It's difficult for me to know what to do when I haven't had your reaction to my re-write. This lack of response, indeed your ignoring of our attempts to contact you, make me think that you are basically uninterested in pursuing the project with me. I feel as though I'm working in a void. Can you please let us know what is going on? Have you met difficulties further up the chain? I know how busy you are, and how many projects you are overseeing. But I too have many demands on my time. The situation has become very demoralizing, and I'm not sure you realize how unproductive it is to alienate your writers in the way that you are alienating me.

Yours (etc).'

A few weeks later another letter arrives, this time from the writer's agent:

Dear Ian,

Neither Alex nor I have heard from you since your call a couple of weeks ago – despite your protestations that you would be in touch again soon. Alex has also tried to call you, and has got nowhere. Therefore we have come to the view that, whatever your initial interest in the project, you no longer want to pursue it. Please confirm by return that the BBC has no further interest, and that the rights in the scripts can now revert to Alex. We will then find a more welcoming and committed home for the drama.

Yours, etc.

These letters are loose imitations of originals.

*

All the Jane Eyres

A Drama Ed Board. Mike Wearing is filling us in on the current slate of serials commissions: 'Andrew Davies has now committed to our *Jane Eyre*. It's a high risk game; he's shifted all his other commitments back to do it for us.' After months of indecision, this most classic of classics has been commissioned by the controller. Mike ponders, 'I wonder how many thousands of other commissions of Andrew's we've knocked sideways'. Charles comments, 'The real question is whether we'll get our *Jane Eyre* made before ITV's.' Another writer, Kay Mellor, is set to write a *Jane Eyre* for ITV, but, says Charles, ITV's drama head, Nick Elliott, hasn't yet committed to it. Petra, a Drama executive, only half jokingly suggests a tactic: 'If we gave Kay the go-ahead on her BBC commission now, we could take her out of the action for writing ITV's Jane Eyre!' Everyone laughs, and they knock the idea around. Mike adds mischievously, 'That's the way we always used to do it . . .' Charles reflects, 'Now, that's a good reason for the BBC keeping a contractual relation with the majority of writers around the country. Hey, I suppose that's what we already do!'

Diary, 1996.

*

Profile and Ratings, High and Low

In the circumstances described, what was the editorial culture of Drama like in the later nineties? As a priority it was impelled to respond to the controllers; and with intensifying competition, and to encourage and consolidate the gains in popular programming, ratings and audience share had become very significant in the controllers' thinking. For BBC1, getting popular drama right had become a central concern. But while dominant, ratings and share were not the sole criteria of success. In general, the main conception of how to justify the output remained one dating back to Reith: that the BBC should be a universal provider, showing the best across the full range of genres, from sitcoms, soaps, variety and game shows to experimental documentaries, challenging drama and political satire.

The controllers' requirements were summed up in the maxim, 'We need both ratings and profile,' the latter a term condensing critical success, press attention, and acclaim or controversy among the cultivated classes. Lower ratings were tolerated if other kinds of attention were achieved, although there was little doubt that competitive ratings were primary, setting the context for exceptions. Moreover, ratings expectations were relative, not absolute; not every drama was expected to achieve the top line. But each commission carried with it an expected rating, and there was consternation when a programme departed greatly from these figures. The drama executives had absorbed the controllers' dictum: they should deliver both 'distinctive' pieces – which stood for high-quality, risky and innovative drama – and ratings-led work. They believed the controllers would still occasionally take a knowing risk, even on BBC1, with shows not designed to bring in the 'numbers'; an example was the Dennis Potter serial *Karaoke* shown after his death in 1996 on BBC1. It was just that this was increasingly rare.

*

The burden of expectation

Programme Review Board: *Karaoke* has begun on BBC1 and is under review. A Documentaries boss opens: 'I fell asleep. The *Guardian* reviewer got it right: it was formulaic, uninspired Potter.' A News chief agrees: 'It was surely not what was anticipated.' Ken Trodd, the producer, owns up to poor ratings – 4.2 million as opposed to the 6 million that the controller, Alan Yentob, hoped for. *Blackeyes*, often considered Potter's worst, got more; *The Singing Detective* got over 8 million. Alan weighs in, saying the critics weren't all bad; even the *Daily Mail* was OK. Peter Fiddick told him it was a work of genius. Ken agrees that it is Potter's best work since the early days. Alan asks the room to suspend judgement: 'Let's not bury this one before it's dead,' and Will Wyatt concurs. They stress the huge burden of expectation carried by this and its twin serial 'because of Potter's death, the Bragg interview, and the cooperation with Channel 4. The pre-publicity was so heavy, it may simply be a victim of too much trailing.' But Ken and Alan reflect, bleakly, that the ratings pattern suggests that the audience is actually being turned off.

Diary, 1996.

*

The play-off

'An interesting aspect of discussions with the controllers about *Our Friends in the North* concerned their expectations for the show, which weren't at all to do with audience size but were absolutely to do with *profile*. I recall a conversation with Alan and Michael in which they said, "If we get two million that's fine; but what we *have* to have is profile – that's what really counts."'

GB: 'This wonderful word "profile": what does it mean?'

'It means getting a lot of newspaper coverage, and winning awards. It means being like *The House*, which only got one or two million, but which nonetheless became a focus for the chattering classes. It has to become part of "the culture" in that curious way. So *The House* got profile rather than audience. There's a kind of play-off between profile and ratings, especially on BBC2. That's part of the public service thing, being able to point to pockets of excellence. I didn't see all the episodes of *The House* – but we're talking about it now, aren't we?'

Producer, BBC Drama, 1996.

*

Success

The walk through *Radio Times* in Programme Review Board. Jo, head of Drama Series, asks the room to join her in congratulating the *EastEnders* team on their adept handling of the culmination of the Aids/HIV storyline: 'It was a tremendous highpoint, very moving and sensitively done.' Will Wyatt asks, cautiously, 'Did anyone find it too much? The Duty Log showed an amazing turnaround. Initial comments were very concerned

328

about the coverage of Aids, but then suddenly the calls were entirely positive and con-vinced.' Another Drama chief comments that at one point the narrative was indeed depressing, holding out no hope of human relationships coming through, but it all came together by the end. Will persists: 'The ratings were certainly good. But was it too tough for the audience?'

Diary, 1996.

*

It is commonly held by commentators and drama producers alike that, histor-ically, two ideological axes ran through the culture of BBC Drama, and they were often aligned. Drama was mainly and aggressively on the political left, and inhospitable to those of other political stripes. At the same time Drama was the locus of a marked cultural hierarchy, with high cultural status attached to those genres identified with literary forms and individual authorial voice – singles, serials and film; while popular drama and continuing series suffered the low status associated with cultural commerce, as though irredeemably lowbrow and lacking in artistic ambition. In this received view, the apotheosis of quality lay in the traditions of leftist social realist and experimental television drama, particularly in singles and serials.

These polarities still haunted Drama Group in the later nineties. But while creative rivalry and competition for commissions were intense, Drama con-tained a more complex and ambivalent interweaving of ideological currents and creative ambitions. A vaguely leftist and humanist social commentary con-tinued to be the default position underlying much of the output. Singles still enjoyed a certain privilege as a genre, its kudos derived from its kinship with theatre and film. Producers proved their credentials by relating how they began work in Singles. And before the 1996 restructuring, Singles, with its devolved funding, retained more commissioning autonomy than the other departments, referring editorially to the controllers without yielding a veto. At the other end of drama, among those working in Series, despite the avowed interest in ratings, there was a barely suppressed anxiety that many of those in charge did not understand popular drama and were tackling it de haut en bas. The 'popular' was elusive; it was always elsewhere, a distance tacitly conceded in executives' earnestly professed desire to learn the tricks of the popular trade. Vestiges of an elitist attitude towards popular drama remained, directed at the Elstree operations devoted to production of EastEnders and Casualty. Their banish-ment to an outer London suburb was taken to symbolise a disdain for popular drama among some corporate and drama chiefs. Yet there was admiration for these 'bankers' in periods of their creative success, and envy for their secure funding, prominence in the schedule and devoted and appreciative audiences. Universally, the greatest admiration was reserved for those shows that combined good ratings with a genuinely inventive take on the genre.

*

Right and left

'When I was a producer, there was a range of us politically, from left to right, with me on the right and people like Ken Trodd on the left. If I'd belonged to a party it would have been the Conservatives, all be it the left wing. Ken needed me as much as I needed him, because the audience could see this was a group of producers with very different political views, all under the same roof. You learned quickly not to voice political views; the rule was you must never use your position as a platform for propaganda. But it's common knowledge that *The Wednesday Play* occasionally changed government policy, that *Edna, the Inebriate Woman* and *Up the Junction* brought to public attention some of the awful conditions that existed in the sixties. And I approved of that as strongly as anybody.

There's a perception that the BBC was very left-wing, but few people, if any, abused their privilege to disseminate party views. But it might not have seemed that way. Take the furore over Potter's *Brimstone and Treacle* in the seventies. Alastair Milne, then managing director of TV, refused to let it go out because he said the response to it was so visceral – and he was right – that there was no universal truth of which that play was the dramatic statement. When he censored it, it was in a sense a measure of the freedom at the time. But we were all outraged. Immediately, everyone in Plays was summoned to a meeting. We were told that none of this would be reported outside the room and were asked to sign a statement that we dissociated ourselves from the appalling interference. I said I wouldn't sign because I didn't think it was a very good play. I said if we were going to nail our colours to the mast, we should do it on a different play, and some colleagues – whom I suppose you could call the right wing – backed me up. Next day the papers had a headline: "BBC Producers and Script Editors Sign Document Complaining . . . A unanimous meeting . . ." That was the sort of thing that went on; it gave the BBC that sobriquet of being leftist and Trotskyist. In fact ,there was a far more varied and dissenting range of views, and that was healthy.'

Former BBC drama producer, 1997.

*

It's dangerous! Developing *Casualty*

'We got the go-ahead for the first series of *Casualty* about ten years ago, and it went out for the first time a year later. In that first January when we were researching it, there was a rash of stuff about the National Health Service in the press; it was that moment in the mid eighties when you suddenly had article after article about violence in casualty departments, low pay and so on, in all the papers, across the board. It was when the NHS was beginning to explode through lack of resources. So we reflected all that assiduously, and it was very exciting: "Look! It's dangerous! It's falling apart!" We'd researched it all so carefully and the stories were all in the right-ish tabloids, so nobody was more surprised than us by the reaction – although a lot of the writers were members of Militant, and in that sense we knew what we were doing. We were electrified by the vehemence of the government's response, particularly as it was a fiction. But by the time it went out the NHS had become the most sensitive issue for the coming general election. We had Norman Tebbit and Edwina Currie ringing up the production office and shouting at us. They were so open! And the BBC got so leaned on that we had to redub over – whatever it was – "Thatcherite junta" and so on. The producer had done *Juliet Bravo* and *The Collectors* before, loads of popular TV – *Juliet Bravo*, of course, with a terrible political bias the other way, presenting the police as warm, nice, festive people. Nobody was particularly happy with the first series. But the Tory government was so livid with the BBC governors that, as I remember it, the reason *Casualty* had a second series was because the BBC couldn't be seen to be buckling to pressure – those glorious days! – they couldn't be seen to be being leaned on by government.'

Executive producer, BBC Drama, 1996.

*

Decoys and dissidents

The tape is off, and the producer I'm interviewing warms up. He tells me how, when Loach and Garnett were filming in the early days of location-based radical drama, they'd set up decoys, people filming elsewhere, to get BBC management off their backs. He comments with relish that Ian Curteis and the other right-wingers who accuse BBC Drama of being a hotbed of leftists are right, that the WRP had many members in Drama in the seventies and eighties, that the left was certainly dominant in recent decades. 'But it only balances the business interests that dominate the other media, right?'

Diary, 1996.

*

Representation

Will Wyatt has come to Drama Ed Board. Avuncularly, he opens by applauding the current slate of winners – Our Friends, Hetty, Hamish. He continues: 'The new charter includes an impartiality clause, and because we're the BBC this will be heavily scrutinised. Some people perceive drama to be less in tune with our need for impartiality than other parts of the BBC. We need to be aware of this, especially when drama depicts real people or events. I haven't come here to lay a heavy hand on you. But everybody pays for the BBC; unemployed miners pay. It's the public's money. We have to reflect this in our output. Yet there are whole areas of social life we don't really touch: small businesses, for example. In the recent EastEnders storyline, it was so obvious that the evil guy had to be the small businessman! Surely we should resist these clichés? Why not have new kinds of representation: a non-cynical policeman, a nice politician, a non-sympathetic black man? We have doctor and nurse script consultants for Casualty, but do we have consultants from hospital management or the regional health authorities? We need a full range of true-to-life experience. Should we advertise in New Scientist or The Economist to find authentic writers from some new scenes?' Someone protests that corrupt and cynical characters are dramatically more interesting, but Will mildly insists on the interest of positive role models. They knock around the problem of diversity: do script editors and readers come from too narrow and nepotistic a circle? Should they be recruited from other areas of life, to feed new experiences into the editorial process? George says the main problem in singles is getting innovative work from writers: 'The most passionate writing seems to be coming from blacks and gays.' Robert comments astutely, 'But what's the point of all this talk of representation if it has no impact on the controllers' commissioning policies?'

Diary, 1996.

*

If representational diversity was a growing concern, its emblem in the later nineties was the regional quota. The aim of the quota was to animate editorial vision by encouraging the representation of diverse British cultures in BBC output. In drama, the regional departments were particularly successful; they worked across the genres, resisting any singularity of purpose, and proved to be a major stimulus for reinvigorating creativity. Yet the character of the regional centres was different, and in symptomatic ways. BBC Northern Ireland in Belfast, centred on a large newsroom operation to cover the Troubles, grew in the nineties a small but lively drama unit which, given the closure of its production base, conceived of itself in entrepreneurial terms, sometimes brokering the other Drama departments' interests in Irish themes or writers, at other times exploiting the tax breaks of the Irish film industry. In these conditions, exploring through television drama the politics of Northern Irish identity was but one priority among others, something remarked on by other figures in the Northern Irish industry. By contrast, BBC Scotland in Glasgow saw itself, from the apex of management down, as primarily engaged in productive cultural dissent from London, informed by diverse notions of Scottish identity, Gaelic fringe and all. Entrepreneurship might be one means to this end. But there was also an awareness of the potential for BBC Scotland, in partnership with commercial rivals Scottish Television and the nascent Scottish independent sector, to nurture a national media industry and boost employment. In Glasgow, stoked by the confidence afforded by devolution, a politics of output was married to a politics of industrial regeneration. In drama, the regional policy widened access to the networks and wrought diversity, forging ahead of other areas of BBC output.

By the later nineties, for much of Drama Group, any simple classification of the genres according to distinctions of high versus low, literary versus populist, had been eclipsed by a subtler, plural and postmodern awareness of the artful possibilities of popular series and sitcoms and of the need for regular recourse to the formulaic, the tried and true, in serials and singles. Each genre benefited from consideration in terms of its own properties, history and expectations, its own highs and lows. Aided by editorial meetings that brought all the departments together, the result was a stormy but cohesive creative culture. Effortfully, the long-standing cultural hierarchies were being reshaped.

*

A cultural thing

GB: 'Why did you gravitate to work in popular drama, in Series? It's a very particular skill . . .'

'. . . Which, despite being an executive producer in Series, I haven't necessarily got. It's odd. All the people who were genuinely interested in and adept at popular television weren't much valued in the BBC. If you look at those people in the earlier days, producers like Geraint Morris and Gerry Glaister, they were expelled by the prevailing culture. It was a cultural thing. That's what led to the great desert of popular drama, because the people in charge were the Michael Wearings and Jonathan Powells – you know, Royal Court, right on – even with their fantastic strengths – *Edge of Darkness*,

Tinker, Tailor, all that amazing work. None of it was *Howard's Way*, your actual popular drama. It was high profile, attention-grabbing, writerly, serials and singles in tone. Then Jonathan became controller of BBC1 and the cheaper popular series, the *Bergeracs*, just weren't there. It takes a long time to build up those series, and they withered. There was nobody new like that being taken on, and nobody left with those series skills once Julia Smith left after *Eldorado*.'

Executive producer, BBC Drama, 1996.

*

'Us' for 'them' versus 'us' for 'us'

'When I became an assistant floor manager in Singles, I became a singles-type person, very different from a series person, as I am now. I was in Singles when it was evolving from working on tape in the studio to being wholly film. I wasn't aware that I *was* a singles person until I became a script editor for *Casualty*. Then I found I had all the prejudices of Singles: that the only intelligent drama came from Singles and Serials, and that anything made for more than five million people in genre and to format cannot have artistic credibility. People in Singles think that what's important is what your peer group and the critics in the Sundays think, rather than what viewers like. I'm detached from Singles now, and they're becoming more ratings aware and doing things they hope will attract ratings. But because they're doing it from a lofty intellectual height it doesn't work. There's a sense of "us" making programmes for "them", whereas here in Series people make programmes they're going to enjoy: it's "us" for "us". We are "them", the audience, and they *are* us. I have an advantage; I don't have to work hard to think what they might enjoy because at my comprehensive every morning I had people saying "that was stupid". I know how sophisticated our audience's responses really are.'

Producer, BBC Drama Series, 1996.

*

What is popular drama?

'That's the frustration I have. I'm a great admirer of George on many levels; but I work with two men who at the end of the day wouldn't know a popular drama if it hit them in the face. They never watch popular drama; they don't like it. They think soap opera is a waste of space. They don't know who the popular stars are. I said to George, "I think we should get Tony Warren to write us a *Screen One*," and he said, "Oh, he invented *EastEnders*, didn't he," and I said, "No, George, he created *Coronation Street*!" Now this is your BBC head of Single drama, and he hasn't got the faintest idea who one of the most important creators – in terms of cultural change – in this country is, and it's terrifying! I said to David once, "We've been offered this great idea for a *Screen Two* about Blur." Now I'm way past *Top of the Pops*, but I know how important musically and in terms of youth culture this group is. And he went, "No, they're not popular. We want Robson Green," and I went. "David, no!" What makes my head swivel about the people I work to is that they don't watch TV. You know, I sit up till three in the morning if I have to, to watch *Peak Practice* or *Casualty*, stuff I hate. But if you don't watch it, how the hell do you know what your audience likes and why? If they admitted they don't know what popular taste is, and they like gritty social realism and that's what they want to make, it'd be fine. But they're scared to admit it. So instead you have endless discussions about "What is popular drama?"'

Script editor, BBC Drama, 1996.

*

Crafts and Trends

Drama's editorial culture centred on two paradoxical principles: that the source of original and inventive drama is the unfettered single authorial voice; and that the heart of the craft is script editing, which improves scripts through repeated scrutiny, often going to five drafts. Scriptwork was a collaborative process between writer, script editor, producer and sometimes director. Its aim was to optimise the telling of the 'story' and to endow it with maximum narrative and psychological coherence, to which end notions of 'truth' were often employed. Script editors felt obliged to work with a moral dimension in mind. In practice such normative preoccupations covered for a set of quite banal concerns: the avoidance of cliché, redundancy, poor style and 'radio writing'. Many script meetings dwelt on attaining psychological realism in the characters. Characterisation must be believable, the back story must make sense, events and implied events in the narrative must follow logically, and the narrative must have rhythm. Dramatisation of a novel, for example, would aim to retain the structure of the book in much attenuated form.

Despite the stress on good script editing, in the casualised employment conditions of the nineties there was little training. It was taught by apprenticeship, a brief course and a dossier of guidelines. But apprenticeship was often cut short and there were strong pressures to 'act up', script editors as producers, recently arrived script readers as script editors – an experience they found bewildering. A trainee script editor confided that she lacked training and relied on informal advice: that there are seven dimensions to address in any script – its premise, themes, writing, plot, structure, characters, and the need for each to have a 'character arc'. The concept of the 'story,' derived from the film industry and specifically figures like Robert McKee who teach successful screenplay-writing, had become almost a fetish in the BBC. Not only in Drama, but in Documentaries, Current Affairs and among the controllers, it served as a shorthand for the desire to achieve strong narrative and filmic qualities. Yet the art of the 'story' was hard to pin down, and the results of scriptwork could be unpredictable.

*

Telling the story

GB: 'Rhodes was full of problems, yet Kate says the early scripts were OK. It was entrusted to a first-rate outfit, but didn't have a BBC script editor attached. Is that why things came unstuck?'

'That had a lot to do with it. The weird thing is, I often wonder whether there's a correlation between the script before we start shooting and what turns up on screen. Look at Pride and Prejudice: when we saw the previews everyone thought it was a load of nonsense. It was so crudely drawn, so hammed up – with that wonderful vicar! But it's a huge success. There's often little correlation between the script handed over to the production team and what comes back.'

GB: 'That's rich coming from a senior script editor! There's this big focus on script development, five drafts and so on, and yet you're saying there's an unpredictability about it.'

'It's true. Take Scarlet and Black: I was so proud of those scripts, we did an immense amount of productive work and adopted a bold way of telling the story. But it didn't get a good response. Certain novels should never be brought to the screen because they work through someone telling you what people are thinking, minute variations of perception and feeling inside people's heads. But TV is a visual medium. With Scarlet and Black it's all about what's going on inside everyone's heads. We had to give the boy someone to talk to, so we could communicate those things to the audience. We gave him Napoleon – a fantasy, only he can see Napoleon. But the audience loathed it. So even though we did a good job, maybe it was the wrong decision to make Scarlet and Black. The thing we concentrate on in script editing is telling the story in the best possible way, though words, scenes, character, visuals. But the director might see it differently, he might come in late and unravel the work done so far. That's part of the unpredictability.'

GB: 'Elsewhere, people don't do as much scriptwork, do they? This is heresy, but is such scrupulous script editing necessary? Or is it a symbolic legacy of the BBC's literary past?'

'It may be that the only reason our job is worth doing is that without it the drama would be even worse! Most ITV script editors have worked for the BBC, and many were trained here; in that sense it's a self-perpetuating culture. It's hard to be objective. I know what can be achieved by going to six drafts; I can spot when it's not been done. And I don't like it.'

Script development executive, BBC Drama, 1996.

*

Moral osmosis

'As script editors we're expected to bring a moral sensibility to the work. The guidelines are common sense – that swearing is boring unless it's going to have an impact; and that unless you're making a statement about sexuality, it's got to have a relationship context. The moral dimension is not explicit; you're just aware of it being there. Learning here is by osmosis; high moral issues seem far removed from what we do day by day. But then, lack of moral intent came up just now in our discussion of ITV's *Moll Flanders*, didn't it?'

Trainee script editor, BBC Drama, 1996.

*

The principle of authorial voice, associated with the history of the single television play, was being destabilised in the nineties. There was a growing awareness of the role of team writing in the best American serials, which were admired for their quality and staying power, and which increasingly filled peak-time on BBC2 and Channel 4. In reality, the authorial ideal was often contradicted; ideas were farmed out to writers, in Singles as much as Series. The BBC soaps were scripted by a number of writers under the guidance of a series editor, and there were attempts at team writing in sitcoms and series, although many remained single-authored. But it was hard to reconcile team writing with the ideal of the individual voice, and there was frank ambivalence about adopting the practice here. Team writing was widely seen as a commercial expedient, diluting integrity and originality. In the later nineties the principle

337

therefore remained intact: authorial vision was the basis of invention; the work of Potter, Bleasdale, McGovern and such recent discoveries as Tony Marchant, William Ivory, Jed Mercurio and Paul Abbott was cited in support. Decades after the collaborative birth of British television drama, the discourse of authorial voice continued to obscure the roles of producer and director in giving life to scripts, and the fact that inspired dramatisations can yield innovative television. If Drama attributed its declining artistic powers to a single cause, it was the attenuation under Birt of the capacity to take risks on the individual writer's voice.[6]

*

Quality, writing, and the truly original voice

GB: 'The view in Drama seems to be that you can find quality across the range, from sitcoms to singles. Or is it a trade-off, with series aimed at grabbing ratings and the better writing going to serials, singles and films?'

'It shouldn't be a trade-off. Very good writing happens some but not all of the time in *Casualty*, *EastEnders* and *Coronation Street*. Series are there to be popular, but there's no reason why they shouldn't be well written. Everyone holds up the early *Z Cars* as a popular series with fine writing from the likes of John Hopkins and Allan Prior, and John McGrath, Ken Loach and others directing. On the other hand there's some very turgid writing in some of the top-end TV films and single plays, with no sense of how to keep an audience. The BBC can allow you this "quality" loophole. I don't see any hard and fast division between what's art and what's popular, between art and commerce. That's not at all what we're about. The supposed tradition of quality BBC drama centred on *Play for Today*, which was meant to be left-wing and focus on social questions, was a bit of a journalist's invention. If you look back there were equal numbers of, I won't say fluff, but not your grinding social realism. They weren't all written by Jim Allen. There's an idealisation of this period. Now, the balance has swung to series and against singles. This may be because singles aren't any good. Whatever, the balance is now towards series.'

GB: 'But if you find good writing in series as well as singles, why does the swing matter?'

'Because to find the truly original voice through series is not as likely as through singles. On *Casualty* you have to write for given characters and follow powerful guidelines. A lot of people who are very good, or crazy, can't conform to the straitjacket that series writing requires.'

Senior executive, BBC Films, 1996.

*

Ensemble USA

'The first year [of Hill Street Blues], Michael Kozoll and I wrote the first eight hours. A couple of writers helped in the middle episodes, then we wrote the last four. But that wasn't typical of how the writing process evolved. We created an ensemble approach. You have so little time to write, and there are so many multiple storylines. We'd get everybody in a room and craft an hour structurally, and we'd give pieces of it to everybody. Then the pieces would come back in and I'd do what they do on NYPD Blue: everything went through my typewriter before it got onstage, because it needed a unifying voice. There were so many writers, someone had to clean it up and do the stitching.'

Stephen Bochco, 1996.

*

Voice-of-the-author led

GB: 'Why are British series shorter than American series? Hill Street Blues, LA Law and ER have more episodes per series, and more series. Why?'

'ITV have kept a lot of theirs going a long time – take London's Burning or Soldier Soldier. But they're not the same quality. In the BBC we're still voice-of-the-author led; we don't do team writing, so we can't refresh things by bringing in new teams. We're not as universally ratings-driven as the States. We believe you should cut while you're ahead, not dilute a series' strength.'

GB: 'But Hill Street and ER went on being great, even though they're team-written?'

'Absolutely. But take Murder One: different writers wrote different bits, and it showed. In the domestic environment, the quality dropped. You felt: that man has never met that child before!'

Producer, BBC Drama Series, 1996.

*

A number of trends characterised the BBC's drama output by the later nineties. Competitive and financial pressures brought a continuation of the long-term reduction in single dramas and serials. In the previous two decades across BBC1

339

and BBC2, the output of singles and serials halved, while series doubled to two-thirds of all drama output. The same period saw a narrowing of thematic content, with police and crime dramas consolidating their grip on BBC1 and ITV. In 1997–8 these themes together with thrillers accounted for almost half of all drama on BBC1 and substantially more on ITV. In the same year, in the wake of The X-Files, sci-fi themes accounted for over half of BBC2's drama output, while over half was American in origin.[7] Singles and serials suffered from a combination of high cost and unpredictable audience response. The drift in singles was towards producing fewer, more costly films that commanded higher profile, evidence of the growing links between television drama and film. After a decade's absence, the classic drama returned with a vengeance from 1994 following a successful dramatisation of Middlemarch. A stream of period dramas began to issue not only from Serials, but Singles and Films, and the search for suitable novels extended through the twentieth century. In 1996 another hit, Our Friends in the North, caused a renewed commitment to contemporary serials.

The BBC's determination to compete in popular drama resulted in increasing numbers of returning series, some of them, like Common As Muck, Ballykissangel and Hamish Macbeth, both ratings and critical successes. Financially, returning series were the holy grail for both in-house and independents, since in competitive times they alone held the promise of continuing income and employment. In-house, the soaps expanded: EastEnders grew new episodes and Casualty begat a spin-off, Holby City. In the drive for ratings, the controllers favoured ideas that came with 'talent attached'. Increasingly, series were built around stars, some of whom received 'sweetheart deals'.[8] The same was true for singles, where any project involving the likes of Judi Dench, Kevin Whately, Billy Connolly or Lenny Henry was considered tantamount to a commission. The impression given by the series mentioned, and others such as Dangerfield and Dalziel and Pascoe, the BBC's unsatisfying answer to ITV's path-breaking Inspector Morse, was that BBC1 was absorbed in attacking ITV on its home ground: either reassuring and lightweight or 'dark and edgy' popular drama. By the later nineties Drama's attention to popular series began to pay dividends: in 1997, BBC1 beat ITV's hit rate in new series.[9] BBC1's single-minded pursuit of share against ITV continued, resulting in 2001 in a higher channel share for the first time since competition began. But the cost was increasingly imitative drama; and while many dramas in each genre were well received, there were also well-publicised flops, such as the serials Nostromo, Rhodes and Ivanhoe and the series Madson and Beck.

To make up funding shortfalls as the controllers set tariffs for commissions below actual costs, high-cost productions now depended on co-financing or co-production deals. But the problem was not restricted to singles and serials; in 1996 an editorial board reported that an astonishing 90 per cent of drama projects required underwriting. Pressure grew on producers to cultivate secondary markets through deals with international distributors or foreign broadcasters and sales of video and other rights. But it would be a mistake to see Drama's increasingly international orientation as driven solely by economic necessity. A distinct prestige accrued to those producers who successfully competed with the Americans at the game of programme exports, or who developed a format for international sale. Editorials routinely included specu-lation on whether A&E, PBS or the Sci-Fi Channel might be interested in a show, or whether an American or Australian star should be cast in order to reel in a co-producer. The need for new markets enforced an internationalisation of the creative imagination, weighing against the development of projects aimed solely at domestic audiences. Producers could be caught between conflicting pressures both to produce for a national audience, the controllers' primary concern, and to secure a range of international markets, mediated by what were often unknown editorial cultures. The effect could be bizarre, as in the £10 million dramatisation of *Nostromo*, shot mainly in Colombia and involving Spanish, Italian and South American interests, the results of which, such as dif-ferent acting styles, were quite garbled. Even European markets favoured American-style romances and fast-cut dramas.[10]

In principle, however, co-production was also enabling, opening up dia-logue across national industries, providing an infrastructure for new kinds of cosmopolitan drama. And not all co-productions resulted in vacuous mid-Atlantic- or Euro-puddings. The international success in the nineties of British films portraying 'British' content, in which Merchant Ivory classics were matched by *Four Weddings and a Funeral*, *Trainspotting*, *The Full Monty* and *East is East*, all made by Channel 4's film arm FilmFour, suggests there was no necessary con-tradiction between global and national markets. This was an awareness nur-tured among drama producers as, with growing convergence between film and single drama, they looked to British film for inspiration.

*

Risk and failure

I've been invited to a preview of *Nostromo* in the basement theatre of Drama Group's Centre House with those involved from Serials and representatives of the European and South American co-producers. I watch two episodes and leave the theatre. Mike

Wearing is in the antechamber having a fag and a coffee. He grins at me in a bemused way and asks, 'What do you make of it, then?' I don't know what to say. On this viewing I find it a co-production mishmash, reeking of compromise. I mumble something about the need to please the co-producers with local star casting, and how I enjoyed his own cameo. He swings away with his enigmatic smile intact. Risks have been taken and spread across co-investors, and they have not come off. Sometimes they do. Mike's demeanour suggests that the risks were not weighed up well.

Diary, 1996.

*

Midnight's Children, episode three – A sprawling saga: the scripts, the funds and the directors

October 16 1996: Pete is meeting the Midnight's Children Indian co-producers, Raj and Mohan. Filming will be in India from February to July next year, with the last few weeks in the UK, particularly if the monsoon makes shooting difficult. Pete voices doubts about the Indian costume designer they've brought in. 'We feel there's a problem, when dealing with a culture as colourful as India, if a designer says he only wants to work in black and white!' They turn to potential difficulties in importing the Indian-made costumes to the UK for the final shoot. They knock it around, till Pete volunteers, 'If there's no other way, I've got a call on the use of a diplomatic bag – actually more like a crate. It's a favour I can't call in too often . . .' Pete says the visas being used by the Britons in pre-production in India must be extended, and soon. Is the Indian bureaucratic process going smoothly? Mohan agrees to check. Raj and Mohan leave, fêted by Pete, who offers to arrange first-class treatment for them at Heathrow. Afterwards, Ed and Pete share concerns. The budget is now £5 million without BBC overheads, and Ruth, the acting Group head, is insisting that they add the full 15 per cent. They complain that this might sink the show, which has already spent a substantial sum. 'Serials are doing lots of projects,' Ed protests. 'We're contributing far more than our share of Group overheads.' If MC falls through Mark Thompson will need an 'event' for autumn 1997, and Ruth will have to find something to fill the London in-house MOG. It will, he says, be an all-round disaster. BBC2 is now offering £4.2 million, the LA alliance £1 million; so Ed has approached Alan Yentob for any funds from 'secret pots.' He sighs, saying this is standard BBC ritual process: everyone plays brinkmanship on money, calls each other's bluff, says they can't go higher, says there's nothing more to cut; and finally, as everything is falling apart, they fudge a compromise.

Next day scriptwork proceeds. Practical exigencies, mainly, have dictated a reduction from six to four episodes. Without consulting Will, the scriptwriter, they have

342

edited episodes two and three into one. Will, apoplectic, has been on to Salman, who has been on to Alan; a 'small nuclear explosion' has reputedly occurred. Script editor John, reviewing their work, cautions that there's a problem of balance: the script mentions 'the corrupt government of Pakistan,' but has nothing on the character of the Indian government. Dan says it'll all come out in the edit. Dan and Jane, a Serials executive, are working on episode four. Dan: 'Is "motherfucker" an anachronism or an acceptable anachronism?' Jane: 'It's about top of the list of unusable expressions' in terms of BBC language policies. Dan confides that Will is a good writer, and his adaptation is sober, almost realist, 'but what we need is a script that translates the book's vulgarian spirit into vibrant filmic terms.' John goes to phone Will to discuss the script changes, and comes back clearly upset. Will rejects the cuts, saying too much of the book will be lost. John says he listed the reasons – practical, financial and dramatic – for the changes, but Will would not concede. It's a stalemate. I ask if this is the point at which they'll have to part company. Gloomily, someone nods.

October 24 1996: The situation is difficult on three fronts: scripts, funds and director. Salman is taking over the scripts from Will. The co-production funds are still not confirmed. Helen, the associate producer, says the budget is down to £4.7 million for two ninety-minute and two fifty-minute episodes if they are filmed on 16mm and not 35mm. Dan is near the brink and has issued an ultimatum: the film must be shot on 35mm; it must be green-lit by tomorrow; and they must go with his directives on the script. Pete is agitated: they will save £140,000 by filming on 16mm; there's no way they can do it on 35mm. They can't be green-lit by tomorrow. And they have above all to keep faith with Salman: if there's conflict over the script, Dan will have to give in. The implication is that Dan may have got himself into a position where he has no alternative but to quit. Pete says he has to force the issue. He phones Dan, clarifying that their positions are incompatible: 'Look, time's incredibly short; we're almost at the point where it's impossible to do. We may have to look for another director.' In fact, Pete has another director, Harry, lined up in the wings. It looks likely Dan will go. Dan has told me that he had to drop another job to take on this project; he will not be pleased at the turn of events. When the others leave I ask Helen if MC will happen; she says probably not, but for the political will behind it because of Rushdie.

December 20 1996: MC is still not green-lit. Clair, the Serials manager, returns from meeting the co-head of Drama, Colin. The consensus is that the only way forward is to ask BBC2 to find the full £5 million. They can't rely on co-production ('It's too public service') and Worldwide has offered a risible £230,000. 'Our line to Mark must be, if he wants it in a year, he has to green-light it today and underwrite the risks.' Clair mentions the need for contingency funds if serious problems arise, but they've allowed for just £100,000, which in her opinion is nowhere near enough, so they might as well have none. The BBC overhead, now £650,000, is seen by Ed and Pete as unreasonable:

'They should operate a realistic overhead.' They tease Clair: 'That's it! We can solve everything by doing it as an independent!' 'With no overhead we'll save £650k!' The jest contains a serious threat. A new director is now attached, no longer Harry but Tom. Tom and Ed agree that Salman's redrafts of episodes two and three need work. Tom says, 'There's a danger that we lose the deep psychological stuff and it becomes a picaresque adventure.' He recalls an exchange with Salman on formats: 'He talks about the novel as "written in thirds", so I asked about writing it as three ninety-minuters.' Tom reports Salman saying he prefers the four-episode format because 'it will stay in the national consciousness longer'. The problem is, the co-producers want three ninety-minuters to strip across a weekend.

2.30 p.m.: There's tension as most of Serials waits in the open-plan department lobby for news of the critical finance meeting between Colin and Broadcast. Pete calls Colin, who says they are now asking the controller for £5.6 million. Pete is aghast: 'Why £5.6? It was £5 million this morning!' Where has the extra £600,000 come from? Is it a contingency? Has the figure been distorted through a process of Chinese whispers? He takes me through the chain of mediators now engaged in negotiations: Pete and Ed, producer and executive producer, talk to Howard, Serials production executive, who talks to Clair, department manager, who talks to Mike, head of Serials, who talks to Keith, head of Drama Finance, who talks to Colin or Alan, co-acting heads of the Group, who talk to Ron Neil, head of Production, or directly to Jill or Kate, channel finance planning managers in Broadcast, who talk to Mark, the controller, who talks to Will Wyatt, CE of Broadcast. 'A crazy, hierarchical structure – with plenty of scope for details to go wrong.' 5.30 p.m.: Pete finally gets a call. Mark will not increase his offer of £4.3 million. Now the only alternative is for the underwriting risk to fall on Production.

Pete and Clair try frantically to contact Alan. Everyone is on tenterhooks. Pete tells Alan's secretary that she can't have his home number, 'because if I don't have a decision before I go home today, I lose half my crew and my designer, and it will be impossible to deliver on time'. Clair reports quietly that Keith has said that if Production won't underwrite, then Drama Group might. It's the first I've heard that Drama has this kind of money – around £1 million – in reserve, or that it might use it to bail out a project. I leave at 6.30 p.m.. There is no decision. Everyone is still waiting.

Diary, 1996.

*

Pitch Culture

How were new dramas conceived and aesthetic considerations addressed in these conditions? In editorial discussions aesthetic issues were rarely articulated in any depth, and seemed most taken for granted. This finding may be a result of the aesthetic being a domain of rich but implicit knowledge in television drama, one that becomes manifest only in the unfolding judgements of the production process. Yet a creative executive from a leading drama independent lamented the absence of a cogent aesthetic language in television drama, linking it to a lack of innovation and to the perpetuation of well-worn aesthetic traditions.[11]

A striking development was the intensifying crossover between drama and documentary, part of a broader reconfiguration of the boundaries of genre that swept through television in the later nineties. On the one hand, drama continued to borrow techniques from documentary, as it had since the inception of social-realist drama in the sixties. This was evident in the continuing quasi-documentary feel of many singles and serials, but also in the trend for low- and mid-budget series shot, like documentary, on the new digital video formats. The BBC2 series This Life, made by Tony Garnett's independent and a notable success of 1996, epitomised this direction and was portrayed by the controllers as a model;[12] Garnett followed it with three powerful series, The Cops, Attachments and Buried, using similar techniques. And the hybrid and controversial genre of drama-documentary continued to have sporadic outings, as in Screen Two's Deadly Voyage and Stonewall. On the other hand, docu-soaps were celebrated as the 'new drama' for their dramatic impact, achieved at lower cost than most series, and for their incursions into drama territories, notably hospital and police operations. The effect was to render drama soaps and docu-soaps in some ways aesthetically equivalent. The controllers' injunction to seek new kinds of low-budget drama was symptomatic of a polarisation of budgets, with singles and serials aimed at international markets stretching up to emulate the production values of film, while many domestic series, competing with docu-soaps, felt the full force of falling budgets.

*

Ambiguity

A Northern club – an insistent rave beat is playing. The filmic look is rough, hand-held, documentary, the sound raw and disjointed. A blonded young woman bursts into a crowded Ladies room, lurches to the sinks and snorts some speed. She looks in the mirror, gnashing gum, as the rush hits her. Her mates giggle and goad her on; one of them passes her a bottle and she takes a swig. Someone calls, 'C'mon, Mel,' and the girls exit into the club crowd, swirling under the coloured lights. The music is louder. One of the women boasts, 'Well, *I* am going to call in sick – it's gone five, you know.' Mel, suddenly agitated: 'What time is it? Fuck.' Mel dashes from the club into the grey dawn. She spots a taxi and says frantically, 'Take me to Wiltchester Gardens – no, wait, what time is it?' 'Half five,' 'Shit. Change that – Christie Road in Stanton.' She's in the taxi, desperately cleaning off her make-up, taking out belly button and nose rings. 'Can you make it before six?' 'Yeah, should do.' She jumps out of the taxi, darts up an alleyway, pulling her hair loose as she runs. The camera is chasing her a couple of feet behind. She gets to a doorway, punches a code into a security machine, and the door opens. Panting, she runs inside the building, down anonymous corridors, tearing off her jacket, her shirt. She enters a room crowded with other people joshing and changing their clothes. She is down to her bra. She throws open a locker and grabs a shirt, swinging it on. A thickset man enters, his back to camera: 'A'right, Mel? Didn't recognise you there. Bin joggin'?' As he turns we catch sight of epaulettes on his shoulders, and on those of others in the room. The shirts are blue or white, the ties black-and-white check. The chat and camaraderie in the locker room come into focus and displace Mel from the centre frame. It's a police station. Mel is a junior policewoman. This is the opening sequence of Tony Garnett's latest reinvention of the police series: *The Cops*.

Diary, 1998.

*

Interesting Times: emulating docs

A Singles editorial: interesting things are thought to be happening in documentary. Don enthuses about the *Modern Times* strand, films like the recent 'Flatmates' and 'Lido'. 'They get three to four million a week, at far lower cost than our stuff. Can't we emulate them and attract similar audiences?' 'They're postmodern, expressive of our times,' says Stuart. Others disagree: 'It's *Marie Claire* TV!' 'It's easy to do something that *seems* to have substance . . .' Don persists: '*Modern Times* is fresh, direct; it finds sexy situations we aren't coming up with.' He reports a chat with celebrated documentarist Molly Dineen about collaborating on a drama. But another executive questions whether documentarists can really make drama. 'The thing about *Modern Times*,' muses a script editor, 'is that they can lay things out without having to find a *meaning*. Here, we always have to arrive at a final meaning,' and the others, pensive, agree. Fay says documentary's real advantage is that it works like the old producer-led drama: 'The film-makers have real autonomy. They can run with one person's vision. Whereas Drama poses huge bureaucratic hurdles and requires lengthy development: that's what our writers can't stand.'

Diary, 1996.

*

Cheap medicine

'BBC1's hospital drama *Holby City* is three weeks old, but it took all of three minutes – and the appearance of Charlie from *Casualty* – for viewers to feel at ease. So this, we realised, is what goes on upstairs of the casualty department at Holby. *Holby City* is a kind of *Rosencrantz and Guildenstern Are As Comfortable As Can Be Expected*. Its human ambience is familiar: a hairdresser from *Corrie* is here, Anna Friel's lesbian lover from *Brookside* is there. As a star we have young doctor Nick Jordan, played by Michael French, formerly an "*EastEnders* love rat". This is casting shorthand, for French plays another love rat here. *Holby City*'s scriptwriters are content to tap out soap-operatic lines such as "We have a serious infection on our hands," or "Some people are their own worst enemy," but we must understand the long hours these junior hospital writers work. The stories are safely unoriginal: hearts are helicoptered in for transplant with seconds to spare. The writers could take a look at ITV's *Trauma Team*, which films the trauma service at the John Radcliffe in Oxford. It is just another docu-soap, but it has a haunting narrative in the case of an animal keeper from Chipperfield's whose left arm was chewed off by a tiger. It is the opposite of paradox to observe that the staff and surgeons seem more real in *Trauma Team* than they do in *Holby City*. But they still aren't as real as they are in *ER*.'

Andrew Billen, 1999.

*

In editorial and commissioning meetings, the way drama projects were conceived and debated reflects directly the forces outlined in this and other chapters, as well as the need, in marketised conditions, to pitch ideas swiftly and winningly. Discussion about what should be produced centred on a group of key, rather crude and surface criteria which together add up to what we might call pitch-talk. First, the genre of a potential drama – series, serial, single or film – and whether it was a period or contemporary piece. Second, the rough tone and generic content of the project: whether it was comic, serious, tragic or fantasy, whether it was another hospital or crime or 'collar' piece, and how it related to others of its ilk, typically as a synthesis of previously successful shows. One such pitch was, 'I see this as a cross between *Prime Suspect* and *Cracker*,' invoking ITV's most innovative dramas of the period; and it was successful, begetting the derivative BBC1 returning series *Silent Witness*. A third criterion concerned the talent: whether the proposal involved a star actor, writer, producer or director, or would be made by a star independent. A fourth set of concerns were the intended channel, season, evening and slot, whether it was pre- or post-watershed, and whether it was an 'event' (intended for Christmas, a bank holiday and so on). Fifth, the source would be considered in relation to the quotas: whether it would be made by London or the regions, in-house or by an independent. Finally, its anticipated cost would be compared with the standard cost of the genre and the tariff attached to the slot, while co-production might also come into the equation.

Pitch-talk made it possible to sketch rapidly the contours of a portfolio of drama output judged according to rough variations of genre, tone and content across the season and schedule, as well as checking production source, talent power and funding. Its twin motors were the sheer volume of drama material to be processed, and the need to satisfy the many scheduling logistics and box-ticking criteria bearing on Drama. An obvious question is whether these criteria came to stand in for subtler judgements of quality and variation in the collective mind. It is as though the culture of the pitch – where even ideas being discussed in the editorial board had to be pitched to colleagues with whom one might otherwise have had another kind of exchange – caused the broad brush strokes and crude generic genealogies characteristic of pitch-talk to take over conceptually.

*

Is it violent?

Drama Ed Board, the lead-in to an Offers meeting with Alan, controller of BBC1. Faced with a folder full of proposals, Charles steers them speedily towards a list of priorities for available slots. He stops only to probe those key criteria that remain unresolved. *Deep Water*: Charles urges George to check how much rights for Patricia Highsmith novels go for before getting too committed. *Little Angels*, a nursing drama from BBC Scotland: are there too many medical series in process? Ruth says BBC Wales also has a 'Little Angels' in development, so Charles tells them to sit down and sort out the clash. *Hetty*: Charles warns that Patricia Routledge will be lost to the BBC if they screw her around any more on this. *McCann*: a drama built around Billy Connolly, but since he's busy for the next year it will have to be held back. *Grown-Ups*: Alan has indicated that he sees this as BBC2 material. *Ivanhoe*: should this be pre- or post-watershed? Charles asks, 'Is it violent?' Someone replies, 'It's got the odd execution . . .' so they move it to post-. *Pie in the Sky*: is this really up to scheduling in the 'kamikaze slot,' against ITV's *Heartbeat*? *Ballykissangel*: Tony points out that there are several other 'collar' pieces in development – *The Collar, Team Spirit*; Charles, with amusement: 'Am I alone in thinking this is a surfeit of vicars?' Andrea picks up the theme of replication: 'We may have another problem: *Miller's Gold* is a Scottish Western, while *Harvest Moon* is a Welsh Western!' At which others jest, 'Well, *Under a Grass Sky* is definitely an Irish Western . . .' 'What next, an Essex Western?'

Diary, 1996.

*

The sway of simplistic thinking in the way ideas were put together was evident in the pitch documents, integrating in-house and independent proposals, produced by Drama Group for Offers and commissioning meetings. Here, veritable haiku set out the premise of each proposal. While these haiku provide only a limited sense of the final dramatic expression of those shows that were eventually made, they condense the core idea. From them can be gleaned a range of strategies for generating dramas in this period, as well as the predictability of those strategies.

The most common, straddling all genres, were stories set in the present or past giving variations on regional experience and roots British life (*Ticket to Ride, The Bowman*). They were often mixed with sagas of working-class existence, family life or universal human dilemmas (*Lucky Cows, Bumping the Odds, Family Butcher*). In series, the police and crime genres had, since *Cracker* and *Prime Suspect*, generated forensic and serial-killer variants (*Without Motive*) and the female detective sub-genre (*Maisie, Beck*). Some ideas blended the ingredients (forensic thriller plus female lead giving *Silent Witness*), while the regional cop show was still hot (*Harpur and Iles, Out of the Blue*). Series also mined docu-soap territory for new subjects (holiday reps in *Reps*, naval recruits in *Navy Blues*). Strategies for singles included the biographical drama (*Petra Kelly, Mr Sex*) and the dramatisation of psychological and medical issues in the public eye (*Rage, The Gift*). Cinematic influence showed up in ideas for singles and serials (*Looking After Jo Jo* out of *Trainspotting, Future Tense* out of *Back to the Future*). Sci-fi drew increasing numbers of ideas (*Invasion Earth, Neverwhere*), and occasional florid proposals mixed and matched (sci-fi plus serial killer plus romance yielding *Future Tense*). Clones and hybrids ruled OK.

*

Ticket to Ride
Mo Quinn remembers her life in a Liverpool suburb in 1963. She was twelve, and the comic, complicated times of the Quinns are seen through her adult eyes. From family life to the looming problem of boys, Mo's world is drenched in the music of the time.

The Bowman
Two young men are locked in a struggle for survival in the fells of modern-day Cumbria.

Lucky Cows
The story of five gutsy, brassy, ballsy women who live on a Manchester housing estate. They don't have jobs. They don't have men. They don't have money. They do have children. John Redwood thinks they are lucky cows. They have different ideas . . .

Bumping the Odds
Two bolshie young women are torn apart by jealousy and loan sharks in this acid comedy about life on the wrong side of Glasgow.

Family Butcher
The lives of three generations of a family butcher shop in rural Aberdeenshire come under examination from the youngest member when their tyrannical grandfather is stopped from working by an accident.

Without Motive
A drama serial about the hunt for a serial killer and its consequences for one policeman and his family. Intended as a searing critique of modern media-dominated society.

Maisie
Maisie Rain teaches detectives how to detect. She's also a fine detective inspector herself. Her individuality wins the speedy respect of her trainees, but sets her at odds with her immediate boss, DCI Susan Askey. A gritty, funny and fast-moving series.

Silent Witness
Silent Witness is about bodies – dead bodies, corpses no longer able to speak for themselves. Dr Sam Ryan is a top-notch forensic scientist with an obsessive crusade against injustice.

Harpur and Iles
Police in a seaport city face an unequal battle with London criminals moving in on their patch, scenting easy pickings. Harpur, an almost straight cop, takes up the challenge, but his real enemy often proves to be his charismatic but virtually mad CID boss, Iles.

Reps
Follows three young English girls during a season as holiday reps on a Greek island. A coming-of-age story set against an exotic world. It's rooted in a uniquely British reality of sexual anxiety and class pride, played out on the battleground of beach and bar.

Navy Blues
Follows a group of young recruits with dreams of sex, travel and adventure as they undergo a baptism of fire into the discipline of Naval life. Their training is gruelling, but in return they discover the team spirit and camaraderie unique to the armed forces.

Petra Kelly
The intense and tangled love story between charismatic radical Petra Kelly and Nato General Gert Bastian, whose double murder shocked the world of peace politics.

Mr Sex
A comedy drama about Al Kinsey, who discovered the clitoris.

Rage
A powerful story about false memory syndrome.

The Gift
A powerful story of the death of a young mother from cancer.

Looking After Jo Jo
It is the early 80s in working-class Edinburgh, and young lovers John Jo and Lorraine have their whole lives ahead of them. A very tough but also savagely funny story of human aspiration involving criminals, lovers, heroin and the police.

Future Tense
Reporter Vincent Keats forms a liaison with Sherilyn, a girl from the future who has been sent back in time by a serial killer determined to hide the evidence of his misdeeds. Their romance is interrupted by her obligatory return to her own time line.

Edited from documents for Offers and commissioning meetings, 1996–7.

*

Formulaic and imitative thinking were therefore pervasive in the conception of new drama. While this was most obvious in popular genres, and continues to be so, it was not limited to them. Dramas of all types were being conceived through crude intra- and inter-generic hybrids. The culture of the pitch threatened to level all judgements since projects had to be pitched with equal fervour or they risked not being considered at all. Executives commented on this state of affairs by parodying standard pitches in Offers meetings: 'Now this one is *really* strong . . .' 'A very *contemporary* piece . . .' '*Very* exciting, just what you've been looking for, Alan . . .' There was an awareness, then, of the tendency for an attenuated pitch-talk to prevail in the collective consciousness, and for the pressures bearing on Drama to crowd out any subtler aesthetic discourse.

*

Small Cinema and Rapid Response

It was in Singles, the putatively high-cultural end of drama, that risk-averse editorial tendencies were the most jarring. Given reduced hours and financial squeezes, Singles faced intense pressure to justify the form and ensure its continuing viability. One response was to get into film. Following government initiatives, British film was primed for expansion in the mid nineties. Influenced by the success of Channel 4's FilmFour operations, itself indicative of television's increasing role in financing European cinema, BBC Films began to co-produce between five and ten features a year, including successes such as *Truly, Madly, Deeply* (1990) and *Priest* (1994).[13] Singles took note of the profile attracted by these activities, and their potential to forge international markets, and was itself drawn into competitive relations with film.

By the mid nineties Singles had adopted film industry mores: rising budgets, the film festival circuit, the search for theatrical release and international distribution. Theatrical film has a long life compared to television. It attracts serious critical attention. Co-financing is easier to find if, through theatrical release, the product gets more than one national airing. As seductive is the glamour of the film scene and the charisma accrued by becoming internationally known. If the BBC's prestige was boosted by its presence in film, the same was true for those producers and executives involved. Directors and writers, employed freelance by the BBC, grew reluctant to commit to single drama and preferred to work in film, with the promise of attaining the status of an *auteur*. But the convergence between television drama and film was also an aesthetic one, fed by the movement of writers and directors between the two. One result was the emergence of a new British cinema, 'a "small" cinema rooted in local realities'.[14] Less creative was the temptation to clone singles from cinematic moulds. Arguably, convergence had the deleterious effect of dissipating single drama's 'capacity to function as a single national event', reducing its provocative directness and the 'immediacy of [its] political outrage'.[15] In this light, singles' capitulation to the higher status of film effectively colluded in its own eclipse.

In addition Singles adopted techniques to reduce risk, developing star vehicles and 'rapid response' dramas: issue-led topical pieces dreamed up in editorial meetings. Relentlessly, Singles executives tracked public affairs to find topics for satirical or serious treatment, for which writers were then sought: the environmental disaster drama, the genetic cloning drama, the child abuse drama, the corrupt Tory drama, the politician-crossing-the-floor drama, the Nick Leeson drama, the rogue cricketer drama. Much of the rest of the singles output cleaved to extant genres: the classic heritage piece (*Persuasion, Mansfield Park, Jude*); the social-realist piece, often with a regional flavour (*Streetlife, The Precious Blood*); the nihilist contemporary youth piece (*Bad Boy Blues, Loved Up, Ruffian Hearts*). To aid marketing, singles were sometimes themed in mini-seasons. Infatuated by film, Singles had closed the door on the tradition of low-budget studio plays, which, although defended by older producers, was widely conceived as outdated. This did not stop some exceptional singles coming from adaptations of theatrical plays, such as *My Night With Reg*, a poignant exploration of the impact of Aids on a group of gay men. But this was uncommon. Contrary to the equation of writerly autonomy with the single play, in some ways singles, formerly the conscience of BBC Drama, had become generic and derivative.

*

Tarantino squared

'You'd think these scheduling johnnies would talk to each other. Last Wednesday BBC1 screened *Bad Boys*, a Tarantino-obsessed drama about dapper, violent thugs. On Saturday BBC2 screened *Bad Boy Blues*, a Tarantino-obsessed drama about dapper, violent thugs. Both were so risibly butch, so casually violent and clumsily constructed as to make you hope that plans for *Floral Dance: The Laura Ashley Story* are well advanced. Where Ian Pattison's comedy-drama had two hoods debating *Pulp Fiction* dialogue, Biyi Bandele's ostensibly more serious work recycled the flashback structure of *Reservoir*

Dogs' heist-gone-wrong so closely that Quentin should have a strong claim to royalties. Not that there will be much of those; this is one of the few of this season's *Screen Two* films not to receive cinematic release. So far, so derivative.'

Stuart Jeffries, 1996.

*

Satire by numbers

'The schedules are awash with single dramas. Guy Jenkin, one half of the *Drop the Dead Donkey* team, did *Mr White Goes to Westminster*. This was the latest example of the most fashionable kind of single: the topical-political. Jenkin has done a few of these now. *A Very Open Prison* was about a kind of Michael Howard in a crisis; *Crossing the Floor* was about a variation of Alan Howarth leaving the Tories to serve under a sort of Tony Blair. Now *Mr White Goes to Westminster* is about a bit of a Martin Bell leaving TV to stand for Parliament against a Neil Hamilton clone. (It seems a safe bet that one of the first things the controllers found on coming back from hols this week was a Jenkin proposal for a play about a cabinet minister – called, say, *John Grass* – whose teenage son is caught dealing drugs . . .)

'Eye TV', 1998.

*

Prêt-à-porter drama

A Singles editorial; they are casting around for new sources of inspiration. One such source is politically hot subjects, fuelling the sub-genre known as 'rapid response'. 'We've just commissioned a script about Haresh Narang, the scientist hounded out for raising the alarm on BSE.' Other topical ideas for possible exploitation are thrown out: after the Bulger killing, violence in children? The kidnapping and sale of babies, following a recent criminal investigation? Date rape, in the wake of several high-profile cases? A script comes up that's focused on an Aids storyline, but Don says he turned it down: 'We're doing too many health-scare, social conscience-type dramas right now.' Tina suggests that, after the success of *This Life*'s take on twenty-something lawyers, they should come up with the 'next profession' for TV to mine. 'How about computer nerds?' 'Or the music biz, or fashion?' 'The Miramax real-life doc on fashion, *Prêt-à-Porter*, was excellent.' 'We've just put ads in all the British sci-fi mags calling for one-page treatments for sci-fi dramas,' a reference to BBC2 controller Michael Jackson's current passion for sci-fi. Someone tells how *This Life* originated when Jackson approached Tony Garnett for a new contemporary series, after which Garnett found Amy Jenkins, the writer, who has a law background: 'They trained a professional up to write!' A script editor notes nervously, 'Writers don't usually like us coming to them with themes; they resent it.' Don: 'But it's appalling how few ideas writers have, when you ask them.'

*

The war-crimes season

George, head of Singles, and his team are meeting a writer and producer, Paul and Colin, who have come in to discuss ideas. George is keen to woo Paul; he has heard that Paul has a script in development with Scottish TV on the Bosnian war crimes. At his urging Paul outlines the story: a British detective goes to Bosnia to find out the truth about the alleged war crimes and meets a Serbian woman translator. The moral complexities of the war are played out against the tragic love affair that ensues. George seems more keen on this idea than on the treatment that Paul and Colin have brought to discuss with him. That one is a touching tale about a young boy and an old woman who meet in Paris and together engage in adventures. Colin, tuning in to George's drift, asks if he is developing a Bosnian war-crimes drama with anyone else. George replies, 'No, but we do have a French war crimes, Second World War idea going: the Catholic Church has hidden a war criminal . . . and so on.' George comes to the point: he asks Paul, 'What would you say to writing the Bosnian drama for us *instead* of the Paris story?' And sending up the potentially tasteless nature of the exchange, and the present tendency to market singles thematically, he chuckles, 'Just think – we could make it a war-crimes season!'

Diary, 1996.

*

Social Realism Grows Old

The dilemmas facing Singles were compounded by the fragile state of the social realist tradition at the heart of British film and television drama, in which aesthetic realism is combined with politicised and crusading social criticism. Recognising the need for more sustained aesthetic debate, in 1996 Drama Group began its own Programme Review, and the lines of a major controversy became clear in discussion of two hit BBC2 dramas, *Our Friends in the North* and *This Life*. *Our Friends* was a nine-part epic portraying British cultural and political history from the early sixties to the nineties through the lives of four working-class friends from Newcastle. Epoch-defining events like the housing corruption scandals of the sixties and seventies and the 1984 miners' strike were dramatised, as well as shifts in urban, class and party politics. Each event was plotted symbolically as part of the larger narrative, with individual psychologies and stories illustrating the historical canvas. This Life, by contrast, was a continuing series centred on a contemporary household of twenty-something yuppie lawyers, in which sexuality, hedonistic pleasures, gay masculinity, office politics and therapy featured as dimensions of multiple open storylines.

Our Friends was a powerful attempt to revivify the political and aesthetic energies of social realism. But it divided its executive producer, Michael Wearing, from the controller, Michael Jackson. Wearing considered it important and innovative; whereas Jackson found it ultimately outdated, even if successful, and instead spoke of series and soaps as the contemporary form: lacking closure, polyphonic, with no dominant narrative line or voice. For Jackson and others, This Life exemplified this fertile trend, while Wearing criticised it for lacking a moral dimension. If this aesthetic stand-off spoke of generational shifts – Wearing the elder statesman, Jackson primus inter pares of the younger executive cadre – it also pointed to a crisis. For despite its manifold strengths, Our Friends bore involuntary marks of pastiche. It suggests that by the later nineties social realism had grown old and inauthentic, resting as it did on heroic conceptions of historical process and moral certainty of a now questionable kind. Ironically, This Life ran out after two series; it was seen as having nowhere to go. The fourteen-year production history of Our Friends, by contrast, attained the status of myth in the television industry, for it epitomised the determination required to overcome the inertia that resists ambition.

Other dramas of the time support this diagnosis of the hollowing-out of social realism, indicating that it had become banalised and was not renewable in the way being attempted by Our Friends. Singles such as Trip Trap and Streetlife, studies in hidden social problems (respectively, domestic violence and the young dysfunctional underclass), married realism and manipulative pathos with an implied reformist zeal. Although in some ways compelling, the narratives centred on cumulative voyeuristic revelations of pathology and abjection. Formulaic in their missionary moralising, and inescapably problematic, these dramas invite a new term: abject realism. One uncomfortable route out of the impasse of social realism was to extremify the voyeuristic horror, as in ITV's drama-documentary No Child of Mine, a harrowing dramatisation of a case of child sexual abuse. Another was to renew social realism's raw power while offering moral ambiguity, as in The Cops. Here, the humanity and venality of both cops and villains (or victims) were explored against the disintegrating social fabric of Britain's North-West, while the line dividing them dwindled to an arbitrary one. A final route took the form of dramas that, suspending moral certainty, dwelt on the difficulty of ascertaining final truths, as in singles exploring notorious issues such as date rape (In Your Dreams) and ritualised child abuse (Flowers of the Forest).[16]

The crisis of social realism, and the need for its aesthetic and political renewal, posed a challenge of which Drama was fully aware. Since it has been so dominant in British film and television drama, and since it bears such high moral seriousness, the implications were grave. Repeatedly, in earnest and in humour, the problem of social realism was aired.

*

Social realism

Drama Ed Board: current ideas are under review. Charles asks Mike Wearing about Family Values, a show we're told is in development even though it's not on the official list. Mike replies, 'It's a little show about the Mafia taking over Britain, buying everything up,' and he continues to draw the outlines of an outrageous comic melodrama. Mark Shivas quips, 'Ah! Social realism, I see,' and, playing on the Drama executives' awareness that they are repeatedly charged with being exclusively interested in social realism, he raises a collective smile. The story could not, of course, be further from social realism, although Mark's arch manner leaves hanging whether, in post-Thatcher Britain, such a story might not in fact be so far removed from reality.

Diary, 1996.

*

Our Friends in the North: a dramatic history

'Our Friends in the North began in 1982 as a stage play. Michael Wearing was a producer at BBC Birmingham at that point. He saw it, pursued Peter Flannery, the writer, and said, "This would make a good serial, why don't you turn it into a four-parter for us?" Peter wrote a four-parter over the next couple of years, by which time the controller who had commissioned it had left. It was now the mid eighties, and the next controller wasn't interested. Michael moved to work in London on single plays, and by then it had become a five- or six-parter finishing in 1979. Michael loyally and doggedly kept hold of the project and tried in the late eighties to commission it up to the present. He was told that the material wasn't legally clearable because it was potentially libellous. The BBC was running scared at the height of the Thatcher crises around privatisation, and to do a highly political drama wasn't going to do any good. Michael Grade was director of programmes, and his emphasis was on ratings and getting *EastEnders* established. So the time was wrong and the project was killed. Then in 1992 it was resurrected by Michael, and he persuaded Alan Yentob to commission more of it, up to the present day.'

GB: 'That date shows interesting political judgement. By then the BBC was beginning to be more confident, although it was still coming up for Charter renewal . . .'

'Yes. But the politics were purely internal at that point, not national. Alan commissioning four scripts from Michael was really just a sop to keep him quiet. It's no commitment; it's probably £40,000, a lot of money, but in the grand scheme of what Yentob has to spend it's peanuts. Yentob never seemed keen on *Our Friends*. The tale – apocryphal or not – is that when he was head of Music and Arts, he met Peter in the Kensington Hilton, the BBC watering hole, and asked what he was doing. And Peter said, "I'm writing a serial for Drama about post-war British housing policy," and Alan never forgot. Certainly, when I first mentioned it to Michael Jackson, when he took over as controller of BBC2, he said he wasn't interested in some history of the Labour Party.

'When I inherited the script it was quite drily political; the love story wasn't there. The whole scripting effort in the last few years, given that it spans thirty years rather than fifteen, has been to write up the soap or saga element. Jackson was a new controller, and he did not get on with Wearing, couldn't fathom him. So he started dealing with me directly. I knew that Wearing threatening to resign was not going to make Jackson do this project. Jackson needed to know about it. It was the biggest drama he was ever going to commit to. I said, "If I was you I'd hand the scripts round to my friends. I'm confident that if you do, they'll say this is something you should make." But I had to do this surreptitiously because I was undermining Wearing's authority. There was a real clash of personality between Wearing and Jackson, right up to finishing the rough cut of episode one. I had Jackson ringing up saying "It's too political," and the next day Wearing would ring and say, "There's not enough politics," then Jackson would ring again. Appalling. So you ignore both of them and do what you think is right.'

GB: 'When Jackson rings with a view like that, is it about his taste or about him as BBC watchdog?'

'It's about his taste.'

GB: 'Michael Jackson, when we spoke, seemed to say that he feels alienated – he didn't use that word – from a certain kind of seventies, eighties social realist political drama. He sees that as the past, as having always characterised BBC Drama. Wearing must embody that for him.'

'Wearing presenting him with *Our Friends* really confirmed his prejudices that here was a drama about post-war housing policy! I had to associate myself as part of *his* generation for it to be even remotely appealing to him. Now, Jackson's terribly complimentary and it's done very well for him, but I suspect it's not entirely to his taste. Before transmission he only saw episode one and an assembly of four.'

GB: 'Why was Michael Jackson sent an assembly of four? Was it particularly controversial?'

'He rang up nervous in midsummer and said, "Is there anything I can see?" So I sent him an assembly of four. That's the police story, the complicated episode about corruption in Scotland Yard, the one he was least comfortable about at script stage. That was the only one I could show him then that was remotely ready. People would get furious if they'd known he'd seen it, because the line here is that controllers should see the finished product, not work in progress.'

GB: 'Had he not seen, for example, the episode on the miners' strike before it went out?'

'Not that I know. I sent him all the tapes, but he said, "I'm going to watch them as they go out." A lot of people "upstairs" saw them. David Berg, the BBC1 scheduler, got hooked on them.'

GB: 'Did the BBC lawyers see them?'

'No. The legal people vetted the scripts – every word, every draft of every script – and indeed the press pack, which I think is a first. On episode one I heard from the top brass, but that's the crucial one because it gets the most reviews and sets the tone. Michael Jackson behaved incredibly well. In the end *Our Friends* cost £8 million, about half his serials budget. There's no co-production in that, nobody was interested. I tried. Worldwide offered £20,000! In truth it was a hard project to sell, because it was about Britain.'

GB: 'But it has a much wider resonance, wider scope . . .?'

'Yes, but nobody, absolutely nobody believed me when I said that. They called it a pitch.'

Charlie Pattinson, producer of *Our Friends in the North*, 1996.

*

Spaces of Invention

If, led by a ratings-attuned commissioning apparatus, formulaic conceptions held sway in Drama Group, this does not capture the complexity of its production cultures. For all the capitulation to the logic of safety, and the exhaustion of social realism, the Drama departments continued to sustain productive spaces of reflection on the character and ongoing evolution of the different genres. Among production staff, and animating everyday editorial and production practices, there remained a resilient commitment to certain core values in a direct line of descent from Drama's history and from Reith: values of serving audiences by extending the imagination, of innovating in a given genre, of mediating wider social changes and political controversies, of dramatising human experience, injustice and oppression. In each department a culture of attempted quality, integrity, innovation and diversity of provision formed some part of the whole, even if it met with limited success. In short, each group retained a striving to make inventive and ambitious drama. It was, then, in producers' reflections on, and invention in relation to, the changing cultural purposes of the BBC, channelled through their creative work, that the clearest expression existed within the corporation of a reconception of its public service ethos. This is a hopeful finding, for it is in the cultures of production and the resulting programmes that any redefinition of public service values must finally impact and be judged.

But these spaces of potential invention only sporadically broke through the prevailing forces for genericism. The evidence of occasional achievements is more remarkable in the output of Series and Serials. Both were engaged in the balancing act decreed by the controllers: to secure audience loyalty by offering sure winners, when possible surpassing ITV in good popular drama; but also to push the genres further through distinctive drama of a kind increasingly left to the BBC and, intermittently, Channel 4. In Series, there were several signs. When developing ideas for a new hospital soap, Project Y, the aim was to position it in new territory, focused more on the experience of orderlies and cleaners than the hospital elite, and to learn from the best US hospital shows in terms of pace, casting and look.

If the melodramatic realism of the existing soaps reached sensational new heights, in BBC Series the sensational was tilted towards moral complexity and educative purposes; while in their characterisation the soaps set out to reflect the changing realities of contemporary Britain through more adequate representations of ethnic and sexual diversity.[17] Series gained much in editorial range from regionally based drama, as evident in shows like Ballykissangel,

Hamish Macbeth and *Tiger Bay*. Most significant was the development in a few series of a post-social-realist language which, equalling the depth of character and social commentary of the earlier tradition, leavened and remixed social realism's 'gritty' and monochrome seriousness with dashes of humour, irony and surreality, while resisting reductive moral certainties. In the new century it seems this development may be breaking the mould of old social realism, creating a new dramatic language that transcends past antinomies, a language at once tragic and comic, real and surreal, multiracial and post-nuclear-family, popular and demanding, pleasurable and gently didactic. Differently inflected, and with roots in the best of the soaps and in exceptional dramas such as *Common As Muck* and *This Life*, something of this can be glimpsed in a trickle of recent series including *Clocking Off*, *Being April*, *Linda Green* and *Paradise Heights* as well as Channel 4's *Shameless*. Meanwhile, in the out-and-out popular stakes, the continuing rewards of BBC Drama's insistent commitment to character and social context can be gleaned by comparing two recent rival shows, ITV's *Footballers' Wives* and BBC1's *Cutting It*.

*

Wisps of dialogue like cigarette smoke in clothes

'Last night Cindy, the Clytemnestra of *EastEnders* (BBC1), snatched her children by assorted fathers and fled the country. Cindy, a bad girl with good cheekbones, had hired a hitman to shoot her husband, Ian. All hell, always on a loose rein in Albert Square, broke loose. Grant and Phil went round 'aving a pop at anybody loosely peripheral to the plot. Big Pat's eagerly awaited wedding was cancelled what with all the guests being in intensive care or helping the police with their enquiries. I have watched thrillers with much less twang than this. Cindy's skin-of-her-teeth escape was excellently scripted and movingly played. If you saw this on a black-and-white set – the good-looking and vicious lovers, the despised husband – you would be reminded of a film noir from the forties. Wisps of the dialogue hang around the mind like cigarette smoke in clothes. "What is it you're after, Cindy?" "No more than anybody else." "Don't you understand? This is what I do. I just let people down. I've made a habit of it all my life".'

Nancy Banks-Smith, 1996.

*

Gulping for a lungful

'BBC1 is repeating the first series of *Common As Muck*, William Ivory's series about Hepworth bin-men. When this first run broke the barrier of the magic 10 million viewership, the BBC couldn't get a second one quickly enough. The second series has, if anything, matured into a more remarkable piece of television. From the opening sequence – Nev's retirement drive-past of veteran garbage trucks – it's clear that both writer and performers are living these characters. This gives the events that follow the emotional resonance that normally only comes from an epic structure. Ivory can turn on a sixpence between rude comedy and tragic melancholy. He is politically sophisticated; not nostalgic for a socialism that never existed, his characters have absorbed the lessons of working-class conservatism, so that their struggles are tinged with entrepreneurial spirit. Sometimes this is treated satirically, but more often it's shot through with dignity as the characters try to find their way in a complex world in which they rarely control the levers of power. Everyone is engaged in a struggle not just to survive, but to survive with decency. Landmark drama can define the moment as well as reflect it. *Common As Muck* will do this for the end of a decade-and-a-half of Tory rule, and the consequences of a crumbling welfare state. It's the most sophisticated treatment of the moral debate facing the nation that we'll see on television: how do people constantly gulping for a lungful of air hold on to their values and their sense of community?'

Ray Cathode, 1996.

*

Multiracial hedonism in Cardiff

'*Tiger Bay* started an 8-week run on BBC1 on Monday. In the shamelessly exploitative opening scene Jodie surrenders her maidenhead to the wicked Roy. "You're 16 and I'm 40," he explains helpfully. "So nothing illegal is going to happen," Jodie replies. The big news in the bay is that the pub is to get a competitor in a floating bar, a converted boat that symbolises gentrification by selling "fancy label lager and unpronounceable grub". I have a feeling we've visited this scenario about 10 years ago, but I assume Thatcher's hedonism arrived late in Cardiff. What is much more intriguing is the unspoken assumption of complete racial integration. By my reckoning there is not a sexual relationship in the show that is not miscegenistic. Charlie is white but both his wives are black. Salim is Asian, his partner white. When Salim lectures the matt-black yob Dan, "You come over here and disturb the peace," he means no more than Dan has come over from the less salubrious end of town. Unless this is multiracial casting gone berserk, we seem to have stumbled on a genuinely multiracial community at ease with itself.'

Andrew Billen, 1997.

*

Never proselytise

'Last night Bianca Butcher, *EastEnders*' flame-haired teen firebrand, decided to termi-nate her pregnancy after 20 weeks. As a result she joined the ranks of soap opera characters who have been put through abortion storylines. Arguably, abortion has become an exploitative staple brought out as soaps become more sensationalist. And this very sensationalism means that mere abortion is not enough – it must be abortion with a twist. Typically, *EastEnders*' abortion was much grimmer than could be dreamt of in [*Channel 4's*] *Brookside*'s current philosophy. Bianca's decision followed an ante-natal scan which showed that her daughter would be born severely handicapped. What was impressive was not the information packed into the week's episodes, which were writ-ten with the collaboration of the Association for Spina Bifida and Hydrocephalus – although this was valuable – but the effective dramatisation of a young, rather dim and deeply uncertain couple struggling to come to a decision and dealing with its conse-quences. This was affecting drama, acted with as much skill as you will witness in a soap. Better than that was the fact that *EastEnders* never proselytised in favour of abortion, but showed sympathetically what can happen to parents who choose that option.'

Stuart Jeffries, 1997.

*

If Series' tentative triumph was to forge popular and substantial routes out of torpid social realism, it was the Serials department that seemed in a fragile way the most creatively autonomous. Freer of the dead hand of market research than Series, Serials' double achievement was to serve up both classy standard adaptations for the heritage market (Middlemarch, Pride and Prejudice) and, in varied ways, to renew the genre by exceeding routine horizons. Serials was blessed with the leadership of the recalcitrant Michael Wearing, who was prepared to criticise senior management to an extent that would cause him, in 1998, to leave. Under his protection its producers had the strength to seek out and exploit opportunities for innovation. Inevitably, if risks were taken, some fail-ures were made. But it was the serial form that uniquely offered writers and directors the chance to work out complex narratives at a length not permitted

363

by film, yet with similar production values. Two of the rare examples of avant-garde television drama, David Lynch's Twin Peaks and Lars von Trier's The Kingdom, were serials made by film directors, both subverting social realism and its characteristic pace. Closer to home the work of David Mercer, Dennis Potter and some of the early output from Channel 4's independent film and video unit stand as beacons of modernist experiment. A telling symptom of the stifling creative conditions afflicting British television drama in the later nineties was the low tolerance for formal innovation: formal experiment simply lay beyond the conceptual bounds. Serials offered little as ostentatiously experimental as the dramas mentioned, with the exception of Potter's last works. But alone of the Drama departments it engaged with this history, fostering dramas that wandered into experimental terrain and made oblique but knowing reference.

*

Look under the bonnet

'There was an odd look on Becky Sharp's face in Vanity Fair (BBC1), as if she were wait-ing for cigarettes to be invented. She was not quite all there. Some of her was here, in the late nineties. She was Natasha-Little-as-Becky-Sharp – amused up to a point, but miffed to find herself marooned in Regency London without cash or parents, in great need of a shag and a caffe latte . . . Vanity Fair seemed to be British television's first ironic period adaptation, and Natasha Little was wearing the first ironic bonnet . . . Sir Pitt Crawley, Becky Sharp's employer, was married to a Page Three girl. Like most of the cast, he could have been a minor figure in The Fast Show. His rottenness and filthiness were parodic, as if to comment on the rotten, filthy characters that all such serials must have . . . This, then, is a production for the late nineties – arch, self-parodying, and a little overexcited by the thought that women as well as men have sex and break wind. But it was a success . . . Perhaps some of the quirks of the late nineties are particularly suited to Vanity Fair and the worldly, knowing, flirtatious and intrusive ways of its narrator . . . And it is a pleasure to look at. The first episode was wan and dour. The director did not demand perpetual sunshine. And there was only one toothless crone in the crowd, which is perhaps the Equity minimum.'

Ian Parker, 1998.

*

Chris Smith's big idea

'"New" Labour seems to be having trouble understanding the BBC. Government is supposed to have an arm's length relationship with the corporation, but culture and heritage secretary Chris Smith has warned the BBC governors that too many costume dramas were appearing in the schedules and that he wished to see more gritty contemporary drama. Smith's television criticism is ill-considered for three reasons. The first is that the best contemporary drama has always been hostile to everything "new" Labour represents. How about more stuff like *Our Friends in the North*, that award-winning attack on Labour corruption in local government? Or perhaps the BBC could phone up Trevor Griffiths or Jim Allen, leftwing playwrights who wrote brilliant plays attacking the last Labour government? ... The second reason Smith is talking bollocks is that one of the reasons the BBC produces so many classic adaptations is the financial position imposed on it. Costume drama is far more likely to attract co-production money. But the third objection to Smith's big idea is the strongest. With uncanny timing he issued his prescription just before one of the best classic adaptations in history, *Our Mutual Friend*, was screened.'

'Eye TV', 1998.

*

Critics accuse the BBC's classic serials of trading on a tradition of heritage 'quality' drama in which 'money shots' conjure up glossy images of the past, at once demonstrating the opulent expense of the production and stoking a nostalgic, unquestioning and reactionary longing. In his invective against postmodern historical pastiche, Fredric Jameson has charged the nostalgia film with denying us the possibility of 'experiencing history in some active way'.[18] But Serials in the later nineties produced a stream of dramas that defied these criticisms and regenerated the form. In both contemporary and historical productions, a range of formal strategies were evident, invariably subtler in their operations than the modernist montages of Potter.

The classic adaptations reworked historical realism, resisting mere gloss, insisting on detail, particularity and interpretation, at times bringing to the fore echoes of contemporary problems, reading the past to disturb our understanding of the present, at others rendering the past strange. A frenetic adaptation of *Tom Jones* made scurrilous use of an in-vision narrator, while recalling the qualities of eighteenth-century literature, 'the marriage of bawdy humour and sophisticated wit; the elision of the sentimental and the genuinely moving; and the recoveries from malevolent shade into sunny optimism'.[19] A purposefully static, beautifully filmed serialisation of *The Tenant of Wildfell Hall* dwelt painfully and with powerful contemporary resonance on the novel's themes of marital and child abuse, and on the fury provoked by male envy and inadequacy, so historicising domestic violence. Dark both filmically and emotionally, it evoked the tones of Victorian landscape painting. A vivacious, cold and parodic *Vanity Fair* achieved a modernist estrangement from heritage-nostalgia, employing leached-out colours and music with a 'sarcastic bounce',[20] and rubbing our noses in Becky Sharp's amorality, in pitiless caricature, and in the tripe feasted on by the lecherous Sir Pitt. If the fantastical *Gormenghast* was mannered and flawed, it was visually haunting. An astonishing adaptation of *Our Mutual Friend* embraced the depths of Dickensian grotesquery and social despair, inviting us to follow a fugue of storylines more complex and morally surprising than any soap, and offering its own, far from reassuring allegory on fate, pity and love. All of this was dealt up with a visual style so dank and sober, with such slow and measured deliberacy in the editing, that it upturned completely the conventions of the genre. Historical serials in this period were marked by incessant imaginative reinvention. The form lived.

Contemporary serials rose as surely to the challenge. Jimmy McGovern's *The Lakes* and BBC Scotland's dramatisation of the Iain Banks novel *The Crow Road*, both with pungent regional settings, explored post-social-realist ground, mixing tragedy and frailty with the hilarious and surreal, the mundane with the melodramatic. Bold formal innovation characterised Tony Marchant's *Holding On*, an eight-part serial commissioned on the tailwind of *Our Friends in the North*. *Holding On* contrived to give a portrait of the social pathologies underlying the surface of London in the nineties. Its devices – centring the narrative by turn on each major character until we knew each intimately; entwining the many stories such that the narrative formed great arcs and loops; having a central, thoroughly unpleasant male character break with naturalism and turn to camera to speak his cynical monologues; a frantic, almost paranoid camera style; above all, the drama's determination to track the disorientating experience of post-Thatcher Britain – created an outstanding drama. A couple of years later, this ambitious legacy was evident in another state-of-the-nation serial, *In a Land of Plenty*, a dramatisation of the Tim Pears novel. Tracing the changing fortunes and internal conflicts of the family of a Midlands industrialist, this drama added a rich and non-naturalistic visual invention by expanding on the place of photography in the narrative to amplify and probe emotional states through slow motion, close-up and photographic framing to capture a child's perception. In these dramas it was the imaginative use of formal innovation that broke the stranglehold of social realism, lifting the works on to fertile new planes. Repeatedly, Serials found ways to do something compelling within given confines, to revivify the language and open up possibilities: arguably all that can be asked of inventive television drama.[21]

*

A river ran through it

'A Dickens adaptation has finally confounded all my expectations. BBC2's *Our Mutual Friend* concluded triumphantly on Monday. This is a book impassioned by anger at capitalism and the literal poverty trap of the workhouse, but Dickens, as usual, lets us off with the consolation of romantic and familial love. The adaptor Sandy Welch chose love as her raft down the rapids of Dickens' swirling narrative. The two main love stories did shine amid the excremental mire but were dimmed by it. The ending was as sinister as it was comforting. The high-society scenes, too often mistaken for the essence of period drama, were increasingly marginalised until they became merely an obtuse chorus to the bacterial life below. A river ran through this piece as a double metaphor. The Thames was a moral sewer, but paradoxically a cleansing agent too, from which the drowned would resurrect themselves as new people. I hail all involved in this masterpiece as Mr Venus' equals. To adapt his boast, they have brought us the smallest bones of a great book and sorted them in a manner that has surprised and charmed us.'

Andrew Billen, 1998.

*

Nineties psychoses

London, the nineties, and the human condition is caught in a frantic narrative circle: the bulimic, self-loathing celebrity restaurant critic who hides in the toilets to stuff crisps; the provincial sisters who indulge in pick-up sex; the elderly mother searching for her schizophrenic son, at loose on the streets due to an indifferent medical system in the wake of 'care in the community'; the desperate tax inspector, driven by moral outrage, engaged in an unequal battle against corporate fraud; and the black kitchen assistant who uses his mother's savings, put aside for education, to set up in pirate radio. Stories of sexual harassment, of madness, of the temptation to jump ship from a public sector starved of resources to the heady world of high finance, of power and its uncheckable abuses. Shots of London's decaying underground, of streets and skylines, black cabs and chauffeur-driven limos, wine bars and line-dancing. Almost everyone, it seems, is only just *Holding On*.

Diary, 1997.

*

Incommensurable Ethics

In adverse conditions, the creative health of Drama Group was, then, fragile. Drama's struggles to meet the many pressures bearing on it, while producing good and popular drama, were doomed often to result in compromise. The complexity of the challenge should not be underestimated. It can be illustrated by Drama's attempts to deal with the intense public concern over the dramatic portrayal of violence. After a series of appalling crimes – the murder of James Bulger, the multiple killings of the Wests, and the Dunblane massacre – the debate was live in the wider drama community, with factions pulling towards both more and less regulation. It was paralleled by one over the representation of violence in factual output. In News and Current Affairs there were precise codes that journalists followed or they risked immediate censure. By contrast, there appeared little consensus over the acceptable limits of violent content in drama. Despite an avalanche of memos from above requiring drama heads to take the utmost care and refer controversial material up, the implementation of that care rested with individual producers. In editorial boards at which the issue was raised, some (male) executives railed against the threat of self-censorship, arguing that top writers would take their work elsewhere if the BBC was seen to be going soft. In part, this was an expression of the libertarian perspective that had held sway in the television and film industries since the sixties; indeed, a determining factor in the increased stylisation of violence in television drama has been the movement of directors between film and television, bringing the aesthetics of Tarantino, Cronenberg or Stone to the small screen.

Yet in informal discussions, several (female) Drama executives argued that it was time to curtail those genres most guilty of graphic violence, often against women, even if the ratings were high; that they had had enough of this dangerous and misogynistic material. In this era the most successful series, ITV's Prime Suspect and Cracker, returned repeatedly to stories centred on prostitute-murdering serial killers. Paradoxically, one of the executives taking the critical line was herself responsible for the BBC's latest spin on the genre, Silent Witness, which she spoke of in this context as a cynical remix. All of these shows, and others of the period, were censured for excessive violence. But in the debates that mattered, in editorial boards and meetings with top management, the 'consensual' face of Drama was entirely defensive: the question of taking greater care on violence was seen as a non-starter and taken as a call for censorship. The internal debate on violence was, then, gendered. Among Drama executives, women who believed there to be a problem were effectively silenced, and a 'male' collective voice denying that there was any problem prevailed.

On this issue of great public sensitivity and creative import, three distinct ethics of accountability therefore stood in tension: that of writerly autonomy, that of popularity, and that of regulating extreme content. The three were incommensurable, and as a consequence of such contradictory pressures, rather than rational deliberation, the debate remained split and undeveloped.

*

Midnight's Children, episode four – Coming together

March 1997: At last *Midnight's Children* has been green-lit, and the finance is in place. Tom, the third director attached to the project, is working closely with Salman, who is still writing scripts. Pete the producer, who will soon leave to take charge of another BBC production, explains: 'It's three years since we bought the option to the book, and we might just be in a position to start. The co-finance contract is signed, a consortium of Indian and American businessmen. If you include BBC overheads, the budget is £6 million, and BBC2 is still putting in £4.3 million. But Serials has two other shows, *Tom Jones* and *Our Mutual Friend*, in financial trouble – short about half a million. The co-production money saves Serials from having to squeeze them.'

GB: 'I hear there's a renewed threat to Salman, that the premium on the fatwa has risen?'

'You used to have to be Muslim, and if you proved you'd killed him, you'd get $2 million. Now you can be anybody and you'll get $2.5 million. It raises the stakes dramatically. According to the press this came from an Iranian splinter group. There's going to be an election in Iran within the year; the current president is not in good shape and is arguably too moderate in a fundamentalist country. So the reason is simple. It's well known that this splinter group is under his control, and if he's seen to be tough that can only help his political standing. In fact both the Iranian and the Indian political situations do not bode well. The Indian government may fall this year; there may be an election at the time of filming, which would be hairy because to create a government you have to have a coalition and placate the Islamic vote. Hence it's not good to be seen to do business with Rushdie. This is potentially a source of difficulty. Then recently, when we were on the verge of getting the Indian officials to agree, which is a heavily bureaucratic process, the BBC pissed India off by appearing to support Pakistan over Kashmir. Because we're all the BBC, our meetings were suddenly cancelled. In the next few weeks we'll hopefully turn that around, but in the meantime it appears the BBC correspondent involved can't return to India. We'll see how we go with this great democracy. It's tricky timing.'

GB: 'I love the coalescence of factors . . .'

'It's good, isn't it, Georgie? You could write a book about it. On the scripts, episode one has gone back to being linear from having been non-linear; Michael wasn't happy with that. But it was a process the script needed to go through. Now it still has the magic-realist elements, but within a straightforward linear narrative which diverges into different things the way the book does, but not as many things, so hopefully it won't confuse the audience. Salman's done it brilliantly. He just loves coming back in for meetings. He was on that edge of either being exceptionally pleased or exceptionally pissed off, you know, "Do we have a green light?" Now I think he's exceptionally pleased, and we're talking about publishing opportunities – the script, the coffee-table book. But there's a sadness because he obviously can't be present at any filming.

'The money from the Indian co-financers replaces the distribution advance because none of the big distributors offered enough. They offered around $1 million where the Indian financers are putting in $2 million. On the same figures, Worldwide offered £270k – ludicrous. Having this co-financing in place creates strong credibility and gives us serious Indian backing. The people in India that can afford to put up this sort of money have major political sway. So it also works as a kind of protection, and not by accident. Hopefully it will help the whole project. We'll see.'

Producer, BBC Drama Serials, 1997.

*

Postscript – Things fall apart

Subsequently, difficulties in the Indian political situation escalated, culminating in a withdrawal of permission to film. The BBC approached Sri Lanka as an alternative, and gained agreement. In due course the Sri Lankan government, sensitive to Rushdie's potentially destablising effects on its Muslim population, also threw up political obstacles. *Midnight's Children* was never made.

*

Partial truths

'I'll tell you what my job is. My job is to tell the truth. Not *the* truth. But my truth. And my truth is partial, in both senses of the word. It is the only truth I know. Which is why the broadcaster's job is to encourage to be made and then shown the widest range of these truths. Over time, as viewers, we will see the world lit up from many points of view and be able to form a rounded, three-dimensional picture. But my job is simpler. It is to say, "This is the provisional sense we have made of this corner of experience. What we are showing you is how it felt to us at the time. What do you think?" As we strive to do well in the face of disappointment and frustration – "How can I persuade them to do that show?" and "How can we get it to be like the one playing in my head?" – it's worth reminding ourselves why what we do is so necessary. There seems to be a human need to make sense of our experiences. The great myths and religions are grand narratives which encompass and account for life itself. We live by stories; they need to be told and retold. The drama we put on the screen is also something else. It assuages our terrible loneliness. Through the empathy and imagination of our writers – and everyone involved in this collaborative act – we catch a glimpse of what it is like to be another. What we do is sometimes important. That it is done is a necessity.

'What worries me is the current culture of macho-management, where fear and loathing are poisoning creativity; everyone is working below potential. We need less management and more creative leadership. The most stifling development this decade has been a centripetal tendency to disenfranchise producers and concentrate decision-making in too few hands. For any category of drama I want to produce, there are two people I can talk to. It is unhealthy for such few sensibilities to be at work. When they start dictating the major elements, they compound the problem. The range of our drama is impoverishingly narrow, and the results too often lifeless and predictable; what is even thought possible shrivels. The changes of the last decade have been hardest on the Beeb. They have made a disaster out of their in-house London operation – yet good work continues to escape. Have senior management asked themselves why no one wants to be head of Drama at the Beeb?'

Tony Garnett, 1997.

*

The Condition of Value

If, in the end, it was neither scriptwriting problems, nor financing, but distant political expediency in the face of swelling religious and social antagonisms that scuppered what promised to be one of the most ambitious television dramas in the history of the medium, then that certainly holds a lesson. But it does not obviate the fact that conditions within the BBC made the life course of *Midnight's Children* tortuous and unstable in the extreme. It would be easy to see the Serials department's stubborn commitment to the project as foolhardy and

371

ultimately wasteful. But it is also possible to see it as a courageous championing of the work of a gifted writer – albeit one with charmed links to Britain's cultural elite – whose persecution and ostracism is one of the most disgraceful episodes in recent cultural history. If some BBC producers imagined they might have the authority to reconfigure this history, who is to say they were wrong to try?

The BBC was founded as a value-imbued public institution. Its strength was to foster the evolution of the ethics and aesthetics driving its programme-making, values that would be manifest in its productions. Whatever the failures and imperfections of earlier eras, the BBC's organisation and management were measured against that overriding purpose. During the Birt period that purpose was undermined and displaced by a tide of other, non-specific values – values not related principally to the BBC's creative integrity. The flood of 'modernising' reforms and structural changes apparently intended to improve the conditions for creativity in reality became so repressively over-bearing and rigid, and their proponents so blind to their destructive effects, that they eroded the conditions necessary for creativity to flourish. The combined effect was to undermine the creative autonomy, the confidence and animation of the BBC's production base. Production departments differed in their ability to withstand these conditions. Drama was particularly damaged, its output made to conform to the multivariate product templates dictated by centralised commissioning according to the ersatz 'accountability' of market analysis and research. Among all the generic product, in the late nineties only scattered signs of creative vitality remained.

Creative values do not thrive in a vacuum. The ethical stance of the BBC's production departments – the commitment to truth-telling, to telling stories about the human condition in pleasurable, challenging or innovative ways, to targeting cutting satire at power-brokers and establishment sacred cows, or to uncovering the bases of injustice or inequality – begins life in the intentions of programme-makers. But the continuing evolution of these values, and their well-being, depend on organisational conditions. They can be blocked, their energies diverted into tangential demands – pitching, selling, accounting, auditing, marketing, politicking. The doctrine of 'value for money' can bully producers' imaginations into submission and conformity. Birt's BBC, with its new managerial credos, undermined the only values that are essential to the BBC, those specific to its core activities: making programmes and running networks. Birtist management knew precisely the price of everything and the value of nothing.

9

Framing Democracy: News, Newsnight and Documentaries

OJ versus Blair

British politics are hotting up as New Labour streamlines its PR operations in advance of a coming general election. Last week an event known inside the BBC as the 'Alastair Campbell debacle' happened. Tuesday 3 October 1995 was the day of the verdict in the OJ Simpson murder trial, which ended with a sensational "Not guilty." It was also the day of Tony Blair's speech to the Labour Party conference. The same day Alastair Campbell, Blair's spin doctor, sent the BBC newsroom a fax pressurising the news editors to put Blair's speech at the top of the *9 O'clock News*, and not second to the OJ verdict. The editors ignored Campbell's injunction and were, are, very angry. OJ nonetheless went lower down the running order. John Birt issued a statement condemning Campbell's action. Campbell issued a rebuttal.

Today I'm discussing access terms with a senior executive from News, and he tells me these events. The editor in the firing line had been furious and wanted to sue; for days they'd discussed whether to sue. This, says the executive, is the kind of heavy and sensitive political business they would not want me directly to observe. I reply that for me to give an accurate as well as a nuanced account of the newsroom, I'd have to have a view of these developments. Could I ask people to report on them right after the event? The reply is evasive: probably, I guess . . .

Diary, 1995.

*

Obsession

'The culture of the BBC is obsessed with scrutinising the British democratic process; it's deep in the BBC's psyche and history. But how much scrutiny do you want about minor rows in constituency parties? As we move towards a global and European perspective, research shows that Westminster politics appear irrelevant to ordinary people, especially young people.'

Senior executive, BBC Radio, 1997.

*

Irony

I've come to *Newsnight* ahead of my fieldwork to meet Jeremy Paxman, one of the presenters, and Jim Gray, a deputy editor. The aim is to see if they are amenable to my study and to discuss terms. When I enter Jeremy's office he is going through some viewers' letters. He thrusts one at me: it's from a sympathiser with the Fairmile road protestors, and it concerns an interview he did last week with three of them the night that Swampy – the hero, the lead tunneller – came up from underground. The letter is hostile, accusing him of bias, being a fascist and so on. It is signed and addressed. Then he shows me a nasty anti-Semitic letter, also signed and addressed.

Jeremy says he gets a lot of letters, including a number of abusive ones, and always writes back when there's an address. Jeremy's Fairmile interview is an interesting one; I had taped it to discuss with my students. How would this most Westminster-focused, establishment-scourging programme deal with environmental protestors, the new politics of the margins, with their basic but canny media savvy? The interview was ambiguous: while 'soft' in Jeremy's terms, it could easily be read as arrogant, aggressive and condescending – which is indeed how my students, largely Fairmile sympathisers, saw it. But in terms of content it was also plain that, when dutifully putting to the protestors the establishment views they vehemently oppose, Jeremy didn't give those views much credence and seemed content for the protestors to bat them away. His bemused demeanour seemed stoked as much by the sheer surreality of the media spectacle of which he was a part, confronting the motley threesome in a muddy field – representatives, perhaps, of a new kind of Englishness, one of Paxman's intellectual passions.

Jeremy and Jim are pleasant. They are concerned whether my presence in the closed 11 a.m. editorial meeting – a high-level strategy discussion between the editor Peter Horrocks or his deputies, the day editor and the presenter – will alter the dynamics. They joke about how rude they are about politicians, how difficult it would be if I quoted out of context or in an unbalanced way. Jeremy adds that their main concern for the programme – the sin they want above all to avoid – is being boring: 'I sometimes think I'm oppositional by constitution.' Both of them talk genially, reflectively, about how ironic it is that *Newsnight* and News and Current Affairs continually make claims for access to private and public institutions in the name of public interest; and yet here they are, querying whether they should grant me access to their 11 a.m. meeting. They don't. I have to make do with attending the more 'public' editorial meeting at 10.30 a.m..

Diary, 1997.

*

Spin, Genre-Bending and the Crisis of 'Politics'

The BBC's journalism is widely seen as the centrepiece of its public service settlement, its intellectual core and the symbol of its independence. By the mid nineties, the BBC and other British media encountered increasingly professionalised political marketing and government public relations. As the Conservatives were engulfed in a cloud of corruption and New Labour groomed itself for power, BBC journalists adjusted to the reversal of political fortunes. Margaret Thatcher's governments had well-honed communications strategies. But New Labour's marketing and news management operations, paralleled by unprecedented party discipline and the makeover of Labour ideology, represented an entirely different order of control. After a brief honeymoon following New Labour's 1997 election victory, in which some editors proposed that a new, productive relationship with government was possible, the journalists' response was an excited determination to match aggressive spin with intensified scrutiny, scepticism and independence. The stand-off fuelled a greater self-consciousness about news management processes and journalists' place in them. Political journalism could never again afford to be naive about its responsibilities to the democratic process and its manipulation by government. With New Labour, media–political relations attained a new, explosive maturity.

If the ascendance of spin and of the public relations state posed challenges to the BBC's journalism, so did the longer-term crisis of democratic participation evident in the growing apathy of the electorate, especially young people, towards conventional politics. These developments were matched by wider public anxieties about the state of the political culture and the impact on it of the increasingly symbiotic relations between the media and political classes. A common view is that forceful spin engenders an over-adversarial journalistic response, that there is too little straight reportage of public affairs and a deficit of the intelligent commentary necessary to support an informed electorate. For other critics, it is the excess of reportage that turns audiences off, while the 'commentary industry' is a sign of a 'degenerating political culture'.[1] Some

375

argue that political coverage is akin to that of a competitor sport, focused on strategy games more than policy, that politics is portrayed in terms of cynical struggles for dominance between political personalities, so fostering a 'culture of contempt'. In the words of Jay Blumler and Michael Gurevitch, these trends amount to a 'crisis of public communication'.[2] The BBC's journalism is inevitably caught up in these controversies. For some it remains too deferential, for others too aggressive. For some it offers too little analysis, for others too much. For some its analytical seriousness covers for cowardice in the face of political pressures; for others the seriousness of BBC journalism is a sign of its resilient health. The contradictory judgements point to the need to attend to the spectrum of journalism now issuing from the BBC.

But voter apathy signals another critical challenge for today's broadcasting: what 'politics' means and where the 'political' resides. The changing conceptions of politics manifest in environmental and identity politics, in anti-globalisation and anti-war movements, made this an incipient theme of internal BBC debate by the later nineties, questioning the exclusive equation often made not only between 'politics' and Westminster, but between 'political' programming and news and current affairs. For some producers, as for some audiences, the BBC's framing of politics was outdated and required to be redrawn. The BBC's democratic duty, in this view, was not only to continue its independent scrutiny of government and of power, but to broaden the character and range of its representations in tune with new social and political times.

The nineties were a period of accelerating change not only for journalism, but for factual television. The BBC's factual output has always ranged from the highest of Himalayan peaks to the humblest of humdrum magazines – The Death of Yugoslavia to Changing Rooms, Newsnight to Watchdog. In the nineties, factual was where the trinity of information, education and entertainment was most being remixed as the corporation met heightened competition with an exponential growth in popular factual programming. A striking trend across all channels was the increasing hybridisation of these genres under the encompassing notion of factual entertainment. In the era of schedule-led commissioning, factual entertainment delivers the requisite audience share at less risk than sitcoms or drama series; it is relatively cheap and relatively reliable. But a blurring of the boundaries of genre was not limited to popular forms. The nineties also saw a mining of the inherently unstable borders between documentary and current affairs, while documentary succumbed to the influence of entertainment and reality formats, and these in turn responded to the ageing of the British sitcom and problems in popular drama. Birt's organisational changes interacted with these genre-bending shifts, to different effect. Documentaries flourished, and the Community Programme Unit continued in striking ways to portray little-represented aspects of social experience. By contrast, Current Affairs was in the doldrums – strangely, as it might have seemed the area with most to gain from Birt's reorientation of the BBC's journalism – and News had to contend with the growth of new formats and outlets.

Once again, the BBC's moves cannot be understood in isolation from wider industry dynamics, foremost among them the intensifying competition for audiences and burgeoning populism of rival broadcasters; but also the political vice that gripped the corporation when, as a consequence, it competed aggressively for audiences to maintain popular legitimacy. For if it took the high road, focused on 'market failure', it risked being condemned as irrelevant and out of touch; if it took the populist low road, it risked being damned as insufficiently 'distinctive'. This tension, both principled and pragmatic, over the positioning of the BBC was repeatedly manifest in its factual output.

*

Mighty public opinion

'Broadcasting brings relaxation and interest to many homes. It does far more: it carries direct information on a hundred subjects to innumerable people who thereby will be enabled not only to take more interest in events which formerly were outside their ken, but who will be in a position to make up their own minds on many matters of vital moment, matters which formerly they had either to receive according to the partial opinions of others, or to ignore altogether. A new and mighty weight of public opinion is being formed, and an intelligent concern on many subjects will be manifested in quarters now overlooked.'

John Reith, *Broadcast Over Britain.*

*

Only one side

'The attitude of the BBC during the [General] Strike caused pain and indignation to many subscribers. I travelled by car over two thousand miles during the Strike and addressed very many meetings. Everywhere the complaints were bitter that a national service subscribed to by every class should have given only one side of the dispute.'

Ellen Wilkinson, Labour MP for Middlesborough, 1926.

*

Democracy and Diversity

The changes to factual in the nineties must be held up against recent thinking on the democratic functions of the media. Discussions of the role of journalism in democratic political systems have taken their cue from the concept of the public sphere developed by Jürgen Habermas. In his account the public sphere is a forum in which contending viewpoints come together and, through rational and critical debate, scrutinise the activities of the state and civil society, thereby forging a consensual public opinion.[3] In Habermas's historical analysis, as in recent democratic theory, the media are thought to play a key part in diffusing a range of opinions and bringing them into dialogue. Indeed, television is often considered the dominant medium of the contemporary public sphere. Habermas's formulation has been criticised for its universalising assumptions, and for taking little account of those differences that cannot be resolved by rational argument. Writers of many persuasions have argued instead for a plural conception of competing and counter public spheres, representing different, sometimes antagonistic and irreconcilable world views; and for a provisional account which acknowledges that, even given a minimal shared commitment to democratic values and procedures, there may be no common perspective from which all others may be judged. In conditions of multiculturalism and globalisation, when the clash of world views fuels violence and confrontation, these issues have real urgency. Once the inequities and inequalities of pluralistic societies are taken on board, the politics of the public sphere become bound to questions of the adequacy of the representation of subordinate and marginalised groups, the recognition of cultural diversity, and the need to foster interaction between incommensurable world views with the aim of reconciliation, or at least mutual toleration.

Britain's television journalism has certainly tried to animate something approaching the public sphere ideal: providing information to nurture a responsible citizenry, staging rational debate with the input of specialist expertise, exercising a critical oversight of the state and other powerful institutions, and encouraging participation in collective debates about common concerns and the public good. However imperfectly, it has achieved this in a pluralistic way not only institutionally, but through the deployment of a range of journalistic tones, from 'heavy' to 'light', the intellectual and investigative to the familiar and domestic. Yet, despite this, the BBC's journalistic culture remains vulnerable to charges of elitism. Two signs are manifest from its earliest decades. The BBC's news values evolved under the imperative that they must avoid all that characterises the popular press: sensationalism, excessive feeling, the vulgar and dramatic. Instead, the BBC saw the role of its news as informative and educative, as embodying tact, good taste and respectability. Before the Second World War these boundaries inhibited the BBC's adoption of innovative journalistic practices, such as live and unscripted reports.[4] They instilled a moralistic split in which news stood for what was rigorous, serious and real, and was duly accorded higher value than mere entertainment, a split between what is adjudged serious and popular, democratic and demotic, that continues to burden News management to the present.

A second symptom became plain as long ago as the General Strike when the BBC through its news bulletins, compiled mainly from official sources and from Reuters, claimed to speak on behalf of the nation, while failing to articulate the perspective of the strikers and those parts of the population in sympathy with them. The resulting 'rhetoric of constitutionalism',[5] spoken jointly by government and the BBC, became a core feature of the corporation's 'mandarin-like conception' of journalism, a 'civil service/professional model which stresses the disinterested mediation of information, the imparting of knowledge and the impartial umpiring of differences of legitimated opinion'.[6] As many studies attest, BBC news and current affairs output has remained heavily reliant on elite and official sources and contacts, to the detriment of less powerful and accredited groups. The BBC's inflection of the ethical foundations of journalism has been coloured, then, by a patrician solemnity and an ambivalent belief in the need to cleave primarily to the political mainstream, whether as exegete or critic. If 'holding power to account' is a watchword of BBC journalism, this has covered for insufficient commitment to giving space to alternative and oppositional voices.

The charge of elitism is encouraged not only by the news culture's adherence to political, social and professional elites for information and expertise, but by the habit of drawing journalists from elite social and educational backgrounds and by the internal view of News and Current Affairs as an intellectual elite within the BBC, one with a fast track to the executive. These propensities were matched in the nineties by audience judgements. The public continued regularly to turn to BBC news; but ethnic minorities, lower socio-economic groups and young people were less engaged.[7] Together, these aspects of the BBC's journalism have laid it open to criticism, such as Rupert Murdoch's infamous attack in 1986 when he linked the accusation that British television paraded the 'prejudices and interests of . . . like-minded people' to a swipe at its 'less than independent, neutered journalism'.[8] The danger of elitism was acknowledged in the 1998 report of the BBC's News Programme Strategy Review, which stated baldly: 'The Threat: We become irrelevant to all but the elite.'[9] A concern to combat any risk of elitism and of being out of touch with audiences was therefore much on the minds of News management.

The pluralistic revisions to public sphere theory direct us to ask how well the BBC's journalism has responded to changing democratic expectations by diversifying the political, ideological and cultural currents aired in its programming, in particular those non-elite and under-represented voices, as Onora O'Neill puts it, 'in danger of being silenced or marginalised'.[10] By the mid nineties, such challenges had become part of the self-understanding of BBC journalists.

Diversity, then, is a theme running through this chapter. Diversity has always been a component of the philosophy of public service broadcasting, but it has several meanings that are often confused. The best known is the broadcaster's duty to offer a diversity of opinion. A second meaning refers to the broadcaster's obligation to represent the social and cultural diversity of the populations it serves. However, the notion of representation itself needs unpacking. It indicates the importance of programmes that reflect the tastes and interests of diverse social groups – programmes made for those groups. But it also refers to the necessity of programming made by such groups, the better to represent their own interests and identities. Representational diversity points not only to reception but to self-expression, the right to participate and to be heard: what in the political context the philosopher Anne Phillips has called the 'politics of presence'.[11]

In structural terms, representational diversity points in two directions: first, to the need for employment policies that draw in and promote ethnic minorities and other marginalised groups. In addition, it raises the organisation of the BBC: the degree of diversity or centralisation in its editorial and production processes and how these influence content. In programme terms, there are two kinds of factual television that invite participation. The first is access programming, which puts the camera and editing decisions directly in the hands of under-represented groups. The second comprises those genres that include some element of non-trivial public participation, such as political discussion programmes, talk shows, phone-ins and interactive websites. The issue, then, is how adequately Britain's publics, its component social groups, are represented not only as audiences, but as producers and participants.

But diversity has a third meaning in relation to public service broadcasting: mixed programming, the provision of a diverse range of genres on mass channels. This is the most neglected facet of diversity, and it points to broadcasting *as culture*, that is, to the importance of formal experimentation and innovation both within each genre and across the corpus. It is this perspective that indicates the limits of the rationalist, 'information-and-education' focus both of narrow models of the democratic purposes of broadcasting and of Habermasian public sphere theory. For both rest on an opposition that poses knowledge and reason against expression and emotion, privileging the former terms. Television, however, with its varied and powerful expressive modes, impels us to move beyond the emphasis on reason and to confront how the aesthetic and affective are central to its capacity to orchestrate a reciprocity of perspectives, to engender empathy and understanding, and so to augment social knowledge and psychological intelligence in its audiences. Whether in the vicarious explorations of other lives offered by observational documentary, or in the daring subversions of common sense given by parodic comedy, or in the resonant imagery and imagined worlds generated by innovative drama, good television condenses a variety of expressive commentaries that extend the way we understand the human condition. It follows that the democratic role of broadcasting includes the responsibility to foster evolution in the cultural properties of each genre, and of the broadcasting mix in *toto*, so as to enrich the imaginative and affective contours of audience experience. Television's aesthetic and expressive dimensions cannot be divorced from its informational role, as they tend to be in notions of the aesthetic as a mere delivery mechanism. The informative/cognitive and the cultural/aesthetic are integral to good television, and at best they co-evolve. Aesthetic vitality is an essential component in the political and cultural value of public service broadcasting.

These principles, immanent in the Reithian ethos, have always been subliminally understood by the BBC, as well as Britain's broadcasting industry. They suggest the importance of examining how the BBC's factual output fared in the later nineties in terms not only of representational diversity, but of aesthetic and expressive invention. Only by looking across the output in these terms is it possible to assess its political and cultural significance, and therefore how well the BBC was fulfilling its democratic promise.

Impartiality and Its Discontents

The BBC's journalism was founded on the twin professional ethics of impartiality and objectivity. Influenced by the ascendance of empiricist epistemology and photographic realism, the journalistic concept of objectivity crystallised in reaction to the growth during the 1920s and 1930s of fascist propaganda and the public relations industry. Objectivity stood as a bulwark against a loss of faith in the prevalence of rationality, truth and progress. Impartiality, however, was the BBC's own special invention. From the outset the corporation set itself the task of acting as an 'impartial arbiter' independent of government, party political and commercial interests. Impartiality was a source of authority and a defence against accusations of partisanship, and it was buttressed by the corporation's claim to position itself within what it defined rhetorically as the moral consensus: 'The BBC cannot be neutral in the struggle between truth and untruth, justice and injustice, freedom and slavery, tolerance and intolerance. It is not only within the Constitution: it is within the consensus about basic moral values.'[12] The limiting point was when impartiality ran counter to what the government defined, usually at times of crisis, as the national interest.

Yet since their inception, the principles of impartiality and objectivity have been subject to criticism. In relation to news, the fact/value distinction at the core of the doctrine of objectivity has been undermined by a recognition that journalism, with its inherent selection and framing practices, cannot attain a neutral, value-free representation of events. From the seventies, the work of the Glasgow Media Group tracked the ideological qualities of news coverage of industrial relations;[13] while studies of the BBC's portrayal of politics showed how the routine attention focused on government/opposition dynamics extended in terms of political diversity only as far as the third national party, marginalising a range of parliamentary and extra-parliamentary movements.[14] Later research probed how the variety of broadcast genres permits greater range. If news has often been closed to all but official angles on such intractable controversies as the Northern Ireland conflict, documentaries and current affairs have encompassed a more open set of political and ideological perspectives.[15] In this take, television is a space in which competing accounts struggle for dominance; yet 'closed' programmes are more frequent and reach larger audiences than those 'open' programmes that portray a wider spectrum of views.

Whatever their status, the doctrines of objectivity and impartiality continue to operate as performative fictions or 'strategic rituals' that bind the professional culture, providing ethical moorings and augmenting its credibility.[16] But by the nineties the changing intellectual climate had also seeped inside the BBC; some journalists had absorbed the critique of television news epitomised by the Glasgow Media Group. The dominant empiricism identified by Philip Schlesinger in his study of BBC news in the seventies, manifest in an absolute distinction between 'the reporting of unadorned fact' and 'comment and interpretation', was being superseded by a more sophisticated grasp of the interpretative nature of journalism.[17]

*

Ideology from the inside out: the current affairs producer's tale

'My family was respectable working class; I went to a grammar school and was the first in the family to go to university. I began a doctorate on politics and the media, looking at the press in Northern Ireland – how they produced the news and used institutional sources, the ideological implications of it all. As a current affairs journalist I'm still interested in that analytical side, in the social production of news; I've always taken an arm's-length view of television. Sometimes I'm not sure why I'm here; at the outset I was angry, I had a hunger in my belly. But now I find it hard to take the medium seriously, seeing it from the inside out. I watch stories being manufactured in a *Drop the Dead Donkey*-ish kind of way and I think, "This is a joke."'

Producer, BBC Current Affairs, 1997.

*

Analysing Falklands coverage: *Panorama*'s editor speaks

'In 1982 I worked on a Channel 4 series, *The Friday Alternative*, which was total anarchy – politically explicit rather than implicit. Its mission was to expose other broadcasters and explain the grammar of TV. We made a programme with the Glasgow Media Group on the coverage of the Falklands War. I'd worked at the BBC so I knew people here. There used to be a weekly private meeting of News and Current Affairs editors to discuss editorial developments, and they'd circulate the minutes around the offices. I was able to get my hands on all the minutes through the course of the Falklands War, which revealed some startling things, like the BBC banned interviews with bereaved relatives. This arose because people were phoning up radio phone-in programmes saying "It's not worth it" and, this being the BBC, it was decided this was not in the national interest. It surprised me that they put material as sensitive as that into the minutes; it never occurred to them that they might be leaked. There's no danger of that now – they're acutely aware of dirty washing. Well, we used the minutes for this Falklands War programme, and the GMG did a study on the language that was used. We turned up all sorts of interesting angles; we did the early work on the Belgrano story, which was to keep coming back. The BBC hated it. At one point they said *The*

Friday Alternative team would be at home working for Goebbels! Unfortunately, *The Friday Alternative* never recovered. Channel 4 reacted to the BBC lobbying. The programme was replaced.'

Steve Hewlett, editor of Panorama, 1997.

*

No one is impartial

'There is no such thing as independent journalism. You're always playing somebody off against somebody else. Take John Ware: he's done incredibly strong work on wrong-doing in Northern Ireland, usually by playing off one part of the security apparatus against another. By cultivating a relationship with Special Branch you may get a story about military intelligence misbehaving, but don't con yourself that you came up with an independent scoop. You didn't: you inevitably served someone's agenda. The only way I can salve my conscience is to say: am I going after the people with real power and influence over people's lives, or people who don't matter? Of course that's full of subjective judgement itself, but it's how I govern what I do. And it's what takes me back to Westminster, because in the end the politicians matter because they shape people's lives.

'There was a phase in the late eighties known here as "contrarian" journalism, embodied by Andrew Neil, which I particularly hated. There was a truth at the heart of it – that British journalism had built up an unhealthy relationship with pressure groups, all of whom have an axe to grind with the holders of power, and had taken handouts from the pressure groups at face value for too long. So Neil said, "Let's attack the pressure groups" – Greenpeace, the Aids lobby. Glenwyn Benson came to *Panorama* in the early nineties with something of that agenda. It resulted in some good TV, and it was a useful corrective. But it meant spending a lot of effort going after small people, and journalistically it was questionable. Yes, Greenpeace is influential, they get their message across unquestioned too often. But ultimately they're not the ones pumping effluent into rivers; they're not framing environmental policy that affects people's lives.'

GB: 'Your point about journalistic critique always coming from a particular position suggests that you're knocking on the head the idea that it's possible to adopt an impartial position.'

'Yes I am. The only thing one can do that's impartial is go after everyone with the same vigour. The BBC can stand obsessive journalists; there's a guy here whose entire mission is to expose Gerry Adams. It's journalistically a big enough organisation to stand that. But if that was the corporation's aim it would be wrong. We spread our cynicism

– or however you describe our approach – around. That's the only sense in which we can be impartial. No one is impartial.'

Assistant editor, Newsnight, 1997.

*

Polarisation: the view from the Nine

I'm with the editor of the *Nine O'Clock News*, who trained at the BBC in the late seventies, went to ITN and worked on *Channel 4 News*, returning to the BBC in the early nineties. He calls ITN 'schizophrenic', with a tabloid approach dominant in all output except *Channel 4 News*. He says Thatcher's 1990 Broadcasting Act caused the ITV companies to compete for franchises, which meant reducing costs. ITN took cuts and was forced downmarket, with a more tabloid agenda and lower budgets for news-gathering, reporting and filming. He speaks of the Birtist 'Revolution of '87' in the BBC's journalism. He can compare before and after, and comments that 'BBC News is still very insular; there's a lot of moaning. What's new is the greater self-consciousness about what we're doing. Someone's always enquiring or writing reports, with rafts of objectives coming down from Birt and Tony Hall.' He says the newsroom culture was very macho in the old days, all about getting good film and 'having been there'. He found it alienating. Now the whole of News is more intellectually driven; the Birtist changes have led to a more analytical approach, in his eyes a big improvement. The *Nine* is the flagship bulletin: it has to be distinctive and significant and embody the public service remit. The newsroom hierarchy is a 'benevolent dictatorship'. He says of his boss, the head of Television News: 'We think alike editorially 99.9 per cent of the time. We've got similar backgrounds – maybe that's why. We both did history at Cambridge; there are loads of Oxbridge firsts in the newsroom.' So, he implies, it works smoothly. He expects the polarisation between BBC News and ITN to continue.

Diary, 1995.

*

The demotic and the serious

'Inside the BBC and ITN – and I've worked for both – people exaggerate the differences between the two, to reinforce the sense of who you are. So if you're inside ITN, BBC News is lumbering, establishment, unexciting, strangled by sobriety, worthy, dull, boring, Oxbridge, mandarin; its producers never watch *Coronation Street*, don't mix with ordinary people and have no understanding of common lives. For a BBC editor, ITN is

385

demotic, ephemeral, vulgar, trivial, obsessively interested in minutiae and human interest, besotted by showbiz, lacks strength in depth, perfectly OK at the quick hits, has no
sustained commitment to serious news values, and its star reporters indulge in clichés.
Well, there are elements of truth in each caricature, but things are more subtle. ITN
does have a commitment to serious news. And even under me the BBC never ran a
Nine O'Clock News that was wholly desiccated. But if you've only got twenty-eight and
a half minutes, that's incredibly compressed airspace – everything needs a privileged
status to get on. So if you look at the *Nine*'s history – the decision to lead with Major's
policy shift on Northern Ireland as opposed to the coach crash in which eleven people
died, or the failure to run the OJ verdict as a lead – it all reminds people what we're
about: that we're *serious.*'

Senior executive, BBC News and Current Affairs, 1997.

*

Mission to Control

John Birt's impact on the BBC's journalism owes much to the 1986 report of
the Peacock Committee which audaciously, given Mrs Thatcher's attacks on the
BBC's journalism, argued that the corporation's news and current affairs
output was the cornerstone of its public service offering and should be protected in the face of escalating competition. Michael Checkland, appointed
director-general in early 1987, announced his intention to strengthen these
areas. A month later he made Birt deputy DG with special responsibility for
overseeing a newly unified, bi-medial News and Current Affairs directorate,
incorporating all radio and television journalism. Birt's appointment and strenuous reorganisation of the BBC's journalism sent out dual messages: increased
resources at the same time as greater discipline and centralised control. Birt,
formerly a producer of LWT's highbrow current affairs series *Weekend World*,
had been highly critical of the BBC's journalism. His criticisms were outlined
in a series of articles written with Peter Jay a decade earlier. In their view, television news propounded a 'bias against understanding' because it ran too
many stories that were bitty and narrow in scope and gave little sense of
context. News, they said, was over-reliant on generalist presenters and lacked
specialists with detailed knowledge of political and economic life. It should be
redesigned so as to devote more time to big stories and put them in the 'fullest
possible context', while current affairs should offer a deeper level of analysis
and increase the number of issue-driven programmes.

On entering the BBC, Birt put this philosophy into practice under the rubric 'mission to explain'. The story count in news bulletins fell and in-depth analysis blossomed, with the result that news stole some of the analytical fire of current affairs. Current affairs features, such as *Panorama*, were required to address significant public issues across the year; and new strands were introduced, backed by four specialist research units focused on economic (*The Money Programme*), political (*On the Record*), foreign (*Assignment*) and social (*Public Eye*) affairs. While ITN was suffering from the ITV companies' drive for ratings in the wake of the 1990 Act, Birt's aim was for the BBC to occupy the journalistic high ground, while attracting the widest possible audience, and to eradicate the journalism that had put the BBC at political risk.

Some commentators welcomed the intellectual solidity of Birt's approach. But it triggered intense criticism. It was argued that the tradition of original and irreverent journalism had been consigned to history as the BBC capitulated to the political pressures behind Birt's appointment. Undoubtedly, the changes brought powerful central controls and a retreat to a more defensible position. The cautious analytical tone was unlikely to draw government ire, and when programmes threatened to cross this line Birt or his deputies intervened. As insidious were other changes to journalistic practice with profound effects on the output. In the name of rigour and efficiency, scripts were to be prepared and the logic of argument fully worked out before filming, which would follow the dictates of the argument. This approach sat uncomfortably with a commitment to impartiality and the need to continue to learn from an unfolding story during production. A critic noted, 'The time-honoured definition of news as something that someone . . . doesn't want to be made public has given way to a new formula in which a kind of intellectual debate is set up to examine the rhetoric of administrative affairs. This rankles with those . . . who prefer to probe the gap in public life between rhetoric and reality.'[18] If Birt steered news and current affairs towards serious analysis, he also introduced conditions that discouraged risk-taking and independence.

*

A very Birtish coup

'In 1987 when Birt arrived, there was a night of the long knives when most of the senior people in News and Current Affairs were booted out. It was brutal, a coup. In Birt's office there was a chart showing the new pyramid. Tony Hall had successfully produced the extended news for the election, and he thought they might make him editor of *Newsnight*, and they made him the boss! Inexperienced people who'd applied to be

Panorama producers were made heads of department. Experienced correspondents like Charles Wheeler were told *Newsnight* was junk; it was "Get rid of the past, get in new people beholden only to us." That's how mad it got. After thirteen years of working in an excellent Current Affairs department, we were presented with a team from LWT, which didn't even have a news service, to run the largest newsgathering service in the world.

'We were told in a big meeting that we didn't know what we were doing, that the award-winning journalism the BBC had done was crap. I'd just spent months in Lebanon being shot at; I'd been mustard-gassed in the Iran–Iraq war, and I'm being told I don't know what journalism is and it's all going to change. And the people telling me say there's only a "mission to explain". In my view of journalism there's a mission to reveal, a mission to investigate, a mission to entertain, a mission to inform, a mission to explain, but most of all there is a mission simply to be there, to show you something you don't know about. TV journalism is about stories, not issues. People want issues with a human face, issues dressed as stories. That's the skill. And they lost it.'

Former executive, BBC News and Current Affairs, 1997.

*

Look, the Shah is going!

'The "mission to explain" view was put by Glenwyn Benson when she famously said of her *Panorama*, "I don't care if only five people watch." She meant that if you want to know about the Maastricht Treaty, we'll explain and it will be a tough watch. Pictures, craft, films played no real role any more. People were recruited not for production skills or for being able to make things accessible, but for their intellectual abilities. Soon no one knew how to make films for a mass audience. They introduced a system called the "three stages of scripting". Researchers researched stories and wrote a script based on what you, as a source, tell them on the phone. The script is then approved and a producer goes out to film and sits down opposite you and says, "Now give me your views on the common agricultural policy." And you say "I think it's pretty awful," and they go "No, cut! You said 'I think it's pretty *scandalous*' – look, it's in the script, that's what you told the researcher." And you say, "Well, I was a little over the top. I've looked into it and it's not as scandalous as I first thought." "No, in the script you say it's scandalous!" So you set up a hypothesis, write the script, somebody approves it, and you go and shoot it.

'There's a story that when Birt did the fall of the Shah in Iran they were convinced at LWT that the Americans couldn't afford to let the Shah go. So the crew arrived with their script and rang back saying, "Look, the Shah is going! He's packing up and heading for the airport. There's some Ayatollah guy in robes flying in, and people are on the streets and the Americans are not coming in!" And back at LWT they said, "Stick with the script." People in the field were saying, "It's not happening," but the decision was *that* is the slant, *that* is what we're going to do. There were moments in the eighties where the BBC came close to writing its own death warrant; there'd been disasters in current affairs. It wasn't faultless. But then Birt rewrote the history.'

Former editor, BBC News and Current Affairs, 1997.

*

Centralising News

Over the nineties the bi-medial management of News and Current Affairs became the model for changes across the BBC. In 1991, Birt followed it by centralising radio and television newsgathering operations in a single Newsgathering department, serving reports to all television and radio outlets. Part technologically driven, part a means of cost savings and job cuts, the aim was also to foster integrated planning and strategy. Many reporters now worked for Newsgathering rather than particular programmes. A common reaction among staff was that the drift towards centralised newsgathering significantly reduced the individuality of news programmes, as they were thought to function more as packaging outlets for pre-delivered content than as editorially independent and distinctive operations.

By the mid nineties bi-mediality was spreading from NCA to all programme areas. The intention was to build coordination between television and radio production in the same genres by co-siting and sharing processes such as research, development and talent management. After 1996, bi-mediality was adopted for commissioning and production in most genres. But it was contentious, particularly among radio staff, since by setting them alongside their better-resourced television colleagues it was believed that radio's autonomy and independent values would be subordinated to television. A notable instance was how, following the bi-medial logic and in pursuit of uniform market disciplines, radio was subject to the same quasi-market commissioning structure as television. Yet the radio production scene is smaller and more intimate than that of television, and the economics of radio entirely different. It was widely held among senior radio staff that radio, unlike television, could not support an expansive independent production sector because the markets, batch runs and returns are too small. In their view the commissioning market in radio begat a bureaucracy that reduced efficiency and undermined creative well-being; rather, the informal cultivation of ideas was the best way to generate good radio.

Another critical phase took place when, in the 1996 restructuring, the World Service's extensive international newsgathering arms were folded into the domestic department. A logical outcome of Birtist policies, the reforms culled the networks of stringers and reporters on which the regional and linguistic subcultures of the World Service had thrived. The plans met concerted public and professional opposition, but they went ahead.[19] Given that the defining values of the World Service were the well-informed local sources of its regional reporting and its greater political and intellectual independence than domestic news, the reforms were seen by critics as a terminal blow to the World Service and to the diversity of BBC journalism. In the opinion of many staff the World Service's autonomy had been irreparably undermined.

Yet further centralisation occurred in 1997 when News management sought to insert a tier of 'supereditors' who would operate bi-medially, coordinate across several news programmes and wield budget controls. Following open dissent among journalists and editors over the way such an extended editorial hierarchy would impact on independence and diversity, Chairman Bland intervened with Birt and Tony Hall, chief executive of NCA. In the resulting compromise the programme editors remained intact, but the layer of executive editors was installed as well. The waves of centralisation evidence the threat to organisational diversity characteristic of the Birt years. If centralised commissioning ruled network programming, centralisation here took in the BBC's very sourcing of information, the core of its democratic functioning.

*

Arts and crafts and Stalinism

'When I started at the BBC in the mid eighties there were four separate sections of news and current affairs: TV News, TV Current Affairs, Radio News and Radio Current Affairs. All might have totally different agendas and coverage; there was a strong sense of competitive editorial drive. Birt was against this. He wanted a more integrated News and Current Affairs. Hence Newsgathering is now bi-medial. That does cut costs. But there are dangers, of an oversmooth, overcontrolled, overunified editorial process, and of the loss of the specific arts and crafts of radio and TV. Radio News is set to move soon from Broadcasting House to be co-sited with TV News at TV Centre. So there'll be a need to watch out for Stalinist pressures to take the "BBC line" editorially. There'll also be a need to guard jealously each programme's culture, their unique possibilities and differences from each other. And there's continuing economic pressure for even more integration; for instance, when they're co-sited, the six o'clock radio and TV news are expected to work together from the same desks. It's a matter of some concern for us.'

Editor, BBC Television News, 1995.

*

Hard and soft, garlic and Dracula

'Public service rhetoric has got perverted; it's being used top-down to justify the DG setting parameters for what programmes do. A series of annual objectives has come down from the DG. In *Newsnight* we were told in a meeting that we had to address ourselves to Significance; then there was Broadening the Agenda, Europe, and Revelation. It was Orwellian; I found myself having to track Revelation in our journalism over a year! David Sells, an old hand, said it was a sad day because for the first time the unwritten rule that programmes have autonomy had been ditched. Now diktats from on high tell us what to do in our journalism. Centralisation has reinforced a normative, macho editorial agenda focused on "hard" news values; public service is being used to defend a white, male, middle-class agenda. "Hard" means "kings and queens"-type reporting, power politics, world events given a macro analysis. "Soft" stories are dismissed as "human interest," too easy – they don't involve flak jackets. But "soft" stories are what people tend to relate to and remember: the Bosnian and Serb couple shot as they tried to cross the line; Jeremy Bowen reporting Irma. But it's "Oh God, we're being tabloid, sentimental! What's happened to our hardness?" It's like holding garlic up to Dracula: public service is used to fend off the "soft" stories the audience might actually want. "Go away! We know what's hard, we know what you need, and it's this!" There's some kind of fear of softness, of femininity.'

Female executive, BBC News and Current Affairs, 1997.

*

Accompanying the changes described were 'efficiency savings'. News and Current Affairs drew no slack from its own management; Hall was widely perceived as more Birtist than Birt. When in 1996 Birt asked the directorate to make 15 per cent savings over five years, news programmes were asked by the News executive for 30 per cent, and in 1997 this was revised to 32 per cent. As well as job losses, which it was claimed would be balanced by openings in the expanding news services, lower budgets translated into less support for reports

391

and filming, foreign coverage and investigative items. For many journalists this was unacceptable. Moreover, the periodic staff cuts placed them under stress; and while the introduction of new technologies appeared to help, it disguised intensifying demands on remaining staff. The transition to digital news and editing systems itself caused problems due, ironically, to lack of centralised oversight evident in the adoption of different systems across the corporation. If the waves of centralisation threatened diversity, they were justified in terms of reducing duplication and achieving economies of scale. In this way, given a flat licence fee income, the repeated reforms were portrayed as the only way to fund new services. Yet for many staff the changes under-writing expansion were destructive of the quality of existing news and current affairs. They were achieved at substantial cost.

*

Sophisticated Sadie, D-Cart, DigiSpot, BASYS and ENPS

GB: 'I hear that ENPS, the new computer system that's supposed to unify the whole of News, is being piloted. But there are also different digital editing systems. Can you explain?'

'I don't know how it's been allowed to happen. The head of daily Radio News admitted at our awayday that it's a complete fuck-up. At Broadcasting House we journalists have been trained on Sadie, a sophisticated digital editing package. Then there's D-Cart, a retrieval system. There are all these different systems in the same building. At the moment I have two computer screens, one that I use to type my script into BASYS, the old news system, and my Sadie screen that I mix sound on. ENPS may help us marry some of those functions, but not with the technology I've been trained in. If you go to the regional newsrooms, they have another digital editing system, which I can't use, so I have to edit manually. And BBC World has DigiSpot, which I can't use either! For all I know there may be yet others. Now why didn't the BBC pilot different types and introduce just one, so wherever I work in the country I can use the same technology? You can't be trained for all these systems! It would never end. For technology as central as this, it's insane.'

Reporter, BBC Radio News, 1997.

*

The internal market in news

'When the internal market was created here in the World Service it led to the News and Current Affairs departments adopting an increasingly tabloid mentality. In Current Affairs we needed to sell material, and you earned credit by selling product to the largest number of internal buyers. If you wrote something that only the Arabic service used you hadn't done well. If you wrote something that got twenty-eight usages out of forty-three language services, that was a very high strike rate. So your agenda became giving people what they wanted. That had a number of effects. People wanted things short and simple, so instead of writing a five-minute guide to what was happening in Rwanda, you'd write two and a half minutes. It seems to me that depth and subtlety become impossible in those circumstances. Another effect was that if there was a Squidgygate-type tape and a massacre in Liberia one day, you knew you'd get far higher usages for Squidgygate, so that would take precedence over the Liberia massacre.[20] A lot of essential current affairs values got lost as a result of the market. In the newsroom there is regulation for core stories, you know: "Even if you lot don't think this is important, we're telling you it is." But for our department it was a buyers' market, and that was destructive.'

Producer, BBC World Service, 1996.

*

Occasional managerial initiatives appeared to weigh against the forces for uniformity. One such initiative concerned Scotland. If the BBC's main historical mode of address was a pious one of serving the British people, it was moderated by reference to Britain's nations and regions. As pressures for devolution gathered pace in the nineties, News management produced a booklet for its 5,000 staff reminding them why 'Scotland is different,' outlining such core elements of that difference as the legal and education systems, and exhorting them to signal this in their journalism. The rhetoric of the 1995 booklet betrays an effortful condescension. By 1998, however, such conciliatory gestures were replaced by heated debate when, backed by a majority of Scottish public opinion, BBC Scotland proposed an 'integrated' Scottish television news – the *Scottish Six* – to replace the BBC's UK-wide *Six O'Clock News*. Changing political realities, it was argued, including the coming Scottish Parliament with its primary legislative powers, diverging policy agendas, and the new multi-layered nature of government in the UK, demanded to be met by new broadcasting arrangements and a rethinking of the BBC's role as a 'national' broadcaster. In the event the governors disagreed, throwing another style booklet, part of a £21 million package and an 11 p.m. Scottish opt-out from *Newsnight* at the problem. Their case was that at the very moment when there was the potential for the UK to fragment, and in the context of a press increasingly segmented along national lines, it became more essential for the BBC 'to reflect the whole of the UK to the whole of the UK'.[21] The issue was to be revisited; but in the meantime, the potential to grant Scotland greater independence and respond to national differences was firmly squashed.[22] If the networks' regional production quota, with its entrepreneurial bent, was tolerated, any substantial democratically ordained autonomy in news was not.

*

Audiences can easily be alienated

'All our network journalists are familiar with the simple fact that "Scotland is different." This leaflet reminds us of some of the many ways in which that is true. Whenever we broadcast a network programme we speak to all parts of the United Kingdom. Sometimes our stories will be relevant to the entire nation, and sometimes only to one or other of the home countries. Audiences can easily be alienated if they feel we don't even recognise when what we are saying does not apply to them. Hence this guide.'

Tony Hall, 1995.

*

Collusive Millbank

A further element in the centralisation of news and current affairs was the opening in 1993 of a large bi-medial Political Programmes unit at Millbank, in Westminster. With Millbank the BBC appeared to respond to the rise of news management at the heart of the political process, as government and parties grew determined to control the way politics is covered. Millbank enabled News management to keep a keen watch over the corporation's political journalism. But for journalists its existence was controversial. Proponents saw it as the symbol of Birt's commitment to disciplined and intelligent political coverage. Critics, in contrast, saw it as a central part of management's strategy to ward off political criticism of the BBC, in two ways: by cultivating incestuous links with the political class, and by ensuring centralised editorial control, so reducing the chances of 'idiosyncratic' reports. For many in NCA, Millbank was compromised by overly close relations with the political establishment. At

the least it encouraged excessive and anodyne coverage of Westminster minutiae or politics presented as melodrama. At the worst it favoured the BBC's
entanglement in spin and neutered its political journalism. For Millbank's
defenders, however, it served no sinister purpose; even under such conditions
integrity could prevail.

*

Outrageous Tories and Labour hacks

'Our job at Millbank is to report politics and Parliament in as wide and varied a way as
possible. Political Programmes, the political weeklies and regional political units all have
a base here, and Newsgathering has about fourteen correspondents. What are their
politics? There are checks and balances. AA and BB are known Tories. I was always cynical about AA; I knew him at Oxford, and he was such an outrageous Tory. But then CC
and DD are Labour; DD is just an old Labour hack. So it all comes out in the end. Are
there too many correspondents? Labour dislikes it, but I'd defend it. If they freeze out
Carolyn Quinn or Nick Robinson it's not going to stop the BBC getting stories because
they rotate around the programmes. We have a huge number and range of outlets.
They can't control what the BBC is broadcasting because they can't control its correspondents. There are just too many of us.'

Executive, BBC Political Programmes at Millbank, 1997.

*

Sleazy Millbank

'*Newsnight*'s breaking of the Tory Eurosceptic debate does not constitute investigative
journalism. It's a good story; it means *Newsnight* are leading the agenda for the press and
other news programmes. But they don't have the resources to put into long-term
investigations, because those are expensive in manpower, time, resources, and – outside reasons of political expediency – there's a bias against them for that reason as
much as anything else. Especially in the new BBC, when they may not, in the end,
achieve results and get on screen.'

GB: 'OK, consumer programmes like *Watchdog* investigate business and industry, in a
soft way; but where does that happen on big political issues?'

'It should happen on *Panorama*. That's its job. But all the big investigative stories of the
last two years have been broken by Westminster press correspondents, the *Guardian*

particularly. For the BBC, you now have a huge operation out of BBC Millbank at Westminster – it employs three hundred people – yet at no stage in the last two years did they ever break a big political story, like the Scott Report, Al-Fayed, Hamilton, sleaze, anything like that.'

GB: 'Why? BBC Millbank is dedicated to politics and to Westminster, yet you're saying it doesn't have this function – so what is its role?'

'Oh, it's a terrible place. It's like a gentleman's club. Guys walk around with their arms around the politicians. They've come from the same universities, the same social background; there is no standing back, no objective role there. It's a cosy working relationship. Even criticisms are couched in such a way as to be deferential. It's completely undemocratic.'

Two producers, BBC Current Affairs, 1997.

*

Incredibly, entirely collusive: the view from Newsnight

'In senior management there's no question: there are a lot of people who spend their time wetting their trousers about us doing difficult journalism and would rather see it banged on the head. The programme editor's job is to fight the inertia of the BBC machine because – and News embodies this more than anything else – there's a kind of "Government Information Service" atmosphere about what we do; you know, "Here's a press release, the government says it's doing this, we tell the grateful nation." Weekly Programmes [i.e. Current Affairs] have always been totally different to that. In the traditional Panorama you didn't do politics often, but when you did you went in there and kicked five or six politicians so badly they never recovered. "Maggie's Militant Tendency" was a classic example, with disastrous consequences. But that was the way Weeklies approached politics. Birt couldn't bear that. He thought, "I can't secure the political future of this corporation on the basis of a group of political programmes that only ever rip the people who are going to determine the BBC's future apart." That's where Birt's analysis was absolutely brilliant: he saw a threatened BBC, up against the wall, so he reorganised News and Current Affairs to create, critically, a massive Westminster unit – BBC Millbank – which fed on all those "decision-makers" and made them feel good about themselves, interviewing them at length. A stroke of genius. Take those regional Westminster units which take all Norwich's MPs seriously and interview them on College Green, and feed it back to Norwich to put on the local news opt-out that night – genius! Because what he administered to Parliament was the most enormous positive stroke. The MPs loved it, and arguably Birt saved the BBC. What he did was extremely clever. The cost of it was to make us incredibly Westminster-centred, with this massive dead weight of news people essentially waiting to report things they've been told to report. Incredibly, entirely collusive. My critique of BBC News would be that it's far too collusive.'

GB: 'You're implying that at *Newsnight* you stand outside that collusive structure . . .?'

'We try to – but of course, we're also built into the organisation.'

Assistant editor, *Newsnight*, 1997.

*

Emasculating Current Affairs

If news was thoroughly centralised, current affairs television fared worse under Birt's reforms. The malaise of current affairs in the nineties was not confined to the BBC.[23] In part, it stemmed from historical changes linked to the 'end of ideology'. With the close of the Cold War, the demise of Thatcherism, the endgame in Northern Ireland and, from 1997, Blairite one-nation politics, what targets remained for critical journalism? A sense of aimlessness prevailed as current affairs adjusted fitfully to the shifting political landscape. To this was added the damage inflicted on the genre at the BBC. Before 1987 the Current Affairs Television department encompassed long-form serious journalism, issue-driven films and popular magazines. The reforms boxed it in, reduced its range and honed rivalries with neighbouring genres. News grew more analytical, leaving less space at the serious end. The film-making skills of Current Affairs fell into disrepair, territory eagerly occupied by an expansive Documentaries department. The lighter output, including consumer affairs shows such as *That's Life* and *Watchdog*, was forcibly moved to Features. Political coverage was directed away from what management perceived as the unruly Current Affairs to the compliant Millbank. In return, current affairs journalists nursed a fulsome contempt for Millbank and what they saw as its collusive relations with the political class.

The identity thrust on Current Affairs centred on cerebral, issue-driven journalism fed by the specialist research units. Vertical controls were introduced following the conflicts with the Thatcher governments; scripts were vetted and an inhibited intellectual tone took hold. In this climate investigative journalism was not welcomed. If budget cuts failed to nobble it, then editorial interventions would. In 1987, 1988, 1991, 1992 and 1994 editions of *Panorama* were pulled, postponed, re-edited or criticised after interventions by top executives. In 1996 a *Newsnight* investigation of alleged dirty tricks by British Airways against Virgin airlines was axed when Birt, a friend of BA chief executive Robert Ayling, criticised its lack of rigour. These incidents sent a message that investigative journalism, always less secure in the BBC than in ITV, was on a short leash.[24]

*

Academic thought police

'Under Birt *Panorama* responded to an internal agenda that was all about arguments, analysis, background – like a fucking academic exercise. Pre-Birt, *Panorama* had come unstuck with a number of programmes, like "Maggie's Militant Tendency," which was almost certainly true; but the BBC was sued for libel, allowed the plaintiffs to get maximum publicity and then settled. A disaster. After 1987 it was all central control, editorial management from the top. They had script conferences where difficult programmes would be referred up to the head of department or Birt. At one time Birt would sit in on *Panorama* script meetings! Now the discipline I come from is different: the script was the last thing you wrote. You spent time ordering your thoughts and structuring and researching the programme; you then wrote the script. Here, they didn't give enough time for thought; they'd come to the script conference and spend seven, ten, twelve hours thrashing it out. I'm a supporter of the mission to explain, but the price they paid in Current Affairs was that key programmes like *Panorama* became desperately unpopular. In the thought-police atmosphere created by the fact that the deputy DG was going to read your script, people were more worried about covering the arguments than whether anyone would understand – that was the last thing on their minds.'

Executive, BBC News and Current Affairs, 1997.

*

They didn't know how to make programmes

'In 1987, the base of film-making skills that existed in Current Affairs was blown away. I arrived in the nineties having learned them on *Nationwide* and *Panorama* and developed them outside the BBC. I talked the language of storytelling, but it was a foreign language here. Before 1987 they made programmes with beginnings, middles and ends, well told as stories. You wanted to know what happened next. Post-1987, the idea of TV as a viewing experience wasn't on the cards. The programme was a space into which you

398

threw facts, argument or polemic; what mattered was whether it was right. It was corporately defensive. The programmes were made by people who could discuss with the most erudite in the land. But they didn't know how to make programmes.'

Editor, BBC News and Current Affairs, 1997.

*

Lip-service

'Every few years News management decide the news isn't investigative enough. They decide they want more off-diary news, stories that aren't pegged to a political story, the staple diet of which follows whatever press release has been churned out by whatever government department. So they started a unit to develop longer-form investigative journalism. I fetched up there, but I found the entire culture here isn't geared to that sort of journalism. It was supposed to be a team of six, but it ended up a couple of us covering a number of major stories. I left. They pay a lot of lip service; they always say, "We want more investigative journalism." But they don't understand. It takes time and money, and in the end you may not get a result. What is classed as investigative journalism in the BBC seems increasingly to be *Watchdog*-type consumer journalism, where you take on small targets, people who are ripping you off. There's a role for that, but now it's everywhere. I once worked at Thames for one of the great current affairs editors, Roger Bolton, a man of remarkable vision who took on the big subjects at the core of the democracy. But in the BBC there's a real sense that editors lack the will to take on the big investigations.'

Producer, BBC Current Affairs, 1997.

*

Current Affairs inhabited a contradiction. Like News, its budgets were ring-fenced and secure, to the frustration of those from Documentaries who believed they could produce better current affairs at less cost. But unlike News it had no guaranteed place in the schedules and had to compete against more entertaining fare to sell its stuff to the controllers. In the nineties these circumstances fuelled a self-fulfilling prophecy: current affairs appeared to continue to exist only via subsidy, and this was linked to its malaise. In the dominant culture of the BBC the commissions market and an entrepreneurial mindset were considered invigorating, and Current Affairs was believed to lack these to its detriment. The new ascetic Current Affairs was stigmatised. As schedule-led commissioning gathered pace, the controllers grew determined either to

399

marginalise or to influence what they saw as this underperforming genre. Current affairs strands were therefore replaced by short series over which the controllers had commissioning controls; those strands that remained could be moved out of prime time.

Within a few years the current affairs output issuing from the 1987 reforms was judged remote and elitist, as reflected in poor ratings. The 'mission to explain' had failed the BBC's long-form journalism, recanted even by those lieutenants charged with making it work. Glenwyn Benson, appointed editor of *Panorama* by Birt in 1992, made a U-turn a year into the job, arguing for more appealing human films. Under her the flagship adopted a more populist and, on occasion, a braver stance. In the words of an insider it was as if 'Birt . . . had sent secret word to Benson that he had been wrong all the time.'[25] By 1993 the ratings had improved and critics wrote of *Panorama*'s recovery. Similar dynamics occurred across the output: dry argument was traded for engaging films, analysis for 'storytelling.' The 'story' became a mantra, the way to boost appeal, expressing envious admiration for the buoyant Documentaries. The changes were symbolised by the appointment of film-maker Steve Hewlett, an 'outsider' who started at the BBC and an able populariser, as the next editor of *Panorama*. In the mid decade Current Affairs moved into populist gear, its energies directed into magazines like *Here and Now* as well as innovative series such as *Leviathan* and *Big Ideas* which offered analysis in a contemporary, individual or 'point-of-view' style. It also pursued diversity via the niche strand *Black Britain*.

Yet for all the efforts, the populist current affairs of the later nineties failed to stem the genre's decline. It continued to be found mediocre in comparison with the stylish and brassy documentary output. The very seriousness, the impartial, authoritative and analytical tone of current affairs were perceived as liabilities, by those both within and beyond the department. Even the relaunched *Panorama* was not safe from the controllers' competitive drive. Towards the end of the decade, budget cuts eroded its airtime and the programme began a migration to the edges of the schedule: from its long-standing Monday mid-evening slot to 10 p.m., and in 2000 to 10.15 p.m. on Sunday night. Ancient rivalries were played out in the simultaneous fall of current affairs and ascent of documentary. As the former emulated documentary, the latter made predatory moves into current affairs territory. Birt's reforms pitched current affairs into precipitate decline. Untouched by Birt, documentary became the sexiest genre on television.

The changing contours of current affairs reveal how closely Birt's policies pursued the political agenda. If the Thatcher governments' threats to the BBC lay behind the reforms that brought the genre to its knees — a sacrificial

offering – then the political thaw of the early nineties under the Major government coincided with its populist turn. Since that government's 1994 White
Paper called for the BBC to become more consumer-aware and commercial,
Birt was once again following the political flavour of the times. These swings
in direction indicate that expediency was dressed as public service principle, at
whatever cost to this critical genre.

*

The anxious structure: docs versus current affairs

'The whole Birt redefinition of News and Current Affairs bypassed us here in
Documentaries, which was remarkable, since *Real Lives* and all the trouble it drew from
the government came from Documentaries. Current Affairs don't benefit from a dialogue with the outside; they could have more independent production in their strands,
and it would be reinvigorating. They're obsessed with rigour; they talk a lot about being
"journalistically sound". It's all in the tone: neutered, authoritative, that "covers the
whole story", that claims some sense of "objectivity", whatever that means. And you
have a much bigger *hierarchy* in Current Affairs than in Documentaries. They have to
refer stuff up, and nobody wants to fall out of line. There's this great chain – the head
of department, then Tony Hall, and it's all connected back to the Policy Unit and Anne
Sloman worrying about the political repercussions of it all. It's an *anxious structure*.
Whereas here there's a smaller chain – just the executive producer, Paul, the head of
Documentaries, and the controller.'

Excutive producer, BBC Documentaries, 1997.

*

A tense relationship: current affairs versus docs

'Documentaries have always wanted to take over Current Affairs; it's a tense relationship. The controllers have assumptions about where the genres play best, and in
Current Affairs we sometimes feel the attitude to our stuff is, "Where can we hide it?"
It will never have some of the brilliant documentary values of a series like *Modern Times*,
because we're obliged to give impartial attention to the argument. Life here is more
complicated. We're not into advocacy or observational journalism; we're into the clash
of big vested interests. It's less glamorous.'

Senior executive, BBC Current Affairs, 1997.

*

Behind the scenes with Lilley and Archer

'The ring-fencing of Current Affairs is a bugbear of mine. In Documentaries we just did a series on the DSS called *The System* which they loved in Current Affairs, even though it was their territory, mainstream politics. Peter Dale made it. One episode was on a pensions bill going through the Commons. I said, "This will be dire." Well, he made a bloody brilliant programme of it! It sung. He had all these engaging characters and machinations; it was fascinating. If Current Affairs had done it, it would have got 0.1; this got 2 million. The minister, Peter Lilley, was involved, but we did things they'd never have done. We got behind the scenes before he gave his speech at the Tory Party conference. He was in some seedy hotel room, and Jeffrey Archer was coaching him. They forgot about the camera, so their slips are down and you see Archer for the slimy git he is, and Lilley as this inadequate. The film speaks more about what makes politicians tick, the Tory Party, the DSS, than any *Panorama*. I can't think of one great Current Affairs series, yet they have millions ring-fenced! I don't have any guaranteed money. We should be allowed to fight those bastards for the money and slots. All I want is to be able to pitch for the territory.'

Senior executive, BBC Documentaries, 1997.

*

Pregnant male seahorses versus black British fostering

Programme Review Board: this week's 'homework' is *QED*, a popular science documentary strand, and *Black Britain*, a new BBC2 current affairs magazine. *QED* is praised: beautifully filmed, it gives an exotic take on the threatened extinction of the seahorse. Mark pontificates about the use of Attenborough as presenter, 'which made it a classic of the genre'. Alan talks as a punter: 'I loved the bit where we saw the male seahorses pregnant, and when they gave birth to ninety seahorse babies!' The men smile, suggesting that the scene gave them an empathic sense of what it might be like to be pregnant and give birth. Alan adds that more could have been made of the politics of conservation. A brilliant success for Science, it got 40 per cent share in peak time.

Black Britain gets a mixed response. Kim says it wasn't focused: a music item, one on Mandela's visit to the UK, one on fostering black kids. June notes that the scheduling is wrong; many of the target audience will be watching *EastEnders*. Giles comments that it had brio, 'but my question is about the constant reference to "we", the black community, as though it's unified, when it needs to look at differences within the community. Take the item on black classical music: it should have been covered with reference to our usual idea of black music – soul, reggae – so how do we see the relationship of classical music to that?' Samir, the only non-white executive here, says it was a good start; the piece on the lack of black candidates in the Labour Party was incredibly important and hasn't been covered by other programmes – *Newsnight*, say. But *Black Britain* is holding back from tackling difficult issues dividing the black community. This *can* be done now, he insists. The producer, who is black, responds. Scheduling is a huge problem, but 'the main thing we've tried to do is avoid taking an overly negative line'. He adds, semi-ironically, 'We've done two programmes without using the word "racism" once! Should we be congratulated?' Alan bats the scheduling issue away: 'We all know that programmes have to stand on their own in the schedule, whatever they're up against.' This critical issue is deftly closed.

Diary, 1997.

*

Driving into markets

'[BBC World exists] to open up markets for the BBC brand. We see World as like a flagship that drives into markets, introduces audiences to the BBC brand, and allows us to internationalise our commercial operations off the back of it. News . . . is what the BBC is known for.'

BBC senior executive, late 90s.

*

News as Product

Birt's arrival at the BBC coincided with fundamental transformations in the nature of television news stemming from the multichannel environment. News, according to the commercial maxim, is a commodity and like all products it can be marketed, branded, formatted and diversified to create new markets.

The history centres on two developments: the advent of rolling news, for which the pioneer was CNN, launched in Atlanta in 1980; and the growth of entertainment-led news formats. In Britain popular news magazines had long existed in shows like *Tonight* and *Nationwide*, and from 1983 the breakfast-time TV-am innovated with a flow of light and friendly human interest stories. The appearance of new formats accelerated from the late eighties, and the BBC took a key role. In 1989 the Sky News channel was launched on satellite, and in 1992 CNN came to Britain. 1991 saw the launch of the BBC's commercial

403

international twenty-four-hour channel, World Service Television News, later rebranded BBC World. In 1994, the BBC launched Radio 5 Live, which offered a 'fun, raw and rough' combination of rolling news and sports; while 1997 saw the launch of the domestic twenty-four-hour channel BBC News 24 and of BBC News Online. For two decades news also expanded across the main schedules: 1980 saw the launch of BBC2's Newsnight, the early eighties BBC1's Breakfast News and Six O'Clock News, and under Birt BBC1 grew a lunchtime news, on-the-hour daytime bulletins and through-the-night news provided by News 24. Multichannel television stoked a massive growth in news services; viewers today can access eight times what was available in 1986.

The expanding markets were underwritten by several wider developments. The appearance of video in the early eighties made filming cheaper and eliminated the need for lengthy film processing. Satellite technology delivered video near instantaneously and allowed its rapid redistribution among many outlets, fostering a market in news footage.[26] Conservative legislation weakened the power of the broadcast trade unions, and as a consequence a multiskilling agreement was adopted in 1988 which enabled all BBC radio and television journalists to be linked electronically for the first time by a computer news system. Over the nineties, digital technologies increased the speed and flexibility of production by integrating all newsgathering functions and allowing news organisations to reuse and repackage their material, thereby boosting further the trade in news material. Together, these developments stoked both the centralisation of news production and the proliferation of news services.

In the BBC the demand to produce news twenty-four hours a day changed the character of journalism. Journalists, always under pressure, had even less time to research or to refresh ongoing stories; they found themselves 'reversioning' material for an escalating number of outlets. With many services competing for the top stories, some were left on hold, and a hierarchy of outlets emerged. The expansion of services might be taken to demonstrate the democratic health of BBC news evident in its increasing diversity; but such a view is superficial, because the expansion was underpinned by the relentless centralisation of news provision. The reality was therefore contradictory: new means of delivery and new formats were countered by greater uniformity of content; an appearance of diversity disguised the considerable pressures for editorial conformity. Yet whatever the controls, some journalists found ways to circumvent them and to carve out small spaces of dissent.

*

Constant demands in a multichannel world

'As a political correspondent I get to Millbank at about six a.m. and do *Today* at six thirty, then the TV *Breakfast News* at seven, then News 24, 5 Live and perhaps the *One*; some days I also do *PM* and the TV *Six*. There's a constant demand on your time because of the expanding outlets. On a major political story, sometimes I don't have time to do more than read the headlines, let alone having time to check the story or ring and speak to the key people involved. It makes me feel I can't do the job properly. I'm utterly squeezed. Often I have too little time to drum up new stories; it has to be purely reactive to the demands of the bulletins. There's a parallel with a doctor who, faced with a roomful of patients, says they're all trivial cases that can wait, and finds later that one of them has died. Sometimes I go home and I *know* I chose the wrong angle. It's troubling.'

Senior political correspondent, BBC Millbank, 1997.

*

Not witnessing events

'The days when you had a television and radio reporter doing the same piece have long gone. Now one or two multiskilled people do it for all the outlets. As a reporter I have no difficulty with that. But there are problems. For evening programmes like *The World Tonight*, if someone is at a story filing all day and you ask for a piece at the end of the day, they're exhausted and so is their material. For reporters it's bizarre: you become a kind of virtual journalist, stuck in a bureau reprocessing material and not actually going out and *witnessing* events, not *experiencing* what you're reporting. Another problem is prioritising the outlets. If I'm being careerist I place my pieces on the programmes with maximum audience and prestige. Beyond that you have to be seen to service all the outlets. But there's a pecking order. *Today* has the largest audience and gets the opinion-formers; it shapes the agenda, how stories are covered. *Today* and *Newsnight* have more resources, so if they want to commission something from a reporter they can offer support. The less prestigious programmes lose out, and radio can lose out compared with TV. But it's limited by negotiated agreements. When 5 Live was set up there were directives that if you're filing breaking news you go there first, then do a news summary, and then service other people. For me the maximum hit is to have a piece on *Today*, the *One* and *Newsnight*. Then you're reaching the programmes with audience and prestige, and the ones that are watched by our managers.'

Correspondent, BBC News, 1997.

*

Regurgitating online

'The bulk of what we do at News Online draws on agency material or existing BBC news material from TV and radio, which we reversion. Our other main source is Newsgathering – reports and live feeds. Our journalism is about selecting elements, packaging and creating background information. Newsgathering is mainly designed to deliver live content for News 24 and 5 Live, and packages for TV and radio news. The typical pre-'97 Newsgathering deliverable was a crafted two-minute-forty package; now correspondents do that as well as loads of live two-ways and Q and As. So they're busy people, delivering several forms of the same material. There is a complaint that we do too much regurgitating agency and BBC copy, and that we should do more value-added stuff – the expert forum, the clickable guide, the "send us your views". It's a debate we need to have: should we do fewer stories and put more into interactive features?'

Executive, BBC News Online, 2001.

*

Stopping the ROT: getting away with dissent

A radio journalist tells me about internal struggles over editorial control. 'When a programme goes out there are usually three records of transmission [ROTs]: a cassette, the original tape if it's not a live show, and an in-studio reel-to-reel tape. As a result there are always tapes of any controversial transmission for the record. However, sometimes, mysteriously, all three tapes go missing.' He makes clear that he's talking about the programme-makers 'losing' the ROTs of programmes that management might want to use to check them out or censure them. 'It'll happen over something like an interview with Chris Patten [then Governor of Hong Kong]. Someone will have dinner at someone's club, they'll hear that we gave Patten a hard time or took an unacceptable angle on the story, and a phone call goes out to BH or Bush. So they try to get hold of the ROTs, but they've gone walkabout, no one can find them [laughs heartily]. Then they ask us, and we say, "Oh, we interviewed him and he said this, I think, and we said that." The heat is off and they can't pin anything on anyone.' In this way, he implies, producers get away with an angle that might have attracted serious flak if those elusive ROTs had not gone missing.

Diary, 1996.

*

406

Responsive News?

Birt's journalistic reforms were, then, profoundly paradoxical. In their initial phase, 'analytical seriousness' was paralleled by the manacling of current affairs and by unprecedented forces for editorial conformity. By the early nineties, as the collective conviction took hold that the news resulting from Birtist analysis was stale, the corporation embraced an entrepreneurial imitation of commercial trends. The drive to build continuous news services reflected a new credo – the inverse of the mission to explain – that, as an observer put it, 'Newsgathering was . . . the future. Our lifestyles demanded information on tap. Our short attention spans meant we were too restless for "issues".'[27] Values of immediacy, of 'see it as it happens', were primary; news had a faster turnover and a shorter life. Now the main preoccupations were with the tone of news, narrative and visual presentation, and there was a questioning of the prominence accorded to mainstream politics. The new approach reflected increased competition as well as trends in US television journalism. The early period of Channel 5's *Five News* was widely taken to be an innovative model, with its youth appeal, relaxed and informal tone and reports focused on individual perspective. This example, in conjunction with criticisms by some reporters during the Bosnian war of the rule of impartiality in the face of extremes of barbarity, fed debates over whether journalism would be enriched by introducing more personal perspective and more varied emotion and tone.

The changes responded also to escalating tensions from the early nineties between News management and the controllers. In their attempts to maximise the success of the schedules, the controllers felt stymied by their lack of control over News and Current Affairs stemming from the ring-fencing of NCA budgets. But this was met by continuing concerns on the part of some journalists over the limited social reach of BBC news services, stoked by dissatisfaction with what were perceived as elitist tendencies in the flagship programmes. In this take, if news was popular, informal or niched, it was no bad thing; such strategies embodied a responsible realism.

In part to placate the controllers, marketing and audience research, which already had clout in other production areas, began to attract belated attention in News and Current Affairs. Branding became a key concern, and from 1993 centralised news production permitted the integrated branding of all bulletins. Meanwhile, journalists spoke increasingly of the need to provide 'useful news' and to be 'audience-centred', based on what research showed were consumers' actual interests and lifestyles. Now NCA would engage with issues relevant to the lives of its audiences, rather than simply impose the putatively universal intellectual values driving its high-end journalism. As indicated in Chapter 7, rather than entailing a commercial orientation, research was seen by its advocates as a means of enhancing NCA's democratic functioning and fostering a responsive BBC.

Attempts to create popular variants of BBC news multiplied. Radio 1's *Newsbeat*, BBC1's *Breakfast News*, Radio 5 Live and News 24 were each portrayed in terms of the need to diversify the tones, techniques and content of news in order to connect with underserved groups – variously 'ordinary people', 'people from different class backgrounds' and 'young people'. Radio 5 Live, for instance, drew on the innovative model of the commercial station LBC to bring a direct, vernacular style to the union of BBC news and sports. If the wider debates about populist journalism centre on criticisms of dumbing down, in the BBC the shifts in output were repeatedly defended as attempts to boost the accessibility, relevance and interactivity of news, and to stem the 'dull and turgid' tendencies of the flagships, rather than any dilution of journalistic values. Quietly, as if there was no contradiction, Birt's doctrine of analytical seriousness was absorbed into the consumer-responsive mix. The problem of positioning remained, as when managers confided that News 24 in its first year had targeted the same audience as Sky News. At such times the insistent question arose: how was the BBC's 'consumer responsiveness' different from that of its commercial rivals?

*

Is this all we should be doing?

'*Newsnight* and *Today* are flagships, but they have such limited audience appeal; *Newsnight* targets a very upmarket audience. The question is: is this all the BBC should be doing? 5 Live has wider appeal and is arguably more innovative than *Today*. When I came to *Breakfast News* a few years ago it was serious, formal and analytical, with nice films. Then it became lighter and the range of stories became broader, although in no sense did its news values radically change. We did more live coverage, getting around the country, fun pieces, quirky regional stories. You can mix these values without diluting them. We introduced interactivity – phone-ins and video diaries. We interviewed ordinary people rather than experts, we had a no-MP rule, and we held *Kilroy*-type debates. The point is, this doesn't have to be "light" at all; it's completely serious.'

Producer, BBC News, 1997.

*

Reaching different people

'Radio 5 Live is a huge success if you match it against what it set out to achieve: reaching people from different class backgrounds and a wider geographical spread, reporting news differently. It does breaking stories really well – look at how they handled Dunblane. The election coverage was accessible and entertaining rather than dull and turgid like the *Nine*. They get different types of people on radio, and they take local material and repackage it for a national audience. It has journalists in all the main regional centres who filter material from local radio and TV, so you hear regional accents and younger people broadcasting. 5 Live stimulates all these possibilities, but here in London I see a lot of snobbery towards it. It's frustrating that people don't see it's a different product, doing what it does well on very little money. Some see it as dumbing down, but 5 Live has range. Let's face it, *The World Tonight* will only ever reach a tiny minority of people.'

Reporter, BBC News, 1997.

*

Rolls-Royce to Newcastle

'The staff here on News 24 are multiskilled; they come mainly from 5 Live and World. The younger journalists are enthusiastic: you've got total control and it's faster. But the people at the top, the strand editors, hate it. They come from *Newsnight* and the *Nine*, programmes with huge resources, where you get in your graphics people and it takes four days, so "How can we possibly do this in two hours?" Here you have to accept that everything can't be of Rolls-Royce quality.'

GB: 'The editor of *Newsnight* tells me unified Newsgathering may cause him to lose his own foreign correspondents, and that digital video means the loss of a higher quality of journalism.'

'He has a point, but then how much do the viewers take in? At News 24 we're universally hated for what we're doing to the traditional news output, but our stuff won't be poor quality. Our mission statement is to report the UK better by breaking news stories quickly and accurately, being unpredictable, and reflecting more of what is going on in the UK. We'll have the relaxed presentation that 5 Live does so well; the men may not wear jackets but they will wear ties. Regionalism will be a key ingredient; if there's a big story in Newcastle we'll go straight to the Newcastle newsroom rather than pontificate from London. In the first year we're targeting ABC1s watching Sky. The format is news, business and sports, but more live than Sky.'

Executive, BBC News 24, 1997.

*

The Dilemma: Ambivalence

The culmination of News management's turn to marketing and audience research was 1997's News Programme Strategy Review, the first audience-research-led review of all news and current affairs output, which aimed for increased understanding of audiences to feed into the changing portfolio.

Partly a response to controller pressure, the PSR was also an exercise in legitimation, a signal that News management was modern, responsive and accountable. Yet it revealed divisions within the directorate between those cleaving to the analytical high-end and those advocating a broader, consumer-sensitive agenda. In the second perspective, the PSR responded to the challenge of connecting with underserved groups, and to evidence that, while multichannel television brought an exponential growth in news output, audiences for news and current affairs were declining and BBC viewing in multichannel homes particularly so. Worryingly, this decline was most pronounced among those groups – ethnic minorities, the less affluent – traditionally alienated from the BBC.[28] The PSR enabled executives to air the dilemma at the heart of the BBC's democratic self-conception: to what extent was the BBC's role to lead public opinion by supplying information that it judged to be of universal value for citizens? To what extent did it mean listening to consumers' ideas of what they want from news? In this stand-off, the consumer-led view became an idiom for expressing discontent with the BBC's univocal news discourse and with the resistance to diversifying the news culture.

The review involved a genuine engagement with the insights of audience research. But for all its democratic intent, the PSR had symptomatic closures that suggest a profound ambivalence to reforming the BBC's journalistic culture. In the research commissioned, and in meetings, although attention was paid to underserved groups, no special resources were devoted to them; ethnic minorities, for example, received no particular focus. And although some of those involved sought to probe the links between the nature of political coverage and disenchantment with conventional politics, senior figures repeatedly closed this discussion down and resisted changes to key political programmes. One battle concerned *Yesterday in Parliament*, the axing of which was put off-limits under putative pressure from Westminster. The division appeared generational: younger executives impatient to rethink 'politics,' the old guard insisting on 'Westminster first.'

The outcome of the PSR was to offer more of the same: both a retention of 'classic BBC values' of accuracy and impartiality, and added consumer-friendly gestures – the use of 'narrative wherever possible', 'clear language' and a 'broad and significant agenda'; both a new policy analysis programme and a popular current affairs weekly; both more investigative journalism and a revamped, regionally attuned *Six O'Clock News*. Branding would clarify the distinctive remit of each service, as well as their collective range.[29] The resolution was, then, both to set the agenda, leading public opinion with high-quality journalism, and to respond to what research suggested were audience desires. Yet a certain complacency was evident in the proposition that changes in language and style alone might appease alienated audiences and could be divorced from deeper changes in news content and values. In short the PSR, despite the voluminous audience research, failed to overturn long-standing BBC tenets about audience 'wants', beliefs that remained undisturbed in the face of the clamorous social and cultural pluralism outside the BBC's doors.

What was glaring about the PSR was the absence of any concerted rethinking of the bounded cultural presuppositions of mainstream BBC journalism. Glaring also was the cynicism of staging such an apparently radical exercise in self-reflection, only for it to result in so little.

*

Indistinguishable!

A meeting of the News PSR steering group. Richard Ayre, deputy head of News, opens by saying he recently saw Birt, who warned them to take audience issues as primary and aim for nothing less than radical change. A strategist outlines recent demographic research as well as some on audience perceptions of TV news. Richard interrupts: 'Did any of you catch *Five News* last night? They had an exclusive on the Manchester airport protests, with a reporter filming on DV from inside a tree house in the protestors' camp when the bailiffs moved in to evict them. Get hold of a tape and watch. The guy had an earring and stubble – he was indistinguishable from the protestors! The audience was invited to identify.' He implies, is this the future?, and leaves it hanging whether he condones or condemns this partial style of journalism. An argument erupts over whether being 'viewer-friendly' and 'story-driven', as Steve Hewlett advocates, will dilute the BBC's cachet of seriousness. Richard comments with gravitas that the authority of BBC news will inevitably decline if they go this route. Steve disagrees: it *can* be done without losing authority. He continues that research in 1995 on the BBC TV news editors showed they all conceived of their audience as identical; they were all going for the same upper-end demographics. 'Just a couple of years ago, News was completely against the audience view; if you'd raised the issues we're raising now there would have been vomiting in buckets.' I am quietly surprised; my contacts in 1995 with the BBC1 bulletin editors showed a varied conception of their audiences.

They alight on a problem thrown up by the demographic research: what is a 'C2DE'? Are pensioners C2DEs? Do classic definitions of the working class still apply? Is class a matter of birth, wealth or occupation? No one knows quite how class is being defined. Steve continues that there's a big beef from the regions about lack of network trailing of the regional news opt-outs after the *Six*. Richard cautions, 'These are intensely political questions crossing three directorates – News, Regions and Broadcast'; so it may prove impossible to make changes in the 6 p.m. to 7 p.m. slot. But Steve says Broadcast are insistent that better ratings must be delivered by this vital slot, the gateway to prime time. Richard Clemmow reports on his team's work on current affairs, outlining a range of positionings of the output: from audience 'wants', the ratings end, to audience 'needs', the old BBC concept of informing and educating. Steve contests his dualistic assumptions: the same informative content can be narrativised and presented better without sacrificing its weight. Sian Kevill concurs, pointing out that audiences perceive little boundary between current affairs and documentaries: 'They really don't see much difference between *Panorama* and *Inside Story*.' Larry, the market researcher, adds: 'The focus groups on current affairs will have as much on Roger Cook, *Oprah* and *Kilroy* as on war-torn zones.'

As the discussion rolls on, Richard Ayre's language hinges on Reithian notions of 'core information and understanding', Steve's on 'stories', format, time of day – a language of schedules, strategies and the seduction of audiences. *Newsnight* comes up; Sian asks, 'Is *Newsnight* too focused on politics?' Steve responds, 'We have to ask who is it for? We think it's for opinion-formers, MPs, captains of industry. But do we know?' Mark Wakefield pursues the theme: 'Can we get the research to explore what audiences mean by "politics"? Is *Panorama* "politics" for them, or *Newsnight*, or *Week in Westminster*? What do they think politics coverage should be? Often it's broadened these days to include health, education, the environment.' Richard Ayre firmly counters: 'Maybe, but *we* know the BBC's main role is to report and analyse the workings of government, Westminster and the party system. We *know* these things are central to BBC coverage of politics, where schools and hospitals are not.' In the break I tell Mark I appreciated his question. He says, 'It's absolutely central, but it's highly sensitive because of Millbank. We need specialist Westminster reports, but how much do we need separate from looking at the policy ramifications on the ground, which bring it alive?'

The meeting draws to a close. Richard Ayre speculates about how, in future, local radio and TV will create their own news programmes simply by clicking and dragging an icon representing a particular item or vox pop. They'll pick and mix from different sources, international and national, and all they'll add will be the presenter. The room is silenced by his unsettling vision. I muse silently that audiences are already creating their own agendas online. Richard draws us back to politics, on his terms: 'I want research on the style of political interviewing, and whether audiences really want Paxman/ Humphrys-type interrogations.' Mark says inconclusive research has already been done on this: some dislike it, others value it; he implies this is too narrow a focus, a dead end. Richard insists: 'I'd like it done again; we've just had a general election and I sense something shifting out there. It's the millennial question: do we want an adversarial style, black and white, right and wrong; or should it be about understanding issues and giving different perspectives? Is there a new approach to broadcast journalism that the BBC should be promoting that deals in complexity and subtlety?' 'But we must keep putting the tough questions to politicians! Mustn't we? . . .' Steve says teasingly, as though to shame them from harbouring any doubts.

Diary, 1997.

*

Newsnight: the critical adjunct

'There's a danger that Newsgathering becomes too reliant on the Palace of Westminster, that the Millbank correspondents get complicit in the political process. People who rely for their livelihood on observing a particular group start to reflect the values of that group; they go native. That makes any outfit that deliberately sets out to probe, like Newsnight, something to be treasured. But instead we're told we're out of line. Birt says, "Don't be so aggressive"; Paxman gets slapped down. It encourages self-censorship.

'A classic example happened recently, the day before a by-election. Michael Crick did a great piece about how all the parties were overspending on their election expenses – a sign of the times. Well, it was deemed controversial, and the head of Daily News went to great lengths to prevent it going out before the ballot. He was being advised that it could be tricky; there was a long argy-bargy involving senior people in the Political Strategy hierarchy. In the end Newsnight ran it and every newspaper picked it up; that could only reflect well on the BBC as it was seen to be doing its job. Now you could say it's healthy for large numbers of BBC managers to be engaged in that kind of process, and the outcome was satisfactory. But what's distressing is that the initial effort to stop Crick came from inside News and Current Affairs, which suggests a cultural attitude. By and large the BBC does a good job; but the overwhelming sense is of an organisation paid by the public to be impartial taking too much account of what politicians and powerful organisations want it to do, and this as its natural response. So the work of being critical and independent,

413

the real journalism, is left to small adjuncts to the centre, like us at *Newsnight*.'

Assistant editor, *Newsnight*, 1997.

*

The badge of honour

'This is the absurd war we have with the people at the top of News: they say *Newsnight* must be different or there's no point. Yet when we do things differently and create trouble, they go "Bloody loose cannon! Who do they think they are? Arrogant, irresponsible . . ."'

Producer, *Newsnight*, 1997.

*

'Casting' Debate: *Newsnight*

Newsnight, BBC2's late-evening programme, is considered, with Radio 4's *Today*, the BBC news analysis programme of record. Well placed to be watched by government and 'opinion-formers', it has a reputation as the intelligent person's guide to the day's key stories, often covered from a provocative angle. In the late nineties, at its best, *Newsnight* was smart, fearlessly probing or relentlessly sceptical, at its worst, sneering, self-regarding, or so bound up in tacit Westminster knowledge as to be unintelligible. Like its presenters, *Newsnight*'s demeanour at times smacked of arrogance and complacency as much as independence. In the culture of *Newsnight*, 'boring' stood for all that was dull, predictable or unintelligent. The programme embodied a contradiction: of all television journalism it was both the most intimate with, and yet the most unsettling of, Westminster mores; like Paxman himself both of, and yet an acute analyst of, the British establishment. Across the BBC *Newsnight* was known as the home of the intellectual elite, the 'officer training corps'; it bred people for top management. In the mid nineties it had a budget of £10 million, but it took the same cuts as the rest of NCA. Falling budgets meant tighter staffing, a declining commitment to investigative journalism, less foreign coverage, less scope to research stories, less film-making and more studio discussion.

Newsnight insistently defined its identity against run-of-the-mill BBC news. Rivalrous with the flagship *Nine*, its staff spoke contemptuously of the bulletins as having been reduced by centralised Newsgathering to mere 'output editing'.

In *Newsnight*'s view they lacked intellectual and critical acuity, while long-form current affairs was relatively slow-footed. *Newsnight* stood partly beyond the standardising reach of Newsgathering and retained its own dedicated reporters for politics and economics. But like the news programmes, it drew its stories mainly from the press, Newsgathering and the official Westminster diary. With Current Affairs, *Newsnight* shared a deep suspicion of BBC Millbank for its complicity with the political class; and within this compromised environment, *Newsnight* conceived of itself as the bastion of integrity, of 'real journalism'. It saw as its main rival *Channel 4 News*, admired as the most intelligent and pug-nacious news show, and journalists crossed between the two programmes. *Newsnight* was a competitive and an elite journalistic culture driven by intense pressures. Some survivors spoke of it as intimidating, driven by fear, even damaging: 'If you weren't told you were a pile of crap you'd probably done all right.' Frequently they drew analogies with public school or Oxbridge: 'There's this terribly public-school-fagging aspect to it: because you were dumped on when you were an AP, people stabbed you in the back and the editors shouted at you, you will do the same.'

*

Sink or swim

'*Newsnight* is very hierarchical. From the internal BBC perspective it's always been like the SAS, the officer training corps, the proving ground. It's understood that you either sink or swim; and if you swim, you can swim anywhere. The parallel that strikes me most is being at public school. It's phenomenally similar: if you aren't one of us, part of the group, you're in desperate trouble and you'll be very unhappy until you either get out or are pushed out.'

Producer, *Newsnight*, 1997.

*

Given *Newsnight*'s flagship reputation, its take on politics was critical for the BBC. If the News PSR provided few leads on changing the BBC's political coverage, how was politics conceived by *Newsnight*? Its staff appreciated the challenges to political journalism posed by intensifying political PR and grow-ing voter and viewer disengagement, and it stood self-consciously on the front line in the battle with spin; a programme aphorism was 'politicians lie'.

As a consequence, in the nineties its self-image centred on aggressive set-piece political interviews conducted usually by Jeremy Paxman or Kirsty Wark, the culmination of the corporation's long march away from the deferential 'neutrality' of earlier decades. Despite its obvious rigour, such antagonistic interviewing was out of line with Birtist 'caution', and Newsnight had been censured publicly by Birt for it. Paxman was famous for fiercely interrogative interviews with prime ministers and other senior politicians in which he persistently attacked evasion, hypocrisy, inconsistent and flawed policy, and ripped the slightest hint of political split apart at the seams. The term for the carefully prepared first question designed to knock one's interviewee off balance was the 'rabbit punch'; and watching through the glass office walls as producers talked Paxman through his tactics prior to 'doing battle' with Michael Portillo or Robin Cook was like observing a boxer being psyched up before a fight. These critical skills were honed in the mid nineties as the Conservatives were repeatedly rocked by sleaze, with Newsnight playing its part. In Paxman's celebrated encounter with Michael Howard in the run-up to the 1997 general election, he asked the then Tory Home Secretary the same question – whether he had threatened to overrule his own director of prisons – fourteen times, refusing to let him off the hook. As New Labour prepared for power, Newsnight took aim both at the disintegrating Tory administration and at the gleaming surfaces of New Labour spin.

Yet Newsnight was also deeply ambivalent about the excessive parliamentary focus of so much BBC news and current affairs, aware that it was losing viewers and turning them off politics as well as fuelling the malaise in media-political relations. The programme embraced the need to rethink political coverage. Repeatedly, comically, in editorial meetings the call was to 'avoid politics', to have 'no MPs on tonight'; yet somehow, repeatedly, the call was overturned. In the face of aggressive spin Newsnight's journalistic ethic was thrown back on 'holding power to account', on the pitiless scrutiny of policies and communications strategies. But in addition, there were attempts to broaden the agenda by covering new political territories. The programme enthusiastically took up the challenge issued by the BSE crisis to cover the politics of science, appointing a dedicated science correspondent whose work won awards. Presciently, it began to probe the complex relations between government and its scientific advisers and quangos, grasping that much that was controversial in contemporary government turned on the handling of sometimes unwelcome scientific counsel. Less successfully, it sought to fill the gap left by the demise of The Late Show, BBC2's innovative strand devoted to culture and ideas.

In practice, certain underlying principles structured Newsnight's agenda in the mid nineties. On the negative side, Newsnight had little interest in covering

European politics; they were treated as dull or ignoble, or treated to a 'mad Brussels bureaucracy' angle. It showed contempt for Britain's third party, the Liberal Democrats, and deplored every minute wasted covering it, ostensibly because the Lib Dems had no chance of getting into power. As media politics themselves became a pressing subject of public concern, in particular Murdoch's influence on New Labour and monopolistic controls over football and satellite television, Newsnight showed great caution about covering these topics, fearing accusations of conflict of interest. On the positive side, Newsnight made some effort to explore the expanding varieties of non-parliamentary and international political and social movements. But this was compromised by a conception of them as 'issue-based', code for not 'real' politics, and coverage was commensurately patronising and unserious. The sense was of the new politics being sealed in a conceptual vacuum rather than being permitted to cross-fertilise and transform the programme's larger conception of politics. Despite ambivalence, Newsnight remained obsessively excited about nosing out splits within, and lies propagated by, government and the main parties.

*

Isolate the scientist: E. coli and Labour splits, March 1997

Newsnight's 10.30 a.m. meeting: Pam, editor of the day, tells the assembled producers that two items are fixed for tonight: a film on the state of Scottish Labour and a story on E. coli and dirty abattoirs, which will probably lead. A damaging report by the government's Meat Hygiene Service was suppressed for a year, and has just been leaked to the Financial Times. It reveals that many British abattoirs are filthy and the meat contaminated with E. coli. Pam says excitedly that the story will focus on the role of the Ministry of Agriculture, Fisheries and Food in suppressing the report. 'We'll try for a three-party sync; Labour will really go for this,' as it highlights Tory government incompetence on food safety, a hot topic. An added twist is that a recent E. coli outbreak in Scotland which caused twenty deaths is currently the subject of a public enquiry. Professor Pennington, running the enquiry, has expressed displeasure that he was not informed about the abattoir report. 'We'll see if there's drama in the House this afternoon, and we'll try Douglas Hogg [the minister] for interview.' Pam solicits ideas for a third item: a holocaust art exhibition in Paris? An EU directive on dogs ('Great pictures!')? The news that Sainsbury's is to sponsor the National Childbirth Trust? Pam likes the last idea: she allocates men to E. coli, women to the NCT, and they move off.

2 p.m.: E. coli will be a film and a discussion, which in Newsnight is called a 'disco'; Susan Watts, Newsnight's science correspondent, is now on it with four producers.

Susan, Sam and Pam plan the disco: ideally they want someone from the abattoirs, someone senior from MAFF and someone worried by the report. Pam tells them to focus on two questions: 'Who is responsible? – someone to be nasty to. And how did this situation arise?' Sam and Susan speculate on the symptomatic nature of the story. The abattoir report came out in 1995; it was probably kept quiet because MAFF knew it would have a hugely negative impact as it coincided with the BSE crisis. It was no doubt a case of news management. Sam reflects that news management on science and public health issues will intensify as coverage gets more dense with twenty-four-hour news. With more channels to fill, health-scare stories will increasingly be splashed all over, but they'll also drop rapidly off the agenda; more headlines, less analysis. Sam teases Susan: 'So the cause of twenty people dying of E. coli earlier this year was the Susan Wattses of this world!' MAFF, he implies, didn't want to face her ilk again over another food scare. Spin is at the root of this story.

3.10 p.m.: Susan and Sam huddle together to 'do a structure', planning how to weave the bits of film and interviews they've set in motion into an argument. They still haven't found anyone for the disco. Steve grunts, 'Yesterday's news tomorrow!,' a self-deprecating reversal of the slogan 'Tomorrow's news today': he's just learned that a local radio station they're talking to broke the story yesterday. 3.30 p.m.: Douglas Hogg gives a statement to the House of Commons on the suppression of the abattoir report, on why it was not 'formally published'. We watch on TV; the story is breaking as we watch. Hogg scapegoats someone called Swann, one of the authors of the report; he says Swann was alone in criticising abattoir standards, and that he refused to revise his position when required to do so. He implies Swann is not representative of the general view given by the inspectors in the report. Labour MP Gavin Strang rises to respond, damning the government for suppressing the report and for secrecy on such matters, and calling for an independent food standards agency. Susan and Sam note which MPs speak on which side.

6 p.m.: Jack is having trouble putting together the disco on E. coli. He can't get a Tory or anyone from MAFF, nor an abattoir owner to speak. No one's available. 6.45 p.m.: things are hotting up. Susan has now talked to Swann, who it turns out was chair of the committee behind the 1995 report, not just one of the authors. Swann flatly contradicts Hogg's statement to the House. Hogg isolated Swann, but Swann has told Susan that the entire committee supported his assessment; they were with him, not against him as Hogg alleged. Pam hears this and cautiously considers potential legal issues. Sam and Susan are intent on steaming ahead: they will interview Swann, who will accuse Hogg of misrepresentation. 7 p.m.: John Morrison, who I'm told is head of Daily News, wanders in. The programme still looks pretty unsteady, but Pam calls gaily, 'Everything's fine!' I ask Susan and Sam who Peter Bell is, since I thought he had taken over recently as head of Daily News. They say wryly that they don't know Bell – 'just another boss far

up the endless chain!' Susan says it's significant that they don't know who Bell is, implying they're unaware, on the floor, of the vast chain of command up through NCA, and don't really want to know.

8 p.m.: Jeremy Paxman walks in; he is mightily miffed because he had to give up going to 'the party of the year' – John Paul Getty Junior's birthday party – to do the programme. He says Peter Snow should have done it; all he had on was some yacht club dinner. 8.30 p.m.: Susan and Sam are in the edit, writing the script and recording Susan's voice-overs as they go, to which the VT editor cuts images, such as pictures of filthy cows' bums snatched from the *Nine*. There's an air of mild panic; the package is late. Professor Pennington has got lost on the way to Radio Nottingham to do a down-the-line interview; they've also lost the line to Nottingham. 9.15 p.m.: they get a line and do the interview; Pennington is very critical of Hogg and MAFF. 10.15 p.m.: the story continues to break: the news agencies are reporting that the Secretaries of State for Wales and Scotland are being openly critical of Hogg's handling of the situation. Excitement explodes: it's *Newsnight*'s holy grail, a government split! Pam sets Jack to find one of them to comment live. Peter Horrocks appears, saying it's unlikely they'll find either Secretary, so they should look for Scottish or Welsh MPs willing to criticise Hogg. 'Hector Munro?' 'No, he's crazy.'

10.30 p.m.: Transmission. They're still editing; a camera goes down in the studio; the taped second item is missing – it's found just in time to get on air. The first item is E. coli; the second a story on Roisin McAliskey pregnant in Holloway Prison, and the threat that her baby may be taken away – the issue is should this happen?; the newsbelt; and the final item is a hard-hitting filmed report on the rejection by Strathclyde's Labour city council of New Labour's public spending plans given that poverty is rife and public services – housing, health – in crisis.

11.30 p.m.: The 'post-mortem': Peter Horrocks warmly congratulates them all on a great programme. Both the E. coli story, 'a Cabinet row breaking', and the Glasgow film were really controversial, 'at the cutting edge of politics. We've been trying for two years to put a story together on a Labour council being critical of New Labour.' Peter says the Glasgow item reveals cracks opening up within Labour in the pre-election period, probably to do with Labour's greater confidence given the opinion polls. 'Perhaps we can do more such stories in the election lead-in.' I reflect that the programme was a perfect formula for *Newsnight*: sophisticated and telling stories on government/party splits, and twice over – a double whammy! But the ultimate accolade, as Peter and all note with pleasure, is that their treatment of the E. coli row has been picked up by the Press Association. *Newsnight* got there first. They have broken news.

Diary, 1997.

*

Notes for new producers: Mr Toad and Mr Snow

'These notes by Jeremy Paxman give an insight into what a presenter expects from you before conducting a discussion. Interviews are *Newsnight*'s bread and butter. By comparison with other programme areas they are cheap and easy to organise. It is the producer's job to provide presenters with a brief which explains the nature of the discussion. The ideal brief includes biographical information, a guide to the subject and an outline of how the interview might progress. For studio discussions, producers should engage prospective guests in conversation to discover areas of agreement and disagreement. The resultant brief might look a bit like this:

Transport policy discussion: The Transport Secretary this afternoon unveiled the latest set of road-building proposals. They include plans to turn the M25 into a fourteen-lane highway, to build another M1 along the existing route, and to double the width of the M62 trans-Pennine route. Environmental groups are outraged (PA 14.30) and British Rail are horrified that the scheme will be partly financed by cutting the remaining rail subsidy (see *Independent* article attached).

We have four guests:
– The Fat Controller. A lifelong British Rail employee, he has devoted his life to railways. Thinks that cutting subsidies will be the death knell of the rail system.
– Mr Toad. One of the best-known motorists in Britain. The motoring convictions which first brought him to public notice are now well behind him and he makes a comfortable living as the acceptable face of the AA.
– Eddie Stobart. One of the most familiar names in trucking. A self-made millionaire from Widnes, Stobart runs a fleet of three hundred lorries. Less well-known is that Eddie is short for Edwina.
– Jon Snow. Presents a little-known news programme on Channel 4. But his main interest in life is cycling. Holder of the coveted yellow anorak for lifetime achievement in the world of pedals, Snow is a forceful advocate of sustainable transport policies.

Suggested areas for discussion: 1) Governments have ducked out of a consistent transport policy for years. Controversial as it may be, isn't any plan an advance on no plan?
– Snow: Don't be ridiculous – this is an abdication of responsibility to the roads lobby.
– Stobart: Absolutely – and it's the right policy.

- Mr Toad: You can't buck the market – people love cars and need somewhere to drive them.
- Fat Controller: Abandoning the railways means more pollution, and it'll all end in tears.
. . . And so on, ideally for five or six suggested topics of discussion.

Some interviewees are unavailable beforehand because they are too important/drunk/ on a plane. But a brief ought to chart how a guest might be interrogated. A note on Achilles' heels is always welcome. Most presenters are grateful for any guidance, so arrange a time to talk the interview through, perhaps with you role playing. Pretending to be Gerald Kaufman need not scar you for life.'

Newsnight: The Essential Guide for New Staff, 1996.

*

Newsnight's Westminster focus was leavened with new currents in the later nineties. If impartiality remained the official doctrine of the newsroom, among some *Newsnight* journalists there were signs of a new, sophisticated self-awareness in relation to the doctrine as well as to their role in mediating public debate. A few spoke of a crisis in the discourse of impartiality, and even of its impossibility. The classic *Newsnight* philosophy – that the programme exists to hold politicians to account and centres on an antagonism to power – was reconceived. It was not possible to approach this from a position of impartiality; rather, the construction of critical perspectives necessarily involved opportunistic alliances with other interests and agendas – but knowingly. The implication was that judgements were being made, with an eye to public interests, about which was the bigger, the more important, target. The admission here of the interested, value-imbued and interpretive nature of journalism amounted to a new realism, an advance in the self-conception of journalists.

In addition, with cuts bringing more reliance on discussions, *Newsnight* journalists stressed their responsibility to orchestrate and enhance critical debate on major public issues. The aim was, by prior analysis of significant positions on any substantive topic, to represent those perspectives in the debate via judicious 'casting'. This was done in one of three ways. Most conventionally, debate brought together representatives of two or three of the main political parties – seen as the lazy option. A second mode was to cast discussions so as to stage the optimal challenge to politicians or the maximum of argumentative fireworks. The third, most progressive mode focused on identifying an advocate for a position that it was judged had been too little articulated in public, that was neglected or stood outside standard discursive circuits, and which therefore demanded to be put. Like impartiality, this new art of orchestrating and augmenting public debate rested on implicit claims to universality, but in a different way. By 'casting' debate Newsnight producers adopted the stance of detached observers with the authority to survey the total-ity of public discourse so as to identify significant positions and gaps. Crucially, this stance accepted the value-imbued nature of journalism, and brought this to bear in a provocative but purposeful way. At times, however, there was a risk of nihilism when the orchestration of debate was driven more by imperatives of provocation, fashion or drama than by other intellectual or representational values.

A related development in the mid nineties stemmed partly from manage-ment edict, partly from internal commitment. The principle was adopted that Newsnight should widen its representational circle so as to include a greater diversity of opinions and perspectives, including those from non-elite and marginalised groups. In producers' daily routines, conspicuous effort went into seeking more women, black and Asian and other non-standard spokes-people to take part in discussions. There were successes and failures. On several occasions I observed the severe problems faced by producers trying to find a 'poor person' or a female expert to take part in an item. This points to the limited social universe of Newsnight's contacts and sources and the blocks to widening representation, despite the avowed commitment to greater inclusion of under-represented groups. Indeed, the less admirable side of Newsnight cul-ture involved a continuing recourse to narrow contact lists in the worlds of politics, business, culture and science, a recourse tinged with excitement at the fleeting power exercised over celebrities and establishment figures, and so a default return to predictable and overexposed faces.

More successfully, a format developed for the 1997 election lead-in staged 'challenges' between politicians and experts on the one hand, and 'ordinary', engaged members of the public on the other, on major electoral issues such as jobs, education and health. As a rule this format produced more astute, informed and varied questioning of policy than any other pre-election pro-gramming. Often, it broke through the well-oiled rhetorical devices by which politicians fend off critical probing. By contrast, in a planning meeting during the election lead-in I observed rationalisations that led to decisions not to take on the politics of race, gay politics and women's politics in the coverage. When it was proposed to cover an issue from the perspective of black voters, the response was that black voters also vote for the main parties, don't they?, the implication being that there was no need to engage with their particular concerns. Both the commitment to wider representation and the capacity to deliver it were, then, halting.

*

'Casting' the poor: Newsnight's poverty item, March 1997

Newsnight's 10.30 a.m. meeting, two months before the general election. Paul, editor of the day, straddles a table surrounded by today's team of eight desk producers. Jeremy Paxman, the presenter, joins the meeting, which proceeds via collective speculation, led by Paul, on potential stories. The desk producers vie, coming up with stories and angles, injecting passion, humour or irony to enthuse their peers. Paul: 'It's a difficult day, unclear what focus we should take. We've got an Evan Davis film. The Grobbelaar football corruption story may break because the court judgement is due. What are the issues?' People respond: 'How widespread is corruption?' 'Increasing commercialisation of the game?' Paul: 'So the angle is: money has corrupted the game. Who shall we talk to?' 'A rep from the FA?' A groan: 'No suits.' 'You want a fan.' 'Nick Hornby?' 'He's terrible in interviews.' 'Not an MP – no MPs.' Jeremy says, 'I doubt corruption is that widespread. A more interesting angle would be that, compared to elsewhere and to other games – racing, whatever – British football's really pretty clean.' Discussion follows. Is this really a lead story? Only if there's a conviction: 'There'll be some drama in it then.'

Other stories are knocked around. Jeremy: 'What about this new C of E poverty initiative? Neither of the fucking parties do anything about poverty – Labour totally ignores it now.' Paul is keen. Jeremy says the figures show that 30 per cent of people are currently living in poverty equal to or greater than the poverty indices from any time this century. He suggests interviews with poor people speaking about their experience. Andy: 'You want something on how the two political traditions that used to care about poverty – one-nation Tory paternalism and Labour radicalism – are both in decline.' There's discussion of going to a city outside London to film poverty: Sheffield? Liverpool? 'No, not Liverpool – if you have that accent, half the audience turns off.' Collectively, they try out various lines: 'Only the Church cares about the poor now . . .'

They search for more stories. The newspapers lie in heaps; everyone is thumbing through, looking for stories to pick up or take in new directions. Paul points to something on German anti-nuclear protests, and they toss it around; the German movement, it seems, has been influenced by British environmental protests. Jeremy says mischievously, 'There's a lot of public sympathy for the road protestors, more for Fairmile than for Newbury – a good reason to attack them?' Alan sparks up: 'I'd like to do something on the cryptosporidium outbreak in the South-West. It's outrageous: the private water companies can't provide clean water.' Paul grimaces and moves on: 'There's a debate at the QE2 conference centre about whether opinion polls are a good thing.' Hilarity erupts over how awful pollsters are: 'They wear nylon socks!' The meeting ends. Producers disperse in twos and threes, hitting keyboards, manning phones. Today's stories will be poverty, the Grobbelaar verdict if guilty, a film on government online, and the German protest.

For poverty, reporter Robin Denselow and a producer are dispatched to Coventry to film. Paul and three others are 'casting' the poverty disco. Politicians from the three parties? There is great reluctance: it will be 'mortally boring'. Or an ex-Labour MP, a Militant sympathiser, now a member of Scargill's party, who is involved in direct action on poverty? He's known to be lively. They plan the graphics, 'serious stuff' with plenty of hard figures to bring 'facticity and edge', while the film may be 'fly-on-the-wall-ish'. They laugh awkwardly at the crudeness of having film of kids with rickets or TB. Paul returns from the 11 a.m. meeting with the editor saying ruefully that they have to use three MPs for the disco. In addition, they decide to have a senior churchman and someone to represent the poor, preferably a woman to balance the genders. The angle is decided: 'The politicians on both sides have forgotten the poor' and the aim is to pin them down.

I sit with Mike, a desk producer. He shows me round the online news system, which contains the Newsgathering prospects for the next day, week and month for both home and foreign. Each morning the producers run this stuff off and check key diary stories 'to see if there are any embargos that can be broken'. Mike continues that Newsnight's agenda is largely driven by what's provided by Newsgathering on this database, and by the press. He comments that they should originate more stories, but they tend not to because of cost. Stories from Newsgathering provide ready-made film to be re-edited, but viewers then risk seeing the same pictures as on the Six and Nine. I ask about the online contacts databases: are they shared between programmes? 'No,' he replies. 'Rudimentary security barriers prevent people crossing into other programmes' files, but you can get through if you want to.' The aim is to ensure that different programmes don't use the same contacts or sources, or the same people would keep turning up. Mike says the forward planning and preparation of stories at Newsnight is weak; he puts this down to falling budgets and an awareness that a story might not get to air. 'Newsnight has taken 7 per cent cuts each of the last two years. Five years ago we prepared five stories each day for a programme with three or four. Now we prepare three or four. It's on the edge; sometimes we're in danger of falling off air.' He bitterly criticises the poor administration in NCA, which has recently screwed up the new Stage 6 building by making it too small: 'They're a parasitical class and their existence means giant overheads are carried by the programmes, which undermines our journalism.'

A couple of hours in Paul asks the poverty team how the disco is going. Mike replies that they've activated their networks, as yet without results; the problem is that organisations working with the poor tend to be suspicious of the media. Tania comes off the phone from a bishop involved in the Church pressure group on poverty, who has agreed to appear, and who is keen to chastise the parties for their inaction on the 'forgotten 30 per cent', as he calls the poor. Tania then sits collecting information on poverty for the graphics package: poverty has grown faster in the UK than anywhere in Europe since 1979; one-quarter of all poor Europeans are British. She gathers statistics on the resurgence of the diseases of poverty, on the growing gap between rich and poor, sharing information with Jill and Mike as they build the argument. Jill responds with queries; she cautions that they'll have to tackle the tricky issue of defining poverty.

4.10 p.m.: The tannoy from Newsgathering announces that the Grobbelaar court case has collapsed; the jury couldn't reach a verdict. Paul considers whether the item can be salvaged: 'It's really just a news spot, isn't it?' 5.10 p.m.: The poverty team still hasn't managed to find a '30 per-center' to come on the programme. Nervously, they joke about finding a '45 per-center' instead, a woman who's articulate and sympathetic but comes from Middle England. I ask what the problem is finding someone poor. Sue says, 'It's always difficult to get hold of members of the deprived classes; they're often reluctant to speak to the media.' Tania jokes, 'They're so deprived they can't string two sentences together!' She says that in the country she comes from 'they simply abolished the welfare state at one stroke!', to which Jack responds, *sotto voce*, 'Only way to do it.' I suggest they try a group representing the unemployed. Mike says, 'The Claimants' Union! That's an idea.' We explain what the CU is to Jill, who hasn't heard of it; she is unenthusiastic.

6 p.m.: Time is getting short and they still haven't found a poor person to appear. Now they're down to trying personal contacts and friends. 7 p.m.: At last, haphazardly, Tania has found a woman for the disco. She's a divorced, disabled single-parent mother of four kids who says she knows all about living near the breadline. On the phone to her Tania gushes, 'Oh I wish you'd come on the programme and say all this! Someone needs to! Jeremy Paxman is lovely, he'll be gentle with you. We'll send a car to collect you and you'll get £50 for coming along,' and the woman agrees. Jeremy comes out of his room. Tania says, 'We've found you a wonderful woman for the poverty debate.' Jeremy: 'Oh great! Is she disabled, with a snotty child with running sores?' Tania, ignoring the sarcasm: 'Yes, she's in a wheelchair, very articulate actually – sounds rather middle-class. And she's bringing along a child for us to look after – can't afford the childcare!' They all smirk as it's so perfectly to formula – which is how they seem to experience the process, as 'cast' according to their needs for the debate. They continue with an ambiguous and self-parodic banter: 'We've had a poor person on before, haven't we?' 'Are you sure we haven't had this woman on before? She sounds vaguely familiar . . .'

Paul tells the poverty team with annoyance, 'The parties won't put up front-benchers!' This is a regular hazard, since *Newsnight* must compete with other outlets for the big political figures, and the prestige of the programme is perceived by them to turn on the star quality of the politicians and celebrities they can command. At present, for instance, Labour shadow minister Robin Cook is refusing to come on the programme due to an earlier clash; too much aggression can tip over into a feud – a technique by which the parties try to keep *Newsnight* in line.

I ask Jack about his team's German anti-nuclear protest story: what are the issues? He lays out several lines of analysis: conflict between south and north Germany, since nuclear power is made in the south and waste is dumped in the north; federal versus regional government, since many *Länder* rejected nuclear power but the federal government developed it; and a 'Nimby' dynamic, whereby locals near the site resent waste being buried in their back yard – an angle Jack relishes, waspishly accusing the activists of hypocrisy. He tells me they went for phone interviews, thinking they'd found people to cover the angles necessary for the argument. But when they did the interviews, the angles people were taking differed markedly from what they thought they'd say. 'We didn't want to hear it! We thought we could change what they were saying, shift it round closer to what we were looking for; but it didn't work! We often do this here – a kind of self-deception, trying to read into the interviewees what *we think* they should be saying. It's crazy.' All this self-critically, reflectively.

8.30 p.m.: I go with Jack to the editing suite; producer David, on loan from Radio 4's *World at One (WATO)*, is also on the item, as is editor Keith. David and Jack stage an argument about the relative value of TV and radio current affairs. Jack taunts that *WATO* has no impact: 'Only mums and old people listen.' David retorts that *Newsnight*'s audience is tiny – 1.1 million? *WATO*'s is 1.4! Jonny corrects him: at best *Newsnight* gets 1.5 million. David, venomous, accuses *Newsnight* of being trite, soundbite-driven, carried by pictures and pace rather than intelligent and sustained analysis, of being obsessed with Westminster and part of a 'dinner party set'. Keith gets on doggedly with the edit, drawing on VTs from the library for images.

10.30 p.m.: Transmission. I watch with the production team from the gallery as the programme goes out. In the poverty disco Lib Dem Simon Hughes is the only MP, when challenged by Jeremy, to make a straight policy offer: his party will put a 50 per cent income tax on those earning over £100,000 and will use it for income redistribution. It draws reactions in the gallery. Jack sneers, 'A Robin Hood! They're going to rob from the deserving rich and give to the indolent poor!' Mike retorts, 'Rubbish!' All are vituperative towards the Labour MP who, addressing Jeremy over the head of Maureen, the 'poor' individual facing him in the disco, talks of the 'dependency state' and uses the language of 'welfare to work' without citing its US origins.

In the German anti-nuclear protest item the Nimby angle is the main one structuring Jeremy's commentary. A guest expert dismisses two women protestors' arguments as dubious idealism that fails to deal with the 'technical' waste problem. Jeremy and he effortlessly belittle the protestors' case, via a collusive condescension. I am left to consider the fact that *Newsnight* almost failed to find a poor person to debate poverty – an indictment of its capacities to include the marginalised and extend the range of social experience that it represents. I muse too that at its best, the programme depends on a kind of reflexive debate between those making it, themselves representative of a range of social experience. Today I note a range of accents and nationalities.

Later, I look at a tape of the programme. What is plain is that any inadequacies of the studio debate are compensated for by the powerful film on Coventry, which both speaks for the 'poor' and allows them to speak. It has mini-narratives – an unemployed father who feeds his family on £40 a week; a health unit registering a rise in infant TB – and a discussion by articulate residents on a sink estate, who state baldly that they know poverty is not on the parties' agenda because there are 'few votes in poverty'. The studio debate is telling too. Jeremy gratuitously cuts across Simon Hughes to say, 'If you *have* a policy, given that you're unlikely to form a government,' and then, to Maureen, 'There's no chance of these guys [*the Lib Dems*] forming a government.' Maureen is formidably articulate. Her final statement, a paean to representation, says it all to the MPs and to *Newsnight*: 'If you want to know why your policies don't work, come to the people who'll tell you, the people at the brunt end of it. Consult us, meet us, talk to us. We're here, we're willing. We're not unable to tell you what the realities are. We *can* contribute.'

Diary, 1997.

*

Puerile anti-PC

A slow *Newsnight* afternoon, and producers Joe and Tim engage in banter. Tim: 'You can't use that woman! I'm using her for my disco. Hands off!' To which Joe responds, in a voice mimicking excerpts from a stupid viewer's letter, 'I'd like to congratulate you for using a woman in your item, and a one-legged, inarticulate black woman too!' As if to outdo him, Tim goes further: 'I'll have you know, this woman represents the black one-legged tarts' association!' They have ad libbed a nasty racist satire on *Newsnight*'s attempts to improve the representation of women, minority and disadvantaged groups, which they seem to see as PC gone mad. Schoolboy-like, they reveal their unease at being asked to deal with those outside their 'normal' social universe.

Diary, 1997.

*

427

In the aftermath of the 1997 election, following open criticism by Birt, senior management decreed that *Newsnight* must move away from its confrontational interview style to match the new, constructive political era heralded by New Labour's ascent to power. *Newsnight* was as much as charged with fostering the 'culture of contempt'. There was a renewed stress on cultural issues, a wider agenda, innovative graphics and sounds, and a new set. A revised Friday edition staged topical debate, aiming to diversify participants, but sometimes degenerated into an upmarket celebrity chat show. Within months, as it became apparent that there was no effective political opposition, the adversarial style was revived as *Newsnight*'s staff came to believe that their role was to hold this government to account. The revival was fuelled by the view that New Labour's spin machinery was the most effective yet encountered. *Newsnight* characteristically believed it had a unique ability, and responsibility, to pierce the spin and probe policies.

The changes at *Newsnight* in the later nineties indicate a shift in the register of BBC journalism towards a more plural, open and nuanced understanding of the social landscape, and of the potential for public debate. However imperfectly, *Newsnight* attempted to put into practice something approaching that reciprocity of perspectives envisaged in recent accounts of communicative democracy. At its best the new approach addressed the need to uncover and animate significant dissensus rather than to confirm consensus; it held the promise of a new kind of debate, transcending Oxford Union bombast and the sterile school-debating-society tendencies of the flagships. At its worst it verged on cynical staging. Despite progress, *Newsnight* had some distance to go in combating the discursive exclusion of minorities, the under-represented, and of non-mainstream politics.

*

Mediating difference: *Newsnight*'s Islam edition, 28 August 1998

I catch an extraordinary and prescient *Newsnight*. The programme is using current events – a new law intended to target foreign nationals conspiring to take terrorist actions abroad, the recent bombings of US embassies in East Africa which killed over two hundred people, retaliatory US strikes on Sudan and Afghanistan – to construct a programme on the question of Islam. The focus is national and global. Kirsty Wark, presenter, opens with an extended 'tease': with the end of the Cold War, is the world more secure? Or is it heading for escalating violence caused by a clash of civilisations between Islam and the West? Does the concept of jihad, holy war, lead irrevocably to

428

terrorism and war? Or does the media's concentration on the actions of extremists make it impossible to see Islam in a more balanced way?

She introduces a satellite feed to Professor Samuel Huntington, author of *The Clash of Civilisations*. Huntington says conflict with Islam is highly probable, and provides reasons why. Kirsty pursues issues ignored by Huntington: isn't the intellectual heart of the conflict in Afghanistan, and hasn't American foreign policy towards Afghanistan, Saudi Arabia and Israel played a large part in fuelling the conflict? Is Islam the new enemy for the US, and isn't the failure on both sides, each misunderstanding the other? Huntington concedes the last point, speaking of American ignorance of the achievements of Islamic civilisation, and adding that it's equally clear that Muslims don't understand the West.

The programme shifts to a film by Mark Urban looking at reactions to the new law, with shots of protests by Islamic youth, followers of jihad, outside the US Embassy in London. Urban says, 'Freedom of speech has made London a magnet for Middle Eastern refugees.' The law will make it possible to prosecute Middle Eastern groups who may be using the UK to plan terrorist acts. He interviews a leading Islamist, who says such groups in Britain will go underground. An Arab journalist argues for more restriction on freedom of speech, particularly incitement to violence.

Kirsty opens what will be the heart of the programme: a studio discussion with two young Muslim intellectuals, representatives of different tendencies within British Islam. Huntington looms from a huge screen behind them. The man, Anjem Choudary, discourses on the misunderstanding of Islam in the West. He distinguishes between 'two struggles': an ideological and political struggle to be waged in all the countries of the world, to bring the people to divine law; and a military struggle which involves the use of violence, in which Muslims are impelled to liberate their lands from occupation, as in Palestine, Kashmir and Kosovo. Muslims, he says, are obliged by the Koran to engage in both these struggles. Huntington comments that these remarks exemplify just what he has written. Kirsty clarifies Choudary's statement, adding that some people 'would be horrified to hear you say that violence is legitimate'.

She turns to the young woman, Ahoda Moorjani. Eloquently, Moorjani is at pains to give another account of Islam. The Koran, she says, does not condone any act of terrorism or violence, although it does state that Muslims have a right to defend themselves. She explains that jihad occurs on two levels: the 'internal jihad', the battle within ourselves against our lower desires; and the 'external jihad', the defence of one's religion and culture. She insistently refuses the view that the Koran supports armed struggle. Kirsty remains cool, facilitative; her interlocutors address her rather than one another. The low-key studio atmosphere is nonetheless electric: *Newsnight* has staged a rare revelation into conflicts within Islam and, three years before 9/11, has witnessed a warning – an astonishing public rationalisation of the case for violent struggle.

Kirsty turns again to Huntington who, in an understated but inflammatory way, comments: 'There are twenty inter-civilisational wars going on in the world today, and fifteen of those involve Muslims fighting non-Muslims – 75 per cent for 20 per cent of the world's population. At this point in history Islam is clearly a militant and often a violent civilisation.' An unknown young British Muslim woman, Moorjani has been positioned by the programme as an alternative voice both to Huntington's dangerous and reductive American fatalism and to Choudary's apologia for violence. With poise and intelligence she shoulders the challenge. It is intensely moving. Moorjani: 'I have to take issue with Professor Huntington's analysis. How do we define Islam? There are many different interpretations of Islam.' She develops an astute critique of Huntington on Afghanistan, arguing that this is no Islamic war but a war caused by resistance to the Soviet Union's invasion of Afghanistan. She cautions against loose notions of Islamic fundamentalism or extremism, which fail to differentiate between distinct histories and agendas within Islam.

Kirsty introduces another film, by Lise Doucet, on Bradford. The premise: has one of the UK's oldest and largest Muslim communities found an accommodation with western secular culture? Bradford, says Doucet, is a 'touchstone for Britain's evolving cultural identity and a barometer of Islamic sensitivity. When they burned The Satanic Verses in Bradford, an explosion of rage and solidarity with Muslims worldwide, Muslims in Pakistan followed their lead.' The film offers rare insight into the city's 70,000 Muslims, some of whom came to Britain fifty years ago. There are images of prayers in the mosque, and cogent reflections by young people on the experience of being British and Muslim. A community leader explains sternly that a letter has been sent to Blair criticising the government for supporting US aggression in Sudan and Afghanistan.

Weaving between film and studio, this Newsnight has found the means to build a fragile bridge between the mainstream media and Muslim communities and intellectuals, to air perspectives likely never before to have been brought into juxtaposition on a mass channel, to explore rising tensions within British Islam and between the Islamic world and American and British foreign policies – that is, to voice and consider incommensurable perspectives on religious and cultural difference that will soon have inconceivably violent and globally destabilising repercussions.

Diary, 1998.

*

A Partial Art: Documentary

If the BBC's journalism only intermittently met the democratic challenge of diversifying the political, ideological and cultural currents represented in its programming, the corporation's documentary television output was less inhibited, rising to the challenge in a variety of ways. The BBC was not alone in mining this rich seam, and the mid nineties were dubbed a 'golden age of documentaries'.[30] New types developed: the long-form series or docu-soap, and fast on its heels, American-style reality programming. The feature-length documentary took on new cinematic life. The advent of digital video and micro-cameras reduced costs and made filming more flexible than ever, broadening documentary's range of subjects.

Three features of documentary were felt to underlie its success. First, the dominance of narrative. The concept of the 'story' became ubiquitous among producers to the point of obsession: 'getting the story right' and 'finding strong characters' were prime concerns. Second, the filmic qualities of documentary, in which the heightened, expressive or exploratory use of visuals and sound can play a key part. As throughout the history of the genre, documentary combined its authoritative realisms with occasional formal experiment; at this time, in some of the output, it was the most fertile of all the genres in fostering aesthetic innovation. Third, documentary allows an enlivening, individual perspective on material, in contrast to the impartiality and balance required of news and current affairs. Documentary's expressive range offered an alternative audience address, one that responded to the sense of fatigue attached to impartiality.

From the mid nineties British television was overwhelmed by the popularity of the rapidly ramifying forms of documentary. Those BBC departments responsible for the output, including Documentaries and History and Bristol Features, enjoyed a period of enormous bouyancy and confidence, overseeing a proliferation of sub-genres in several inventive directions. The confidence stemmed from their widely acknowledged successes, shown in ratings and awards, at both ends of the output: popular, as in prime-time BBC1 docu-soaps like Children's Hospital, Animal Hospital, Driving School, Airport and Hotel; and high-end, as shown by strands such as BBC2's Modern Times and Storyville, serials like The System, The House, Breaking Point, The Gulf War and The Death of Yugoslavia, and history series including The Nazis: A Warning From History, People's Century and Cold War.

As in its drama output, but more so, BBC documentary showed contradictory tendencies: both innovation and increased genericism. The commissioning mentality reflected in the tariff-based programme funding model, in response to heightened competition and budget squeezes, targeted popular documentary and factual entertainment, genres that delivered more audience, more reliably, for less cost. Driving School drew 12 million viewers to BBC1; and where serious drama might cost £600,000 an hour, high-end documentary cost £130,000 and docu-soaps the same or less. Compounded by the production departments' hunger for commissions to fund their staffing, this logic led to an explosion of populist programming – docu-soaps, leisure and lifestyle programmes, game shows – and to escalating hybridisation of these genres, as well as imitation of formats across channels. The nadir was when, in 1998, BBC1 and ITV screened the clones *Neighbours at War* and *Neighbours from Hell* one hour apart. Previously found on BBC2, Channel 4 and in daytime, factual entertainment rapidly colonised the prime-time schedules of BBC1 and ITV.

The proliferation of documentary sub-genres represented an unprecedented diversification. But the sub-genres themselves exhibited both standardisation, shown not only in formulaic docu-soaps but in some high-end documentaries, and a strong presence of innovative and occasionally experimental work. The coexistence of generic and innovative tendencies was particularly striking in the intensely competitive dynamics operating between key strands on BBC2 and Channel 4, *Modern Times* against *Cutting Edge*, *Storyville* against *True Stories*.

The departments making documentaries were at this time the sole areas in BBC production functioning well in organisational terms in supporting creativity. In Documentaries, in a remarkable exception to the rule of centralised commissioning, power lay with the executive producers, some of them overseeing strands – BBC1's *Inside Story*, BBC2's *Modern Times* – others one-off series. Each ran a small team, and they were in competition with one another, making relations uneasy. The executive producers enjoyed substantial autonomy in commissioning, drawing on both in-house and independent film-makers. They benefited from trusting relations with the controllers, who looked to them for their expertise, for cultivating relations with talent, and for quality control over the films being made. At the BBC, the success of docu-soaps triggered fierce competition for commissions among departments, including Science and the Community Programme Unit, as well as from the independents. But serious forms also continued to be made. At ITV, in contrast, the rise of popular factual was matched by a sharp decline in serious documentary; the output of the flagship *Network First* strand halved between 1995 and 1997, and the strand ended soon after.[31] A strange effect of hybridisation was the tendency for increasing aesthetic equivalence – for a similar look, feel and pace to cross between the genres.

*

Red matter

8.30 p.m., a weekday: BBCI has the docu-soap *Children's Hospital*, BBC2 the zany cookery show *Two Fat Ladies*. I switch from the former, focused on a heart operation, a sustained sequence in which internal organs are handled by a surgeon and which zooms in on visceral material, so that red, bloody organic matter fills the screen, to the latter, in which a fresh sauce is being prepared in close-up, with tomatoes pulped by plump hands and poured into a basin, so that red organic matter splatters and burbles in the bowl. I zap between them. The imagery is the same – a sensual viscerality. Red splattering matter fills the screen.

Diary, 1997.

*

Dirty gritty realist things

The ping-pong imitation ruling the schedules bridges documentaries and fiction. Tonight late on BBC2 I catch the drama *The Cops*, with its dirty, gritty realism and grey, bleached-out palette. I switch to Channel 4 where *Staying Lost*, a low-cost documentary, is playing. The two not only have similar subject matter – the seamy side of Northern poverty; drug cultures, their criminal overspill and human cost – but an uncannily similar visual style. Unsteady camera; dark and grimy, flat colours. A new, shared and ambiguous kind of realism.

Diary, 1999.

*

Tasty and nice and easy

'I'm exec-ing a series called *Manchester Stories*, the follow-up to *Soho Stories*. I'm iffy about it, making twenty-four half-hour programmes in nine months. It was "We've done *Soho Stories*, where next?" and Manchester was the happening place. We employ multiskilled APs to film, and someone then moulds it into good stories, using it like plasticine to make it into something in the cutting room.'

GB: 'It raises the formula-spinning mode of commissioning. There's a lot of carping about the imitation effect between *Cutting Edge* and *Modern Times*, people chasing similar kinds of film . . .'

'Oh God, yes. We're very guilty of making the same thing over and over. It's the system. If something works they want more. In commissioning meetings it's, "I want more of *X Cars*, but without the cars," "I want more of *Children's Hospital*, but no hospitals." More of the same, but different. *Soho Stories* was new and clever. And departmentally, these series are useful because they're a solid amount of work, a training ground, they get good figures – who's going to argue with that? On the other hand they're absolutely generic, completely formulaic, however well they're made. And there's a certain voyeurism. An awful lot of TV is middle ground, middle England, and that's what gets commissioned. Most of it doesn't involve any serious or fresh analysis. It creates strong characters and narrative, and you just hope you hit the bulls-eye. It's "us" looking at "them" and making it very palatable, bite size chunks – tasty and nice and easy. What gets me is the quantity of it all. The risk is that it pushes out all sense of innovation.'

Executive producer, BBC Documentaries, 1997.

*

Docusoapia

As the concept of factual entertainment took hold, three developments sig-nalled its ascendance on all channels. They indicate the power of inter-generic hybridisation across these genres. One was the rapid expansion of lifestyle and leisure programming evident in the reinvention of advice and magazine shows in traditional areas: cookery, gardening, home decoration, antiques, hobbies, fashion, holidays and travel. Another was the creation of spin-off sub-genres by mixing these shows with 'challenge', makeover, quiz, or celebrity formats on the same topics. These sub-genres represented a new inter-generic space, part entertainment, part factual, part education. As the original craze for docu-soaps waned, they offered the controllers another relatively cheap and reliable replacement: long-run series that could be 'stripped across the schedule' in prime time.

The third major trend was the rise, following American formats, of cheap reality programming based on CCTV, amateur footage or reconstructions, usually on a crime, law or medical theme. From the quasi-reality show *Crimewatch UK* to *999* and *X Cars*, from courtroom relays and police reconstruc-tions to the docu-soap-like coverage of eccentric lifestyles, this expanding way of filling the schedules toyed with the status of serious documentary or current affairs. It appeared to deliver public sphere functions, for example by giving inside views of closed legal or medical institutions. But these were counter-balanced by the genre's voyeuristic, intrusive and prurient qualities, as well as by its contributions to generating extremes of exhibitionism in its willing participants. In these shows, investigative journalism and docu-soap were evoked, pastiched and crossed with confessional television. One source of the intertextual power of reality television was its resonance with several epiphanic events in public consciousness caught on video footage – Rodney King's beating by the Los Angeles police, the kidnapping of James Bulger, the OJ Simpson motorway chase and televised murder trial. As digital techniques brought the veracity of visual images into question, the apparently banal truthfulness, the indexical and evidential status of reality footage, offered a reassuring but illusory sense of being in unmediated contact with the world. Reality television extended the territory occupied by crime and medical shows into 'real-life' drama-documentaries: as the saying went, 'documentary is the new drama'.[32]

By the end of the nineties these trends had spawned the entirely constructed 'reality' genre of group-dynamic game show epitomised by *Big Brother*, *Castaway*, *Survivor* and, at its most debased, *Temptation Island* and *The Villa*. In these shows, quasi-sociological insights drawn from a vacuous behaviourism were added to the spurious claims of reality television; and with its 'interactive' elements, *Big Brother* was hailed as a breakthrough by the television industry. Reality television, whether 'social' game show or CCTV fest, lost any pretence to narrative art. *Big Brother*'s dramatic qualities were the narrative equivalent of watching paint dry. But the vast ratings drew the BBC to join Channel 4, ITV and Sky One in screening the genre. Given their unpalatable underbelly, the corporation could reconcile itself to reality shows only by smearing them with informative or educational veneers; and while the obsession with developing docu-soaps and reality shows was a measure of the 'enterprising' spirit unleashed inside the BBC, they could be excused as cross-subsidising more expensive and serious documentaries.

It was popular factual formats that provided the basis for the growth of a number of powerful independents selling to the BBC. While it was commonly held that the independents' success derived from entrepreneurial acumen, in contrast to what were seen as the sluggish BBC production departments, in reality many of the independents were led by ex-BBC producers. But a more sinister development erupted in this same period, highlighting the tenuous nature of documentary's truth claims in the age of reality television. In 1998, an unprecedented fakery crisis rocked British television when it transpired that an ITV documentary made by Carlton, *The Connection*, was falsified. It was matched by revelations that talk shows on both BBC1 and ITV had used fake guests, that one Channel 4 documentary contained staged scenes while another was a hoax, and that a woman who was secretly filmed when injured in a road accident for a 'live emergency' show was to sue the production company for invasion of privacy.[33] The regulator fined Carlton £2 million, criticising the duplicities of the production team and the company's culture, and the BBC issued revised Producer Guidelines, stipulating thorough research and tougher codes for filmed reconstructions. The rise of such unethical practices can be traced to a potent mix of factors: a blurring in documentary of the boundary between fact and fiction, as well as casualisation, the decline in training, rampant competition and falling budgets. But for one critic the crisis pointed to history: 'A decade of editorial loosening, cost-cutting and ratings-chasing in British television is being challenged. The ITC has issued a long-distance rebuke to Thatcherism' for the deregulation that resulted in a climate of unfettered sensationalism.[34]

If The Connection represented its degradation, less obvious was the erosion of documentary's ability to offer subtle insight into its subjects due to the banalisation of the genre. For docu-soaps, which initially appeared to give comedic voice to non-elite groups, became through sheer repetition a burlesque in which we laughed at, rather than with, its quaint examples of humanity.

*

Criminal lottery

'Crimewatch UK's policemen are well-polished middle managers – you can barely see them through the haze of public relations. The traditional TV policeman is shabby, dysfunctional and impassioned. He takes a drink or two. (He can currently be found in The Vice, where Ken Stott and Anna Chancellor have somehow made watchable drama out of a sorry stock of cop clichés). Abrasive slob or Crimewatch's suited businessman? People watching the fine documentary series Mersey Blues will have seen scores of policemen not sure which of these TV roles to take up. A couple of them have turned to corruption ("It's the contradictory imagery, Guv") . . . On Crimewatch, for all the suits, there is still a tension between the police and the assured, handsome broadcasters. There is an edginess, perhaps laced with class suspicions; and a suggestion that Nick Ross could at any moment be banged up on the charge of being a soft, lippy ponce. But out of this confusion comes calm. We are led to believe that the BBC and the police have got everything in hand . . . The programme suggests shared village values, and a fiercely powerful network of amateur informers. Famously, at the end of each show, Ross invites his viewers not to have nightmares. And throughout you sense his intelligent concern at finding a balance between prurience and responsibility, empathy and voyeurism . . . And we watch it as a kind of criminal lottery. Like the National Lottery, you can be confident that the programme will change someone's life. And like the *Lottery* programme, it is hard to give up hope that the programme's interactive element will somehow embrace you. When, in a reconstruction ("Shut up, or I'll have to kill you!"), they tell of a witness who has yet to come forward, and Nick Ross says: "Was that you?," it doesn't matter that the person being sought is the wrong age and sex. You still think: was I there? And then it's back to the studio to hear of "a number of sightings", "a tremendous response", and see a room full of policemen wearing make-up.'

Ian Parker, 1999.

*

Trading bullshit for Nazi gold

'In the early-evening soaps, like *Animal Hospital*, you learn a lot – in *Animal Hospital* about veterinary care, in *Children's Hospital* about paediatrics and Great Ormond Street. We're careful to make it into intelligent popular programming, with educational stuff you won't find in prime time on ITV. *X Cars*, our biggest hit this year, had public safety info about cars and road procedure, whereas ITV's *Police Camera Action* was all high-speed car chases. Well, we had high-speed chases too, but we had *Crimewatch*-type public service commentary as well . . .'

GB: [*laughing*] 'Your face! I'm confronted with a somewhat sceptical face . . .'

'Because it's bullshit! Actually, we do all that to keep the governors happy. We were trying to make very popular programmes and compete with the other side. But these shows also act as valuable commissioning loss-leaders; they give me a lever to get through more serious stuff. Right now we're making a special on Nazi gold. It's inves-tigative, a dynamite story, front-page stuff, and very expensive to make. It's one of those things that might wither on the vine in this new BBC. Well, *X Cars* got me the money to do it. Likewise, two years ago, *Children's Hospital* got me the money for the Solzhenitsyn piece. They were reluctant to give me the money this year, but I got it, and the show will bring huge profile. It's a trade-off; it really is trading.'

Senior executive, BBC Documentaries, 1996.

*

Making fun of the lumpen proles

'There's no such thing as ideas-led documentary any more. It's all "stories" out there, in both the BBC and Channel 4. Channel 4 will do *Doctor in Trouble*, you know: true story, doctor with a ten-year waiting list, can't cope, we follow him around, fly-on-the-wall. Molly Dineen did it with Tony Blair last night. There's been a narrativisation of documentary. That's the cost of keeping docs in prime-time. It was also the cost of putting on covertly socially critical docs in the eighties. You couldn't say the Tories were bastards; what you could show was people in grinding poverty or difficult circumstances who'd lost control of their lives. You got a lot of sad stuff like that which was meant to point the finger not at the feckless poor but at an uncaring government. And it was relatively successful. But the film-makers also discovered how to make stories out of the lumpen proletariat, the mainstay of current documentary. Maybe it's documentary coming clean about looking down your nose at the proletariat. Now you just make fun of them.'

Independent documentary producer, 1997.

*

The denial of complexity

'People have been inventing things in documentaries for years. Robert Flaherty, the American documentary pioneer, was also a pioneer of staging them. In *Man of Aran* he wanted to see the islanders hunting basking sharks. Unfortunately this tradition had died out – so he taught them how to do it. Documentary has never been a literal medium. It has always valued meaning more than facts. As a documentary-maker someone pays you to find out about your subject in great and unusual detail and to interpret that experience for your audience. It's a moral responsibility.

'In 1990, the government decided that winning an ITV franchise shouldn't depend on a sizeable reputation but on a sizeable cheque. Suddenly all the challenging ITV documentaries began to disappear. As gold fever led to a land-grab for ratings, big audiences weren't a bonus – they were a necessity. Then one day someone invented the docu-soap, bastard child of the "important" documentary. One of my favourites is *Vets in Practice*, a world in which everything's for the best. The controller must have registered the audience figures with satisfaction: eight million for a fraction of the price of a sitcom. What's wrong with this kind of television is not that it's popular. It's the way it's made. There's no time and no point in doing research. Any relationship between producer and subject is impossible. A producer told me that accurate portrayals were not part of the ethos. The whole exercise was the avoidance of ambiguity, the denial of complexity. It's hard not to see this approach as fundamentally dishonest – more so than Flaherty's fabrications. But docu-soap's real crime is that a generation of film-makers has been weaned on it. They're trained to find subjects that conform to middlebrow sensibilities, as though storylining *Neighbours*. No wonder there's a crisis in this industry.'

Peter Dale, 2000.

438

*

Accessing Truths

Docu-soaps offered only ersatz participation to those whose lives were being filmed. It was left to one small outfit within the corporation, known colloquially as the 'conscience of the BBC', to pursue the politics of presence in television. The Community Programme Unit, founded in 1973 in the mould of Canadian, American and British experiments in access cable television, invited individuals and groups to make films about their lives, opinions and passions under their own editorial control, with BBC support. One principle guided the CPU's work: 'sharing representational power', that is, enabling people to represent themselves.[35] In pursuit of diversity, the focus was primarily on those little known, dissenting or excluded perspectives that answered back to received views or that lay outside television's standard representations.

The CPU's natural territory was the point-of-view documentary. As docu-soaps and other low budget forms took off, and given its long experience of access production and digital technologies, the unit's potential in the stringent competitive climate of the later nineties should have been great. Its established strands *Open Space*, *Video Diaries* and *Video Nation* continued to offer remarkable insights via self-portraits by individuals from diverse walks of life, extending the representational range of British television in unparalleled ways. At the heart of the CPU's output was the shock of recognition, of truth, afforded by the unmediated, rough and real qualities of its filmic self-representations; and the grain of these films, resisting television's converging aesthetics, made such shock all the more powerful and necessary.

As low-cost, hand-held, point-of-view DV documentary expanded across the schedules – the avant-garde end of the reality-television spectrum – the CPU's output remained exemplary and cutting edge. But in the BBC of the mid nineties, under the grip of entrepreneurial values in which nothing that was not competitive was accorded significance, the CPU was unfashionable. Its status was low, its budgets tiny and, while apparently valued, it gained scant attention from the controllers. Thrust unprotected into the internal market, the CPU was forced to compete for commissions to fund its staffing and resources. The effect was to encourage it to head for the centre-ground of programming with proposals for run-of-the-mill docu-soaps or quirky spin-offs, rather than to expand its unique varieties of access television, far more developed than on rival channels. Innovation was not absent, however, as shown by series like *Israel Shorts* and *Living with the Enemy*, the latter a precursor of the later *Wife*

Swap-style formats; and some years after, the influence of the CPU can be gleaned in debased form in the BBC1 format, *One Life*. But in the nineties, the CPU had an increasingly fragile existence; it suffered successive rationalisations. Contradicting its importance to the BBC, the department's structural autonomy ended in 1998 when it lost its head and became a subsidiary of Documentaries. In 2000, it was further subsumed within the giant Factual and Learning Group. Despite the potency and viability of its films, the CPU was scandalously undervalued. Ironically, and pointing to the inversion of the BBC's values in the nineties, this most 'public service' of production departments was stigmatised by that very fact.

*

Natalie's baby

Natalie, who became pregnant at fourteen, has filmed a *Teenage Diary* over the months before and after her baby's birth. Both challenging and confirming stereotypes, her film gives her particular view of teenage motherhood. It opens with stepfather Phil criticising Natalie in the family kitchen: 'Under sixteen you shouldn't be having a baby. I don't know how many times I've told you!' Natalie: 'You think I should have got rid of it – killed a little life? It was an accident!' Phil: 'You should be at work.' Natalie: 'Where am I going to get a job? I ought to be at home with my baby.' Cut to the title, 'Natalie's baby,' over a bleak outside shot. Natalie alone, thoughtfully, standing by a baby's cot: 'I was expecting lots of abuse from people. They haven't, though there are a few people, you know: "You shouldn't be having a baby at your age!" The thing people don't seem to understand is: all the girls I know are sleeping with their boyfriends. I had an accident. But there's a responsibility there, and I realise that. People should at least admire the fact that I'm taking on the responsibility, not just for a few months but for the rest of my life . . . Keith and I had been together for some time when we decided we wanted to sleep together. Mum wasn't happy, but she took me to the doctor to ask for the pill. My doctor flatly refused, saying it was illegal to have sex at fourteen . . . From the moment I knew I was pregnant, there was a bond between me and my baby. I never considered having an abortion, although Mum and Keith said they'd support me whatever I wanted to do . . . My sister Sam lived in a council flat nearby with her two-year old son Nicholas. She had him at seventeen and had a rough time being on her own with a baby.' Natalie films an exchange with Sam: 'Do you find it difficult with Nicholas now?' Sam: 'He's calmed down a bit . . .' 'How about coping on the money you get?' 'It's difficult. It's not enough money to go around, to pay your bills and shopping.'

Later Natalie, alone to camera, says she didn't want to turn out like her sister; she wanted to be a child psychologist. Now she realises she won't be. Arguments break out between Keith and her mum and stepfather over Keith's dog. Keith and Natalie go to live in one room of Sam's damp and dilapidated flat. The birth arrives; Natalie is fine and bonds with baby Christopher. They return to Sam's flat. Keith is out a lot. Natalie gets increasingly tired and isolated. The flat is cold. Her mum offers to have her move back home. She refuses. Natalie's relationship with Keith deteriorates. She determines to get out in the day and visits a centre for teenage mothers. With her mum's help, she and Keith share a crazy teenage night out with friends. The dog is messing all over Sam's flat; Sam wants Keith and the dog to leave. Natalie is threatened with intervention by the social services. She and the baby move back to live with her mother. When she is sixteen, she says, she will be able to get a council flat and live with Keith as a proper family, as she wants.

Natalie has made a non-sensational portrait of the stigma, the hardships and small pleasures of teen motherhood, of the kindness of female kin, of dealing with fate's hand and poverty with self-respect and fortitude. In its highly personal, clumsy directness, her film also varies the tone of documentary, de-naturalising the relentlessly smooth, desensitising surfaces of populist factual television.

'Natalie's baby', BBC2, 1998.

*

Autonomy, Aesthetics, Invention

If the access films of the CPU expanded the diversity of voice on British television, the high end of BBC documentary made a different contribution to diversity in the later nineties by cultivating documentary as art. The output continued to mine three dominant traditions. The first, in the mould of *The World At War*, was the analytical series that emulated the objective journalistic stance of current affairs. Often employing the methods of oral history, these series provided increasingly complex and multi-stranded accounts, as in *The Gulf War*, *The Death of Yugoslavia*, *People's Century*, *The Nazis* and *Provos*. *The Gulf War* made news by offering, just five years after the events, an analysis of the propaganda behind the war and why it was fought. The second tradition, in the lineage of Kenneth Clark's *Civilisation*, Jacob Bronowski's *The Ascent of Man* and David Attenborough's natural history programmes, was the series hung on the authority of an expert presenter. Examples were Robert Winston's *The Human Body* and Attenborough's *The Life of Birds*. These most costly and prestigious series, however, sometimes bore the marks of international co-production in their dilute intellectual content and coffee-table appeal.

It was the third major category, observational documentary, fuelled since the sixties by repeated innovations in lightweight film technologies, which saw the most movement. The expansion of docu-soaps and reality television took the lead from earlier developments, generating the 'intimate fly-on-the-wall' film in the mould of Paul Watson's 'The Family' and the 'crisis' film focused on the drama of extreme events.[36] The Grierson tradition of authored, sociologically informed observational documentaries continued strong. The BBC2 series Nurses, for example, in its wilfully slow-paced portrait of the training of a cohort of Newcastle student nurses dissected the parlous state of the National Health Service at the end of eighteen years of Conservative rule, a parable for the underfunded neglect of Britain's welfare state.

But observational documentary also saw energetic innovation. In a direct line of descent from Roger Graef's ground-breaking series Police, a new sub-genre scrutinised the workings of powerful institutions from within: 'power fly-on-the-wall'. By turns serious social criticism and scurrilous gossip, series such as True Brits on the diplomatic service, The House on the Royal Opera House and The System on the Department of Social Security illuminated via telling micro-portraits the macro-politics of power in Britain. As significantly, observational documentary in this period fostered a reinvigoration of documentary poetics. The BBC2 strand Modern Times, its editorial autonomy sustained by the delegation of commissioning powers, focused on 'distinctive', 'authored' films and encouraged film-makers to take creative risks. A striking result was to unleash aesthetic experimentation: a definitive element in the history of the genre, but one often inhibited by documentary's incorporation into televisual realism. Another effect was to generate forays into reflexive film-making in which, in the manner of cinéma-vérité, the film-maker undermines the codes of narrative objectivity by putting herself in the film and revealing the artifice in its production.

*

Conversation and authorship: running Modern Times

'The joy of being a strand editor is that I have a great deal of flexibility. In a huge organisation with commissioning power concentrated at the top, this is the one bit where they delegate it. A lot of my role is conversations with film-makers. Often I commit to a film without having agreed a definite idea; explaining lets them discover whether they're really keen. Once they're making the film, I see my job as someone they feel they've got to talk to. Some people show you films close to how they want it to go out;

others show me it in a complete mess. I don't just see the film at the end.'

GB: 'It feels as if Documentaries is more *auteur*-ish than other places in the BBC; I mean Drama is too, but here there's a smaller team, it's pared down.'

'It is *auteur*-ish. When documentarists direct drama, the surprise is how much control they lose. They have to worry about the producer, writer, actors – it's a heavier apparatus. Here we encourage authorship. I want people to come up with something distinctive, to find a signature; to carve out something that means their films are films that only they could have made.'

Stephen Lambert, editor of Modern Times, BBC Documentaries, 1997.

*

Emblematic of the experimental aesthetic, Lucy Blakstad's 'Lido' was a sensuous exploration, via a portrait of a south London open-air swimming pool, of the texture of everyday life in cosmopolitan Britain. In the film Blakstad allowed her presence to be glimpsed at the margins, responding to or initiating dialogue. Noise and action were periodically suspended, spliced with slow-motion sequences of water splashing, bodies swimming, heat rising, balls bouncing, the images underpinned by a pulsing minimalist soundtrack – the whole evoking the qualities of intensely co-present, sun-saturated urban experience. It was Seurat's *Bathers at Asnières* re-worked for Britain today.

A number of inventive films deployed the new stylistics to achieve a new engagement with their subjects, wringing art and politics out of inauspicious material. As though informed by the latest thinking in academic social anthropology, they traced the 'social life of things' across global and national landscapes, noticed formerly hidden or unnoticed areas of life, tracked social hierarchies and testified to alternative viewpoints and modes of experience.[37] *The System* was a multifaceted, aesthetically experimental account of the state benefits system and its symbol, the giro cheque, from all sides – clients, operatives and political masters. The series probed equally the ugly *hauteur* of those civil servants charged with finding cuts in the escalating budgets of the welfare state by the brittle minister, Peter Lilley, and the desperation and pathos of the recipients, framed by the prison-like screens of the benefits office. It revelled in revelatory asymmetries, swinging between Whitehall grandeur and Sheffield's and Glasgow's poorest. It blasted us with understated insight: £47.90 as the basic income support deemed sufficient by the Conservative government to support one adult for one week; 20 per cent of Britons as dependent on benefits, caught in the poverty trap. Apparently and ambiguously empathic, it peeled back the minister's dilemmas, failed policies and contradictions. All of this was augmented by the use of rhythmic and repetitive music and images of the bureaucracy of care to break the flow and pace the tale: the clatter of millions of giros being printed; the Hogarthian faces of the underclass; row upon vast row of storage racks packed with claimants' files. The stylisation lifted The System into a new aesthetic space, reflective, purposefully complex and resisting easy judgement.

'Mange tout' used the device of the luxury vegetable to trace the ruthlessly exploitative web spun between the Tesco supermarket chain, its client supplier farm in Zimbabwe, and its customers in the guise of a Home Counties dinner party. Punctuated with beautifully composed images of the laboured perfection of the mange tout, enriched by its portrayal in their own words of the existential dilemmas of two farm workers, and a study in the mutual imagination by Zimbabwean rural poor and British financiers of each other's lives, the film gave as cogent, humanising and haunting an account of the abstractions of global capitalism as can be found in any medium. These were films on contemporary power and the effects of power, eschewing polemic and dry didacticism and embracing visual and aural experiment, a new poetics integral to new observational forms.

In a variety of ways, these and other films broke new expressive ground, engendering new kinds of imaginative and emotional connection on the part of audiences. They evidence precisely that commitment to the progression of documentary aesthetics necessary for the co-evolution of producers' and audiences' engagement with the genre, the basis of its continuing cultural vitality. By the later nineties, with imitative populism dictating the terms of British television, this fertile corner of documentary was the sole area in which aesthetic and expressive invention, essential ingredients in the democratic functioning of television, were fully unleashed.

*

Editing Zog: Which genre is this?

I'm watching Peter Dale edit his film, The Return of Zog, with John Dinwoodie, a freelance editor. It's week four of a six-week edit; they're preparing a cut to show executive producer Stephen Lambert. Peter tells me it's ninety minutes long, and the final cut must be 48.5. Peter's humour is so deadpan as to be almost indecipherable; 'I just carry on until the deadline and then ask for one more week.' Peter made The System. He has been at the BBC for twenty years. His life is good, he says, supported to make the films he wants to make, by contrast with his independent friends who have to 'hang about Horseferry Road with a suitcase from which they hawk their brooms.' He believes in the public service ethic and thinks it is operative in his and others' work.

Peter's present film is about a referendum held in Albania a few months ago, at the same time as a parliamentary election, on whether the monarchy should be restored. The would-be king is Leka Zog. It was shot over a three-week trip to Albania by Peter and cameraman Roger Chapman. Peter tells me it was a strange film to make. They had an opening to go to Albania and thought they could hang something interesting on the referendum and election. But at times it felt as if they were getting nothing; they could barely make contact with Zog. It got funny at times. He wants the film to convey something of this experience. Peter explains that the Albanian monarchy fell in 1939 when the Italians invaded. King Ahmed, Leka's father, and his family went into exile; Leka Zog was two days old. He has lived for the last twenty years in South Africa. Peter says he and John are doing something tricky: trying to make Peter look naive so it seems he's being manipulated by the film's protagonists, Zog and his entourage. 'Then gradually we reveal who this man is.' I gather Zog is networked with bizarre and powerful international figures. Peter says the art is in making these revelations subtly. They are perusing newsreels from the thirties and forties of King Ahmed, of Zog as a baby, of royal banquets, of the royal cavalry – all the paraphernalia of a developed monarchical system prior to Communist rule.

John uses a digital editor with three screens; one has a huge list of tagged bits of film. They are orchestrating how to interweave the various Albanian political interests, and how to introduce the Monarchy Party spokesman, who says ominously that his party is 'above politics' and that there will soon be no need for a democratic process. They put the structure together as they work; they don't cut to a written plan. John likens the process to sculpting: 'You keep moulding, cutting bits off, till the form eventually emerges.' Today they go over and over about five minutes of film, reordering, splicing in new entries and exits. Peter writes a script as they go.

Two days later Stephen Lambert is here for the first of three screenings for his feedback. Peter speaks his script over the images; and there's some music, a version of 'Getting to know you' from Rodgers and Hammerstein's The King and I. Early on Peter's voice-over explains the origins of the monarchy when Ahmed, a dictator, declared himself king in 1928. At last I begin to understand. The film is about the resurgence of 'golden age' mass fantasies after the fall of Communism; but this monarchical 'golden age' is a constructed mythology born of dictatorship – now being resurrected by Leka Zog. We meet the ninety-year-old mother of the leader of the Monarchy Party, who says she hates the Communists as 'there was lots of killing' under them. In this potent logic, the monarchy is loved and revered because it stands opposed to a murderous Communism. It is this logic that Peter's film aims to disturb. We meet a local paramilitary 'commander', Nihat Kula, and see his weapons stockpiles; he is wanted for murder. We see him striking a deal with Zog. We meet his paramilitaries, boys of twelve years old and more, who hold Kalashnikovs – 'the best guns in the world!' The film stops and Peter explains a missing archive section which will impute that Ahmed was an arms dealer. Back to the film: a rally of royalists on referendum day. The focus is on Ali, a senior policeman and Zog's bodyguard. Ali's family were sent to a collective farm by the Communists, where Ali was forced to work in the fields aged ten. 'So much suffering,' he says heavily. Ali speaks of the burden of uncertainty his people bear. Since the Communists fell in 1990 there have been seven governments, but nothing changes. Each government smashes everything built up by the previous one.

We arrive at the film's climax. An earlier motif has been Peter and Roger's efforts to speak to Zog; this has an understated hilarity, as they chase his car in a taxi without success. They finally get an interview. And it is strange. Zog talks evasively, chain-smoking, of 'duty' as his motive for wishing to become king. He blocks further discussion of his intentions, and of the history of the monarchy. A humorous scene follows in which Peter asks to accompany Zog to the final campaign rally. The bodyguards debate: should they take the Porsche, the Mitsubishi? It's about prestige goods, the trappings of power. I reflect that the film is as much a comic narrative about access to power, and note uncanny parallels with my BBC experience. In the film, Zog ends the interview after a few minutes saying he has another meeting that can't be moved. This is just how it was when I finally interviewed senior BBC executives after weeks or months of waiting.

When the film finishes, Stephen says it's great on the whole. Peter says the problem is finding the balance between a knowing and an unknowing stance, where things are revealed. I am amazed to learn the artifice in the narrative: the whole build of this edit is to the interview with Zog near the end. But Peter says they met him just after they arrived, though they were kept at arm's length throughout the visit. So this narrative arc is entirely constructed to build tension and humour. Stephen probes the distinction between the constructed 'real' in the edit, and what really happened. He asks: 'Can you make any more of the characters? Of Ali?' He says there's little depiction of the desperation and poverty: could it be clearer? Peter and John respond by pulling up footage of a ruined colliery, in which former workers' families are squatting without electricity or water. A woman speaks of having nothing: no money, no hope, of trusting no one. They pull up another sequence, this one of a police roadblock, and of families searching at the roadside for their missing sons, while dead bodies are piled nearby – 'a stench of death'. Peter speaks of a dilemma. They'd cut these scenes because such 'generic' scenes of poverty, decay and death have been seen so many times before; they call up a 'repertoire of clichés.' And they took power away from the king-focused core story. At Stephen's urging they reinsert the 'generic' scenes early on. Now they work through from the top, looking at unused film. Stephen says 'I got a bit bored here,' 'I like that pace,' or 'That scene is funnier here.' They discuss whether 'it gets too wedgy' if they take a piece of commentary and plonk it in earlier; they want to avoid having 'wedges' of information intercut with present actuality as the form of the film.

Five days later the film is down to fifty-five minutes. They're working on the interview, which is cut more rapidly, with fewer longueurs. The would-be king seems stronger, less awkward; but is this right? Should they reinsert some of the silences to convey the tensions? We watch a 1979 newsreel of a press conference in Rhodesia at the time that Leka Zog, who lived in Spain under Franco for seventeen years, was thrown out after Franco's death. Leka speaks of using a private army and propaganda to achieve the liberation of Albania; the aim is to topple Hoxha's Communist regime. He boasts of owning arms depots around the globe. It is revelatory footage. Peter and John want to insert it late in the film in the sequence on voting. Zog, then, has long been a central figure in anti-Communist operations with international right-wing backing. Today I'm left wondering: how will they use this stuff? Will we gain an understanding of these coordinates in the final cut?

We do. The broadcast film ends with election day and its aftermath. Enver Kula, brother of the gangster commander, invites Peter to film the voting in his village. He is one of the returning officers. Images of tanks, gun-toting, militias shooting into the air – of intimidation and fear. We are inside the polling station: the papers are being counted – 'Monarchy . . . Republic . . .'. The machinery of democracy is revealed as vulnerable and exposed; everyone can see in this small community who has voted for whom. The commander turns up: he tells his brother to stop fooling around with the election and man the roadblocks. Two days later the votes are still being counted amid rumours that the Monarchy Party has been defeated. The mood among Zog's gang turns ugly. The next day it is announced that they have indeed lost; the Socialists have won a landslide victory. Zog calls a press conference in which he accuses the Socialist leadership of rigging the ballot. He emerges in military gear. His men brandish weapons; the atmosphere is nasty, seething. There are scenes of crowds, violence, shooting. One person was killed and several injured, say the final credits, in shootings outside the Albanian Electoral Commission. Days later Leka Zog left Albania in a private plane, vowing to return.

In the end *The Return of Zog* is knowingly ambiguous, an experiment in remixing the terms of foreign documentary. The film evokes in turn the conventions of the serious foreign report, the political thriller and the elite political interview; with comedic touches like the car chase and staged photo calls it teeters on the edge of parody – *Carry On Commander* – or even, more sinisterly, a 'Documentary of the Absurd.' Above all, it resists the generic pull of the hard-hitting current-affairs report on post-Communist disintegration. Instead, the film adopts the contours of a mystery, filling in as it unfolds the historical roots of Albania's murky, anarchistic *realpolitik*, the poignance of its impossibly fragile forays into democracy. It is as much ethnographic as current affairs. The film doesn't denounce the agents of violent lawlessness. Instead, we meet the paramilitaries; Peter takes a drink with them, asking about their activities and lives. We are given minute and telling observations of the everyday operations of power and terror. Peter has taken risks; some critics judge the film a failure.

Diary, 1997.

*

Emotion, imagination and the extension of concern

'If emotions are suffused with intelligence, and contain an awareness of value, we will have to consider emotions as part of the system of ethical reasoning. If we think of emotions as essential elements of human intelligence, this gives us especially strong reasons to promote the conditions of emotional well-being in a political culture: for without emotional development, a part of our reasoning capacity as political creatures will be missing . . . An education for compassionate citizenship should also be a multicultural education. This means not just learning facts about classes, races, nationalities, sexual orientations other than [one's] own, but being drawn into those lives through the imagination, becoming a participant in those struggles . . . What I am advocating, what I want from art and literature, is empathy and the extension of concern.'

Martha Nussbaum, *Upheavals of Thought: The Intelligence of Emotions.*

*

Mixes and Boundaries

If representational diversity was part of the thinking in the BBC of the nineties, the assessment in this chapter portrays a mixed reality. The pincer movement applied by Birt to news – centralisation and commodification – had the effect of diminishing editorial bravery and originality, reinforcing 'institutional caution'[38] and homogenising news content ready to be repackaged for new outlets. Across news and current affairs there was a reduction in generic range: less investigative journalism; less, and less prominent, serious current affairs; less foreign coverage; and a growth in populist current affairs crossing over into the territory of documentary and reality television. These deep structural trends were countered by the attempt to diversify presentational tones and styles in the new twenty-four-hour and online news services. Despite the conviction that Westminster-centric political journalism was causing audiences to turn off, and the felt imperative to reconceive 'politics', in practice the corporation's journalism was able only fitfully to connect with new political phenomena beyond the given parliamentary framework. Similarly, despite the growth of a sophisticated self-awareness in *Newsnight* of its role in mediating public debate, and an avowed commitment to extending the representational circle beyond the standard cast of establishment and experts, the ensuing shift was ambivalent, unsteady and partial.

Yet beyond its journalism, the rich mix of the BBC's factual programming did respond to the challenges of representational diversity. In the nineties it was in documentary that BBC television developed, more than in its journalism but in a way that *complemented* its journalism, diversity of representation in all its dimensions. One lesson to be drawn from the state of BBC documentary in the nineties, in contrast to drama, is that intense competition in conjunction with creative autonomy and aesthetic buoyancy in a particular genre – even given the demand to achieve relative ratings targets – can stimulate a virtuous circle of invention. Outside the essential but limiting paradigm of impartial reportage, the historical lineages and contemporary developments described testify to documentary's ability not only to explore in depth little known and little seen facets of social experience – the lives of the poor and the oppressed; what has been rendered private or secret; the effects and workings of power – but, in the access films of the CPU, to enable the participation and self-expression of those groups and individuals otherwise unheard. In these ways documentary had an unmatched capacity to diversify the ideological and political currents aired by television. But those lineages also evidence documentary's imaginative and expressive potential, not only in the astonishing range of its subjects but, as or more importantly, in the attempts to integrate new perspectives on social life with formal innovation.

By moving us emotionally while extending the aesthetic grounds of our imaginative engagement, documentary stimulated our compassionate receptivity; it developed more than other genres the emotional intelligence and social knowledge of its audiences. This capacity of good television, to adapt the philosopher Martha Nussbaum, demands that we acknowledge its 'vital political function, even when [its] content is not expressly political – for [it] cultivates imaginative abilities that are central to political life' and to the development of an 'independent and passionate citizenry'.[39] By exemplifying how television's expressive power is dependent on aesthetic renewal, and how audiences readily connect with such aesthetic shifts, documentary in the nineties provided a singularly important lesson – one often forgotten in relation to what is a cultural form like any other. In as much as it enhances the social, informative, expressive and aesthetic range of television, documentary plays a central part in its democratic functioning.

There was, however, a powerful counter-tendency. The corporation's 1997 deal with the Discovery channel signalled that high-cost documentary, like drama, had become increasingly reliant on co-production. This was especially true of natural history and history output, but also the BBC's last ethnographic film strand, *Under the Sun*. Discussion of projects to be co-financed by American distributors revealed editorial pressures that led in sensational, populist and standardising directions. But internal forces also caused the extraordinary flowering of documentary genres to be short-lived. In the late nineties the controllers announced that docu-soaps had run their course; in fact, refor-matted often as voyeuristic social experiments, they continue to bulk out factual entertainment. More alarmingly, high-end documentary declined precipitately on all channels. *Modern Times* and *Inside Story*, the successful single-documentary strands, were wound up. The justification was to return commissioning powers to the controllers and focus marketing on one-off series. Strands were out of favour; they devolved too much creative control. The effect was to eviscerate high-end documentary's autonomy, its space for invention. The BBC's documentary output settled into a double act in which expensive middlebrow 'events' for the international market – *Walking with Dinosaurs*, *Blue Planet* – dotted the reality and leisure programming now flooding the schedules.

Despite the magisterial scale and scope of the BBC's news and factual programming in the nineties, it is instructive to discern its boundaries, its constitutive 'outside'. Then and now, there are limits to the BBC's diversity of representation. Two telling genres mark the boundaries, and they remain, more generally, marginal to television. On the one hand are those aesthetically experimental films that might be considered to take too far their questioning of documentary's core techniques – narrative, interview, authoritative voice-overs – by parody or ironic play. On the other hand are those directly political forms of reportage thought to veer too close to impassioned activism and radical politics. In relation to both, the due moderation and conventionalism considered seemly in BBC programming, which continue to bind the corpora-tion to its deferential and paternalist past, are put under strain, reframed, perhaps, as inhibition, incuriosity, insularity or cowardice. Such genres threaten to destabilise due moderation by other values: imagination, partiality and risk-taking; they continue to be uncomfortable for the corporation. If representational diversity means anything for the BBC today, it means overcoming these boundaries and embracing risk as a productive value.

*

The other news: the Alt News debate

It's the 2001 Edinburgh International Television Festival, a debate titled 'Alt News' between mainstream news organisations and representatives from those activitist media suppliers that exist outside the mainstream and use the Internet, radio and video to spread alternative news. There is no one here to represent the BBC. The chair, Robert, asks Maria Luksch, director of Ambient Information Systems, to start. 'I provide a Speakers' Corner for the media age: we work across all media, selecting one appropriate to the job when someone can't get access to the mainstream.' She describes an impressive network of media activism crossing South-East Asia. Alan Hayling goes next, from production company MBC. 'I'm here as the old lefty. The current wave of radicalisation evident at Genoa and Seattle is similar to what I was involved in post-May '68. I helped form the Newsreel Collective, ex-BBC people who thought the BBC wasn't covering the struggles against fascism in Spain and Portugal, and rejected the coverage of Northern Ireland. Our Portugal film was shown all over the UK in public forums – trades unions, Women's Institutes. We were national in outlook, where the new generation of media activists have a global politics. The problem is distribution: the Genoa activists didn't want their films shown next to factual entertainment, or on the corporatised web.' He plays a clip from a seventies film made by the Newsreel Collective of the Grunwick strike, which shows extremes of police violence against striking Asian women. Robert asks, 'Were these images ever seen on TV?' Alan: 'Never'.

Graeme Bowman from production company Wark Clements speaks next: 'I became aware of all sorts of news material that wasn't getting on the main channels; I wanted to help get it on.' He shows a clip from *AltWorld*, the Channel 4 slot he edits. '*AltWorld* gives people a taster of alternative film-making. Then they can go to our website, from where we have links to indie sites, so there's a chain taking users through. The responses are very positive: there's a huge audience that thinks mainstream media are not telling it all. It's borne out by the low turnout at the last election.' Robert turns to Chris Cramer, chief of CNN Networks, ex-head of BBC Newsgathering. There's a clip of CNN coverage of the Genoa protests which features a heavy police attack on the 'anarchists' who came to 'provoke violence'. Chris doesn't defend the clip; 'It was one of three reports. Look, you've shown us militant journalism; its critical function is to stop us in the mainstream from being lazy. But big isn't bad! Journalists in CNN and the BBC don't lose their desire to change the world.' He says he would have shown pro-activist films of Genoa on CNN had he had access to them, 'and CNN's website allows us to give more access to raw footage . . .'

Paul O'Connor from Undercurrents speaks last. 'We use film-making to advance justice and social change. We train people to make their own films; we trained activists at Genoa.' He shows a Genoa clip: images of a peaceful multinational demo, then violent police actions. 'We offered this to the BBC and PATV. They wouldn't take it. The story was activist violence.' Chris: 'We'd have run it! Next time offer it to us, OK?' Nick Pollard, head of Sky News: 'We'd have run it too! But activists are often hostile to the mainstream . . .' Paul counters, 'We debate this regularly. But nothing changes. Only *Channel 4 News* is broadening its agenda.' Winding up, Alan says investigative journalism is disappearing: he cites a film on the death of young black men in police custody that no one will show. Maria argues that the days of one-to-many media are over. Paul challenges, 'In the eighties the Channel 4 workshops supported alternative media. Who does now?'

Diary, 2001.

*

At the end of the Birt era, BBC News and Current Affairs confronted an uncomfortable reality. The huge growth in the supply of television news via new channels and services had been met by a striking reduction in news viewing. For all the market-research-fuelled attempts to reach underserved audiences, ethnic minorities, younger viewers and lower social classes – the same groups alienated from mainstream politics – remained disenchanted with news. The take-up of rolling and Internet news services nowhere near offset the decline. One result was an industry-wide debate, informed by the shift to 'partisan' news on American networks like Fox, about whether Britain's impartiality codes should be relaxed.[40] The inescapable message for the BBC was that the Birtist reforms and new services had failed to re-engage and to reverse the decline in these audiences. The resurgence of a braver, more original journalism had to wait for the next turn of the wheel.

An unanticipated effect of Birt's straitjacketing of BBC journalism by wave upon wave of rationalisation was to unloose, under his successor Greg Dyke, a volatile derepression. As that derepression encountered the Labour government's experienced public relations machinery, set to work to justify an unpopular and controversial war, the consequences were explosive. Proving that the practices underpinning the perceived impartiality and independence of BBC journalism remain a pillar of the legitimacy of public service broadasting, in 2003 the most serious clash between the government and the BBC in decades erupted over errors made by one journalist, Andrew Gilligan, in reporting sources that questioned the government's justification for war.

Dyke's BBC, Hutton, the Digital Challenge, and the Future

The lost report: the politics of truth (I)

I'm talking to a senior producer in the World Service. I mention the attempts being made by chiefs on the sixth floor at Television Centre to renegotiate the terms of my BBC study midway through, and my fears that, whatever is agreed on paper, they may try and find a way to prevent publication. My contact reflects, 'Yes, you're right to be anxious. A woman came a few years ago to do a study of the World Service. She'd done research on the NHS, and her aim was comparative – to see how two public bodies were dealing with similar restructurings. When she'd drafted her report I went through it, checking things. I said, "Make sure I see a copy of the final thing, not through someone else; give it to me directly." It was fairly critical, and interesting. Somehow the report never came out. It went to some managers; but when I asked it was always lost, unavailable. It was squashed – no doubt because it was critical.'

Diary, 1997.

*

6.07 a.m.

JOHN HUMPHRYS: 'The government is facing more questions this morning over its claims about weapons of mass destruction in Iraq. Our defence correspondent is Andrew Gilligan. This in particular, Andy, is Tony Blair saying they'd be ready to go within forty-five minutes . . .?'

ANDREW GILLIGAN: That's right, that was the central claim in his dossier which he published in September . . . What we've been told by one of the senior officials in charge of drawing up that dossier was that actually the government probably knew that

that forty-five-minute figure was wrong, even before it decided to put it in. What this person says is that a week before the publication date of the dossier, it was actually rather a bland production. The draft prepared for Mr Blair by the intelligence agencies didn't say very much more than was public knowledge already and Downing Street, our source says, ordered a week before publication, ordered it to be sexed up, to be made more exciting and ordered more facts to be, er, to be discovered.'

Today, BBC Radio 4, 29 May 2003.

*

All of you killed him

'In their argument with the BBC to clear Alastair Campbell's name, did Downing Street, did Alastair Campbell, did Geoff Hoon push Dr Kelly into a position so exposed and difficult that he couldn't cope with it? That's the main allegation against them. Alastair Campbell is a decent man who will be extremely upset by what's happened tonight. I have to say I would be very, very surprised if, after this, he has an enormous appetite to stay in the job for much longer . . . The question for the BBC is, in declining to say whether or not Dr Kelly was the source, did the BBC carry on piling the pressure on to him? All round Westminster, people are starting to blame each other and say, "It couldn't have been us, it was really the other guys." I think, throughout the country, as people look on – at journalists, politicians and officials – they will probably say, "A plague on all of you. You are part of this. It was your game that dragged this man, who was a civilian in your war, into it, and probably in the end all of you killed him."'

Andrew Marr, 17 July 2003.

*

Why the BBC is losing

'If the Hutton inquiry vindicates the *Today* programme, Tony Blair is history. But the calm of the Blairite circle suggests total confidence that the judge will come down on their side. Alastair Campbell is so much the creation of hostile journalists that it's tempting to wonder if he is a fictional character. He is everywhere discussed and reviled. It was therefore a shock to watch the monster of media imagination spend five hours giving unspun evidence to Lord Hutton and emerge at the end as a calm figure. You could hear the same self-assurance in the voices of the other Blairite witnesses – Jonathan Powell, the PM's chief of staff, and Sir David Manning, his former foreign policy adviser. There is no trepidation in their voices. All stick with absolute confidence to a truth they hold to be self-evident: the BBC got it wrong. Alastair Campbell did not over-ride the protests of the intelligence services to insert the false or highly questionable claim that Iraq could launch chemical and biological weapons within forty-five minutes. To curious British citizens, their openness is beside the point. They wonder why there isn't an investigation into how the public came to be told there were weapons of mass destruction in Iraq when there were none worthy of the name. They wonder why Britain went to war. The Hutton inquiry hurries past these large issues. They are raised only to be left hanging in the air, as the court concentrates on its narrow remit to inves-tigate the events that led to the death of Dr Kelly.'

Nick Cohen, August 2003.

*

A War, a Death, a Report, and their Repercussions

In 2003 and 2004, events occurred which may prove to be decisive for the future of the BBC. The entanglement of the BBC, government and civil service in the death of the scientist Dr David Kelly, the inquiry into and report on Kelly's death by Lord Hutton, and the ensuing resignations of the director-general Greg Dyke and chairman Gavyn Davies will go down in the annals as one of the most serious crises in relations between the BBC and government. In the aftermath of the 2003 Iraq war, Kelly, Britain's foremost expert on Iraq's weaponry, spoke secretly to several BBC journalists including Today's Andrew Gilligan and Newsnight's Susan Watts expressing disquiet about the misuse of intelligence on weapons of mass destruction by the Labour government as a foundation of its public case for war. When Gilligan used Kelly's opinion as a basis for a series of reports on BBC radio and in the Mail on Sunday newspaper, the government rounded on Gilligan demanding to know his source. Pressure mounted on Kelly, and three days after an appearance before the Foreign Affairs Committee Kelly was found dead, apparently from suicide.

During the war, and in the context of widespread public opposition before the war began, the government had led an attack on the BBC's news coverage with a 'snowstorm of complaints' of alleged anti-war bias.[1] One target of the criticisms was Gilligan's journalism. Ironically, research comparing coverage of the war by different British news organisations shows that the BBC's tone was far from anti-war or critical of the government. The BBC made greater use of official British and American government and military sources and reported less on Iraqi citizen casualties than other broadcasters, although overall, Sky News's coverage was the most pro-war. Adopting a characteristic cautious pragmatism in the face of controversy, the BBC focused mainly on the progress of the war, an approach favoured by the embedding of journalists with the military, rather than examining the case for war. The sole exception to this tenor of reporting was that, on the question of Iraq's weapons of mass destruction (WMD), the BBC was a little more likely to challenge Iraq's WMD capability than other news organisations – a scepticism vindicated in the period after the war.[2]

The Hutton inquiry threw up intriguing symmetries: the government leaking Kelly's name to the press, Gilligan leaking to MPs on the Foreign Affairs Committee that Kelly was Watts's source; the government resting its forty-five-minute claim on one Iraqi source, Gilligan resting his reports about the 'sexing up' of intelligence on the single source of Kelly. The inquiry provoked productive soul-searching by the journalistic profession on the imperfect reality of its practices, on the insight that 'all journalism, struggling against deadlines and inevitably incomplete information, is flawed'.[3] In another irony, the widely differing reporting of the inquiry proceedings itself demonstrated the inescapability of journalistic interpretation. Most striking, as many commentators have argued, is the fact that Hutton's narrow remit, defined by Downing Street and backed by unprecedented and dramatic evidence of formerly hidden governmental and editorial processes, drew the public mind away for a critical few months from bigger questions about the legitimacy of the government's case for war. By expiating the wrongdoings of the Kelly affair, the effect of Hutton was to ward off awareness of larger possible misdemeanours.

There is another symmetry in the structural changes revealed by Hutton in relation to both the Labour government and the BBC that underlay each institution's operations in this period, changes that in both cases can be traced circuitously back to the impact of the Thatcher era. Labour's eighteen years in opposition led it to pursue aggressive party discipline and image management. What the extraordinary plethora of evidence presented to Hutton revealed is how, since achieving power in 1997, such full-throttle management had leaked out to infect the broader substructures of government, resulting in the politicisation of the senior civil service. In the words of the report of the Phillis inquiry, set up in 2003 to look into public concerns about the abuse of spin, there is a 'three-way breakdown of trust between government and politicians, the media and the general public'. Key to this breakdown, according to Phillis, are the erosion of civil service impartiality and a blurring of the lines between government and party communications, causing a vicious circle of mutual recrimination and distrust between government and media.[4] Published just before Hutton's findings, Phillis diagnosed not only the conflict at Hutton's core, but a wider malaise afflicing Britain's democratic process. 'The upper echelons of Whitehall appear Blairite to a man and a woman because they know what their political masters are looking for . . . [and] have absorbed the managerial culture of Blairism. So John Scarlett [*chairman of the Joint Intelligence Committee*] could tell Lord Hutton on 26 August: "No worries of any kind were expressed to me at any stage . . ." Of course not. In the eyes of his subordinates, he was one of them.'[5] An entry in Alastair Campbell's diary of 8 July 2003 describes how senior civil servants, officials and press officers joined him to pen a press release about Gilligan's source. As one critic asks: 'This begs the question: what were the chairman of the JIC, the Prime Minister's chief of staff and the permanent secretary at the Ministry of Defence doing hunched over the computer, writing a press release?'[6]

As worrying is the intense pressure exerted by the government on the BBC before and during the Kelly affair, including attacks on the governors. 'Threats, veiled and not so veiled, from "government sources" to take revenge on the BBC by reducing its funding, removing its director-general, and changing its charter have been reported frequently,' wrote the chairman, Gavyn Davies, causing the Prime Minister to phone asking him to retract his account.[7] The Hutton inquiry uncovered insistent letters from Campbell to the BBC director of News, Richard Sambrook, from as far back as November 2001, containing stinging criticisms of BBC coverage and of specific reporters' stories. Out of the public eye, the arm's-length relations between the corporation and the government intended to guarantee the independence of the BBC was ditched by the government in the face of sustained conflict.[8] One writer reflects, 'The expectations of the BBC are laid out in its charter, but guidelines on how the government should behave towards the BBC have never been written down. They are based on vague "understandings" which are increasingly unacceptable in business or public life.'[9] In relation to both civil service and BBC, the government stands accused of ignoring vital boundaries designed to prevent the abuse of power.

*

Forever a dull moment in the very busy life of Honest Tony

'Tony Blair got away with it. Like the hero of some fiendish computer game, he survived the rolling boulders and gobbling monsters to make it to the next stage. But the game is not over yet. He arrived promptly at the inquiry, sat down and gave Lord Hutton a little smile, perhaps to put him at his ease. He began well. Where had he first heard of the allegations on the *Today* programme? "I was in Basra, with British troops." (Thanking our brave lads for their sacrifice, while the wretched Gilligan was peddling his lies, we were supposed to think.) The gist of his defence was, and I paraphrase, "Look, I'm a pretty straight sort of guy. If I'd lied, I'd resign, but I didn't. I'm also very busy, so I had plenty on my mind. I agreed to release Dr Kelly's name because I thought it would have been wrong to keep it from MPs. That's because I'm a pretty straight sort of guy." He didn't seem nervous, except when questions reached the period after Dr Kelly had admitted talking to the BBC. At this point – how did he decide to name Dr Kelly? – his language began to go haywire, in that it flew all over the place, tangled up and then sprang apart again, liable to poke its user's eye. He started to wave his hands in strange shapes and patterns. Us old-time Blair-watchers know that this indicates a "Why won't you believe me?" kind of agitation.'

Simon Hoggart, August 2003.

*

The truth is darker than Gilligan

'Gilligan's most important error was to give the impression that one man, Campbell, was responsible. The truth is more dark. This was the work of the whole of Downing Street and the Joint Intelligence Committee, operating in tandem to turn unimpressive and hedged raw intelligence into something more definitive for public consumption. The top people were behind the plan. The broad parameters of Hutton's report have been set. The proceedings suggest that the conclusion will criticise the September dossier, namely the JIC and its intimate relationship with the No. 10 press office. It will criticise the Ministry of Defence and its treatment of Kelly. All this will be tempered with criticism of BBC journalistic practice and its procedures for dealing with complaints. Blair knew what his people were doing in Downing Street. He chose them. He encouraged them, if not in their every decision, then in their broad strategy. He is guilty by association. But in a court, that is not enough to convict.'

John Kampfner, September 2003.

*

The Thatcher governments' hostility to the BBC was indirectly responsible also for the state of the BBC's journalism at the time of the Iraq war. In response to political fire, Birt had centralised ruthlessly and built strong editorial controls in the name of accuracy and analytical rigor. On becoming director-general in

2000, Greg Dyke's instinct was energetically to supersede the editorial inhibitions instilled by Birtism. As a former ITV boss, his view was that in comparison with ITV's best investigative traditions, exemplified by *World in Action*, the BBC lacked investigative nous and courageous journalism. Dyke and his advisers grasped the deleterious effects of the shift away from editorial autonomy towards anxious hierarchies embodied in added layers of management, and he wanted to encourage people to take independent and creative editorial directions. His news supremo, Richard Sambrook, came in advocating original and distinctive journalism, as well as the need to connect with younger audiences through unusual approaches. Getting headlines and breaking stories became goals. One of Dyke's first acts as DG was to 'de-layer', axing the 'supereditors' imposed in 1997. Another was to junk bi-mediality, restoring separate Radio and Television News divisions. Roger Mosey, head of Television News, stressed the benefits of a flatter structure: 'I want people to take imaginative decisions. I don't want to suffocate editors under a bureaucratic structure. Editors edit. That's the whole point.'[10]

Andrew Gilligan's hiring by the editor of the *Today* programme, Rod Liddle, was emblematic of the culture change. Liddle, known as a maverick, was suited to the new climate. Having successfully reinvented *Today*, Liddle left the BBC in 2002 when, following a controversial *Guardian* column in which he expressed antipathy to the Countryside Alliance and, by implication, Britain's Tories, he was asked by the corporation to choose between *Today* and his column.[11] Gilligan was hired from the *Sunday Telegraph*; as a reporter he was thought to work in unorthodox but original ways, 'more like a print than a broadcast journalist'.[12] To the culture change was added the 'battery-farm journalism' of Newsgathering. On the day of his report based on Kelly as a source, Gilligan did nineteen broadcasts. It was only in the first, live, unscripted two-way at 6.07 a.m. on *Today* that Gilligan made the ill-judged assertion that the government 'probably' knew the forty-five minute claim to be wrong. The story was, however, elaborated in his *Mail on Sunday* article, in which he named Campbell as responsible for 'sexing up' the intelligence. During the Hutton inquiry it emerged that, in the context of clamorous government complaints, Gilligan's actions were compounded by several instances of less than scrupulous care in managerial and regulatory procedures. The *Today* editor, Kevin Marsh, considered the work to be a good piece of investigative journalism but later judged that it was marred by flawed reporting, sending a critical email to the head of Radio News, and no action was taken on this judgement. Dyke failed to examine the case thoroughly before supporting his journalists, waiting four weeks before closely checking the report. The governors backed Dyke without due independent investigation, elevating their role of protecting the BBC from government interference over their other critical regulatory function.

The Kelly affair might seem singular. But similar flaws were evident in the handling of the Oryx case a year earlier, when journalistic error was magnified by managerial misjudgement. The origins of this case lay also in Dyke's culture change. In summer 2001, the *Ten O'Clock News* editor charged his reporters with making the news by breaking big stories. In the wake of September 11, in the words of a commentator, 'this approach went exponential'.[13] An external source purported to have found links between Oryx, a diamond-mining firm, and Osama bin Laden. This triggered an investigation leading to a broadcast. But the story centred on a basic mistake. There was no link. The BBC took a long time to admit the error, and eventually ran an apology, while pursuing aggressive damage limitation. The corporation was sued for defamation, had no defence, and settled before the court hearing, paying a large sum in compensation.[14] It would be short-sighted, however, to see these cases as a *post hoc* vindication of Birt's policies. As an executive commented, 'In taking risks and being more editorially creative, you inevitably run the risk of making mistakes and offending people.'[15] Both cases, and the BBC's susceptibility to failures both editorial and of managerial and regulatory process, were later acknowledged by senior figures; they accepted that risk-taking journalism must be met by impeccable editorial standards and rock-solid self-regulation.

For all the complexity of the Kelly affair, there are strong grounds for rejecting a symmetrical reading of the culpability of the BBC and government. None of the faults in Gilligan's or the BBC's actions invalidate the thrust of Gilligan's original story, which was strengthened by the complete lack of evidence after the war, to date, of the existence of Iraqi WMDs. This was clarified when, days before Lord Hutton reported, David Kay, the US official charged with leading the hunt for WMDs, resigned from the post saying candidly, 'I don't think they existed.'[16] As one observer puts it, 'BBC journalists had discovered a legitimate story of huge public significance: that within the intelligence services, there were real doubts about the strength of the information published in the September dossier, which was the basis on which Britain went to war with Iraq.'[17] But detailed evidence given to Hutton also supports Gilligan's case. Despite Susan Watts' conviction that there were 'significant points of difference' between Gilligan's report and her *Newsnight* reports and that her own exchanges with Kelly did not support the conclusions reached by Gilligan,[18] Kelly's statements in the transcript of Watts' phone call with him on 30 May 2003, the day after Gilligan's controversial report, support Gilligan's claims.

Moreover, it is hard to see the difference between Gilligan's claim that Campbell sexed up the dossier and Campbell's contention that he made only presentational changes as anything other than specious. Cabinet memos exchanged between Campbell and Scarlett submitted to Hutton show Scarlett agreeing to Campbell's request to strengthen the language in the dossier in a few crucial respects;[19] while Jonathan Powell, the PM's chief of staff, also requested changes in the dossier, which were duly made.[20] The public interest served by Gilligan's reporting is plain. The Kelly and Oryx affairs suggest the need for robust complaints procedures and regulatory reform, but not of a kind that would weaken the BBC.

*

Synonymous

SUSAN WATTS: 'OK just back momentarily on the forty-five-minute issue I'm feeling like I ought to just explore that a little bit more with you the um, er . . . So would it be accurate then, as you did in that earlier conversation, to say that it was Alastair Campbell himself who . . .?'

DAVID KELLY: 'No I can't All I can say is the Number Ten press office. I've never met Alastair Campbell so I can't –'

WATTS [interrupts] 'They seized on that?'

KELLY: 'But I think Alastair Campbell is synonymous with that press office because he's responsible for it.'

Transcript of recorded interview, 30 May 2003.

*

The Hutton inquiry came in the most critical phase in the BBC's life cycle, the period of deliberation on renewal of the BBC's Charter. The stakes could not have been higher. Lengthy debate preceded the 2003 Communications Act as to whether the BBC should come fully under the responsibility of Ofcom, the new media regulator. This did not occur. But later that year, as the Hutton inquiry proceeded, the Culture Secretary announced no less than four overlapping initiatives to feed into Charter review: the most comprehensive review ever of public service broadcasting in Britain, to be carried out by Ofcom; a 'roots and branches' independent review of the BBC led by Lord Burns, addressing all aspects of its existence including its licence fee funding; a review of the BBC's online services; and a review of the BBC's new digital television and radio networks. The implication of the coincidence of these events was plain. Depending on Hutton's findings, and the extent to which the governors' role in the Kelly affair was found wanting, the government might use Charter review to exact revenge, whether by bringing the BBC under the New Labour-inclined Ofcom or by altering its funding basis.

Pre-empting the publication of Hutton's report and acknowledging its errors, the BBC clamped down on its journalists writing for outside publications. It published revised editorial guidelines intended to make controversial stories more robust. It announced a shake-up of its complaints procedures and the appointment of a deputy director-general to head them up.[21] A week before Hutton reported, a provocative *Panorama* on the Kelly affair, containing criticisms of both BBC and government, demonstrated the BBC's capacity for impartiality even on this crisis in which it was hotly implicated. Its production was kept strictly separate from Dyke, Sambrook and others at the centre of the Hutton inquiry. The programme aired clips from an unbroadcast interview in which Kelly stated that Saddam's WMDs posed an 'immediate threat'. However, it did not show the full interview in which Kelly added that the threat was less than before the first Gulf War, and that Saddam was likely to use WMDs only as a last resort if Iraq was invaded.[22] The programme also probed the role of the Murdoch-owned *Times* which, in the lead-in to the Ministry of Defence's 'clue-rich' statement about the identity of Gilligan's source which finally caused Kelly's name to become public, dripped information into the public domain on the as yet unidentified Kelly.

In the event, the Hutton report confounded expectations. On the eve of its publication in January 2004, the same evening that the government won by a majority of only five its vote on the second reading of the controversial Higher Education Bill, another Murdoch organ, the *Sun*, pushed this near defeat to the edges of the headlines by leaking Hutton's findings. Rather than, as widely anticipated, finding fault with both Downing Street and the MoD for their handling of Kelly, and with the BBC for its contribution to the mounting pressures on Kelly, Hutton exonerated the government, mildly chided the MoD and heaped blame on the BBC. His criticisms centred on Gilligan's infamous 6.07 a.m. broadcast, which was judged to have made unfounded allegations against the government's integrity. From this, Hutton radiated out to excoriate the BBC's editorial systems, complaints procedures and the actions of management and governors. The blatant imbalance of Hutton's findings caused public consternation, including accusations that the inquiry amounted to a whitewash.[23] The impression was strengthened when Alastair Campbell held a triumphalist press conference to press home his accusation that it was not the government that lied, but the BBC.

In rapid succession Davies, Dyke and Gilligan resigned; as they went, Davies and Dyke made statements querying the report. Dyke's going was enforced; he had offered his resignation to the governors expecting them not to accept. But with Davies gone the acting chairman and a majority of governors shifted ground. Within hours of Dyke's departure, they issued the fulsome apology demanded by the Prime Minister. In unprecedented and impassioned scenes, thousands of BBC employees demonstrated around the country in support of Dyke. Two days after the report's publication, those visiting the BBC website found, for a few hours, a surreal headline, evidence of the depth of anger among BBC staff: it read 'Alastair Campbell has been appointed the next director-general of the BBC.' A day later 4,000 staff paid for a full-page statement in the Daily Telegraph defending Dyke's championing of 'brave, independent and rigorous BBC journalism that was fearless in its search for the truth'. It continued, 'We are determined to maintain his achievements and his vision for an independent organisation that serves the public above all else.'[24] Two weeks later, Mark Byford, the acting director-general, who had been Birt's favoured successor, announced an internal review into the issues raised by Hutton. When published in May 2004, it concluded of the controversial Today report that 'a core script was properly prepared and cleared in line with normal production practices . . . but was then not followed by Andrew Gilligan.' Every other individual involved was cleared.[25]

As many commentators noted, the outcry that followed the Hutton report did not so much reflect the view that the criticisms of the BBC were ill-judged, but the absence of any similarly forensic explication of the government's part in the events leading to Kelly's death. In the words of Conor Gearty, 'Things were simply too perfect, too beautifully and compassionately managed at too many levels of government for the report to be believable . . . [T]here was a war fought on an apparently false basis, a scientist who seemed to have tried to point this out was dead, and nobody responsible for the war or that death – not a single minister – has paid a political price. The contrast with the way Lord Hutton treats the BBC is brutal.'[26] As Gearty points out, Hutton drew an astonishing ruling from his analysis of the 6.07 a.m. broadcast, one that, if followed rigorously, could manacle investigative journalism in Britain. Even before Hutton reported, a leading broadcaster warned that 'the systematic attempt by the government and some in the press to exaggerate the flaws in Gilligan's original reports, and in the way the BBC reacted to the government's complaints', could lead to this outcome.[27] Hutton's ruling was that 'The right to communicate [information on matters of public interest] is subject to the qualification . . . that false accusations of fact impugning the integrity of others, including politicians, should not be made by the media.'[28] 'Imagine a BBC,' Gearty asks, '[that] refuses to broadcast anything that might conceivably pose such a risk . . . There would be calm, certainly, and quiet reportage of minis- terial achievement, but there would not be democracy as we know it.' Hutton's rule, he concludes, is 'transparently repressive' and does not represent the law 'as it is or as it ought to be'.[29]

The Kelly affair and Hutton report are likely to remain controversial. At the time of writing, the fundamental issue of the legality of the government's case for war is unresolved. In February 2004, days after Hutton reported, under pressure following David Kay's resignation as chief of the Iraq Survey Group, President Bush yielded to calls for an independent commission into why the intelligence on Iraq's WMDs appeared to have been so flawed. A day later, after months of resistance, Tony Blair followed suit and announced the Butler inquiry into the same issues in the UK, to be held in secret and with no remit to address 'the actions of individuals'. Like Hutton's, Butler's remit was criti- cised as too narrow; in due course both opposition parties refused to give it their support. In subsequent weeks critical questions continued to pour forth: did the Prime Minister not know, as his Defence Secretary did, that the forty-five-minute claim in the government's September dossier referred to battlefield rather than strategic weapons? If, as has become public knowledge, the legal team advising the Attorney-General believed the war to be illegal, did the Attorney-General also take this stance when advising the Prime Minister before war began?[30] Entrenched public doubts about the government's actions in going to war look unlikely to be assuaged without full disclosure of the cir- cumstances behind the decision to go to war.

For the BBC post-Hutton, the danger is overreaction in journalistic terms, through a return to Birtist inhibitions, and in terms of structural reforms that could damage the essential political independence of the BBC. The situation gives cause for concern. On the one hand the corporation appears determined to resist such an outcome. Challenged in October 2003 by the Home Secretary, David Blunkett, days before the transmission of The Secret Policeman, an exposé of institutional racism in the Greater Manchester Police, the corporation stood firm. The programme went out on BBC1, was lauded, and led to the resignation of six police officers. But the same month, following a clash with Lambeth Palace after John Humphrys asked the Archbishop of Canterbury on Today about the morality of the Iraq war, the editors cut a section deemed controversial. Following the Hutton report, a renewed flow of complaints by the government about the 'anti-war agenda' led to timidity. The day after Humphrys probed Defence Secretary Hoon on possible discrepancies between two of his statements, *Today* broadcast an extraordinary two-minute 'clarification' by Hoon. In general, 'correspondents admit that ministers have been largely successful in driving WMD off the agenda';[31] and editorial caution is not confined to Iraq. In the early months of 2004, the signs were of a BBC more prone to censorship, with Byford issuing a directive calling for an end to exclusives, although, as one observer put it, 'there remain pockets of recalcitrant and vigorous journalists who won't be cowed'.[32] As seriously, it was a BBC riven by dissent over the governors' decision to kowtow to the government by sacking a highly-respected and popular director-general. In a revealing twist, Lord Hutton let it be known that he had not expected his report to trigger any resignations at the BBC and did not condone them.[33] It seems that Campbell's acquittal speech, government signals and sensational media coverage combined to make the BBC governors panic and offer Dyke's head in an exaggerated gesture of atonement.

*

The disappearing email: the politics of truth (II)

30 March 2001: I have an article published in the *Guardian* on the reasons behind consumer resistance to the government-backed transition to digital television. I criticise the government's overriding concern with competition policy in relation to the changing broadcasting industry. And I note in passing the contradictions stemming from the gaping absence of regulatory response to the anti-competitive strategies of Murdoch's BSkyB. I receive a number of emails from readers, mostly in support of my arguments. One, friendly at the top, rapidly develops into something else, part dissension and part sell:

> Dear Dr Born, I enjoyed your article in the *Guardian* this morning. I just wanted to clarify a few points with you. I expect the deadline for your article came too late to take into account this week's ITC report stating that 30 per cent of homes now have digital TV. The 35 free-to-air TV and 37 radio channels available on digital satellite, with free equipment and no obligation to subscribe (one-off installation cost only) have helped this figure get to this level in just over 2 years. The barriers to entry could not be lower with the cost of installation – £100 without a subscription or £40 with one – being just a third of the average cost of a new TV which people tend in any case [*sic*] every six years . . . I am baffled by your remark about 'anti-competitive strategies of Rupert Murdoch's BSkyB television company' (a company in which News Corporation has a 37.4 per cent share and minority representation on the

Board) . . .

Abruptly, eleven paragraphs down, the email stops with no closing cadences. I glance at the heading and find that it came from 'Julian.Eccles@bskyb.com' at 16.54. At 16.55 I receive the following email, again from Julian Eccles at BSkyB: 'Eccles, Julian, would like to recall the message, "Article".' I muse that this is no doubt a code intended to cancel the previous email – but it failed.

Friday 27 April 2001, 7 p.m.: I scan my emails for the last time before stopping work for the weekend. 'You have new mail' pops on to the screen. The message is from Nicholas Hellen, media editor for Murdoch's *Sunday Times*. Hellen has been chasing me for four years, trying to get hold of my BBC research in order – it seems clear – to run a negative story on the BBC. At times friendly and wheedling, at others threatening and hostile, he has tried everything, and it has been unpleasant. At one point he admitted on the phone, almost apologetically, that he would love to drop the story, but his editor is determined that he should get hold of my material. In periods when he has phoned persistently, I have not felt able to answer the phone, and we have gone ex-directory. He has phoned the head of my former department threatening to expose that I have had a quarter of a million pounds of public money and have done nothing with it.[34] While I have tried to keep away from him, occasionally I have been naive and have held a conversation, hoping to placate him. In 1999, I wrote a report on my study for the ESRC, the public body that funded my research. It circulated among academic colleagues, industry figures and some of my BBC informants, the Department of Culture, Media and Sport, a couple of influential Labour think-tanks, the Independent Television Commission and, in shortened form, the Culture Select Committee. It also went to Greg Dyke via his head of strategy. The report is critical of Birtist management but supportive of the BBC's continuing role. In his email tonight Hellen says he has a copy of my report and will run a story on it this Sunday.

His email is perfectly timed: it comes too late on Friday for me to seek advice from my normal sources. Hellen does run a story apparently based on my study, including inaccuracies and a hilarious 'anthropological' spin, which is pure fabrication: 'The corporation's traditional values are said to have been eroded by the ascent of a new species of "corporation man", promoted under a series of dominant male leaders, including the director-general, Greg Dyke, and his predecessor, Lord Birt.' Hellen's article does, however, represent some of my critical material accurately. It ends with a spurious quote from ape expert Desmond Morris. I never learn who leaked the report, and I later reflect whether it can be coincidental that, after four years, Hellen ran his story just weeks after my *Guardian* criticisms of BSkyB.

*

An overall and a hat

'If you want organisations to change you have to carry the staff with you. I chaired a report for government on the NHS a few years ago. One of the things I said was, "The staff have had political-initiative overload. If you can't get them back onside, they're not going to take any notice." As part of the exercise, I wanted to be a porter for a night. So I went to the Whittington in North London to A & E on a Friday in an overall and a hat. It was an amazing night. A kid was born in the car park. A bloke hit one of the nurses. The idea that I was going to go up to these nurses and say, "Do you think you've met your charter standards? . . ." The only thing to say was, "How do you survive this every night?" The problem in the health service was that the people at the coalface thought they did it despite the management, not because of it. That was the biggest change you had to make. It's the same here. Somehow John had lost contact, [his] relationship with the people who work here. That's most of what I spend my time doing.'

Greg Dyke, 2000.

*

A new vision

'In the nineties, one of the stated aims of the BBC was "to be the best-managed organisation in the public sector". I have to admit that wouldn't have got me out of bed in the morning. So let me offer you a new vision. We want the BBC to become the most creative organisation in the world, and I don't just mean in the production and programme areas, I mean right across the BBC, everywhere – including the commercial parts, finance, strategy, public policy and HR. Creativity is as important in those areas as in the obvious areas like production.'

Greg Dyke, 2002.

*

Change the Organisation

When Greg Dyke came to the BBC in 2000, he demonstrated as deep an understanding of the ecology of public service broadcasting and the BBC's role in that as any BBC-born-and-bred executive. Known as a canny ITV entertainment mogul, lampooned as the man who gave the world Roland Rat,[35] Dyke was expected above all to make the BBC compete. In the event, he showed additional skills. Indeed, his skills and achievements testify to the continuing strength and vitality of that shared culture in British broadcasting based on a common, evolving vision of the architecture and values of public service broadcasting. Dyke was fortunate to inherit a huge potential stock of goodwill as the organisation emerged from the clouds of Birtism. He inherited also Birt's two most productive legacies. First, the fruits of Birt's lobbying for a rise in the licence fee to fund digital expansion. Birt had asked for £700 million a year for seven years. But in 2000 the government awarded just £200 million rising to £300 million a year over the same period, requiring the corporation to find another £1 billion in savings and extra earnings. Seven years of Birtist management, with its mantras of efficiency and accountability, apparently failed to deliver a financially transparent organisation. Chris Smith, the Culture Secretary responsible for the 1999–2000 review of the BBC's finances, was said to be 'horrified' by the differing accounts given during the review.[36] Second, Dyke inherited the outlines of an ambitious digital strategy, its roots established by the rapid flourishing of BBC Online and the launching of two as yet unsuccessful side channels. Dyke pinpointed forensically those aspects of the BBC's post-Birt functioning in urgent need of attention. But he also exhibited a genuine feel for people. His model as DG was Hugh Carleton Greene, an iconoclast identified closely with his programme-makers, and widely credited in the 1960s as 'the creator of the new BBC as Reith had been the creator of the old'.[37] Dyke's was a dual strategy taking in both organisational and programming change in the service of creativity; he saw that the two were inextricably linked.

The organisational changes set out in 2000 were sweeping. Under the banner 'One BBC,' Dyke dismantled the Broadcast/Production split and bi-mediality in many genres, curtailed the excesses of the internal market, and scrapped the Corporate Centre and Policy and Planning units. One thousand jobs were to be cut, although it is unclear how far this was achieved. One hundred and ninety business units were reduced to fifty-three. The number of corporate accounting systems was reduced from eleven to one, vesting control in a single external centre, reducing by 75 per cent the volume of internal trading and cutting the costs of financial management in half. Corporate functions like strategy were pared to their essentials. Dyke's twin aims were to create a flatter, less hierarchical and bureaucratic, less divided and internally competitive organisation, and to make massive savings on bureaucracy. Where 24 per cent of licence fee income had been spent running the BBC, he pledged to reduce this to 15 per cent, taking out 'a complete level of management' and ploughing the £200 million saved each year into programme-making and digital services. By 2003 the running costs had dropped to 13 per cent. In Dyke's first

year an additional £100 million was spent on production, with
going to BBC1, drama and the regions. In his first two years spend
grammes rose by £450 million, the largest increase in the BBC's hi
stressed a new ethos of trust and common purpose, creative collab
good working relations. The new 'petal'-shaped corporate structure centred
on four programme divisions, and a new executive committee shifted the
balance towards the creative, production and channel interests of the BBC.
Collaboration was enhanced by cross-department initiatives designed to foster
the sharing of ideas. Curiously, for all this, he was unforgiving of internal complaints, and was considered by some to tolerate productive dissent – surely a
precondition for trust – even less than Birt.

Above all, Dyke saw clearly the extremely low ebb to which in-house production departments had been brought by Birt's policies. Perceiving the
critical place of in-house production in maintaining the BBC's creative well-
being, and its strategic importance in justifying the BBC's existence, Dyke
aimed to reverse that situation. Courageously, and against the politically expedient market- and competition-oriented grain, he stated openly that in-house
production would be favoured over outsourcing via independents, although
the independents' contributions would still be valued. The Independent
Commissioning Group, charged with championing independent production
in the BBC, was abolished. At the same time in-house departments, including
the regional centres, were given output guarantees and longer-term commissions, thereby boosting their stability, power and prestige, enabling better
planning and a focus on creativity. In revising the commissioning process,
which had been entirely centralised in the controllers' hands under Birt, Dyke
made a crucial shift by introducing genre commissioners who held the budgets in drama, factual, entertainment and arts, creative experts with an
overview of production in each genre across all channels. However, all commissions had also to be agreed by a controller, making it a 'dual tick' system.
The precise balance of forces in each genre was decided pragmatically; in
some areas such as Current Affairs and Drama Serials the same person acted as
both head of production and genre commissioner, restoring the putative
'conflict of interest' that Birt's Broadcast/Production split had been elaborately and expensively designed to avoid. Dyke's commissioning structure
was at first considered even more laborious and complex than Birt's. Yet over
time it proved a well-judged solution, restoring as it did a central decision-
making role to those expert in each genre, as well as more equal access for
regional production, which had been lost under Birt's restructuring. Indeed it
is hard to see how else commissioning could now be organised, since the

BBC's expanded portfolio of channels, each with a particular strategic identity, introduces new planning and production complexities which demand that production in any genre be coordinated across the portfolio as a whole.

The last plank of Dyke's organisational reforms concerned diversity. He announced a drive to overcome the poor representation of ethnic minorities in the BBC's workforce, declaring frankly a year into the job that 'the BBC is hideously white'.[38] The target for ethnic minority staff was raised from 8 to 10 per cent, and for management from 2 to 4 per cent, with financial bonuses for achievements towards reaching the targets. Dyke was not new to these issues; at LWT he helped to found the first black and Asian unit in British television. He correctly linked the issue of diversity in employment directly to the BBC's long-standing difficulties in reaching out to the cosmopolitan young and to those from ethnic minority communities: 'I want a BBC where diversity is seen as an asset . . . a BBC open to talent from all communities and all cultures, a BBC which reflects the world in which we live today . . . Young Britain buzzes with the energy of multiculturalism, yet most broadcast media do not reflect [this].'[39] Under Dyke, programming initiatives sought to normalise ethnic diversity on screen, raising the profile of black and Asian actors in both mainstream and niche dramas, sitcoms and comedy output. The results were additional core black and Asian characters in EastEnders, Holby City and Merseybeat, mixed casting on dramas such as The Canterbury Tales, as well as 'multicultural' shows like Three Non-Blondes, Babyfather and Motherland. The digital strategy added another dimension, with the launch in 2002 of two digital radio services for black and Asian Britain. The Asian Network, previously broadcast to the Midlands, relaunched as a national station. It offers a mix of music and speech for both first and second generations, and includes local material in a range of South Asian languages. IXtra is a black music station encompassing a range of mainstream, new and eclectic styles, with journalism and debate aimed at the concerns of black British youth. If the strategy had results in programming, it also stoked controversy. While The Kumars at No. 42 was widely appreciated, black media professionals criticised The Crouches as patronising, and parts of the black community continue to berate the BBC for failing to give space to black programme-makers.[40]

Following the report of the Stephen Lawrence inquiry, in 2000 the broadcasting industry formed a Cultural Diversity Network to monitor and increase the employment of ethnic minorities in British broadcasting. Two years later the figures had worsened, with Channel 4's employment of ethnic minorities falling, in a period of economic downturn, from 13.5 per cent in 2000 to 6.6 per cent in 2001; while in 2002 seven ITV franchises had no ethnic minorities in management at all. These figures led Bectu, the broadcasting union, to accuse British television of being 'institutionally racist'.[41] In 2003 Dyke took on chairmanship of the CDN, signalling his ongoing commitment; and by 2004 the BBC had met Dyke's higher targets, causing him to raise them higher still, with a focus on getting minorities into management.[42] What impact this and other initiatives will have in modernising the cultural address of British broadcasting and bringing diversity to the screen remains to be seen. Despite signs of continuing internal strife over racial discrimination, the BBC under Dyke for the first time made a determined start.[43]

*

Something momentous

'Something momentous in the history of British television is taking place before our eyes. In the past 14 weeks, BBC1 has moved ahead of ITV1 to become the UK's most popular channel. The turnaround has happened so fast that even BBC executives are surprised at their own success. It is looking as if Greg Dyke, the ultra-competitive director-general, has succeeded in re-establishing BBC1 almost too well.'

Maggie Brown, 2001.

*

Values from the marketplace

'A flagship public service channel that takes its values from the marketplace is deluding itself. And doing a great disservice to its viewers, its programme-makers and its public service competitors. A more commercially focused BBC reduces the scope – and funds – for ITV1, Channel 4 and Channel 5.'

David Liddiment, ITV director of programmes, 2000.

*

Compete to Win

Dyke did not disappoint in boosting the BBC's competitiveness. He was aided by an advertising recession which from 2001 squeezed the finances of commercial broadcasters at the same time that the BBC saw its first rise in real income in two decades. Dyke set as a priority restoring the fortunes of BBC1, investing an extra £110 million. With the new BBC1 controller, Lorraine Heggessey, the first woman ever to hold this position, he engaged in a series of daring moves to give the channel competitive edge. He exploited ITV's continuing indecision over the scheduling of its late evening news, which had been moved from its 10 p.m. slot. Having first announced a year-long transition, in October 2000 Dyke declared boldly that BBC1's flagship Nine O'Clock News would move in just two weeks to 10 p.m.. The move took competitors unawares and drew the censure of the Culture Secretary. But it proved a master stroke, securing a higher audience while ITV's late news took years to stabilise, and freeing up the 8 p.m. to 10 p.m. schedule for popular programmes and films.

A substantial proportion of BBC1's new funds were poured into popular dramas, some entertaining and inventive (Clocking Off, Linda Green, Cutting It, Spooks, Bedtime), others aping ITV's midweek staples (Merseybeat a humdrum variant of The Bill). In August 2001, a fourth weekly episode of EastEnders was introduced, while Casualty ran for forty episodes a year. Ninety-minute dramas like Judge John Deed were designed, in the mould of ground-breaking ITV dramas Inspector Morse and Prime Suspect, to occupy the space opened by the move of the news. High end drama scored occasional hits, with singles cleverly marketed as a series in The Canterbury Tales and daring satire on New Labour's relations with journalism in State of Play. Sitcoms such as My Family and All About Me, featuring a disabled lead character, did well, as did 'events' like Walking with Dinosaurs and Blue Planet. Panorama was shunted to late on Sunday, while arts programmes were temporarily mislaid and the long-running Omnibus strand was cut. Outright populism was evident in Fame Academy, cloned from the ITV hit Popstars; and the 'national-cultural' role of the BBC took on a new guise in gently didactic, participatory shows like Test the Nation and its BBC2 equivalents, Great Britons and The Big Read. The result was a rich mixed schedule on BBC1, but one tightly focused to compete, with the odd remarkable popular drama, sitcom or comedy in compensation.

As part of his commitment to broadcasting as a socially unifying force, Dyke reversed Birt's declining investment in top sports broadcasting. He understood that sports are a critical part of the licence fee settlement; they reach groups otherwise distanced from the BBC and significantly boost audience appreciation. Dyke brought sports into one division and poured new funds into renewing the coverage. In his first year the highlights of Premier League football were lost to ITV, but live coverage of the FA Cup was won jointly with BSkyB, though the BBC failed to win the rights to live Champions League football when the sponsors chose ITV because of the corporation's sponsorship ban. In 2002 the BBC screened the Commonwealth Games and the football World Cup, trumping ITV's sports audiences. In 2003 the Premier League highlights were snatched back, allowing the popular *Match of the Day* to return after a three-year break. In 2004 the FA Cup, Six Nations rugby, Euro 2004, Wimbledon and the Olympics will all be available on the BBC.

BBC2 also gained competitive drive under controller Jane Root, with *The Simpsons* and *The Weakest Link* stripped across the week in early evening. It aired the innovative cult US serial 24 and the powerful drama *Band of Brothers*. Occasionally it offered original hits, like *Marion and Geoff* and *The Office*, with the best transferring to BBC1. While complaints arose over the relaunch in 2004 of the international current affairs strand *Correspondent* as *This World*, they were placated by a bigger budget, a longer slot and improved scheduling. As part of a channel review, BBC2 was repositioned in 2000 to 'stop chasing the youth audience' associated with Channel 4 and appeal to an older, 'more mainstream, suburban audience.' The strategy, centred still on a 'wall of leisure' and lifestyle programming in mid evening, brought ratings success.[44]

The result of these tactics was that for the first time since competition began in 1955, in the last quarter of 2001 BBC1 edged ahead of ITV1 in the ratings. At the end of 2003 BBC1 was maintaining a lead over ITV1, and BBC2 over Channel 4, and a quarter of all viewing was going to multichannel television; while in multichannel homes, where 40 per cent of viewing went to cable and satellite, the BBC channels were neck and neck with their rivals.[45] Dyke's populist agenda for the main channels performed as intended. But ratings success came with serious political dangers. Howls of rage issued from rival broadcasters. Columnists berated Dyke for selling out on public service broadcasting and making life difficult for commercial competitors.[46] The paradox at the heart of the BBC burst once again on to the centre of Britain's political stage: success was OK, but not too much. The BBC countered by pointing to the range of its services, and to the need to ensure that its channels are popular, that licence fee payers get programmes they want to watch. Dyke saw clearly that at this critical juncture of transition to digital television, if the BBC's popularity had not been demonstrated, it could have been shunted into a 'market failure' siding, forced to vacate the popular ground and retaining only that minoritarian, 'cultured' remit that its antagonists would prefer. By daring to remain true to, and to modernise for today's ruthless business environment, the Reithian vision of a necessary mix of popularity and aspiration, Dyke took on an unavoidable confrontation, one central to the BBC's capacity to flourish in new times.

Dyke also inherited from the nineties the heavily generic commissioning and production dynamics in drama and factual described in earlier chapters, which, encouraged by Birt's restructurings and by the internal market, outlived Birt. Indeed, under Dyke they were honed even further. But the BBC is not alone: the generic dynamics remain dominant across British television, to the point where the industry itself has begun to question the derivative and formatted nature of much fare, particularly in factual and reality programming, and the extent to which, with the accelerating recycling of genres, as a scheduler put it, 'TV is eating itself.'[47] Creativity was ill-served for a few years when Documentaries were subsumed under the huge Factual and Learning division, with little creative leadership. A striking recent development is the intensifying use of hybrids, of genre-bending, not only in factual entertainment (*What Not to Wear, Would Like to Meet*) but in high-end genres, through the insistent imposition of narrative and dramatisation. History, increasingly popular from the later nineties, has been diversified to exploit its popularity further. In addition to the classic authored piece, notably Simon Schama's *The History of Britain*, itself spiced with dramatised interludes, and the straight docudrama, such as *Conspiracy* and *Dunkirk*, and influenced also by the computer-animation-based quasi-documentaries *Walking with Dinosaurs* and *Walking with Beasts*, have come ancient history docudramas of varying quality like *Pyramid*, *Colosseum* and *Pompeii — The Last Day*, all involving speculative use of character and drama. Dramatised history is even edging out classic drama, as in *Charles II — the Power and the Passion* and *The Private Life of Samuel Pepys*. Hybridity rules also in arts and science documentaries and current affairs, where time has been manipulated in another sense by offering futuristic quasi-docudramas, as in *If . . .*, *Smallpox 2002*, and *The Day Britain Stopped*. In arts, *Dickens* and *Frankenstein: Birth of a Monster* evidence yet more outings for the historical docudrama, the latter, despite the lurid title, a portrait of the life and work of Mary Shelley.

In 2001, two events occurred which subdued the collective mood inside the corporation. That year's general election saw the lowest turnout since 1918 – just 59 per cent of the electorate voted; while the BBC's election coverage, designed to be user-friendly and to avoid alienating viewers, saw dramatically reduced audiences compared with 1997 and, even more so, 1992. Although the cause of the low turnout was diagnosed by the Electoral Commission as a failure of the campaign to connect with the electorate, the BBC decided to tackle the situation by undertaking a comprehensive review of all its political coverage with a focus on audience research.[48] The results gave insight into the disillusion and disengagement of young people, who perceived politics as 'bland, boring and corrupt' and saw BBC politics coverage as 'white, middle-class, middle-aged men being badgered by other white, middle-class, middle-aged men in a secret shared language.'[49] The review's outcome was unconvincing: the predictable shedding of some long-standing political programmes and launch of new ones, including the enjoyable, personality-led *This Week* and the supposedly youth-friendly *The Politics Show*. More convincing was the arrival on the networks of a generation of sharper, more interesting and distanced political commentators, including the new political editor Andrew Marr, Mark Mardell and, on Radio 5 Live, John Pienaar. Like Birt's News PSR, the politics review initially fudged the challenge of reconceiving how the passionate 'issue' politics central to those it researched might be covered. The second event to change the mood was September 11 2001. In itself 9/11 had the powerful effect within the corporation of recalling the value and the necessity of serious, international and investigative current affairs journalism – a value marginalised in the late Birt years. Experienced journalists, the World Service's contribution and its network of regional correspondents and experts, 'intelligent, mediated journalism' – all were suddenly back high on the agenda and have, with concerted attempts to reinvigorate current affairs, remained there.[50]

Competitiveness was unleashed also on the commercial front. Under Dyke and Rupert Gavin, CE of BBC Worldwide since 1998, the corporation proved itself no longer commerce-averse. Through its publishing, licensing, merchandising and distribution activities, Worldwide's revenues grew so that a £53 million cash flow back to programme-making in 1997 reached £123 million by 2003. New ventures such as BBC America, the USA's second fastest growing cable channel, were predicted to move into profit in the next few years. In 2003 the BBC-Discovery global co-production partnership was extended for ten years, while further partnerships and joint ventures were in development.[51] Worldwide's expanding activities were helped by the government granting an unprecedented £350 million borrowing facility. Naturally, such energetic growth attracted criticism from commercial rivals who charge the BBC with overaggressive entrepreneurship, unfair trading and with prioritising populist content that sells well in international markets. As controversial, however, was the BBC's core 'public service' plan to use £150 million of licence fee income to create an online digital curriculum for all schools to replace traditional schools broadcasting, the centrepiece of Dyke's educational strategy. The government backed the plan, but opposition soon swelled from educational software companies, who complained of being kept out of the market by a dominant BBC. In response, the government announced a £50 million fund for schools to spend in the private sector, a compromise gesture considered inadequate by the opposition.[52] Such run-ins accelerated in direct proportion to the BBC's entrepreneurial successes, and look set to continue.

Not all partnerships were commercial. Dyke fostered innovative, long-overdue initiatives to strengthen the BBC's role as the hub connecting and mediating a network of educational and cultural institutions. New links were forged with the Open University, and a partnership was built with four universities to make the corporation's science programming available on broadband for students in further and higher education. More ambitious still is the plan to make the BBC's Creative Archive in radio and television, produced with public funds, publicly accessible for the first time via the Internet. Where the BBC owns the rights to content, the aim is to make it freely available for anyone in the UK to download, adapt and use for non-commercial purposes.[53] Dyke built these important foundations; it is to be hoped that yet more is done by the next regime to position the BBC as the central animator of Britain's public culture writ large.

Given innovation on many fronts, and given long-standing criticisms, it is surprising that Dyke and his chairman, Gavyn Davies, fudged the opportunity to offer up substantial reforms of the BBC's governance. Davies took office in 2001 announcing that he would make the BBC 'more directly accountable to the public than ever before'.[54] In early 2002 he set out a modest modernising package centred on improved clarity about the different roles of executive and governors, greater focus in monitoring performance against objectives, more accountability through statements of programme policy for all services, and a new department to provide the governors with independent advice and support.[55] Unsurprisingly, the reforms did not quell the critics. Nor did they go far enough for the BBC's own good.

The lessons that emerge from Dyke's tenure as director-general are salutary. The BBC must indeed be popular, but it must be more. It is in that crucial addendum that the BBC's problems lie, and they will only be solved by a combination of resisting the temptation to be ratings-led in every slot on the main channels, creative leadership, and attracting back talented programme-makers in key genres. Despite Dyke's attempts to make the BBC a congenial place to work, creatives continued to flood out from the corporation, drawn by the soaring salaries on offer elsewhere. In addition, the commissioning heads need to remember that all hybridity is not innovative, and that all invention does not take the form of laboured hybridity. When pursued relentlessly, genre fusion itself becomes a mere device, something viewers cynically nose out. Currently, the BBC shows symptoms of following the lemming-like tendencies of the industry as a whole, affecting not just specific genres but the way such genres are 'refreshed'. What is needed is a restoration of the awareness of the different historical roots, aesthetic trajectories and values of particular genres, and of how they can be further inventively fostered. When, as at present, documentary-makers have been led to believe that it is unthinkable to cut a film to any other rhythm and pace than the extreme rapidity of the drama soaps – "fourteen cuts per half-hour," as an executive told me – things are at a pretty pass. Everything converges and much is lost – not a nostalgic cry this, but one about due latitude and historical depth in creative renewal.

Given the success of the main channels under Dyke, and the accusations that BBC1 has 'vacated any serious aspirations at all', Dyke's successors would be well advised to cut derivative programming and[56] take some decisive 'public service' risks, for example by moving *Panorama* to a prime-time BBC1 slot, or by restoring an innovative cultural review of the kind missing since the demise of BBC2's *The Late Show*. Yet Dyke's focus on popularity had a critical justification. The reach of all BBC services was 92.7 per cent in 2002–3, with BBC1's reach the highest at 82.9 per cent and BBC2's second at 67 per cent. The singular importance of the two channels is that they allow the BBC to address the vast majority of the British people with the same programmes and in an integrated way. This will be an even more important function of the BBC in the digital era.

But if BBC1 is labelled populist, how to describe the output of the commercial broadcasters in today's climate? Following the deregulation at the start of the nineties, and even in conditions of economic growth, Britain's commercial broadcasters faced turbulent competition as more players competed for the limited pie of advertising and subscription revenues. One effect was that Sky One, Channel 5 and Channel 4 converged on the profitable youth and upmarket demographics favoured by advertisers. Exacerbated by laissez-faire regulation, and by the lax controls on satellite and cable channels, the late nineties saw populism and sensationalism sweep across the output. A blatant symptom was a crass sexualisation of content unprecedented in British television history. BBC1's populism pales, then, in comparison to the callow and insatiable populism devouring its competitors.

*

Sky diving

'Sky One is . . . going back to its roots of risqué 16 to 34-skewed programming as it attempts to fend off [*the new Channel 4 digital entertainment channel*] E4, which launches today. Channel chiefs have called for more, longer-running "tits 'n' bums-style programming" to appeal to "younger, post-pub" viewers and have dumped plans to turn the channel into a mainstream competitor to ITV and BBC1. As a result, budgets have been slashed for entertainment and factual programmes – which, along with acquired US programming, make up the backbone of Sky One ... Sky has asked for programmes to be made for around £90,000 an hour, instead of the usual £130,000 to £150,000. . . . "Sky One has swung from being a tits 'n' bum channel to a mainstream channel and back to tits 'n' bums again," said [a supplier].'

Colin Robertson, 2001

*

Channel 5: bottom-feeding

'It is hard not to admire Channel 5. From the day it opened its doors it became pretty much the only British broadcaster to do exactly what it said on the tin. Channel 5 chief executive Dawn Airey, much as she hates the "films, fucking and football" epitaph, cut the crap long before Greg Dyke drew out his scissors. Channel 5 met audience targets, it met financial targets and it continued to exist, much against the odds. Kevin Lygo [director of programmes, who has announced he is "braining up" the channel] has started from the reasonable assumption that Channel 5 has always managed expectations at a brilliantly low level. It has gone unchided by the highbrows as they have never expected it to deliver them a service. One can see why Airey is wary of any [notion] of braining up, when bottom-feeding has suited [Channel 5's] agenda so well. . . . The only problem for Lygo and Airey is keeping expectations low enough that Channel 5 will continue to exceed them.'

Emily Bell, 2002.

*

Channel 4: the bottom line

'Last week's leader [in the trade weekly Broadcast] failed to acknowledge that Channel 4 is bucking the trend of declining terrestrial ratings. In multichannel homes you reported that "the greatest casualties are still ITV and BBC1", but you neglected to mention that C4's share in multichannel homes has increased over the past year by 4.5 per cent. . . . Advertisers choose Channel 4 because we attract what they consider valuable audiences: ABC1s, the so-called upmarket viewers; and 16–34s, the young audience. Channel 4 has increased the most commercially important and hardest to reach audiences, 16-34s, up by 9 per cent and the ABC1 audience, up by 4 per cent.'

Claire Grimmond, head of Market Planning, Channel 4, 2001.

*

Endemol's finest

A plenary at the 2001 Edinburgh International TV Festival: John de Mol, president of Endemol Entertainment, the company selling *Big Brother* around the world, has come to share his wisdom with the industry. He is hailed as one of the foremost creative innovators in global broadcasting. He talks in a self-congratulatory way about creativity, diversity, the astonishing growth of his business: 'Endemol . . . is driven purely by creativity.' While he talks, the videos behind him show various degrees of nakedly (as it were) exhibitionist and sexualised reality television, 'culturally diverse' breasts, buttocks and penises from Germany, Sweden, Portugal, Switzerland . . .

Diary, 2001.

*

From Sky to BBC2 to Channel 5: from sex to veil to sex again

When we write about television, we don't often write about what we actually see. Tonight I'm watching late night television after a current must-see, Channel 4's *The West Wing*, a drama set inside the White House in Washington in which the high art of American quality drama is employed to serve the bathos of contemporary American patriotism. The particular poignancy of *The West Wing* is that the start of this run overlapped with the debacle that was the 2000 American presidential election. In *The West Wing* President Bartlett, played by Martin Sheen, has a running spiritual love affair with a series of black men in his service, who consistently symbolise the pure, noble, wise and transcendent. Meanwhile, in another televised set piece in Florida, one apparently dealing in actuality, rank corruption in the American political process has disenfranchised thousands of Floridian blacks. In *The West Wing*, the fictional White House is peopled by press secretaries, speech writers and presidential advisers who turn to their consciences so often that collective ethical reflection is the routine accompaniment to sandwich lunches, corridor clinches and friendly late night poker games with the President. Meanwhile, in actuality, ex-President Clinton is accused of disbursing pardons in return for monetary gifts, while the newly elected George Dubbya sends bombers to Baghdad at the drop of a pretzel.

It is nearly midnight, and on my cable set strange things are happening on channels 2, 3 and 4 which – perplexingly – give me Sky One, BBC2 and Channel 5. On Sky One, the naughty narrative of *The Villa* is coming to its climax. Eight or so young Brits have been sent to a holiday villa in a hot Mediterranean country. They are being filmed con-

479

stantly while they booze, do karaoke, eat, chat, snog and shag. The fun is in the turnover of partners as they swap around and speculate on who will fuck whom and when. A woman sits on a man's lap and they poke their tongues into each other's mouths, breaking off only to leer into the camera and wipe the saliva away. In a perverse sexualised synthesis of *Blind Date* and *Big Brother*, the camera lurks and catches them at it in the hammock or by the pool. Hilarity is invited when, each morning, the camera moves inside the bedrooms and under the duvets to reveal who has slept with whom. The climax arrives: from the start, each person had been secretly paired with another, and now we learn whether they have scored the right partner. As in some teen sexual fantasy, we have been set up as voyeurs of the crudest debauchery, while yet cleaving to an illusion of romantic destiny. My little daughter is asleep upstairs and I wonder whether, by the time she is a teenager, she will have been taught such ugly promiscuity and what it will mean for her in a post-Aids world.

I zap along and find that BBC2 has *Langan Behind the Lines*, a low-budget documentary in which our narrator, the plucky Sean Langan, has gone to Baghdad to report on ordinary lives and everyday opinions inside Saddam Hussein's Iraq. It is in the genre of whacky male adventurers, for which the prototype is Louis Theroux's zany travel series. Like Theroux, Langan wears trendy glasses and smiles nonchalantly through threats and dangers, as if he'd just wandered into the darker reaches of Camden Lock. Filmed on a lightweight digital video camera, presumably smuggled in by Sean and his companion, the film gives a rare and intimate *vérité* portrait of the city, its spaces and moods and inhabitants. I have never seen anything like this on Iraq before. I have never had the chance to hear ordinary, elderly Iraqi men in a Baghdad café express off the cuff, through a translator, their support for Saddam and their condemnation of western democracies for their aggressive bombing.

Langan wanders into a gigantic central mosque; he watches devoted thousands at prayer. He is given the chance to talk to a leading ayatollah from the mosque, and is led into a side room where he sits with the ayatollah on the floor. Reasonably, the ayatollah beseeches him to speak the truth about the suffering in Iraq, to act responsibly with the information he has gained, and he asks God to help Langan achieve these tasks. Langan comes gaily back with, 'That's quite a job you've given me!' Next we get shots of a magnificent religious complex in classical Islamic style, the buildings decorated richly in blues, golds and reds. It is a sacred shrine peopled by pilgrims from all over the Arab world. Sean wants to talk to them, but we learn that he has gained some minders – 'Not one, not two, but three minders' – and they have advised him not to speak to anyone. With understated irony Langan reports, 'I asked them why I can't speak to people. They wouldn't tell me. So then I asked what questions they didn't want me to ask, so I could avoid them.' Next Sean is standing awkwardly in an anonymous road with the shrine in the distance. His sunny countenance is wearing thin and he speaks about what it's like to move around and film with the minders there. 'It's boring, so boring – I've had the worst afternoon.'

Leaving Langan, I flip to Channel 5: here what is called a documentary is underway. Its sole premise is that a group of strippers are touring Australia in a bus and we are to follow their progress. The poorest of the poor in televisual conception, it's a cheap travelogue crossed with soft porn. Very soon it is plain that all we are doing is waiting for the next flash. The aching tedium of the links and fillers is worse than in the soft porn this is pretending not to be; it lacks even the usual apology for a storyline. The strippers are packing up to leave a small town where they have performed; a group of drunken men are filmed outside the venue about to return home. With fixed ear-to-ear smiles, they are straining to tame their aggressive sexual disinhibition for the camera. Each carries a rolled-up poster as a trophy which they prod suggestively in the air saying, 'Wait till I get home!' and 'The missus will know what's coming to her!' The girls have arrived to visit an elderly miner, a man whose excitement when surrounded by bare-breasted girls is clearly uncontained. Is the filmic condescension to this man an affectionate one as it presents itself, or a cruel one masquerading as playful? A thin thread of narrative is resurrected as one of the girls preens almost naked on a rock, smothering her breasts in oil, preparing for a photographer: they are shooting a glamour calendar en route and the photo shoots punctuate the journey. Now the bus is heading for Alice Springs where the strip show will take place in a bar. From behind the girls we see the baying crowd, as well as experiencing the sexual thrill of the swaying bodies themselves – we are set up to be voyeurs of the voyeurs. When the credits roll, I note with amazement that the film has been co-produced by the Australian Film Finance Board.

As I escape Channel 5 in a frenzy of zapping, the balance of viewing between the channels in British television is made plain: against a common *vérité* mode of address, we cut from shagging, to behind the scenes of Muslim life, to oiled tits, and back again. From debased flesh to veiled, black-covered flesh to debased flesh.

Diary, 2001.

*

I don't even want it!

I've just left 1997's Television Show in Islington, where debate focused on the technical difficulties thrown up by the start of Channel 5. I find a taxi and mention to the driver that I've come from a TV event. He launches in: 'Just show me someone from Channel 5 and I'll give them a kicking!' He tells a horror story about his video player going wobbly due to interference from the test transmissions. He contacted Channel 5. They stood him up, then they couldn't put it right. 'My point is, I didn't ask for Channel 5. I don't even want it! We don't need new channels. We've got more television than we can use already. So why do they force it on us?' He mourns the takeover of sports by Sky. He says the BBC were highly skilled at sports broadcasting – good camerawork, great commentary. ITV is naff in comparison, but Sky is even worse. He berates the creation of a US-style multichannel TV environment, and dislikes the heavy use of US imports, with odd exceptions like *Friends*. He goes on that Thatcher's changes, by creating greater competition, forced up the price of sports on TV, pushing the BBC out of coverage of major events. Labour will be no different, he says. Politicians are 'all the same'.

Diary, 1997.

*

Sky's the Limit

The final element of Dyke's tenure as director-general was to establish the BBC's digital services. Once again, the achievements were substantial. If BBC1 was shamelessly revamped to grab the popular audience, it is the corporation's digital strategies which evidence subtle and imaginative thinking about the digital future and the BBC's role in optimising that future for contemporary Britain, and which mark out an ocean of clear blue water between the BBC's ambitions and those of its rivals. They evidence also a necessary pragmatism about renewing the BBC's relationship with younger generations. It is in digital that the pay-off of the BBC's public funding compared with advertising-funded public service broadcasters becomes achingly plain. The story of digital television (DTV) is instructive, and the background was inauspicious. In 1999, as technological convergence gathered pace, the Culture Secretary issued a decree setting out twin goals: the industry must achieve a transition to DTV between 2006 and 2010, and public service broadcasting must remain at the core of Britain's digital ecology. The goals were reiterated in a White Paper, which announced also the plan to merge Britain's five telecommunications and media regulators into the 'light touch' Ofcom. In advocating DTV, the government was driven by larger public policy interests, which included a desire to put Britain at the forefront of the digital economy and to stimulate the domestic market for information and communication technologies. A shift to DTV would permit the lucrative sale of the analogue spectrum. Moreover, if it became universally available, DTV was seen as a platform to deliver universal Internet access, so mitigating the 'digital divide'. In the government's eyes these developments would in turn help to combat social exclusion and political apathy.[57]

In dictating a tight framework for the switchover to DTV, the government had little to say about incipient consumer resistance to the presiding pay-television model, nor about the difficulties thrown up by the existence of three platforms – digital cable, digital terrestrial and digital satellite, the latter dominant and in the hands of Murdoch's BSkyB. To the industry, three platforms brought the risks and costs associated with lack of standardisation and with Sky's market dominance. To consumers, they brought market fragmentation and fears of obsolescence which, together with rising subscription costs, further fuelled resistance. Given BSkyB's hold on distribution and its anti-competitive tactics, through vertical links to Sky channels, premium movie and sports content, a central government aim was to ensure pluralism by identifying a rival universal platform.[58] DTT was the main candidate, and in 1998 ITV took up the challenge, announcing a DTT venture, OnDigital. But in 2001 Britain hit economic downturn. Commercial broadcasters faced a severe advertising recession while being expected to expand their digital proposition; more than ever they were led to conceive of DTV as a source of revenue growth. Multi-revenue business models were adopted in the Sky mould, and subscription channels were identified as the most likely means of profitability.[59] In reality, the economics of digital channels were fragile and in 2001 several folded, including those backed by large corporations. OnDigital, meanwhile, failed to provide a platform service to rival BSkyB and, with climbing debts, it collapsed in early 2002 leaving no effective competitor for BSkyB. Consumer resistance bedded down, with take-up of DTV stalling in 2002 at 40 per cent of households. Repeated surveys suggested that such resistance was not passing. A consensus grew in industry debates on the need for high-quality content to drive digital take-up; the Consumers' Association argued that, for the government to achieve analogue switch-off, the public service broadcasters should play a key role by developing attractive free-to-air digital services to draw the 'refuseniks'.[60]

However, the advertising-funded public service broadcasters were in neither the position nor the frame of mind to offer free-to-air services. The thinking behind Channel 4's DTV strategies can illustrate. Throughout the nineties Channel 4 was expansive. After 1993 its high advertising profits were ploughed into new services and the soaring costs of its hit American imports. In the later nineties the channel was redefined as a cross-platform media company and sought to expand commercially. Michael Jackson, chief executive from 1997, argued that public service broadcasting was outdated and that commercialism could be synonymous with the innovation central to the channel's remit. Two digital subscription channels were launched – FilmFour and

E4, a youth entertainment channel – as well as Internet and interactive operations. With *Big Brother* from 2000, the channel pioneered multi-platform programming in the UK. E4 and the main channel focused increasingly on profitable youth demographics, and more recent expansion included a joint-venture interactive horse-racing channel, At the Races. The aim was clear; as an insider put it, 'It's all about tapping into betting revenues. There's an argument that with interactive television, the one thing that will really make money is betting.'[61]

Channel 4 based its digital strategies on market analysis and research, offering a series of rationales for the new services. They included a concern to increase and diversify its revenue streams, ostensibly to protect the public service channel; the need to build audience share, strengthen the brand and enter the pay-television economy; and the need to attract younger people to the channel, and to innovate in content delivery. Behind the rationales lay controversial assumptions, including the notion that pay television was becoming the norm in Britain, and that niche viewing represented the future for all viewing. Striking was the use of research on existing multichannel households, the majority of them Sky subscribers, to project models of universal future behaviour – a self-fulfilling prophecy, as Channel 4 then built its strategies on that projection, with the effect of further influencing markets in this direction. The assumptions are therefore teleological and coercive: they bring about what they purport merely to reflect. Other controversial aspects of Channel 4's changing culture included the conviction that the concept of minorities was no longer meaningful, and that universality was no longer required of Channel 4. As recession bit, the subscription channels struggled, eating up investment and causing a budget freeze, job losses and the closure of Channel 4's esteemed film arm. For a period the pay channels were subsidised by the public service channel, the opposite of what was intended. In short, changing political and market conditions in the nineties, compounded by lack of regulatory intervention by the ITC, caused Channel 4 – supposedly Britain's most experimental and innovative broadcaster, committed to diversity and minority provision – to commercialise, and in the process lose touch with its founding remit.[62]

*

Micro-communities to the Pompidou Centre

'The digital strategy arrived at by Greg and Mark Thompson emerged from several years of improvisation and rapid-feedback learning. The commercial digital television strategy had been sorted first. We identified a need for the licence fee archives to be exploited properly; that led to UKTV and the Flextech joint venture. Then there was News 24, brought into existence to protect the BBC's brand reputation in that area. There was BBC Choice, initially a side channel which sat between BBC1 and BBC2 and offered follow-on programming, deepening the experience of the main channels. Similarly, BBC Knowledge was conceived in a blaze of enthusiasm for interactivity and digital education. But for all three, the BBC hadn't fully thought through how we would populate them as linear TV networks. And they were poorly funded, because we were working to a limit of 10 per cent of income investment on digital projects. Those services were running by 1999. Two things were clear. One, they weren't adding sufficient value and they weren't clear in what they were offering. And two, there was a more complex, long-term digital vision called Hever being built at the same time, a project developed by John with strategy teams across the BBC. This was a bold, intellectually rich, intensely conscientious, ramified vision for public service in the digital age. The idea was to use digital to serve micro-communities alienated from the BBC, to create a large public digital space reaching hundreds of different underserved communities and interests. It was linked to the famous 100 Tribes research, an attempt to put flesh on it in service terms. So by the end of the decade we had a long-term vision, underfunded services actually on air, and not much linkage between the two.

'When the 2000 licence fee settlement came, it was good but not sufficient to fund Hever. And there was a change of leadership. Swiftly, there was a radical simplification of the digital plan, particularly in television. Mark Thompson was the prime mover. The idea was that in the medium term, digital allows us to establish a shape for BBC television which is more substantial and rich than in the analogue age, and which is similar to what we ended up with after half a century of development in radio. A lot of thought was given to what the BBC did when it reworked its radio networks in 1970. The broad mix of networks established then, with the addition of 5 Live, has stood the BBC in good stead by serving a wide range of audiences reasonably well. That gave Mark his breakthrough: he identified four television channels as the right core mix, with daytime used for the children's services. This, with News 24, created a "thus far and no further" vision, allowing us to say this is clearly added value, but it's not a relentlessly aggressive march into every territory. We saw that BBC4 had to focus on factual, education and culture, BBC3 on audiences seeking something different, slightly younger and more entertaining than usual for the BBC. They were always mixed-genre; moving from quasi-niche brands like Choice and Knowledge to numeric channels signalled their upgrading to mixed-genre, public service networks, albeit with different positioning and feel. In his Banff speech Mark said we hadn't taken sufficient account of what was happening to multichannel audiences. The problem is the uncertainty in how audiences will change. It may well be that they want niche channels to be niche channels and the BBC to be the BBC. But the two can be complementary. If we get it right, BBC4 could have the impact of something like the Pompidou Centre in cultural Paris: a huge, exciting, publicly funded space with a thriving commercial gallery sector all around it.'

Senior executive, BBC digital channels, 2001.

*

Digital Visions

Dyke's digital strategies were based on completely different assumptions to those of Channel 4. Birt's instinct had been to deploy digital for polar ends: on the one hand commercial expansion, and on the other pure public service purposes by attempting to reach underserved communities. Dyke adopted a similar philosophy but took a more mainstream if resolutely public service orientation, one peppered with pragmatism. To the Reithian mission to inform, educate and entertain, Dyke added 'connect'. The BBC's strategies were less coercive than Channel 4's. They did not assume that pay television and niche viewing were the future. Instead, they built in flexibility so as to respond to the way new markets and audience tastes actually develop over time. To ensure that analogue viewers were not disadvantaged, for example, and that the direction of children's viewing habits was not predetermined, programmes for the new BBC children's channels were shown also on the analogue channels. The aim was to 'future-proof': to tempt viewers by enabling them to see what digital offers, without pre-empting the future pattern of viewing, while creating a presence in the new markets for children and young people so as to resist any possible marginalisation. The BBC bequeathed by Dyke resists the proposition that pay television is inexorably becoming the norm, and it resists this at the level of distribution, channels and content. It resists the assumption that universality and minority provision are no longer salient. Plainly, it is freed from such coercive assumptions by its public funding. But the point is deeper: it is that the BBC's strategies evidence an entirely different construction of the future of DTV and of digital media, one sensitive to the variety of audience experiences, with a responsible awareness that Britain's future digital ecology will be powerfully conditioned by its own new activities.

Dyke's proposals advanced a portfolio of five new digital radio networks, including the two stations targeted at ethnic minorities, and four complementary free-to-air DTV channels: BBC3, a mixed-genre, entertainment-led youth channel; BBC4, a channel for culture, science, the arts and ideas; and two children's channels. The majority of the new networks began operating in 2001 and 2002. The DTV proposals included core public service dimensions lacking in Channel 4's offering: the provision of mixed-genre channels of range and diversity; the challenge of universality and of serving a range of audiences, mass and minority; and the need to plan subtly the complementarity between services, essential in an age of convergence. Controversy arose over the repositioning of BBC1 and BBC2 when Mark Thompson, then director of television, appeared to float a reduction in their genre mix. But this was later retracted, and a commitment was given that the main channels would remain generalist and cover a wide range of genres, albeit in a focused way. The new channels are seen as testing grounds for new ideas and talent, with successful shows crossing from BBC3 to BBC1 and BBC4 to BBC2.

The plans were decidedly not driven by a market failure conception of the BBC's role. Behind the children's channels and BBC3 was market research showing a growing alienation among young people towards public service broadcasting. The aim was to resist this trend by rebuilding the relationship on the multichannel territory that young people increasingly favour, laying the basis for future generations. The BBC emphasised three factors that would distinguish its DTV channels from commercial rivals. They would be free-to-air and without advertising; they would contain a high proportion of original British programmes, with budgets higher than the norm for DTV; and each channel would contain a range of genres, in contrast to the niche-channel pay-TV model. The BBC took the view that it was legitimate to position the channels in competitive markets because such interventions would serve audiences and assist Britain's economic success by raising standards in DTV.[63] Its rejection of a market failure rationale was powerfully vindicated when Nickelodeon, a leading commercial supplier of children's channels, reacted to the BBC channels by significantly increasing its commitment to British production and the budgets for those productions.[64] This augurs rising quality in children's television.

It is too early to assess the performance of the DTV channels, the audiences for which, as with all such channels, are small. Yet questions remain. The channels are said to 'embody a new set of contemporary, believable public service values' and multiculturalism is stressed by executives as central to the remit of both BBC3 and BBC4.[65] But it is not clear to what extent the claims have translated into programming. While greater representation of minorities in staffing the new channels and its suppliers must be a key factor, executives are inarticulate about how this can be achieved. Stuart Murphy, controller of BBC3, portrays the channel as intelligent but populist, edgy and reckless, and as 'assuming multiculturalism'. But he admits that the tone of BBC3 is in tension with the BBC's reigning middle-class values, and wonders openly whether BBC3 will achieve this tone, seeing it as a critical test of the corporation's ability to update and diversify its own culture. BBC4 has become a home for international news, film and documentary in the *Storyville* strand, sustained arts output, drama, history and ideas, with cult viewing in the parodic US sitcom *Curb Your Enthusiasm*. The signs are that it is hitting its stride. BBC3's strengths are also emerging. It has ventured boldly into new comedy with *Little Britain*, *Three Non-Blondes* and *Nighty Night*, sitcom with *Coupling*, low-budget single drama with *The Announcement*, and risky series with the acute NHS drama *Bodies*. A new irreverent tone is evident in science with *Body Hits* and in documentary with *Little Angels*, but the main news bulletin has failed to locate a youth-oriented vein. BBC4 has been charged with becoming a ghetto for low-rating 'public service' genres, enabling BBC1 and BBC2 to maximise ratings. This is too simple, and relations between the channels involve more overlap, and more collaboration. But it is something to be watched.

Dyke's final move, having launched a slate of free-to-air DTV channels, was to tackle BSkyB's dominance in DTV platforms. In autumn 2002, the BBC launched Freeview in partnership with BSkyB and Crown Castle, the successor to ITV's defunct DTT service. Freeview suits those consumers willing to pay a one-off charge to get DTV but wanting to avoid pay television, and who are satisfied with a wider but limited range of digital channels. By paying well under £100 for a decoder box they gain free access to about thirty channels. Freeview proved immensely popular, particularly among those consumers previously resistant to DTV. Within a year of its launch, it became BSkyB's main competitor, pushing the take-up of DTV to over 50 per cent of households.[66] In early 2003 Dyke announced another coup. The BBC withdrew from BSkyB's satellite encryption service, saving £85 million. Carriage had been negotiated with an alternative satellite and the BBC channels were to be offered free-to-air. The implications were profound. Dyke had created the possibility of a 'Freeview-on-satellite' which might eventually break BSkyB's hold on this superior, potentially universal platform; and in 2004, with Ofcom's support, the corporation followed through with a formal proposal for a 'freesat' service, arguing that this alone would solve the government's problem of achieving digital transition.[67] Proving how devastating were the BBC's moves, just two months later BSkyB was impelled to hit back with its own 'freesat' proposal.[68]

In new media and in old, Dyke's contention was that the BBC's role will be more important in the digital era, because commercial media face increasing market fragmentation and audience segmentation; as a result they will be less able to afford to support even their former services. He outlined three roles for the BBC: international, particularly in providing independent information and mediating opinion in the post-9/11 climate; national, in terms of fostering social integration through the main networks; and regional or local, especially given the consolidation and commercialisation of ITV and its consequent with-drawal from regional services.[69] At each level the BBC's digital activities, branded BBCi, now enhance what is offered. Crucial is the way new media extend the variety and range of the BBC's mode of address to its audiences and publics, inviting participation. To exemplify, I want to sketch four contrasting BBC initiatives, each utilising digital potential to highly innovative ends. Two of them are content-based, and the other two are experiments in which the BBC is acting to animate interactive connections, in this way fostering public media spaces.

The first is the use of cross-platform links to populate a thematic event. In 2003 the BBC staged an Asylum Day, in which standard linear factual and fictional programmes on television and radio were linked to online activities and archives, sources of information on charities and NGOs, heated debate and advice. On the website, moving personal testimonies of current and past asylum seekers and migrants – online video diaries – sat side by side with pro- and anti-asylum polemics. Later in 2003 another thematic event, marked by programming on all the BBC's platforms, was Black History Month. A second initiative is the use of interactivity to enhance linear broadcast forms. One such experiment was Radio 4's *The Dark House*, a drama linked to a site where listeners could develop and opt for alternative narratives, and could follow the story through the experience and inner thoughts of any one of the three main characters.

A third experiment, a belated outcome of the review of political programmes, takes off from the recognition of the crisis in political communication and of citizens' disengagement with formal politics. In a departure from the Westminster-centred political journalism of impartiality, and responding to the new forms of political imagination and connection engendered by the Internet, a new website, iCan, is being designed in the mould of a bulletin board for extra-parliamentary issue-based and activist politics. The aim is to assist campaigning and to animate new political communities by offering resources such as databases on pressure groups, local councillors, MPs and NGOs, and the means to create links to like-minded activist individuals and groups. The site depends on user-generated content and will evolve through its use. It is mainly locally oriented; a pilot engages local radio and television teams in Bristol, Sheffield, Leicester and other cities. A productive spin-off may be to generate grass-roots news stories to be fed into newsgathering, enriching the news agenda and the local relevance of news.[70] We might call iCan a facilitative online space for political self-representation and self-organisation. The subtext is the reinvigoration of civil society via citizen empowerment. The vision of the changing political functions of the BBC immanent in this experiment heralds a new maturity in its journalistic culture and, potentially, radically revises its philosophy of journalism: it is an immense departure.

The fourth and most ambitious initiative is the BBC's development in Hull via a public–private partnership with Kingston Communications and regional and city agencies of a broadband-based, local-radio-backed pilot for a wired city. Named BBC Hull Interactive, the BBC has invested £25 million over five years in the project. It encompasses unprecedented levels of interactivity and opportunities for local production of content and programmes, a new dedicated local television news service, a centre providing free ICT skills and multimedia training, and the delivery of broadband learning packages for schools and home-based adult education. The pilot acts as a test site where the corporation can try out and gauge responses to a range of new media services, such as a navigation tool enabling the legitimate downloading of and interaction with audio-visual content from a variety of sources. Research in Hull suggests that television consumption in the broadband context is polarised: on the one hand 'apathetic' or 'ambient TV' use, on the other the desire, modelled on the capacity to rework digitised music online, for controls that allow consumers to play with and rework audio-visual material. The micro-community-building idea has re-emerged in Hull in the guise of experiments enabling users to create their own television content, trading technical quality for a highly localised or targeted peer-to-peer service.[71]

Commentaries on the contemporary BBC rarely take in the extraordinary renewal and greater ambition of its public service vision evidenced by these developments. Dyke grasped the opportunities afforded by digital media at several complementary levels: platforms, channels, old (linear) and new (non-linear and cross-platform) content. He did this in order to exploit the public service synergies so obtained and to enable innovation to occur across different platforms. In this way Dyke forged the architecture and etched the philosophical outlines of a free-to-air public service system in digital media, delivering an alternative to pay media and their commercial lock-ins for those seeking a continuation of the public service experience. The BBC's inspiration under Dyke was to see that it should work across these several fronts and at different levels in transforming its activities and audience address; and to use digital to answer major challenges posed by the co-evolving political and media ecology: the need to raise political consciousness and respond to new political forms, to rejuvenate the civic culture, to encourage connection and participation, and to innovate in content. In these and other ways Dyke's BBC made substantial inroads into that reinvention of public service broadcasting demanded by contemporary conditions.

*

Collective learning

'One of the major roles of the BBC in the past has been as a focus for the collective learning of British broadcasting. If the BBC was a private firm it might paradoxically be easier to recognise just how much it depends on its corporate culture. It might be easier to ask how to nurture loyalty and foster an ethos of quality and high trust between its employees. The introduction of a more internally competitive culture might be constrained by the fear that [it] would threaten this valuable asset by setting creative workers against each other, and emphasising personal interest over the interest of the corporation as a whole. Broadcasting, like other cultural industries, is innovative or it is nothing. It must continually generate new ideas. [The goal should be] to create a community of employees, one that chatters, invents and criticises. Excessive marketisation limits the collective innovation that comes from a free flow of information. In the market paradigm it is assumed that competition will fuel innovation. Now we know that it is much harder to create an innovative environment and much easier to destroy it than anyone imagined.'

Geoff Mulgan, 1993.

*

A Creative Ecology

For anyone wishing to understand the media environment and its relationship with contemporary culture, two fundamental truths should be at the forefront. They have been alluded to throughout this book. First, contrary to the reductive idea of sovereign consumers central to neo-liberal thought, broadcasting shows us that audience tastes do not exist in some pristine state, arriving perfectly formed in the marketplace. Audience tastes are not autonomous. They are cumulatively and historically conditioned by interaction with what is produced. In the ecology of broadcasting, production precedes, conditions and sets limits to consumption. This point is often confused with an elitist defence of

491

'producer interests', but it is no such thing. It is first and foremost an empirical truth applying to all forms of culture, and one that in broadcasting applies to the most popular as well as esoteric programming. More generally, broadcast culture exists in a double relation with wider cultural and ideological movements: in a centripetal motion it draws them in, selectively metabolising them in its operations; and in a centrifugal motion it sends them out, refracted in its programming. But this truth also grounds a broader principle. Even if it was possible to construct a mechanism to feed audience tastes directly into production, the more perfectly to mirror their existing desires, it would not result in the best nor the most democratic of media worlds. For in all genres, creativity requires that producers exceed and confound the expectations of audiences, the better to renew their desires and interests.[72] Despite the limited insights of audience research, and the reality of audiences' power variably to interpret what they receive, producers shoulder both creative power and responsibility and we lose sight of the necessary autonomy of producers at our peril. The more inventively and responsibly that creative autonomy is deployed, the more it is benign.

The second truth, which follows, is that the BBC is unavoidably influenced by the broader media ecology. Because it must be popular, and because of the wider conditioning of tastes by what is prevalent in the broadcast culture as a whole, the BBC must emulate the character of popular programming put out by its rivals, or risk becoming isolated from the general drift of programming and so from public tastes. Two critical points ensue. First, it is not sufficient to regulate only the BBC for public service. The intensely symbiotic nature of the media ecology means that each broadcaster must be required to uphold these standards, so as benevolently to condition audience tastes. Britain's pre-1990 regulatory structure embodied exactly this principle. It was this principle that Dyke articulated in 2003 when, in order to ensure an ecological balance in the UK in favour of public service, he rejected the call for ITV to be 'liberated' from public service obligations.[73] Second, to enable the BBC to withstand and counteract the populist drift, it must have a considerable market presence across all genres and significant platforms. In this way it will be empowered to influence the wider industry towards high-quality services and richer cultural goals and, most importantly, to impact substantially on audience tastes.[74] It is this latter function that is commonly overlooked in discussions of the BBC's role in the digital future. Without it the low-cost, lower-quality programming issuing from many commercial providers will meet little resistance in establishing the framework of public tastes and expectations. In such circumstances the BBC's offerings will become increasingly exceptional in the public mind, bringing about just that marginality its rivals would prefer. The result of this vicious circle is likely to be a further degradation of Britain's media ecology.

The strongest recent market-led vision of Britain's digital media environment, by Barry Cox, the government's digital television 'tsar' and deputy chairman of Channel 4, proposes that people should in future relate to broadcasting as a 'digital bookshop' in which they pay only for what they wish individually to consume. The vision is predicated on the arrival of broadband and the Personal Video Recorder, which allows viewers to record and store many hours of material. Both technologies are equated with a more perfect market mechanism and the growth of fragmented 'on-demand' viewing. Their existence is seen as leading to the demise of the 'cultural tyranny', the scheduled mass channels and messy mixed economy of public service broadcasting.[75] The same model, propounded in the 1986 Peacock report, has long been cogently criticised on both economic and cultural grounds.[76] Despite this, it carries great weight in policy circles, in part due to mechanisms outlined in relation to Channel 4's digital strategies. In a breathtaking teleology, fuelled by technological determinism, the assumption is made that market research on existing digital households gives access to future trends for all viewers; policies and business models are then designed which will drive markets further in the same commercial direction.

In fact, after fifteen years of multichannel television, a majority of British households reject Cox's model, refuting predictions of the decline of mass channels and of swelling hostility to the public service paradigm. Seventy-five per cent of viewing in all homes now goes to the five public service terrestrial mass channels; in multichannel homes the figure falls to 60 per cent, but in Freeview homes, those resisting a pay model in DTV, it is 84 per cent.[77] Having determined a transition to DTV, the government became alarmed by the scale of consumer resistance and the consequent political dangers of being seen to impose it. Independent research in 2003 commissioned by the government in light of its concerns fills out the nature of this resistance. Of six focus-group derived 'mindsets' characterising people's attitudes to DTV, five were dissatisfied with or saw negative consequences stemming from multichannel and digital television, including family fragmentation and the growth of extreme and amoral content. DTV was equated by resistant consumers with pay television, itself associated with a profusion of cheap, poor-quality, entertainment-driven American programming and with the degeneration of British television.[78] For this vast body of consumers, the BBC has thus far been tasked single-handedly with delivering government policy by offering free-to-air DTV options in distribution and high-quality channels. The public continues to hold Britain's public service broadcasting in high esteem. Alone, the BBC is fostering a non-coercive, non-pay transition to digital.

If the aim of Cox and others to drag reluctant Britons into a pay-on-demand digital heaven seems ill-conceived, how, then, can creativity be nurtured in the digital age? If production is prior to consumption, the critical issue is the quality and diversity of the programmes and services available to audiences, services that will in turn condition the future direction both of audience tastes and of broadcast markets. It is producers' intentions in combination with the conditions bearing on production that together determine the quality of pro-grammes and services. Both high ambition among producers and supportive conditions are necessary for the realisation of high-quality output, and neither is sufficient. But where ambition will be thwarted and suppressed by adverse conditions, benevolent conditions may well encourage the emergence and development of talent and invention. If 'organisations depend as much on their guiding values, and their culture, as they do on formal structures',[79] pro-ducers' creative responsibility must be led by such values. In this vein, several writers have attributed quality in television to whether or not its production 'is governed by an ethic of truth-telling',[80] or more broadly to whether 'the system as a whole [regards] the pursuit and elevation of programme quality as a priority goal',[81] while stressing that such aims will find plural expression in different genres.

The BBC's ethos has epitomised such values in media organisations, and these are important insights. But they say little about the conditions that con-strain and mould programme-makers' intentions and that have corroded not only the BBC's ethos but those of its sister broadcasters. A central purpose of this book has been to demonstrate, via Birt's BBC, how powerfully such an ethos, and such intentions, are influenced by the conditions bearing on pro-duction. These conditions are both internal, such as the complex structures of control and dependence in commissioning processes, and external. It is impos-sible, again, to understand the populism exhibited by BBC channels in recent years without linking this directly to the pressures created by the dive down-market of rival channels, themselves responding to excesses of competition and market fragmentation caused by political acts of deregulation. The chain of causation is inescapable. These are pressures that, within the BBC, can override the integrity and creative potential of its production cultures.

Both externally and within the organisation, as shown in this book, con-ditions in the nineties were far from favourable. By taking the collective mind elsewhere, by elevating values of competition, entrepreneurialism, efficiency, financial probity and management 'best practice' over those of good programme-making and commonality of purpose, the BBC's power was misdirected. Certainly, Birtist concerns were an alternative interpretation of the BBC's corporate responsibility, and many observers argue that they were overdue. In their effects on production, however, these values were far from neutral. They were actively destructive of the space and the climate for creativity. Together with fierce competition in the industry, they eroded the BBC's capacity to fulfil its primary public responsibility: creativity.

If we turn around the negative image given by Birtism, aspects of a well-functioning creative ecology come into focus. Changing conditions could enable the BBC to rebuild its ethos, revivified by contemporary values, as Dyke began with his stress on pluralism and civic participation. Obstructive marketisation and contractualism, corrosive casualisation, and excesses of bureaucracy and auditing must be wheeled back. Training and career development, and thereby deep identification with the organisation's overarching aims, must be boosted. Risk-taking must be nurtured. Dyke reduced the BBC's inherent segmentation, fostering collaboration across departments and communication across boundaries. If audience research and accountability procedures under Birt offered only phoney solutions to the BBC's sometimes arrogant introversion, the corporation now appears more outward-looking and genuinely responsive to those it serves. Research, when demoted from being the engine of creative decision-making, no doubt has a productive part to play in informing high-level strategy and investment. But there is much to do to make accountability more than a mantra, given shape in the pages of an annual report that only critics and media journalists read.

Above all, there is a need for two major, related shifts in political and public discourse. The first is the challenge of rebuilding collective trust in the benign power vested in our professional bodies – not artificially, but founded on a real confidence in the exercise of professional skill, integrity and responsibility.[82] The second change, already in the wind, is the need to recover a belief in the benefits of large and integrated public organisations, with their virtues of scale, scope, training, integrity and cooperation, and their ethically-imbued corporate being. This is particularly so for industries like broadcasting and new media that form both the infrastructure of our national political and cultural life, and a key element in Britain's international competitiveness.

*

The purpose of government

January 2003: Labour's Culture Secretary, Tessa Jowell, is giving a keynote speech to a major conference on the future of public service communications. She opens: 'People often ask me what is the purpose of government. And I reply that it is to promote competition.' She continues by trailing the Communications Bill to be passed later this year which rests on the powers of the new super regulator, Ofcom, and which elevates competition regulation over the content regulation at the heart of public service broadcasting. The Bill will profoundly liberalise media ownership in Britain, for the first time allowing non-EU foreign conglomerates to buy a consolidated ITV, and enabling Murdoch to buy a terrestrial station, Channel 5, subject to a public interest test. It is widely acknowledged that such liberalisation will necessitate more strenuous content regulation than in previous eras, yet that is in tension with the Bill's basic philosophy. It emerges that of Ofcom's 880 posts, just 60 are devoted to content and standards while 326 deal with markets; and that the 'light touch' Ofcom, intended to promote efficiency, will cost 27 per cent more than the five regulators it replaces. Jowell also announces a slate of reviews of the BBC's digital and other services, in addition to the existing review of News 24, in the lead-in to Charter renewal.

Diary, 2003.

*

The great corrupter

'Pretending Channel 5 needs investment is absurd: its principal shareholder is five times the size of Granada and Carlton put together. But to Murdoch it would be invaluable. He could buy up sports rights for both terrestrial and satellite, outbidding all comers, cross-promoting across his newspapers and two TV platforms. With Murdoch behind it, Channel 5 could destroy ITV. John Major, desperate to assuage the wrath of Murdoch's press, gave him all he wanted in the new digital universe. Now here we go again, Tony Blair handing over the last prize to Murdoch, whose papers repay him handsomely. Murdoch is the great corrupter of politicians. Politicians fear they need this bully's patronage. Whenever they cave in, his grip on politics tightens.'

Polly Toynbee, 2003.

*

What took them so long?

'Tessa Jowell, the Culture Secretary, has announced an independent review of BBC

496

News 24. But in the multichannel era, it is surely absurd that the BBC should be asked to justify a 24-hour news service. A more pertinent question is, what on earth took them so long? If there is one mandatory obligation which ought to be written into the BBC's Charter, it is the duty to exploit its investment in journalism, its 45 foreign bureaux, its network of specialists and regional correspondents and its tie-up with BBC World in a round-the-clock news service. It would be a scandalous waste of public money if such a rich resource were not made freely available.'

Steven Barnett, 2002.

*

Governing by numbers

'We like to make sure we always have one review [of the BBC] in process and two pending.'

Bill Bush, special adviser to the Culture Secretary, 2003.

*

Auntie's Nanny

There is a puzzle at the heart of BBC–government relations. If the government is relying on the BBC to deliver core policy objectives by fostering the transition to DTV and encouraging Britons to go online, how, then, to make sense of its accelerating reviews of the BBC's operations, commercial and otherwise? In the daily barrage of commentary, it is hard to discern the larger pattern. For what emerges in the last decade is a curious set of recursive forces. In 1994, as part of Charter renewal, the Conservative government published a White Paper that required the corporation to expand into new media and to become more commercial, in order to make up its financial shortfalls and to forge a bridge-head for British media into global markets. The BBC readily complied. These developments generated a furious reaction from the BBC's commercial rivals who, citing competition law, charged the corporation with abusing its privi-leged position and distorting the markets in which it operates. It is from this date that accusations of unfair trading became focal for those attacking the legitimacy of the BBC. Since then BBC Online, BBC News 24, BBC3, the new children's channels, the move of BBC1's 9 p.m. news to 10 p.m. – all have been the target of such accusations by competitors, and some of the complaints were pursued legally through the British and European courts (although none reached a hearing). In turn, these conflicts caused the government to engage in an escalating series of interventions requiring the BBC to justify publicly both its commercial and public service expansions. The interventions included repeated calls for public consultations, annual reporting to the Secretary of State, ministerial approval of new commercial activities, tough tests for the approval of new public services, and external auditing arrangements and assessments of the BBC's compliance with competition rules. In sum, government instructions dictated BBC policies, which provoked competitors' hostility, which in turn elicited government sanctions against the BBC.

A variant of the same cycle is seen in the history of digital television. The government determined a transition to DTV. Sky was in a position of market dominance and the government required competitors to maintain pluralism, while many consumers were unhappy with the pay-DTV model. The BBC, funded appropriately, designed free-to-air alternatives. In reaction, commercial competitors protested at the BBC's 'inappropriate' entry into digital markets. As a consequence, the BBC became subject to searching government-directed reviews. The BBC cannot win: commercialise and compete, but not too well, while the government behaves towards the corporation as a hectoring nanny.

In the event, in 2001 the government ruled on the BBC's DTV plans, passing all of them except BBC3 because of its potentially detrimental effect on E4 and Sky One, whose market share, analysts argued, would be likely to fall. The debate over BBC3 set a worrying precedent in that competition issues – the interests of commercial rivals – threatened to prevail in government thinking over the larger question of the public interest in youth channels. In late 2002 a revised proposal for BBC3 was passed, with stringent public service conditions attached. It is notable that, for all the criticisms of the BBC's fair trading procedures, when reviewed in 2001 for the government by an eminent competition lawyer, he concluded that they compared 'favourably with those of other undertakings. Indeed, I am not aware of any organisation that is subject to as much scrutiny – internal and external – to ensure compliance with Competition Law.'[83]

The recursive forces demonstrate the incoherence of neo-liberal policy in this area. Rather than censure the BBC for delivering what it itself has judged to be in the public interest, government might be advised to define, and then defend, appropriate boundaries to the BBC's operations. Here it is useful to distinguish between the BBC's essential and non-essential public service activities. Its non-essential activities include merchandising, publishing and other add-ons or extensions of its core services, and these should be subject to the rigorous application of competition law. Its essential public service activities are those related to its central information, education, entertainment and cultural roles in media markets where it is likely to have a substantial presence. This category encompasses the online services and digital public service channels, and in these markets the BBC's dominance may even be tolerated because of its benign functions of standard setting, minority provision and relative autonomy from commercial pressures. Both European and domestic competition law stipulate exceptions that can be justified in relation to such services on the grounds of the BBC's special public service mission. The corporation should not be treated equivalently to other market players without such a mission; the government should establish rules and then respect the BBC's capacity to act innovatively.

Nowhere is the vacuity of the present rhetoric of competition more apparent than in the attitude of the government towards independent production. The stakes rose when in 2004 the independents' trade body called for the BBC's independent quota to rise to 50 per cent, a position echoed by Ofcom.[84] Policies have rightly been put in place to enable independents to grow as businesses, but it is widely foreseen that this will go along with further concentration of an already concentrated independent sector, while for years even Channel 4, established to support a diverse independent sector, has favoured large, established independents in its commissioning. Current policies therefore carry great costs: the loss of that emphasis on diversity and innovation, on encouraging new entrants and new voices, that was the core purpose of the sector. They favour consolidation over the sector's animating principles. The indications are that as the independents grow, their culture changes to focus more on the commercial bottom line of bulk commissions and raising the rate of profit than on risk-taking. Moreover, as large players in international markets, the commitment to imaginative production oriented solely to domestic audiences wanes. The question is: where are the policies to ensure real diversity and to nurture and sustain the viability of new entrants and small independents?

When the BBC's commercial practices serve rather than drive its public service activities, there are significant benefits: expanding sales and foreign revenues which flow back and enhance national, free-to-air services. The corporation acts responsibly when it adds value for licence fee payers by commercially exploiting its unmatched programme rights. Beyond a certain scale, however, commercial activities risk overwhelming the BBC's public service orientation and undermining its legitimacy. They should represent only a limited proportion of its total operations, although their scale may nonetheless be considerable. Such limits, moreover, would create predictability for competitors and yield opportunities for them to exploit. The BBC's standard-setting role has great importance for the media ecology not only culturally but economically. By setting standards through a significant scale of operations nationally and internationally, the BBC progressively influences the markets in which it operates. The beneficial effects of the BBC being enabled to pursue its ambitions accrue not just to the BBC but to the entire British media and beyond.

The government's intrusive interventions in recent years point to a deeper pathology, one heightened by the events around the death of David Kelly: that is, a reduction in the BBC's independence from government. From the encouragement of Birtist micro-management, to the repeated reviews of services, to ministerial criticism of the move of the main evening news, to the rapid escalation of hostilities prior to Hutton, the government arrogates to itself a continuous power of surveillance and demands an inappropriate intimacy with the corporation's workings. Little institutional autonomy remains. It is no surprise that these developments coincide with the BBC's lack of satisfactory resolution of its governance arrangements. The two are closely linked as, ostensibly, the government intervenes because it cannot trust the governance. In reality, its drive to curb the BBC seems fuelled as much by its ideological discomfort with a creative and powerful public sector, and its insalubrious political interest in appeasing Murdoch's press.

A series of structural reforms are urgently needed. Bringing the BBC fully under Ofcom, given the latter's economistic orientation and closeness to New Labour, would be unproductive. Alarmingly, the problem of political placemen has migrated from the BBC governors to Ofcom, while Ofcom is already proving quixotic in discharging its statutory duties. In its first review of public service television in 2004, it trails potentially explosive reforms by altering, less than a year after the Communications Act, how it proposes to assess public service broadcasting. Where the act specifies a range of necessary types of programming, Ofcom has outlined deregulatory moves away from detailed requirements on ITV and Channel 5. Rather than work with the effective historical model that has underpinned Britain's exceptional broadcast traditions and expertise, Ofcom hubris – not unlike the hubris demonstrated by Downing Street before the Iraq war when it disregarded expert diplomatic opinion – wills that it is time fundamentally to rethink the framework. Yet its documents are dotted with contradiction and the evasion of interpretation; contradiction in that, while Ofcom doctrine espouses evidence-based regulation based on tight definitions and quantitative data, basic issues appear simply as articles of faith. The statement '[In] a fully digital world . . . consumers will have access to much greater choice'[85] begs the crucial and opaque question of just how 'choice' in broadcasting is defined or even measured. And while it is reported, citing the BBC's Newsnight and Horizon, that 'audiences for more challenging types of programming fell sharply in multichannel homes between 1998–2003',[86] this critical finding hangs, with ominous fatalism, uninterpreted: does it signal a 'rational' consumer judgement that such programmes are of little value, or that this programming has declined in quality? Or could it reflect the fact that the first wave of multichannel adopters were attracted precisely because they were susceptible to the greater populism of the offering, and that their TV tastes have, by virtue of the conditioning consequent on their exposure, been drawn further in this direction?

In this light, it is essential to retain an element of regulatory pluralism in the British system. The BBC must reform its self-regulation, instituting a real and effective separation between the executive and governors. A strong, genuinely independent self-regulatory body for the BBC would bring a virtuous circle of benefits: augmenting the authority and the legitimacy of its self-regulation, creating greater insulation from government intervention, increasing the corporation's independence, and providing a robust and independent oversight of the executive – the function lamentably missing in the Birt period. In place of the part-time, amateur, 'great and good' Board of Governors, the new body should be full-time; it should include representation of creative expertise as well as other relevant professional experience; it should democratise and make transparent its system of appointments; and it should have sufficient resources including an independent research base to inform and support its judgements.

But the independence of the BBC can be bolstered further. To prevent the potential abuse by the government of its powers to set the licence fee, Britain should learn from Germany, where an independent Broadcasting Finance Commission exists to monitor the sector and recommend the level of the licence fee for the two public service broadcasters. A final measure, to ensure that the government's backstop regulatory powers rest on coherent and consensual principles, is to provide a definition of public service communications in law. The 2003 Act offers a broad-brush Reithian definition for television, one that is productively updated by stipulations that cultural activity in Britain and its diversity are reflected in and stimulated by a range of genres, and that the output should reflect the lives and concerns of different communities and cultural traditions within the UK.[87] However, controversially, it is a definition that will be applied to the system as a whole rather than, as before, to each channel; it is this that apparently gives Ofcom the green light to completely redraw the map of the broadcasters' public service commitments. Much is therefore left to interpretation by Ofcom. It is a matter for enormous concern that the act does not set out core principles by which to adjudge whether Ofcom's interpretation adheres to them, principles that would also enrich Britain's constitutional culture.[88] Taken together the steps outlined would be likely to depoliticise the current situation, enhance the BBC's regulation and independence, diminish its vulnerability to government and strengthen Britain's democracy.

*

Who do you know?: the politics of truth (III)

My main BBC fieldwork is long past and, as instructed by the funding body, my research report has been sent to a range of public bodies with the aim of having some impact on policy. Today I've followed my report to the relevant government department, the DCMS, and am meeting an official who has expressed interest in my work. I'm here to explore whether there is any way the findings, or my skills, can be of service, and for guidance on how one might pursue the insights higher up the policy chain. I assume this is an ideas-led, expertise-led issue, and that the official will see it the same way. As the meeting progresses, and a vaguely empty pair of eyes wander in and out of vision, while stacks of policy documents are pushed across the desk in my direction, I realise that I'm being toyed with. There's no real interest in developing a relationship.

My interlocutor seems to grow a little intrigued, however, by my sheer, innocent determination, along with the lack of understanding on my part of the implicit ground rules of the game we are apparently engaged in. Finally, as though in a last effort to bring the meeting to its resolution, the curtains to the secret inner sanctum are swept back. He leans towards me with a sympathetic, only slightly less condescending smile, and asks very pointedly, cutting the crap: 'Look: who do you *know*?' For a long moment I'm speechless; I don't understand what he's talking about. Then, instantaneously, I'm ashamed of my naivety, which has outlasted the baptism into political realism of my fieldwork. I grasp the cue: it's about politics, power, contacts in government, the DCMS, the ITC, the IPPR, Demos – anywhere and everywhere, that is, that matters. I will, he tells me, get somewhere – doors will open to further uses of my research, possibly, he implies, to public appointment – if I have, or can cultivate, patronage from someone who matters in the seething inner circle of Labour policy-niks. James Purnell, for instance: whizz-kid former IPPR media policy researcher, then BBC fast-track Corporate Centre audit executive, then Downing Street Policy Unit broadcasting man, now Labour MP. James Purnell: the man who, when still at the BBC, and after several approaches on my part, agreed to be interviewed in three months' time as he was so busy reviewing Performance Review, and who, when that date arrived, had left the BBC. The IPPR or Demos, for instance: both of which I'd offered my BBC report to publish, but neither of which quite wanted it. I thank the official for the inside tip, and am reinforced in my determination to write a book that will reach beyond this circle. The funding council's injunction to get real, inform industry and government, has met that obscure and immovable object of desire – power. It's not what you know, but who you know.

Diary, 2000.

*

After Hutton

For the BBC, the long-term fall-out from the Hutton crisis is difficult to predict. In some eyes, the BBC emerges bruised and cowed, no longer the fearless organization devoted to bearing witness to uncomfortable truths of the sort required more than ever by the present disastrous deterioration in international relations. But for others, despite Hutton's judgement, or even because of its blatant biases, the BBC's insistence on its independence and on maintaining its questioning of government have been vindicated a thousand times over since the Kelly affair. In this view, the BBC emerges chastened but unbowed, its vital democratic role strengthened.

The interregnum was ended and the outlook clarified, however, by the appointment in April 2004 of Michael Grade as the new chairman of the BBC. Grade is one of the most experienced and successful figures in broadcasting, with tenures as controller of BBC1 and chief executive of Channel 4, and the first television professional to be appointed chairman. He immediately made three crucial interventions. First, he made it known that the BBC had 'done our apologising'. He then stated that 'the editorial independence of the BBC is paramount', pledging that it would remain an 'independent, universally available, value for money public service broadcaster' and that he was committed to the licence fee.[89] Finally, in a move both politically astute and principled, he let it be known that he would prioritise the biggest reforms of the BBC governors in their history, likely to be along the lines mentioned earlier, in particular by separating the roles of management and watchdog and making the governors a fully independent body with its own support staff, and by altering its makeup to include media experts.[90]

Weeks later, Grade announced the appointment of Mark Thompson as director-general, a BBC trained, long-standing and talented BBC executive with extensive experience as an editor of news and current affairs, BBC2 controller and director of television, who from 2001 had taken time out as chief executive of Channel 4. The apologetic habit of recent decades of drawing DGs only from outside the BBC was ended, and the Thompson–Grade duo was hailed as a 'dream ticket' and as potentially a more talented combination even than Dyke and Davies. A beneficiary of the Newsnight/Panorama route to high office, Thompson rose through the ranks in the Birt regime without adopting its ideological mien, and when controller of BBC2 showed a keen eye for colour and range in drama, documentary and comedy and for a well-judged Reithian mix. As director of television and Dyke's right-hand man, he was responsible for devising the corporation's ambitious and nuanced digital broadcasting strategy.

Adopting as his motto 'public value', Thompson took office in June 2004 with a pledge to continue cutting excessive overheads, and with a new clarity about the BBC's purposes manifest in streamlined management boards dedicated to the BBC's creative, journalistic and commercial activities. He gave a commitment to the continuing place of investigative journalism, but cautioned that 'ratings are never the most important thing in our journalism. Nor . . . in any of our other services.'[91] A report on BBC journalism after Hutton, published the next day, reiterated the 'publisher' responsibilities of programme editors, stressed the need for better training and career development, to be achieved partly via an in-house 'college of journalism', and signalled a major overhaul of the complaints procedures.[92] Thompson's statement made plain his debt to Dyke and other talented peers, including Alan Yentob. On three crucial fronts, each the subject of an immediate review and each with as much long-term importance as the journalism reforms, Thompson laid out his stall. Commercially, he asked, where should the BBC's activities begin and end, and with which partners? Creatively, he lightly chided Dyke for not completely overturning Birt's 1996 production/channel and commissioning split, stating unequivocally that 'the best work comes from the closest possible creative dialogue and I'm not sure the current set-up . . . helps'.[93] At last, it seems, the central pernicious myth of the Birt era – that the gains from close cooperation between channel and production visions underpinned by a unified public service ethos are outweighed by the benefits of 'clean' market transactions – may be revoked. Thompson's third commitment was to see through Dyke's decision to move a major part of the BBC's operations out of London and into other parts of the UK, boosting the contribution of the Nations and Regions and showing an awareness of the critical importance of both cultural and organizational diversity and decentralization to the future BBC. Whether measured in term of sober journalistic acumen designed to keep future Campbells and Huttons at bay, flair for the BBC's cultural aspirations and cutting-edge entertainment, strategic intelligence and social awareness, or rhetorical art when addressing the industry and political forums that matter, Thompson promises much.

But for all this, unless the political perils besetting the BBC are tackled, it may have little meaningful autonomy by which to navigate its future. It is by confronting the vexed issues of governance and self-regulation, which lay at the heart of the BBC's escalating political difficulties in recent years, that chairman Grade can attempt to put right two of the most significant problems that remained unaddressed by both Birt and Dyke and their chairmen. By bringing in extensive reforms of the kind outlined, he would tackle the political bullying exemplified by the Kelly and Hutton crises and responsible for the loss of the most talented director-general in generations. By radically changing the rules of engagement, the reforms can be expected to insulate the BBC further not just from government but from Ofcom. But such reforms would also correct the lack of effective oversight of the executive manifest in the governors' collusion with Birt's politically-expedient managerialism, a collusion complicit in the political subordination of the BBC, without which the damage of the Birt years might have been limited. Moreover, with distinguished professionals among their ranks, the governors would benefit from the collective expertise evident in the broadcast traditions that have enriched and amused Britons over the last eighty years. These are people who will need to navigate with vision the endemic uncertainties of the contemporary media world; and we can hope that they are not the kind to know the price of everything and the value of nothing.

In these ways, in the hypercompetitive times that beckon, the reforms would set the BBC's governance on a footing likely to enable the organization to flourish relatively unburdened by political diktats in the future. The net outcome may, then, be a stronger BBC. Yet when all is considered, it would be unrealistic to think that the political crisis of the BBC is over, or that it can ever be over. There is blood on the lens, there are vast commercial interests ranged against the BBC, and the stakes at the core of the relationship between public service broadcasting and democracy continue inexorably to rise.

Uncertain Vision

Re-imagining the Nation

Orwell in Aarhus

I am in a hotel room in Aarhus, Denmark. With hours to kill I am watching the international channel BBC World on a set suspended near my bed. The programming is strange, episodic, with longueurs in between programmes in which flags fly and a repetitive music theme sounds. The hourly news slot is interspersed with quarter- and half-hour programmes, their insubstantial nature perhaps intended to reflect the distracted state of today's international traveller. The channel speaks of a kind of limbo, which echoes perfectly my own state.

I switch to its twin, BBC Prime, an entertainment channel with back to back light drama and sitcoms: *Casualty*, *EastEnders*, an old *Dr Who*, the *Jools Holland Show*. An ad comes on for BBC World. It has an uncanny resemblance to the Turner Prize-winning video art of Gillian Wearing. Her video has people speaking other people's words, for example switching children's and parents' voices, so that the wrong voice issues from each person. Here, in the BBC World ad, a series of multicultural figures – black, white, Indian, Chinese, kids and adults – speak in each others' voices, all jumbled up. It's eery, chaotic, disturbing. Then comes the punchline: 'But truth speaks with one voice'. Suddenly the multicultural figures speak with their own voice; tension is relaxed and 'reality' restored. The implication is clear and the message emotional and powerful: the BBC's global services – and BBC World – speak truth, and it's a truth that all can understand, whatever their colour, age or ethnicity. The BBC avows for itself a global role of truth-speaking. The ad is electrifying; I am utterly slain. But perhaps the message is too powerful, too propagandistic. Should the BBC use such Orwellian language? Should it dare to propose for itself such a universal role?

Diary, 1997.

*

Outside is inside

'Europe today has been cosmopolitanised from within. There are roughly seventeen million people in Europe today who can't possibly fit the ethnocultural definition of European-ness due to their skin colour or religion, but who nevertheless understand themselves, identify and organise themselves culturally and politically as Europeans. Thanks to transnational obligations and interconnections, Europe, like the rest of the world, has been turning into an open network with blurring boundaries, where outside is already inside. Europe is if anything in the vanguard of this process.'

Ulrich Beck, 2003.

*

Not by reimposing a homogeneity which has long since departed

'Broadcasting now has a major role – perhaps the critical role – to play in "re-imagining the nation": not by seeking to reimpose a unity and homogeneity which has long since departed, but by becoming the "theatre" in which [Britain's] cultural diversity is produced, displayed and represented, and the forum in which the terms of its associative life together are negotiated. This . . . remains broadcasting's key public cultural role – and one which cannot be sustained unless there is a public service idea and a system shaped in part by public service objectives to sustain it.'

Stuart Hall, 1993.

*

What should the role of Britain's public service broadcasting be in a world of conflictual pluralism, concretised in the 'war on terror'? How should it respond to the changing shape and scale of political community given by the parallel realities of Europeanisation and devolved government? When Britain no longer contains a single political public and has become a multinational state? When 'Britishness' is being reconceived along new lines by those many citizens – the British-Asian, British-Welsh, British-Jamaican, British-Moslem – who live daily the condition of dual or multiple identity? Timothy Garton Ash writes of cosmopolitan Britain at the dawn of the 21st century as a Janus with four faces, its identity straddling 'island' and 'world', Europe and America. Bearing the legacies of its historical adventures, Britain today, he contends, is a 'world island';

stubbornly insular and relentlessly internationalist, it 'is an especially clear case of the modern world'.[1] In the light of tectonic shifts in political, social and cultural realities, it is perplexing that policy debates on the future of public service broadcasting are often parochial, dwelling on the political flavours of the moment. Too often they miss the cues that come from addressing these shifts, and their implications for the emerging media landscape.

Broadcasting has many functions in our lives. Increasingly it can compound our isolation, attenuating co-presence, while holding out the ambiguous consolation of mediated substitutes for human exchange and the obligation to witness others' distant suffering.[2] It proffers experiences from the soporific to the electrifying, from simple pleasures to discomforting truths and complexities. This is its banality and its power. But a public service broadcaster like the BBC has an overriding duty to respond to the redrawing of Britain's constitutional and social contours and to developments in the world, and to allow them to inform and enrich its cultural, political and moral stance. A Britain and a Europe 'cosmopolitanised from within' demands that public service broadcasting finds a new engagement with its publics, one that meets head on the formidable challenges of a progressive pluralism. Such a claim does not amount to a call for an unthinking multiculturalism, nor for the fixing or exacerbation of ethnic and cultural differences. It entails two complementary assertions: that mutual cultural recognition and the expansion of cultural referents, as opposed to assimilation, are dynamics essential to the well-being of pluralist societies;[3] but that this does not obviate the need for integration – for the provision of common information and experience and the fostering of common identities, just as it does not gainsay the inevitable syncretisms and hybridities that occur across cultural and religious boundaries.

Public service broadcasting in this context has a singular importance. For in the face of international conflicts and domestic tensions, it offers precisely that independent arena for staging a 'politics of complex cultural dialogue' that is required in order to cultivate commonality, reciprocity and toleration.[4] It does so by providing three fundamental preconditions: not only common platforms for public reasoning and exchange, and astonishingly powerful expressive and imaginative forms which underpin the growth both of empathy and of unified experience, but means for the self-representation and self-expression of diverse groups. For where reasoned deliberation may fail to conciliate, aesthetic appreciation may succeed, in the process building empathic identification. The dialogical and reciprocal operations of broadcasting, then, are not confined to reason and cognition; its expressive and affective dimensions have both cultural and political value. In these ways public service broadcasting can mitigate the potentially divisive tensions between solidarity and diversity.[5] But it can also help to cultivate a 'proper distance', that is, 'enough knowledge and understanding of . . . the other culture to enable responsibility and care . . . to be close but not too close, distant but not too distant'. Such a stance resists the representation of others as beyond our humanity and compassion or, at the other extreme, as exactly like us – the 'immorality of identity'.[6] In the age of *Big Brother* it may seem a bitter joke, but broadcasting can extend and deepen our humanity.

In 1993 Stuart Hall issued a call to public service broadcasting to embrace cultural diversity and to become a forum for the negotiation of Britain's common life. A decade later, the commercialisation of Channel 4 and the vac-illations in the minority remits of both Channel 4 and the BBC suggest that Hall's challenge to the broadcasters remains potent. But the BBC's task is now bigger. More than at any time in its history, as Dyke understood, it must suc-ceed in mediating not only national, regional and local, but transnational and international cultural and political currents. The BBC's capacity to reinvent itself, a capacity put to work repeatedly in its eighty year history, faces unprecedented tests given the new political and cultural complexities.

In two inward directions, it has faltered. In relation to Scottish devolution, it has been hampered by the structural misfit between political devolution and cultural nationalism set against a centralised, London-based BBC and the reser-vation of political controls over broadcasting by Westminster. 'London's torpe-doing of the *"Scottish Six"* in 1998 remains an object lesson well learned in Queen Margaret Drive.'[7] Notable is the lack of will in Broadcasting House to devise innovative organisational forms responsive to the new, multidimen-sional political space. And with the availability of spectrum via digitalisation, why is it not possible to offer a Scottish television news, sourced from Glasgow, to run in parallel with the news services from London? In relation to ethnic minorities, as I have argued throughout this book, the BBC's record on repre-sentation in the linked terms of perspectives and cultural expressions aired and equity of employment and promotion within the organisation is unsatisfactory; but there are stirrings of improvement. In this and the case of Scotland, the issue is that of attaining a redistributive justice within and across the UK that is at once cultural and economic, encompassing content and employment, images and industry. The BBC – in its dual being as social organisation totemic of the public sector, and as animator of Britain's democratic conversation and public culture – has an obligation to show the way. Its output will only benefit.

Just as the BBC has been ambivalent towards devolution, it has yet to respond adequately to the arguably more difficult challenge of the European Union, a political formation that remains both contested and unsustained by any unified political culture. The poverty of the political debate about Europe in Britain is certainly not just the fault of the BBC. Yet the corporation has failed to discern a way of covering Europe that gives its institutions due significance and fosters intelligent criticism, thereby encouraging informed public debate, and that builds on the considerable historical foundations to nourish such a political culture. This is an indictment of its political and cultural invention, and of its continuing narrow focus on Westminster politics.

But if such arguments are pertinent in the national context, different reasoning should prevail externally. Of greater significance for international relations than the income promised by commercial international channels are the extraordinary international reach and appreciation of World Service radio and the BBC's Internet services. Under the rubric of fair trading, complaints arose in recent years that because the publicly-funded online news operations were freely available outside the UK, the corporation was again squeezing the space for private initiative. In reply, the BBC devised two versions of its news website, for domestic and overseas users; non-UK users are identified, and the marginal costs of the international edition are met from World Service funds. This is an appropriate solution to what is in reality a political and moral opportunity, and it is a sign of the dominance of one-dimensional market thinking that this was not perceived in the earlier controversy. For the true nature of these global activities in information and culture is redistributive in another sense: they are Britain's gift to the world; and in gift economies, as anthropology tells us, giving accrues prestige, while receiving entails a moral debt and the expectation to reciprocate. It is through these activities, now expanded on the commercial plane, that the BBC has become a global model, extending Britain's influence.

On occasion cleaving to, at other times distanced from its old allegiance to the rituals of national life, while laboriously coining new integrative media rituals to bind society, the BBC is adjusting fitfully to the new political and social geography. For the present, the corporation's attempts under Dyke to pluralise and modernise its audience address oscillate uneasily with the sanctimonious nationalism that has always been a formative part of its makeup. A striking change in recent years, reflecting the wider ebbing of deference, is the corporation's unsteady achievement of greater objectivity and self-critical edge in its treatment of the major organs of state, notably the monarchy and parliament. I have stressed in this book that while the loss of certainty and rise of scepticism towards old universals – whether Britishness, or impartiality – brings risks, it augurs a new maturity and openness, an advance on past pieties.

*

One of us

CONTINUITY: *'It's Easter day, and Shula and Jennifer are coming out of church in. . .*
The Archers.'
[THEME MUSIC] *Dum di dum di dum di dum; dum di dum di da da . . .*
SHULA: *'Morning, Jennifer – happy Easter!'*
JENNIFER: *'And to you too. Good sermon, wasn't it?'*
SHULA: *'Oh yes! What Janet said about the Queen Mother was very well judged.'*
JENNIFER: *'Yes, wasn't it? She's quite right. Of course it's sad; but such a full life..'*
SHULA: *'. . . Should be celebrated as well!'*
JENNIFER: *'Mum was full of memories last night.'*
SHULA: *'Oh, not the only one, I expect.'*
JENNIFER: *'She remembers her visiting the East End during the war to see the effects of the*
Blitz. "It was wonderful", she said, "She was one of us – it gave everyone a boost and united
the country!" That's why it meant so much to her going to the hundredth birthday tribute . . .
Mum and Jack had such a good time. They've kept some of the rose petals showered on the
crowd – it was just before the Queen Mother spoke . . .'
SHULA: *'Oh, what a nice memento!'*
JENNIFER: *'Yes. As Jack said, it's a special memory of a very special person.'*

The Archers, BBC Radio 4, 31 March 2002.

*

(Dis)respect

'The Prince of Wales pointedly chose an ITN crew to record a protocol-breaking television eulogy to his "darling grandmother" yesterday, as the royal family privately
expressed anger at the BBC's coverage of her death. Royal sources suggested the
choice was a snub to the BBC, which has been criticised for the alleged lack of respect
in its coverage. Peter Sissons, who anchored the BBC television coverage in the aftermath of the Queen Mother's death, was criticised for not wearing a black tie, and for
alleged intrusive questioning. Sissons is privately furious: he was following BBC guidelines by wearing a sombre burgundy tie and believes he has been caught up in a
vendetta between the corporation and anti-BBC newspapers. For his broadcast, the
Prince sat in front of two framed photographs of the Queen Mother, one addressed in
faded ink: "From granny with much love, 1976".'

The *Guardian* front page, 2 April 2002.

*

Getting it wrong

'When the BBC announced it would not be commissioning another series of *Babyfather* we were told: "Don't worry, there will be more black programmes." Along came *The Crouches*: a black sitcom with a stellar black cast. But many were surprised to learn that the writer behind Britain's newest black sitcom is a white Scottish man. This wouldn't be an issue if it were not so patently obvious to anyone who watched the first show that it was written by someone who was not in touch with black people and the way we live. BBC director-general Greg Dyke famously said the BBC was "hideously white". Are there really no black writers out there who could have done a better job? Black people pay the licence fee like everyone else. Are we to be grateful when the Beeb comes up with a show for us and keep quiet when they get it so badly wrong?'

Comment, *New Nation*, 2003

*

Point Counterpoint

It is a truism to claim that the nation state is in retreat under the impact of supranational economic and political restructuring. If we conceive of the nation as a 'community of communicators',[8] and if the collective identities that underpin nationhood are in a continual process of recomposition – sometimes under an illusion of timeless continuity, sometimes, as at present, explicitly in flux – then public service broadcasting's task in mediating the processes of nationhood has become infinitely more problematic in the 21st century. This is not only due to the challenge of responding to the different political orders mentioned before, and to the realities of multi-ethnic, multi-cultural and multi-faith societies, but because of the changing contours of imaginary identification wrought by transnational media as they cut across and reconfigure national media spaces. Public service broadcasting has since its inception taken a leading part in both maintaining and reshaping the boundaries that define the national community. It has done so in four ways: by its power to orchestrate, via its representations, the processes of inclusion and exclusion that define that community, arbitrating between contesting definitions, between 'community from above' and 'community from below'; by its articulation, particularly in the era of monopoly, of the substantive contents and boundaries of the nation's cultural life; by both fomenting civil society and forming a vital part of civil society; and by its orchestration of 'the dialectic between internal and external definitions',[9] its authoritative role in playing the nation back to itself, and to the world outside. Broadcasting has a critical role in the temporal dimension of these processes by constructing both our vivid social present and our social memory. In its visceral visual immediacy, television produces history through a series of heightened media events; while in its unrelenting 'present-ness' and narrativisation, it can desensitise us to the many modes of time passing and can obscure historical understanding.[10]

Broadcasting's contribution in the contemporary context is not only its unequalled reach as a space for orchestrating community and for exhibiting and experiencing diversity. It is also its potential, by virtue of the constant juxtaposition of genres and perspectives on mass channels, to relativise different kinds of knowledge and expression, sharpening its audiences' capacity for comparison and judgement. This dynamic is greatly magnified by the multi-channel and new media environment. Today, the BBC's output is itself relativised as it jostles for attention alongside competing media outlets, whether international news and entertainment channels, alternative online news sites, or transnational satellite networks and minority media with their often pronounced ethnic, territorial and ideological allegiances. Such media plenitude forms a clamorous counterpoint to the old national media culture.[11] It brings new blessings and new dangers; present political and cultural complexities are compounded by the propensities unleashed by the new media.

Two transnational media can illustrate, both in principle productive, but in practice ambiguous, with distinct troubling effects. In both, public service communication's functional purposes – its truth-seeking, reason-developing, empathy-enhancing, community-growing qualities – are destabilised and thrown into relief. Transnational satellite television has become associated with two tendencies. On the one hand it unlooses new degrees of global commercialisation by favouring those 'universal' genres – sport, movies, pop music, pornography – that most readily cross cultural boundaries. On the other, it encourages new kinds of particularism by feeding migrant and minority communities, in whichever society they live, evocative images of an idealised homeland that can reinforce their sense of isolation and disconnect them from their immediate locale. For some young British Asians, for example, national networks fuel a sense of relative deprivation, while the sexualised content of non-BBC channels creates a barrier to viewing. In contrast, Zee TV and other South Asian-based entertainment channels hold out an alternative 'imagined community', a fantasy identification eased by the experiential gap between their actual lives and the realities of the society depicted; in turn this identification stokes their alienation, a vicious circle that compounds the fracturing of Britain's social fabric.[12]

The Internet, too often idealised as an anti-authoritarian instrument herald-ing freedom of information and expression, has become equally a mechanism for the proliferation of enclaves of extreme opinion and the dissemination of disinformation. Its segmented, non-editorialising nature makes the net an unprecedented means for encountering the different and unknown and for exploring an ocean of primary sources, but also for self-enclosure and the pursuit of unsubstantiated rumour and damaging obsessions. It poses anew problems of verification, of judging reliability, of ascertaining the origin of information – problems magnified by the ease of digital image and audio manipulation. One manifestation of these issues is the move among broadcast-ers, given the ease and speed of distribution, to use the net to support an online market for the re-sale of news packages and film material. An industry discus-sion on the topic exhibited an astounding lack of concern with the distance opened up between journalistic origins and final use, and with how the outlets buying such 'off-the-peg' material could verify its source and accuracy.[13] The net, then, flattens differences in authority and tests both truth and trust.[14] The online presence of the BBC in such a context has a critical function, for its long-established ethos of accuracy and impartiality merits at least a reasonable degree of trust and provides an anchor of veracity. In this way the BBC, along with other authoritative news providers, helps strenuously to shape what can otherwise be, for many users, simply the noise of the net.

Against this background, the challenge of achieving a benign national media ecology becomes increasingly difficult, while the need for a superven-ing vision becomes more pressing. Government's foremost tool for positive intervention has been public service broadcasting. Only non-commercial public service broadcasting – in Britain, the BBC – can be delegated by govern-ment to exercise a critical and creative oversight of such developments and of the national media space, and to develop considered interventions in it – as Dyke's BBC showed so well with Freeview. In the UK, only the BBC at present can be required to undertake systematic strategic analysis of current trends so as to moderate the excesses of the transnational and commercial media and design powerful networks and services in response *under no other imperative than the public interest* – a point-counterpoint dynamic necessitated by the speed of the commercial mining of technological change, as the recent history of digital television illustrates. This oversight, and the orchestration of a benign media ecology, occurs in the national media space; but due to the 'overspill' charac-teristics of new media its effects can be far wider. If democracy is as much a social, cultural and ethical phenomenon as a political one, then its further development depends on government perceiving that the delegation of this oversight to public service broadcasting – in Britain, to the BBC – is vital for the progressive evolution and re-imagination of our democracy. Public service broadcasting is therefore engaged in a dialectic with government, delegated by it to secure the conditions for democracy's expanded well-being. However public funding is not the sole condition for oversight in the public interest; the 2003 Communications Act mislaid the lesson from history that the best in public service broadcasting stems from well-funded but limited competition across all its ambitions, not from thinly parcelling out its functions among different providers. Policy debate today has also mislaid the truth that regulating for pluralism in broadcasting has little to do with giving more of the pie to independent production as it is currently constituted – increasingly concentrated, commercially-driven, its employment practices and commitment to training unimpressive – and everything to do with regulating for diversity in channels and commissioning. Optimally, Channel 4 should be funded to compete with and complement the BBC in fulfilling its public functions – as it has not been for the past decade.

How, then, should the BBC look ahead to the media future? Should it adopt a universalistic or particularistic logic? For all the talk of diversity in this book, the existence of a unified public culture requires that minoritarian perspectives be brought together and made available for the majority. The goal must be to ensure the existence of channels for counter-public to speak to counter-public, as well as for their integration into an (always imperfect) unitary public sphere. The alternative is the extreme segmentation characteristic of commercial media in the United States where 'the logic of segmentation emphasizes the value of difference over the value of commonality'.[15] Public service media cannot only be about a proliferation of micro publics, but about achieving a unifying space in which are displayed and in which mutual encounters take place between expressions of the sometimes incommensurable component cultures of the nation.

What is striking, when we look at the BBC's recent initiatives, is the sophistication of the conception, buttressed by the new possibilities given by interactive, cross- and multi-media. It is possible to draw out from the variety of current strategies a typology of five structural forms of mediated exchange, each critically important, which together flesh out the 'complex cultural dialogue' demanded by present circumstances. The BBC is not alone in developing such initiatives, nor are they equally well developed. But together they add up to a generative vision about how the corporation's remarkable assets can be deployed to public service ends in coming years – how it can orchestrate a pluralist communicative ethics. The first three are structural variations on the encounter among and between social 'majority' and 'minorities'. The first is the established form in which the majority hosts divergent and contesting minority perspectives. It is well suited to mass broadcast networks, and comes close to the long-standing orthodoxy in which 'diverse opinions' are presented for debate on current affairs, politics or talk shows. A second form is when minority speaks to majority and to other minorities: inter-cultural communication. It is well served by both broadcasting and the Internet. This is the function of cultural-diversity-in-unity: universal channels become the means of exposure to and connection with others' imaginative and expressive worlds. It encompasses minority programming on mass channels, such as black and Asian sitcoms, drama or current affairs; access programming, like the *Video Diary* format on television or the web; and cross-platform events engaging the experience of minorities, like the BBC's Asylum Day. A third form is when, via radio, video, cable and satellite television or the net, minority speaks to minority (or to itself): *intra*-cultural communication. Examples are the diasporic networks and ethnic minority niche media which at their best foster reflection, association and solidarity among minorities. For the BBC, its Asian and black music digital radio stations are a bold venture in this direction. But the innovative Australian national network SBS, a continuous flow of niche broadcasts serving each minority community by turn, offers another model.

The last two of the five forms of communicative exchange are variants of mediated community. The fourth comprises territorially-based local and regional community networks; they can be served by all media, as exemplified by the BBC's Hull interactive project and, less elaborately, by experiments in online local democracy. A fifth form is when issue-based, non-territorial communities of interest are linked by point-to-point networks. This is a development primarily associated with the net, and it is a potential facilitated by the BBC's iCan activist website, as well as by the countless self-generated activist networks.

These wide-ranging experiments affirm the BBC's inventiveness in orchestrating a plural public media space, and in enabling Britons to benefit from the possibilities offered by the expanding media ecology. Highly local and 'universal', weaving connections without closure, the vision is both 'individuated and collective, . . . inclusive, participative and connective'.[16] It is one that will be massively enhanced when the Creative Archive releases the BBC's programming riches into the public domain – the multi-media equivalent of open source software – enabling Britons to rework content in an open and iterative process of recreation.[17] There is, of course, much more to do. Some of the experiments are in their infancy; some will fail, others will take their place. What matters is the quality of invention.

In rethinking the future of public service communications, I have proposed that we can learn from the BBC's suggestive strategies, many of them championed under Dyke. The BBC continues to provide a fertile model for those democratic and newly democratising polities willing to invest in the cultural and political development of their citizenry. John Dewey's insights at the time of the BBC's birth into the social nature of knowledge, the importance of dissemination and of the aesthetic – the 'arts of presentation' – provide an eloquent justification for the existence and the universal address of mass broadcast channels.[18] The challenge for public service communications in an age of diversity is to develop both instanciations of Dewey's 'Great Community', or Hall's 'theatre' of the associative life of the nation, as in the universal orientation, the moral and often consensual address of generalist public service channels and of 'impartial' news functions; and to offer a rich array of communicative channels for the self-representation, participation and expressive narrativisation of minority and marginalised groups, addressed both to and among those groups and to the majority. In this way, public service communications will encompass both a politics of ideas and a politics of presence, and will contribute to the formation of a more adequate communicative democracy than we have yet seen.

The BBC's role can no longer be primarily to represent a unified nation, as Reith believed. It is to provide a unifying space in which plurality can be performed, one in which the display and interplay of diverse perspectives can animate and reshape the imagined community of the nation. It is a space in which plurality not only of information and opinion, but of expression, of aesthetic and imaginative invention, must have full reign. The BBC's task, now as always, is to be hopeful. The realisation of its vision will be uncertain; but the vision must be inspired.

*

Past into future

31 December 1999, 5.15 a.m.: I'm riding the lift to the 8th floor cafeteria in Broadcasting House. I am here as one of three presenters of Radio 3's millennium eve special, *The Unfinished Symphony*, an overview of two thousand years of western music. It's a project of astonishing scale conceived by the producer, Antony Pitts, aided by executive producer Graham Dixon. I'm told I was asked to present because I can keep talking – meaning, I suppose, that I'm verbose. The show is eighteen hours of live radio. My co-presenters are Geoffrey Smith, critic and presenter of *Jazz Record Requests*, and music and cultural historian Roderick Swanston. In fact I knew both before. Roddy

taught me memorably when as a child I attended the Royal College of Music, and Geoffrey and I met when I played jazz cello in Mike Westbrook's big bands. We will start at 6 a.m. and continue until the chimes of midnight. The past will see us into the future.

On the 8th floor I collect bacon and egg and toast. I have left Geoffrey and Roddy down in the basement studio where we will do the show. I'm fond of this cafeteria; it reminds me of the wafting gravy and custard odours of municipal Britain in the 60s and 70s, of school lunches at my Paddington primary school in the days of the LCC. Looking out, it has unparalleled views across central London, a metaphor for the BBC's panoptic vision of British life, its central place in that national life. Looking in, I recall many a coffee break watching goings-on in the cafeteria, a place that offers unique insight into 'all human life' at the BBC. There are the middle-aged British black and Asian women serving food at all hours; the reception staff and commissionaires taking breaks, hunched over teas. There are the loud-voiced, ambitious thirty-something ex-Oxbridge producer-intellectuals draped around their meal trays, oblivious to others, earnestly discussing internal politics, a pitch, or the preparation of the Albert Hall for an OB. There are the pretty girls of all hues and types, attracted by and attractive to the media bosses: will this clever secretary move into production? Will this studio manager get to train as a script editor? Then the management and policy types, of whatever age, with their middle-aged haircuts and suits, reading the paper alone, blank faced. Wait a minute: is that Jeremy Bowen over there, balancing a tray with one hand while he fiddles with a mobile phone with the other?

I'm called back to the reality of the marathon show. For months we have prepared it mainly via emails. It has a structure like a rose unfurling. At 6 a.m. we begin with a hypothetical reconstruction of western music in the year zero. At 10.00 we hit 1000 AD. At 15.00 we get to 1500, and to the present by midnight. So each century gets more time: the 16th century half an hour, the 20th century ninety minutes. For each century we have debated at length which composers, pieces and performers we would want captured on the only surviving CD, shot into space, when some millennial apocalypse hits the world. If you had just one hour to represent the entire musical output of the 18th century, what would you choose? We don't want to be slavish to canons, but personal and quirky. Yet somehow many canonic works appear on Antony's playlist. For the dawn of 20th century modernity, to show its parallelisms, I have asked Antony to pair Charles Ives's 'Decoration Day', a personal favourite, with some film music. He chooses the *Casablanca* rendering of the classic song, 'As Time Goes By', one that captures in a central trope the nature of American popular culture – an African-American man singing, by proxy, a love song for a white European woman caught up in a narrative of flight, divided loyalty and moral ambiguity. For my tastes we have too little popular music counterposed against the 'great tradition' in the programme, and it is weaker for the lack of this historical dialectic. But tomorrow, the whole day is devoted to world music, in some ways balancing out today's focus.

Preparation accelerates in the final weeks, wreaking havoc with my family's Christmas break in Germany. As we leave for the holiday days before the show, I'm given Antony's final tapes with the running order and asked to prepare my links. I set up a laptop in my kids' hotel bedroom, with a primitive cassette player and earphones. I'm worried about my scripts and want to run them past Antony, but how can I send him my drafts? There is no email link at our small hotel. I phone Graham, who tells me there will be a way – 'The BBC always finds a way'. An hour later he calls back. In this hamlet in the Black Forest, Graham has located via the Internet a hotel with its own website. He has phoned, explaining our problem. When the BBC was mentioned the staff bent over backwards to be helpful. As I trudge through the snow to the hotel day after day, it becomes clear that the owners believe this is the start of a wonderful friendship – that BBC executives will soon be flooding in to holiday in Saig.

We are on air. I've done my stint as lead presenter for the 13th to 16th centuries. I've busked my way in conversation and debate with Roddy and Geoffrey through the 17th to 19th centuries. Jenny Abramsky, head of Radio, has dropped by, full of enthusiasm. Roddy has emerged as the leader in historical knowledge, Geoffrey as the relaxing, imaginative interlocutor, and I try to ask the odd intelligent question or make provocative points. I try, above all, not to be 'too academic', a cardinal radio sin. We are being inundated with emails from listeners; the pace has grown over the hours. When music is playing, Antony comes into the studio from the control room waving the printouts and plonks them down in front of us. We have them all: expressions of delight, relief that something this ambitious is being broadcast on this day, complaints at the amount of plainchant and sacred music in the programme's early hours, criticisms, corrections, questions. We read them out and try to reply. It's interactive! Missing my children because of the absences caused by weeks of work, I get an email from them at a neighbour's home – they are listening between millennium eve parties. We hit the 20th century: my last big stint as presenter, and I am in my element – this I know something about. I am enjoying it immensely, the music, the adrenaline, the combined intelligence that is making the programme work, the company real and virtual, the sense of realtime connection with discerning but appreciative listeners, some of whom I now know individually by name. Time speeds up; the final two hours rush past in a blur. We hit midnight, the chimes of Big Ben. The news. The next programme. Champagne. Roger Wright, controller of Radio 3, has kept a benign eye on us through the day and is with us now. I do not sleep until 5 a.m. and wake at midday in my BBC hotel room to a somnolent, hazy London, and a world perched on the brink of – what?

Diary, 1999.

*

519

The Arab BBC

'In the first five years of its existence, Al-Jazeera has become the most watched satellite channel in the Arab world and has infuriated every government from Libya to Kuwait. . . What draws the viewers is not soaps, millionaire quizzes . . . but news and political debate of a kind that the Arab world had never seen until the channel started in 1996. It has become the channel that Arabs turn to for big events – such as the Palestinian intifada or the Afghan conflict – though in some countries they are technically breaking the law if they do. Some describe it as the "Arab BBC", which is not surprising, given its origins. They lie in the mid-90s when the BBC set up an Arabic-language TV channel and contracted – unwisely as it turned out – with a Saudi satellite company to transmit its programmes to the Middle East. It was not long before the Saudis, unhappy with the content, pulled the plug. That would have been the end of it had the Emir of Qatar not offered $100 million . . . to fund a new and independent-minded TV station. Ready-trained staff from the BBC channel joined it en masse, bringing – as they see it – BBC values with them.'

Brian Whitaker, October 2001.

*

Radio-controlled peace?

As we drive from Bagram airbase towards Kabul, I eye suspiciously the cluster of unexploded bombs which are far too close to the road for anybody's comfort. They may well be routine for BBC Newsgathering, but we aren't Newsgathering, we're a bunch of BBC bureaucrats, here for the UN – a team to draw up a report on what's needed for the reconstruction of the media in Afghanistan, to be put to a conference of major donors in Tokyo. The UN asked the BBC to do this because it is so well placed. The corporation has been broadcasting on radio to this region for 60 years in Persian, and for 20 years in Pashto, the other major Afghan language. As well as the news and current affairs of the main World Service, the BBC's Afghan Education Service makes the now-famous soap, New Home, New Life, and a range of adult and children's educational programming. A recent addition has been a five-days-a-week programme of lifeline information for those newly displaced by the war, organised by the BBC World Service Trust. The Trust channels funds from outside sources into communications projects – usually for educational or health programmes, or training, for developing countries.

The media need to be completely rebuilt. The broadcasting infrastructure is either ancient or destroyed. Radio is going to be the key medium. A very large percentage of

Afghanistan's population is illiterate, and the overwhelming majority are far too poor to own a television. But there is a huge hunger for media. When the team's taxi stopped for petrol, the attendant had his radio propped on the pump (listening to the BBC). Anyone who questions whether the media should be a priority in a country with millions displaced, facing famine, should hear what the Afghans themselves have to say. The problems have all been caused by politics, so a political settlement is the essential foundation of any reconstruction. Repeatedly, we hear that there needs to be a cultural change, from one of war and division to one of peace and communication. The media are seen as a key factor in these issues. And Afghans are not sitting around waiting for the world to act. At least four newspapers – typically two sides of a single sheet – have appeared since the fall of the Taliban. Radio and TV Afghanistan is on the air for a few hours every day. Even more remarkably, there is a broad consensus on the shape of the reconstructed media, particularly broadcast media. A national broadcaster is seen as vital to prevent stations being factional and divisive, as, it seems, is the pattern even now, with local warlords controlling stations in provincial cities. Everyone we heard in the interim authority, and most journalists, want an editorially independent national broadcaster. So our report recommends a massive training programme to create a robustly independent journalism, support for the national broadcaster, along with a framework to guarantee its independence.'

John Tuckey, February 2002.

*

Civil war and cricket

'In my years in Afghanistan, I occasionally saw groups of small boys playing cricket in the street with whatever they could use for bat and ball, as in so many other countries. But I'd never seen a proper game being played there until one day nearly four years ago. On a wide open space near the middle of Kabul, there it was. I was astounded. I think the only previous time there'd been a cricket match in Afghanistan was when the British army occupied Kabul for a short period in the early 1840s – before they were forced out of the country in one of the worst military defeats of all time. I stopped and watched, enjoying every minute. There in front of me were a whole group of Afghans totally absorbed in having fun, at a time when there was so little other entertainment in Afghanistan. Cinemas, television, music and so many other things had by then been banned by the Taliban. Before long we were chatting away, and the players pointed out they had very little equipment. They used an old tennis ball wrapped in plastic tape. The stumps and bats were home-made and the ground was rough. Would it be possible, they asked, for me to get them some proper kit? I said I'd try, knowing it would be difficult. They explained they were practising for the first serious match ever to be played in Kabul. I joked about my fellow-countrymen playing in Afghanistan all those years ago. Ah, they said, we look forward to playing against England. And they asked if I could report next week's match on the BBC. I said I would be delighted.

At least 60 per cent of Afghans listen to the BBC, which broadcasts daily in their own languages of Pashto and Persian. And when the day came for the match I had more fun writing about the cricket than anything for a long time – it made a change from covering the fighting. That evening they heard about their game over the airwaves. Weeks later I met two English businessmen, Stuart and Michael, who'd arrived in Afghanistan to start installing the country's telephone system. While I was showing them around Kabul, I asked if they would like to watch some cricket. They laughed, thinking I was joking. Before long, my Afghan friends were trying their luck again in their quest for some decent equipment. What I didn't know was that Stuart was a keen cricketer and a member of the most famous cricket club in the world – the MCC in London.

Stuart returned to England the next day, and to my astonishment I received a message from him a few days later saying the MCC had promised to send several sets of cricket equipment. The day came for a presentation by Stuart when he was next in Kabul. When he handed over the bats, balls, pads and other new equipment, the Afghan cricketers couldn't believe their luck. In the distance we could hear the thump of artillery fire from the front line about 30 kilometres north of the capital, as the match got underway. The players themselves were just ordinary Afghans – a carpet salesman, a few students, many with no jobs at all. Cricket has become their life. While they have few resources, they showed their gratitude in style. They presented special Afghan rugs to Stuart and the MCC official who had made the supplies possible. In the middle of each rug was woven a cricket pitch, and around the edges their names – with a message of thanks.'

William Reeve, *From Our Own Correspondent*, BBC Radio 4, October 2001.

*

Glossary

A word on departmental titles: the BBC's departments and directorates have repeatedly been reorganised and renamed in past years. For clarity, I use throughout the book a consistent name that relates to the main function of the section in question. For example, the title News and Current Affairs (NCA) is used for the combined directorate, which, however, was rebranded BBC News in mid-1996; and while current affairs television programming came from a department within that directorate called Weekly Programmes, I refer to it as Current Affairs, and to the news departments as News.

BBC – directorates and departments:

CPU / DPU – the joint Community Programme Unit and Disability Programme Unit, shortened in this book to the CPU.

Current Affairs / Weekly Programmes – the latter was the title of the Current Affairs department under Birt. For clarity, the name Current Affairs is used instead throughout the book.

Documentaries and History – a joint department in the mid-late nineties, shortened in the book to Documentaries; although documentary production was spread across a number of departments, including Bristol Features, Music and Arts, Science and the CPU/DPU.

Regions and Nations – the directorate responsible for those parts of the BBC outside the ambit of the main corporate operations in London; terms used also for any BBC activities occurring in the BBC's bases in the regions and nations of Britain. Often shortened simply to 'regions' and issues of 'regionality'.

NCA / News – from 1987 the BBC's combined News and Current Affairs directorate, in 1996 re-branded BBC News. For clarity the title NCA is used throughout the book to refer to the combined directorate.

Online / BBCi – the BBC's Internet, interactive and new media arms, branded BBC Online from 1997, rebranded BBCi in 2002.

Worldwide – the BBC's commercial arm, known before 1994 as BBC Enterprises.

BBFC   British Board of Film Classification, the regulator of film content.

BSC   Broadcasting Standards Commission: content regulator for British tele-
                    vision and radio, 1996 to 2003.

BSkyB   British Sky Broadcasting, company operating Britain's main digital
                    satellite television platform, Sky Digital; owners also of 11 television
                    channels including Sky One, Sky News and sports and movie channels.

Channel 4   Britain's second major public service television network, a publisher-
                    broadcaster launched in 1982 with a remit to complement ITV and to
                    experiment and innovate.

Channel 5   Britain's second mainstream commercial television network, a pub-
                    lisher-broadcaster launched in 1997; in 2000 re-branded Five.

DCMS   Department of Culture, Media and Sport: the government department
                    charged with overseeing broadcasting and other media.

DG   Director-general of the BBC.

Demos   A think tank that has been influential on New Labour.

DTV   Digital television.

GMG   University of Glasgow Media Group, collective authors of a series of
                    influential critiques from the mid 1970s of British television news and
                    current affairs.

IBA   Independent Broadcasting Authority: from 1972 to 1990 the regulator
                    overseeing commercial television and radio in Britain.

ITA   Independent Television Authority: from 1954 to 1972 the body regu-
                    lating Britain's first commercial television network, ITV.

IPPR   Institute of Public Policy Research: a leading New Labour think tank.

ITC   Independent Television Commission: from 1990 to 2003 the regulator
                    for commercial television in Britain, including terrestrial public service
                    TV.

ITV   Independent Television: Britain's first and largest commercial public
                    service television network, which began operating in 1955. (ITV)
                    Network Centre: the commissioning body for the ITV network.

Ofcom   From 2004 the UK's communications regulator, with oversight of broadcasting, telecommunications and new media in Britain (with the exception of the BBC).

PACT   Producers Alliance for Cinema and Television: the British trade association for independent film and television companies.

PSB   Public service broadcasting.

PSR   Programme Strategy Review: the rubric for the BBC's periodic, large-scale internal audits.

Dramatis Personae

The BBC's senior employees change roles and job titles quite frequently. It may therefore seem as though there is little consistency in the book, but the explanation for changing titles and roles is usually that the individual in question has been promoted, that s/he has moved to a new job, or that a different individual has come to fill that role.

Richard Ayre   Deputy head of News and Current Affairs 1996 to 1999.

John Birt   Deputy director-general 1987 to 1993; director-general of the BBC 1993 to 2000.

Christopher Bland   Chairman of the BBC Board of Governors 1996 to 2001.

Michael Checkland   Director-general of the BBC 1987 to 1992.

Peter Dale   BBC documentary film-maker until 1998; head of Documentaries for Channel 4 1998 to the present.

Gavyn Davies   Chairman of the BBC Board of Governors 2001 to 2004.

Charles Denton   Head of BBC Drama Group 1993 to 1996.

Greg Dyke   Director-general of the BBC 2000 to 2004.

George Faber   Head of Single drama, BBC Drama Group 1993 to 1996; founding director of independent production house Company Pictures in 1998.

Michael Grade   Controller of BBC1 1984 to 1986; managing director (designate) BBC Television 1986 to 1988; chief executive of Channel 4 1988 to 1997; chairman of the BBC, 2004 to the present.

Tony Hall   Editor of Television News and Current Affairs 1987 to 1993; managing director of BBC News and Current Affairs 1993 to 1997; chief executive of BBC News 1997 to 2000; director of News 2000 to 2001.

Steve Hewlett Editor of *Panorama* 1995 to 1997.

Peter Horrocks Editor of *Newsnight* 1995 to 1997; editor of *Panorama* 1997 to 2000; head of Current Affairs 2000 to the present.

Marmaduke Hussey Chairman of the BBC Board of Governors 1986 to 1996.

Michael Jackson Controller of BBC2 1993 to 1996; director of television and controller of BBC1 1996 to 1997; chief executive of Channel 4 1997 to 2001.

Stephen Lambert Editor of *Modern Times* in BBC Documentaries from 1994 to 1999; director of programmes at RDF Media 1998 to the present.

Mark Shivas Head of BBC Drama Group, 1983 to 1993; head of BBC Films department 1993 to 1997.

Mark Thompson Assistant editor of *Newsnight* 1985 to 1988; editor of the *Nine O'Clock News* 1988 to 1990; editor of *Panorama* 1990 to 1992; head of Features 1992 to 1994; head of Factual Group 1994 to 1996; controller of BBC2 1996 to 1998; head of Nations and Regions 1998 to 2000; director of television 2000 to 2001; chief executive of Channel 4 2001 to 2004; director-general of the BBC 2004 to the present.

Michael Wearing Head of Serials, BBC Drama 1989 to 1993; head of Series and Serials 1993 to 1994; head of Serials 1994 to 1998.

Will Wyatt Managing director of Network Television 1991 to 1996; chief executive of BBC Broadcast 1996 to 1999.

Alan Yentob Controller of BBC2 1987 to 1992; controller of BBC1 1992 to 1996; director of programmes in BBC Production 1996 to 2000; director of Drama, Entertainment and Children's 2000 to the present.

Full references for narrative quotations

The author and publishers gratefully acknowledge permission to quote extracts from the following:

FRONT MATERIAL

John Dewey, *The Public and its Problems*, New York: Henry Holt, 1926, edited from Chapter 5, 'Search for the great community', pp. 166-184. Charles Dickens, *Hard Times*, Cambridge: Cambridge University Press, 1996 (1854), edited from Chapter 36.

PROLOGUE

Guy Barker, jazz trumpeter, interviewed on *Jazz Line Up*, BBC Radio 3, 14 October 2000. Report on Burundi civil war on the *Today* programme, BBC Radio 4, 30 December 2000. Boris Johnson, 'Blast the Beeb's bilge', *Daily Telegraph*, 19 August 1999. David Cox, 'Dyke is just Birt with a grin', *New Statesman*, 29 January 2001. Media diary, *Private Eye*, 6 October 1995.

CHAPTER 1

Robin Foster, ITC head of strategy, economy and finance, *Broadcast*, 16 February 2001.

CHAPTER 2

Tom Burns, *The BBC: Public Institution and Private World*, London: Macmillan, 1977, pp.218, 220. David Docherty, BBC deputy director of Television and director of New Services, BBC Broadcast, interviewed on *Boxing Clever*, BBC Radio 3, 14 April 1998.

CHAPTER 3

Anthony Smith, former BBC producer and Director of the British Film Institute 1979 to 1988, quoted in S. Barnett and A. Curry, *The Battle for the BBC*, London: Aurum, 1994, pp. 101–2. Paul Fox, former managing director of BBC Television, quoted in S. Barnett and A. Curry, *The Battle for the BBC*, p. 102.

CHAPTER 4

Peter Bazalgette, chairman of Endemol UK, the 1998 MacTaggart memorial lecture, Edinburgh International Television Festival, August 1998.

CHAPTER 5

Alex Graham, chief executive of Wall to Wall Television: 'The BBC: A coherent organisation?', in W. Stevenson (ed.), *All Our Futures*, London: British Film Institute, 1993, p. 77. Beverley Barnard, deputy chair of the Commission for Racial Equality, speech to the BBC governors' seminar: 'The BBC: Reflecting the cultural richness of the UK', July 2000. Stuart Hood, former controller of programmes, BBC Television: 'Creativity and accountancy', in E. G. Wedell (ed.), *Structures of Broadcasting: A Symposium*, Manchester: Manchester University Press, 1970, p. 71, (quoted in R. Paterson, 'New model BBC', in G. Mulgan and R. Paterson (eds.), *Reinventing the Organisation*, London: British Film Institute, 1993, p. 18.)

CHAPTER 6

BBC, *Our Commitment to You: BBC Statement of Promises to Viewers and Listeners, 1997–1998*. BBC, *Our Commitment to You: BBC Statement of Promises to Viewers and Listeners, 1998–1999*. BBC, *Our Commitment to You: BBC Statement of Promises to Viewers and Listeners, 1999–2000*. Tom Burns, *The BBC: Public Institution and Private World*, p. 33. Marmaduke Hussey, *Chance Governs All*, London: Macmillan, 2001, pp. 245–6. Lord Tedder, from 1950 governor and from 1951 vice-chairman of the BBC, quoted in A. Briggs, *Governing the BBC*, London: BBC, 1979, pp. 156–7.

CHAPTER 7

Seamus Heaney and Faber and Faber, 'Glanmore Sonnet VII' from *Field Work*, London, 1979, reprinted in *Opened Ground*, London, 2000; 'Perfect Day' © Lou Reed 1972, 2000; Paddy Scannell and David Cardiff, *A Social History of British Broadcasting 1922–1939*, Oxford: Basil Blackwell, 1991, edited from pp. 374–380. Tom Burns, *The BBC: Public Institution and Private World*, edited from pp. 137–144.

CHAPTER 8

Laurie Taylor, 'Desert menu', *New Statesman*, 19 March 2001. Stuart Hood, *A Survey of Television*, London: Heinemann, 1967, pp. 49–50, quoted in T. Burns, *The BBC: Public Institution and Private World*, p. 151. BBC Radio network controller, speaking in c. 1973, quoted in T. Burns, *The BBC: Public Institution and Private World*, p. 244. W. Stephen Gilbert, 'The absence of censorship', *Sight and Sound*, March 1998, edited from p. 33. Tod Gitlin, *Inside Prime Time*, London: Routledge, 1983, edited from p. 63 and pp. 84–85. Edited from Matt Wells, 'Keep it real', *Media Guardian*, 14 May 2001. Mark Lawson, 'A big fat mess', the *Guardian*, 16 August 1999. Stephen Bochco, originator and executive producer of *Hill Street Blues*, interviewed by John Willis, National Film Theatre, London, 1996. Andrew Billen, 'Weak medicine', *New Statesman*, 29 January 1999. Stuart Jeffries, 'Super cool blues', the *Guardian*, 3 June 1996. 'Eye TV', by Square Eyes, *Private Eye*, 9 January 1998. Nancy Banks-Smith, 'Cindy breaks for the border', the *Guardian*, 18 October 1996. Ray Cathode,

'The box', *Sight and Sound*, December 1996. Andrew Billen, 'Miscegeny, suicide, polygamy and jail', *New Statesman*, 25 July 1997. Stuart Jeffries, 'Sensitive slant on issue drama', the *Guardian*, 28 November 1997. Edited from Ian Parker, 'Look under the bonnet', *The Observer Review*, 8 November 1998. 'Eye TV', by Square Eyes, *Private Eye*, 20 March 1998. Andrew Billen, 'Gold stars all round', *New Statesman*, 3 April 1998. Tony Garnett, drama producer, speech to the Drama Forum, November 1997.

CHAPTER 9

John Reith, *Broadcast Over Britain*, London: Hodder and Stoughton, 1924, quoted in P. Scannell and D. Cardiff, *A Social History of British Broadcasting*, p. xvi. Ellen Wilkinson, Labour MP for Middlesborough, in a 1926 letter to the *Radio Times*, quoted in P. Scannell and D. Cardiff, *A Social History of British Broadcasting*, p. 33. Tony Hall, chief executive of BBC News and Current Affairs, 'Introduction' to Scotland leaflet for NCA staff, June 1995. BBC senior executive, quoted in Alison Preston, *The Development of the UK Television News Industry 1982–1998*, PhD thesis, University of Stirling, 1999, chapter 6, p. 184. BBC *Newsnight* programme, *Newsnight: The Essential Guide for New Staff*, April 1996, pp. 19–20. Edited from Ian Parker, 'You've been Nicked', *The Observer Review*, 31 January 1999. Peter Dale, head of documentaries for Channel 4, 'Private lives, public television', speech to the Institute of Contemporary Arts, London, 2000. BBC Community Programme Unit, 'Natalie's baby', *Teenage Diaries*, BBC2, 12 October 1998 (original transmission 1993). Peter Dale (director), *The Return of Zog*, BBC2, 29 October 1997. Martha Nussbaum, *Upheavals of Thought: The Intelligence of Emotions*, Cambridge: Cambridge University Press, 2001, edited from pp. 1, 3, 432.

CHAPTER 10

Live two-way between John Humphrys and Andrew Gilligan, *Today*, BBC Radio 4, 6.07 a.m., 29 May 2003. Andrew Marr, BBC political editor, speaking on the 10 O'Clock News, BBC1, 17 July 2003. Nick Cohen, 'Why the BBC is losing', *New Statesman*, 25 August 2003. Simon Hoggart, 'Forever a dull moment in the very busy life of Honest Tony', the *Guardian*, 29 August 2003. John Kampfner, 'The Prime Minister will survive the Hutton inquiry', *New Statesman*, 29 September 2003. Transcript of Susan Watts's recorded interview with Dr David Kelly, 30 May 2003, submitted as evidence to the Hutton inquiry. Greg Dyke interviewed by Janine Gibson, Edinburgh International Television Festival, 31 August 2000. Greg Dyke, 'One BBC: Making it happen', speech to BBC staff, 7 February 2002. Maggie Brown, 'Getting One over', *Media Guardian*, 19 November 2001. David Liddiment, ITV director of programmes, the 2000 MacTaggart memorial lecture, Edinburgh International Television Festival, August 2000. Colin Robertson, 'Sky One back to basics', *Broadcast*, 19 January 2001. Emily Bell, *Broadcast*, 22 February 2002. Claire Grimmond, Channel 4 head of Market Planning, letters page, *Broadcast*, 12 January 2001. Geoff Mulgan, 'Reinventing the BBC', in G. Mulgan and R. Paterson (eds.), *Reinventing the Organisation*, edited from pp. 76–80. Polly Toynbee, 'The threat to our TV from this corrupter of politicians', the *Guardian*, 30 April 2003. Steven Barnett, 'Unfair competition? BSkyB is an expert at it', the *Observer*, 31 March 2002. Bill

Bush, special advisor to the Culture Secretary and the Department of Culture, Media and Sport, speaking at the Oxford convention on Public Service Communications, January 2003.

EPILOGUE

Ulrich Beck, 'Cosmopolitan Europe', lecture delivered to the London School of Economics, January 2003. Stuart Hall, 'Which public, whose service?', in Wilf Stevenson (ed.), *All Our Futures: The Changing Role and Purpose of the BBC*. London: British Film Institute, 1993, pp. 36-7. *The Archers*, BBC Radio 4, 31 March 2002, the episode following the death of the Queen Mother. Matt Wells and Stephen Bates, 'BBC sidelined as Prince Charles speaks of "magical grandmother"', the *Guardian* front page, 2 April, 2002. 'Why keep quiet when the Beeb gets it so wrong?', Comment, *New Nation*, 15 September 2003, p. 2. Brian Whitaker, 'Battle station', the *Guardian* supplement, 9 October 2001, p. 2. John Tuckey, 'Radio-controlled peace?', *Media Guardian*, 21 February 2002, p. 7. William Reeve, former BBC correspondent in Kabul, *From Our Own Correspondent*, BBC Radio 4, 6 October 2001.

Notes

PROLOGUE

1. Andrew Rawnsley, *Servants of the People: The Inside Story of New Labour*, London: Penguin, 2000, p. 377.
2. Rawnsley, *Servants of the People*, p. 377.
3. *BBC Annual Report and Accounts 2002–03*, London: BBC, 2003. Reach is defined as the percentage of the national audience viewing or listening to a specified service for 15 consecutive minutes per week.

CHAPTER 1

1. From Reith's letter to the Prime Minister, Winston Churchill, 12 May 1926, cautioning the government against commandeering the BBC in the General Strike: John Reith, *Into the Wind*, London: Hodder and Stoughton, 1949, p. 108.
2. Paddy Scannell and David Cardiff, *A Social History of British Broadcasting 1922–1939*, Oxford: Basil Blackwell, 1991, p. 6.
3. John Reith, 'Memorandum of information on the scope and conduct of the broadcasting service', 1925, p. 3. Quoted in Scannell and Cardiff, *A Social History of British Broadcasting*, p. 7.
4. Matthew Arnold, *Culture and Anarchy*, Cambridge: Cambridge University Press, 1996, p. 70.
5. Reith, 'Memorandum of information', p. 4. Quoted in Scannell and Cardiff, *A Social History of British Broadcasting*, p. 7.
6. Scannell and Cardiff, *A Social History of British Broadcasting*, p. 11.
7. Scannell and Cardiff, *A Social History of British Broadcasting*, p. 10.
8. Jean Seaton, 'Reith and the denial of politics', Chapter 8 in James Curran and Jean Seaton, *Power Without Responsibility: The Press and Broadcasting in Britain* (5th edition), London: Routledge, 1997, p. 118.
9. Raymond Williams, 'Programming: distribution and flow', Chapter 4 in *Television: Technology and Cultural Form*, London: Fontana, 1974. For a recent take, see Stephen Heath, 'Representing television', in Patricia Mellencamp (ed.), *Logics of Television*, Bloomington, Indiana: Indiana University Press, 1990.
10. Simon Frith, 'The pleasures of the hearth: The making of BBC Light Entertainment', in James Donald (ed.), *Formations of Pleasure*, London: Routledge, 1983.
11. Scannell and Cardiff, *A Social History of British Broadcasting*, pp. 269–273.

12. From The Whitley Document of 1932, written by Reith and J. H. Whitley, which first defined the governors' duties; quoted in Asa Briggs, *Governing the BBC*, London: BBC, 1979, p. 59.

13. Briggs, *Governing the BBC*, p. 14.

14. Seaton, 'Reith and the denial of politics', pp. 118–9.

15. References from Ian McIntyre's *The Expense of Glory: A Life of John Reith*, London: Harper Collins, 1993, pp. 145–147. The phrase 'notorious syllogism' comes from Scannell and Cardiff, *A Social History of British Broadcasting*, p. 33.

16. Seaton, 'Reith and the denial of politics', pp. 115–6.

17. Both quotations from Seaton, 'Reith and the denial of politics', p. 121.

18. Seaton, 'Reith and the denial of politics', pp. 125 and 126.

19. Scannell and Cardiff, *A Social History of British Broadcasting*, p. 69.

20. Scannell and Cardiff, *A Social History of British Broadcasting*, p. 71.

21. Scannell and Cardiff, *A Social History of British Broadcasting*, pp.177 and 178.

22. Scannell and Cardiff, *A Social History of British Broadcasting*, p. 23.

23. John Tulloch, 'Policing the public sphere: The British machinery of news management', *Media, Culture and Society* 15, 1993, p. 373.

24. Meltem Ahiska, *An Occidentalist Fantasy: Turkish Radio and National Identity*, Chapter 4. Unpublished PhD thesis, Goldsmiths' College, University of London, 1999.

25. Scannell and Cardiff, *A Social History of British Broadcasting*, pp. 278–9.

26. Asa Briggs, *The History of British Broadcasting in the United Kingdom: The Golden Age of Wireless*, Vol. II, Oxford: Oxford University Press, 1965, p. 31.

27. Anthony Smith, *Television: An International History*, Oxford: Oxford University Press, 1995, p. 84.

28. Report of the Annan Committee, 1977, p. 16, cited in Peter Goodwin, *Television Under the Tories*, London: British Film Institute, 1998, p. 17.

29. Jeremy Isaacs, the 1979 MacTaggart memorial lecture, quoted in Stephen Lambert, *Channel Four: Television with a Difference?*, London: British Film Institute, 1982, p. 91.

30. John Birt, speech published as 'Freedom and the broadcaster', *The Listener*, 13 September 1979, pp. 336–8; quoted in Lambert, *Channel Four: Television with a Difference?*, p. 92.

31. On the black workshops, and the 1981 Workshop Declaration which made them possible, see Karen Ross, *Black and White Media*, Chapter 2, Cambridge: Polity, 1996.

32. On the 'Supergun' *Panorama*, see Steven Barnett and Andrew Curry, *The Battle for the BBC: A British Broadcasting Conspiracy*, London: Aurum, 1994, pp. 162–3, and on the 'Sliding Into Slump' *Panorama*, pp. 169–70.

33. Unpublished BBC Charter Review Task Force report, 'The BBC: the Entrepreneur'; quoted in Peter Goodwin, *Television Under the Tories*, London: British Film Institute, 1998, p. 128.

34. Quoted in Goodwin, *Television Under the Tories*, p. 136.

CHAPTER 2

1. Antonio Gramsci, *Selections from the Prison Notebooks*, London: Lawrence & Wishart, 1971, p. 258.

2. Andrew Barry, Thomas Osborne and Nikolas Rose (eds.), *Foucault and Political Reason: Liberalism, Neo-Liberalism and Rationalities of Government*, London: UCL Press, 1996.

3. *The Media Guide 1996.* London: Fourth Estate, 1996, p. 161.
4. *BBC Annual Report and Accounts 2002–03,* London: BBC 2003.
5. Both quotations from Geoff Mulgan, *Politics in an Anti-Political Age,* Cambridge: Polity, 1994, p. 151.
6. John Birt, the Fleming Lecture, March 1993, quoted in Barnett and Curry, *The Battle for the BBC,* p. 194.
7. Personal communication, expert source, 2001.
8. Quoted in Briggs, *Governing the BBC,* pp. 30–1.
9. Burns, *The BBC,* p. 192.
10. Burns, *The BBC* , p.221.
11. Burns, *The BBC,* p. 32.
12. Burns, *The BBC,* p.217.
13. Barnett and Curry, *The Battle for the BBC,* p. 102.
14. Burns, *The BBC,* p. 240.
15. Burns, *The BBC,* p. 239.
16. Burns, *The BBC,* p. 257.
17. E. Bell, 'Birt role beggars belief', *Broadcast,* 8 June 2001, p. 13.

CHAPTER 3

1. John Birt, the Fleming Lecture, March 1993, quoted in Barnett and Curry, *The Battle for the BBC,* p. 194.
2. Both quotations from government Green Paper, *The Future of the BBC,* November 1992; cited in Goodwin, *Television Under the Tories,* p. 129.
3. Roger Thompson, quoted in Barnett and Curry, *The Battle for the BBC,* p. 181.
4. Richard Paterson, 'New model BBC', in Geoff Mulgan and Richard Paterson (eds.), *Reinventing the Organisation,* London: British Film Institute, 1993, p. 26.
5. Simon Deakin and Stephen Pratten, 'Quasi-markets, transaction costs and trust: institutional change in broadcasting', ESRC Centre for Business Research, Working Paper, University of Cambridge, 1998.
6. *Broadcast,* 8 June 2001, p. 14.
7. British Film Institute Centre for Audience and Industry Research, *Television Industry Tracking Study,* interim results, 1998.
8. Bob Franklin, *Newszak and News Media,* London: Arnold, 1997.
9. *Broadcast,* Editorial, 8 June 2001, p. 13.

CHAPTER 4

1. Indeed Producer Choice was followed in 1998 by the setting up of BBC Resources Ltd., a wholly-owned trading subsidiary of the BBC encompassing the corporation's production, technical and craft services.
2. See, *inter alia,* Ian Hargreaves, *Sharper Vision,* London: Demos, 1993; Richard Collins and James Purnell, *The Future of the BBC,* London: IPPR, 1996; Richard Collins and Christina Murroni, *New Media, New Policies,* Cambridge: Polity, 1996.
3. Richard Saundry, 'The limits of flexibility: the case of UK television', *British Journal of Management,* v. 9, 1998, pp. 151–162, especially pp. 157–161.
4. On this inflation and Birt's response, see Chris Barrie, 'Pay TV warning for "all live sport and top shows"', *The Guardian,* 6 November 1998. The powerful indepen-

dents were named as Hat Trick, Ginger Media, Bazal, Mentorn Barraclough Carey, Talkback, Tiger Aspect and Planet 24.

5. On the inflated market in talent, the BBC's need to respond, and the BBC Talent initiative launched by Alan Yentob, see Peter Bazalgette, 'The great talent hunt', *Media Guardian*, 10 April 2000.

6. On the BBC's insistence on taking the majority of rights in its independent productions from middle-sized and small independents and refusing to do licensing deals, see *Broadcast*, 8 June 2001, p. 13. On the BBC's exertion of pressure on small independents to yield their rights in programmes, see *Broadcast*, 1 March 2002, p. 15.

7. An example is Channel 4's moving of a highly successful history programme from a small independent to a large production company after its first series. The original, *David Starkey's Henry VIII*, the first series to use historian David Starkey, was made by Convergence Productions; the second series, *The Six Wives of Henry VIII*, also fronted by Starkey, was commissioned from United Productions, part of the Granada group. See *Broadcast*, 28 March 2002, front page.

8. This analysis is similar to the economists' 'Hotelling effect'; see Richard Collins, 'Too much of a good thing?', in D. Tambini and J. Cowling (eds.), *From Public Service Broadcasting to Public Service Communications*, London: Institute of Public Policy Research, 2004, p. 138 (and n. 12).

9. The fakery scandals broke in 1998 and 1999 and caused the most serious public crisis over the professional and ethical standards of British broadcasting in decades. The first and most serious arose following revelations of staging in the documentary *The Connection*, which led to the production company, the ITV subsidiary Carlton, being fined £2 million by the ITC. There followed charges of defrauding by the BBC1 talk show, *Vanessa*, and the ITV talk show, *Tricia*.

10. It is plausible that Carlton's *The Connection* sprang from similar conditions. The commissioning broadcaster, Central, had a close relationship with Carlton, and for this reason compliance controls may have been light.

11. Rupert Gavin quoted in J. Harding, 'Moving Four Forward', *Financial Times Creative Business*, 29 January 2002.

12. For an analysis of the balance of trade, and recommendations arising, see David Graham and Associates, *Building a Global Audience: British Television in Overseas Markets*, London: Department of Culture, Media and Sport, 1999.

13. Shirley Dex *et al*, 'Workers' strategies in uncertain labour markets: Analysis of the effects of casualisation in the television industry', paper presented at the Work, Employment and Society conference, Cambridge, September 1998, p. 3.

14. See Goodwin, *Television Under the Tories*, Chapter 11, esp. pp. 161–2, and Saundry, 'The limits of flexibility'.

CHAPTER 5

1. *The House*, directed by Michael Waldman (Double Exposure, trans. BBC2, 1996). The origins of this sub-genre can be traced to Roger Graef's pioneering documentaries on powerful institutions, notably *Police* (1982).

2. Quoted in Gillian Ursell, 'Labour flexibility in the UK commercial television sector', *Media, Culture and Society*, v. 20, n. 1, 1998, p. 134.

3. Figures taken from Ursell, 'Labour flexibility in the UK commercial television sector', pp. 136–7; Goodwin, *Television Under the Tories*, pp. 158–160; British Film Institute Centre for Audience and Industry Research, *Television Industry Tracking Study*, Third Report, 1999, p. 17; and from the 2000, 2001 and 2002 censuses of employment patterns in the audio-visual industries by Skillset, the official training body for the broadcasting and film industries. Skillset defines freelance employment as any contract of less than one year's duration, and employee status as any contract of more than one year's duration. BBC Drama Group figures from 1996 show that 48% of employees were on 'continuing contracts', 19% on contracts of a year or more, while 33% were on shorter, freelance contracts (BBC Drama, 1996 Annual Performance Review).

4. In the absence of official figures from the BBC, the employment figures for the BBC are estimates supplied in 2001 by BECTU, the BBC's main trade union. The overall figure of between 7,000 and 10,000 job losses derives from comparing the 1990 membership of the BBC's pension scheme, approx. 23,000, with the equivalent figure for 2000, approx. 16,000. This figure cannot show jobs converted from permanent to freelance status.

5. On the growing training deficit in the television industry and its causes, see Richard Saundry, 'Producer Choice: Casualisation and creativity at the BBC', Centre for Industrial Policy and Performance, University of Leeds, September 1995, pp. 16–18.

6. The phrase is taken from an account of the effects of casualisation in Rachel Murrell, 'Taking it personally: Women and change in the BBC', in Mulgan and Paterson (eds.), *Reinventing the Organisation*, p. 57.

7. On the intensification of work in television with casualisation and multiskilling, see Saundry, 'Producer Choice: Casualisation and creativity at the BBC', p. 10.

8. Quotes from 'Black talent base in north', *EqualiTV* – Network Television's equal opportunities magazine, n. 19, April 1996, p. 8.

9. However it was not obvious in the early nineties that such a transformation would be achieved, and many of the same equal opportunities issues faced women as continue to face ethnic and disabled minorities. For a history and an analysis, see Murrell, 'Taking it personally: Women and change in the BBC'.

10. *BBC Annual Report and Accounts, 1998–99*, London: BBC, 1999, p. 63.

11. The McPherson report into the murder of the black teenager Stephen Lawrence and the failures of the police investigation into the murder, published in 1999, made a number of recommendations aimed at challenging racism. Coining the term institutional racism, it began a major public debate on the pervasive forms of racism and race-related inequalities in Britain's major social and political institutions. See *The Stephen Lawrence Inquiry: Report of an Inquiry by Sir William McPherson of Cluny*. London: Stationery Office, 1999.

12. Taken from British Film Institute Centre for Audience and Industry Research, *Television Industry Tracking Study*, Second Interim Report, 1998, and Third Report, 1999; and Shirley Dex et al, 'Workers' strategies in uncertain labour markets: Analysis of the effects of casualisation in the television industry', paper for the Work, Employment and Society Conference, University of Cambridge, September 1998.

CHAPTER 6

1. The phrases are taken from Michael Power, *The Audit Society: Rituals of Verification*, Oxford: Oxford University Press, 1997, Chapter 1.
2. This analysis is drawn from Power, *The Audit Society*, esp. Chapter 3.
3. Department of National Heritage, quoted in Goodwin, *Television Under the Tories*, p. 133.
4. *Broadcast*, 8 June 2001, figure quoted by Emily Bell, p. 13. See also the BBC *Annual Report and Accounts 1998–99*, which confirms for that year a spend of £60m. on Corporate Centre and £31m. on 'restructuring', or a total of £91m.; and the BBC *Annual Report and Accounts 1999–2000*, London: BBC, 2000, which cites for the same functions £57m. and £25m. respectively, or £82m. in total.
5. See BBC *Annual Report and Accounts 1999–2000*, p. 37; BBC *Annual Report and Accounts 2000–01*, London: BBC, 2001, p. 41.
6. Barnett and Curry, *The Battle for the BBC*, p. 209.
7. Figures from Ben Potter and Rebecca Barrow, 'Protests as BBC spends £22m. on advisors', *Daily Telegraph*, 7 August 1999, p. 1, and Jason Deans, 'BBC consultancy spend tops £28m.', *Broadcast*, 10 September 1999, p. 1; quoted in Stuart MacDonald, 'The cost of control: speculation on the impact of management consultants in the BBC', *Prometheus*, v. 22, n. 1, 2004, p. 51. Some estimates are far higher: a senior BBC executive gave the figure of £74m. per annum as the consultancy spend in the late Birt years.
8. MacDonald, 'The cost of control', p. 51, citing *The Economist*, 'A very Birtish coup', 30 August 1997.
9. MacDonald, 'The cost of control', p. 54.
10. The assertion that there have been no successful sitcoms that did badly in their first series is contentious; for an alternative view see R. Paterson, 'Friends, Fools and Horses: British television fiction in 1996', p. 88, in M. Buonanno (ed.) *Imaginary Dreamscapes*, Luton: Libbey, 1998. Paterson cites *Only Fools and Horses* as one example among others.
11. From 'Measuring the BBC's Performance', a speech given to the Foundation for Performance Measurement by Robin Foster, Director, Strategy and Channel Management, 19 March 1998, p. 3. Foster later occupied senior roles at the ITC and from 2003 at Ofcom, Britain's unified communications regulator.
12. Foster, 'Measuring the BBC's Performance', p. 12.
13. Foster, 'Measuring the BBC's Performance', p. 25.
14. Foster, 'Measuring the BBC's Performance', p. 24.
15. Foster, 'Measuring the BBC's Performance', p. 15.
16. On the reorientation of Radio 1, its new philosophy and its impact on the output, see David Hendy, 'Pop music radio in the public service: BBC Radio 1 and new music in the 1990s', *Media, Culture and Society*, v. 22, n. 6, 2000.
17. Power, *The Audit Society*, p. 12.
18. All quotations in this section are taken from BBC Press Service statement 'Listening to the Public', 1999.
19. Figures from *Our Commitment to You: Statement of Promises to Viewers and Listeners*, 1999–2000.

20. Michael Power, *The Audit Explosion*, London: Demos, 1994, p. 11.

21. On these points, see Marilyn Strathern, 'From improvement to enhancement: an anthropological comment on the audit culture', *Cambridge Anthropology*, v. 19, n. 3, 1996–97, esp. p. 4.

22. This resonant phrase is taken from Marilyn Strathern, 'A case of self-organisation', unpublished ms., University of Cambridge, 1996, p. 3, note 5.

23. Pierre Bourdieu developed his theory of symbolic violence in a number of works; see, *inter alia*, *Outline of a Theory of Practice*, Cambridge: Cambridge University Press, 1977; *Reproduction in Education, Society and Culture*, London: Sage, 1990; and *Language and Symbolic Power*, Cambridge: Polity, 1991.

24. Barnett and Curry, *The Battle for the BBC*, p. 153.

25. See the case studies given by Briggs in *Governing the BBC*, Chapter IV, pp. 187–233.

26. See, for example, Briggs, *Governing the BBC*, Chapter V, and Burns, *The BBC*, pp. 27–33.

27. See Barnett and Curry, *The Battle for the BBC*, Chapter 10.

28. See Jeremy Paxman, *Friends in High Places*, London: Penguin, 1990, Chapter 4, quoting Lord Shawcross, p. 136, note 11.

29. Executive, BBC Corporate Centre, 1997.

30. Desmond Christy, 'The Provos are all very nice, but…', *The Guardian*, 1 October 1997.

31. Quotations and summary taken from Asa Briggs, *The BBC: The First Fifty Years*, Oxford: Oxford University Press, 1985, pp. 151–2, drawing from W. A. Robson (ed.), *Public Enterprise* (1937), and Robson's article in the *Political Quarterly* devoted to broadcasting in 1935.

32. On the threats to creativity in cultural organisations posed by excessive demands for accountability, see Matthew Evans, 'The economy of the imagination', the New Statesman Arts Lecture, London, 27 June 2001, published in the *New Statesman*, 2 July 2001.

CHAPTER 7

1. *The Draftsman's Contract*, directed by Peter Greenaway, 1982.

2. BBC Network Television Marketing Plan, 1996–97, p. 1.

3. BBC Network Television Marketing Plan 1996–97, p. 2.

4. On the history of Radio 1's repositioning, see Simon Garfield, *The Nation's Favourite: The True Adventures of Radio 1*, London: Faber and Faber, 1998; and Hendy, 'Pop music radio in the public service: BBC Radio 1 and new music in the 1990s'.

5. Before going to Channel 5, Corinne Hollingworth had been executive producer of BBC1's most successful soap, *EastEnders*.

6. Scannell and Cardiff, *A Social History of British Broadcasting*, p. 375. It was just a year earlier, in 1935, that George Gallup established the first independent professional opinion polling organisation, the American Institute of Public Opinion, which was followed by the British Institute of Public Opinion in 1937.

7. Asa Briggs, *The History of Broadcasting in the United Kingdom: Competition 1955–1974*, Vol. V, Oxford: Oxford University Press, 1995, n. 29, p. 21, and ch. 1.

8. Ien Ang, *Desperately Seeking the Audience*, London: Routledge, 1991; M. Allor,

'Relocating the site of the audience', *Critical Studies in Mass Communication*, v. 5, n. 3, 1988: pp. 217–233.

9. E. E. Evans Pritchard, *Witchcraft, Oracles and Magic Among the Azande*, Oxford, 1937.

10. Patrick Barwise and Andrew Ehrenberg, *Television and Its Audience*, London: Sage, 1988.

11. Jurgen Habermas, *The Structural Transformation of the Public Sphere*, Cambridge: Polity, 1989, ch. 24 and p. 240.

12. From 'A Scheduling Policy for BBC1 and BBC2', BBC Network Television, February 1996, p. 5.

CHAPTER 8

1. 'Bearing in mind the cost of the service, you have to think very very hard before you put on a programme that is of interest, say, to one million as against six million... The BBC attitude to figures . . . can be very honest and very democratic, but it can also be used as a stick to beat everything that doesn't command a large audience'. Burns, *The BBC*, quoting a BBC executive, pp. 152–153.

2. Burns, *The BBC*, p. 241.

3. BBC1 1996 Commissioning Brief for Drama 1998–99, pp. 22–23.

4. BBC1 strategic overview meeting for Drama 1998–99: presentation.

5. BBC2 1996 Commissioning Brief for Drama 1998–99, p. 8.

6. By the 2000s, US-style team writing had become more common: it was used for the series *Merseybeat*, and lay behind the sitcom *My Family*. There were plans to use it more widely for long-run shows. See *Broadcast*, 26 July 2002, p. 15.

7. Data on long-term drama trends from Steven Barnett and Emily Seymour, "*A Shrinking Iceberg Traveling South*": *Changing Trends in British Television*, London: Campaign for Quality Television, 1999, Chapters 4 and 5.

8. *Hetty Wainthrop Investigates*, for example, was built around Patricia Routledge, *Hamish MacBeth* around Robert Carlyle, *Silent Witness* around Amanda Burton, *Beck* around Amanda Redman, *Sunburn* around Michelle Collins, *Harbour Lights* around Nick Berry.

9. William Phillips, 'Auntie's runners', *Broadcast*, 24 January 1997.

10. Barnett and Seymour, "*A Shrinking Iceberg Traveling South: Changing Trends in British Television*", p. 65, citing a producer.

11. The opinion came from Sophie Balhetchet, a leading independent drama producer and executive producer with Tony Garnett's independent, World Productions.

12. *This Life*, conceived as potentially the first continuing series for BBC2 and intended to bring a young audience to the channel, cost £230k an hour, a relatively low budget for drama, and one comparable to the BBC soaps.

13. John Hill and Martin McLoone (eds.), *Big Picture, Small Screen: The Relations Between Film and Television*, Luton: John Libby, 1996, chapters by Mark Shivas and John Hill.

14. John Hill, 'Enmeshed in British society but with a Yen for American movies', in Hill and McLoone (eds.), *Big Picture, Small Screen*, p. 230.

15. John Caughie, 'The logic of convergence', in Hill and McLoone, *Big Picture, Small Screen*, p. 220.

16. Ray Cathode, 'The box', *Sight and Sound*, November 1996.

17. Christine Geraghty, 'Social issues and realist soaps: a study of British soaps in the

1980s-1990s', in R. Allen (ed.), *To Be Continued … Soap Operas Around the World*, London: Routledge, 1995.

18. Fredric Jameson, *Postmodernism, or The Cultural Logic of Late Capitalism*, London: Verso, 1991, p. 21.

19. Ray Cathode, 'The box', *Sight and Sound*, December 1997.

20. Desmond Christy, 'A heroine for our mercenary times', *The Guardian*, 2 November 1998.

21. See John Caughie, 'Art television: authorship and irony', Chapter 5, esp. pp. 129–131, in J. Caughie, *Television Drama: Realism, Modernism and British Culture*, Oxford: Oxford University Press, 2000.

CHAPTER 9

1. Ian McWhirter, 'When false prophecy usurps faulty politics', *The Observer*, 3 September 1995, quoted in Brian McNair, 'Current trends in political journalism', unpublished paper, 1997. I draw extensively on McNair's paper in this section, with gratitude.

2. Jay Blumler and Michael Gurevitch, *The Crisis of Public Communication*, London: Routledge, 1996. For similar arguments regarding the American situation, see Tod Gitlin, 'Public sphere or public sphericules?' in Tamar Liebes and James Curran (eds.) *Media, Ritual and Identity*, London: Routledge, 1998.

3. Habermas, *The Structural Transformations of the Public Sphere*.

4. Paddy Scannell and David Cardiff, 'News values and practices', Chapter 6 in *A Social History of British Broadcasting*.

5. Scannell and Cardiff, 'News values and practices', p. 111.

6. James Curran, 'Crisis of public communication: a reappraisal', in Liebes and Curran (eds.), *Media, Ritual and Identity*, pp. 195–6.

7. BBC News Domestic Strategic Review, Phase Two, April 22 1998: p. 40.

8. Rupert Murdoch, the 1989 MacTaggart memorial lecture, quoted in Barnett and Curry, *The Battle for the BBC*, pp. 126–7.

9. BBC News Domestic Strategic Review, Phase Two, 22 April 1998, p. 71.

10. Onora O'Neill, 'Practices of toleration' in Judith Lichtenberg (ed.), *Democracy and the Mass Media*, Cambridge: Cambridge University Press, 1990, p. 173.

11. Anne Phillips, 'Dealing with difference: a politics of ideas or a politics of presence?', in Seyla Benhabib (ed.), *Democracy and Difference: Contesting the Boundaries of the Political*, Princeton, NJ: Princeton University Press, 1996; and *The Politics of Presence*, Oxford: Oxford University Press, 1995.

12. Edited from BBC Principles and Practice in News and Current Affairs, 1972 edition, p. 8, quoted in Philip Schlesinger, *Putting 'Reality' Together: BBC News*, London: Methuen, 1978.

13. The University of Glasgow Media Group have authored a series of critical studies of news including *Bad News*, London: Routledge and Kegan Paul, 1976; *More Bad News*, London: Routledge and Kegan Paul, 1980; *Really Bad News*, London: Writers and Readers, 1982; *War and Peace News*, Milton Keynes: Open University Press, 1985; and John Eldridge (ed.), *Getting the Message*, London: Routledge, 1993; and most recently, *Bad News from Israel*, London: Pluto, 2004.

14. Schlesinger, *Putting Reality Together*; Stuart Hall, Ian Connell and Lydia Curti, 'The "unity" of current affairs television', in Tony Bennett et al (eds.) *Popular Television and Film*, London: British Film Institute, 1985.

15. See, for example, Philip Schlesinger, Graham Murdock and Philip Elliot, *Televising Terrorism*, London: Comedia, 1983; Brian McNair, *Images of the Enemy*, London: Routledge, 1988.

16. Gaye Tuchman, 'Objectivity as strategic ritual: an examination of newsmen's notions of objectivity', *American Journal of Sociology* v. 77, n. 4, 1972. For a recent discussion, see Judith Lichtenberg, 'In defence of objectivity revisited', in James Curran and Michael Gurevitch (eds.), *Mass Media and Society* (3rd edition), London: Arnold, 2000, pp. 238–254.

17. Schlesinger, *Putting 'Reality' Together*; for a discussion of the 'limits of change' in relation to these issues in the 1970s, see Chapter 9.

18. Bob Wolfinden, 'Has BBC journalism lost its spirit of enquiry?', *The Listener*, 10 March 1988, quoted in Bryan McNair, *News and Journalism in the UK*, London: Routledge, 1994, p. 88.

19. See the many articles in and letters to the national press in June and July 1996. Several newspapers ran a campaign against the World Service reforms.

20. Transcriptions of the 'squidgy' tape, a recording of conversations between Princess Diana and her lover James Gilbey, were published by the tabloid press at the height of the British royal scandals in the early nineties: hence 'Squidgygate'.

21. Senior executive, BBC Scotland, 2004.

22. Philip Schlesinger and Damien Tambini, *Taking Stock: Broadcasting and Devolution in Scotland and Wales*, briefing paper, Stirling University: Media Research Institute, 1999.

23. For an analysis of the wider crisis in current affairs television, see Barnett and Seymour, *"A Shrinking Iceberg Traveling South": Changing Trends in British Television* Chapters 2 and 3.

24. Bob Franklin, *Newszak and News Media*, London: Arnold, 1997, pp.191–2; Brian McNair, *News and Journalism in the UK*, Chapter 5.

25. Richard Lindley, *Panorama: Fifty Years of Pride and Paranoia*, London: Politico's, 2002, p. 362.

26. Alison Preston, 'The marketisation of television news', Chapter 4 in *The Development of the UK Television News Industry 1982 – 1998*, PhD thesis, University of Stirling, 1999.

27. John Kampfner, 'The callow youths on our screens have had their day in the sun', *Media Guardian*, 5 November 2001, p. 9.

28. See Ian Hargreaves and James Thomas, *New News, Old News*, London: ITC/BSC, 2002, Chapter 5; BBC News, 'News and Current Affairs Audiences: Emerging Messages 1996–97', August 1997.

29. Summary of News PSR results taken from the booklet *BBC News: The Future – Public Service News in the Digital Age*, London: BBC, 1998.

30. Roger Bolton, 'Don't take the vision out of telly', *The Observer*, 14 January 1996.

31. John Mulholland, 'What's up docs?', *The Guardian*, 26 January 1998.

32. Andrew Billen, 'Documentary is the new drama', *New Statesman*, 24 October 1997.

33. On staging in C4's *Staying Lost*, Janine Gibson, 'Film of street children "set up"', *The Guardian*, 19 August 1998; on Channel 4's *Daddy's Girl* as a hoax, 'From Hitler diaries

to Vanessa Feltz', *The Guardian*, 13 May 2004; on the emergency show, Christopher Reed, 'Crash victim sues over secret TV film', the *Guardian*, 5 March 1998.

34. Mark Lawson, 'Carlton is being fined a weighty £2 million', the *Guardian*, 19 December 1998; see also John Willis, 'The faking of real TV', *Media Guardian*, 11 May 1998.

35. This section draws on Giles Oakley, 'The quest for TV quality: the documentary – people representing themselves', speech to the Prix Italia Forum, June 1996.

36. See Brian Winston, *Claiming the Real: The Documentary Film Revisited*, London: British Film Institute, 1995, p. 154.

37. Arjun Appadurai, *The Social Life of Things*, Cambridge: Cambridge University Press, 1988.

38. Blumler and Gurevitch, *The Crisis of Public Communication*, p. 199.

39. Martha Nussbaum, *Upheavals of Thought: The Intelligence of Emotions*, Cambridge: Cambridge University Press, 2001, p. 433.

40. Ian Hargreaves and James Thomas, *New News, Old News*, London: ITC/BSC 2002; Peter Keighron, 'Telling the same stories', *Broadcast*, 15 November 2002; Patrick Barrett, 'The news gets personal', *Broadcast*, 9 May 2003.

CHAPTER 10

1. Mark Thompson, 'We need more whistle-blowers', *Media Guardian*, 29 September 2003.

2. Justin Lewis and Rod Brookes, 'How British television news represented the case for the war in Iraq', in Stuart Allen and Barbie Zelizer (eds.), *Reporting War: Journalism in Wartime*, London and New York: Routledge, 2004.

3. Peter Wilby, 'Baghdad burns while London spins', *New Statesman*, 25 August 2003.

4. The Phillis Report, *An Independent Review of Government Communications*, London: Cabinet Office, January 2004, p. 2.

5. Anne Perkins, 'The Banquo at the Hutton inquiry is Sir Andrew Turnbull, cabinet secretary', *New Statesman*, 1 September 2003.

6. John Kampfner, 'The Prime Minister will survive the Hutton inquiry', *New Statesman*, 29 September 2003.

7. Gavyn Davies, 'These threats to the BBC are serious and sinister', *Daily Telegraph*, 27 July 2003.

8. Peter A. Hall, 'Media accuracy is vital, but its freedom is even more so', the *Guardian*, 17 January 2004.

9. Martin Sims, 'Government pressure meets intransigence from BBC', *Intermedia*, December 2003.

10. Roger Mosey quoted in Maggie Brown, 'All hell is set to break loose', *Media Guardian*, 17 January 2000.

11. 'Focus: The Today row', *Observer*, 29 September 2002.

12. Executive, BBC Current Affairs, 2003.

13. Jamie Doward. 'Auntie's £10m ego trip', the *Observer*, 21 July 2002.

14. The BBC paid Oryx £0.5 million compensation and £300 thousand in costs (the *Guardian*, 28 November 2002).

15. Senior executive, BBC News and Current Affairs, 2003.

16. Duncan Campbell and Patrick Wintour, 'Survey chief resigns saying Iraq never had stockpiles', the Guardian, 24 January 2004.

17. Steven Barnett, 'Opportunity or threat? The BBC, investigative journalism and the Hutton Report', in Stuart Allen (ed.), Journalism: Critical Issues, Milton Keynes: Open University Press, forthcoming, 2004.

18. Letter from Susan Watts' solicitors, Finers Stephens Innocent, to BBC Litigation department, 11 July 2003, p. 2, submitted to the Hutton inquiry as evidence, ref. SJW/1/0082.

19. See Campbell's memo to Scarlett of 17 September 2002 in which Campbell requested fifteen changes in the dossier. Scarlett replied a day later agreeing to some of the changes and rejecting others. Hutton inquiry website, daily evidence, 19 August 2003, morning session, references: Cab/11/0066 and Cab/11/0067. On this, see Andrew Sparrow, 'Documents show Campbell urged change to WMD text', Daily Telegraph, 21 August 2003.

20. Barnett, 'Opportunity or threat?'

21. Matt Wells, 'BBC acts to head off Hutton rebuke', the Guardian, 11 December 2003; Matt Wells, 'BBC tightens rules on single-source stories', the Guardian, 15 December 2003.

22. Richard Norton-Taylor, 'The emperor is left without a stitch', the Guardian, 23 January 2004.

23. See, for example, the Independent, front page, 29 January 2004.

24. 'The independence of the BBC', the Daily Telegraph, 31 January 2004, p. 9.

25. BBC Press Office, 'Due process – statement', 10 May 2004.

26. Conor Gearty, 'A misreading of the law', London Review of Books, 19 February 2004, p. 3.

27. Mark Thompson, 'We need more whistle-blowers'.

28. Statement by Lord Hutton on 28 January 2004, paragraph 53 (2), summarising paragraph 291 of the Hutton Report, January 2004.

29. Gearty, 'A misreading of the law', p. 5.

30. See the leader, 'We must have the truth on Iraq', the Observer, 29 February 2004.

31. John Kampfner, 'Don't mention the war', Media Guardian, 16 February 2004.

32. Steven Barnett, speech to the 'After Hutton' conference, University of Birmingham, March 2004.

33. David Hencke and Michael White, 'Top BBC resignations astonished Hutton', The Guardian front page, 4 March 2004.

34. I received an Economic and Social Research Council grant of £134,000 to fund my BBC research for three years.

35. Dyke began his executive career in the early eighties by taking over the ailing TV-am morning news show, where he replaced Peter Jay's upmarket agenda with the glove puppet Roland Rat (made by Anne Wood, later responsible for creating the BBC's Teletubbies), cartoons and female-friendly items.

36. Janine Gibson, 'Blow for BBC means Dyke must get tough', The Guardian, 22 February 2000.

37. Briggs, The History of Broadcasting in the United Kingdom: Competition 1955–1974, Vol. V, p. 318.

38. Dyke speaking on BBC Radio Scotland, *The Mix*, 7 January 2001.

39. BBC Press Office, 'Greg Dyke makes ethnic diversity a top priority at the BBC', 7 April 2000, citing Dyke's speech to the Race in the Media Awards, London.

40. Jacqueline Asafu-Adjaye, 'Why television has to change', *Broadcast*, 24 October 2003; and see the reports in *New Nation* 21 July 2003, 15 September 2003 and 27 October 2003.

41. Jamie Doward and Burhan Wazir, 'British TV accused of institutional racism', *The Observer*, 25 August 2002.

42. Owen Gibson, 'BBC hits ethnic minority recruitment target', the *Guardian*, 26 January 2004.

43. On two recent cases of racial discrimination, see Joy Francis, 'BBC still showing its "hideously white" face', *Media Guardian*, 13 May 2002.

44. Maggie Brown, 'Second to none', *Media Guardian*, 15 April 2002.

45. Annual percentage shares of viewing figures for all households in 2003 are from BARB: BBC1 25.6%, ITV 23.7%, BBC2 11.0%, C4 9.6%, C5 6.5%, and multichannel viewing 23.6 %. In multichannel households, shares of viewing for the week ending 25 April 2004 were: other 41.6%, BBC1 19.3%, ITV1 19.8%, BBC2 7.1%, C4 6.9%, C5 5.2%. *Broadcast*, 14 May 2004.

46. See for example Jamie Doward, 'Tuned in for the big fight', *The Observer*, 6 January 2002.

47. Quoted in Danny Cohen, 'Time for a bit of originality'; see also Patrick Barrett, 'Old wine in new bottles', both in *Broadcast*, 14 November 2003.

48. Jay Blumler and Michael Gurevitch, 'Public service in transition? Campaign journalism at the BBC, 2001', in J. Bartle et al (eds.), *Political Communications: The General Election of 2001*, London: Frank Cass, 2002; John Plunkett, 'TV's new political agenda', *Broadcast*, 15 March 2002; Steven Barnett, 'So long to the bloke in the suit', *Media Guardian*, 17 June 2002.

49. Sian Kevill, *Beyond the Soundbite: BBC Research into Public Disillusion with Politics*, London: BBC, February 2002.

50. John Kampfner, 'The callow youths have had their day in the sun', *Media Guardian*, 5 November 2001.

51. Gautam Malkani, 'Worldwide domination', *Financial Times*, 4 March 2003; BBC *Annual Report and Accounts 2002–03*, London: BBC, 2003.

52. Raymond Snoddy, 'Who will set the lessons?', *The Times*, 1 March 2002.

53. Greg Dyke, Dunn speech to the Guardian Edinburgh International Television Festival, 24 August 2003.

54. Interview with Gavyn Davies, *Broadcast*, 28 September 2001.

55. See BBC *Governance in the Ofcom Age*, London: BBC, 26 February 2002.

56. Steven Barnett, 'The BBC is seriously wicked', *The Observer* business section, 2 December 2001.

57. Independent Television Commission, *Investing in UK Culture*, paper for Smith Institute seminar, London, 2001.

58. On BSkyB's anti-competitive tactics, see Matt Wells and Maggie Brown, 'Rupert bared', *Media Guardian*, 13 May 2003.

59. Independent Television Commission, *Investing in UK Culture*.

60. Consumers' Association, *Turn On, Tune In, Switched Off: Consumer Attitudes to Digital TV*, London, 2001.

61. Interview with Andy Anson, Channel 4, 2001.

62. See Georgina Born, *Uncertain Futures: Public Service Television and the Transition to Digital – A Comparative Analysis of the Digital Television Strategies of the BBC and Channel 4*, London: Media@LSE Working Papers, n. 3, 2003; Georgina Born, 'Strategy, positioning and projection in digital television: Channel Four and the commercialization of public service broadcasting in the UK', *Media, Culture and Society*, v. 25, n. 6, 2003.

63. *BBC Submission to the Government Communications Review*, London: BBC, 4 July 2000.

64. Source: *Broadcast*, 5 October 2001.

65. Quotation from *BBC Television in the Multichannel Environment: Strategy 2001–2004/5*, London: BBC, April 2001.

66. Matt Wells, 'Digital TV at turning point as converts top 50%', *The Guardian*, 17 December 2003.

67. Emily Bell, 'BBC breaks free from Sky', *Media Guardian*, 17 March 2003; Dan Milmo, 'BBC calls for satellite Freeview', *The Guardian*, 27 April 2004.

68. Matt Wells, 'Sky offers free 200-channel satellite deal to fight off soaring BBC service', *The Guardian*, 10 June 2004. The BSkyB announcement is interpreted as part of a tactic intended eventually to bring 'freesat' customers to the company's pay-TV deals.

69. Greg Dyke, 'One BBC – Making it happen', speech to staff, TVC London, 7 February 2002.

70. Owen Gibson, 'A portal for the people?', *Guardian New Media*, 10 November 2003.

71. Greg Dyke, 'The BBC: connecting locally', speech at the Ferens Art Gallery, Hull, 10 October 2001; Ashley Highfield, 'Interactive revolution', *Television*, November 2003.

72. On this, see Steve Neale, *Genre*, London: British Film Institute, 1980.

73. On the 'liberation' of ITV from public service obligations see Damien Tambini, 'The end of public service TV?', *Media Guardian*, 22 December 2003.

74. For a similar argument see Andrew Graham and Gavyn Davies, *Broadcasting, Society and Policy in the Multimedia Age*, Luton: Libby, 1997; and Richard Collins, 'Public service broadcasting: an agenda for reform', *Intermedia*, v. 26, n. 1, 1998.

75. Barry Cox, 'The coming of freesheet television', 'The reformation of the BBC', 'Paying the piper but not calling the tune' and 'Towards 2014': four lectures published in the *Guardian*, 28 January 2003, 4 February 2003, 11 February 2003 and 18 February 2003; and Barry Cox, 'Truth, lies, and public service broadcasting', speech to the Programme in Comparative Media Law and Policy, Oxford University, 7 August 2003.

76. See, *inter alia*, Graham and Davies, *Broadcasting, Society and Policy in the Multimedia Age*.

77. *Broadcast*, 12 December 2003; Tambini, 'The end of public service TV?'

78. Scientific Generics, *Attitudes to Digital Television*, draft report for the DTI and DCMS, 19 December 2003.

79. Geoff Mulgan, 'Reinventing the BBC', in Mulgan and Paterson (eds.), *Reinventing the Organisation*, p. 76.

80. John Mepham, 'The ethics of quality in television', in Geoff Mulgan (ed.), *The*

Question of Quality, London: British Film Institute, 1990, p. 69.

81. Jay Blumler, 'Vulnerable values at stake', in J. Blumler (ed.), *Television and the Public Interest*, London: Sage, 1992, p. 31.

82. Onora O'Neill, 'Called to account', lecture 3, the 2002 BBC Reith Lectures, *A Question of Trust*, BBC Radio 4, May 2002.

83. Richard Whish, *Review of the BBC's Fair Trading Commitment and Commercial Policy Guidelines*, para 6.1, April 2001.

84. Jane Martinson, 'PACT seeks 50% BBC quota', the *Guardian*, 23 April 2004.

85. 'Ofcom publishes Phase 1 Report of the Public Service Broadcasting Review', London: Ofcom, 21 April 2004, p. 3; and Ofcom, *Ofcom Review of Public Service Television Broadcasting: Phase 1 − Is Television Special?*, London: Ofcom, April 2004, 'The conceptual framework in a digital age', para. 154, p. 74.

86. 'Ofcom, 'Ofcom publishes Phase 1 Report of the Public Service Broadcasting Review', p. 2. The same message is given in the full report thus: 'Some of the more serious and challenging programme types were most affected by multichannel competition. *Horizon, Newsnight* and *The South Bank Show* all had a viewing share more than 50% lower in multichannel homes compared with [terrestrial-only] homes'. *Ofcom Review of Public Service Television Broadcasting: Phase 1 − Is Television Sepcial?*, 'Impact', p. 6, and see Figure 28, p. 46.

87. See Communications Act 2003, paras 264 (6) (b) and 264 (6) (i).

88. For an attempt to outline such principles, see Georgina Born and Tony Prosser, 'Culture and consumerism: citizenship, public service broadcasting and the BBC's fair trading obligations', *The Modern Law Review*, v. 64, n. 5, 2001.

89. Jason Deans, 'Grade vows to defend BBC independence', the *Guardian*, 2 April 2004.

90. Matt Wells, 'Grade plans shakeup to take on BBC's foes', the *Guardian*, 15 May 2004.

91. Mark Thompson, speech to BBC staff, 22 June 2004, p. 4.

92. *BBC Journalism, the Neil Report*, London: BBC, 23 June 2004.

93. Mark Thompson, speech to BBC staff, 22 June 2004, p. 6.

EPILOGUE

1. Timothy Garton Ash, 'The Janus dilemma', *The Guardian*, 5 June 2004, p. 3, p. 5.

2. See John Thompson, *The Media and Modernity*, Cambridge: Polity, 1995, esp. Chapter 3, on the rise of 'mediated quasi-interaction'; Luc Boltanski, *Distant Suffering*, Cambridge: Cambridge University Press, 1999.

3. James Tully, *Strange Multiplicity: Constitutionalism in an Age of Diversity*, Cambridge: Cambridge University Press, 1995, p. 5.

4. Seyla Benhabib, *The Claims of Culture: Equality and Diversity in The Global Era*, Princeton, N.J.: Princeton University Press, 2002, p. 75.

5. David Goodhart, 'Discomfort of strangers', *Prospect*, February 2004.

6. Roger Silverstone, 'Regulation, media literacy and media civics', *Media, Culture and Society*, v. 26, n. 3, 2004, pp. 444–5.

7. Philip Schlesinger, 'No escape from politics', in *The Future of the BBC: Perspectives on Public Service Broadcasting in Scotland*, Glasgow: BBC Scotland, 2004, p. 10.

8. W. J. M. MacKenzie, *Political Identity*, Manchester: Manchester University Press,

1978, p. 165, quoted in Philip Schlesinger, *Media, State and Nation*, London: Sage, 1991, p. 156.

9. Schlesinger, *Media, State and Nation*, p. 173.

10. Paddy Scannell, 'Television and history', in Janet Wasko (ed.), *Blackwell Companion to Television*, Oxford: Blackwell, forthcoming 2005.

11. I take the fertile notion of counterpoint in media cultures from Roger Silverstone, 'Contrapuntal cultures: From minorities to moralities in European media', paper presented to the MODINET conference, University of Copenhagen, October 2003; this in turn is derived from Edward Said's *Culture and Imperialism*, London: Vintage, 1994, and other of his writings.

12. Nabila Saddiq, *Young British Muslims and the Media*. Unpublished MPhil dissertation, University of Cambridge, 2004.

13. The industry conference mentioned was Broadcasters Online: TV and Radio Internet Innovations, London Business School, 10 September 1999.

14. Onora O'Neill, 'Freedom of the press and intellectual interchange', in B. S. Markesinis (ed.), *The British Contribution to the Europe of the 21st Century*, Oxford: Hart, 2002.

15. Oscar Gandy, 'Dividing practices: Segmentation and targeting in the emerging public sphere', in W. L. Bennett and R. M. Entman (eds.), *Mediated Politics: Communication in the Future of Democracy*, Cambridge: Cambridge University Press, 2001, p. 157.

16. Don Redding, on behalf of the NGOs 3WE and Public Voice, 'A vision of a BBC that serves citizens to 2016', *The Future of the BBC*, London: Westminster Media Forum Projects, April 2004.

17. Eddie Gibb and David Lee, 'Towards an "open source" BBC?', *The Future of the BBC*, 2004.

18. John Dewey, *The Public and its Problems*, Chapter 5, 'Search for the great community', New York: Henry Holt, 1926.

Index

A&E Channel 167, 168, 170, 341
Abbott, Paul 338
Abramsky, Jenny 519
accountability 31, 77, 91, 107–8, 129, 214,
    230–3, 495
An Accountable BBC (1994) 230
accountancy, and accountability 107–8;
    availability of finance 97–9; awareness of cost
    123–5; and balancing of accounts 122–7; and
    bounded discipline 107–8; budgets 103, 105,
    137–8; cross-subsidies 114; development
    money 120–1; and efficiency savings 109,
    127–8, 306–7; internal reorganisation of
    101–5; lack of financial management 104; as
    morality 106–9; and necessity of foresight 108;
    overheads 137–8; in practice 101–6, 110–14,
    116, 118–21; production 97–9;
    profligacy/overspends 97, 102–5, 106, 108,
    123; rationalisation 100; realities of 124–5;
    reduction of systems 468; resistance to methods
    108; scales of operation 105; virtual money
    122–8; wars 114–22, *see also* funding
ACTT 42
Adam Smith Institute 50
Adams, Colin 321, 343, 344
advertising *see* marketing
aesthetics 75, 84–7, 344–5, 353, 368, 381,
    441–8, 450, 517
Afghanistan 520–2
African-Caribbean Programme Unit 201
Airey, Dawn 478
Airport 431
Al-Fayed, Mohammed 35
Al-Jazeera 520
All About Me 472
All Creatures Great and Small 167
Allen, Jim 338, 365
'Allo, 'Allo! 296
AltWorld 451
The Ambassador 275
American Visions 290
Andrews, Leighton 57
Anglia TV 255
Animal Hospital 173, 291, 437
Annan Committee (1974–77) 43–4
Annan, Lord 47

The Announcement 488
Annual Performance Review (APR) 234, 236–7,
    240–1, 249–51, 271
Ant and Dec Show 95
Applebaum, Anne 53
Archer, Jeffrey 402
The Archers 160–1, 511
Arena 97–8
Ariel 65
Aristotle 80
Armchair Theatre 38
Arnold, Matthew 27
Arts Council 41
Arts for Labour 52
The Ascent of Man 247, 441
Asher, Jane 246
Askey, Arthur 30
Assignment 387
Asylum Day 489, 516
At the Races 484
Atkins, Anne 89
Attachments 345
Attenborough, David 441
audience 64, 75, 341; alienation of 394;
    competition for 37–8, 39; consultation with
    89; feedback 41; figures 90; liking for 265;
    long-term studies 223; minority/universal
    broadcasting paradox 54–5; for news 405;
    reaching 477–8; reaction to niche channels
    485–6; respect for 85; share 223–4; targeting
    266–7; variety of 45; young people 91, 262,
    263, 265, 267, 297, 298–300, 473
audience research *see* Chapter 7 *and* 29–30, 254–5,
    256, 407, 495; '100 Tribes' project 284–6;
    ambivalence/resistance towards 274–8;
    historical 269; intensification of/commitment
    to 272–3; listening/responding to 270–2; and
    the news 407–8, 410; and News and Current
    Affairs directorate 281–4; placement of 258; as
    political tool 280–1; power of 273–81;
    qualitative 274, 286–7; reassurance engendered
    by 273–4; reliance on 278–9, 286–8;
    technology use in 272; and what makes good
    drama 275–7
audit, auditing 72, 77, 214–15, 224–5;
    accountability for trust 230–3; doubts

548

concerning 242; as intimate bureaucracy 233–5; in practice 235–41; recursive 234–5; as symbolic violence 238–9; unknown participants 235
Australian Broadcasting Corporation (ABC) 170
Australian Film Finance Board 481
authorship, authoring channels 75, 288–93, 337–9, 442–3
avant-garde television 46
The Avengers 38
Ayre, Richard 88–9, 284, 411–13

Babyfather 470
Back Up 275
Bad Boy Blues 353
Bad Boys 291
Bad News 200
Baker Bates, Rodney 124, 216
Ballykissangel 90, 266, 274, 276, 291, 340, 348, 360
Band of Brothers 473
Band of Gold 276, 277, 278
Band Waggon 30
Bandele, Biyi 353
Banks-Smith, Nancy 361
Bannister, Matthew 164, 247, 260, 262, 263–5, 288, 300
Barnard, Beverley 208
Barnett, Steven 497
Barwise, Paddy 286
BASYS 392
Bates, Simon 300
Bazal Productions 147, 166
Bazalgette, Peter 161
'The BBC: The Entrepreneur' (1991) 60
BBC 80, 473; affection for 1–3; alienation from 10; anthropologist in 12–13, 14–17, 19; autonomy of 500, 505; background 5; campaigns against 10; censorship in 33; concern with quality 269; creation of national culture 34; crisis at 6–8, 49, 62–4; criticism of 4–5, 47, 48, 48–9, 62; as cultural state 66–7; cynicism in 82; democratic aspects 10, 33, 34–5; demoralisation in 134; dumbing-down 4, 11; essential/non-essential activities 497–8; ethos 494; expense accounts 83; Golden Age 319–20; government relationship 497–503; hierarchical nature 65–6, 67; high standards 30; history of 26–31; identity 183, 210; importance of selling its brand 53; influences on 494–5; innovations 37–8; as institutionally racist 471; internal divisions 72–3; internal market 60; internal reflection 35; investment in 52–3; market failure vs universality/mixed programming 63; as metonym for establishment 93; middle brow tone 29–30, 87; monopoly of 29; moral authority/self-importance of 70; morale in 109; non-commercial/public partnerships 476; openness in 17–18; paranoia in 18; political aspects 6, 8–9, 31–5, 49–50, 51–2, 62, 69; populist 30,

494; possibility of privatisation 49–50; problems/failures 10–11; propaganda skills 33–4; public service orientation 498–500; rituals of inclusion 87–96; rivalries in 78–9; role of 517; satirisation of self 30; schizophrenic nature 114; self-regulation 60–1, 229–31, 501–2; service reach 477; skills/erosion 3; social/ethical purpose 81–2, 86–7; success/achievements of 9, 11; tensions 31; vilification of 9–10; weaknesses in 87
BBC Afghan Education Service 520
BBC Asian Network 470
BBC Audience Research 269
The BBC Beyond 2000 (1998) 230
BBC 1Xtra 470
BBC Birmingham 319
BBC Bristol 189
BBC Choice 485
BBC Club 137–8
BBC–Discovery joint-venture partnership 171–2, 450, 475
BBC Enterprises 59
BBC Experience exhibition 65
BBC governors 31, 47, 49, 60–1, 62, 232, 242–9, 252, 331, 365, 437, 457, 462–3, 465, 476, 501, 503, 505
BBC Hull 490, 516
BBC Knowledge 485
'The BBC Listens' 232
BBC Manchester 188, 189
BBC Millbank 95, 394–7, 412, 413, 415
BBC News 24 231, 497
BBC Newsgathering 451
BBC Northern Ireland 136, 177–8, 319, 323, 324, 332–3
BBC Online 9, 112, 128, 219–20, 227, 255–6, 461, 468, 497
BBC Prime 506
BBC Radio Nottingham 199
BBC Scotland 135, 136, 177–8, 283, 319, 323, 324, 333, 393–4
BBC Video 160
BBC Wales 13, 136, 319, 323, 324, 348
BBC World 392, 403, 404, 506
BBC Worldwide 475
BBC/ITV duopoly 62, 102–3; complacency of 43; critics of 43; early days 37–9; funding 50; golden opt-out 40; sport 25
BBC1 88, 90, 118, 124, 143, 167, 174, 259–60, 266, 276, 289, 291, 314
BBC2 41, 73, 75, 86, 88, 90, 91, 95, 96, 118, 144, 159, 167, 174, 175–6, 179, 184, 259–60, 264, 279, 289, 290, 294, 295, 297, 298–9, 314, 473
BBC3 485, 486, 488, 497
BBC4 485–6, 488
Beck 340, 349
Beck, Ulrich 507
Bectu 471
Bedtime 472
Being April 361

Bell, Emily 478
Bell, Peter 418–19
Benn, Tony Wedgwood 102
Benson, Glenwyn 176, 199, 384, 388, 400
Berg, David 359
Berkeley Square 276
Best, George 295
bi-media policy 99, 110–11, 132, 134, 135, 136, 194–6, 386, 389–90, 468
Big Bang/Year Zero 135
Big Brother 315, 435, 479, 484
The Big Read 472
Big Strong Girls 315
The Bill 276, 291, 292, 472
Billen, Andrew 347, 363, 367
Billington, Rachel 246
Bird, John 140
Birmingham 136
Birt, John 14, 62, 103, 124–5, 176, 218, 220, 241, 243, 247, 338, 373, 413, 428, 466; accountability of 129; accounting under 306; and BBC as command economy 67–8; and Broadcast/Production split 112–14; and combining of radio and TV 110–11; divisions/rivalries under 77; downsizing, redundancies, casualisation under 181; election to director-general 49; and erosion of creativity 304; and genre-bending 376–7; impact on news/journalism 385, 386–9, 394, 396–8, 403, 404, 448, 452; introduction of internal market 60; legacy of 468, 504, 505; managerial initiatives 214–15, 227; and 'mission to explain' 57–8, 407; negative legacy of 494–5; on pluralist fourth channel 45; and political subordination 6, 458, 463–4, 473, 493, 495, 500, 502, 505; rationalisation/reforms under 6, 99–106, 222–3; on rights issue 163, 164; savings claims 127–8; tenure at root of present crisis 6; values under 372; vision of marketisation 64
Black Audio 205
Black Audio Film Collective 46
Black Britain 201, 400, 402–3
Black History Month 489
Black Londoners 202
Black Workers' Group 206
Blackeyes 327
Blair, Tony 23, 24, 35–6, 56, 57, 95, 438, 453–4, 457–8, 464, 496
Blakeway Productions 144
Blakstad, Lucy 1, 95, 443
Bland, Sir Christopher 247, 390
Bleasdale, Alan 338
Blind Date 298
Bloomfield, Sir Kenneth 247
Blue Planet 450, 472
Blumler, Jay 376
Blunkett, David 464
BMG 159–60, 168
Board of Governors 31, 49, 231, 242–51
Board of Management 69, 220

Bocho, Stephen 339
Bodies 488
Body Hits 488
Bolland, Mike 135
Bolton, Roger 399
Boot Camp 315
Boult, Adrian 30
Bourdieu, Pierre 238
Bowen, Jeremy 518
The Bowman 349, 350
Bowman, Graeme 451
Boxtree 168
Boyle, Danny 250
Boyle, James 110
Boys from the Blackstuff 68, 296
Bradbury, Malcolm 170
Bradley, Richard 174
The Brain 174
branding *see* marketing
Brass Eye 85–6
Breakfast News 198, 404, 408
Breaking the Bank 168
Breaking Point 431
Brecht, Bertolt 30
Bridgewater, Carl 94
Briffa, Ed 227
Briggs, Asa 68, 69
Brimstone and Treacle 309, 330
Bristol Features 431
Brite 168
British Association of Film and Television Awards (BAFTA) 93
British Broadcasting Company (BBC) *see* BBC
British Film Institute (BFI) 41, 53
British Interactive Broadcasting (BIB) 227–8
Brittan, Leon 49
broadband 490
Broadcast (BBC directorate) 24, 88, 247, 277, 344, 412, 466; conflicts over ownership/sale of rights 162–5, 169; continuing problems 176–7; financial/restructuring aspects 123, 126–7, 132, 134, 135, 136, 138–9; as rationally planned/market-led 307; and supervision of legal/financial compliance 151–6
Broadcasters' Audience Research Board (BARB) 93, 270, 272, 273
broadcasting, best practice in 150; deregulation of 50–2, 61, 64; as entertainment 29; financial profligacy 102–3; increasing productivity 150; mixed programming 29; opening up of 43; programme requirements 52; in public interest 28; quality in 51–2; rebuilding trust in 495; self-absorption of 70; training/employment anxieties 186; universality of 28–9; uplifting approach 29–30
Broadcasting Acts 24; (1990) 50–2, 58, 62, 99, 101, 180, 385; (1996) 61–2
Broadcasting House 16, 89, 110, 200, 392, 517
Broadcasting Research 270–2, 281
Broadcasting Standards Council (BSC) 248
Bronowski, Jacob 247, 441

Brookside 75, 291, 324
Brown, Gordon 57
Brown, Maggie 471
Browne, Colin 217
BSkyB 25, 48, 59, 61–2, 73, 227–8, 465, 466, 472, 483, 488
Buddha of Suburbia 290
Bugs 275
Bumping the Odds 349, 350
Buried 345
Burns, Lord 461
Burns, Tom 65, 69, 70, 72, 270, 307
Burundi 3–4
Bush, Bill 497
Bush, George W. 464, 479
Business Affairs 136
Butler enquiry (2004) 464
Butler, Sir Robin 1

cable and satellite channels 47–8, 52, 59, 61, 64, 73, 80, 255, 292, 403, 477
Calderwood, Andrea 167, 249–50, 348
Caleb, Ruth 250, 251, 302, 321, 342, 348
Cameron, Colin 135
Campaign for Quality Television 51–2
Campbell, Alastair 373, 454, 457–9, 458, 461–3, 465
Can't Cook Won't Cook 315
Canterbury, Archbishop of 464
The Canterbury Tales 470, 472
Capaldi, Peter 140
Capital radio 262
Cardiac Arrest 168, 276
Cardiff, David 33
Carlsberg 161
Carlton 435–6, 496
Cash for Questions scandal 35–6
Castaway 315
Castle, Barbara 23, 55–7
casualisation 180–5, 197
Casualty 90, 167, 168, 250, 276, 291, 314, 320, 329, 331, 332, 335, 338, 472, 506
Cathode, Ray 362
Catliff, Nick 174
CBS 315
Ceddo 46, 204–5
Central Television 80
centralisation 304–10, 306–10; decentralisation project 504; of news 389–94; of newsgathering 414
Centre House 68
Centre for Policy Studies 207
Chain Reaction 176
Chalmers, Judith 102
Chancellor, Anna 436
Changing Rooms 147, 184, 315, 376
Channel Five 10, 24, 51, 73, 127, 142, 148–9, 255, 266, 477, 478, 481–2, 496
Channel Four 41–2, 44–7, 50, 51, 62, 64, 73, 80, 86, 95, 104, 131, 133, 142, 143, 144, 145, 146, 159, 187, 190, 202, 205, 267, 289,

294, 299, 315, 361, 435, 467, 473, 477, 484
Channel 4 News 198, 385
Charles II - the Power and the Passion 474
Charter 31; renewal 101, 157, 158, 231, 461, 462, 496, 497
Chatham House Rules 73, 89
Checkland, Michael 49, 57, 59, 62, 101, 103, 106, 244, 386
Children In Need campaign 258
Children's BBC 90, 95, 174
children's channels 486, 487, 497
Children's Hospital 174, 431, 433, 437
Choudary, Anjem 429, 430
Citizen Smith 296
Citizen's Charter 214
civil service 32, 69, 456–7
Civilisation 441
Clarissa 296
Clark, Kenneth 441
Clash of the Titans 296
Clemmow, Richard 110–12, 283, 412
Clinton, Bill 479
Clocking Off 361, 472
CNN 59, 403, 451
co-productions 162, 165–72, 291, 340–1, 450, 481
Cohen, Nick 455
Cold War 431
Colosseum 474
Commercial Policy Guidelines 158, 161, 233
commercialisation 72, 100, 213, 292; and accusations of unfair trading 497–9; background 57–60; competitiveness of 439, 475–6; and digital media 493; paradox of 54–5; in practice 60–4, 156–61
Commission for Racial Equality (CRE) 207
commissions, commissioning 72, 174, 290, 296, 354–5, 376; and audience research 277; bi-medial logic 389–90; briefs 310–11, 312; calculated 90; centralisation of 289, 304–10, 306–10, 389–90; debates/discussions 347–9; documentaries 431–2; generic dynamics of 473–4; in-house vs independent production 59–60, 130, 144, 145, 148, 183; legal/financial compliance 151, 152; populist 184–5; reform of 469–70; as schedule-led 399–400; tariff-based funding model 306, 308, 431
Commodities 42
Common As Muck 168, 340, 361, 362
communication 375; diversity of opinion 516; failure of 72; inter-cultural 516; internal 65; intra-cultural 516; five structural forms of 515–16; territorially-based local/regional networks 516
Communications Act (2003) 461, 496, 500
Community Programme Unit (CPU) 12, 16, 77, 79, 112–14, 173, 175–6, 184, 185, 246, 377, 432, 439–41
competition see Chapter 4 and 11, 48, 439, 494; effect on creativity 38–9; government rhetoric

497–503; increased 471–82; paradox of 54–5;
in practice 37–9, 58, 62, 64, 70, 73, 133,
307–8, 314; research in 271
conflict of interests 131–2, 149
The Connection 435
Connolly, Billy 340, 348
Conrad, Joseph 296
Conservatives 36, 43, 48–9, 180, 331, 395, 497
Conspiracy 474
consultants, consultancy 71, 100, 124, 132, 133,
221–30, 258; cynicism/distrust of 218–19; on
the fringes 228–30; introduction of 217–20,
221–2; negative conception of BBC 226–8;
reliance on 213–14; and value for money
221–2, 224
Consumers' Association 483
controllers 72, 78, 117, 129, 255, 277–8, 281,
289, 308, 314, 327, 407
Cook Report 299
Cook, Robin 57, 426
Cool FM 298
Cooper, Robert 166, 250, 267
Coopers & Lybrand 100
Coote, Anna 24
Co-production 119–20, 139, 162–72, 303,
341–3, 441, 475
The Cops 345, 345–6, 356, 433
Coronation Street 38, 52, 126, 150, 276, 292, 334,
338
Corporate Affairs Directorate 216
Corporate Centre 77, 121, 122, 123, 134, 159,
169, 213, 216, 224, 227, 235, 241, 244, 250,
260, 284, 306, 468
Corporate Strategy Unit 216–17
Correspondent 473
Countryside Alliance 459
Coupling 488
Cox, Barry 493
Cox, David 5, 10, 59
Cracker 275, 276, 277, 278, 291, 368
Crawford Committee (1925) 67
Creative Archive 476, 516
creativity 16, 59, 67, 70–1, 81, 82, 87, 100, 101,
210, 250, 372, 474, 479; and casual/freelance
employment on 181–3, 191, 197, 210–11; and
centralisation 306–10; devolution of 305; effect
of competition on 38–9; erosion of 304, 306,
495; freedom of 305; greater opportunities for
45; importance of 467, 468; innovations
needed 477; loss of personnel 476;
marginalisation of 224; multi-layered 256; and
privatisation of ideas 190–3; and suspicion
towards research 271; rising standards in 39;
and uncertainty 209–11
Crick, Michael 413
Crimewatch UK 434, 436–7, 437
Cronenberg, David 367
cross-media ownership 61
Crossing the Floor 354
The Crouches 470
The Crow Road 289, 366

Crown Castle 488
Crown Prosecutor 13, 275
CTE 168
Cuban missile crisis 39
Culloden 95
Cultural Diversity Network (CDN) 470, 471
Culture Select Committee 231, 466
Cunningham, Jack 53
Curb Your Enthusiasm 488
Current Affairs 16, 57–8, 336, 396, 469; control
of 397–8; decline in 398–9, 400–1; effect of
Birt on 398–9; emasculation of 397–403;
identity of 397; malaise of 397, 399–403; and
mission to explain 400, 407; no guaranteed
schedule slot 399; as populist storytelling 400;
relationship with Documentaries 401; ring-
fencing of budget 399, 402
Currie, Edwina 331
Curteis, Ian 246, 331
Cutting Edge 73, 74–5, 314, 433
Cutting It 361, 472

Daily Express 36
Daily Mail 36, 328
Daily Mirror 75
Daily Telegraph 463
Dale, Peter 74, 438, 444–8
Daley, Janey 246
Dalton, Hugh 67
Dalziel and Pascoe 167–8, 168, 275, 340
Damazer, Mark 93, 96
Danger Man 38
Dangerfield 90, 166, 250, 274, 275, 291, 302,
311
Dann, Trevor 264
Dark Heart of Africa 171
The Dark House 489
Darling Buds of May 276
Davies, Andrew 170, 326
Davies, Gavyn 5, 457, 463
Davis, Evan 423
The Day Britain Stopped 474
Deacon Brody 119
Deadly Voyage 345
Deasy, Frank 290
The Death of Yugoslavia 91, 296, 376, 431, 441
Deep Water 348
Degrees of Error 91, 290
Deloitte 100
democracy 28, 373–4, 378–81, 505
Demos 176, 502, 503
Dench, Judi 340
Denton, Charles 12, 13, 63, 81, 104, 116, 118,
118–21, 135–6, 164–5, 166–7, 182, 212, 235,
239–41, 266, 267, 280, 321, 326, 357
Department of Trade and Industry (DTI) 41, 47
Dewey, John ix, 517
Dickens, Charles xi, 367
digital cable 227–8, 483
digital radio 461, 486
digital satellite 227–8, 483

digital technology 111, 392, 435, 439, 442, 445, 468, 470

digital television (DTV) 61, 63–4, 80, 231, 461, 465, 473; attitudes to 493; background 482–6; broadband-based local wired city 490; challenge to BSkyB 488; contain range of genres 487; cross-platform links 489; free-to-air 487, 488, 490–1, 497; government attitude/ interventions 497, 498–9; Hever strategy 485; high proportion of British programmes 487; initiatives 489–90; interactivity 489; introduction of 482–91; political engagement 489–90; questions concerning 487–8; strategy 486–92

digital terrestrial television (DTT) 227–8, 483

digital video (DV) 196–7, 345, 409, 411, 431, 439, 480

Dineen, Molly 346, 438

'The Dinner Party' 74

Dinwoodie, John 444–8

director-general (DG) 49, 78, 90, 101, 103, 216, 244, 251, 391, 468

Directorate Implementation Group (DIG) 201

Directorate of Policy and Planning 216

Disability Programme Unit (DPU) 112–14, 184

Discovery Channel 163, 171–2, 175, 255, 292, 450

Diverse 144, 187

Diverse Reports 45

diversity 378–81, 450, 515, 516–17; ideological 307–8; and minority groups 470–1; and mixed programming 380–1; mixed-genre channels 379–80,487; Newsnight and 421–6, 427–9; of opinion 380, 516; political 329–32; of representation 380–1, 449, 450; social/cultural 380

Dixon, Graham 517, 519

Docherty, David 79, 216, 217, 271, 284

Documentaries 16, 17, 112–14, 174, 176, 186, 336, 397, 401, 431, 440, 443

documentary 73, 74–6, 84, 90, 91, 92, 95, 376, 377, 440–47, 448; access documentary 439–41; analytical 441; as art 441–8; contradictory tendencies 431–2; crisis of faking in 438; democratic function 450; docu-soaps 431, 432, 433, 434–8; dominance of narrative 431; emotional/aesthetic aspects 440–41, 449–50; enlivening/individual perspective 431; expert presenter 441; filmic qualities of 431; formula-spinning mode of commissioning 433–4; golden age of 431; gritty realism 433; hybridisation of 432; inventiveness in 443–8; negative effects on 450–2; observational 442; proliferation of sub-genres 432; reality 431; reflexive film-making 442

Double Your Money 38

Doucet, Lisa 430

Dr Who 506

The Draftsman's Contract 258

Drama 12, 126, 152, 163, 204, 240–1, 273, 275–7, 290, 336, 341, 346, 368, 372

Drama Editorial Board 68, 106, 135–6, 166, 191, 192, 239–41, 249–51, 302, 310, 321, 324, 332, 348, 357

Drama Finance 115, 116, 119–21

Drama Group 12–13, 15, 16, 18, 66, 76, 78, 104, 106, 241, 250, 266, 277, 289, 296; adoption of film mores 352–5; ambiguities 345–6; APR 249–51; audit in 235; and authorial voice 337–9; budgets 324; and classic adaptations 365–8; and co-production deals/rights sales 162, 166–8; cohesiveness in 333–4; commissioning 304–10; consultant in 212; crafts/trends 335–7, 339–42; and creative autonomy 325; creativity in 368, 371–2; culture of 327; difficulties in 320–1; and editorial control over independent production 153–6; effect of restructuring on 135–7; emulating documentaries 346; financial aspects 114–15, 116, 122, 125, 126, 133–4, 139–40; financing 303; funding 325; history of 319–20; hostile conditions in 321; impoverished/narrow 371; and independent quotas 322–4; job losses/redundancies 190; leadership of 321; and logic of safety 313; making a profit 164–5; meetings 321; moral sensibility 337; obsession with hit popular dramas 223; ordering/scheduling of programmes 310–13; pitch culture 344–51; political/cultural diversity 329–32; and popular drama 334–5; in practice 319; problems/difficulties in 319–22; ratings/expectations 327–9, 360; and regional quotas 324–5, 332–3; reorganisation of 182; risk-averse tendencies 341–2, 352; rivalries in 319; and social realism 355–9; and spaces of invention 360–7; and straddling of genres 349; and trust 215–16; and values 372; and violence 368–9; and writer alienation 325–6

Drama Overview meeting 164–5, 289–92

Drama Production Centre 116

Driving School 174, 431

Drop the Dead Donkey 354

The Dual 176

Dubs, Lord 246

Dunkirk 474

duopoly see BBC/ITV duopoly

Dyke, Greg 10, 14, 144, 452, 466, 504, 505; and education strategies 475–6; focus on popularity 477; increases BBC competitiveness 471–82; and introduction of BBC's digital services 482–91; and the Kelly affair 459–60, 462–3, 465; lessons learnt from 476–7; new vision 467; news reforms under 459; organisational reforms 466–69; resignation of 5, 455; skills/achievement 467–71

E4 484

Ealing Studios 106–7

East is East 341

EastEnders 78, 90, 127, 161, 167, 224, 250, 291, 314, 320, 329, 334, 338, 361, 363, 402, 470, 472, 506

Eaton, Mick 42
Ebony 202
Edge of Darkness 68, 333
Edinburgh International Television Festivals 44–5,
    74–6, 309, 451, 479
Edmonds, Noel 4
education 53–4, 475, 475–6
efficiency 48, 58, 59–60, 77, 100–1, 109, 113,
    127–8, 131, 178, 256, 391–2, 494
Ehrenberg, Andrew 286
Eldorado 62, 223, 334
Electoral Commission 474
Elliott, Nick 73, 83, 326
Elstein, David 10, 24, 25
Emergency Ward 10 38
Emery, Dick 171
Emma 291
Emmerdale 291
employment 67; and best practice 201;
    casualisation of 180–90, 197; conditions 82;
    contracts 182–3, 186–9, 192–3; effect on
    creativity 181–3, 191, 197, 210–11; and
    exchange/privatisation of ideas 190–3; and
    flexibility 183; freelance 186–90, 191, 211;
    insecurity of 186; insider/outsider status
    197–201; and institutional identity 209–10; job
    losses/redundancies 58, 107, 109, 113, 133,
    179; minority representation/equal opportunity
    201–8; recruitment strategies 43, 78, 80–1;
    revolving door phenomenon 185; skilling,
    reskilling, multiskilling 193–7; staff appraisals
    17–18; uncertainties in 210–11
Endemol Entertainment 146, 147, 166, 314, 315,
    479
ENPS system 111, 392
Enterprises (BBC directorate) 163
Entertainment Group 16, 104, 129, 135, 169, 223
entrepreneurial activities 60, 191, 332–3, 475–6,
    494; development of 172–6; evangelical nature
    of 176–8; and independent producers 147,
    149; libidinalisation of 173
ER 75, 250, 276, 339, 347
Ernst & Young 100, 218
Esther 113
ethics 86, 368–71
Europe Express 187
Evans, Chris 263, 264, 288, 300
Evans, Kim 95, 296, 402
Express newspapers 255
Extending Choice (1992) 63, 260
Extending Choice in the Digital Age (1996) 60, 63–4
External Services 71

Faber, George 13, 81, 118–21, 175, 241, 332,
    334–5, 348, 355
Factual programming 163, 169, 176, 296, 474
Factual Entertainment 126
Factual Group 104, 112, 113
Fair Trading Audit Committee 232
Fairmile, Jeremy 374
Falklands War (1982) 47, 383–4

Fame Academy 472
The Family 249
Family Affairs 127
Family Butcher 349, 350
Farr, Sue 14
The Fast Show 161
Features 112–14, 397
'Fermat's Last Theorem' 91
Fiddick, Peter 249, 250, 328
Film 114, 352
film movements 41–2
FilmFour 352, 483
films 46, 78, 104, 106, 116, 338, 340, 352
Finance 116, 138
finance see accountancy; funding
Financial Planning 103
Finch, Nigel 98
Fine Cut 91
Five News 407
Flaherty, Robert 438
Flextech 175, 292–3, 485
40 Minutes 74, 75, 210
Footballers' Wives 361
For Love or Money 187
Foreign Affairs Committee 455, 456
Foreign Office 32
Forgan, Liz 63
formats 145–7, 167–8, 191–2, 290–91, 313–15,
    404, 422
Fortune, John 140
Foster, Robin 47, 217
Foucault, Michel 66
Four Weddings and a Funeral 341
Fox Entertainment 255, 315, 452
Fox, Paul 105
Francis, Karl 13
free-market economics 7–8, 45, 49–52, 101
freelancers 16, 107, 134, 181–3, 191, 197,
    210–11
Freeview 488, 493, 514
French, Michael 347
The Fresh Prince of Bel Air 207
The Friday Alternative 383–4
Friends 75
The Full Monty 341
funding 4–5, 9, 11, 81–2, 515; and commercial
    enterprises 59; development 134, 136–7; for
    the fourth channel 45, 46; increased 471–2,
    472–3, 475; justification of public 54–5; small-
    scale film finance 41; squeezing of 48; through
    advertising 49–50; through commercial
    activities 156–61, see also accountancy
Furneaux, Charles 74–6
The Future of the BBC, Green Paper (1992) 60, 101;
    White Paper (1994) 60, 214, 232, 497
Future Tense 349, 351

Gaby Roslin Show 95
Gardam, Tim 144, 199
Garnett, Tony 331, 345, 346, 354, 370–1, 371
Garton Ash, Timothy 507

Gavin, Rupert 162, 475
Gearty, Conor 463–4
General Strike (1926) 31–2, 243, 377, 379
generic television 312–15, 430–31, 475
genres 292, 333, 382; access programming 73,
    84, 439–41, 516; arts 73, 84, 95; avant-garde
    364; bending 376–7; bundling/trilogies 290;
    children's 159; classic drama 172, 175, 290,
    291, 353, 365–6; comedy 84, 90, 255, 297;
    contemporary serials 366; creative renewal
    needed 477; crossing 85–6, 92; current affairs
    84, 376; docu-soaps 76, 172, 174, 307, 347,
    349, 434–8, 438; docudramas 474;
    documentaries 73, 74–6, 84, 90, 91, 92, 95,
    376, 377; drama 73, 84, 90, 91, 105, 117–18,
    127, 129, 133, 159, 168, 290, 291; drama
    documentary 86–7, 435; entertainment 38, 76,
    84, 90–1, 133, 142, 376; factuals 142, 315–16,
    376–7, 432, 435, 435–6, 449; features 90; fly-
    on-the-wall 179, 264, 438, 442; game shows
    307; history 474; hybrids/clones 173, 312–13,
    349, 432, 434, 474; lifestyle/leisure 94, 142,
    172, 307, 316, 434, 450; outflow of talent
    from 133; popular drama 90, 142, 334–5, 376,
    472; reality TV 307, 313–14, 376, 434–5, 435,
    439, 442, 450; recycling of 474; regional
    drama 360–1; sci-fi 349, 354; science 84;
    serials 168, 290, 291, 363–4; series 168;
    singles 290; sitcoms 91, 376, 472; soaps 360;
    social realism 353, 355–9, 361; spin-offs 314;
    sports 10, 24–5, 48, 61–2, 84, 90, 91, 95, 291;
    sub-genres 434; thrillers 349; unlimited
    313–16; violence 368–9, see also programmes
Getting Hurt 170
Ghostbusters 91
The Gift 349, 351
Gillespie, Dizzy 2
Gilligan, Andrew 452, 453–4, 455–63
Glaister, Gerry 333
Glasgow Media Group (GMG) 200, 382, 383
Gold, Susie 167–8
Golden Rose award (Montreux) 93
Goodwin, Daisy 94
governance 9; challenges 243; consulting the
    public 246–8; Davies' and Dyke's reforms of
    474–5; internal processes 248–51; out of touch
    244–5; problems/criticisms 242–3; and public
    accountability 476; reforms 505; rifts in 49;
    vague 243
Governing Today's BBC (1997) 230
government, and commercialisation of BBC
    47–60, 497–9; competition rhetoric 497–503;
    and DTV 498; and independent production 499;
    intrusive interventions 498, 500; relationship
    with BBC 497–503; state control 31–2, see also
    Conservatives; New Labour; media-political
    relationship
Grade, Lew 37
Grade, Michael 46, 62, 89, 358, 503
Graef, Roger 442
Graham, Alex 200–201

Graham-Dixon, Andrew 184
Gramsci, Antonio 66
Granada 126, 275, 278, 496
Grant, John 244
'The Grave' 75
Gray, Jim 374–5
Great Britons 472
Greene, Hugh Carleton 319, 468
Greenpeace 384
Greer, Ian 36
Gregory, Philippa 86
Grierson, John 442
Griffiths, Trevor 365
Grimmond, Claire 478
Ground Force 147
Grown-Ups 348
Guardian newspaper 298, 327, 459, 465, 466
The Gulf War 431
Gulf War (1991) 58
Gurevitch, Michael 376
Gutteridge, Tom 247

Habermas, Jürgen 287, 378
Hall, Stuart 507, 509, 517
Hall, Tony 111–12, 123, 385, 387–8, 390, 401
Hamann, Paul 17, 92, 94, 95, 113, 174–5, 180
Hamilton, Neil 35–6
Hamish Macbeth 90, 168, 249–50, 276, 340, 361
Hammond, Eric 244
Hancock's Half Hour 38
The Hanging Gale 250
Happily Ever After 296
Harding, Philip 247
Hare, David 241, 246, 249–50
Hargreaves, Ian 246
Harman, Harriet 56
HarperCollins 168
Harpur and Iles 349, 350–1
Harris, Rolf 173–4
Harrison, Suzan 175
Harvest Moon 349
Hatch, David 101
Have I Got News For You 153, 290
Hayling, Alan 451
HBO 168
Heaney, Seamus 254
Heart of Darkness 296
Heartbeat 276, 291, 302, 320, 348
Heath, Edward 69
Heffer, Simon 53–4
Heggessey, Lorraine 92, 94, 95, 173–4, 472
Hellen, Nicholas 466
Hello Girls 291
Henry, Lenny 340
Hetty Wainthropp Investigates 90, 168, 275, 278, 332,
    348
Hever 485
Hewlett, Steve 88–9, 283, 400, 411
Hi-de-Hi 296
Highsmith, Patricia 348
Hill Street Blues 87, 339

Hillsborough 25
Hillsborough 324
History of British Art 184
The History Man 68
Hobson, Dorothy 249–50
Hodgson, Patricia 216, 227, 247
Hogg, Baroness 246
Hogg, Douglas 417, 418, 419
Hoggart, Simon 458
Holby City 340, 347, 470
Holding On 290, 366, 367
Holiday 102
Hollingworth, Corinne 127, 266
Holtham, Gerry 24
Home Front 94, 184
Hood, Stuart 209
Hoon, Geoff 454, 464–5
Hopkins, John 338
Horizon 91, 501
Horrocks, Peter 23, 35–6, 199, 419
Hotel 431
The House 90, 91, 289, 328, 431, 442
House of Elliot 167–8
Howard, Michael 95, 416
Howard's Way 296, 334
Howe, Lady 246
Hughes, Simon 427
Hull Interactive 490, 516
The Human Body 441
Human Rights Act (1998) 231
Hummingbird Tree 322
Humphrys, John 453–4
Huntington, Samuel 429, 430
Hussey, Marmaduke 49, 57, 101, 213, 243, 244
Hutton inquiry 5, 454–65, 503–6
Hutton, Lord 5

I Love Lucy 46
I Will Not Complain International Inc 229–30
iCan 489, 490
If . . . 474
impartiality 32, 43, 78, 381–2, 407, 411, 462;
   crisis in discourse of 421–22
In a Land of Plenty 366
In the Red 170
in-house production 59–60, 77, 469; financial
   aspects 134, 136, 156; relationship with
   independents 130, 133, 137–42
Independent Advice Panel 249–50
Independent Broadcasting Authority (IBA) 44, 51
Independent Commissioning Group 469
Independent Film and Video Unit (at Channel 4)
   46
Independent Filmmakers Association (IFA) 41
Independent newspaper 26
independent production 50–1, 80, 130, 131–2,
   133, 276, 310, 312, 432, 469, 497–8;
   bargaining power 142; changes in 141; choices
   made by 144–7; coercive situations 140–1;
   consolidation within 142–3; costs 141–2;
   creative/financial incentives 151; and editorial

compliance 152–6; effect of dependence on
   broadcasters 148–9; as entrepreneurial/
   innovative 149; funding 145, 147; government
   attitude towards 499; and informal networking
   148; international takeovers 147; and making of
   porn 147; policing of market 151–2; proxy
   company 139–40; quota 44–6, 58, 59–60, 78,
   99–100, 130, 131, 133, 141, 177, 180, 322–5;
   regional 322–5; relationship with in-house
   production 138–42; size of companies 142,
   144–5, 146; staffing 145; structure of 148;
   talent in 141–2, 148, 149
Independent Television Authority (ITA) 37
Independent Television Commission (ITC) 47,
   51–2, 64, 466, 484
Independent Television News (ITN) 39, 198, 385,
   387
India 303, 316–17
information technology (IT) 137
Inside Story 432, 450
Inspector Morse 340, 472
interactive services 80
international markets 58, 165, 168, 341, 345,
   450, 475
Internet 484, 514, 516
Invasion Earth 349
IPPR 24, 502, 503
IRA 49, 247–8
Iraq 453–65, 479, 480, 500
Isaacs, Jeremy 44
Israel Shorts 439
It Ain't Half Hot, Mum 296
ITEL 168
ITV 37–9, 46, 51, 58, 86, 90, 133, 143, 159,
   180, 276, 289, 291, 314, 356, 361, 368, 432,
   470, 473, 482, *see also* BBC/ITV duopoly
ITV Network Centre 73, 302
ITV1 9, 473
Ivanhoe 340
Ivory, William 338, 362

Jackson, Michael 14, 19, 74, 86, 90, 91, 93, 94,
   118, 143, 144, 158, 159, 176, 201, 206,
   240–1, 259, 264, 289, 290–2, 294, 295,
   295–7, 354, 356, 358–9, 483
Jackson, Paul 129
James, P.D. 246
Jane Eyre 326
Jardine, Lisa 247
Jay, Margaret 24
Jay, Peter 386
Jazz Line-Up 2
Jeffries, Stuart, 353–4, 363
Jenkins, Guy 354
Johnson, Boris 4, 10, 53
Johnson, Clare 42
Joint Intelligence Committee (JIC) 457, 458
joint-venture partnerships (JVP) 171–2, 175
Jones, Jack 56
Jools Holland Show 506
Jordan, David 199

journalism 8, 375–6, 378–81, 430–1; analysing
  Falklands coverage 383–4; centralisation of
  389–94; contrarian 384; as critical/independent
  413–14; and diversity of representation 449;
  and emasculation of current affairs 397–403;
  eye-witness reportage 33; failings in 26; and
  ideology 383; imaginative independence/
  expedient conformity 33; impact of Birt on 385,
  386–9, 407, 452, 458–9; as impartial 32–3,
  381–6, 413, 449; investigative 397, 399, 414,
  448, 475; need for standards/self-regulation
  460; new self-conception of 421; objectivity of
  381–2; original/distinctive 459; personal
  perspective 407; political 415–17, 448–9, 489;
  publisher responsibilities of 504; reform of
  407–8, 410–14, see also news
Jowell, Tessa 496
Jude 353
Judge John Deed 472
Juke Box Jury 38
Julien, Isaac 205
Juliet Bravo 331

Karaoke 327
Kaufman, Gerald 56
Kavanagh QC 277
Kavanagh, Trevor 36
Kay, David 460, 464
Keating, Roly 293
Kelly, David 5, 8, 454–65, 500, 503
Kensington House 98, 99
Kevill, Sian 412
King Lear 170
The Kingdom 364
Kingston Communications 490
Kinsley Lord 100
Kiss FM 261, 300
Koch, Anne 282
Kozoll, Michael 339
KPMG Management 218
The Kumars at No.42 470
Kung Fu Monks 172

LA Law 339
The Lakes 13, 366
Lambert review (2002) 231
Lambert, Stephen 17, 74–6, 180, 445, 446
Langan Behind the Lines 480
Langan, Sean 480–1
The Late Show 416, 477
Lawson, Mark 316
Lawson, Nigel 58
LBC 408
Leggo, Mike 92
Lewis, Jeffrey 87
licence fee 49–50, 52, 58, 59, 61, 64, 81, 82–4,
  92, 134, 156, 161, 232, 461, 468, 485, 499
Liddiment, David 63, 471
Liddle, Rod 459
'Lido' 1, 443
Life After Life 249

The Life of Birds 441
Lilley, Peter 402, 443
Lime Grove 57–8, 99
Linda Green 361, 472
Lion Television 174–5
Listener Research Unit 29–30, 251
'Listening to the Public' 232
Little Angels 488
Little Britain 488
Liverpool One 314
Living with the Enemy 439
Loader, Kevin 175
Lloyd, David 145
Loach, Ken 331, 338
local radio/TV 30, 412–13
London Weekend Television (LWT) 144, 386,
  388–9
London's Burning 276, 302, 339
Long, Bob 173, 176
Looking After Jo Jo 290, 349, 351
Loved Up 353
Lucky Cows 349, 350
Lygo, Kevin 150, 478
Lynch, David 364

McGovern, Jimmy 13, 324, 338, 366
McGrath, John 338
MacCabe, Colin 53–4
Macintosh, Charles Rennie 296
McKee, Robert 336
McKinsey 71, 132, 218, 219–20, 221–2, 227–8,
  258, 293
McPherson of Cluny 208
McQuarrie, Ken 135
Macdonald, Adam 295, 297
MacShane, Denis 53
MacTaggart Lecture (1979) 44–5
Maddox, Brenda 246
Madson 275, 340
MAI 255
Mail on Sunday 455, 459
Maisie 349, 350
Major, John 57, 61, 214, 496
Making Babies 94
management, best practice 494; and compliance
  confusion 154–6; consultation processes 88–9;
  criticisms of 179; effect of restructuring on 181;
  failure of 133; financial 71; and introduction of
  new personnel 181; managerial caution 58;
  naming/renaming 65–6; as neutron bomb
  135–7; new managerial vision 63–4; news
  initiatives 393–4; overhaul of 468–9;
  politically-expedient 505, see also new public
  management
Manchester Stories 433
'Mange Tout' 74, 444
Manning, Sir David 454
Mansfield Park 353
Marchant, Tony 338, 366
Mardell, Mark 26, 36, 475
Marion and Geoff 473

market research 86, 264, 278, 280, 281–4, 287, 297, 412, 493, *see also* audience research; marketing
market-based economics 7–8, 9–10
marketing 407, 410; '100 Tribes' project 284–6; advertising 39, 50, 75, 293, 332; American influence 255–7; BBC brand 403; and brand values 267; branding campaigns 259–60; branding the real 265–9; and channel identities/consumer expectations 292–3; and channel perception 267; and creativity 256; and cross promotion 255–6; and danger of artificiality 268; delusions fostered by 287; development of 300–1; escalating importance of 258–9, 268; ethnographic research 286, 297; focus groups 86, 264, 278, 280, 287, 412, 493; multichannel values 288–92, 301; and news research 281–4; on-air promotion 267; planning/strategy 259–60; revamping/risk-taking 260–5; and scheduling tasts 2947; and technological progress 255–6; and threat to creativity 287–8; trailers 266–7; and understanding young people 298–300; values 258–65, *see also* commercialisation
marketisation 47–8, 58, 59–60, 99–101, 106, 108–9, 178, 179, 181, 210, 495
Marks & Spencer 161
Marr, Andrew 454, 475
Marsh, Kevin 459
Match of the Day 473
MCC 522
Meacher, Michael 41
media 89, 91; and audience taste 491–2; criticism 49; ecology 491–7, 514, 516; influences 492–5; initiatives 489–90; policy 8–9, 131–2, 491–500
The Media Show 187
media-political relationship 53–4, 57, 375–7, 456–65, 490–1, 493, 496–7
Mellor, Kay 326
Mentorn Barraclough, Carey 247
Mercer, David 364
Mercurio, Jed 338
Meridian 255
Merseybeat 470, 472
MIDAS 122
Middlemarch 68, 340, 363
Midnight Hour 282
Midnight's Children 290, 302–3, 316–19, 342–4, 369–70
Miller's Gold 349
Mills, Jeremy 174
Milne, Alastair 49, 62, 330
Milne, Paula 309
Ministry of Defence (MoD) 457, 458, 462
Ministry of Information (MoI) 33
minority groups 10, 45, 46, 54, 84, 91, 112–14, 114, 247, 400, 402–3, 470–1, 515, 516
The Missing Postman 168
Mitchell, Steve 110–11
Modern Times 1, 17, 73, 74–5, 91, 95, 180, 210, 289, 314, 346, 401, 431, 432, 433, 442–3, 450
Moerzoff, Eddie 74
Mol, John de 479
Moll Flanders 127, 290, 291, 337
The Money Programme 387
The Monocled Mutineer 296
Monopolies and Mergers Commission 59
Moonie, Lewis 24, 25
Moore, Peter 74
Morris, Chris 85–6
Morris, Desmond 466
Morris, Dominic 227
Morris, Geraint 333
Morris, William 296
Morrison, John 418
Morse 277
Mosey, Roger 459
Motherland 470
Movie Magic 239
Mr Sex 349, 351
Mr White Goes to Westminster 354
The Mrs Merton Show 90, 297
MTV 255
A Mug's Game 90
Mulgan, Geoff 491
multichannel television 63, 290, 404, 405, 410, 473, 493, 497, 501, 513
The Munsters 46
Murder One 94, 339
Murdoch, Rupert 10, 11, 24, 48, 49, 61–2, 73, 105, 379, 462, 465, 483, 496, 500
Murphy, Stuart 487–8
Murroni, Christina 24
Music and Arts 176, 184–5, 293
My Family 472
My Night With Reg 353

9/11 475
Natalie's Baby 440–1
National Broadcasting and Advisory Councils 231
national community, BBC's role in orchestrating 508, 512–17
National Health Service (NHS) 467
National Lottery 436–7
Nations and Regions *see* regions, regionality
Nationwide 403
Natural History Unit 171
Natural World 171
Navy Blues 351
The Nazis: Warning from History 431, 441
Neighbours at War 432
Neighbours from Hell 432
Neil, Andrew 246, 384
Neil, Ron 112, 113, 129, 175, 344
Network Centre 126–7, 302
Network First 432
Network Radio 164
Network Radio Research 264
Network Television Review of the Year 87

Network TV 89–92, 103, 116, 213, 215, 216, 217, 221
Neverwhere 349
The New Entrepreneurs 176
New Labour 6, 7–9, 10, 131, 176, 283, 375, 416, 472, 500; lack of interest in arts, culture, BBC 52–3; party conference (1996) 23–6, 35–7, 52–4, 55–7; pensions debate 55–7
Newman, Sydney 320
'New Music First' 226, 260–1
new public management 213–15; and accountability 251–2; bureaucratic 213; business for culture 224–30; corporalist tendencies 213; and culture of integration 212; cuts and resentments 215–17; disfunctional 220; governance issues 242–51; pitching 212; self-audits under 233–6; self-regulating policies 231–2; strategy 221–4; success of 253; use of consultants 217–20, 221–2; use of key performance indicators (KPIs) 225–6; values 224–30, *see also* management
New Writer's Award 93
News (BBC directorate) 12, 16, 26, 33, 38–9, 39, 57–8, 77–8, 88–9, 194–6, 390, 399, 407, 410, 412
news, 497; as analytical 397; centralisation/commodification of 448–9; civil service/professional model of 379; competition in 407; as consumer-responsive 407–9, 410–13; core information/understanding vs stories, strategies, seduction of audience 412; democratic expectations 380; demotic/serious 385–6; as elitist 379–80; getting headlines/breaking stories 459, 460; hard/soft stories 391; immediacy/as it happens 407; impartiality in 452; internal market 393; and mission to explain 388, 407; polarisation between BBC/ITV 385; political collusiveness 394–7; as product 403–6; public sphere ideal 378–9, 380; regionalism as key ingredient 409; reinvigoration of 475; and representational diversity 380–1, 450; ring-fencing of budget 399; values 379, *see also* journalism
News and Current Affairs (NCA) 78, 88–9, 93, 99, 110–11, 217, 379, 383, 386, 413; audience decline 452; branding 407–8; criticisms of 424; efficiency savings 391–2; Millbank unit 394–7; redundancies in 387–8; reorganisation of 396–7; research into 281–4; ring-fenced budgets 407
News Information 108
News International 36, 61, 255
News Online 406
News Programme Strategy Review 16, 110–12, 410–13, 475
News of the World 298
News 24   79, 112, 408, 409, 485, 497
Newsbeat 408
Newsgathering 99
Newsnight 3, 15–16, 23, 25–6, 35–6, 56–7, 78, 79, 91, 176, 198, 202, 203, 374–5, 376, 387–8,

394, 395, 404, 405, 408, 412, 413–14, 449, 455, 460, 501; aggressiveness of 416–17; as bastion of integrity/real journalism 414–15; E. coli/Tory spin story 417–19; effect of cuts on 414, 421; hierarchical 415; and impartiality 421; Islam edition 428–30; mode of discussion on 421–2; new approach of 428–9; notes for presenters 420–1; political coverage 415–17; politician/expert vs ordinary public 422–3, 427; poverty item 423–7; as programme of record 414; and widening of representational circle 422
Newsreel Collective 451
Nickelodeon 90, 487
Nighty Night 488
Nine O'Clock News 292, 385, 386, 409, 414, 472
No Bananas 291
No Child of Mine 356
Noel's House Party 90
Noggin the Nog 159
Nolan Committee 231
Northern Ireland 47
Nostromo 322, 340, 341
Nurses 442
Nussbaum, Martha 448

Oakley, Giles 8, 173, 176, 402
Oasis 171, 262
O'Connor, Paul 451–2
Odone, Christina 246
Ofcom 496, 499, 500, 501–2
Offers 66, 72; meetings 175–6, 184, 185, 192, 312, 348, 349, 352
The Office 473
Office of Fair Trading 231
Oftel 228
Olympic Gold 185
One Life 440
O'Neill, Onora 380
Omnibus 472
On the Record 199, 387
OnDigital 483
One Foot in the Grave 255
One O'Clock News 36
Open Broadcasting Authority 44
Open Space 439
Open University 475–6
Oprah 295
Oranges Are Not the Only Fruit 290
Orbach, Susie 297
organisation, business units/cost centres 107; common interests/rivalries with external broadcasters 73; complexity of 72–3; creative/administrative split 70–1; divisions/conflicts in 70; engineering/technical staff 71; fission and fusion 77–9; hierarchical 69; institutional analogies 69–70; personnel functions 71; planning of programmes 71–2; reorganisation of 71–2; restructuring of 6, 100, *see also* management
Oryx case 460, 461

Our Friends in the North 68, 90, 91, 168, 241, 289, 290, 328, 332, 340, 355–6, 357–9, 365
Our Mutual Friend 68, 365, 366, 367
Out of the Blue 314
Out on Tuesday 46

PACT (Producers Alliance for Cinema and Television) 142–3, 145, 499
Paddington Green 314
Painted Babies 172
Panama Row 13
Panorama 49, 58, 78, 88, 105, 198–9, 283, 291, 388, 395, 400, 402, 412, 462, 472, 477
Paradise Heights 361
Parfitt, Andy 264
Parker, Ian 364, 437
Parnell, Val 37
Parsons, Charlie 314, 315
partnerships 475–6
Patten, Chris 406
Pattinson, Charlie 13, 357–9
Pattison, Ian 353
Pawlikowski, Paul 74
Paxman, Jeremy 35–6, 374–5, 413, 414, 416, 420, 423, 425
PBS 341
Peacock, Alan 49–50
Peacock Committee/Report (1986) 50, 386, 493
Peak Practice 276, 291, 335
Pears, Tim 366
Pearson 168
Pebble Mill 3, 202, 302, 319, 323–4, 324
Peel, John 261, 300
The People's Account 204
Pennies From Heaven 309
People and Programmes (1995) 63
People's Century 431, 441
'Perfect Day' video 256–7, 258
Performance Review 223, 226, 241
Perkins, Geoffrey 129
Persuasion 90, 103, 353
Petra Kelly 349, 351
Phillips, Anne 380
Phillips, Mark 74, 169, 170–1
Phillips, Melanie 207, 246
Phillis, Bob 59
Phillis enquiry (2003) 456–7
Picture This 91
Pie in the Sky 168, 348
Pienaar, John 475
Pilkington Committee (1962) 43
pitch, pitching 13, 131, 175–6, 213, 250, 308, 372; pitch culture 344–52
Pitts, Antony 517, 519
Planet 24 315
Plantin, Marcus 302
Planning 66, 77, 105, 118, 122, 161, 167, 216, 284, 468
Play for Today 309, 338
Play UK 293
Plowman, John 129

Police 442
Police Camera Action 437
policies, bi-medial 99, 132, 134, 135, 136, 386, 389–90, 468; centralisation 30, 103, 121; commitment to new technologies 47; editorial 77; fair trade 157, 158; and globalisation 47; market competition/economic efficiency 47
Policy and Planning Unit 77, 247, 284, 401, 468
Political Programmes 394–7
The Politician's Wife 309
politics 95, 375–7, 378–81, 394–7, 410, 412–13, 422, 448–9, 474–5, 481–2, 489–90, 496–7, see also media-politics relationship
politics of complex cultural dialogue 508–9
politics of presence 380, 517
The Politics Show 475
Pollard, Nick 452
Polygram 160, 168
Pompeii – The Last Day 474
Pompidou Centre 486
Popstars 472
popular television 11, 52, 54–5, 62–3, 73, 81, 85
populism (in UK TV) 64, 148, 178, 314, 444, 472, 477, 494
Post Office 26, 27
Potter, Dennis 62, 93, 309, 327–8, 330, 338
Powell, Enoch 53
Powell, Jonathan 223, 271, 454, 461
Power, Michael 214, 230
The Precious Blood 353
Prescott, John 57
PriceWaterhouse 100
Pride and Prejudice 68, 90, 266, 336, 363
Priest 91
Prime Suspect 275, 276, 277, 291, 368, 472
Prior, Allan 338
The Prisoner 38
Private Eye 12, 149
The Private Life of Samuel Pepys 474
private sector 67–8
Producer Choice 60, 78, 99–100, 213, 252, 306; cultural effects 124; described 101–5; divisiveness of 109; financial aspects see accountancy; impact of 131–4; introduction 99–101; irrationalities of 108–9; and job losses/redundancies 181; management problems 116; pilot system 106–7; in practice 110–15; problems/difficulties 122–8; profits/losses resulting from 126; reactions to 129; and reframing/redescribing of BBC 107–8; rivalries/conflicts 117–22
Producer Guidelines 91, 233, 436
producers 65, 70, 86–7, 92, 93, 94, 105, 126, 131, 133, 150, 153, 254–5, 261, 280, 287, 307–8, 329, 341, 494
Production (BBC directorate) 91, 100, 372, 469; conflicts over ownership/sale of rights 162–5, 169; continuing problems 176–7; financial/restructuring aspects 112–14, 132, 134, 135, 136, 138–9; and monitoring of editorial compliance 152–6

production departments 77, 112–14, 469
professionalisation 108
Programme Board 35
Programme Complaints Unit 232, 248
Programme Finance Committee (PFC) (in Drama Group) 76, 104, 115, 119, 120, 235
Programme Planning 30
Programme Review Board 35, 87, 92–6, 322, 327, 328, 402
Programme Strategy Reviews (PSR) 63, 88–9, 234, 281, 284, 410, 415, 475
programmes/programming 495; autonomy of 391; children's 90; closed 382; and editorial taste 85; effect of competition on 38; ethics/aesthetics 84–7; funding for 340–1; mixed programming 29; imitative/safe 148; increased spending on 469; and independent quotas 177; ordering 310–13; outsourcing 58; pricing 90; production 90; quality of 76, 80, 111, 135, 144, 178; records of transmission (ROTs) 406; rivalries/divisions 77–9; schedules 13, 72, 91; secondary value of 145; standards 126, *see also* genres, commissioning
The Proms 295–6
Provos 248, 441
public corporations 67
Public Eye 282, 387
public opinion 377, 410
public relations (PR) 89, 214
public service broadcasting 7, 9, 40, 43, 64, 114, 256, 260, 440, 452, 468, 505; ambitions for 490–1; BBC model 515–17; and challenge of EU 509–10; commercial 483–4; communication structure 515–17; and cultural diversity 509, 512; definition of 79; dialectic with government 515; and digital services 482; in favour of 80; fulfilling 67; future of 506–17; global activities 510; held in high esteem 494; importance of 508–9; and market competition 52; marketplace values 471; mixed economy of 493; and the national community 512–15; as nebulous idea 47; and online digital curriculum for schools 475–6; pluralistic model 44–7; proposals 27; rationale 80; redefinition of 252; Reithian view 27–9; rhetoric 391; role of 507–8; sceptical view of 50; values 83
public sphere theory 378–9, 380–1
Purnell, James 502–3
Puttnam, David 40, 53
Pyramid 474

QED 402
'Quality Time' 74
'Quality, Values and Standards' governors' seminar 246–8
Quinn, Carolyn 395

Radcliffe, Mark 300
Radio 71, 72, 110–12, 124, 132, 217, 247, 262, 271, 281
Radio Current Affairs 390

Radio International 170–1
Radio 5 Live 404, 406, 408, 409, 475
Radio Luxembourg 30
Radio News 390, 459
Radio Times 59, 94–5, 96, 328
Radio 1 16, 225–6, 260–2, 263–5, 268, 293, 297, 298, 299–300
Radio 3 16, 77, 110, 517–19
Radio 4 77, 110, 304
Rage 349, 351
Rampling, Danny 300
Rantzen, Esther 296
ratings 54–5, 62–3, 73, 74, 75, 76, 86, 93–4, 250, 274, 327–35, 435, 472–3, 473
RDF 144, 145
Ready Steady Cook 147, 161
reality TV and reality programming 146–7, 314–16, 434–5, 442, 479
Real Lives 49, 401
Record Review 110
Reed, Daniel 74
Reed, Lou 256–7, 258
Rees-Mogg, William 49
Reeve, William 522
Reeves and Mortimer 90, 93
regions, regionality 30–1, 101, 124, 135, 136, 322–5, 332–3, 360–1, 412, 469
Reith, John 11, 27–9, 31, 63, 70, 243, 245, 360, 468
Reithian 81–2, 84, 85, 96, 274, 381, 412, 473, 486, 501
representation, diverse 380–1, 448, 449, 450, 512–17; minority 201–8; widening of 422
Reps 351
Resources Review 102
A Respectable Trade 86–7
restructuring 129, 131–4, 135, 136–7, 258, 288; apparent incoherence of 129; based on marketisation concept 99–106, 132–3; bi-medial policy 99, 389–90, 468; and co-production 156, 162, 165–8, 169–72; collaborative 469; and control of rights 156–61, 169–72; financial overhaul 106–14; and flexible specialisation 132; and growth of self-competition 156, 162–4; impact of 181; and in-house/independent production confusion 138–41; and the independent sector 131–2, 133, 148; and internal conflicts 162–5; as misguided/self-destructive adventure 178; and new accountancy 114–22; organisational reforms 468–70; in practice 122–9; problems/disaffections arising from 134–8, 154; as rationalisation programme 99–106; secretiveness of introduction 132; and supervision of legal/financial compliance 151–6, *see also* accountancy; Producer Choice
The Return of Zog 444–8
Reynolds, Gillian 74–5
Rhodes 152, 276, 291, 336, 340
Rhythm of Life 171, 172
Rich Deceiver 90

rights 162–5, 166, 168, 169
Rights Agency 163, 164, 169
Rights Archive 157, 158
rituals of inclusion 87–96
Robertson, Colin 478
Robinson, Nick 395
Robson, W.A. 251
Root, Jane 187, 473
Ross, Nick 437
Rough Justice 94
Roughnecks 249
Routledge, Patricia 278, 348
Royal Opera House 179, 442
Royal Television Society 65
RSGB 282–4
Ruffian Hearts 353
Rusbridger, Alan 35
Rushdie, Salman 290, 302–3, 316–19, 342–4,
    370

Salmon, Peter 150
Sambrook, Richard 457, 462
Sankofa 46, 205
Satanic Verses, The 303, 430
satellite television see cable and satellite television
'Saturday Night' 74
SBS 516
Scannell, Paddy 27, 33, 270
Scarlet and Black 336
Scarlett, John 457, 461
schedules, scheduling 255, 262, 277, 288–93,
    294–7, 311–13, 348–9, 353–4, 376, 399–400,
    434, 472–3
Schlesinger, Philip 382–3
Sci-Fi Channel 341
Science 112–14, 402, 432
Scottish Six 393, 509
Screen journal 42
Screen One 118, 119, 170
Screen Two 118, 335, 345
scripts 13, 76, 82, 335–9, 342–3, 347, 354–5,
    358, 389, 397
script editing 335–7
Scruton, Roger 207
The Sculptress 90, 291
Seaton, Jean 32
Second World War 33–4
The Secret Policeman 464
self-competition 162
Sells, David 391
Sergeant Bilko 46
Serials 78, 118, 175, 240, 302, 319, 334, 340,
    342, 344, 366–7, 369
Series 78, 118, 119, 140, 319, 333, 337, 360,
    363
sexualised television 479–81
Shah of Iran 388–9
Shah, Samir 95, 96
Shameless 361
Sharma, Sarinda 207
Sharman 291

Shelley, Mary 474
Shipwrecked 315
Shivas, Mark 106, 116, 357
Short, Clare 26
Signs and Wonders 290
Silent Witness 90, 158, 167–8, 168, 235, 291, 349,
    350
The Simpsons 473
Singer, Aubrey 41
The Singing Detective 327
Singles 78, 114, 117–19, 121, 140, 175, 319,
    334, 335, 337, 340, 346, 352, 352–3, 352–5,
    356
Six O'Clock News 393, 404
Sky 227, 228, 255, 409, 482, 483
Sky News 228, 452, 455
Sky One 84, 435, 477–8
Sky Television 10, 24, 73
Skytext 80
Sloman, Anne 401
Smallpox 2002 474
Smart TV initiative 91, 92
Smith, Anthony 99
Smith, Chris 8–9, 365, 468, 472, 482
Smith, Geoffrey 16, 517–19
Smith, Julia 334
Snow, Jon 420
Soho Stories 289, 433
Soldier Soldier 291, 339
Somalia 3
Spectator 10
spin 8, 36, 57, 375–7, 416, 418
Spooks 472
sport 10, 48, 61–2, 90, 91, 95, 291, 295, 296,
    482, 521–2; BBC/ITV duopoly 25; cricket
    521–2; debate on 24–5; football 472–3; new
    funds for 472–3
Sports Federation 25
Sportsview 105
Star Trek 290
Starks, Michael 227
State of Play 472
Statement of Promises 232–3, 246
Staying Lost 433
Stephen Lawrence inquiry (2000) 470
Steptoe and Son 38, 296
Stone, Oliver 368
Stoneman, Rod 42
Stonewall 345
Storyville 431, 432, 488
Stott, Ken 436
Strategic Communications Unit 8
strategy 91–2, 132, 133
Strategy and Planning Overview meeting 167
Streetlife 249, 353, 356
Sun newspaper 36, 462
Sunday Telegraph 459
Sunday Times 466
Survivor 314
Swann (E.coli report) 418
Swanston, Roderick 16, 517–19

The Sweeney 80–1
Sykes Committee (1923) 27
The System 431, 442, 443–4

24 473
Taggart 277
Tait, Richard 198
Take Your Pick 38
Talking to Susie 297
Talks 33
Tarantino, Quentin 353, 368
Tarkovsky, Andrei 98
Taylor, Laurie 52, 304
Taylor, Peter 247
Tebbit, Norman 4, 331
Tedder, Lord 245
Telefonica group 147
teletext 65
Television 15, 71, 72, 132, 258–9, 266, 271, 281, 288
Television Centre (TVC) 13, 65, 66, 90, 92, 103, 138, 259, 271, 295, 390, 453
Television Corporation 146
Television Current Affairs 390
Television Film Services 106–7
Television News 385, 390
Television Show 127
Television Training Trust 201
Temptation Island 435
Ten O'Clock News 460
The Tenant of Wildfell Hall 365–6
Tesco 161
Test the Nation 472
Thames Television 59
That Was The Week That Was (TW3) 38
Thatcher Government (Thatcherism) 7, 45, 47, 49–52, 58, 61, 358, 397, 400, 456, 458
Thatcher, Margaret 6, 40, 44, 54, 180, 243, 375, 386
That's Life 397
The House 179, 289, 328, 431, 442
Thérèse Raquin 296
Theroux, Louis 480
They Think It's All Over 90, 160
This Life 91, 96, 167–8, 289, 290, 296, 345, 354, 355, 361
This Week 75, 475
This World 473
Thompson, Mark 144, 176, 199, 289, 298, 302, 342, 484, 485, 487, 503–4
Three Non-Blondes 470, 488
Ticket to Ride 349, 350
Tiger Bay 361, 362–3
Till Death Us Do Part 38
The Times 49, 462
Tinker, Tailor 334
Tiswas 159
Titchmarsh, Alan 2
Today 3–4, 405, 408, 453–4, 455, 459, 463, 464–5

Tom Jones 168
Tonight 39, 403
Top of the Pops (TOTP) 90, 161
Townsend, Peter 23
Toynbee, Polly 246, 496
trade unions 41, 42, 46, 103, 200
Trainspotting 341
Trauma Team 347
Travis, Dave Lee 263, 300
'100 Tribes' project 284–6
Tribune 26
Trier, Lars von 364
Trip Trap 356
Trisha 314
Trodd, Ken 93, 310, 327, 330
Trollope, Joanna 246
True Brits 442
True Stories 432
Truly, Madly, Deeply 352
trust 3–4, 97, 210, 213, 215–17, 220, 230–3, 268, 495
Tuckey, John 521
Tully, Mark 62
Turkish Service 34
Twin Peaks 364
Two Fat Ladies 433

UK Arena 293
UK Gold 59
UK Horizon 293
UK Style 293
UKTV 292–3, 485
Under the Sun 172, 450
Undercurrents 451
Union World 46, 202
Unfinished Symphony, The 517–19
universality, availability 28; genre and mixed programming 29; social/cultural commitment 28–9
University of Glasgow Media Group see Glasgow Media Group (GMG)
Up the Junction 330
Up Pompeii 296
Urban, Mark 429

value for money 221–2, 223–4, 224, 372
values, Birtian 372; drama 371–2; marketing 258–65, 267; marketplace 471; multichannel 288–92, 301; new public management 224–30; news/journalism 379; public service broadcasting 83
Vanessa 314
Vanity Fair 364, 366
Venables, Terry 296
A Very Open Prison 354
Vets in Practice 438
The Vice 436
Video Diaries 176, 184, 439
Video Nation 184, 246, 247, 439
video production 46

The Villa 435, 479–80
Vine, Jeremy 56
Virgin radio 262
Virgo, Tony 250, 302, 324
Vive La Différence 187

Wakefield, Mark 88, 227, 282, 284, 412–13
Walking with Beasts 474
Walking with Dinosaurs 450, 472, 474
Wall, Anthony 98
Wall to Wall 144, 187, 188
Wallace and Gromit 91
Ware, John 384
Wark Clements 451
Wark, Kirsty 26, 56, 416, 428–30
Watch With Mother 159
Watchdog 291, 376, 395, 397
Watkins, Peter 95
Watson, Paul 442
Watts, Susan 417–19, 455, 460, 461
The Weakest Link 473
weapons of mass destruction (WMD) 455, 456,
    460, 462, 464, 465
Wearing, Gillian 506
Wearing, Michael 68, 114, 127, 136, 240–41,
    249, 250, 303, 326, 328, 357, 358–9, 363–4
The Wednesday Play 38, 330
Weekend World 386
Wells, Matt 315
The West Wing 479
Westwood, Tim 264
WGBH 168, 170
What Not to Wear 474
Whately, Kevin 340
Whelan, Charlie 57
Whiston, John 296
White City building 17, 169, 173, 174, 227, 246
White Paper (1994) see The Future of the BBC
White, Susanna 74
Whitehead, Philip 88
Whitelaw, William 44, 45, 46

Wife Swap 439
Willemen, Paul 42
Williams, Paul 83
Williams, Raymond 29
Willingale, Betty 83
Willis, John 74
Winston, Robert 94, 441
Without Motive 349, 350
Wives and Daughters 170
The Works 95
Workshop Declaration 41
The World at One 194, 426
The World At War 441
World Productions 167
World Service 4, 9, 16, 71, 79, 108, 124, 136,
    390, 453, 475
World Service Television News 59, 404
World Service Trust 520
The World Tonight 110, 111, 199, 282, 405, 409
Worldwide 9, 59, 91, 100, 157, 158, 170, 171,
    296; conflicts over ownership/sale of rights
    162–5, 166, 168, 169
Wright, Jo 250, 328
Wright, Roger 519
Writing on the Wall 291
Wyatt, Will 14, 24, 25, 90, 91, 92, 93, 94–6,
    247, 277, 332, 343, 344

X Cars 437

Yentob, Alan 12–13, 53, 63, 66, 85, 90, 92, 98,
    129, 136, 137, 170, 176, 179, 192, 250, 271,
    274, 276, 278, 303, 310, 321, 327, 327–8,
    342–4, 348, 352, 358, 402
Yesterday in Parliament 410
Young Conservatives 49
Young, Mal 127
Young, Stuart 50

Z-Cars 38, 338
Zenith 152